THE CAMBRIDGE HISTORY OF
THE AGE OF ATLANTIC REVOLUTIONS

*

VOLUME I

The Enlightenment and the British Colonies

Volume I offers an introduction to the Enlightenment, which served as the shared background for virtually all revolutionary turmoil, and the American Revolution, which inaugurated the Age of Revolutions. Beginning with a thorough introduction, the volume covers international rivalry, the importance of slavery, and the reformist mindset that prevailed on the eve of the revolutionary era. It addresses the traditional argument on whether the Enlightenment truly caused revolutions, concluding that the reverse is more apt: revolutions helped to create the Enlightenment as a body of thought. The volume continues with a regional and thematic assessment of the American Revolution, revealing how numerous groups in British America – including Black and Indigenous people – pursued their own agendas and faced interests at odds with the principles of the revolution.

WIM KLOOSTER is Professor and the Robert H. and Virginia N. Scotland Endowed Chair in History and International Relations at Clark University. He is the (co-)author and (co-)editor of twelve books. His monograph *The Dutch Moment: War, Trade, and Settlement in the Seventeenth-Century Atlantic World* won the Biennial Book Award of the Forum on Early-Modern Empires and Global Interactions and the Hendricks Award of the New Netherland Institute.

THE CAMBRIDGE HISTORY OF
THE AGE OF ATLANTIC REVOLUTIONS
Edited by
WIM KLOOSTER

In three volumes, *The Cambridge History of the Age of Atlantic Revolutions* brings together experts on all corners of the Atlantic World who reveal the age in all its complexity. The Age of Atlantic Revolutions formed the transition from an era marked by monarchical rule, privileges, and colonialism to an age that stood out for republican rule, legal equality, and the sovereignty of American nations. The seventy-one chapters included reflect the latest trends and discussions on this transformative part of history, not only highlighting the causes, key events, and consequences of the revolutions, but also stressing political experimentation, contingency, and the survival of colonial institutions. The volumes also examine the attempts of enslaved and indigenous people, and free people of color, to change their plight, offering a much-needed revision to R. R. Palmer's first synthesis of this era sixty years ago.

The Cambridge History of the Age of Atlantic Revolutions, Volume I: The Enlightenment and the British Colonies
EDITED BY WIM KLOOSTER

The Cambridge History of the Age of Atlantic Revolutions, Volume II: France, Europe, and Haiti
EDITED BY WIM KLOOSTER

The Cambridge History of the Age of Atlantic Revolutions, Volume III: The Iberian Empires
EDITED BY WIM KLOOSTER

THE CAMBRIDGE HISTORY OF
THE AGE OF ATLANTIC REVOLUTIONS

*

VOLUME I

The Enlightenment and the British Colonies

WIM KLOOSTER
Clark University, Massachusetts

Shaftesbury Road, Cambridge CB2 8EA, United Kingdom

One Liberty Plaza, 20th Floor, New York, NY 10006, USA

477 Williamstown Road, Port Melbourne, VIC 3207, Australia

314–321, 3rd Floor, Plot 3, Splendor Forum, Jasola District Centre, New Delhi – 110025, India

103 Penang Road, #05-06/07, Visioncrest Commercial, Singapore 238467

Cambridge University Press is part of Cambridge University Press & Assessment, a department of the University of Cambridge.

We share the University's mission to contribute to society through the pursuit of education, learning and research at the highest international levels of excellence.

www.cambridge.org
Information on this title: www.cambridge.org/9781108476034
DOI: 10.1017/9781108567671

© Cambridge University Press & Assessment 2023

This publication is in copyright. Subject to statutory exception and to the provisions of relevant collective licensing agreements, no reproduction of any part may take place without the written permission of Cambridge University Press & Assessment.

First published 2023

Printed in the United Kingdom by TJ Books Limited, Padstow, Cornwall

A catalogue record for this publication is available from the British Library.

Library of Congress Cataloging-in-Publication Data
NAMES: Klooster, Wim, editor.
TITLE: The Cambridge history of the age of Atlantic revolutions / Wim Klooster.
DESCRIPTION: Cambridge, United Kingdom ; New York : Cambridge University Press, 2023. | Includes bibliographical references and index.
IDENTIFIERS: LCCN 2022058499 (print) | LCCN 2022058500 (ebook) | ISBN 9781108476034 (v. 1 ; hardback) | ISBN 9781108469432 (v. 1 ; paperback) | ISBN 9781108475983 (v. 2 ; hardback) | ISBN 9781108469326 (v. 2 ; paperback) | ISBN 9781108599405 (v. 2 ; eub) | ISBN 9781108475969 (v. 3 ; hardback) | ISBN 9781108469319 (v. 3 ; paperback) | ISBN 9781108598248 (v. 3 ; epub) | ISBN 9781108567671 (v. 1 ; epub)
SUBJECTS: LCSH: Revolutions–History–18th century. | Social change–History–18th century. | Revolutions–History–19th century. | Social change–History–19th century. | History, Modern–18th century. | History, Modern–19th century.
CLASSIFICATION: LCC D308 .C36 2023 (print) | LCC D308 (ebook) | DDC 940.2/7–dc23/eng/20221207
LC record available at https://lccn.loc.gov/2022058499
LC ebook record available at https://lccn.loc.gov/2022058500

ISBN – 3 Volume Set 9781108567817 Hardback
ISBN – Volume I 9781108476034 Hardback
ISBN – Volume II 9781108475983 Hardback
ISBN – Volume III 9781108475969 Hardback

Cambridge University Press & Assessment has no responsibility for the persistence or accuracy of URLs for external or third-party internet websites referred to in this publication and does not guarantee that any content on such websites is, or will remain, accurate or appropriate.

Contents

List of Figures   viii
List of Maps   ix
List of Contributors to Volume 1   x
Preface   xi

Introduction   1
WIM KLOOSTER

PART I
ENLIGHTENMENT AND CULTURE

1 · Enlightenment and the American Revolution   53
CAROLINE WINTERER

2 · Enlightenment and the French Revolution   80
JOHNSON KENT WRIGHT

3 · Enlightenment and the Ibero-American Revolutions   106
BRIAN R. HAMNETT

4 · Cultural Practices and Revolutions, c. 1760–1825   132
NATHAN PERL-ROSENTHAL

PART II
THE BRITISH COLONIES

5 · The Revolution in British America: General Overview   161
MARK PETERSON

Contents

6 · The Myth of "Salutary Neglect": Empire and Revolution in the Long Eighteenth Century   *189*
HOLLY BREWER

7 · The British Atlantic on the Eve of American Independence   *207*
PATRICK GRIFFIN

8 · Cities and Citizenship in Revolution   *228*
JESSICA CHOPPIN RONEY

9 · The Other British Colonies   *248*
TREVOR BURNARD

10 · The Participation of France and Spain   *269*
GONZALO M. QUINTERO SARAVIA

11 · Britain, Ireland, and the American Revolution, c. 1763–1785   *296*
STEPHEN CONWAY

12 · A Contest of Wills: The Spectrum and Experience of Political Violence in the American Revolution   *318*
WAYNE E. LEE

13 · Recovering Loyalism: Opposition to the American Revolution as a Good Idea   *344*
LIAM RIORDAN

14 · White Women and the American Revolution   *373*
AMI PFLUGRAD-JACKISCH

15 · Blacks in the British Colonies   *398*
JAMES SIDBURY

16 · Life, Land, and Liberty: The Native Americans' Revolution   *422*
COLIN G. CALLOWAY

17 · Shaping the Constitution   *448*
MAX M. EDLING

Contents

18 · Reform and Rebellion in Spanish America at the Time of the American Revolution   474
ANTHONY MCFARLANE

19 · International Warfare and the Non-British Caribbean   500
WIM KLOOSTER

20 · Interpreting a Symbol of Progress and Regression: European Views of America's Revolution and Early Republic, 1780–1790   519
LLOYD KRAMER

Index   542

Figures

1.1	The Phoenix, or the Resurrection of Freedom "1776".	62
2.1	The transfer of Voltaire's remains to the Panthéon, 1791.	81
10.1	Cartoon printed in Amsterdam, c. 1781.	276
10.2	The British lion engaging four powers, 1782.	284
10.3	The capture of Yorktown, 1781.	291
12.1	The Somerville powder house, from where British troops stole 250 barrels of gunpowder in 1774.	323
12.2	Retreat of British troops from Concord, 1775.	327
12.3	A prison hulk.	335
13.1	New York printer James Rivington publicized his own symbolic execution by a New Jersey mob in his *New York Gazetteer*, 20 April 1775.	350
13.2	Portrait of Loyalist Claims Commissioner John Eardley-Wilmot by Benjamin West.	370
14.1	A Society of Patriotic Ladies, at Edenton, North Carolina, 1775.	381
14.2	Nancy Hart defending her home against British soldiers.	384
15.1	Four Continental Army soldiers at the siege of Yorktown, 1781.	407
20.1	Declaration of Independence, painting by John Trumbull, 1819.	537
20.2	"The Old Plantation," South Carolina, c. 1790.	538

Maps

5.1	British North America, 1763.	175
11.1	The British Isles, 1775.	298
16.1	Indigenous nations on the eve of the revolution.	424
16.2	Sullivan's expedition, 1779.	435
16.3	The Shawnee migrations, 1774–1794.	440

Contributors to Volume 1

Holly Brewer
Trevor Burnard
Colin G. Calloway
Jessica Choppin Roney
Stephen Conway
Max M. Edling
Patrick Griffin
Brian R. Hamnett
Johnson Kent Wright
Wim Klooster
Lloyd Kramer
Wayne E. Lee
Anthony McFarlane
Nathan Perl-Rosenthal
Mark Peterson
Ami Pflugrad-Jackisch
Gonzalo M. Quintero Saravia
Liam Riordan
James Sidbury
Caroline Winterer

Preface

I thank Debbie Gershenowitz and Cecelia Cancellaro at Cambridge University Press for the smooth and pleasant collaboration. I would also like to express my gratitude to the three scholars who made up an advisory board that assisted me in choosing the contributors: Rafe Blaufarb, Ben Weider Eminent Scholar in Napoleonic Studies at Florida State University, Patrick Griffin, Madden-Hennebry Professor of History at the University of Notre Dame, and Gabriel Paquette, Professor of History at the Johns Hopkins University. All three have also written a chapter in this book.

About a dozen of the chapters were first presented at the workshop "Black Men and Women in the Age of Revolutions" in January 2020. I thank Yale University for providing an excellent venue for the workshop and Mark Peterson for making arrangements.

Some contributors contracted Covid-19, whereas others were affected by lockdowns. I thank them all for their perseverance. Although a number of invited authors reneged on their contractual promise to write a chapter far into the project, I am confident that the age of Atlantic revolutions has been covered sufficiently in the pages that follow.

Wim Klooster

Introduction

WIM KLOOSTER

Sixty years ago, R. R. Palmer published his two-volume *Age of the Democratic Revolution*, in which he described a "revolution of Western Civilization," that, he argued, had occurred in the years between 1760 and 1800. These decades, Palmer went on, saw numerous agitations, upheavals, and conspiracies on either side of the Atlantic, that arose out of specific or universal conditions, not simply as the result of the French Revolution. What Palmer outlined was what we now call the Age of (Atlantic) Revolutions, a theme that has been and continues to be the inspiration for high-quality publications, in part because this period in history supposedly laid the foundations for the countries shaped in the aftermath of these revolutions, and in part because of the need to explain the unusual political activity and social upheaval on display in this era. Virtually absent from the countless monographs, articles, and edited volumes is an overview of this important period in Atlantic history. Many specialists work within their own subfield, writing and conducting research on, for example, the American Revolution without closely following the newest trends in scholarship on the revolutions in France or Latin America. The aim of this book is to bring together current scholarship for the first reference work dedicated to the age of revolutions. Jointly, the chapters that make up this book will reveal the era in all its complexity. They will reflect the latest trends, discussing more than simply the causes, key events, and consequences of the revolutions by stressing political experimentation, contingency, and the survival of old regime practices and institutions. The time is ripe for analyzing these matters in a way that does justice to both the local nature of the revolts and their much wider Atlantic context.

Most scholars of the Age of Revolutions no longer share Palmer's geographic and temporal frameworks. They include the quarter-century (or more) after 1800 and look beyond western Europe and the United States to Haiti and Latin America. No general agreement exists, however, on the exact start and end dates, nor on its confinement to the Atlantic world. The periodization advocated by C. A. Bayly, who has made a case for the timeframe 1760–1840, is about the same as that adopted in this *Cambridge History of the Age of Atlantic Revolutions*.¹ Like any time limits, these are somewhat arbitrary. One could push the outer boundary to 1848. By that year of revolution, however, so many new factors and forces had emerged on the various national political scenes – including full-fledged liberalism and nationalism, and capitalism's working class – that there is more reason to see them as elements of a new era.

Although the geographic scope of these three volumes is vast, it has been my choice not to include all instances of rebellion, but to focus on coherence. What ties the numerous rebellious movements on either side of the Atlantic basin together in the half-century between the shots fired at Lexington and Concord (1775) and the Spanish loss at the siege of Callao, Peru in 1826 is more than just the, often violent, transitions from old to new regimes. The common glue is what marked these transitions: the questioning of time-honored institutions in the name of liberty; the invention and spread of a politics of contestation at local and national levels; the unprecedented experimentation with new forms of democracy; the abolition of numerous forms of legal inequality; and last but not least the aspiration to universal rights. These were processes in which plebeians, elites, and members of middling groups all participated. These phenomena were not experienced wherever in the world riots and rebellions broke out. They were largely absent, for example, from the Ottoman empire, although it was in great turmoil during the age of revolutions, especially in the years 1806–1808, when two sultans were deposed and thousands of people killed.²

What the age of revolutions brought was hope for fundamental change, a scarce good in the early modern world. Any criticism of authorities had previously been forbidden and heavily punished. It was only during periods of unrest that peasants in Europe could express their dissatisfaction without fear of reprisal. In such times, there are also glimpses of the hidden transcript of enslaved men and women throughout the Americas, which reflected the

---

¹ C. A. Bayly, *The Birth of the Modern World, 1780–1914: Global Connections and Comparisons* (Oxford: Oxford University Press, 2004); C. A. Bayly, "The Age of Revolutions in Global Context: An Afterword," in David Armitage and Sanjay Subrahmanyam, eds., *The Age of Revolutions in Global Context, c. 1760–1840* (Houndmills: Palgrave Macmillan, 2010), 209–17: 217.
² Ali Yaycioglu, *Partners of the Empire: The Crisis of the Ottoman Order in the Age of Revolutions* (Stanford: Stanford University Press, 2016), 158.

awakening of their hopes.³ A historian of the Russian Revolution has written that "revolutions disrupt assumptions that the future can only appear along the straight tracks where the present seems to be heading, and so challenge how we understand time and history ... Utopia is this open disruption of the now, for the sake of possibility, not a closed map of the future. It is the leap not yet the landing."⁴ This leap was made time and again by the oppressed. On the eve of the French and Haitian Revolutions, writes **John Garrigus** (Volume II, Chapter 23), many enslaved residents of Saint-Domingue "believed change was possible, whether that came through applying new laws or actively confronting the master class." For the 1790s, no fewer than forty-seven slave revolts and conspiracies have been documented for the Greater Caribbean, a number much larger than ever before or afterwards. Similarly, the years 1789–1802 saw 150 mutinies on single ships and half a dozen fleet-wide mutinies in the British, French, and Dutch navies, which meant that between 67,000 and 100,000 mobilized men were involved in at least one mutiny.⁵

Hope in the American Revolution often took the form of millennial expectations, which were so intense "during the early years of the revolutionary war that numerous patriots foresaw the final destruction of Antichrist and the establishment of the Kingdom of God within the immediate future." One revolutionary on Long Island saw the millennium as "the happy period when tyranny, oppression, and wretchedness shall be banished from the earth; when universal love and liberty, peace and righteousness, shall prevail."⁶ The French Revolution aroused hope, both at home and abroad, that tended to be secular in nature. After arriving in France in 1792 as the United States' Minister Plenipotentiary, Gouverneur Morris wrote in a letter that he was delighted to find "on this Side of the Atlantic a strong resemblance to what I left on the other – a Nation which exists in Hopes, Prospects, and Expectations. The reverence for ancient Establishments gone, existing Forms shaken to the very Foundation, and a new Order of Things about

---

³ Martin Merki-Vollenwyder, *Unruhige Untertanen: Die Rebellion der Luzerner Bauern im Zweiten Villmergerkrieg (1712)* (Luzern: Rex Verlag, 1995), 121–2; James C. Scott, *Domination and the Arts of Resistance: Hidden Transcripts* (New Haven: Yale University Press, 1990).
⁴ Mark D. Steinberg, *The Russian Revolution 1905–1921* (Oxford: Oxford University Press, 2017), 292–3.
⁵ David Geggus, "Slave Rebellion during the Age of Revolution," in Wim Klooster and Gert Oostindie, eds., *Curaçao in the Age of Revolutions, 1795–1800* (Leiden: KITLV Press, 2011), 23–56: 41–3; Nyklas Frykman, *The Bloody Flag: Mutiny in the Age of Atlantic Revolution* (Oakland: University of California Press, 2020), 10.
⁶ Ruth H. Bloch, *Visionary Republic: Millennial Themes in American Thought, 1756–1800* (Cambridge: Cambridge University Press, 1985), 79, 81.

to take Place in which even to the very names, all former Institutions will be disregarded."⁷ The imagined new order caused tremendous optimism on the part of enthusiasts for the French Revolution. Norwegian-born Henrik Steffens recalled in his memoirs that when he was sixteen and living with his family in Copenhagen, his father came home one day, deeply impressed by the French Revolution, and told his three sons: "Children, you are to be envied, what a happy time lies ahead of you! If you don't succeed in gaining a free independent position, you have yourselves to blame. All restrictive conditions of status, of poverty will disappear, the least will begin the same struggle with the most powerful, with the same weapons, on the same ground. If only I were young like you!"⁸ Steffens experienced the time that followed as not simply a French but a European revolution that was planted in millions of hearts: "The first moment of excitement in history ... has something pure, even sacred, that must never be forgotten. A boundless hope took hold of me, my whole future, it seemed to me, was planted in a fresh, new soil ... From then on my whole existence had taken on a new direction ..."⁹

Rights

If revolutionaries were guided by ideas emanating from the Enlightenment, did the Enlightenment produce the revolutions? No, answers **Johnson Kent Wright** (Volume 1, Chapter 2), at least not in the case of France. "Had 'enlightened' criticism of the Bourbon monarchy been sufficient to have launched the Revolution, it ought to have occurred some two decades earlier than it did." And yet, Wright adds, the French Enlightenment was essential to the way the revolution unfolded. Likewise, enlightened ideas helped steer the revolutions in the Ibero-American world, but, as **Brian Hamnett** argues (Volume 1, Chapter 3), the Enlightenment did not lead inevitably or automatically to support for revolution. In New Spain, for example, the outbreak of insurrection in 1810 divided its proponents into hostile camps.

Rights were an essential element of the sometimes baffling transformations that took place during the age of Atlantic revolutions. Rights used to

---

⁷ Cited in Philipp Ziesche, "Exporting American Revolutions: Gouverneur Morris, Thomas Jefferson, and the National Struggle for Universal Rights in Revolutionary France," *Journal of the Early Republic* 26:3 (2006), 419–47: 426.
⁸ Henrich Steffens, *Was ich erlebte: Aus der Erinnerung niedergeschrieben* (Breslau: Josef Mar und Kompanie, 1840), vol. 1, 362–3.
⁹ Steffens, *Was ich erlebte*, 364–5.

be privileges, granted to someone for the common good. Every male had rights commensurate with his station in life, which thereby confirmed the hierarchical organization of society. They were accompanied by obligations that forced the rights' holders to use their powers for the common good. The new notion that gradually took shape – and remained unfinished – was that humans' own moral power allowed them to stake their claims and relate their own rights to those of others. Rights transcended all structures of authority and were thus common to humankind. Human equality now trumped any differences in rank, nationality, or culture.[10] The US Declaration of Independence – the first revolutionary document to invoke rights – echoed this new idea by positing the existence of a supreme law against which positive law could be measured and, if needed, changed.[11] The French Declaration of the Rights of Man and Citizen served the same function, for which it was criticized by supporters of liberalism as metaphysical.

Once formulated, these catalogs of rights could inspire groups who had not been among the intended beneficiaries to claim parity. Just like Black people could argue that their humanity sufficed to negate their status as slaves, some women pressed for their equal rights. The authors of two Belgian pamphlets, who predicted that the current tide of revolutions would bring an end to "seventeen centuries of masculine abuse," called for a national assembly, half of whose members were to be women. If their demand was ignored by the nation's leaders, women would withdraw from society.[12] Adversaries of such rights, however, used the same language of natural rights to oppose these demands. Woman's nature, male French revolutionaries argued, made her unfit to exercise political power.[13]

The invocation of a higher law coexisted in the age of revolutions with the continued emphasis on ancient positive rights by men and women challenging the social order. In many places across the Atlantic world, as **Stephen**

---

[10] Knud Haakonssen, "From Natural Law to the Rights of Man: A European Perspective on American Debates," in Michael J. Lacy and Knud Haakonssen, eds., *A Culture of Rights: The Bill of Rights in Philosophy, Politics, and Law – 1791 and 1991* (Cambridge: Cambridge University Press, 1991), 19–61: 21, 32, 35–6; Simon Middleton, *From Privileges to Rights: Work and Politics in Colonial New York* (Philadelphia: University of Pennsylvania Press, 2006), 5–6.

[11] Andrew J. Reck, "Natural Law in American Revolutionary Thought," *The Review of Metaphysics* 30:4 (1977), 686–714: 712.

[12] Janet L. Polasky, "Women in Revolutionary Belgium: From Stone Throwers to Hearth Tenders," *History Workshop* 21 (1986), 87–104: 93.

[13] Annelien de Dijn, *Freedom: An Unruly History* (Cambridge, MA: Harvard University Press, 2020), 226.

Conway argues in Volume I, Chapter 11, "the events associated with Palmer's 'democratic revolution' began as a conservative reaction to the reforming endeavors of rulers, not as a grassroots desire to extend popular participation." Ireland's Protestants, he shows, were looking backwards "in seeking to reclaim their autonomy." "Most of them were not interested in a democratic transformation of Ireland." **Janet Polasky** (Volume II, Chapter 14) writes that one of the groups challenging Austrian rule in Belgium "wanted to restore the medieval constitutions and reestablish the rule of the three Estates. Instead of natural rights, they referred to 'the eternal rights of man,' meaning something quite different from the enlightenment ideal. Instead of the 'rights of the People,' they referred to the privileges of the 'nation belge.'" In the (Swiss) Helvetic Republic, a document presented to the authorities of Zurich in 1794 that has been labeled the *Stäfner Memorial* demanded both the restoration of old privileges and a constitution that defended individual human rights.[14]

The introduction of rights was no straightforward process, as can be illustrated by the uncertain status of the right to profess one's religious belief. The tone was set by the Virginia Declaration of Rights, which stipulated that "all men are equally entitled to the free exercise of religion, according to the dictates of conscience."[15] Although it has been argued that religious freedom was achievable in Protestant places such as Virginia where tolerance had already been practiced, its adoption was usually a matter of controversy. In Pennsylvania's constitutional debate of 1776, one side – made up of Protestants – opposed religious leniency, which they feared would put them at the mercy of the alien creeds of Islam, Catholicism, and Judaism. Likewise, although Massachusetts' constitution may have guaranteed the exercise of religion in private, it contained an injunction to the legislature to support Protestant teachers.[16] Nor was such intolerance the exclusive domain of elite politicians in the age of revolutions. A series of Catholic relief bills proposed

---

[14] Urte Weeber, "New Wine in Old Wineskins: Republicanism in the Helvetic Republic," in Joris Oddens, Mart Rutjes, and Erik Jacobs, eds., *The Political Culture of the Sister Republics, 1794–1806: France, the Netherlands, Switzerland, and Italy* (Amsterdam: Amsterdam University Press, 2015), 57–64: 62.

[15] Daniel L. Dreisbach, "George Mason's Pursuit of Religious Liberty in Revolutionary Virginia," *The Virginia Magazine of History and Biography* 108:1 (2000), 5–44: 16.

[16] Charles D. Russell, "Islam as a Danger to Republican Virtue: Broadening Religious Liberty in Revolutionary Pennsylvania," *Pennsylvania History: A Journal of Mid-Atlantic Studies* 76:3 (2009), 250–75: 251; Eduardo Posada-Carbó, "Spanish America and US constitutionalism in the Age of Revolution," in Gabriel Paquette and Gonzalo M. Quintero Saravia, eds., *Spain and the American Revolution: New Approaches and Perspectives* (London: Routledge, 2020), 210–23: 217.

by the British government threw into sharp relief the existence of a popular Protestantism that defined itself in opposition to French Catholicism and eventually led to the Gordon Riots (London, 1780).[17]

The antipluralist tendency was, however, stronger in the Catholic world, even in France, where the Catholic faith lost its status as state religion and where Protestants and Jews were emancipated. Political culture proved hard to change.[18] And so it could happen that a small town in Alsace decided in 1794 that the Jews had to shave their beards, and could no longer carry their Decalogues in public or show any other signs of their religion.[19] It was not different in the colonies. When the planters of Saint-Domingue sought protection from the British king in 1793, proposing some articles of government, they insisted on the exclusivity of the Catholic religion.[20] Soon, of course, French revolutionary intolerance went beyond the insistence on Catholicism, when the adoption of the Civil Constitution of the Clergy led to discrimination against the millions of people who clung to the old Church.

The influential constitution of Cádiz stated unambiguously that the religion of the Spanish nation was and would always be the only true Roman Catholic one. When the legislators gathered in Cádiz voted for press freedom in 1810, they followed it up by setting up boards of censorship that would make sure that published works did not threaten religion. Three years later, they went one step further by decreeing the death penalty for anyone suggesting the implementation of a policy of tolerance vis-à-vis non-Catholics.[21] At the same time, as **Roberto Breña** notes (Volume III, Chapter 3), the constitution "tried to control what up to that moment was an almost exclusive role of the Church in public education, publishing, and public discourse." Javier Fernández Sebastián has convincingly argued that "the overwhelming preponderance of Catholicism in the Hispanic world explains how difficult it was to conceive of religion and politics as separate spheres, and the correlative difficulty of regarding 'religion' as an abstract category of a general nature, capable of embracing several 'religions,' in the

---

[17] Brad A. Jones, "'In Favour of Popery': Patriotism, Protestantism, and the Gordon Riots in the Revolutionary British Atlantic," *Journal of British Studies* 52:1 (2013), 79–102.
[18] Bronislaw Baczko, *Politiques de la Révolution française* (Paris: Gallimard, 2008), 62–3.
[19] Claude Muller, "Religion et Révolution en Alsace," *Annales historiques de la Révolution française* 337 (2004), 63–83: 76.
[20] J. Marino Incháustegui, ed., *Documentos para estudio: Marco de la época y problemas del Tratado de Basilea de 1795, en la parte española de Santo Domingo* (Buenos Aires: Academia Dominicana de la Historia, 1957), 640.
[21] Juan Pablo Domínguez, "Intolerancia religiosa en las Cortes de Cádiz," *Hispania* 77:255 (2017), 155–83: 164, 178.

plural." Since Catholicism was the foundation of the nation's identity, tolerance meant "disunion, illegitimacy, even civil war."[22] This sentiment was shared by the priests of central Switzerland when the constitution of the Helvetic Republic was promulgated, which meant that irreligiosity and heresy were no longer punishable.[23]

Residents of the Catholic world would not have viewed religious exclusivity as a form of inequality. As members of the Christian community, every individual enjoyed an equal status by virtue of their baptism. Their ties were governed by brotherly love. At least, that was the case in theory. In practice, it remained an ideal, pursued by Hidalgo and other priests involved in the Mexican uprising of 1810. The early Church fathers rather than Enlightenment *philosophes* were the inspiration for Hidalgo, who stated that his goal was to build a society in which all were recognized as equal children of God.[24] Likewise, the 1797 republican conspiracy in Venezuela, writes **Cristina Soriano** in Volume II, Chapter 28, "argued in favor of social harmony between whites, *pardos*, Indians, and blacks, because all these racial groups were seen as 'brothers in Christ.'"

Not all Catholic leaders were bent on continuing the exclusivity of their religion. Some sought to introduce a measure of tolerance. The difference between tolerance and religious freedom was expressed by the "Jews, settled in France" in a petition to the National Assembly a few months after the Declaration of the Rights of Man and Citizen had been adopted. "The word tolerance," they wrote, "which after so many centuries and so many *intolerant acts* seemed to be a word of humanity and reason, no longer suits a country that wishes to establish its rights on the eternal basis of justice.... To tolerate, indeed, is to suffer what one would have the right to prohibit." Under the new conditions, the dominant religion had no right to prohibit another religion from humbly placing itself by its side.[25] But religious inequality was not to vanish, while tolerance – that typically early modern phenomenon – was still a viable option in Europe and the Americas. The

---

[22] Javier Fernández Sebastián, "Toleration and Freedom of Expression in the Hispanic World between Enlightenment and Liberalism," *Past & Present* no. 211 (May 2011), 159–97: 162–3, 186, 188.

[23] Eric Godel, "La Constitution scandaleuse. La population de Suisse centrale face à la République helvétique," in Andreas Würgler, ed., *Grenzen des Zumutbaren: Erfahrungen mit der französischen Okkupation und der Helvetischen Republik (1798–1803)* (Basel: Schwabe Verlag, 2011), 29–44: 32.

[24] Laura Ibarra García, "El concepto de igualdad en México (1810–1824)," *Relaciones* 145 (2016), 279–314: 287.

[25] "Pétition des juifs établis en France, adressée à l'Assemblée Nationale," 28 January 1790, in *Adresses, mémoires et pétitions des juifs 1789–1794* (Paris: EDHIS, 1968), 17–18.

Polish constitution, writes **Richard Butterwick** (Volume II, Chapter 20), began "with a stirring preamble and an article maintaining the prohibition against 'apostasy' from the Roman Catholic 'dominant and national religion,' while assuring freedom of worship and the protection of government to all creeds." Similarly, the Organic Law that saw the light in Pernambuco, Brazil in 1817 said that the state religion was Roman Catholicism, while the other Christian sects of any denomination were tolerated.[26] In early independent Colombia, a campaign for religious toleration failed to achieve its goal. Foreigners could still not hold Protestant services in public in spite of sustained criticism of the Catholic clergy, which was held responsible for blocking new ideas.[27] The most radical constitution adopted in a Catholic country was that issued by Jean-Jacques Dessalines in 1805. While Toussaint Louverture's constitution of 1801 had declared Catholicism the official state religion, that of Dessalines (although short-lived) introduced religious tolerance.[28]

Sovereignty and Public Opinion

Many historians have assumed that a form of self-government was already in place in Britain's North American colonies. These are considered to have thrived in a long era of "salutary neglect." When that era ended in the aftermath of the Seven Years' War, a revolution became thinkable. In Volume I, Chapter 6, **Holly Brewer** shows that "salutary neglect" was largely a myth: "The political, legal and economic situations in the colonies were constantly negotiated in a struggle for power that was occurring not only on the level of empire but in England itself ... To the degree that such 'salutary neglect' existed ... it was part of this negotiation and struggle over the meaning and terms of power. While some could escape the power of empire in the short term, it was constantly tugging at their sleeves. One could take up land in the 'wilderness,' for example, ... but the only way one owned it was by getting a legal title – and that demanded negotiation with all the ligaments of colonial authority, from surveyor and courts to secretary of

---

[26] Leonardo Morais de Araújo Pinheiro, "Análise da Lei Orgânica da Revolução pernambucana de 1817 à luz dos direitos fundamentais," *Revista Brasileira de História do Direito* 4:2 (2018), 114–34: 130.
[27] David Bushnell, *The Santander Regime in Gran Colombia* (Westport, CN: Greenwood Press, 1970 [1954]), 210, 215.
[28] Lorelle D. Semley, "To Live and Die, Free and French: Toussaint Louverture's 1801 Constitution and the Original Challenge of Black Citizenship," *Radical History Review* 115 (2013), 65–90: 78.

the colony. How one could develop it, and what one could grow, how one could pass it on, were often regulated by laws that might emerge in the colonies but were subject to Royal veto. Other regulations were imposed directly by imperial authorities."

Revolutions are always a struggle for sovereignty. Despite the widely shared support for popular sovereignty, opinions were divided on the people's postrevolutionary political role. A prominent monarchist member of France's National Assembly opined that while all powers emanated from the people, their well-being depended on leaving the exercise of these powers to the king to prevent the chaos of anarchy.[29] In continental British America, **Max Edling** remarks (Volume 1, Chapter 17), the ideology of the American Revolution "introduced a nebulous concept of popular sovereignty, which somehow existed both at state and at national level." "Several of the new constitutions incorporated Congress's declaration of independence in whole or in part, thus illustrating how legitimate authority was based on popular sovereignty simultaneously expressed at national and local level." In Spanish America, it was unclear whether self-rule extended to a town's immediate vicinity or whether administrative centers could claim to govern vast areas. The assumption of sovereignty in Spanish America implied a return to nature. As Clément Thibaud has explained, that meant not a return to a Hobbesian world of lone individuals but *pueblos*, peoples in the sense of free communities. If indeed the *pueblo* was the repository of sovereignty, opinions differed on the *pueblo*'s identity, at least in New Granada. Was it the town, the province, or all of New Granada?[30] Federalists in many parts of the Atlantic world, often inspired by the United States and opposed to the horrors to which centralism had allegedly given rise in Jacobin Paris, usually found support outside traditional political centers. To legitimize the dispersion of political power, Dutch federalists used the climate argument – according to which each land had its own character and was therefore entitled to its own legislation – to plead for separate laws for each of the seven small provinces. Another argument was that the distance between the population and its rulers was much smaller on

---

[29] His name was Jean-Joseph Mounier. Nicolai von Eggers, "Popular Sovereignty, Republicanism, and the Political Logic of the Struggles of the French Revolution" (Ph.D. dissertation, University of Aarhus, 2016), 216.
[30] Clément Thibaud, "Des républiques en armes à la République armée. Guerre révolutionnaire, fédéralisme et centralisme au Venezuela et en Nouvelle-Grenade, 1808–1830," *Annales historiques de la Révolution française* no. 348 (2011), 57–86: 63; Isabel Restrepo Mejía, "La soberanía del 'pueblo' durante la época de la independencia, 1810–1815," *Historia Crítica* 29 (2005), 101–23: 102–5.

a provincial level. Such democratic reasoning had its limits, though, because the federalists' emphasis on the preservation of provincial laws and customs was at odds with the new egalitarian spirit.[31]

Penetrating everywhere, that new spirit changed the nature of political debates, which were no longer confined to elite venues. **Javier Fernández Sebastián** points out in Volume III, Chapter 12 that the "increase in the pace of publication of newspapers and readers' insatiable demand for news rapidly accelerated the circulation of new concepts and multiplied the uses, often contradictory, of basic political terminology." To succeed in achieving political goals, the mobilization of public opinion became indispensable, as in the Dutch Republic, where Patriot newspapers were not just sold widely but also carried many readers' letters, showcasing public opinion.[32] Public opinion, which rebels constantly invoked, came to be seen as an enlightened court with universal authority.[33] In order to expose the French king to this new "court" and remove him from the royal court in Versailles, plebeians forced Louis XVI to settle in Paris, where he would be surrounded by "the people." In Venezuela, conversely, several representatives proposed to move the seat of Congress away from Caracas and avoid the crushing weight of the capital's public opinion. Their adversaries opined that at least in Caracas, some Enlightenment may be found. One of them argued: "Public opinion is not power, but the sum of all opinions that cannot be formed without knowledge. And could it be that they exist among shepherds, farmers or peasants, who don't even know the name of those who govern them? Public opinion, in matters of government, resides only in the big cities and not in the villages and shacks, especially in America, where the previous government has always kept under a black veil even the inhabitants of the capital city."[34] And even in the big cities, only a small group of men were zealots for liberty, Genevan native Étienne Dumont noted when he arrived in Paris on the eve

---

[31] Peter A. J. van den Berg, *Codificatie en staatsvorming: De politieke en politiek-theoretische achtergronden van de codificatie van het privaatrecht in Pruisen, de Donaumonarchie, Frankrijk en Nederland, 1450–1811* (Groningen: Wolters-Noordhoff, 1996), 306, 307, 314, 319.

[32] Nicolaas van Sas, "The Patriot Revolution: New Perspectives," in Margaret C. Jacob and Wijnand W. Mijnhardt, eds., *The Dutch Republic in the Eighteenth Century: Decline, Enlightenment, and Revolution* (Ithaca, NY: Cornell University Press, 1992), 91–120: 102–3.

[33] Keith Michael Baker, *Inventing the French Revolution: Essays on French Political Culture in the Eighteenth Century* (Cambridge: Cambridge University Press, 1990), 186, 193–6.

[34] Véronique Hébrard, "Opinion publique et représentation dans le Congrès Constituant Vénézuélien (1810–1812)," *Annales historiques de la Révolution française* no. 365 (2011), 153–75: 162 (quote), 167, 170–1.

of the revolution: "There are in the immense population of this metropolis about fifteen or twenty thousand persons, who consider the meeting of the Estates-General as a matter of the utmost importance, and who anxiously watch all the measures of the court; these men, being to be found everywhere, in coffee-houses, at the theatres, in private companies, and in public places, may be said to form the public opinion."[35] That most delegates at the Estates-General and National Assembly would have agreed with Dumont is suggested by the highly centralized polity they set up. **David Andress** argues in Volume II, Chapter 1 that the revolutionaries expected only obedience from locally elected leaders, did not introduce intermediary bodies outside Paris, and opted not to set up institutional checks on the legislature.

To focus single-mindedly on the politically active members of a society would obscure the politicization on a vast scale – inside and outside France – of ordinary people, who appropriated the official rhetoric that was expressed in official documents and proclamations, and employed it when they thought it useful.[36] A new democratic culture emerged in the countries neighboring France, characterized by newspapers, pamphlets, societies, republican catechisms, and civic feasts which featured freedom trees and Phrygian hats.[37] In Italy, writes **John A. Davis** (Volume II, Chapter 17), "freedom of the press, official and unofficial newspapers, pamphlets and broadsheets offered unprecedented platforms for public debate, while the newly created consultative and executive committees, public assemblies, the drafting of constitutions, the debates on the procedures and formalities of government, the organization of plebiscites and formalized civic and public ceremonies gave opportunities to experience active citizenship, as did the political clubs and societies."

Essential to the process of cultivating peoples bound together by horizontal ties of citizenship and shared visions of revolutionary transformation, writes Michael Kwass, was material culture "as legislators, producers, and

---

[35] Richard Whatmore, "Étienne Dumont, the British Constitution, and the French Revolution," *The Historical Journal* 50:1 (2007), 23–47: 32.

[36] Jean-Luc Chappey, "Révolution, régénération, civilisation. Enjeux culturels des dynamiques politiques," in Jean-Luc Chappey, Bernard Gainot, Guillaume Mazeau, Frédéric Régent, and Pierre Serna, eds., *Pour quoi faire la Révolution* (Marseille: Agone, 2012), 115–48; Maxime Kaci, *Dans le tourbillon de la Révolution: Mots d'ordre et engagements collectifs aux frontières septentrionales (1791–1793)* (Rennes: Presses universitaires de Rennes, 2016), 288; Eugenia Molina, "Politización y relaciones sociales en Mendoza (Argentina) durante la década revolucionaria (1810–1820). Conflictos y consensos en la configuración de un nuevo orden," *Boletín Americanista* 58 (2008), 251–71: 253.

[37] Annie Jourdan, *La Révolution, une exception française?* (Paris: Flammarion, 2004), 271–2.

consumers imbued everyday objects with revolutionary meaning. More than merely reflecting political ideas and aspirations, material objects mediated their very expression ..."[38] In one rural part of the Dutch Republic in the 1780s, all sorts of everyday objects demonstrated one's allegiance on both sides of the political divide: crockery, pottery, drinking utensils, sugar-casters, cookie boards, scent bottles, and tobacco and snuff boxes.[39] Just as cultural objects were invested with a revolutionary meaning, cultural *practices* underwent a transformation. They served, argues **Nathan Perl-Rosenthal** (Volume I, Chapter 4), as vehicles for new political ideas and practices. These cultural practices, such as letter-writing, were not in themselves revolutionary, and could be used by the revolutions' opponents, but in the hands of revolutionaries they were given new forms.

Politicization was not by definition, or at least not exclusively, ideological. **Joris Oddens** contends in Volume II, Chapter 13 that "in some rural areas [of the Dutch Republic] passions ran high, but what was at stake seems to have been a long-running tribal conflict rather than an ideological divide dating to the revolutionary era itself: rival factions in a village sided with the Patriots or with the Orangists, but more particularly *against* each other, or the entire population of one village sympathized with one camp because the people of a neighboring town politically or economically dwarfing them supported the other." This phenomenon existed everywhere. Preexisting disputes or grievances often conditioned the choice for revolution or status quo. If a large town in Spanish America embraced revolution, nearby smaller towns seeking greater autonomy would remain faithful to the old regime. Similarly, the feuding Anglicans and Presbyterians ended up on opposing sides in the American Revolution in good part to avoid each other. Yet another example can be found in Africa. Shortly after Brazil declared its independence, the elite of Benguela (Angola) used the crisis of the Portuguese empire to try to break away from its subordination to Luanda, join Brazil, and become a province attached to Rio de Janeiro. **Roquinaldo Ferreira** reveals in Volume III, Chapter 22 that this was no surprise move. Benguela and Rio were linked through the transatlantic slave trade, the Benguela elite sent its sons to study in Brazil, and it had regularly imported foodstuffs from Brazil in time of need.

---

[38] Michael Kwass, *Consumer Revolution, 1650–1800* (Cambridge: Cambridge University Press, 2022), 198.

[39] Jouke Nijman, "Politieke cultuur en volkscultuur in de Patriottentijd," *Groniek* 30 (1997), 417–31: 425, 426.

Rhetoric was, of course, also largely strategic. No fewer than 227 towns in France petitioning the National Assembly to reassign lawcourts and other institutions to them adopted egalitarian language.[40] Similarly, in German cities, writes **Michael Rowe** (Volume II, Chapter 18), "demands that had previously been couched in the familiar language of historic rights and privileges now included references to the universal liberties triumphant in France." Elsewhere, old and new regime values mixed, as in the case of a free merchant of color from Guayaquil who petitioned the Cortes of Cádiz in 1820 for both citizenship and recognition as an *hidalgo*.[41] And in the hinterland of the Swiss canton of Zurich, the language of reform was combined with an insistence on inalienable rights. This pragmatic republicanism, writes **Marc H. Lerner** (Volume II, Chapter 11), was typical of Switzerland in the age of revolutions.

The defenders of the status quo responded to revolutionary activity in various ways, appealing to the public themselves in person or in writing, or simply muzzling the press, as the viceroy of New Spain did in Mexico City, an act he defended by alleging that press freedom had led to an "extraordinary number of seditious and insulting publications."[42] Nor were the revolutionaries, once in the saddle themselves, content with an alternative opinion being expressed. During the American Revolutionary War, Patriots bullied printers into retracting contentious statements. In other instances, they seized and destroyed the entire print run of pamphlets they considered dangerous. In addition to book burnings, there were monetary rewards for the capture of certain pamphleteers. Amid such escalating levels of violence, Loyalists found it increasingly hard to make their voices heard.[43]

Not everyone engaged in political contestation. Many peasants and urban workers were indifferent to the revolutions as long as they could maintain such a stance. Farmers in Chile were only gradually drawn into the political conflict as they were mobilized on either side of the divide through ties of clientage. Indifference could also give way to outright opposition to the state,

---

[40] Wim Klooster, *Revolutions in the Atlantic World: A Comparative History*, new edition (New York: New York University Press, 2018), 173–4; Ted W. Margadant, *Urban Rivalries in the French Revolution* (Princeton: Princeton University Press, 1992), 157.

[41] Federica Morelli, *Free People of Color in the Spanish Atlantic: Race and Citizenship, 1780–1850* (New York: Routledge, 2020), 127–8.

[42] Juan Ortiz Escamilla, *Calleja: Guerra, botín y fortuna* (Xalapa: Universidad Veracruzana; Zamora: El Colegio de Michoacán, 2017), 112.

[43] Holger Hoock, *Scars of Independence: America's Violent Birth* (New York: Crown Publishers, 2017), 38–9. See also Harry M. Ward, *The War for Independence and the Transformation of American Society* (London: Routledge, 1999), 59–65.

as it did in the Dutch province of Friesland, where those who were largely interested in issues that were of their immediate concern such as food prices or high taxes ended up turning their back on the Batavian Republic when the electorate was forced to sign a declaration signaling their resistance to any form of rule by stadtholders, aristocrats, or autocrats.[44]

Democracy

Most thinkers and activists conceived of freedom as the ability to live under laws that the inhabitants of a country made themselves.[45] The revolutionaries agreed that the regimes they built had to be supported by some form of popular control over the government. Only a political system that reflected the people's voice – which was often, but certainly not always, called democracy – could supplant aristocratic or monarchical rule. That voice was to be expressed through representation, which was inseparable from suffrage.[46]

Who constituted the people? At least a section of the adult population, and usually – in line with classical republicanism – those who had taken up arms to defend the revolution. The 1826 constitution of Bolivia said that Bolivians included "those who fought for liberty in Junín or Ayacucho," the sites of two battles that had doomed the Spanish empire in South America.[47] Similarly, the French constitution of 1795 singled out "veterans of one or more campaigns for the establishment of the Republic" as citizens who did not have to qualify financially in order to cast their vote.[48] The earlier French constitution of 1791, which was never implemented, had even granted suffrage to every adult male, a decision replicated only in

---

[44] Igor Goicovic Donoso, "De la indiferencia a la resistencia: Los sectores populares y la Guerra de Independencia en el norte de Chile (1817–1823)," *Revista de Indias* 74:260 (2014), 129–60: 136; Jacques Kuiper, *Een revolutie ontrafeld: Politiek in Friesland 1795–1798* (Franeker: Van Wijnen, 2002), 517.

[45] De Dijn, *Freedom*, 177–8.

[46] Minchul Kim, "Pierre-Antoine Antonelle and Representative Democracy in the French Revolution," *History of European Ideas* 44:3 (2018), 344–69: 351. Earlier forms of representation were now abandoned. Cf. Joaquim Albareda and Manuel Herrero Sánchez, eds., *Political Representation in the Ancien Régime* (London: Routledge, 2019).

[47] Constitution of Bolivia, 22 November 1826, in J. R. Gutiérrez, ed., *Las constituciones políticas que ha tenido la República Boliviana (1826–1868)* (Santiago: Imprenta de "El Independiente," 1869), 4–5.

[48] Andrew Jainchill, "The Constitution of the Year III and the Persistence of Classical Republicanism," *French Historical Studies* 26:3 (2003), 399–435: 418.

Paraguay (1813).[49] Some constitutions extended voting rights not to every male, but the vast majority of men. That of Cádiz (1812) enabled many inhabitants in the Spanish empire to cast their vote. In Mexico City, for example, 93 percent of the adult male population was enfranchised. Likewise, the Brazilian constitution of 1824 incorporated in the electorate vast numbers of small urban and rural proprietors as well as tenant farmers and sharecroppers, although it did not give the vote to journeymen and free men who lived from piecework or who were not regularly employed.[50] Formal exclusion did not necessarily mean the inability to take part in the election process. In both France and Spain, communities were represented by well-known individuals, who received the vote after days of deliberation, during which anybody could chime in. Commoners who could not vote were still believed to be *virtually* represented through their public demonstrations of support or rejection of elected candidates.[51] North American Patriots, of course, scoffed at the notion of virtual representation. During the crisis that preceded the American Revolution, Britain's insistence that Americans were represented in Parliament despite their inability to vote had alienated numerous Americans from the metropole.

In most parts of the Atlantic world, representative democracy was introduced sooner or later, but without citizens resigning themselves to the reduced role that would later become the norm, when their input became largely limited to the periodic casting of votes. Many North Americans left little leeway to the delegates, whom they saw as "mere agents or tools of the people" who could give binding directions "whenever they please to give them."[52] During the Cortes of Cádiz, Spanish newspapers as well as politicians invoked the demand that the people control their representatives very closely, reserving for themselves the last say in expressing the general will.[53]

---

[49] Richard Allan White, *Paraguay's Autonomous Revolution, 1810–1840* (Albuquerque: University of New Mexico Press, 1978), 56.

[50] Jaime E. Rodríguez O., *The Independence of Spanish America* (Cambridge: Cambridge University Press, 1998), 105; Cecília Helena de Salles Oliveira, "Contribuição ao estudo do Poder Moderador," in Cecília Helena de Salles Oliveira, Vera Lúcia Nagib Bittencourt, and Wilma Peres Costa, eds., *Soberania e conflito: Configurações do Estado Nacional no Brasil do século XIX* (São Paulo: Editora Hucitec, 2010), 185–235: 214.

[51] Jean-Clément Martin, *Nouvelle histoire de la Révolution française* (Paris: Perrin, 2012), 208; François-Xavier Guerra, "The Spanish-American Tradition of Representation and Its European Roots," *Journal of Latin American Studies* 26:1 (1994), 1–35: 7.

[52] Gordon S. Wood, *The Creation of the American Republic, 1776–1787* (Charlotte: The University of North Carolina Press, 1969), 371.

[53] Javier Fernández Sebastián, "Democracia," in Javier Fernández Sebastián and Juan Francisco Fuentes, eds., *Diccionario político y social del siglo XIX español* (Madrid: Alianza Editorial, 2002), 216–228: 218.

Militant Parisians known as Enragés, who were wrongly portrayed at the time as forming a movement, considered direct democracy the only option for their city. They agreed with Rousseau that sovereignty could not be delegated. The people should have the right to sanction the laws and if there were to be delegates, they must be revocable at will.[54] A form of direct democracy was actually established in one city 400 kilometers to the north. In 1796, voters in Amsterdam received the right to send proposals to the municipal government. If two-thirds of the electorate backed a proposal, it would be binding.[55]

The man who crucially intervened in the French Revolution on more than one occasion, the Abbé Sieyès, disagreed with the view that delegates should be kept on a leash by the voters. He summarized the legislative process as follows: "The members of a representative assembly ... gather in order to balance their opinions, to modify them, to purify some through others, and to extract finally from the *lumières* of all, a majority opinion, that is to say, the common will which makes the law. The mixing of individual wills, the kind of fermentation that they undergo in this operation, are necessary to produce the result that is desired. It is therefore essential that opinions should be able to concert, to yield, in a word to modify one another, for without this there is no longer a deliberative assembly but simply a *rendez-vous of couriers*, ready to depart after having delivered their dispatches."[56]

Sieyès did not simply favor representative democracy; he also introduced the distinction between active and passive citizens that was adopted in France. Fulfilling income or property requirements, the first group was allowed more extensive participation in political life. Sieyès' distinction was soon copied in other new regimes. By virtue of Brazil's 1824 constitution, for example, citizens were all males of age at least twenty-five years who lived on their own and did not work as domestic servants. They also had "a yearly net income above a hundred thousand reis derived from real estate property, industry, trade, or employment." These men could vote in the parochial assemblies, which chose the provincial electors. Electors, however, could

---

[54] Albert Soboul, "Audience des Lumières. Classes populaires et Rousseauisme sous la Révolution," *Annales historiques de la Révolution française* 34:170 (1962), 421–38: 425.
[55] Thomas Poell, "The Democratic Paradox: Dutch Revolutionary Struggles over Democratisation and Centralisation (1780–1813)" (Ph.D. dissertation, University of Utrecht, 2007), 91.
[56] Murray Forsyth, *Reason and Revolution: The Political Thought of the Abbé Sieyes* (Leicester: Leicester University Press; New York: Holmes & Meier Publishers, 1987), 134.

only be members of the active citizenry, made up of all men with an income of at least 200,000 reis, who had not been freed from slavery.[57]

Underlying this division was a difference between the people as conceptualized by Enlightenment thinkers and the actual population. The abstract people were a source of legitimacy, whereas the real people were deemed ignorant and superstitious by the elites.[58] The natural representatives of the people, d'Holbach and Diderot had taught, were those who were the best informed and educated.[59] Where revolutionaries succeeded in toppling a regime, they commonly began the process of enlightening the vast mass of the population. Delegates presented themselves as moral guides in a society that allegedly had become corrupt, which meant that it would take time for civilization to become rooted. The moral decay that he accused Spain of bringing to its colonies at the same time made Simón Bolívar oppose the establishment of a genuine democracy. The people, he maintained, were simply not ready yet for a political role. He was not alone. Six days before the storming of the Bastille, one deputy of the Third Estate wrote that the revolution – a term he presciently used – should be postponed by ten years, allowing the people to educate themselves.[60] To the Italian intellectual Vincenzio Russo, representative democracy was a temporary stage that should last as long as popular education was needed. Once that goal had been achieved, direct democracy could be introduced.[61]

Thomas Paine asserted, on the other hand, that the educational effect of representative democracy would be immediate. "[T]he case is," he wrote, "that the representative system diffuses such a body of knowledge throughout a nation, on the subject of government, as to explode ignorance and preclude imposition ... Those who are not in the representation, know as much of the nature of business as those who are. An affectation of

---

[57] Márcia Regina Berbel and Rafael de Bivar Marquese, "The Absence of Race: Slavery, Citizenship, and Pro-slavery Ideology in the Cortes of Lisbon and the Rio de Janeiro Constituent Assembly (1821–4)," *Social History* 32:4 (2007), 415–433: 416, 425.

[58] Valérie Sottocasa, *Les brigands et la Révolution: Violences politiques et criminalité dans le Midi (1789–1802)* (Ceyzérieu: Champ Vallon, 2016), 363.

[59] Jonathan Israel, *A Revolution of the Mind: Radical Enlightenment and the Intellectual Origins of Modern Democracy* (Princeton: Princeton University Press, 2010), 66.

[60] Adrien Duquesnoy, *Un révolutionnaire malgré lui: Journal mai–octobre 1789*, ed. Guillaume Mazeau (Paris: Mercure de France, 2016), 137. See for the changing meaning of the term "revolution" in those days: Keith Michael Baker, "Enlightenment Idioms, Old Regime Discourses, and Revolutionary Improvisation," in Thomas E. Kaiser and Dale K. Van Kley, eds., *From Deficit to Deluge: The Origins of the French Revolution* (Stanford: Stanford University Press, 2011), 165–97: 191–6.

[61] Luciano Guerci, *"Mente, cuore, coraggio, virtù repubblicane": Educare il popolo nell'Italia in rivoluzione (1796–1799)* (Turin: Tirrenia Stampatori, 1992), 112–13.

mysterious importance would there be scouted. Nations can have no secrets; and the secrets of courts, like those of individuals, are always their defects. In the representative system, the reason for everything must publicly appear. Every man is a proprietor in government and considers it a necessary part of his business to understand."[62] Although Jacobins embraced it, this conviction was not widely shared. While they may have hoped for a rapid enlightenment of the masses, most revolutionary regimes adopted constitutions that included a literacy requirement. This was necessary, explained French lawmaker Boissy d'Anglas, because a man "is only truly independent when he does not need anyone to enlighten him about his duties and to convey his ideas."[63] The leaders of the new Spanish American republics shared the Enlightenment ideal of popular education, many of them embracing the system of mutual education invented by the Englishman Joseph Lancaster. In that way, writes **Karen Racine** (Volume III, Chapter 15), large numbers of people could become literate in a short amount of time. The goal of education, however, was to train not participatory citizens, but moral subjects who were economically useful.

Even so, urban crowds made up of literate and illiterate residents alike often performed an important legitimizing function for revolutionary elites. Leaders of Central American revolts, writes **Timothy Hawkins** (Volume III, Chapter 6), "relied on the energy of subaltern groups, in particular the urban masses, to advance their causes. In not a few cases, these uprisings arose from popular demands for redress of traditional grievances, which suggests a disconnect between the priorities of the leadership and the protesters." Some of the watershed moments in the age of revolutions saw the intervention of vociferous crowds that had been invited to show up. One such occasion was the popular response in Bogotá to the refusal of the viceroy of New Granada to form a junta that would be the local government. The crowd's anti-Spanish demonstrations on 20 July 1810 forced the viceroy to change his mind. Agents working for the rebel elite had used various methods to urge the plebeians to make their way to certain downtown sites, where they energized them. These agents were scribes and other middle-rank local officials who mingled with working men and were known to the elite because of their positions.[64]

---

[62] Thomas Paine, *The Rights of Man for the Benefit of All Mankind* (Philadelphia: D. Webster, 1797), 31.
[63] Jainchill, "The Constitution of the Year III," 421.
[64] Manuel Pareja Ortiz, "El 'pueblo' bogotano en la revolución del 20 de julio de 1810," *Anuario de Estudios Americanos* 71:1 (2014), 281–311: 283–4, 287, 291.

When crowds were not manipulated but operated autonomously, they instilled fear in the elites. **Anthony McFarlane** writes in Volume I, Chapter 18 that elites in Quito and Arequipa (both in the viceroyalty of Peru) backed local revolts against Spanish policies until they "took fright at plebeian mobilization and rallied to defend the established order," terrified of a breakdown in social discipline.[65] John Adams feared that new claims would arise. "Women will demand a Vote. Lads from 12 to 21 will think their Rights not enough attended to, and every Man, who has not a Farthing, will demand an equal Voice with any other in all Acts of State. It tends to confound and destroy all Distinctions, and prostate all Ranks, to one common Levell."[66] Although such arguments were usually self-serving, they also expressed a sense of reality, as **Howard Brown** argues in Volume II, Chapter 7: "Actually implementing democratic ideals meant dismantling existing structures of authority and risked unleashing less appealing impulses across all social strata. Too often, notions of liberty, equality, reason, and progress acted as bellows on the glowing coals of resentment and jealousy."

Pursuing their own agendas, peasants and urban plebeians nonetheless achieved many of their loftier goals. In France, **Noelle Plack** (Volume II, Chapter 3) notes, "for four years the peasantry rose in waves of protest and insurrection which ultimately forced legislators in Paris to abolish once and for all the feudal regime. These actions should not be underestimated as it has been argued that without them, peasants in France would most likely have been responsible for feudal dues until at least the middle of the nineteenth century." She adds that "[t]ax revolt, in the form of petition, riot, resistance, and noncompliance was far more prevalent in the French Revolution than many historians realize. Popular refusal to pay taxes was as important an aspect to bringing down the *ancien régime* as subsistence riots and attacks on seigneurial chateaux." The balance sheet looked different in Brazil, where the struggles of the popular classes ended in defeat. A dozen years into the construction of the new independent polity, the goal of most legislators was to obtain more local autonomy and an increased federalization of the provinces instead of more social participation in politics. The social structure was consequently left largely untouched, which set off riots

---

[65] See, for Buenos Aires, Gabriel di Meglio, "Un nuevo actor para un nuevo escenario. La participación política de la plebe urbana de Buenos Aires en la década de la revolución (1810–1820)," *Boletín del Instituto Argentina y Americana "Dr. Emilio Ravignani,"* 3rd series, 24 (2001), 7–43: 32–3.

[66] Cited in Joan Hoff, *Law, Gender, and Injustice: A Legal History of U.S. Women* (New York: New York University Press, 1991), 62.

and revolts of those whose demands did not find an expression on the parliamentary level.[67] Their defeat, however, writes **Hendrik Kraay** (Volume III, Chapter 20), does not mean "that these struggles were unimportant; rather, they were what made independence such an uncertain and contingent process and these years such a dynamic period in Brazilian history." **Gabriel Paquette** (Volume III, Chapter 16) adds that by contrast with preceding years, the decades after Brazilian independence "were characterized by tempestuous relations between the capital and the provinces, between urban and rural areas, between landed proprietors and their subalterns, between masters and slaves." At independence, "the destruction of the Old Regime was incomplete, perhaps not even yet under way."

Women

Women's contributions to revolutions and counterrevolutions have often gone unheralded. In France and Spanish America, more than a few examples have been found of women who actually took part in the armed struggles, sometimes disguised as men.[68] More frequently, their role was that of noncombatants, as **Ami Pflugrad-Jakisch** mentions in Volume I, Chapter 14. During the American Revolution, thousands of poor women "followed both the British and the continental armies as cooks, washerwomen, seamstresses, nurses, scavengers, and sexual partners." American women were also active on the political front, engaged in boycotts of British goods or in spinning bees, producing cloth to substitute for British manufactures. In numerous ways, women shared the plight of men. Loyalist women in South Carolina, for instance, were "verbally abused, imprisoned, and threatened with bodily harm even when they had not taken an active role in opposing the rebel cause." Those women who did help the British armies

---

[67] Andréa Slemian, "Os canais de representação política nos primórdios do Império: Apontamentos para um estudo da relação entre Estado e sociedade no Brasil (c. 1822–1834)," *Locus: Revista de história* 13:1 (2007), 34–51: 49–51.

[68] Claude Guillon, "Pauline Léon, une républicaine révolutionnaire," *Annales historiques de la Révolution française* 344 (2008), 147–59: 150–1; Christine Peyrard, *Les Jacobins de l'Ouest: Sociabilité révolutionnaire et formes de politisation dans le Maine et la Basse-Normandie (1789–1799)* (Paris: Publications de la Sorbonne, 1996), 231; Evelyn Cherpak, "The Participation of Women in the Independence Movement in Gran Colombia, 1780–1830," in Asunción Lavrin, ed., *Latin American Women* (Westport, CN: Greenwood Press, 1978), 219–34: 221–2; Alberto Baena Zapatero, "Las mujeres ante la independencia de México," in Izaskun Álvarez Cuartero and Julio Sánchez Gómez, eds., *Visiones e revisiones de la Independencia Americana: Subalternidad e independencias* (Salamanca: Ediciones Universidad de Salamanca, 2012), 115–35: 121.

also suffered physical abuse.[69] When their husbands fled, Loyalist women often stayed behind and, as one historian has argued, "seized this moment to exert a new form of independence. War shook up the existing social order and provided women with a brief moment to act independently of existing gender restrictions."[70]

Shortly after the French commissioners put a de facto end to slavery in Saint-Domingue, women in the southern part of the colony who benefited from emancipation contested the new labor regime under which they had to toil. Along with their male counterparts, the women protested the regulations that the same commissioners introduced in an attempt to keep the plantation economy afloat. On more than a few occasions, only women expressed their displeasure by refusing to work or working less than was expected from them.[71]

The small group of revolutionaries who championed women's rights in Europe, writes **Jennifer Ngaire Heuer** in Volume II, Chapter 10, "were often politically marginal, or only intermittently engaged with the issue," adding that Olympe de Gouges and Mary Wollstonecraft are probably better known today than they were in their own time. Gerrit Paape, a rare male activist for women's rights, still remains virtually unknown to this day. This prolific Dutch writer sketched the outlines of a Batavian Republic 200 years in the future, in which women were educated and had the same rights as men. Their inborn intelligence and their ingenuity were no longer "smothered in kitchen smoke." As Batavian citizens, they helped build a better world.[72]

In France, the revolution did entail a number of new rights for women, which Heuer sums up as follows: "Women acquired a decree of legal autonomy, were able to sign contracts and enter in justice in their own names, marry without parental authorization once they reached the age of majority, divorce their husbands, and inherit equally with their brothers." Women actively campaigned for equal rights within the family, presenting equality in petitions as a natural right. But they also invoked a moral

---

[69] Jim Piecuch, *Three Peoples, One King: Loyalists, Indians, and Slaves in the American Revolutionary South, 1775–1782* (Columbia, SC: University of South Carolina Press, 2008), 61.

[70] Kimberly Nath, "Left Behind: Loyalist Women in Philadelphia during the American Revolution," in Barbara B. Oberg, *Women in the American Revolution: Gender, Politics, and the Domestic World* (Charlottesville: University of Virginia Press, 2019), 211–28: 223.

[71] Judith Kafka, "Action, Reaction and Interaction: Slave Women in Resistance in the South of Saint Domingue, 1793–94," *Slavery and Abolition* 18:2 (1997), 48–72.

[72] Gerrit Paape, *De Bataafsche Republiek, zo als zij behoord te zijn, en zo als zij weezen kan: Of revolutionaire droom in 1798: Wegens toekomstige gebeurtenissen tot 1998* (Nijmegen: Vantilt, 1998 [1798]), 77–9.

language to question the traditional gender hierarchy in the family.[73] Bringing up changes in gender roles was still anathema around the Atlantic world. In the early American republic, both men and women saw women's discussion of their natural rights as dangerous because they feared that women would give up their domestic tasks.[74]

Politicians and intellectuals in the Iberian world took every effort to exclude women from public affairs. Those who thought otherwise were ignored. **Nuno Gonçalo Monteiro** (Volume III, Chapter 17) mentions that Portugal's parliament did not even vote on the proposal by one deputy to at least allow the mothers of six legitimate children to take part in elections. **Mónica Ricketts** contends in Volume III, Chapter 13 that in Spanish America "much like in France after the Revolution, women's participation in war and politics was seen as a sign of disorder and anarchy, for it was believed that their passions made them prone to corruption." If women were to remain aloof from politics, some politicians expressed their desire to see women educated. However, the goals of education did not differ from colonial days. Women were to be prepared for marriage, motherhood, and domestic skills.[75] One could argue that women in the Americas were not as a rule excluded from political rights due to sexual discrimination, but because, just like two other categories that were excluded – children and domestic servants – they belonged to the family as a political unit. As such, they were presumed to share the interests of the male members of their households.[76] In British North America, **Jessica Choppin Roney** explains (Volume I, Chapter 8), citizenship denoted the performance of duties for the benefit of the community, especially military protection. Since women were viewed as incapable of performing such duties, they could not be citizens and their "political personhood was subsumed under that of the male head of her household."

Economic Equality

If inequality of birth was a major target for revolutionaries, that cannot be said for inequality of property. **Lloyd Kramer** (Volume I, Chapter 20) cites

---

[73] Suzanne Desan, "'War between Brothers and Sisters': Inheritance Law and Gender Politics in Revolutionary France," *French Historical Studies* 20:4 (1997), 597–634: 624–6.
[74] Rosemarie Zagarri, "The Rights of Man and Woman in Post-Revolutionary America," *The William and Mary Quarterly* 55:2 (1998), 203–30: 217.
[75] Cherpak, "Participation of Women," 230.
[76] Anne Verjus, *Le cens de la famille: Les femmes et le vote, 1789–1848* (Paris: Bellin, 2002), 19–22.

the French Marquis de Chastellux, who became concerned during his travels in the early American republic about the political consequences of unequal wealth. He "identified a socioeconomic threat that could soon weaken or even destroy the institutional structures of republican equality." Although economic considerations were conspicuously absent from most political debates and writings in the age of revolutions, there was no lack of thinkers who proposed considerable economic reforms. In his *Agrarian Justice*, Thomas Paine cried out: "The present state of civilization is as odious as it is unjust ... [I]t is necessary that a revolution should be made in it. The contrast of affluence and wretchedness continually meeting and offending the eye, is like dead and living bodies chained together."[77] Charity, which had been the traditional response to poverty, would no longer do. The French revolutionaries made a serious effort to provide poor relief, as shown by fifty-six decrees enacted within just a year by the Legislative Assembly that targeted this issue.[78] Besides, the Convention adopted a maximum limit on the prices of a wide array of staples.

In *Du contrat social*, Rousseau had already warned of the dangers of economic inequality. "As for wealth," he wrote, "no citizen should be so rich that he can buy another, and none so poor that he is compelled to sell himself." When that happens, those who are less advantaged may be forced to follow the will of someone else rather than their own. In other words, dependence will lead to a loss of freedom.[79] The idea that equality must extend to the economic realm was articulated by a special deputy to the French National Assembly from a town in Auvergne: "In the division of benefits, poverty alone has rights, and wealth must be repulsed; legislators must remove all the means that can produce extreme wealth and extreme poverty. Equality must be the goal of all their institutions and all their laws, because from equality alone is born happiness, which is the purpose of all societies."[80] Why was it, one French author asked, that one person received more land than his fellow men? Since their needs are the same, why would enjoyment be different? Such a law can only derive from force. Another one

---

[77] Thomas Paine, *The Complete Writings of Thomas Paine*, ed. Philip S. Foner (New York: Citadel Press, 1969), vol. 1, 617.
[78] Alan Forrest, *The French Revolution and the Poor* (New York: St. Martin's Press, 1981), 23.
[79] Frederick Neuhouser, "Rousseau's Critique of Economic Inequality," *Philosophy & Public Affairs* 41:3 (2013), 193–225: 197.
[80] Margadant, *Urban Rivalries*, 164–5.

agreed. The common good had become a source of pillage.[81] Such sentiments were not limited to France. Around the same time, a schoolteacher in Delaware named Robert Coram stressed economic equality by arguing that God had given the earth in common to all and for the benefit of everybody. Each person was therefore born with the natural right to enough land to survive.[82]

The question was how to achieve such equality. The naïve idea, adhered to by some North American politicians, that equal opportunity was the panacea did not find support among small farmers and marginal artisans in the early American republic.[83] Was a leveling of property a good idea? Jacob Green, a Presbyterian minister and advocate of the American Revolution, welcomed an equality of estate and property, but believed it could not be expected. Georg Forster, the prominent German revolutionary, admired the American constitution, which, he wrote, allowed for only one aristocracy, namely that of wealth. That, however, could not be removed without implementing an impracticable Spartan community. The French militant politician Jacques-Nicolas Billaud-Varenne agreed that, especially in a large country, the "balance of fortunes" could not be just and immobile.[84] The French Jacobins nonetheless did consider imposing a limit on the accumulation of property in response to a demand by the *sans-culottes*, but failed to take that step when push came to shove.[85]

Some authors living in parts of Germany unaffected by revolutionary turmoil, where practical changes were out of the question, proposed radical solutions. Since every person had the same right to the earth's goods, private property had to be abolished, argued Carl Wilhelm Frölich. It militates

---

[81] Antoine de Cournand, *De la propriété, ou la cause du pauvre: Plaidée au tribunal de la raison, de la justice et de la vérité* (Paris, 1791), 5; Pierre Dolivier, *Essai sur la justice primitive, pour servir de principe générateur au seul ordre social qui peut assurer à l'homme tous ses droits et tous ses moyens de bonheur* (Paris, 1793), 15.

[82] Seth Cotlar, "Radical Conceptions of Property Rights and Economic Equality in the Early American Republic: The Trans-Atlantic Dimension," *Explorations in Early American Culture* 4 (2000), 191–219: 193.

[83] Ruth Bogin, "Petitioning and the New Moral Economy of Post-Revolutionary America," *The William and Mary Quarterly* 45:3 (1988), 391–425: 392.

[84] S. Scott Rohrer, *Jacob Green's Revolution: Radical Religion and Reform in a Revolutionary Age* (University Park: Pennsylvania State University Press, 2014), 203. Georg Forster to Therese Forster, Arras, 21 August 1793, in Klaus-Georg Popp, ed., *Georg Forsters Werke: Sämtliche Schriften, Tagebücher, Briefe: Briefe 1792 bis 1794 und Nachträge* (Berlin: Akademie-Verlag, 1989), 425. Citoyen Billaud-Varenne, *Les élémens du républicanisme: Première partie* (Paris, 1793), 57.

[85] Massimiliano Tomba, "1793: The Neglected Legacy of Insurgent Universality," *History of the Present: A Journal of Critical History* 5:2 (2015), 109–36: 120.

against the fulfillment of the needs of everyone. For his part, the philanthropist Heinrich Ziegenhagen proposed the organization of small-scale agricultural colonies based on communal property in which children of the poor and the rich would be raised together to become sociable beings.[86] These plans had in common with contemporary radical French proposals that they did not reflect the rapidly changing economies of western Europe. Far from taking into account the reality of industrialization, they revered subsistence agriculture and idealized peasant simplicity.[87] If these were lone voices, a popular belief in genuine economic equality did take root in Italy. Various authors took up their pens to address the population and convince them that their ideas were mistaken and that they had to content themselves with equality before the law. Economic differences were the logical consequence of differences in natural abilities.[88]

Nor were the rural dwellers insisting on economic change in New York and Virginia looking for equalization of property. Confronted with unfair taxes and economic constraints, they simply tried to end their status as tenants and become part of a reformed society based on landownership. Revolutionary elites did not meet such demands but they made land available in the western parts of their states, thereby easing tensions.[89] In the Río de la Plata, José Artigas organized an agrarian reform, as **Gabriel di Meglio** writes (Volume III, Chapter 9). He distributed vast rural properties from the enemies of the revolution among free blacks, free *zambos*, Indians, and poor creoles. The independence war in northern Spanish America had no comparable outcome. Simón Bolívar's land policy was more concerned with preserving the support of the *caudillos* – the warlords who controlled regional supplies and soldiers – than with offering hope to the rural poor. The caudillos could thus form a new landowning elite who benefited from confiscated property and public land.[90]

---

[86] Helmut Reinalter, *Die Französische Revolution und Mitteleuropa: Erscheinungsformen und Wirkungen des Jakobinismus. Seine Gesellschaftstheorien und politischen Vorstellungen* (Frankfurt am Main: Suhrkamp, 1988), 126–8.

[87] R. B. Rose, "The 'Red Scare' of the 1790s: The French Revolution and the 'Agrarian Law,'" *Past & Present* no. 103 (1984), 113–30: 125. Inside and outside France, these values retained their strength into the nineteenth century. Cf. Giorgio La Rosa, "La représentation dans la pensée politique d'un jacobin italien. Luigi Angeloni (1759–1842)," in *Le concept de représentation dans la pensée politique* (Aix-en-Provence: Presses universitaires d'Aix-Marseille, 2003), 313–20.

[88] Guerci, *Mente, cuore, coraggio, virtù repubblicane*, 131–9.

[89] Thomas J. Humphrey, "Conflicting Independence: Land Tenancy and the American Revolution," *Journal of the Early Republic* 28:2 (2008), 159–82: 174, 182.

[90] John Lynch, "Bolívar and the Caudillos," *Hispanic American Historical Review* 63:1 (1983), 3–35: 25.

Introduction

If equalizing property may have ultimately been unachievable anywhere, the French Revolution did accomplish a comprehensive transformation of property. In Volume II, Chapter 2, **Rafe Blaufarb** explains what the famous abolition of feudalism entailed. In 1789–1790, the French revolutionaries did away with the old system of property and replaced it with an entirely new one. "Feudalism," Blaufarb writes, was "not a special form of property-holding specific to the nobility, but rather *the system* of real estate itself, a system whose essence was to produce a hierarchy of multiple claims to single parcels of land." By blurring public power and private property, feudalism blocked the establishment of national sovereignty. Feudalism was replaced by the national domain, which became the repository of confiscated ecclesiastical properties and properties that had belonged to the royal domain. The sale of these *biens nationaux* was a long, drawn-out process that benefited numerous groups in French society, including, as **Philippe Bourdin** mentions in Volume II, Chapter 9, "the *petite bourgeoisie* (innkeepers, butchers, and merchants, whose numbers were increasing), the stockjobbers who sometimes acted as intermediaries for families of the old nobility, and the state creditors." However, a law of 1796 that forbade the sale of *biens nationaux* in small lots shut the door to the small and medium-sized peasantry, which had fervently hoped to acquire more land since the start of the revolution.[91]

Violence

Revolutions are not straightforward affairs. The search for freedom never leads directly to emancipation, but brings about a crisis in which the revolutionaries are presented with different solutions.[92] The initial claims to autonomy in Spanish America following the king's resignation in Bayonne, writes **Stefan Rinke** (Volume III, Chapter 1), "were not hard revolutionary ruptures, but rather events in which the elites cautiously groped their way into unknown territory and gradually expanded their own ideas and demands." Independence was not yet on the horizon. Revolutions could gain momentum when many plebeians suddenly stopped resigning themselves to the old hierarchical civic order and became aware of the potential power of the joint

---

[91] Bernard Bodinier and Éric Teyssier, *L'événement le plus important de la Révolution: La vente des biens nationaux (1789–1867) en France et dans les territoires annexés* (Paris: Société des Études Robespierristes, 2000), 383–98.

[92] Federica Morelli, "Guerras, libertad y ciudadanía. Los afro-descendientes de Esmeraldas en la independencia," *Revista de Indias* 76 (2016), 83–108: 84.

efforts of like-minded people. That was a nightmare scenario for the champions of the status quo. When the Haitian revolution broke out, one planter believed his class might need to kill half of the enslaved workforce to stop the "epidemic" and replace those killed with new imports from Africa.[93]

While polarization was deadly in Saint-Domingue, the middle ground was also lost sooner or later in other revolutionary theaters. In Mexico, any reluctance to support one side was seen as a sign of sympathy for the other.[94] Similarly, Patriot authorities in North America summoned, secured, or confined anyone suspected of being "unfriendly to the rights of America."[95] After the end of the revolutionary war, John Jay explained to Peter Van Schaack that the latter had been mistaken to try to maintain his neutrality: "No man can serve two masters: either Britain was right and America was wrong; or America was right and Britain was wrong. They who thought Britain right were bound to support her; and America had a just claim to the services of those who approved her cause. Hence it became our duty to take one side or the other."[96] **Liam Riordan** (Volume I, Chapter 13) cites Massachusetts Governor Thomas Hutchinson, who wrote in 1776 that "under the present free government in America, no man may, by writing or speaking, contradict any part of this Declaration, without being deemed an enemy to his country, and exposed to the rage and fury of the populace."

One of the features of the revolutions was the amount of violence that accompanied them. In Ireland, **Thomas Bartlett** writes (Volume II, Chapter 16), "the extreme violence witnessed during the 1798 rebellion, and during the run-up to it, bears comparison to that perpetrated in the Vendée, and later in Spain during the Peninsular War. As in these theaters, irregular combatants were simply not recognized as legitimate fighters and therefore the normal ethical constraints on soldiers' conduct could be ignored." In Mexico, another historian has suggested, the rebellion created "a political space for the emergence of violent men of little principle and

---

[93] Philippe Girard, *Toussaint Louverture: A Revolutionary Life* (New York: Basic Books, 2016), 125.

[94] Timo Schaefer, "Soldiers and Civilians: The War of Independence in Oaxaca, 1814–1815," *Mexican Studies/Estudios Mexicanos*, 29:1 (2013), 149–74: 168. As exemplary punishment, at least in Oaxaca, both sides also tended to set fire to villages. Ibid., 172.

[95] Christopher F. Minty, "'Of One Hart and One Mind': Local Institutions and Allegiance during the American Revolution," *Early American Studies: An Interdisciplinary Journal* 15:1 (2017), 99–132: 115.

[96] T. H. Breen, *The Will of the People: The Revolutionary Birth of America* (Cambridge, MA: The Belknap Press of Harvard University Press, 2019), 146.

large ambition."[97] During Hidalgo's revolt and the following counterinsurgency, thousands of people were executed. **Juan Ortiz Escamilla** writes in Volume III, Chapter 5 that the military dictatorship set up by the royalists in Mexico, which lasted six years, "was a period characterized by assassinations, plundering, arbitrary executions, exemplary punishments, the burning of villages, and the raping of women." In other parts of Spanish America, the death toll was initially relatively small, but as **Ernesto Bassi** tells us (Volume III, Chapter 8), northern South America was where the low-intensity confrontation first mutated into violent warfare under the banner of "war to the death." Bassi adds that in the same region, the Spanish recapture of most of South America was launched and took its most violent form. Chile and Upper Peru also registered a large mortality. A census held in La Paz in 1824 after hostilities had ceased revealed a very small number of men between ages fifteen and twenty-five.[98] Even by then, the end to violence was not in sight in Spanish America. **Juan Luis Ossa Santa Cruz** argues in Volume III, Chapter 7 that "the following decades witnessed countless armed conflicts, transforming violence into a daily and legitimate political practice that, with ups and downs, lasted for the rest of the century."

Was the French Revolution notoriously violent or has the violence unleashed in France been exaggerated? **Marisa Linton** writes (Volume II, Chapter 8): "The received opinion is that the French Revolution was unique in its time in its recourse to political violence. Yet comparisons with the death toll in the English Civil Wars (that stretched throughout the British Isles) and 'revolutions' of the seventeenth century, with the American Revolution, and with the suppression of the revolt in Ireland in 1798, suggest that it would be more accurate to see revolutionary violence in the context of wider factors such as fear, repression, and the degree of retaliation, rather than as the consequence of a specific ideology unique to the French Revolution." Revolutionary Saint-Domingue offers another example of widespread violence, and certainly not only on the part of enslaved insurgents. White residents, as **Bernard Gainot** shows (Volume II, Chapter 24), engaged in lynching and mutiny. These so-called "patriots" were driven by a violent rejection of equal rights.

---

[97] Eric Van Young, *The Other Rebellion: Popular Violence, Ideology, and the Mexican Struggle for Independence, 1810–1821* (Stanford: Stanford University Press, 2001), 196.

[98] Karen Racine, "Death, Destiny, and the Daily Chores: Everyday Life in Spanish America during the Wars of Independence, 1808–1826," in Pedro Santoni, ed., *Civilians in Wartime Latin America: From the Wars of Independence to the Central American Civil Wars* (Westport, CN: Greenwood Press, 2008), 31–53: 36.

The American Revolution was indeed remarkably violent as well. The British Army left in its wake landscapes that were so affected that it seemed they had been hit by a tornado or earthquake. "Rape," writes one historian, "was endemic within the British Army."[99] Areas that could not be held by either side were pillaged relentlessly, such as, for example, Westchester County, just north of New York: "From 1775 through 1782, the county became a no man's land whose four thousand families enjoyed neither personal security nor freedom from plunder. Contending armies, militias, and partisan bands took farm surpluses and left families with too little to last through winter. They raided friend and foe alike to pilfer personal property, steal livestock, burn barns and houses, and cut trees and fences for firewood. Soldiers and criminal gangs looted what armies and militias left behind."[100] Violence was also of central importance on the Patriot side, studied by **Wayne Lee** in Volume 1, Chapter 12. He notes that "the American revolution and the accompanying war included a wide set of categories of political violence, all of which occurred within the same overall clash of wills." And in most cases, those categories were also *stages*. Lee distinguishes between violence that was "intimidative and catalytic," "regular and logistical," and "retaliatory."

Violence was not the monopoly of warring armies. In revolutionary Pennsylvania, acts of violence were often committed by those frustrated about the lack of decisive action on the part of politicians whose rhetoric they shared. Such violence required the revolutionary elites to take the rebels' grievances seriously.[101] The peasant revolts across early revolutionary France were part of a similar dynamics with massive consequences, since they helped bring about the end of "feudalism." In France, violence away from the battlefield continued in the years to come. Howard Brown has explained that "the Revolution not only destroyed the institutional constraints on popular violence, it eroded many of the cultural ones as well. This included the diminished role of the clergy in community life, the decline in deference accorded social status, the disruption in patronage patterns, and the reduced primacy of the local community."[102] There was a transatlantic continuity in

---

[99] Hoock, *Scars of Independence: America's Violent Birth*, 131, 170 (quote).
[100] Allan Kulikoff, "Revolutionary Violence and the Origins of American Democracy," *The Journal of the Historical Society* II:2 (Spring 2002), 229–60: 236.
[101] Kenneth Owen, "Violence and the Limits of the Political Community in Revolutionary Pennsylvania," in Patrick Griffin, Robert G. Ingram, Peter S. Onuf, and Brian Schoen, eds., *Between Sovereignty and Anarchy* (Charlottesville: University of Virginia Press, 2015), 165–86: 180–1.
[102] Howard G. Brown, *Ending the French Revolution: Violence, Justice, and Repression from the Terror to Napoleon* (Charlottesville: University of Virginia Press, 2006), 50.

French violence, as one historian has argued. It was no coincidence that the French campaign in Saint-Domingue of 1802–1803 resembled that in the Vendée in its goal to exterminate the enemy. Contemporaries already referred to the "colonial Vendée" as they laid (at least partial) blame for both on the British enemy. As if to confirm this connection, the Directory appointed as its agent in Saint-Domingue one of the generals who had "pacified" the Vendée.[103]

Royalism

The Vendée's opposition to the revolution was symbolized from the start by white cockades worn in public, which gave expression to the rebels' adherence to royalism. Yet royalism did not necessarily denote a progressive or conservative ideology. Neither the revolutionaries in the Americas nor those in France started out as republicans. Only when King George did not live up to the expectation of orators and writers to reclaim the royal privileges that his predecessors had lost did a republican solution become a possibility in North America. It was at that juncture that Thomas Paine's *Common Sense* came out, condemning the "royal brute of Britain."[104] Monarchist members of the French Assembly favored the revolution, but more as a set of early achievements than as a seemingly endless movement. They hoped to entrust the king with sovereign powers, assisted by a bicameral parliament that would provide counsel. After this constitutional project was rejected, they tried to maintain a centrist position between revolution and counterrevolution.[105] **Caroline Winterer** (Volume I, Chapter 1) stresses that during their revolution, North Americans were impressed by Europe's enlightened despots, who mixed monarchical rule with Enlightenment. And **Matthew Rainbow Hale** (Volume II, Chapter 5) notes that there was an intimate relationship between monarchy and democracy that proved to be resilient. What exerted a particularly powerful force in the 1790s on both sides of the North Atlantic was the allure, derived from monarchies, of indivisible sovereignty.

---

[103] Malick Ghachem, "The Colonial Vendée," in David Patrick Geggus and Norman Fiering, eds., *The World of the Haitian Revolution* (Bloomington: Indiana University Press, 2009), 156–76.

[104] Eric Nelson, *The Royalist Revolution: Monarchy and the American Founding* (Cambridge, MA: The Belknap Press of Harvard University Press, 2014), 33, 57–8, 63.

[105] Pascal Simonetti, "Les monarchiens. La Révolution à contretemps," in Jean Tulard, ed., *La contre-révolution: Origines, histoire, postérité* (Paris: Perrin, 1990), 62–84.

Nor were the political elites of Spanish America who assumed sovereignty after the forced abdication of Fernando VII in Bayonne natural republicans. Their intention was not to repudiate the monarchy, but to redefine it in a constitutional framework that was dictated locally and not in Cádiz. Before they embarked on independentist projects, the elites aimed to consolidate governmental rule and maintain the basic laws in a Hispanic structure.[106] Individuals and groups across the Atlantic world, then, continued to display allegiance to their hereditary rulers, from whom they sought protection and the concession of privileges.[107] Slaves in New Granada often understood the republican fight for independence as an attempt of their owners to limit the authority of the king. At the same time, they tried to have their defense of the king's power expressed in the form of individual or collective advantages.[108] Many enslaved freedom fighters in Saint-Domingue also supported a distant European king, carrying royalist banners and proclaiming that they wanted to restore Louis XVI to his throne after they had heard about his arrest.[109] Other rebels sided with Spain, in part because, as **Robert D. Taber** writes in Volume II, Chapter 22, "Spain also offered a king, a potent symbol of good government." Monarchism survived the revolution in Saint-Domingue and was alive and well in independent Haiti. Dessalines was crowned Emperor Jean-Jacques I, while Henry Christophe later led the kingdom of Haiti as King Henry I. And even the republic that Alexandre Pétion established, in which universal male suffrage was introduced, was "an oligarchy with a democratic veneer," writes **Erin Zavitz** (Volume II, Chapter 26).

In Latin America, too, monarchism remained a viable option after independence. One reason, as **Gabriel di Meglio** contends in Volume III, Chapter 9, was the Congress of Vienna's condemnation of governments created by revolution. That influenced the debate in Buenos Aires about postrevolutionary rule, in which some fancied a constitutional king, who could maintain order and put an end to local turmoil. In Brazil, the outcome of the independence process was an imperial state. Besides, writes **Jurandir**

---

[106] José M. Portillo Valdés, *Crisis atlántica: Autonomía e independencia en la crisis de la monarquía hispana* (Madrid: Fundación Carolina, Marcial Pons, 2006), 147–53.

[107] Hannah Weiss Muller, "Bonds of Belonging: Subjecthood and the British Empire," *Journal of British Studies* 53:1 (2014), 29–58: 57–8.

[108] Marcela Echeverri, *Indian and Slave Royalists in the Age of Revolution: Reform, Revolution, and Royalism in the Northern Andes, 1780–1825* (New York: Cambridge University Press, 2017), 60.

[109] Jeremy D. Popkin, *You Are All Free: The Haitian Revolution and the Abolition of Slavery* (New York: Cambridge University Press, 2010), 94, 104, 129–30.

Introduction

Malerba in Volume III, Chapter 18, regent prince Dom João, who had moved the Portuguese court to Rio de Janeiro, played an important role in the independence process: "willingly or not, by coopting the Brazilian upper classes through his patriarchal and enticing policy, the sovereign helped decisively define the profile of the new elite that was formed in Brazil during the thirteen years he spent in Rio de Janeiro." When the unpopular first emperor, Dom Pedro, suddenly abdicated in 1831, a fresh opportunity was presented to radical leaders of the liberal opposition, writes **Jeffrey Needell** in Volume III, Chapter 19. The parliamentary leadership, however, "interwoven with the families and interests of the elite," balked. Instead, they chose, again, to support the vision of a constitutional monarchy that they had been trying to force upon Dom Pedro since 1823. Faced with radical republicanism, with its associated, clear threat of socioeconomic and national destabilization, they chose, again, the hope of constitutional, balanced partnership with a "unifying, charismatic national leader." Dom Pedro II thus started his reign as the new emperor.

Monarchical leadership also marked the start of Mexican independence. Cultivating close ties with the local elites, Agustín de Iturbide worked out the Plan of Iguala, which declared "the absolute independence of this kingdom," but also extended an invitation to Fernando VII or one of his family members to govern New Spain.[110] After the Spanish government declined, Iturbide assumed command and, supported by the Mexican elite, was enthroned as Emperor Agustín I. José de San Martín also strongly favored organizing independent states as monarchies, while even the committed republican Simón Bolívar had begun to flirt with monarchism by 1825. A British diplomat quoted him as saying in a private conversation: "Of all Countries South America is perhaps the least fitted for Republican Governments. What does its population consist of but Indians and Negros who are more ignorant than the vile race of Spaniards we are just emancipated from. A country represented and governed by such people must go to ruin." It would, however, take a while, he believed, for the inhabitants of the former Spanish colonies to embrace the notion of a new king.[111] Bolívar was not the only one during his presidency of Colombia to advocate a constitutional monarchy. A French agent wrote that the clergy, the army, and the common

---

[110] Jaime E. Rodríguez O., *"We Are Now the True Spaniards": Sovereignty, Revolution, Independence, and the Emergence of the Federal Republic of Mexico, 1808–1824* (Stanford: Stanford University Press, 2012), 253–63.

[111] Harold Temperley, *The Foreign Policy of Canning 1822–1827: England, the Neo-Holy Alliance, and the New World*, 2nd edition (London: Frank Cass & Co., 1966), 557–8.

people all favored that option. Some wanted Bolívar himself to be crowned, while others debated his possible succession, if he died, by a foreign prince.[112]

On the whole, royalists belonged to the counterrevolutionary camp, those desirous to maintain the status quo or pursue their goals without overthrowing the government. In Central America, people across the social spectrum steadfastly clung to Spain during the 1810s, when in all other parts of Spanish America people began to aspire to independence. **Timothy Hawkins** (Volume III, Chapter 6) notes that this was "despite exposure to the widespread political ideas of this revolutionary age and the kind of persistent internal grievances that united to spark and fuel independence movements in other colonies. Combined with a colonial administration single-minded in its dedication to root out dissent, this broad consensus helped marginalize and suffocate the few substantive challenges to the colonial order that did arise during this decade." More generally, writes **Marcela Echeverri** in Volume III, Chapter 10, "even within a position of loyalty, all subjects in the Atlantic empires embraced and produced radical lasting change."

In British America, royalists did not automatically adopt certain views. The only matter on which Loyalists agreed was the need to defend royal rule.[113] Royalist disunion in Spain during that country's constitutional triennium (1820–1823) even led to confrontations between different royalist factions, as **Juan Luis Simal** tells us in Volume III, Chapter 4. The constitutional monarchy was challenged by ultraroyalists, who engaged in guerrilla activities with the support of a rural population that resented taxes, conscription, and recent socioeconomic changes.

Loyalists in North America included members of ethnic and religious minorities who perceived the Crown as "a buffer against the tyranny of the majority."[114] Likewise, Indians in Spanish and Portuguese America sought to uphold the time-honored colonial pact, on account of which they paid royal tribute, and thus contributed to Crown income, in exchange for assuring themselves of the possession of their lands and the preservation of their way

---

[112] C. Parra-Pérez, *La monarquía en la Gran Colombia* (Madrid: Ediciones Cultura Hispánica, 1957), 95, 105, 129, 323.

[113] Maya Jasanoff, *Liberty's Exiles: American Loyalists in the Revolutionary World* (New York: Vintage Books, 2012), 189.

[114] David J. Fowler, "'Loyalty Is Now Bleeding in New Jersey': Motivations and Mentalities of the Disaffected," in Joseph S. Tiedemann, Eugene R. Fingerhut, and Robert W. Venables, eds., *The Other Loyalists: Ordinary People, Royalism, and the Revolution in the Middle Colonies, 1763–1787* (Albany: State University of New York Press, 2009), 45–77: 50.

of organizing their community.¹¹⁵ Indian tributaries in the Spanish colonies had different demands than their caciques, who were exempt from tribute payments, and enjoyed the privilege to ride horseback and use arms. One feature of Túpac Amaru's revolt in Peru was the rift in many communities between caciques, who remained loyal to the Spanish Crown, and their tributaries, who supported the uprising.¹¹⁶ The end of the colonial pact could be devastating. In Argentina, **Gabriel di Meglio** explains in Volume III, Chapter 9, "the end of tribute and juridical inequality meant that those villages no longer had rights to their common land, which they had used to pay the tribute, nor to maintain their ethnic leaders, who were in charge of the tribute. Thus, many villages lost their lands, which were sold out." Even the term "Indian" was being erased. The liberal Mexican politician José María Luis Mora proposed to the Congress of his country to do away with that term, since "the Indians should not continue existing" as a social group subject to special legislation. Nonetheless, the term was used throughout the 1820s, although at times the indigenous population was labeled "the so-called Indians."¹¹⁷

To the degree that the age of revolutions challenged royal authority, contemporary movements in Africa have been described by some historians as parallel. John Thornton has advanced the argument that Kongo's political system contained an absolutist concept that bestowed all power on the king. In the eighteenth century, absolutism was challenged by a movement (mislabeled "republican" by Thornton) that stressed the need for popular consent to royal rule.¹¹⁸ Even more forcefully, Paul Lovejoy has made a case for the great significance of jihad in west Africa, especially in the central Bilād al-

---

[115] María Luisa Soux, "Rebelión, guerrilla y tributo: Los indios en Charcas durante el proceso de independencia," *Anuario de Estudios Americanos* 68:2 (2011), 455–82: 458; Mariana Albuquerque Dantas, "Os indios 'fanáticos realistas absolutos' e a figura do monarca português: Disputas políticas, recrutamento e defesa de terras na Confederação do Equador," *Clio* 33:2 (2015), 49–73: 50, 56.

[116] Alexandra Sevilla Naranjo, "'Al mejor servicio del rey.' Indígenas realistas en la contrarrevolución quiteña, 1809–1814," *Procesos. Revista ecuatoriana de historia* no. 43 (2016), 93–118: 111; David T. Garrett, "'His Majesty's Most Loyal Vassals': The Indian Nobility and Túpac Amaru," *Hispanic American Historical Review* 84:4 (2004), 575–617: 597. Caciques in New Spain did not collect tribute, nor did they enjoy the same social standing as their counterparts in the viceroyalty of Peru: Aaron Pollack, "Hacia una historia social del tributo de indios y castas en Hispanoamérica. Notas en torno a su creación, desarrollo y abolición," *Historia Mexicana* 66:1 (2016), 65–160: 71.

[117] Laura Ibarra García, "El concepto de igualdad en México (1810–1824)," *Relaciones* 145 (2016), 279–314: 306.

[118] John K. Thornton, "'I Am the Subject of the King of Congo': African Political Ideology and the Haitian Revolution," *Journal of World History* 4:2 (1993), 181–214: 187.

Sūdān (south of the Sahara) between 1804–1808 and 1817. In response to the despotic rule of warlords, Islamic governments "based on religious leadership and consensus among Muslim officials" were established. How revolutionary west African jihad actually was remains to be seen. What is clear is that the universalist strain of the revolutions in Europe and the Americas was absent. Debates about slavery focused on the illegitimacy of enslaving Muslims, while ending slavery for non-Muslims never came up.[119] In other words, Islamic west Africans had arrived at the point that Christian Europeans had reached in the late Middle Ages, when they ended slavery, but only among their own.

Counterrevolution and Banditry

Ideologies that challenged the revolutions were not exhausted by royalism. Revolts that were directed against revolutions, such as that in the Vendée, had in common their communal character; rural dominance; the importance of religious sentiments; their spontaneous nature; and the opposition to the politics of progress defended by the state that jeopardized the beliefs, structures, and functioning of traditional rural societies.[120] Across Europe and even in Spanish America, the fear of French influence and its ability to dramatically change traditional societies was enormous. Typical is the judgment of the Spanish Inquisition in late 1789 when it forbade the printing of materials that referred to the events in France: these works were produced by a new race of philosophers, who were men with a corrupted spirit. By posing as defenders of liberty, they actually plotted against it and destroyed the political and social order.[121] Spain's Secretary of State, the count of Floridablanca, did all he could stop the flow of information arriving from France. In Volume III, Chapter 2, **Emily Berquist Soule** writes that he "placed more Spanish troops on the border with France in order to deter unsanctioned crossings of people and goods. He implemented a policy of strict censorship designed to keep out all news of the events in France;

---

[119] Paul E. Lovejoy, *Jihād in West Africa during the Age of Revolutions* (Athens, OH: Ohio University Press, 2016), 90, 245–6.
[120] Jean-Pierre Poussou, "Les autres 'Vendées,' jalons pour une thématique des 'Vendées,'" in Yves-Marie Bercé, ed., *Les autres Vendées: Actes du colloque international sur les contre-révolutions paysannes au XIXe siècle* (La Roche-sur-Yon: Éditions du Centre vendéen de recherches historiques, 2013), 299, 304.
[121] Gonzalo Añes Álvarez de Castrillón, "España y la Revolución francesa," in Almudena Cavestany, ed., *Revolución, contrarrevolución e Independencia: La Revolución francesa, España y América* (Madrid: Turner Publicaciones, 1989), 17–39: 20.

forbidding French newspapers, and even employing Inquisition officials to inspect mail coming across the Pyrenees."

British American Loyalists, writes **Trevor Burnard** (Volume I, Chapter 9), "especially those of higher social status, feared that the wild ideas of liberty thrown about by revolutionaries would have a leveling tendency and by promoting lawless anarchy" were harming the empire. Anarchy was projected onto the new republican regimes because of their commitment to democracy. Revolutionaries tended to believe that only republics, ruled as they were by laws and not the royal will, could resist the tendency of men to pursue only their own, personal interest.[122] Counterrevolutionaries rejected the way in which these laws took effect. The large mass of people, asserted a priest from Guayaquil in the viceroyalty of Peru, cannot judge for themselves their own interests unless they put themselves in the hands of a single individual. A Dutch thinker who supported the antirevolutionary Orangists wrote in the same vein that the "people" was incapable of acting by itself. Since they were dependent on a few among them, democracy was in practice always a struggle between various groups of demagogues.[123] The quest of revolutionaries to erect a new society was chimerical in the eyes of their opponents, who rejected the fictitious state of nature. The natural, transcendent order established by God could not be changed.[124]

While prominent rebels and conservatives created the script for each revolution, the vast mass of people involved in the revolutions were motivated by their own individual or group goals, as the abovementioned motives of peasants, slaves, and Indians make clear. In northern South America, **Ernesto Bassi** argues in Volume III, Chapter 8, "support from the *pardos* [the light-skinned free people of color] was highly contingent and depended on the fact that they tended to see political independence or continued allegiance to Spain not as an end in itself but as a means to achieving a more

---

[122] Anthony Pagden, *Spanish Imperialism and the Political Imagination: Studies in European and Spanish-American Social and Political Theory 1513–1830* (New Haven: Yale University Press, 1990), 136.

[123] Victor Samuel Rivera, "José Ignacio Moreno. Un teólogo peruano. Entre Montesquieu y Joseph de Maistre," *Araucaria. Revista Iberoamericana de Filosofía, Política y Humanidades* 15:29 (2013), 223–41: 238. Wyger R. E. Velema, "Elie Luzac and Two Dutch Revolutions: The Evolution of Orangist Political Thought," in Margaret C. Jacob and Wijnand W. Mijnhardt, eds., *The Dutch Republic in the Eighteenth Century: Decline, Enlightenment, and Revolution* (Ithaca, NY: Cornell University Press, 1992), 123–46: 138.

[124] Serge Bianchi, *Des révoltes aux révolutions: Europe, Russie, Amérique (1770–1802). Essai d'interprétation* (Rennes: Presses universitaires de Rennes, 2004), 447.

important aim: legal equality. The same assertion is valid for slaves, although in their case the goal was to secure freedom."

Principle often combined with opportunism to persuade people to join or oppose the revolution. **Liam Riordan** writes in Volume 1, Chapter 13: "The complex web of circumstance and opportunity that informs allegiance in times of uncertain change and military mobilization is necessarily shaped by perceptions of self-interest." In Mexico, Hidalgo's rebellion "encouraged certain marginalized and semi-marginalized Mexicans to employ violence in order to adjust deeply held grievances against the regime, provincial administrators, and members of the propertied classes who had long enjoyed the benefits of power, and it presented to many others an opportunity to get rich-quick, or at least to stake out for themselves a place in any new society."[125] These men engaged in guerrilla warfare, as **Juan Ortiz Escamilla** explains. Violent raids on towns and habitual looting of haciendas were their trademarks. Their leaders, often locally born, saw to the distribution of booty and captured livestock among their supporters. Italy's bandits engaged in robbery and armed revolt as a form of revenge against a society that had marginalized them. They found common cause in attacking the privileged classes, fighting government bureaucracy, as well as the French invaders. Those invaders' insults of personal or family honor convinced many a peasant to take up arms.[126] Besides, peer pressure and a search for adventure must have played a role as well.[127]

The distinction between rebellion/counterrebellion and banditry was often blurred, either because ordinary bandits sided with the royalists or the patriots, or – particularly in countries in which Napoleon's armies lived off the land and introduced mass conscription – because banditry doubled as resistance, but also because guerrillas on both sides often engaged in crimes that had no political dimension. At the same time, authorities were eager to label counterrevolutionary attacks as brigandage since that served to discredit the enemy's political demands. In France, the term "brigand," which had initially both caused aversion and won admiration among the members of the National Assembly, was increasingly defined negatively in the course of the Revolution, especially after the start of the war in the Vendée. In their

---

[125] Christon I. Archer, "Banditry and Revolution in New Spain, 1790–1821," *Bibliotheca Americana* 1:2 (1982), 58–89: 59, 88.

[126] Massimo Viglione, *Le insorgenze: Rivoluzione & Controrivoluzione in Italia, 1792–1815* (Milan: Edizioni Ares, 1999), 96–7; Michael Broers, *Napoleon's Other War: Bandits, Rebels, and Their Pursuers in the Age of Revolutions* (Oxford: Peter Lang, 2010), 110.

[127] Van Young, *The Other Rebellion*, 105–6.

subsequent fight against insurgents in countries occupied by France, lawyers and gendarmes ceased to distinguish between bandits and guerrilla fighters.[128]

Bandits – with or without a political agenda – used the breakdown of law and order that was the result of revolution. Chilean banditry, for example, was encouraged by the anarchy of the civil war between republicans and royalists, as many poor people were displaced or otherwise affected.[129] In northern South America, the disruption of the colonial state and colonial institutions opened the door to the caudillos, military leaders who drew to them the *llaneros*. These plainsmen lived by plunder and lacked any political objectives. They followed "the first caudillo who offers them booty taken from anyone with property. This is how Boves and other bandits of the same kind have been able to recruit hordes of these people, who live by vagrancy, robbery, and assassination."[130] Such bandits may have been able to fill the political vacuum left by the disappearance of the old government, but in turn they prevented a new civilian government from taking hold. The Thirteen Colonies in North America fell prey to banditry – which included the stealing of slaves – that was hardly political in nature. As historian Holger Hoock observes, by 1780, "large swaths of the American lower South presented a scary scene – a virtually permanent little war of raiding and plundering between Patriot and Loyalist militias, prisoner abuse, even outright murder. In addition, armed gangs unaffiliated with any real military units operated in the semi-lawless wasteland between the lines."[131] Many of the smaller bands "operated independently, though often in the guise of serving one side or the other."[132] Nor can the Maroons who refused to remain on their plantations during the Haitian Revolution and retreated into the interior be categorized as counterrevolutionaries. As **Philippe Girard** writes (Volume II, Chapter 25), the Maroons distrusted all elite actions vying for control of Saint-Domingue, opposing "whichever side was dominant to preserve their freedom and autonomy."

---

[128] Sottocasa, *Les brigands et la Révolution*, 60, 146, 289; Broers, *Napoleon's Other War*, 55, 102–3.

[129] Leonardo León, "Montoneras Populares durante la gestación de la República, Chile: 1810–1820," *Anuario de Estudios Americanos* 68:2 (2011), 483–510: 487–8, 492.

[130] John Lynch, "Bolívar and the Caudillos," *Hispanic American Historical Review* 63:1 (1983), 3–35: 5.

[131] Hoock, *Scars of Independence*, 309.

[132] Matthew P. Spooner, "Origins of the Old South: Revolution, Slavery, and Changes in Southern Society, 1776–1800" (Ph.D. dissertation, Columbia University, 2015), 62.

Ideology, then, was just one of many factors motivating individuals. On both sides of the American Revolution, desertion was rampant. One historian has written, "A steady stream of Loyalists deserted, as they were converted to the American cause, discouraged because of limitations placed on looting, disheartened by the ever-lengthening conflict, enticed by the colonial lifestyle, or simply out of boredom." Patriots also deserted, "many of them for the same reasons as the Loyalists, because of uncertainty of the rightness of their cause, because the changing seasons meant they were needed for work on their farms, or because the war was not the adventure or sure meal ticket they had thought it would be."[133] If many men changed their minds, others avoided choosing sides as long as possible. Their lack of affiliation did not mean indifference. Instead, their personal or group goals might or might not align with the two main adversaries. Tenants in the northern Hudson Valley whose goal was to own the land on which they worked put off a choice for either side in the war until they could no longer avoid it. For their part, indigenous groups in Upper Peru often withdrew to their communities and only did the absolute minimum to satisfy patriots and royalists, waiting to see which side was gaining the upper hand.[134]

Nor did enslaved men and women in the Thirteen Colonies automatically take side with one of the two main sides. **James Sidbury** contends (Volume 1, Chapter 15) that "the Revolutionary War offered Blacks in North America many potential opportunities, but none that were reliable, so it is unsurprising that different people living in different places pursued different strategies." Still, 20,000 of them actually ran to the British armies during the course of the war, attracted by vague promises of freedom; 8,000 to 10,000 of them survived and managed to leave the United States, as Sidbury writes, "to live the rest of their lives as free people."

International Dimensions

Textbook accounts of revolutions tend to obscure their strong international dimension. The American Revolution, for example, cannot be understood without acknowledging the role of the French colonies of Martinique and

---

[133] Anne Pfaelzer de Ortiz, "German Redemptioners of the Lower Sort: Apolitical Soldiers in the American Revolution?," *Journal of American Studies* 33:2 (1999), 267–306: 290.

[134] Thomas J. Humphrey, *Land and Liberty: Hudson Valley Riots in the Age of Revolution* (DeKalb: Northern Illinois University Press, 2004), 93; Soux, "Rebelión, guerrilla y tributo," 458.

Saint-Domingue and the Dutch island of St. Eustatius, as **Wim Klooster** stresses in Volume I, Chapter 19. As for Spain's role, **Gonzalo M. Quintero Saravia** argues in Volume I, Chapter 10, that when its government joined the French war effort against Britain in 1778, it "not only tipped the balance of the conflict, giving France and Spain numerical superiority both at land and at sea, but also profoundly changed the general strategy of the war ... This clear superiority opened up new theaters in this now truly global war, spreading British resources thin. Britain would be forced to abandon a purely American perspective of the conflict and adopt a more global view of the war ..." France's support for the American Revolution was accompanied in the same years by its defeat, alongside Bern and Savoy, of Geneva, where an insurrection had taken place against the magistrates. Geneva was unfortunate, writes **Richard Whatmore** (Volume II, Chapter 12), that in 1782 the strength of France was at a peak unparalleled since the 1680s. French invasions of foreign countries may have stopped during the early stages of the French Revolution, but the fear of an international conspiracy aimed at defeating the revolution helped forge a parliamentary majority in Paris in favor of war in 1792. From then on, warfare was a permanent feature of French life until the Battle of Waterloo, conquest of neighboring territories doubling or masquerading as liberation.[135]

The Spanish American independence movements were even more borderless than those in Europe. Troops from Buenos Aires were deployed not only in battles against Spanish forces in Chile and Upper Peru, but also outside the viceroyalty of the Río de la Plata in Peru. Similarly, natives of New Granada were instrumental in ending the Spanish regime in Peru. In addition, the independence movement in Spanish America was entangled with that in Brazil, as **João Paulo Pimenta** shows in Volume III, Chapter 21. One element of this braided history was the repeated Portuguese and later Brazilian interventions in the Banda Oriental, starting in 1811, which were predicated on fear of the successive revolutionary governments in Buenos Aires. These military incursions ended only with the creation of Uruguay in 1828.

International connections were not just military in nature. What gave the revolutionary age coherence was the spread of ideas and ideals, inspiring both enthusiasm and aversion. Pimenta notes that through "newspapers, as well as diplomatic reports, official and private correspondence, and the

---

[135] T. C. W. Blanning, *The Origins of the French Revolutionary Wars* (London: Longman, 1986).

circulation of people, rumors, and news, Spanish America became increasingly familiar in Brazil, arousing interest, fears, and expectations, and provoking reactions." All around the Atlantic world, the North American Declaration of Independence and the constitutions spawned by the new nation and its component states became powerful documents in the hands of rebels in other locales.[136] The French Declaration of the Rights of Man and Citizen and the French constitutions of the first revolutionary years served the same purpose. In Hungary, **Orsolya Szakály** writes in Volume II, Chapter 19, the radical Society of Liberty and Equality "called for a democratic republic of equal citizens in Hungary with references to the French Revolution." Political awareness in several Spanish colonies was also stimulated by the French Revolution. In Volume II, Chapter 6, **Clément Thibaud** shows that members of Spanish American elites could derive inspiration from the French Declaration as much as slaves and free people of color, as they both did during the French revolutionary decade and the Spanish imperial crisis after 1808. No explicit reference could be made to the French example, but, writes Thibaud, "between 1811 and 1813, all constitutional projects in Spanish America included a section on the Rights of Man and of the Citizen." The French model did not arrive alone, mingling with that of the Haitian Revolution to form a potent mixture of revolutionary ideas, slogans, and practices. In the 1790s, **Cristina Soriano** writes (Volume II, Chapter 28), the new revolutionary language "that arrived on the coast of the Spanish Main challenged the already tense relations that existed among different socioracial groups. The majority of the white population interpreted this revolutionary narrative as a violent torrent that sought to destroy their political system and social order, while many free and enslaved people of African descent saw this as their opportunity to achieve social justice and emancipation from the system of slavery, or to at least renegotiate their labor conditions and political roles." One free man of color in Spanish Louisiana expressed his admiration for French rule in Saint-Domingue, where, he said, men like himself enjoyed civil equality. "We can speak openly, like any white person and hold the same rank as they." It is unjust that we don't enjoy equality in Louisiana. Anticipating a line from Martin Luther King's famous speech, he added: "Only their method of thinking – not color – should differentiate men."[137]

---

[136] George Athan Billias, *American Constitutionalism Heard Round the World, 1776–1789: A Global Perspective* (New York: New York University Press, 2009).

[137] Kimberly Hanger, "Conflicting Loyalties: The French Revolution and Free People of Color in Spanish New Orleans," *Louisiana History* 34:1 (1993), 5–33: 26.

Among German radicals, debates revolved around the French catalog of rights, which they saw as the foundation for social order. The French example still resonated internationally when, in France itself, Thermidor set in and principles of natural law were no longer considered the foundation of liberty but denounced as an arsenal for anarchists and levelers which had produced the Terror.[138] The international impact of the ideas spawned by both the French Revolution and the American Revolution, as well as those associated with the Enlightenment, has often been presented as ideological absorption. It was, however, not the force of these ideas themselves that enabled them to spread to certain locales. As one historian has argued, ideas can make history only when they successfully process reality and offer ways out of a social impasse. Crises make those seeking solutions look for appropriate intellectual and political instruments.[139] And once a revolutionary situation is unfolding, creative energies are unleashed that produce new ideas and ideals.[140]

As had happened under the influence of the Revolution in France, a surge of politicization also occurred under the influence of the constitution of Cádiz of 1812, at least in the Iberian world. **Jane Landers** writes in Volume III, Chapter 11 that this constitution "reversed long-promulgated racial prohibitions and decreed that 'Spaniards of African origin' should be helped to study sciences and have access to an ecclesiastical career." The new constitution, Landers continues, was read in plazas across the Atlantic, to enthusiastic crowds that included free and enslaved Blacks. After the constitution reached Cuba, a series of slave revolts swept through the island, as hope born of debates in the Cortes and British Parliament helped launch rumors about abolition decrees authored by authorities as diverse as the king of Spain, the Spanish Cortes, the king of England, the king of Haiti, and the king of Kongo. Those debates did not create such beliefs but activated the often deep-felt conviction of Black men and women of the illegality of their enslavement. News from afar was not necessary to trigger such ideas, as suggested by the impact of the constitution of Antioquia (New Granada), which was saturated with the metaphor of liberty, on a group of slaves who

---

[138] Yannick Bosc, *La terreur des droits de l'homme: Le républicanisme de Thomas Paine et le moment thermidorien* (Paris: Éditions Kimé, 2016); Günther Birtsch, "Naturrecht und Menschenrechte. Zur vernunftrechtlichen Argumentation deutscher Jakobiner," in Otto Dann and Diethelm Klippel, eds., *Naturrecht – Spätaufklärung – Revolution* (Hamburg: Felix Meiner Verlag, 1995), 111–20: 119–20.

[139] Peter Blickle, *Von der Leibeigenschaft zu den Menschenrechten: Eine Geschichte der Freiheit in Deutschland* (Munich: Verlag C. H. Beck, 2006), 15.

[140] Kristin Ross, *Communal Luxury: The Political Imaginary of the Paris Commune* (London: Verso, 2015), 6–7.

claimed to represent more than 10,000 fellow bondspeople. Convinced of the existence of a liberating decree, they approached the tribunal of justice in Medellín, only to be arrested.[141]

The movement to abolish slavery was one that transgressed boundaries. In Volume II, Chapter 4, **Erica Johnson Edwards** shows that the French Society of the Friends of the Blacks and its successor organization, the Society of the Friends of the Blacks and the Colonies, enjoyed membership from both sides of the Channel and both sides of the Atlantic. In another sense, abolitionism also extended across international borders. As **Seymour Drescher** details in Volume II, Chapter 15, Great Britain sent a large fleet to Algiers, which succeeded in liberating many enslaved Europeans, victims of the Barbary corsairs, took great pains to stimulate international condemnation of the transatlantic slave trade, and made recognition of the new Latin American countries dependent on a commitment to abolish the slave trade. News about the termination of slavery in foreign lands was not always a welcome boon for abolitionists. Abolition in Saint-Domingue in 1793, sanctioned by the French Convention the following year, made antislavery activists both in Great Britain and in the United States lose ground in their struggle. **Ashli White** demonstrates in Volume II, Chapter 29 that those bent on upholding slavery in the United States spread the fiction that Black people in Saint-Domingue were fighting a war of revenge against their former masters after they had been set free thanks to false philanthropists.

The Haitian Revolution also proved to be a major source of inspiration among those living in bondage in the New World's many slave societies, while the French Revolution found resonance among both whites and nonwhites. That was in part due to the initiatives of Victor Hugues, France's most senior representative in the years 1794–1798, whose revolutionary troops were composed largely of former slaves. This massive force, **Jessica Pierre-Louis** tells us in Volume II, Chapter 27, "forced the British to recruit and emancipate more enslaved conscripted soldiers to cope with the increase in French troops. Thus, general French freedom also generated, albeit to a lesser extent, emancipation in the British colonies."

Separating the reception of the closely intertwined French and Haitian revolutions is not easy. In Brazil, **Alejandro Gómez** asserts (Volume III, Chapter 14),

---

[141] María Eugenia Chaves, "Esclavos, libertades y república: Tesis sobre la polisemia de la libertad en la primera república antioqueña," *Estudios Interdisciplinarios de América Latina* 22:1 (2011), 81–104: 87–9. Cf. Wim Klooster, "Slave Revolts, Royal Justice, and a Ubiquitous Rumor in the Age of Revolutions," *The William and Mary Quarterly* 71:3 (2014), 401–24.

Introduction

both the revolution in Saint-Domingue and the support of revolutionary activity by the French colonial regime in Guadeloupe affected the city of Salvador, where conspirators in 1798 criticized the "monarchical yoke" and praised the "freedom, equality, and fraternity" of the French.[142] The impact of these two revolutions on the Americas was dissimilar, David Geggus has argued: "If the French Revolution proclaimed the ideals of liberty and equality, the Haitian Revolution demonstrated to colonized peoples that they could be won by force of arms. Plantation societies built on bondage, prejudice, and inequality were peculiarly vulnerable to the ideology of revolutionary France, but the dramatic example of self-liberation offered by Saint-Domingue's transformation into Haiti brought the message much closer to home."[143]

In Spanish America, writes **Clément Thibaud** (Volume II, Chapter 6), the legacy of the French or Haitian revolutions was not explicitly invoked, but hiding in plain sight. Revolutionaries had a thorough grasp of what the French assemblies had accomplished and adopted several institutions that had originated in France. It would also be impossible to imagine the revolutionaries' acceptance of racial equality without the shadow of the Haitian Revolution.[144] And then there was the Haitian republic, a vivid reminder of the successful revolution, which officially maintained its neutrality, but provided crucial support to rebels in Caribbean South America. **Ernesto Bassi** writes (Volume III, Chapter 8) that the obvious sympathies for the Spanish American revolutions of Alexandre Pétion (the president of one of Haiti's two polities at the time) led to the characterization of his republic by Spanish officials as "the receptacle of all the adventurers."

Like the Haitian Revolution, that of France was particularly influential in its own hemisphere. In nearby Switzerland, for example, both intellectuals and peasants who had suffered under the remnants of feudalism responded enthusiastically in the first months after the storming of the Bastille, while in rural areas in western Germany peasants refused to pay tithes or perform the *corvée*, the unpaid labor owed to their lords.[145] Usually, however, the

---

[142] See also Luiz Geraldo Silva, "El impacto de la revolución de Saint-Domingue y los afrodescendientes libres de Brasil. Esclavitud, libertad, configuración social y perspectiva atlántica (1780–1825)," *Historia* 49:1 (2016), 209–33.

[143] Geggus, "Slave Rebellion," 27–8.

[144] David Geggus, "The Sounds and Echoes of Freedom: The Impact of the Haitian Revolution on Latin America," in Darién J. Davis, ed., *Beyond Slavery: The Multilayered Legacy of Africans in Latin America and the Caribbean* (Lanham, MD: Rowman & Littlefield, 2007), 19–36: 25.

[145] Marc H. Lerner, *A Laboratory of Liberty: The Transformation of Political Culture in Republican Switzerland, 1750–1848* (Leiden: Brill, 2012), 79; T. C. W. Blanning,

revolution's supporters were small in number and to be found among radical city-dwellers, who often pinned all their hopes on a French invasion. Joseph Schlemmer, a German lawyer, wrote in 1792: "The happiness of half the world depends on the luck or misfortune of French arms. For if they win, the subject can hope for equity and justice, for better laws to protect him. If they lose, the most terrible slavery in monarchical states is inevitable."[146] The French, indeed, brought freedom, introducing various degrees of rural emancipation in Belgium, the Helvetic Republic, several parts of northern and western Germany, and the Grand Duchy of Warsaw. These French policies also led to preemptive emancipation in German states that were not invaded.[147]

Despite the changes wrought, bitterness and opposition eventually prevailed in the areas subdued by French arms. In Volume II, Chapter 21, **Annie Jourdan** writes: "In view of the political, economic, and social consequences, the so-called sister republics were a flagrant failure. Their alliance with the French republic brought them continuous disorder, increased taxation, military violence and depredations, and infinite abuses of power." Italian territories were particularly badly affected. In Milan, the French provoked outrage by billeting soldiers in private homes, establishing a National Guard for which all able-bodied men between sixteen and fifty-five were recruited, and eliminating religious festivals and sacred wall paintings on public buildings.[148] Apart from strong local cultural and religious traditions, the French invaders were confronted with deep-rooted judicial cultures which challenged their uniformist impulse.[149] Sooner or later, although not universally, the French presence descended into boundless military violence, which inspired counterviolence.[150] **John A. Davis** (Volume II, Chapter 17) nuances this picture. Even brutal features of the French presence, he writes,

---

Reform and Revolution in Mainz 1743–1803 (Cambridge: Cambridge University Press, 1974), 306.

[146] Jörg Schweigard, Aufklärung und Revolutionsbegeisterung: Die katholischen Universitäten in Mainz, Heidelberg und Würzburg im Zeitalter der Französischen Revolution (1789–1792/ 3–1803) (Frankfurt am Main: Peter Lang, 2000), 155.

[147] John Markoff, "Violence, Emancipation, and Democracy: The Countryside and the French Revolution," The American Historical Review 100:2 (1995), 360–86: 383.

[148] Laura Gagliardi, "Il volto della Rivoluzione: Milano di fronte all'invasione francese (1796–1799)," in Cecilia Nubola and Andreas Würgler, eds., Ballare con nemico? Reazioni all'espansione francese in Europa tra entusiasmo e resistenza (1792–1815) (Bologna: Società editrice il Mulino; Berlin: Duncker & Humblot, 2010), 23–34.

[149] Luigi Lacchè, "L'Europe et la révolution du droit: Brèves réflexions," Annales historiques de la Révolution française no. 328 (2002), 153–69: 162.

[150] Jean-Clément Martin, Violence et révolution: Essai sur la naissance d'un mythe national (Paris: Éditions du Seuil, 2006), 289–91.

"were not sufficient to reduce the republican experiments of 1796–1799 to a mere narrative of military oppression. The attraction of the promised new republican order had been evident when in April 1796 Bonaparte was greeted enthusiastically in Milan as a liberator. Republican sympathizers and political exiles from Naples, Rome, and Piedmont flocked to the city where political clubs and associations were founded, and newspapers and journals were launched." The response was similar in other parts of the Italian peninsula. Besides, Davis argues, the popular anger that did erupt in 1799 – on a scale vaster than the insurrection in the Vendée – "was in many respects a continuation of insurrections and unrest that had been evident throughout the peninsula from much earlier, but existing discontents had been exacerbated by the impact of the revolution, the military occupation, and the new republics."

In some countries, the fear of a French invasion caused officials to stoke fear about the baneful presence of imaginary Frenchmen. In Saxony and Austria, French agents were accused of stirring up the population or preparing a coup d'état.[151] Nowhere, though, was the fear of French emissaries so great as in Spanish America in the first years after Fernando VII and Carlos IV surrendered to Napoleon in 1808. A tremendous amount of bureaucratic energy was spent on detecting unknown travelers and checking the countless reports about their alleged activities.[152] In reality, Napoleon did send some agents to Spanish American shores, but they remained harmless.

By the time Napoleon seized power, France rarely served as a beacon of hope anymore, at least in Europe.[153] In the eyes of numerous commentators, who now looked to Great Britain for inspiration, the French Revolution had failed, and its supporters were simply terrorists and anarchists.[154] If books by

---

[151] Jirko Krauß, *Ländlicher Alltag und Konflikt in der späten Frühen Neuzeit: Lebenswelt erzgebirgischer Rittergutsdörfer im Spiegel der kursächsischen Bauernunruhen 1790* (Frankfurt am Main: Peter Lang, 2012), 411; Helmut Reinalter, "Gegen die 'Tollwuth der Aufklärungsbarbarei': Leopold Alois Hoffmann und der frühe Konservatismus in Österreich," in Christoph Weiß, ed., *Von "Obscuranten" und "Eudämonisten": Gegenaufklärerische, konservative und antirevolutionäre Publizisten im späten 18. Jahrhundert* (St. Ingbert: Röhrig Universitätsverlag, 1997), 221–44: 227–8.

[152] Timothy Hawkins, *A Great Fear: Luis de Onís and the Shadow War against Napoleon in Spanish America, 1808–1812* (Tuscaloosa: The University of Alabama Press, 2019).

[153] By contrast, liberals and conservatives at the Cortes of Cádiz tried to learn lessons from the early stages of the French Revolution. José M. Portillo, "El poder constituyente en el primer constitucionalismo hispano," *Jahrbuch für Geschichte Lateinamerikas* 55 (2018), 1–26. In addition, as seen above, radicals in the Spanish colonies continued to be inspired by French revolutionary thought and practice.

[154] Richard Whatmore, *Terrorists, Anarchists, and Republicans: The Genevans and the Irish in Time of Revolution* (Princeton: Princeton University Press, 2019), 349–50.

Voltaire, Rousseau, and Raynal had always been banned in the Catholic world, publications associated with the revolution in France were seen by moral guardians of monarchical regimes as equally impious, seditious, or obscene. It was not even necessarily a book's content that was judged – authorship by a disreputable person sufficed for a work to be condemned. Censors in Brazil in the 1810s prohibited the sale of the innocent-sounding *Liberty of the Seas* because its author, the former Jacobin Bertrand Barère, had been "one of the most bloodthirsty associates of the monster Robespierre." And although the *philosophe* Gabriel Bonnot de Mably had died in 1785, his works were blacklisted because his doctrines of equality and liberty were found to have contributed much to the French Revolution.[155]

Whereas anti-French feelings abated, anti-Spanish sentiment in Spanish America grew after 1808, as the fight between patriots and royalists intensified. In Buenos Aires, a series of repressive measures against the *peninsulares* commenced with the May revolution of 1810, although persecution was limited to those who openly rejected the new regime. It became much more comprehensive after the discovery of an antigovernment conspiracy with Spanish ringleaders.[156] At the tail end of the independence process, there was also a reckoning for Spanish natives in both Peru and Mexico. Their massive expulsion caused so much ill-will on the part of the Spanish government that it embarked on an unsuccessful reconquest of Mexico in 1829–1830.[157] Like in other former colonies, Brazil also initiated measures against natives of the former metropole. **Hendrik Kraay** (Volume III, Chapter 20) asserts that these policies were not simply aimed at eliminating an enemy ethnicity. Anti-Portuguese rhetoric and violence were also about political choices and local power struggles. Besides, "expelling Portuguese-born office holders also conveniently opened up spaces in the civil and military bureaucracy for Brazilian patriots."

The French themselves, meanwhile, were not above excluding foreigners, who were seen by the Jacobins as treacherous enemies of the revolution. Months after the outbreak of war with Britain, all British nationals were arrested, and their property was confiscated. Englishmen soon stood accused

---

[155] Lúcia Maria B. P. das Neves and Tânia Maria T. B. da C. Ferreira, "O medo dos 'abomináveis princípios franceses': A censura dos livros nos inícios do século XIX no Brasil," *Acervo* 4:1 (1989), 113–19: 116.

[156] Mariana Alicia Pérez, "¡Viva España y Mueran los Patricios! La conspiración de Álzaga de 1812," *Americanía. Revista de Estudios Latinoamericanos* special issue (May 2015), 21–55.

[157] Harold Dana Sims, *The Expulsion of Mexico's Spaniards, 1821–1836* (Pittsburgh: University of Pittsburgh Press, 1990).

Introduction

of "lese humanity." War to the death was consequently declared on them.[158] Such policies stood in stark contrast to the universalism the revolutionaries had professed in the first years of the revolution. As late as January 1793, *Le Moniteur Universel*, the government's official newspaper, had invoked "the bonds of universal fraternity which the French have extended to all peoples and on which they stake their lives."[159] Universalism did not disappear once France's armies began to cross the country's boundaries, although its adherents were now usually to be found elsewhere. In his *A Letter to the People of Ireland* (1796), Irishman Thomas Russell connected the plight of those countrymen of his who had been impressed by the Royal Navy not only to the oppression of Catholics in Ireland but also to that of enslaved Africans. Impressment, after all, enabled Britain to wage wars that aimed at continuing the Atlantic slave trade.[160] Russell thus tapped into the remarkable popular success of Britain's abolitionist movement. **Seymour Drescher** writes (Volume II, Chapter 15): "Unlike its counterparts in France and America it endured for half a century as a national social movement. Its participants were initially aroused by what they deemed violations of the 'principle of humanity.' Their intended beneficiaries were not their own fellow Britons nor even residents of their own colonies. They differed from the enslaved in race, color, religion, or culture."

If imperialism did not raise its head in France until a few years into the revolution, the American Revolution was more blatantly imperialist from the very start. In Volume I, Chapter 16, **Colin Calloway** contends that "the Revolution was also, quite simply, a war over Indian land. Speculators like George Washington had worked long and hard to get their hands on the best western lands; western settlers sought to rid lands of Indian neighbors, and Congress and the individual states needed land to fulfill the bounties and warrants they issued in lieu of pay during the war." Those Indian neighbors paid the price for westward expansion. Calloway relates that the Cherokees sued for peace after a genocidal campaign had been waged against them. At the peace treaties they signed, they lost more than 5 million acres. The indigenous plight throws into relief the apparent contradiction discerned by **Patrick Griffin**

---

[158] The rebels in the Vendée, who were officially excluded from the nation – not humanity – were treated the same way: Sophie Wahnich, *L'impossible citoyen: L'étranger dans le discours de la Révolution française* (Paris: Éditions Albin Michel, 2010), 11, 359.

[159] Rachel Rogers, "The Society of the Friends of the Rights of Man, 1792–94: British and Irish Radical Conjunctions in Republican Paris," *La Révolution française* (2016), 1–26: 6, http://lrf.revues.org/1629.

[160] Anthony Di Lorenzo and John Donoghue, "Abolition and Republicanism over the Transatlantic Long Term, 1640–1800," *La Révolution française* (2016), 14, 48–9, http://lrf.revues.org/1690.

(Volume 1, Chapter 7). The creoles of British North America, he writes, were "a people of paradox: anti-imperial when it came to the metropole and imperial when it came to dominance at home." Westward expansion continued after the peace treaty with Britain was signed in 1783, but, as **Mark Peterson** notes (Volume 1, Chapter 5), the Confederation Congress (the body that initially governed the new republic) was ill-equipped to manage claims on western lands. It was in part to solve this problem that a constitutional convention was convened that ended up creating a new form of national government.

The Realm of Freedom

Some revolutionaries, even those who stood to benefit more than others, had always doubted the possibility of introducing a new order.[161] The German "Jacobin" Joseph Görres believed in a four-stage development that had begun with the transition from barbarism to society, which was followed by that from a despotic to a representative regime. Next, a pure democracy would arise that would eventually give way to the period of "anarchy," during which people no longer needed a government. This progression took time, however. To move from the second stage to the third, as the French revolutionaries had tried to accomplish by introducing the constitution of 1791, did not make sense. That constitution came thousands of years too early. A long process of popular education was first required.[162]

Still, the upheaval of the late eighteenth and early nineteenth centuries created new regimes that often bore no resemblance to the old ones. These regimes made a start, however incomplete and reversible, and more in some places than others, with the emancipation of the many men and women who previously had been voiceless. And yet the belief, generated by the revolutions around the Atlantic world, in an imminent entry into the realm of freedom was proven to be misplaced. In the course of the revolutions, goals that had been embraced in the early stages mutated into ideological phrases that lacked urgency.[163] What gained currency was, once again, the idea that change would come only gradually. For most residents of the Atlantic world, true liberty would have to wait until a distant future.

---

[161] Domenico Losurdo, "Vincenzo Cuoco, la révolution napolitaine de 1799 et l'étude comparée des révolutions," *Revue Historique* 281:1 (1989), 133–57: 151.

[162] Joseph Görres, "Mein Glaubensbekenntnis (Juni/Juli 1798)," in Axel Kuhn, ed., *Linksrheinische deutsche Jakobiner: Aufrufe, Reden, Protokolle. Briefe und Schriften 1794–1801* (Stuttgart: J. B. Metzler, 1978), 240–50: 242–3.

[163] Stefan Greif, "Das Diskontinuierliche als Kontinuum. Aufklärung und Aufklärungskritik im Werk Georg Forsters," *Georg-Forster-Studien* 15 (2010), 77–93: 87.

PART I

★

ENLIGHTENMENT
AND CULTURE

I

Enlightenment and the American Revolution

CAROLINE WINTERER

A French sympathizer of the American Revolution imagined this charming scene. "They say that in Virginia the members chosen to establish the new government assembled in a peaceful wood, removed from the sight of the people, in an enclosure prepared by nature with banks of grass, and that in this sylvan spot they deliberated on who should preside over them."[1] Michel René Hilliard d'Auberteuil had no local knowledge of Virginia, so there is perhaps too much Rousseau and not enough Richmond in his portrait. But still he captured some essential truths about the ideals of enlightenment in the American Revolution: the appeal to nature as a primal origin for human society; the deliberate choice of government by representatives of the people; and, above all, the optimism that drove the formation of new governments on principles of kingless republicanism. The core ideal of the new, transatlantic idea of enlightenment was that human reason could understand, change, and improve the world. Its relationship to the phenomenon we call the "American Revolution," however, has always been controversial.

How do we even begin to approach so grand a topic as enlightenment and the American Revolution? It helps to listen to what eighteenth-century Americans themselves said about it. To do that, we have to set aside – or at least be aware of – some of what has been said about the topic over the last seventy years.

Since the Cold War era, scholars of the United States have wrapped the topic in a warm cloak of approval that sometimes tells us more about their own concerns than those of the eighteenth century. Surveying the destructions of the Second World War and anxiously eyeing the Soviet Union, American historians looked to the founding era as a bulwark against

---

[1] Michel René Hilliard d'Auberteuil, *Essais historiques et politiques sur la Révolution de l'Amérique Septentrionale* (Paris: self-published, 1782), 119.

totalitarianism. They offered a new label – "The American Enlightenment" (a term unknown in the eighteenth century) – as an ideological bomb shelter against Nazism, communism, and fascism. And because their modern concerns were political, they collapsed the broad intellectual movement of enlightenment into the narrowly political project of the American Revolution.[2] As Henry Steele Commager put it in 1977, enlightenment ideas were "imagined" in Europe and then "fulfilled" in the American Revolution.[3] For over half a century, this Cold War story has given a satisfying, triumphal cast not just to "The American Enlightenment," but to the American Revolution itself. It proves irresistible even today.[4]

By contrast, people living in eighteenth-century America used only the lower-case terms "enlightened" and "enlightenment." To them, enlightenment was process, not product. It was not the culmination of European ideas in a political event across the sea, but rather an ongoing, never-completed effort to establish happy human societies based on reason. These ideas came not just from eighteenth-century Europe, but through a long-term transatlantic exchange of ideas. For people in the eighteenth century, enlightenment also involved a vast range of topics beyond politics: science, religion, art, literature, history, ethnology, political economy, and more.[5] Enlightened ideas appealed to and were articulated by both the educated elite and those

---

[2] Recent historiographical overviews include Caroline Winterer, "What Was the American Enlightenment?," in Joel Isaac, James Kloppenberg, Michael O'Brien, and Jennifer Ratner-Rosenhagen, eds., *The Worlds of American Intellectual History* (Oxford: Oxford University Press, 2016), 19–36; John M. Dixon, "Henry F. May and the Revival of the American Enlightenment: Problems and Possibilities for Intellectual and Social History," *William and Mary Quarterly*, 3rd series 71:2 (2014), 255–80; Nathalie Caron and Naomi Wulf, "American Enlightenments: Continuity and Renewal," *Journal of American History* 99:4 (2013), 1072–91; Sebastian Conrad, "Enlightenment in Global History: A Historiographical Critique," *American Historical Review* 117:4 (2012), 999–1027.

[3] Henry Steele Commager, *The Empire of Reason: How Europe Imagined and America Realized the Enlightenment* (Garden City, NY: Anchor, 1977), xi. See also Henry May, *The Enlightenment in America* (New York: Oxford University Press, 1976); Donald Meyer, *The Democratic Enlightenment* (New York: Putnam, 1976); Ernest Cassara, *The Enlightenment in America* (New York: Twayne, 1975). More recent interpretations include John M. Dixon, *The Enlightenment of Cadwallader Colden: Empire, Science, and Intellectual Culture in British New York* (Ithaca, NY: Cornell University Press, 2016); Susan Manning and Francis Cogliano, eds., *The Atlantic Enlightenment* (Aldershot: Ashgate, 2008); Lee Eric Schmidt, *Hearing Things: Religion, Illusion, and the American Enlightenment* (Cambridge, MA: Harvard University Press, 2000); Ned Landsman, *From Colonials to Provincials: American Thought and Culture, 1680–1760* (New York: Twayne, 1997).

[4] Jonathan Israel, *The Expanding Blaze: How the American Revolution Ignited the World, 1775–1848* (Princeton: Princeton University Press, 2017).

[5] Caroline Winterer, *American Enlightenments: Pursuing Happiness in the Age of Reason* (New Haven: Yale University Press, 2016).

with less access to power and privilege.⁶ The uniting thread for all these people and arenas of thought was the hope that reason could light the path forward to a better tomorrow.

As a process rather than as a product, the eighteenth-century idea of enlightenment involved uncertainty and anxiety. The barriers could seem insurmountable in a world of pain, ignorance, error, oppression, and despotism. Anachronistic modern labels (such as "Radical Enlightenment" or "Moderate Enlightenment," which were never used in the eighteenth century) judge efforts at enlightenment according to whether they meet our modern criteria of long-term success or failure. These labels fail to capture the real ambivalence that characterized efforts at enlightenment around the Atlantic. Like others in Europe and Spanish America, revolutionary Americans mixed hope with doubt about whether enlightenment could ever be achieved. It loomed like a distant summit, in sight but difficult to reach. "My friend," wrote the French economist Pierre Samuel du Pont de Nemours to his friend Thomas Jefferson after the American Revolution, "we are snails and we have a mountain range to climb. By God, we must climb it!"⁷

Some of this uncertainty involved whether airy ideas could cause a revolution in government. Rather than taking sides in a debate that continues to this day, we can start with the opinions that eighteenth-century observers themselves hazarded: that the revolution was revolutionary precisely because it showed the reality of enlightenment. The term "American Revolution" was coined as early as 1777 to describe the political break with Britain. But it took the first histories of the "American Revolution," written in the 1780s, to claim that the American Revolution showed evidence of the progress of humanity toward a better world of reason, rights, and government by the people. That this interpretation seems familiar to us is exactly the point: the first histories of the American Revolution were themselves the product of an enlightened view of the world. Thus, in some way, the whole concept of an "American Revolution" resulted from the ideal of enlightenment. John Adams insisted upon the efficacy of ideas in causing what he called the "real" American Revolution. "But what do We mean by the American Revolution? Do We mean the American War? The Revolution

---

⁶ James Delbourgo, *A Most Amazing Scene of Wonders: Electricity and Enlightenment in Early America* (Cambridge, MA: Harvard University Press, 2006).

⁷ Pierre Samuel Du Pont de Nemours to Thomas Jefferson, 18 August 1816, in Gilbert Chinard, ed., *The Correspondence of Jefferson and Du Pont de Nemours, with an Introduction on Jefferson and the Physiocrats* (Baltimore, MD: Johns Hopkins University Press, 1931), 1.

was effected before the War commenced. The Revolution was in the Minds and Hearts of the People ... This radical Change in the Principles, Opinions Sentiments, and Affection of the people, was the real American Revolution."[8]

It is not enough, then, to describe the role of enlightened ideas in the American Revolution, as though taking attendance with a clipboard. For the "American Revolution" itself was a narrative frame imposed in the 1780s and later on a string of otherwise inchoate events by people who yearned to see the forces of enlightenment at work. The long-term results of their efforts remain visible today. R. R. Palmer's *The Age of Democratic Revolution* crafted an ambitious, celebratory Atlantic genealogy for the American Revolution that has inspired decades of scholarship (including the *Cambridge History of the Age of Atlantic Revolutions*). Palmer's genealogy cast the American Revolution – and the subsequent "Age of Atlantic Revolutions" (another post-Second World War coinage) – as the cradle of twentieth-century democracy and even, as Palmer styled it, "Western Civilization."[9]

As these Cold War genealogies become artifacts of history rather than present ideology, the topic of "enlightenment and the American Revolution" demands two approaches. The first is to document how eighteenth-century people themselves understood the ideal of enlightenment in the project of political independence and republican nation-formation. The second is to show how these ideas laid the groundwork for our present understanding of the American Revolution. This chapter is organized around four major concepts – nature, progress, reason, and revolution – which offer a sketch map to a body of thought so vast and diverse that it defies complete representation. Still, they can point to a few of the main lines of thought that animated Americans and their contemporaries around the Atlantic in the last decades of the eighteenth century.

The North American Context of Enlightenment

Eighteenth-century North Americans shared many ideas about what it meant to be enlightened with other people around the Atlantic. They held in

---

[8] John Adams to H. Niles, 13 February 1818, Founders Online, National Archives, accessed 11 April 2019, https://founders.archives.gov/documents/Adams/99-02-02-6854.

[9] Robert Roswell Palmer, *The Age of Democratic Revolution: A Political History of Europe and America, 1760–1800*, vol. I: *The Challenge* (Princeton: Princeton University Press, 1959), 5 ("The Revolution of Western Civilization"); Robert Roswell Palmer, *The Age of Democratic Revolution: A Political History of Europe and America, 1760–1800*, vol. II: *The Struggle* (Princeton: Princeton University Press, 1964).

common the new idea that human reason could understand the world using empirical data from the five senses (rather than revelation or superstition), and that this understanding could then be used to improve the world. According to people who considered themselves enlightened, the future should be better than the present and the present better than the past. Properly harnessed, all human efforts could point to a golden future of human happiness.

Many historians used to argue that enlightened ideas were born in Europe (chiefly in France) and then migrated to America. We can call this the "diffusion" hypothesis. Today, owing in part to the digitization and widespread availability of archival documents from the colonial periphery, opinion has shifted to the view that enlightenment ideas emerged from many points and circulated widely. "Network" rather than diffusion is now the organizing paradigm to describe this process (though the textile metaphor was not used in the eighteenth century to describe it). At any rate, the vehicles for circulation included every manner of published media as well as a lively trade in objects, ranging from moose pelts to microscopes. All these lit up conversations across thousands of miles of water and land. National and regional strands of enlightenment emphasized certain ideas and attitudes.[10]

Late eighteenth-century North America was one regional variation within this Atlantic world of ideas. By comparison with Europe – with its princely patronage of universities, academies, museums, and libraries – colonial America was thin on institutions of enlightenment. Still, by the late eighteenth century Americans enjoyed high literacy levels, buoyed by a steady stream of books imported from Europe (and especially London), as well as locally published magazines and newspapers that reprinted the latest opinions and conjectures. By the 1760s, there was enough intellectual infrastructure in colonial North America – colleges, printing presses, libraries, a few museums and academies – to support the intensive written communication networks on which the American Revolution ultimately hinged.[11]

---

[10] Caroline Winterer, "Where Is America in the Republic of Letters?," *Modern Intellectual History* 9:3 (2012), 597–623. See also Roy Porter and Mikuláš Teich, eds., *The Enlightenment in National Context* (Cambridge: Cambridge University Press, 1981); John Robertson, *The Case for the Enlightenment: Scotland and Naples 1680–1760* (Cambridge: Cambridge University Press, 2005).

[11] Overviews include Robert Ferguson, *The American Enlightenment, 1750–1820* (Cambridge, MA: Harvard University Press, 1994); Michael Warner, *The Letters of the Republic: Publication and the Public Sphere in Eighteenth-Century America* (Cambridge, MA: Harvard University Press, 1990). For the book trade, see Hugh Amory and David D.

For this would be a revolution by document. As the first of what are today called the "Atlantic revolutions," the American Revolution launched what would eventually become so normalized that it can easily slip from view: the publication and widespread international circulation of documents not just to provoke revolutionary activity, but to embody the meaning of revolution itself. Although the late eighteenth century was still an oral culture (as the "Declaration" of Independence reminds us), the legalistic formulation of universal principles on which the American and later revolutions hinged could be achieved only in the more permanent medium of writing.[12]

And so writing there was. By the 1760s, colonial American "committees of correspondence" were linking distant colonists in a common project of information-gathering and eventually shadow governance. The first state constitutions, the Declaration of Independence, and the federal Constitution emerged from the hope that documents – especially published documents – would form bulwarks against despotism. The Declaration of Independence and the state constitutions were immediately translated and published in France, facilitating further circulation. (Though in their exuberantly varied translations of keywords such as "mankind," the French also gave the lie to enlightened dreams of finding a universal natural language.)[13]

By raising sight above the other senses, Americans celebrated their revolutionary documents as exempla of clarity. One proponent of the new federal Constitution claimed that it was a "luminous body" whose "light ... was so

---

Hall, eds., *A History of the Book in America*, vol. 1: *The Colonial Book in the Atlantic World* (Cambridge: Cambridge University Press, 2000); Robert Gross and Mary Kelley, eds., *A History of the Book in America*, vol. II: *An Extensive Republic: Print, Culture, and Society in the New Nation, 1790–1840* (Chapel Hill: University of North Carolina Press, 2010); Richard Sher, *The Enlightenment and the Book: Scottish Authors and Their Publishers in Eighteenth-Century Britain, Ireland, and America* (Chicago: University of Chicago Press, 2006); David Lundberg and Henry F. May, "The Enlightened Reader in America," *American Quarterly* 28 (1976), 262–93. On letter writing, see Sarah Pearsall, *Atlantic Families: Lives and Letters in the Eighteenth Century* (Oxford: Oxford University Press, 2008); Konstantin Dierks, *In My Power: Letter Writing and Communications in Early America* (Philadelphia: University of Pennsylvania Press, 2009). On manuscript culture, see David Shields, "The Manuscript in the British American World of Print," *Proceedings of the American Antiquarian Society* 102:2 (1993), 403–16.

[12] Jay Fliegelman, *Declaring Independence: Jefferson, Natural Language, and the Culture of Performance* (Stanford: Stanford University Press, 1993).

[13] Elise Marienstras and Naomi Wulf, "French Translations and Reception of the Declaration of Independence," http://chnm.gmu.edu/declaration/marien.html. See also Mary M. Slaughter, *Universal Languages and Scientific Taxonomy in the Seventeenth Century* (Cambridge: Cambridge University Press, 1982); Umberto Eco, *The Search for the Perfect Language* (New York: Blackwell, 1995).

clear that nothing more was wanted."[14] They also pioneered new visual forms that might uncover the truths that the rigidly sequential syntax of prose concealed or distorted. Tables, questionnaires, timelines, pie charts, and diagrams promised clear windows into truths that could topple illegitimate authority. Americans also reached for optical metaphors to understand their new representative governments: were they mirrors or miniatures of the people?[15]

But doubts lurked amid the optimism. James Madison wondered whether mere "parchment barriers" could restrain the accumulations of power that led to tyranny.[16] Language itself resisted the clarity to which enlightened Americans aspired. Even as he defended the words of the Constitution that he had just helped to draft, Madison pondered the limits of human language and therefore all human knowledge in *The Federalist*. God spoke clearly, but the "cloudy medium" of human language muddied meaning. As human and therefore necessarily imperfect creations, the Constitutional convention and the Constitution itself could only wallow in "obscurity."[17]

Forms that promised clarity merely cast new shadows. The major documents of the American Revolution are all either literally enumerated lists (in that they have actual numerals, whether Roman or Arabic: these include the state and federal bills of rights; the Articles of Confederation; and the federal Constitution) or unenumerated lists (the grievances against King George III in the Declaration of Independence). Like diagrams and tables, enumerated lists – especially lists of rights – sought political safety in visibility.

But by announcing presence, enumeration also exposed absence. The Ninth Amendment confronted the problem without resolving it: "The enumeration in the Constitution, of certain rights, shall not be construed to deny or disparage others retained by the people." Critics quickly seized on the problems of this amendment. James Iredell of North Carolina called the Bill of Rights a "snare" rather than a "protection." He imagined a distant future in which the omitted rights – the potential infinity of rights left out of the enumerated rights – came back to haunt them. "No man, let his ingenuity be

---

[14] 23 March 1796 (HR), *Annals of Congress*, 4th Congress, 1st Session, 5: 688; 22 March 1796 (HR), *Annals of Congress*, 4th Congress, 1st Session, 5: 657. Library of Congress, *A Century of Lawmaking for a New Nation: US Congressional Documents and Debates, 1774–1875*, http://memory.loc.gov/ammem/amlaw.lwac.html.

[15] Lorraine Daston and Peter Galison, *Objectivity* (New York: Zone Books, 2007); Anthony Grafton and Daniel Rosenberg, *Cartographies of Time: A History of the Timeline* (Princeton: Princeton Architectural Press, 2010); John Bender and Michael Marrinan, *The Culture of Diagram* (Stanford: Stanford University Press, 2010).

[16] *The Federalist*, 48.   [17] *The Federalist*, 37.

what it will, could enumerate all the individual rights not relinquished by this Constitution. Suppose, therefore, an enumeration of a great many, but an omission of some, and that, long after all traces of our present disputes were at an end, any of the omitted rights should be invaded, and the invasion be complained of; what would be the plausible answer of the government to such a complaint?"[18] It was typical of the anxious open-endedness of this era's frame of mind that the problem would be phrased as a question.

Nature

The word "nature" is everywhere in the political texts of the American Revolution. Americans invoked natural law, natural man, natural rights, human nature, and the state of nature. In the 1760s and after, the appeal to nature became a way to delegitimize claims to authority that rested on other foundations: history, custom, divine access, and lineage. Nature was now seen to come before all of these. Before King George III, before Parliament, before Magna Carta, before Christianity, before the first biblical kings, before the Egyptians, before Adam himself: there lay nature.

The words "Nature and Nature's God" in the Declaration of Independence remind us that nature and God were not sharply differentiated. Nature could simultaneously be both the creator and the product of God's creation. Both God and nature were transcendent, creative forces operating from time immemorial. Now, after the Scientific Revolution, religion itself began to be infused with ideas taken from the scientific study of the natural world. "Natural laws" like those documented by Isaac Newton attested to God's desire that humanity should use reason in all realms of life, including some matters of faith. Miracles seemed increasingly implausible.

Humans stood upon an isthmus between mundane and divine nature. They were both a product of God's creation but also possessed of a shared "human nature" (another new term) that, like the trees and planets, was subject to empirical investigation. People could inspect their own psychology, as David Hume did in his *A Treatise of Human Nature* (1739). Still, some parts of humanity remained opaque. One was "conscience" as a faculty of the mind, an inner sanctum of morality or even divinity. It was now walled off from state power and state observation. Thomas Jefferson

---

[18] James Iredell, "North Carolina Ratifying Convention," 28 July 1788, in Philip B. Kurtland and Ralph Lerner, eds., *The Founders' Constitution*, 2 vols. (Chicago: University of Chicago Press, 1987), vol. 1, 476.

eventually reached for a metaphor of both physical and optical blockage – a wall – to affirm his support for the separation of church and state.

Early in the 1760s, Americans seized on one of these new nature ideas to frame their growing discontent with British taxation: the "state of nature." This hypothetical origin of all human societies emerged from the political struggles of seventeenth-century Britain that pitted absolutist kings against Parliament. Theorists such as Thomas Hobbes, John Locke, and others sought a cradle for rights that was independent of monarchical largesse. By "rights" they meant entitlements to property, life, liberty, and other desirables that had a long English history stretching even beyond Magna Carta in the thirteenth century. But now, with the fiction of a "state of nature," rights could transcend English history and find a universal appeal as the common birthright of humankind. John Locke's description of the state of nature in his *Two Treatises of Government* (1689) resonated with American colonists eager to justify the universality of their rights claims. "Man being born, as has been proved, with a Title to perfect Freedom, and an uncontrouled Enjoyment of all the Rights and Privileges of the Law of Nature, equally with any other Man, or Number of Men in the World, hath by Nature a Power ... to preserve his Property, that is, his Life, Liberty and Estate, against the Injuries and Attempts of other Men."[19]

Although the state of nature was widely understood to be a useful fiction (Rousseau thought it "no longer exists, perhaps never existed, and will probably never exist"), Locke drew many of his examples from the native peoples of North America.[20] As Secretary of the Board of Trade and Plantations and to the Lords Proprietor of Carolina, Locke had read extensively about the American Indians. "Thus in the beginning, all the world was America," he announced in a Genesis-like formulation in his *Two Treatises*. (That Locke's understanding of Indian polities was empirically incorrect was for later commentators to establish and publicize.) Locke's equation of America with natural political origins became part of the background noise of the revolutionary era. It helped to encourage a local strand of nationalism in which the United States became nature's nation. This would be realized most fully in the nineteenth century, but its seeds were sown much earlier.

The "state of nature" opened the door to another new idea: "society." Today we take for granted that human beings live in societies. But the idea of

---

[19] John Locke, *Two Treatises of Government*, 4th edition (London: John Churchill, 1713), 246.
[20] Jean-Jacques Rousseau, *A Discourse on Inequality*, ed. Maurice Cranston (1755; New York: Penguin, 1985).

Figure 1.1 The Phoenix, or the Resurrection of Freedom (1776). Allegory depicting the death of liberty in Europe and its new home in America; a temple, lettered "Libert. Americ.," stands on a distant shore beyond which stretches a fertile landscape; in the foreground, on the left, Father Time casts flowers on the remnants of Athens, Rome, and Florence, while on the right, a figure representing British liberty lies on a tomb mourned by seventeenth-century republicans Algernon Sidney, John Milton, Andrew Marvell, John Locke, and James Barry, the artist who made this print, himself; a man with shackled ankles stands in front of the tomb with a tattered copy of Habeas Corpus protruding from his coat. Courtesy of British Museum.

society as the primordial, prepolitical container for human activity emerged only in the seventeenth and eighteenth centuries. The term "society" had previously existed to refer to smaller, voluntary associations, such as London's Royal Society, the major British scientific institution of its day. But it now acquired powerful political uses. Referring to a community with shared customs, laws, or institutions, the new use of society first of all presumed that human beings were fundamentally social: to live in society was "human nature." Society was thought to be shaped by natural laws of human behavior and organization that could be observed and categorized. Properly understood, society would be the great engine of human progress. "What a man alone would not have been able to effect," explained the Abbé Raynal in one of the first histories of the American Revolution, "men have executed in concert ... Such is the origin, such the advantage and the end of all society."[21] The thickening concept of society led to the proliferation of other new terms, such as the "social contract," "civil society," "social happiness," "science of society," and eventually "sociology."[22]

Following the logic of the state of nature was the new idea that government was a contract between ruler and ruled. All humans lived in society. Only by choice, and through consent among equals, could governments be formed from society. Government therefore became not a God-given reality, but a human-created contract among consenting equals. Government by consent implied that the contract could be broken if certain conditions were met (which the Declaration of Independence achieved by positing "a long train of abuses and usurpations"). This political rupture could result in the most drastic break of all: revolution.

The major state-of-nature theorist for American revolutionary politics was "the celebrated Montesquieu" (as Americans almost invariably called him). A French nobleman who had once lived in London and deeply admired the balanced British constitution, Charles-Louis de Secondat, Baron de la Brède et de Montesquieu was the author of the widely known and translated book, *De l'esprit de loix* (*The Spirit of Laws*). Published in 1748, it was soon translated into English and had enormous influence all over Europe and the Americas. Its popularity was in some sense remarkable. The book was poorly organized, aphoristic, and often opaque. "What does he mean by a Man in a State of Nature?" wondered John Adams when he read Montesquieu in 1759.[23] Still, Montesquieu's name was held in such high regard that even the arrival of his grandson in revolutionary Philadelphia as part of the French military corps was duly noted.[24]

Montesquieu gave revolutionary Americans a framework for understanding the natural origin and major types of society and government over time and place. In his view, governments were not entities given by God,

---

[21] Guillaume Thomas François Raynal, *The Revolution of America* (London: Lockyer Davis, 1781), 35.
[22] Keith M. Baker, "Enlightenment and the Institution of Society: Notes for a Conceptual History," in W. Melching and W. Velema, eds., *Main Trends in Cultural History* (Amsterdam: Rodopi, 1994), 95–120; Mary Poovey, "The Liberal Civil Subject and the Social in Eighteenth-Century British Moral Philosophy," in Patrick Joyce, ed., *The Social in Question: New Bearings in History and the Social Sciences* (New York: Routledge, 2002), 44–61.
[23] *Diary and Autobiography of John Adams*, vol. 1: *1755–1770*, in *The Adams Papers Digital Edition*, ed. Sara Martin (Charlottesville: University of Virginia Press, 2008–2019).
[24] James Madison to Joseph Jones, 5 December 1780, in *The Papers of James Madison Digital Edition*, ed. J. C. A. Stagg (Charlottesville: University of Virginia Press, 2010).

but instead institutions created by human beings according to the "humour and disposition" of the particular people who created them.[25] Accessible to reason, government could be comprehended, categorized, and also reformed.

Observing the diversity of regimes around the world over time, Montesquieu divided them into three kinds, each with its own principle or "spirit": republican (resting on virtue); monarchical (resting on honor); and despotic (resting on fear). One of the greatest dangers to government was the desire for power, which Montesquieu believed formed part of human nature. The only remedy was to check that power – or as Montesquieu put it: "it is necessary, from the very nature of things, power should be a check to power."[26] In Book 6, Montesquieu laid out the scheme for which Americans in the Constitution-making era admired him: separation of the three powers of government (legislative, executive, and judicial) to block the tyrannical growth of power in any one of them. "There would be an end of every thing, were the same man, or the same body, whether of the nobles or of the people, to exercise those three powers, that of enacting laws, that of executing the public resolutions, and of trying the causes of individuals."[27]

State-of-nature arguments made a dramatic early appearance in British America in the wake of the Sugar Act (1764) and the Stamp Act (1765). Massachusetts lawyer James Otis' *The Rights of the British Colonies Asserted and Proved* (1764) was the first colonial pamphlet to respond to British policies by asserting rights derived not from human institutions, but instead from a state of nature governed by natural law and God. Citing Locke, Otis posited a "state of nature" governed by a "law of nature." Only by giving their "consent," could people leave the state of nature to form "civil government." The only good governments were those founded on "human nature, and ultimately on the will of God, the author of nature."[28] This scene-setting permitted Otis to proceed to his primary claim: that all British subjects born in America were "by the law of God and nature, by the common law, and by act of parliament ... entitled to all the natural, essential, inherent and inseparable rights of our fellow subjects in Great-Britain."[29]

---

[25] Charles Louis de Secondat, Baron de Montesquieu, *The Complete Works of M. de Montesquieu*, 4 vols. (London: T. Evans, 1777), vol. 1, https://oll.libertyfund.org/titles/837#Montesquieu_0171-01_108.
[26] Ibid., https://oll.libertyfund.org/titles/837#Montesquieu_0171-01_874.
[27] Ibid., https://oll.libertyfund.org/titles/837#Montesquieu_0171-01_883.
[28] James Otis, *The Rights of the British Colonies Asserted and Proved* (London: J. Almon, n.d. [1764]), 6, 7, 13, 15.
[29] Otis, *The Rights of the British Colonies*, 52.

Enlightenment and the American Revolution

The idea gained traction quickly, in part because it supplied a more universal language for rights claims than those offered by British history alone. John Adams was soon thundering about nature as a primordial source of rights in his 1765 opposition to the Stamp Act. "I say RIGHTS, antecedent to all earthly government – Rights, that cannot be repealed or restrained by human laws – Rights, derived from the great Legislator of the universe."[30] The state of nature had become commonplace in colonial rhetoric by the time Thomas Jefferson invoked it in his *Summary View of the Rights of British America* (1774). In many ways, this was a traditional document: it took the ancient and venerable form of a petition to the king, and it was grounded in historical precedents stretching back to the Anglo-Saxons. But sprinkled throughout was the new language of the state of nature as the ultimate origin of colonial – and universal – rights. Americans "possessed a right which nature has given to all men," he began, of "establishing new societies under such laws and regulations as to them shall seem most likely to promote public happiness."[31]

The new state constitutions drafted after the mid-1770s contained bills of rights that reflected both their specific origin in British common law and the fashionable new appeal to nature. Virginia's Declaration of Rights, written by George Mason in June 1776, opened with soaring rhetoric about rights emerging from a primordial state of nature. "That all men are by nature equally free and independent and have certain inherent rights, of which, when they enter into a state of society, they cannot, by any compact, deprive or divest their posterity; namely, the enjoyment of life and liberty, with the means of acquiring and possessing property, and pursuing and obtaining happiness and safety." One historian has called this "a jarring but exciting combination of universal principles with a motley collection of common law procedures."[32] It was indeed exciting enough that Thomas Jefferson drew on Mason's universalizing rights language in the Declaration of Independence. And it became the constant refrain through the war years that by throwing

---

[30] John Adams, "A Dissertation on the Canon and the Feudal Law," No. 1, 12 August 1765, https://founders.archives.gov/documents/Adams/06-01-02-0052-0004. See also Daniel Rodgers, *Contested Truths: Keywords in American Politics since Independence* (New York: Basic Books, 1987), 45–79; Eric Slauter, "Rights," in Edward G. Gray and Jane Kamensky, eds., *The Oxford Handbook of the American Revolution* (New York: Oxford University Press, 2013).

[31] Thomas Jefferson, "A Summary View of the Rights of British America," in Merrill D. Peterson, ed., *Thomas Jefferson: Writings* (New York: Library of America, 2011), 105–6.

[32] Gordon Wood, *The Creation of the American Republic, 1776–1787* (Chapel Hill: University of North Carolina Press, 1969), 271.

off British rule, Americans had entered into a state of nature – understood in the new, abstract philosophical sense of the term. "And yet at this time the people were in a great degree in a state of nature, being free from all restraints of government," wrote the secretary of Congress to John Jay in 1781.[33]

The idea of natural law and a state of nature gave Americans a new political language with which to frame their opposition to British taxation and ultimately to justify resistance and revolution. The language played a large role in the first state constitutions and bills of rights. As time passed, the explicit political appeal to the language of nature receded, ultimately playing a minor role in the federal Constitution-making era. By that time, the idea of nature had become so thoroughly normalized as a way of thinking about political origins and justifications that it was usually assumed without further need of articulation and embellishment.

Progress

A second major assumption of enlightened people was progress. A new and powerful interpretation of history, the idea of progress asserted that with reasoned human effort everything should get better. Progress was a bracing new vision of human potential that contrasted and ultimately displaced the two other major historical interpretations dominant for over two millennia. The biblical narrative had emphasized a Fall from Eden due to human sin in a cosmic drama whose meaning lay largely outside the span of a human life. Classical history involved ever-repeating cycles of political rise and fall that hinged on civic virtue and civic vice. Progress instead implied an ever-improving state of affairs largely by and for the people.

The highest goal of progress was happiness. Today we talk about happiness in personal terms, as self-fulfillment. The eighteenth century further emphasized another, more expansive meaning of happiness: what they called "public happiness" and "social happiness." Nations and peoples enjoyed public or social happiness when they were shielded by wise leaders against internal threats and external enemies. "Politicks is the science of social happiness, and the blessings of society depend entirely on the constitutions

---

[33] To John Jay from the Secretary of Congress (Charles Thomson), 11 July 1781, in *The Selected Papers of John Jay Digital Edition*, ed. Elizabeth M. Nuxoll (Charlottesville: University of Virginia Press, 2014–).

of government," John Adams explained in 1776.[34] This political meaning of happiness made it a frequent partner of the word "safety." The French vice admiral d'Estaing invoked this meaning to George Washington after the disastrous siege of Newport, Rhode Island. "The happiness and safety of America is your own work."[35] (Today the term "national security" retains some of this eighteenth-century flavor.) The opposite of public or social happiness was not sorrow but anarchy or despotism. And the Declaration's "life, liberty, and the pursuit of happiness" may have referred less to personal fulfillment than to the right to a collective political state of security.

The young republic faced formidable barriers to progress. Revolutionaries wondered where the new United States – as a sovereign nation – stood in the scale of civilization. This seems like an obscure worry to us today, but in the eighteenth century it had everything to do with political survival. The idea that all societies progressed through a series of stages from savagery to civilization had gained widespread popularity in the eighteenth century and was eagerly taken up by Americans. It was the special concern of a group of Scottish thinkers, including Adam Ferguson, John Millar, Lord Kames, and William Robertson. Using "data" (a new term from this era) collected from European empires around the world, as well as much somber reflection from the safety of their own Scottish armchairs (which is what made this kind of history "conjectural"), they proposed that all societies, in all times and places, developed upwards along a staircase of increasingly complex and sophisticated organization. They used material circumstances – what Marxists (whom the Scots deeply influenced) would later call "the mode of production" – as their guides to their categories. Thus, all societies moved from nomadic, animal-chasing "savagery" to settled agriculture ("barbarity"), and finally reached so-called "civilization" embodied in its highest form in commercialized eighteenth-century Europe. European imperialism could be justified as a civilizing process for savage and barbaric peoples. But as a former colony in a region still heavily populated by nomadic "savages," the United States faced skepticism about its capacity for ascent on the scale of civilization.[36]

---

[34] Papers of John Adams, vol. IV, February–August 1776, in *The Adams Papers Digital Edition*, ed. Sara Martin (Charlottesville: University of Virginia Press, 2008–2019).

[35] Vice Admiral d'Estaing to George Washington, 26 October 1778, in *The Papers of George Washington Digital Edition*, ed. Theodore J. Crackel (Charlottesville: University of Virginia Press, 2008).

[36] Winterer, *American Enlightenments*, Chapters 3, 4, 7. On eighteenth-century Scottish thought, see Gladys Bryson, *Man and Society: The Scottish Inquiry of the Eighteenth*

Part of the solution hinged on climate. In the eighteenth century, climate was thought by influential theorists to be the major agent shaping human societies and governments. Climate could account for human diversity within the biblically sanctioned story of monogenesis, or descent from a single pair in Eden. Much to the concern of American revolutionaries, however, some European naturalists, such as the Comte de Buffon and Cornelius de Pauw, had asserted that the allegedly cold, humid climate of the Americas shriveled all life forms – plants, animals, and humans. It even diminished Europeans who dared to settle there.[37] Revolutionary Americans anxiously eyed the other civilizations of the Americas to determine where they stood vis-à-vis the nomadic Indians of North America ("savages") and the urbanized Aztecs of central America ("semi-civilized").[38] Thus, a major question for American revolutionaries was whether their new nation, led by inexperienced statesmen born or now living in an unfavorable climate, could ever ascend to full civilization in the eyes of Europeans.

Thomas Jefferson's *Notes on the State of Virginia*, written in the early 1780s and published in France, Britain, and the United States later in that decade, exemplified the anxious uncertainty plaguing white Americans about where the new nation would stand in the scale of civilization. The "state" in Jefferson's title is a pun: it refers both to the political entity of Virginia (formerly a colony, now a state), as well as to its fluctuating climatic condition. The two meanings were related: would a republican state create a favorable climate? and was the climate of Virginia favorable for successful republican government?

Like so many other texts of this era, the *Notes on the State of Virginia* takes the form of an enumerated list. The list consists of Jefferson's responses to the queries of François Barbé-Marbois, the secretary of the French legation in Philadelphia. Barbé-Marbois wondered about the condition of the new American states recently seceded from Britain. Jefferson filled his text chock-a-block with tables assuring his French audience that American plants and animals were as large as or larger than those in Europe.[39] And so were

---

Century (Princeton: Princeton University Press, 1945); Silvia Sebastiani, *The Scottish Enlightenment: Race, Gender, and the Limits of Progress* (New York: Palgrave, 2013); Samuel Fleischacker, "The Impact on America: Scottish Philosophy and the American Founding," in Alexander Broadie, ed., *The Cambridge Companion to the Scottish Enlightenment* (Cambridge: Cambridge University Press, 2003), 316–37.

[37] Antonello Gerbi, *The Dispute of the New World: The History of a Polemic, 1750–1900*, trans. Jeremy Moyle (Pittsburgh: University of Pittsburgh Press, 1973 [1955]).

[38] Winterer, *American Enlightenments*, Chapters 3 and 4.

[39] Lee Dugatkin, *Mr. Jefferson and the Giant Moose: Natural History in Early America* (Chicago: University of Chicago Press, 2009).

the people: Jefferson was at pains to argue that the American Indians, though native to the American climate, could ascend the scale of civilization since their current inferiority was the result "not of a difference of nature, but of circumstance."[40] The new republic would create a favorable climate for civilization, which would then civilize the Indians. Jefferson's "Empire of Liberty" hinged on this climatic theory, which he pursued as president through the Louisiana Purchase and other policies.[41]

The question of United States' civilization was also debated at the international level – or, in the terminology of the era, as part of the "law of nations." Like so many areas of political thought in the revolutionary era, this one drew from the idea of natural law. Beginning in the seventeenth century, as European empires expanded across land and sea, a cadre of European jurists tried to determine how law governed the actions of whole nations in relationship to one another. Eighteenth-century Americans were familiar with theorists such as Samuel von Pufendorf, Hugo Grotius, and Jean-Jacques Burlamaqui. They were especially drawn to Emer de Vattel, whose *Le droit des gens* (*The Law of Nations*, 1758) derived an idea of relations between sovereign states from a prior conception of natural law and human governments formed out of a state of nature.[42] Vattel believed that the law of nations was a science accessible to human reason. "There certainly exists a natural law of nations, since the obligations of the law of nature are no less binding on states, on men united in political society, than on individuals."[43]

Vattel's ideas were relevant because American diplomatic failures after 1776 had dramatically revealed to them that recognition of a new nation in the system of the "law of nations" was earned and not a given. The federal Constitution emerged not just from domestic concerns, but in an international context where a "law of nations" based in natural law was thought to govern the interactions of "civilized" nations.[44] In the legal case of *Rutgers*

---

[40] Thomas Jefferson, *Notes on the State of Virginia* (London: John Stockdale, 1787), 100.
[41] Anthony F. C. Wallace, *Jefferson and the Indians: The Tragic Fate of the First Americans* (Cambridge, MA: Belknap Press of Harvard University Press, 1999); Peter S. Onuf, *Jefferson's Empire: The Language of American Nationhood* (Charlottesville: University of Virginia Press, 2000).
[42] Frederick G. Whelan, "Vattel's Doctrine of the State," in Knud Haakonssen, ed., *Grotius, Pufendorf and Modern Natural Law* (Aldershot: Dartmouth Publishing, 1999), 403–34.
[43] Emar de Vattel, *Le droit des gens*, 2 vols. (London, n.p.: 1758), vol. 1, 3. English translation from Liberty Fund edition, preface, https://oll.libertyfund.org/titles/vattel-the-law-of-nations-lf-ed.
[44] Daniel M. Golove and Daniel Hulsebosch, "The Law of Nations and the Constitution: An Early Modern Perspective," *Georgetown Law Journal* 106 (2018), 1593–658.

v. *Waddington* (1784), mayor James Duane of New York explained his reverence for the law of nations as an obligation for newly independent Americans to learn and cultivate:

> Profess to revere the rights of human nature; at every hazard and expence we have vindicated, and successfully established them in our land! and we cannot but reverence a law which is their chief guardian – a law which inculcates as a first principle – that the amiable precepts of the law of nature, are as obligatory on nations in the mutual intercourse, as they are on individuals in their conduct towards each other ... What more eminently distinguished the refined and polished nations of Europe, from the piratical states of Barbary, than a respect or a contempt for this law.[45]

Lurking in the background of the new "progress talk" was the fear that economic progress would cause a decline in the civic virtue on which the new republic rested. Traditional thinking about republics, inherited from the Greeks and Romans, identified farming as the source of such virtues as self-sacrifice that upheld republics. But as the United States "progressed" up the ladder of civilization – with more manufactures, commerce, cities, and other markers of "civilization" – what would become of those sturdy agricultural virtues? The fears worsened with the westward expansion across the Appalachians in the decades after independence. To some, national expansion was an undeniable sign that the empire-rejecting republic had now become an empire in its own right.[46]

Thus, the idea of progress was from the first a double-edged sword. It filled Americans with hopes for a happy future of progress toward civilization. It provided a frame for filling with higher meaning their political break from Britain. But its linearity – its insistence that all movement through time must necessarily be either progress or degeneration – became an interpretive trap that remains with us today.

Reason

Revolutionary Americans thought a lot about how their own minds worked. They could not improve the world unless they understood their own perceptions of what was true and good. But the Declaration's "self-evident" truths masked a real question about how fallible humans could discern truth.

---

[45] Golove and Hulsebosch, "The Law of Nations," 1608.
[46] Drew R. McCoy, *The Elusive Republic: Political Economy in Jeffersonian America* (Chapel Hill: University of North Carolina Press, 1980).

The dark conspiracies allegedly brewing in Whitehall heightened colonists' desire to find a path to truths that were not in fact self-evident at all.

The political texts of the American revolutionary era reflect their concerns about the mind's capacities to grasp external realities. Like others at this time, American revolutionaries held up "reason" as a universal human attribute that could discern empirically valid conclusions based on information delivered to the mind through the five senses. John Locke's *Essay Concerning Human Understanding* (1689) and the works of Scottish philosophers such as Frances Hutcheson and Thomas Reid were mainstays of British American reading. These books explained how the mind formed ideas about reality from sensory perception mixed with reflection. As a property common to all humanity, this way of reasoning was termed "common sense."

The mind's powers included not just cold calculation but also a "moral sense" based in part on sensory perceptions such as pleasure and pain. This moral sense – variously called the affections, sensibility, or sympathy – formed the basis for human social action, connecting self and society.[47] Sensibility was "the great cement of human society," as one Scottish philosopher put it.[48]

In 1776, pain and pleasure joined reason in a new political calculus. The Declaration of Independence raised not just happiness but pain to a high pitch of political significance. The colonists endured three versions of suffering (suffer, sufferable, and sufferance), along with tribulations that were both "uncomfortable" and "fatiguing." Earlier that year, Thomas Paine in his bestselling pamphlet *Common Sense* (1776) had both popularized and politicized Scottish epistemology. Paine's achievement was to pair "common sense" with republican government. The pamphlet's title announced that a shared commitment by ordinary people to overthrowing British rule was the only reasonable conclusion available from an appraisal of sensory data regarding trampled rights and liberties. No special knowledge or erudition was required: Paine's text deliberately lacked footnotes. He would offer nothing more than "simple facts, plain arguments, and common sense."[49]

---

[47] Sophia Rosenfeld, *Common Sense: A Political History* (Cambridge, MA: Harvard University Press, 2011); Sarah Knott, *Sensibility and the American Revolution* (Chapel Hill: University of North Carolina Press, 2009); Jessica Riskin, *Science in the Age of Sensibility: The Sentimental Empiricists of the French Enlightenment* (Chicago: University of Chicago Press, 2002).

[48] Henry Home, Lord Kames, *Essays on the Principles of Morality and Natural Religion* (Edinburgh: R. Fleming, 1751), 17.

[49] Thomas Paine, *Common Sense* (Philadelphia, PA: R. Bell, 1776), 17.

But common sense raised as many political questions as it answered. Alexander Hamilton singled out the "important question" in the first essay of The Federalist: "whether societies of men are really capable or not of establishing good government from reflection and choice, or whether they are forever destined to depend for their political constitutions on accident and force."[50] Did "the people" as a whole possess enough reason and common sense to govern? And which individual people possessed those traits? These emerged as two of the most fiercely debated questions of the revolutionary era.

The struggle led to one of the great unexpected and ironic outcomes of enlightened thought: the new, hierarchical categorization of humanity based largely on reasoning capacity. Women, children, slaves, and Native Americans among others now entered a period of major reassessment as a result of the new ideal of a reason-based republic.[51] We can consider African Americans and women more closely here.

For African Americans, the American Revolution represented two linked achievements: the largest flight by slaves since the first Black slaves had arrived in English North America in the early 1600s, and the occasion for the first rights-based articulations of African American liberty. There were approximately half a million African and African American slaves in the United States in 1776; the small free Black population clustered largely in urban areas. In the years leading up to independence, free Blacks in the north moved quickly to apply the idea of natural rights to their personal enslavement, mirroring the language free white colonists used to describe political enslavement to Britain. With access to print through white sympathizers such as John Woolman and Benjamin Rush, they could more broadly spread the critique of Black enslavement on the grounds of natural rights. Some slaves in Boston also petitioned the legislature for emancipation using the language of rights.

In the decades after 1776, the language of nature and rights pervaded the new movement of antislavery activism. The movement gained support from the fact that ultimately approximately 9,000 African Americans served in the war against Britain. In Fairfield and Stratford, Connecticut, a band of slaves

---

[50] The Federalist, 1.
[51] For children, see Holly Brewer, By Birth or Consent: Children, Law, and the Anglo-American Revolution in Authority (Chapel Hill: University of North Carolina Press, 2005).

petitioned the wartime legislature in May 1779, asserting a common human nature.

> [R]eason and revelation join to declare that we are the creatures of that God, who made of one blood, and kindred, all the nations of the earth ... We can never be convinced that we were made to be slaves ... Is it consistent with the present claims of the United States to hold so many thousands of the race of Adam, our common father, in perpetual slavery? Can human nature endure the shocking idea? ... ask for nothing but what we are fully persuaded is ours to claim.[52]

Many northern states passed emancipation acts in the wake of independence that allowed for the gradual liberation of slaves.

Yet enlightened ideas about republican participation based on reason also worked against African American claims to equality. For centuries, the Genesis story of Creation, in which all humanity had descended from an original pair, had served to maintain the idea that all humans ultimately formed part of the same human family. Differences in appearance and behavior could be attributed to climate or custom. American slaveholders in the post-independence era, however, fearful that rights-based claims to equality would lead to widespread slave emancipation, began to argue that African Americans were by nature intellectually inferior to Whites. They emphasized that this intellectual inferiority did not result from climatic effects so much as from unchangeable heredity. Lacking the full complement of reason necessary for participation in republican governance, African Americans should therefore either remain in servitude or, if freed, be colonized elsewhere.

Thomas Jefferson's *Notes on the State of Virginia* contained the American revolutionary era's most detailed catalog of Black inferiority. A Virginia slaveholder who over the course of his life held approximately 600 slaves, Jefferson cited "the real distinctions which nature has made" – that is, permanent Black intellectual, physical, and moral inferiority to Whites.

---

[52] Gary Nash, *The Unknown American Revolution: The Unruly Birth of Democracy and the Struggle to Create America* (New York: Viking, 2005), 320–21. For works on antislavery ideas that make reference specifically to the goal of enlightenment, see Andrew S. Curran, *The Anatomy of Blackness: Science and Slavery in an Age of Enlightenment* (Baltimore, MD: Johns Hopkins University Press, 2011); Justin Roberts, *Slavery and the Enlightenment in the British Atlantic, 1750–1807* (Cambridge: Cambridge University Press, 2013). The classic formulations are Winthrop Jordan, *White over Black: American Attitudes toward the Negro, 1550–1812* (Chapel Hill: University of North Carolina Press, 1968); David Brion Davis, *The Problem of Slavery in the Age of Revolution, 1770–1823* (Ithaca, NY: Cornell University Press, 1975).

Jefferson's essay was among the first to propose that Black inferiority was due to innate difference, lodged in inheritable bodily characteristics that would not change with climate.[53] Thus, the revolutionary era produced both the first claims to common humanity based on "natural" rights, but also the first arguments that "nature" itself created immutable inferiorities.

White women in the United States also lodged new claims for reasoned participation in the republic. Women had long been thought of as deficient in full mental capacities, though this had generally formed part of a larger biblical argument about the sin of Eve. Now, republicanism's claims to the equality of all human beings put the question of women's natural reasoning capacities squarely on the table. Judith Sargent Murray's "On the Equality of the Sexes" (1790), published in the *Massachusetts Magazine* when women's publication was still rare and often condemned, demanded to know the empirical basis for assertions of female inferiority. "Is it indeed a fact, that she hath yielded to one half of the human species so unquestionable a mental superiority?"[54]

Because it remained difficult to argue for women's civic participation and education as an end in itself, women instead pointed out that the need to educate republican men for citizenship required schools for future mothers.[55] Female academies for young women were founded beginning in the 1780s. Some of the earliest included Sara Pierce's Litchfield Academy, founded in 1792 in Litchfield, Connecticut. They offered a curriculum designed to educate both "reason" and "the affections." Though making concessions to female capacities to reason, the academy curricula offered a different array of courses to that of male-only colleges such as Harvard and Yale. Few offered Latin and Greek (which were thought to be virilizing preparation for citizenship, and therefore inappropriate for girls), and they generally focused on

---

[53] Jefferson's claims, because they potentially contradicted the monogenesis story of Creation, were the subject of fierce attacks at the time, especially by ministers such as Samuel Stanhope Smith, president of Princeton. See Mark Noll, *Princeton and the Republic, 1768–1822: The Search for Christian Enlightenment in the Era of Samuel Stanhope Smith* (Princeton: Princeton University Press, 1989).

[54] Judith Sargent Murray, "On the Equality of the Sexes," in Sheila L. Skemp, ed., *Judith Sargent Murray: A Brief Biography with Documents* (Boston, MA: Bedford Books, 1998), 177.

[55] Linda Kerber, *Women of the Republic: Intellect and Ideology in Revolutionary America* (Chapel Hill: University of North Carolina Press, 1980); Rosemarie Zagarri, "Morals, Manners, and the Republican Mother," *American Quarterly* 44 (1992), 192–215; Sarah Knott and Barbara Taylor, eds., *Women, Gender and Enlightenment* (New York: Palgrave, 2005).

geography, arithmetic, history, French, and needlepoint.[56] Some of the first publications just for women, such as the *Lady's Magazine*, offered a mashup of news, fiction, and reprints of European and American publications. These included the radical British writer Mary Wollstonecraft's *Vindication of the Rights of Woman* (1792), which had extended the idea of rights to women, arguing for their legal, social, and educational disabilities under current practices. Still, after the revolution, a backlash occurred that reasserted female difference in both body and mind, stalling claims to equal rights of citizenship for many decades to come.[57]

Revolution

During the late eighteenth century, the word "revolution" changed political meaning. In the past it had usually meant a cyclical return to a political origin point, as when the Earth has completed its journey around the Sun. In the theories of Aristotle and Polybius, the three kinds of government – monarchical, aristocratic, and democratic – all eventually degenerated into their baser versions (tyranny, oligarchy, and mobocracy), at which point the cycle of politics would begin anew. But beginning in the later eighteenth century, the term "revolution" began to refer much more often to the forcible establishment of a wholly new form of government, and even a new social and cultural order.

What made a revolution revolutionary was this new horizon of possibility, the sense that time itself was accelerating into a better tomorrow.[58] New mottos captured the temporal rupture: the American Revolution's "Novus Ordo Seclorum" (new order of the ages) and the French Revolution's "ancien régime" to refer to the era before 1789. The Abbé Raynal declared that the American Revolution fundamentally ruptured history itself. "The present is about to decide upon a long futurity," he wrote in *The Revolution of America* (1781). "All is changed ... A day has given birth to a revolution. A day has transported us to another age."[59] The first history of the American

---

[56] Mary Kelley, *Learning to Stand and Speak: Women, Education, and Public Life in America's Republic* (Chapel Hill: University of North Carolina Press, 2006), 16–19, 47.
[57] Rosemarie Zagarri, *Revolutionary Backlash: Women and Politics in the Early American Republic* (Philadelphia: University of Pennsylvania Press, 2009).
[58] Reinhart Koselleck, "Historical Criteria of the Modern Concept of Revolution," in *Futures Past: On the Semantics of Historical Time*, trans. Keith Tribe (Cambridge, MA: MIT Press, 1985), 39–54.
[59] Raynal, *The Revolution of America*, 80.

Revolution written by an American – David Ramsay's *The History of the American Revolution* (1789) – also announced the opening of "an Era in the history of the world, remarkable for the progressive increase in human happiness!"[60]

In *On Revolution* (1963), the political theorist Hannah Arendt equated this new meaning of revolution with modernity itself. "Historically, wars are among the oldest phenomena of the recorded past while revolutions, properly speaking, did not exist prior to the modern age; they are among the most recent of all major political data."[61] Yet the major political data of revolutions are not always transparent. Amid the bombastic rhetoric of new nationalism, Americans quietly expressed ambivalence and doubts about whether republicanism in fact yielded enlightenment. The US House of Representatives spent precious hours debating the matter in 1796. Some representatives hoped to announce to Europe that the United States was the most enlightened nation in the world. Others declared that idea a fool's errand. Not only would it irritate more militarily powerful European powers, but they could not agree on which "political data" would in fact confirm that the United States had achieved enlightenment through republican government.[62]

One data point was clear: the ongoing political importance of monarchy. Thomas Paine had relegated monarchy to a mist-shrouded barbaric age in *Common Sense*. But, in fact, nearly all of Europe and the Americas were still governed by monarchs, and would be for many decades to come. "American Ministers are acting in Monarchies, and not in Republicks," John Adams noted correctly from Paris in 1783.[63] Nor were those monarchies the sinister agents of barbarity on which American revolutionary propaganda rested. Quite the opposite. For centuries, European monarchies had often acted as

---

[60] David Ramsay, *History of the American Revolution*, 2 vols. (Philadelphia, PA: R. Aitken, 1789), vol. II, 356. See also Karen O'Brien, *Narratives of Enlightenment: Cosmopolitan History from Voltaire to Gibbon* (Cambridge: Cambridge University Press, 1997); J. G. A. Pocock, *Barbarism and Religion*, 6 vols. (Cambridge: Cambridge University Press, 1999–2015); Johnson Kent Wright, "Historical Thought in the Era of the Enlightenment," in Lloyd Kramer and Sarah Maza, eds., *A Companion to Western Historical Thought* (Oxford: Blackwell, 2006), 123–42; Caroline Winterer, "History: Narratives of Progress," in Jack Censer, ed., *A Cultural History of Ideas in the Age of Enlightenment*, vol. IV: *A Cultural History of Ideas in the Age of Enlightenment*, vol. eds. Sophia Rosenfeld and Peter Struck (London: Bloomsbury Academic, 2022), 183–97.
[61] Hannah Arendt, *On Revolution* (New York: Penguin, 1963), 12.
[62] Winterer, *American Enlightenments*, 246–9.
[63] John Adams to Abigail Adams, 27 February 1783, Papers of John Adams Digital Edition.

major cultural and intellectual brokers. They sponsored scientific societies, museums of all kinds, and patronized individual artists and intellectuals. A glance backward into their own history would have revealed to Americans that King George II had helped to found four universities: three, including Princeton, in his North American colonies; and one at Göttingen in his Germanic territories. This fact was conveniently forgotten amid revolutionary iconoclasm, when republican names replaced royal ones (as when King's College became Columbia).

And lacking a clear sense of what a republican executive should look like, Americans also observed the recent phenomenon of enlightened despotism with interest. Emerging from divine-right monarchy, eighteenth-century rulers such as Catherine the Great of Russia, Charles III of Spain, Gustav III of Sweden, the Holy Roman Empress Maria-Theresa, and Frederick the Great of Prussia all to varying degrees adjusted their mandate to the intellectual climate of their era. They claimed – by their actions, publications, and policies – that it was possible to mix formidable executive power with reforms aligned with the new ideal of enlightenment.[64] They reformed law codes and criminal justice, encouraged greater religious toleration, restructured education, and promoted arts and culture. To Americans watching from across the Atlantic, these monarchs provided widely known, dynamic, modern examples of how to mix monarchical rule with the new goal of enlightenment. Unlike the absolutist monarchs of the previous century, who could swat away kingless republican rule as a momentary infatuation, enlightened despots operated in an era when popular opinion and republican government were becoming lived realities.

Nowhere was Americans' serious interest in enlightened despotism clearer than in their admiration of Frederick the Great of Prussia, the war hero, political philosopher, and reformer. During his nearly half-century reign, from 1740 until his death in 1786, King Frederick became a relentless public advocate for enlightened reform engineered through powerful monarchical rule. A scholarly ruler who collected philosophers like butterflies at his Prussian palace Sans Souci, Frederick the Great published numerous works on his version of enlightened monarchical rule that were read by revolutionary Americans seeking to build a republic for the age of enlightenment. He read Rousseau on the social contract, Montesquieu on mixed government,

---

[64] Derek Beales, *Enlightenment and Reform in Eighteenth-Century Europe* (London: I. B. Tauris, 2005); Hamish M. Scott, ed., *Enlightened Absolutism: Reform and Reformers in Later Eighteenth-Century Europe* (Basingstoke: Macmillan, 1990).

and corresponded frequently with Voltaire, and even co-authored a refutation of Machiavelli's *The Prince* (called *The Antimachiavel*) that was widely read by Americans. Frederick's main platform, expressed in his *Antimachiavel* and elsewhere, was that a powerful, virtuous monarch could promote the state and the enlightened well-being of his subjects within the context of single-person rule.[65] Americans pondered this species of executive as they set about inventing the monarch-like presidency from whole cloth in Article II of the Constitution.[66]

Frederick's Prussia was the context for what has today become the most celebrated manifesto of enlightenment: Immanuel Kant's "An Answer to the Question, What Is Enlightenment?" ("Beantwortung der Frage: Was ist Aufklärung?," 1784). This essay was unknown to revolutionary Americans, as Kant himself largely was until the early nineteenth century. But the essay's core questions were both familiar and relevant to them: under what political conditions does a people emerge from a state of intellectual dependency to one of independence and enlightenment? Which species of government was best aligned with the goal of enlightenment? Over the next decades, an answer to the question of "what is enlightenment?" remained elusive as Europe and the Americas lurched from monarchy to republicanism and back again. "What is enlightenment?" one of Kant's exasperated contemporaries wondered. "This question, which is almost as important as what is truth, should indeed be answered before one begins enlightening! And still I have never found it answered!"[67]

By the 1780s, the new dream of enlightenment had already created a particular story of America's break with Britain. This event, now called the "American Revolution," would be no local rupture but instead a new order of the ages, a world-historical event in the grand ascent of universal human rights. The new United States would "illumine the world with truth and liberty," declared the Connecticut minister Ezra Stiles in 1783. "This great american revolution, this recent political phænomenon of a new sovereignty

---

[65] Caroline Winterer, "Enlightened Despotism and the American Revolution: The Political Thought of Frederick the Great of Prussia," in Ben Lowe, ed., *Political Thought and the Origins of the American Presidency* (Gainesville: University Press of Florida, 2021), 98–124; Tim Blanning, *Frederick the Great: King of Prussia* (London: Allen Lane, 2015).

[66] Jack Rakove, *Original Meanings: Politics and Ideas in the Making of the Constitution* (New York: Knopf, 1996), Chapter 9.

[67] Immanuel Kant, "Beantwortung der Frage: Was ist Aufklärung?," *Berlinische Monatsschrift* (1784), 481–94; James Schmidt, "The Question of Enlightenment: Kant, Mendelssohn, and the *Mittwochgesellschaft*," *Journal of the History of Ideas* 50:2 (1989), 272.

arising among the sovereign powers of the earth, will be attended to and contemplated by all nations."[68]

Yet even as the new interpretative frame of the "American Revolution" settled into place by the 1780s, doubt, ambiguity, and open-endedness lingered. This can be difficult for us to see, given our commitment to finding a "real" American Revolution, a brute fact independent of interpretation, awaiting only our discovery, as though we had finally freed ourselves from the progressive interpretation of history embedded in the very idea of an "Age of Atlantic Revolutions." Immanuel Kant captured the uncertain frame of mind by putting a question mark at the end of his title. In his final letter before his death, Thomas Jefferson turned to the progressive tense to describe the unfinished project of enlightenment in America. "All eyes are opened, or opening, to the rights of man," he wrote in 1826. "The general spread of the light of science has already laid open to every view the palpable truth, that the mass of mankind has not been born with saddles on their backs, nor a favored few booted and spurred, ready to ride them legitimately, by the grace of God. These are grounds of hope for others."[69]

Jefferson recognized that there were grounds for hope. But eyes were still opening. Enlightenment had not yet been achieved.

---

[68] Ezra Stiles, *The United States Elevated to Glory and Honor* (New Haven, CT: Thomas & Samuel Green, 1783), 52, https://digitalcommons.unl.edu/etas/41.

[69] Thomas Jefferson to Roger Weightman, 24 June 1826, in Peterson, *Thomas Jefferson: Writings*, 1517.

2
Enlightenment and the French Revolution

JOHNSON KENT WRIGHT

"Je suis tombé par terre, c'est la faute à Voltaire, / Le nez dans le ruisseau, c'est la faute à ..." So sings the street urchin Gavroche, toward the end of *Les Misérables*, as he scrambles over the barricades during *les Trois Glorieuses* in 1830, picked off by a rifle shot before he can get out one more "Rousseau." Hugo's ditty parodied what had long been conventional wisdom in reactionary circles about the origins of the French Revolution – seemingly confirmed, of course, by the *panthéonisations* of Voltaire and Rousseau in 1792 and 1794, respectively. If the notion of an umbilical connection between philosophy and the Revolution was never confined to the right, few would doubt its special appeal for thinkers on that side of the political spectrum. Variations on the theme echoed throughout the long nineteenth century, from Burke's fiery invective at the start of the Revolution, and Constant's post-mortem for "ancient liberty" early in the Restoration, to Tocqueville's lamentations over the "abstract, literary politics" of the *philosophes* during the Second Empire. The Third Republic launched, Taine expanded on Tocqueville, tracing the new regime's deplorable program of *laïcité* to the cold-hearted, irreligious rationalism of the Grand Siècle, original source of the "revolutionary spirit." On the eve of the First World War, Cochin issued a blunt reminder: "Before the bloody terror of 1793, there was, from 1765 to 1780, a dry terror whose Committee of Public Safety was the *Encyclopédie* and whose Robespierre was d'Alembert."[1] By the interwar period, however, the trope seemed to have run its course. The war itself, and its dénouement in Russia, had ushered in a new political world; the routines of settled scholarship had blunted older passions. In *Les origines intellectuelles de la Révolution française*, published in

---

[1] Augustin Cochin, "Les Philosophes," a lecture delivered in 1912; cited in Darrin McMahon, *Enemies of the Enlightenment: The French Counter-Enlightenment and the Making of Modernity* (New York: Oxford University Press, 2001) – a fundamental work of intellectual history.

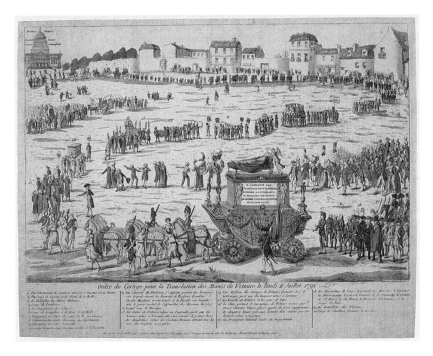

Figure 2.1 The transfer of Voltaire's remains to the Panthéon, 1791. © Reproduction Benjamin Gavaudo/CMN.

1933, the literary historian Daniel Mornet sought to give a decent burial to Tocqueville, Taine, and Cochin alike. Meticulous reconstruction of the political thought of the *philosophes*, and of the diffusion of their ideas, Mornet argued, showed that their outlook was essentially pragmatic and reformist, not revolutionary. The *"esprit critique"* of Montesquieu and Voltaire, Rousseau and Raynal had indeed weakened the Old Regime. But it was responsible neither for its ultimate collapse nor for what ensued: "A Lenin, a Trotsky wanted a particular revolution; first they prepared it; then they carried it out, then they directed it. Nothing like that occurred in France. The origins of the Revolution are one story, the history of the Revolution is another."[2]

There was another respect in which Mornet's *Les origines intellectuelles de la Révolution française* marked the end of an intellectual era. For all the interest

---

[2] Daniel Mornet, *Les origines intellectuelles de la Révolution française, 1715–1787* (Paris: Armand Colin, 1933), 471.

of the above record, it actually preceded the emergence of the notion of "the Enlightenment" as a widely recognized historical category. In most European languages, the definite article became fixed to the noun only at the end of the nineteenth century, English last of all. In French, the concept of *"les lumières"* has remained stubbornly plural to this day. As Lynn Hunt and Margaret Jacob have argued, the birth of "Enlightenment Studies" as we know it came later still, well into the interwar period. It was the achievement of a series of distinguished scholarly victims of fascism – Ernst Cassirer, Paul Hazard, Franco Venturi, Peter Gay – for whom identification with their object of study was at one with the defense of "modernity" itself.[3] The result, for much twentieth-century writing on the Enlightenment, was to preclude automatic or intimate association with the French Revolution. In France, Hazard approached the topic with "the crisis of European consciousness" in mind. The *telos* of Cassirer's *The Philosophy of the Enlightenment* was not the Declaration of the Rights of Man and of the Citizen, but Kant's *Critique of Judgment*. The major mid-century synthesis in the Anglo-American world, Gay's *The Enlightenment: An Interpretation*, concluded with a profile of the American Revolution, rather than the French, as the consummate political expression of the Enlightenment.

It was only at the end of the century that this scene altered, thanks to two successive historiographical developments. First, came the ascendancy of the Revisionist interpretation of the Revolution, which upended what was taken to be Marxist–Jacobin "orthodoxy" about its origins with sweeping restatements of the themes of Tocqueville, Taine, and Cochin. The French Revolution marked not the advent of capitalism, but the triumph of a radically egalitarian ideology, whose key meaning for modern history lay in the awful warning of the Terror. Far more consequential and surprising, however, has been Jonathan Israel's cyclopean recasting of the entire problematic, with his multi-volume history of "Radical Enlightenment" – a comprehensive worldview, descending from Spinoza, which, Israel contends, can be regarded as the "one 'big' cause," not just of the French Revolution, but of the Atlantic convulsions as a whole. Israel's political outlook, based on rapturous identification with "Radical Enlightenment," initially made his interpretation look very different from that of Revisionism, as if two centuries of commination had suddenly capsized into celebration. But the appearance was deceptive. Far more important has been what they share intellectually – an aggressive

---

[3] Lynn Hunt, with Margaret Jacob, "Enlightenment Studies," in Alan Charles Kors, ed., *Encyclopedia of the Enlightenment* (Oxford: Oxford University Press, 2003), vol. 1, 418–30.

reassertion of the independent causal weight of *ideas* in modern history, rendering the Enlightenment, in Israel's view above all, a kind of *primum movens* of "modernity" itself.[4]

On the whole, historians have greeted Israel's project with skepticism – admiring his industry and stamina, while tending to regard his central thesis as a grandiose myth of origins. But few have been tempted to offer an alternative narrative of similar scope and scale. The main critical response thus far has been either to retreat to more diluted, "pluralist" conceptions of the Enlightenment, restoring a kind of *status quo ante*, or simply to dispense with the category altogether.[5] One alternative, of course, would be adopt the position that Israel himself regards as the scandalous antithesis of his own, encapsulated in Roger Chartier's suggestion that: "[i]n affirming that it was the Enlightenment that produced the Revolution, the classical interpretation perhaps inverses the logical order: should we not consider instead that it was the Revolution that invented the Enlightenment by attempting to root its legitimacy in a corpus of texts and founding authors reconciled and united, beyond their extreme differences, by their preparation of a rupture with the old world?"[6] Better still, perhaps, might be to try to combine the positions of Israel and Chartier in some fashion, such that the relations between the Enlightenment and the French Revolution can be understood not just as "causal" – in either direction – but as forming an intelligible whole within the wider flow of Atlantic history. Something like that will be attempted here, in necessarily stenographic form.

The Anglo-Dutch Future

An obvious starting point is to try to approach our topic from a more long-term perspective than is customary. An older tradition has, in fact, always encouraged us to see the Enlightenment as in some sense the heir to the two

---

[4] Indeed, as if to confirm suspicions, in the latest volume of his series, Israel records his belated discovery that the coiner of the term "Radical Enlightenment" was none other than Leo Strauss; see Jonathan Israel, *The Enlightenment That Failed: Ideas, Revolution, and Democratic Defeat, 1748–1830* (Oxford: Oxford University Press, 2019), 29–31.

[5] It is striking, for example, that in his two magisterial volumes, *Before the Deluge* and *Sans-Culottes*, Michael Sonenscher, the leading historian of the intellectual origins of the French Revolution in Anglo-American scholarship, should have found virtually no use for the idea of "the Enlightenment" – treated largely as an unhelpful historical anachronism: cf. Michael Sonenscher, *Sans-Culottes: An Eighteenth-Century Emblem in the French Revolution* (Princeton: Princeton University Press, 2008), 55.

[6] Roger Chartier, *The Cultural Origins of the French Revolution*, trans. Lydia G. Cochrane (Durham, NC: Duke University Press, 1991), 5.

pan-European intellectual movements that preceded it – indeed, as simultaneously the *culmination* and *cancelation* of the Renaissance and the Reformation.[7] Neoclassical architecture and neorepublican politics show that the Enlightenment remained deeply indebted to the earlier recovery of the cultural heritage of classical antiquity.[8] Yet the eighteenth century marked precisely the moment when any lingering notion of the superiority of the Ancients over the Moderns was left behind for good. The Enlightenment assault on the intellectual authority of Christianity was more dramatic still: in effect, the Protestant critique of Catholicism was now extended to religion itself. What made this dual "emancipation from self-incurred tutelage" – Kant's famous definition of the Enlightenment – possible? It owed everything, on this account, to one more intellectual movement, whose very name, the "Scientific Revolution," was an invention of the Enlightenment, whose leading thinkers all agreed in tracing the proximate origins of their ideas to a specific set of ancestors – above all, Bacon, Descartes, Spinoza, Locke, Newton. The Enlightenment, according to this view, was just that: the process by which the most advanced thought of the seventeenth century was popularized and disseminated in the course of the eighteenth century.

But if such is a plausible intellectual ancestry for the Enlightenment, that leads us to a further issue, crucial for the question of its relation to the French Revolution. Why should France have played so central a role in the movement – comparable with that of Italy in the Renaissance and Germany in the Reformation? Any answer will take us beyond the history of ideas proper and into the wider currents of early modern political and economic history. Only a few broad and familiar brushstrokes are possible here. But few will dispute that at a world-historical level, the major development of the Renaissance epoch was the start of the long and complicated transition to capitalism in Europe, the climax of which would be the Industrial Revolution that unfolded in Britain at precisely the moment that France was engulfed in its political revolution. Despite, or perhaps because of, the sheer volume of recent work on the history of capitalism, there is no scholarly consensus on the exact shape of the transition – save perhaps in one respect. Nearly every major account agrees in assigning France a marginal or secondary role in that history. This was indeed a cherished theme of the most celebrated historian

---

[7] For an example, see the Introduction to Norman Hampson's unjustly neglected book, Norman Hampson, *The Enlightenment* (Harmondsworth: Penguin, 1968), 15–40.

[8] There is at last a study of "classical republicanism" in eighteenth-century France worthy of the topic: Ariane Viktoria Fichtl, *La Radicalisation de l'idéal républicain: Modèles antiques et la Révolution française* (Paris: Classiques Garnier, 2020).

of both: "Is it perhaps both France's tragedy and the secret of its charm," Fernand Braudel famously asked, "that it has never really been won – what is called won – over to capitalism?"[9] For Braudel, it was the sheer size of France, by comparison with its more compact rivals, that explained why capitalism tended to develop *around* the country, its cutting-edge moving from the city-states of Renaissance Italy to the succession of "world cities" – Venice and Genoa, Antwerp and Amsterdam, and, finally, London – whose domination of Mediterranean, Atlantic, and then global trade laid the foundations for the new civilization. A different, more substantial explanation was first suggested by Braudel's *Annales* colleague Marc Bloch, in his earlier *French Rural History*: what distinguished the French developmental path was the persistence of smallholder property after the end of the Middle Ages. Bloch contrasted this pattern to the dispossession of the English peasantry by large gentry landowners, as well as with the imposition of the "second serfdom" in eastern Europe – the triangular comparison that was later to serve as the basis for Robert Brenner's enormously influential account of the transition, with the emphasis it places on the precocious development of *agrarian* capitalism in the Low Countries and, especially, England.[10] There are, of course, many other approaches to the history of capitalism – but it is difficult to think of any that fails to portray France as a kind of perennial laggard at every stage in its emergence and development.

Obviously, it took a very long time for historical dynamics of that kind even to start to become visible to contemporaries – indeed, we can date the dawning realization that France was being overtaken by more economically advanced rivals very precisely to the Enlightenment. Harder to miss were the fortunes of the French *state* in the early modern period. Like its Habsburg, Tudor, and Vasa counterparts, the Valois monarchy was a creation of the Renaissance. But it was the era of the Reformation that marked the real watershed in the history, not just of French absolutism, but of the state-form in general. On the one hand, the Bourbon re-founding of the monarchy, in the wake of the most savage episode of confessional strife of the age, brought the long and arduous process of absolutist state-construction in France to an apparently triumphant conclusion. At the beginning of the "personal rule" of Louis XIV in 1661, the Bourbon monarchy was by far the largest and most

---

[9] Fernand Braudel, *The Identity of France*, vol. II: *People and Production*, trans. Siân Reynolds (New York: HarperCollins, 1991), 666.

[10] For characteristically acute comments on Braudel, Bloch, and Brenner, see Perry Anderson, "Fernand Braudel and National Identity," in Perry Anderson, *A Zone of Engagement* (London: Verso, 1992), 254–6.

populous state in Western Europe – the model for all other absolutisms, and seemingly poised to overtake its Habsburg rival at last. If that was never to be – if the menace of a Gallic "universal monarchy," which still haunted the early Enlightenment, was never realized – the reason is clear. The seventeenth century also saw the first great revolutionary breaches in the absolutist political order, with the success of the Dutch bid for independence from Habsburg rule, formally conceded in 1648, and the final overthrow of Stuart absolutism in Britain, secured by the "Glorious Revolution" of 1688. Recent historiography has provided us with any number of different ways of understanding the Dutch Revolt and the English revolutions: Wim Klooster's *The Dutch Moment* is the outstanding study of the consequences of the former; Steve Pincus' *1688: The First Modern Revolution* on the meaning of the latter; while Jonathan Scott, weaving together the Dutch Revolt, English Civil War, and North American independence into a single overarching narrative, offers an explanation for nothing less than *How the Old World Ended*.[11] Meanwhile, in a book that at least suggests that reports of the death of the traditional notion of "bourgeois revolution" may have been premature, Neil Davidson has argued that the Dutch Revolt and English revolutions marked the moment of "systemic irreversibility" for preindustrial capitalism, hitherto often halted in its development, thanks to the capture of *states* themselves for the first time.[12]

These are deep waters, of course. But at more fathomable depths, we can perhaps glimpse here the elements of a long-term ancestry not just for the Enlightenment, but also for an explanation of French primacy within it. If the Dutch Revolt and English revolutions were indeed the first "modern revolutions," their credentials look strongest on the economic–geopolitical level on which the accounts just cited focus.[13] Politically and ideologically, what they contributed to the cycle of upheavals that began a century later with the American and French revolutions, and ended with Latin American independence, seems less obvious. In fact, neither their political example nor their intellectual–cultural impact should be underestimated. We will return to the

---

[11] Wim Klooster, *The Dutch Moment: War, Trade, and Settlement in the Seventeenth-Century Atlantic World* (Ithaca, NY: Cornell University Press, 2016); Steve Pincus, *1688: The First Modern Revolution* (New Haven: Yale University Press, 2011); Jonathan Scott, *How the Old World Ended: The Anglo-Dutch–American Revolution, 1500–1800* (New Haven: Yale University Press, 2020).

[12] Neil Davidson, *How Revolutionary Were the Bourgeois Revolutions?* (Chicago: Haymarket Books, 2012).

[13] To which one might well add Giovanni Arrhigi, *The Long Twentieth Century: Money, Power, and the Origins of Our Times*, 2nd edition (London: Verso, 2010).

first, and to the centrality of the English model of "ancient constitutionalism" to the French Enlightenment, in particular, below. For the moment, what is most crucial is what might be described as the unintended *intellectual* consequences of the Dutch Revolt and the English revolutions. The ideological inspiration for both was confessional, of course. However, as with the Renaissance before it, the practical result of the Protestant appeal to a distant past was to hasten the arrival of an unexpected future. For it was the Dutch Republic and that "republic disguised as a monarchy," as Montesquieu described the United Kingdom, that provided the staging ground for the essential relay linking the Renaissance and the Reformation to the Enlightenment. The traditional name for that relay descended from the Enlightenment itself – the "Scientific Revolution," a historical category whose recent scholarly fortunes have oscillated violently, confident declarations of its nonexistence a generation ago even more confidently overturned in our time.[14] Just as striking is the way in which its temporal edges have been extended and blurred. At one end, Anthony Grafton has devoted much of his career to a comprehensive demonstration of the intricate linkages between Renaissance humanism and the emergence of modern science and historiography. At the other, among Jonathan Israel's great and lasting achievements must be counted his insistence on tracing the origins of the Enlightenment to the era of the "Scientific Revolution" – even if that is too narrow a term.

For what is beyond dispute is that the major thinkers of the Enlightenment all joined in paying tribute to a gallery of immediate ancestors, who, in their majority, were connected to the Anglo-Dutch perch, taking advantage of the margins of freedom and toleration it afforded – "scientists" like Newton or Harvey, of course, but any number of other polymathic figures: Descartes, Spinoza, Leibniz, Grotius, Hobbes, and Locke. If we are looking for the proximate origins of the Enlightenment, we could do worse than to date them to what Paul Hazard classically called the *"crise de la conscience européenne"* – essentially, the moment when French thinkers, more or less suddenly aware of the intellectual efflorescence of contemporary Holland and Britain, began the process of translating, interpreting, and appropriating its harvest. This was a role that only Francophones could play, possessing the combination of means – command of the first vernacular language to

---

[14] For the first, see Steven Shapin, *The Scientific Revolution* (Chicago: University of Chicago Press, 1996); for the second, David Wootton, *The Invention of Science: A New History of the Scientific Revolution* (New York: Harper, 2015).

challenge Latin as the principal vehicle for intellectual communication in Europe – and motives – the need to overcome the "self-incurred tutelage" of sociopolitical and intellectual backwardness – that captured the essence of "enlightenment" in the century that followed. It is no accident that scholars should have so often selected, as the inaugural effort in this enterprise, Pierre Bayle's *Dictionnaire historique et critique*, the work of a French Huguenot, published from Dutch exile in 1697.

Renaissance, Reformation, and the Enlightenment

The news from the Anglo-Dutch future arrived, however, in a thought-world and political scene that was still dominated, in very many ways, by the Renaissance and the Reformation. For an explanation of why the French Enlightenment – and with it, the Revolution – might be regarded as a kind of grand finale to the former, we need look no further than to Dan Edelstein's *The Enlightenment: A Genealogy*, perhaps the most effective of all the scholarly ripostes to Jonathan Israel.[15] For Edelstein, the Enlightenment was just that, a "genealogy" – that is, an epochal category, whose original matrix was the late seventeenth-century *"querelle des Anciens et des Modernes."* The great paradox of the Enlightenment's *"esprit philosophique,"* Edelstein argues, in what amounts to an ingenious updating of Peter Gay's interpretation of the Enlightenment as a form of oxymoronic "modern paganism," is that the key figures in its elaboration all tended to fall into the camp of the "ancients" – testimony, à la Grafton, to the enduring contribution of Renaissance humanism to the formation of modern thought. Meanwhile, the role that the French Reformation played in shaping the Enlightenment was, if anything, even more consequential, for reasons laid out in one of the masterpieces of the historiography of early modern France, Dale Van Kley's *The Religious Origins of the French Revolution*.[16] The Bourbon monarchy, born out of searing confessional strife, forged a uniquely intimate cultural–political bond with Catholicism in the course of the seventeenth century – but at a very high price. The costs included not just the Revocation of the Edict of Nantes (1685), now a byword in the history of self-inflicted calamity, but also the fateful rift that had opened *within* the French Church by the end of the reign

---

[15] Dan Edelstein, *The Enlightenment: A Genealogy* (Chicago: University of Chicago Press, 2010).

[16] Dale K. Van Kley, *The Religious Origins of the French Revolution: From Calvin to the Civil Constitution, 1560–1791* (New Haven: Yale University Press, 1996).

of Louis XIV. The monarchy's attempt to crush Jansenism, the crypto-Calvinist form of Catholicism around which opposition to the Bourbon regime now gravitated, backfired spectacularly, in Van Kley's view. The result was to drive Jansenism and traditional Gallicanism together, into a common defense of "constitutional" limits to royal authority, focused on two institutions that were critical to the fiscal well-being of the state – the upper courts of legal appeal, or *parlements*, and the General Assembly of the Clergy. But the escalating collisions between the Crown and a significant section of the judicial *noblesse de robe*, which came to a head in the second half of the century, had crucial intellectual consequences as well. For it was precisely this battle over apparently anachronistic theological issues, Van Kley argues, that was responsible for giving the French Enlightenment itself a uniquely antireligious and anticlerical stamp.

However, in order fully to grasp these dynamics – the ways in which the dual legacies of the Renaissance and Reformation gave specific shape to the Enlightenment in France – we need to step back for a more panoramic view of this landscape. Obviously, a full account of what was unique to the French Enlightenment would require both a comparative analysis of the movement as a whole, extending across the entire European world, including its projections overseas, as well as an account of its institutional underpinnings. For the first, Anglophone readers happily enjoy an embarrassment of riches, with only slightly less sweeping surveys added annually to Israel's six volumes, most recently by David Wootton, Margaret Jacob, and Ritchie Robertson.[17] As for institutions, it is already clear that William Sewell's recent *Capitalism and the Emergence of Civic Equality in Eighteenth-Century France* will galvanize their study, owing, in particular, to his recuperation of the most encompassing institution of all, when it comes to history of the Enlightenment – the "bourgeois public sphere" theorized long ago by Habermas, which Sewell remodels into a "commercial" one.[18] But for our purposes, looking ahead toward the Revolution, what is most crucial is to try to get a sense, at least, of the development of Enlightenment *political* thought in France. Readers of Jonathan Israel will be familiar with his own account.

---

[17] David Wootton, *Power, Pleasure, and Profit: Insatiable Appetites from Machiavelli to Madison* (Cambridge, MA: Belknap Press of Harvard University Press, 2018); Margaret Jacob, *The Secular Enlightenment* (Princeton: Princeton University Press, 2019); Ritchie Robertson, *The Enlightenment: The Pursuit of Happiness* (London: Allen Lane, 2020).

[18] William H. Sewell, Jr., *Capitalism and the Emergence of Civic Equality in Eighteenth-Century France* (Chicago: University of Chicago Press, 2021).

The eighteenth century, his story roughly goes, saw a long contest between two very different kinds of French "enlightenment": a reformist "moderate mainstream," committed to pragmatic accommodation with throne and altar; and a "radical" alternative, whose combination of materialist ontology, egalitarian ethics, and democratic politics made it inherently "revolutionary." Long confined to the margins, "Radical Enlightenment" made its first "breakthrough" into the wider public sphere in the 1750s and 1760s, with the appearance of the *Encyclopédie*. By the end of the 1780s, Israel argues, it had completed the "revolution in mind" that made the overthrow of the Old Regime possible, which duly began with the storming of the Bastille and the issuing of the Declaration of the Rights of Man and of the Citizen – the latter an enduring monument to the revolutionary leverage of "Radical Enlightenment."

It is not hard to see the attractions of Israel's account, even, or especially, reduced to a bare formula. The alternative briefly sketched here is not infinitely distant from it, but owes more to Mornet's *Les origines intellectuelles de la Révolution française*, as well as to an even older study, Elie Carcassonne's *Montesquieu et le problème de la constitution française au XVIIIe siècle*.[19] Mornet's basic argument was delivered in the form of a *periodization* of the development of political thinking over the course of the century, similar to that of Carcassonne, in terms of three phases, defined by major changes in the wider political history of the Bourbon monarchy. Each of these periods, it can be argued, saw the emergence of a novel current of "enlightened" political criticism – novel to France, that is: each owed crucial debts to sources from outside the Hexagon. Each also pointed to specific programs of political reform, which traced an arc, over time, from a "conservative" to a more "radical" posture – though the terms remain anachronistic, precisely because none were "revolutionary," in Israel's sense of the term. Indeed, what is striking about the evolution of political thought in eighteenth-century France is that its drift in a more "radical" direction went hand in hand with a deepening pessimism about the prospects for reforming state or society, as

---

[19] Elie Carcassonne, *Montesquieu et le problème de la constitution française au XVIIIe siècle* (Paris: Presses universitaires de France, 1927). The brief sketch of the development of Enlightenment political thought that follows owes much to Keith Baker's enormously influential typology, distinguishing among three distinct "discourses" ("judicial," "administrative," and "political" – that is, discourses of "law, reason, and will"), whose initial statement was also inspired by Carcassonne; see Keith Michael Baker, "French Political Thought at the Accession of Louis XVI," in *Inventing the French Revolution: Essays on French Political Culture in the Eighteenth Century* (Cambridge: Cambridge University Press, 1990), 109–27.

if in a grand demonstration of the *impotence* of "enlightenment" alone to effect political change.

The early Enlightenment in France unfolded during a lull in the "Second Hundred Years' War," between the Wars of the Spanish and of the Austrian Succession, when steerage of the state, after the Regency, was assumed by an able and cautious cardinal, Fleury. Against this backdrop, what shape did "enlightened" political thought begin to take? What springs to mind first are the critical mirrors held up to Bourbon absolutism by Montesquieu's *Persian Letters* (1721) and Voltaire's *Philosophical Letters* (1734) – an imaginary Persian one in the first, an idealized English in the second. But both performances owed something to a more consequential intellectual development taking place to the side of the stage. That was a very striking revival of the debate over the "fundamental laws" of the monarchy – its unwritten "ancient constitution" – of a kind that had flourished in the sixteenth century, then lapsed during the Bourbon reconstruction. By the 1730s, a very contentious scene had emerged, which featured a face-off between a *thèse royale*, defending an absolutist reading of the monarchy's constitution, and two competing versions of a *thèse nobiliaire*, assigning historical priority in constitutional history to one of the two types of French noble, martial "Sword" or judicial "Robe." That this was the French version of the wider "ancient constitutionalism" that Jacob Levy has recently contended was central to the emergence of liberal constitutionalism in modern history is obvious enough.[20] Indeed, the debate itself, in which reference to the British model of "ancient constitutionalism" was ubiquitous, was the incubator for what proved to be the major work of political thought of the century, and not just in France – Montesquieu's *De l'esprit des lois*, published in 1748. The *Divine Comedy* of the eighteenth century, Montesquieu's masterpiece had something in it for everyone, from his famous interpretation of the English constitution in Book XI, to intimations of forms of political thinking that would dominate the next two phases of the Enlightenment – on the one hand, a sketch of the emergent science of political economy; on the other, gestures toward the kind of republicanism fleshed out by Rousseau or Mably. Montesquieu himself was no republican, however, but rather a conservative monarchist, who opposed any further leveling of the "intermediate powers" that he regarded as essential to the preservation of liberty. The political message of *On the Spirit of Laws* was summed up in the existential warning that

---

[20] Jacob T. Levy, *Rationalism, Pluralism, and Freedom* (Oxford: Oxford University Press, 2017), esp. Chapters 5, 6.

Montesquieu issued to both sides in the debate over the "fundamental laws" of the realm: "No monarch, no nobility; no nobility, no monarch."

By the time *On the Spirit of Laws* was published, however, the relatively tranquil context in which it was composed had begun to crumble away, succeeded by two decades of geopolitical defeat and domestic tumult. Internationally, no sooner had Fleury exited the stage than traditional military adventurism resumed, the results of which evolved quickly from disappointing – the War of the Austrian Succession (1740–1748) – to calamitous – the Seven Years' War (1756–1763). By the end of the latter, the Bourbon monarchy had again been bested in its continental rivalry with the Habsburgs; far more importantly, it had seen Britain strip away its colonial holdings in North America and India. Domestically, the 1750s and 1760s featured a series of escalating collisions between the court and the *parlements*, building to a *va-et-vient* climax: the expulsion of the Jesuits in 1763, a symbolic victory for the Jansenist–parlementary camp, was then followed by the Maupeou "coup" of 1770–1771, which saw the monarchy's new chancellor attempt a top-to-bottom remodeling and rationalization of the entire upper judiciary – which was then undone, restoring the traditional parlementary system, at the accession of Louis XVI in 1774. Superficially, this looked like a triumph for political reform à la Montesquieu, the successful defense of what he regarded as the pivotal "intermediate power" of the realm. On Dale Van Kley's reading, however, the apparent victory was classically pyrrhic. For so successful was the parliamentary side in tarring the Bourbon monarchy with the brush of "despotism" that it ended up contributing to the mutual ruin of monarchy and *noblesse de robe* alike. Not only that, Van Kley argues, but it is precisely here that we can trace the decisive impact that this "religio-political" contest had on the shape of the French Enlightenment. For it was in the midst of this combination of dramatic setbacks in international competition and ideological–political uproar at home that the Enlightenment reached its maturity in France. Its flagship enterprise was the *Encyclopédie* edited by d'Alembert and Diderot, accompanied by a noisy crowd of self-described *philosophes*, figures such as Helvétius or Holbach at center stage, La Mettrie or Morelly in the wings, most fitting the bill of Israel's "Radical Enlightenment" closely enough. In Van Kley's view, it was the relentless scapegoating of the *philosophes* by both sides in the Jesuit–Jansenist fracas – a triangular contest unique to the French scene – that drove the French Enlightenment (or, at least, its "radical" cutting-edge) into the embrace of a militant atheism and hostility toward Christianity that had no equivalent elsewhere in Europe.

For all the drama of this frontal collision between belief and unbelief, however, the major intellectual development of the period actually lay elsewhere, in a sphere seemingly remote from religion. For the two decades after 1750 also saw the flowering for the first time of a French tradition of *political economy*. With roots in the early Enlightenment, among thinkers in direct contact with the Anglo-Dutch thought-world, including Cantillon, Montesquieu, and Melon, political economy in France now made a dramatic entrance into the Enlightenment "public sphere" in two waves: first, a circle that formed from the late 1740s under the inspiration of Vincent de Gournay, coiner of the terms *laissez-faire* and *bureaucratie* alike; and then the emergence of the imposing "school" of physiocracy, which joined a sophisticated theoretical analysis of markets to an aggressive campaign for the development of an English-style *agrarian* capitalism in France. For William Sewell, in the most important recent study of the economic origins of the Revolution, the coming out of political economy in the 1750s and 1760s was itself an effect of the development of "commercial capitalism," the acidic "abstraction" of the market already melting away Old Regime social hierarchies, paving the way for the advent of "civic equality" announced by the Declaration of Rights.[21] In the short term, however, as a program for "enlightened" political reform, political economy proved to be even more impotent than Montesquieuean "ancient constitutionalism." Where the latter sought to stop or reverse the leveling effects of Bourbon *political* centralization, Gournay's followers and the Physiocrats both attempted to harness the powers of the state for deliberate projects of *economic* development, with the need to overcome France's laggard status vis-à-vis Britain never far from sight. Both efforts – an initial experiment, inspired by Gournay, in lifting controls over the grain trade in 1763–1764, and then the more comprehensive program of liberalization spearheaded by Turgot as controller-general in 1774–1776 – were spectacular failures. Not only that, but the latter, of course, coincided with the restoration of the traditional structure and powers of the *parlements*, as if in a graphic display of the manner in which the two major projects of political reform generated by the Enlightenment to this point had canceled each other out.

---

[21] For something like the opposite, Brennerite argument, stressing the failure of all efforts to import capitalism prior to industrialization and, especially, the "non-capitalist" character of the French Revolution itself, see Xavier Lafrance, *The Making of Capitalism in France: Class Structures, Economic Development, the State and the Formation of the French Working Class, 1750–1914* (Leiden: Brill Academic, 2018).

For Mornet and Carcassonne, the accession of Louis XVI marked the start of the third and final phase of the development of Enlightened political thought. In Carcassonne's view, the undoing of Maupeou's judicial reforms meant that "Montesquieu had now been overtaken by Mably" – that is, a new player had now taken center stage, the *republican* alternative represented by the Abbé de Mably and, above all, Jean-Jacques Rousseau. This strand of thinking was certainly more "radical" than what had come before it, but it also attracted far less attention to itself in the Enlightened public sphere than had either the defenders of the *parlements* or the promoters of physiocracy. As early as the end of the 1750s, Mably had embraced a Lockean conception of popular sovereignty and actually sketched what Keith Baker famously called "a script for a French revolution," which envisioned parlementary resistance leading to a convocation of the long-defunct Estates-General, which would then bestow a new, republican constitution on the country – but in a text that remained unpublished until the Revolution itself.[22] Rousseau's *Du contrat social* (1762), represented a different order of achievement altogether, invoking Hobbes, instead of Locke, to develop the first fully *democratic* theory of sovereignty in modern political thought. Yet this was also the least read of all of Rousseau's major works, with virtually no discernible effect on French politics before the Revolution. Like Mably, Rousseau produced a premonitory critique of what might be termed the "market fundamentalism" of political economy, as it took shape in France.[23] But when it came to practical politics, Rousseau confined his attention entirely to an abortive intervention into Genevan affairs, followed by utopian sketches for agrarian republics on the periphery of European civilization – Corsica, Poland. Mably, meanwhile, wrote copiously on France and French politics, with his attention consistently focused on the prospects for a convocation of the Estates-General, as the sole plausible path toward the creation of a national representative assembly. But Mably's optimism for such an outcome vanished permanently with the Maupeou "coup." Neither the restoration of the *parlements* nor the arrival of a *"ministre philosophe"* such as Jacques Necker at the head of state finances, nor even the model of "actually existing republicanism" on display in British North America in these years, could alter Mably's conviction that the chances for what he

---

[22] See Baker, "A Script for a French Revolution: The Political Consciousness of the Abbé Mably," in *Inventing the French Revolution*, 86–106.

[23] For the finest sounding of the depths of Rousseau's criticisms, see Céline Spector, *Rousseau et la critique de l'économie politique* (Bordeaux: Presses universitaires de Bordeaux, 2017).

had termed a *"révolution ménagée"* in France – a willful, orderly process of regime change – had been passed by. At his death in 1785, the sole prospect that Mably could envisage for France had a Spanish shape: for the foreseeable future, the country would remain a paralyzed giant in the throes of irreversible decline.

Yet within five years, the Revolution had begun, the result of a sequence of events that corresponded almost exactly to the scenario that Mably had sketched thirty years earlier – parlementary protest leading to a convocation of an Estates-General, which duly transformed itself into a National Constituent Assembly. However, if Mably's final pessimism was thus confounded, it nevertheless conveys a broad truth about the relationship between the Enlightenment and the start of the French Revolution. Had "enlightened" criticism of the Bourbon monarchy been sufficient to have launched the Revolution, it ought to have occurred some two decades earlier than it did. The fairest chances for *philosophes*, "radical" or otherwise, to have somehow toppled the monarchy on their own came between 1765 and 1775, when the aftermath of defeat in the Seven Years' War coincided with the peak of parlementary resistance to the crown. Ample commentary from the period, much of it literally invoking the specter of "revolution," attests to the extent to which philosophic criticism had weakened the ideological props on which Bourbon legitimacy had rested.[24] By the time of the accession of Louis XVI, however, it seemed evident to all observers that the monarchy had weathered the philosophic storm – had even, in the eyes of many, made a new beginning. In a very real sense, "enlightenment" had failed – not least because no united front had proved to be possible between the two major oppositional currents to have emerged from the early Enlightenment. After a joint appearance in the pages of *De l'esprit des lois*, these diverged sharply, pointing toward very different destinations: on the one hand, an English-style "ancient constitutionalism," gesturing at a French 1688, and, on the other, a program for state-led economic modernization, aimed at galvanizing the French countryside. Both projects stymied or stalled, the late Enlightenment saw the maturation of a third current of political thinking, "republican" or "patriotic" in character – whose ultimate goal, the transfer of sovereignty to a national representative assembly, was declared unthinkable or impossible by its own major thinkers. French political thought was not completely becalmed in the last decade before the Revolution. In the view of

---

[24] For samples, see Baker, "Inventing the French Revolution," in *Inventing the French Revolution*, 214.

Carcassonne, Mornet, and William Sewell alike, it was in these years that the conditions for the eventual triumph of the principle of "civic equality" were finally assembled. But when it came to any plausible means of its realization, Mably was far from alone in concluding that the goal remained further from sight than ever.

The Radicalization of the Enlightenment

That judgment, mistaken as it was, returns us to Mornet's dictum: "The origins of the Revolution are one story, the history of the Revolution is another." By any sober reckoning, the Enlightenment played no more than a secondary role in those origins. If it is necessary to specify what Jonathan Israel calls "one 'big' cause" for the Revolution, that is to be sought, of course, not on the *ideological* plane, among philosophical "radicals" plotting regime change, but in the *geopolitical* arena – in the long sequence of failures in international and inter-imperial warfare, which produced the bankruptcy revealed to Louis XVI in August 1786. It was that dismal record, and, behind it, the dawning sense of the economic backwardness of the country, that were in large measure responsible for provoking "enlightened" criticism in the first place. However, if the Enlightenment was thus insufficient to have "caused" the Revolution, that does not mean that it played a similarly marginal role in what Mornet called its "history." On the contrary, once the trigger of bankruptcy was pulled, the French Enlightenment turns out to be absolutely necessary to any explanation of the way that the French Revolution actually unfolded, across some twenty-five years of political and social upheaval. More than that, there was an uncanny sense in which its major phases, down at least to Thermidor, corresponded more or less exactly to the sequence of reform projects generated by the Enlightenment in the course of the century – each, however, now "radicalized" by admixture with the later currents, before being surpassed in a succeeding phase.

First, the entire course of what was later termed the "pre-Revolution" was dominated by a sudden and intense reactivation of the struggles over the "ancient constitution" of the monarchy that had initially emerged during the Regency and then reached a noisy climax in the years before the Maupeou "coup." The final contest between the *thèse royale* and the *thèse nobiliaire* was short and sharp – and different from what had come before in two crucial respects. On the one hand, as the shape of the fiscal and political reforms introduced by Calonne and Loménie de Brienne demonstrate, the promoters of the first had now fully embraced the latest wisdom of modern political economy. The package of a basic land tax, economic deregulation, and a consultative "Assembly of Notables" was plainly a belated version of the program for "enlightened despotism" advocated three decades before by the Physiocrats. On the other hand, not only had the Estates-General – an institution never once mentioned in *De l'esprit des lois* – now completely supplanted the *parlements* within what might be called the "constitutional imaginary," but when the endgame arrived, the defenders of an anti-absolutist constitution now divided into two antithetical camps, which Carcassonne dubbed "aristocratic" and "national." The victory of the latter, committed to Sewell's "civic equality" as a baseline principle, was sealed months before the Estates actually met by the ideological *coup d'état* of Sieyès' *Qu'est-ce-que le Tiers Etat?* In this final showdown, the Bourbon monarchy's "ancient constitution" achieved its greatest feat of the century, the convocation of an Estates-General – whose first move, once transmogrified into a National Assembly, was to abolish the constitution, together with the entire "feudal regime." As if in confirmation of the truth of Montesquieu's maxim, nobility itself followed, scarcely a year later.

For Jonathan Israel, the program of "national regeneration" launched in 1789 should be seen as a victory for "Radical Enlightenment," which had now completed its long journey from the Anglo-Dutch periphery to the very heart of the continental Old Regime, above all by giving voice to long-simmering "social grievance." No doubt there were some bona fide Spinozistic "monists" in the revolutionary ranks; and the municipal revolts and rural unrest of July were obviously pivotal in propelling the work of the National Assembly forward. But it is perhaps more accurate to describe the results of the Assembly's labors over the next two years as *fundamentally* an embodiment of the hopes and principles of the "moderate mainstream" of the Enlightenment – tricked out with elements of "radical" ornamentation, to be sure, but falling far short of any thoroughgoing rupture with the political and social order it challenged. The rhetorical fireworks of August 1789 tell their own story. What could be more "radical" than the bonfire of "privilege" effected on the Night of 4 August, followed by the declaration, a week later, that "the National Assembly entirely destroys the feudal regime"? Far more consequential in the lives of ordinary citizens, however, was the sweeping overhaul of the entire administrative structure of the state completed a year later – dividing French territory into rationally defined departments, districts, and communes, overseen by locally elected officials – a lasting triumph, if ever there were one, for the principles of "moderate" Enlightenment. Meanwhile, the Assembly spent much of the rest of August 1789 composing a tremendous ideological overture, the "Declaration of the Rights of Man and of the Citizen." Fourteen of its seventeen articles were devoted to the civil liberties cherished by the Voltairean high Enlightenment. Of the three provisions that touched on politics, only the sixth, declaring law to be "the expression of the general will," owed anything at all to "radicalism"; the appeal to "national sovereignty" in the third, and the salute to the "separation of powers" in the sixteenth, were the work of the most conservative wing of the Assembly.[25]

Little wonder then that the constitution crafted by the National Assembly in conformity with these principles proved to be the compromise-formation that it was. The decisive rejection of a bicameral legislature in early September put an end to the political project of the *Monarchiens* – the heirs to Montesquieu who had aimed at an English-style "mixed government," combining a double chamber with a strong royal executive. Far from any kind of republic, however, the result was, in the consecrated phrase, a *"monarchie républicaine,"* which combined a hereditary royal executive power, armed with a "suspensive" (rather than absolute) veto over a unicameral legislature, whose indirect mode of selection reduced the effective electorate to around 45,000 propertied men. The lines of continuity from the political articles of the *Encyclopédie* – most of them not the work of any kind of "radical," but of the conservative jurist Jaucourt – through the whole series of reforms proposed by *ministres philosophes*, from Turgot to Calonne, are obvious enough.[26] It is true that the constitutional monarchy was furnished with fiscal foundations – the creation of a novel financial instrument, backed by nationalized ecclesiastical real estate – that it seems difficult to describe as anything other than "radical." Yet the *assignat* scheme, far from being any kind of bolt from the blue, was the product of nearly a century of fully "enlightened" speculation and debate about the financing of public debt – the burden, indeed, of one of the most commanding recent accounts of the intellectual origins of the Revolution, Michael Sonenscher's *Before the Deluge*. Not only that, but the entire project was in the service of the most conservative of ends, the National Assembly's decision to assume the Bourbon

---

[25] See J. K. Wright, "National Sovereignty and the General Will: The Political Program of the Declaration of Rights," in Dale K. Van Kley, ed., *The French Idea of Freedom: The Old Regime and the Declaration of Rights of 1789* (Stanford: Stanford University Press, 1994), 199–233.

[26] For the indispensable work in English on politics in the *Encyclopédie*, see Henry C. Clark, ed., *Encyclopedic Liberty: Political Articles in the Dictionary of Diderot and D'Alembert*, trans. Henry C. Clark and Christine Dunn Henderson (Indianapolis, IN: Liberty Fund, 2016).

monarchy's debts in order to facilitate a rapid return to the arena of international and inter-imperial warfare. A similar combination of surface rupture and structural continuity can be seen, finally, in the companion-piece to the *assignat* scheme, the remodeling of the Church that followed on the nationalization of its landed property. Indeed, the fundamental lesson of Dale Van Kley's *Religious Origins of the French Revolution* is that the "democratization" of Catholicism effected by the Civil Constitution of the Clergy was the expression of a deeply traditional Gallicanism, rendered *à la page* by the transfer of sacral sovereignty from king to Nation – a shift that owed far more to Jansenism than to "Radical Enlightenment."

If the political and social order created by the Revolution of 1789 can thus be seen as a kind of epitome of the aims of the French Enlightenment's "moderate mainstream," how shall we describe the regime presided over by the National Convention elected in the wake of the revolution of August 1792? That the First Republic, the Jacobin phase in particular, can be regarded as a revolutionary incarnation of the "classical republicanism" for which Rousseau and Mably had been the standard-bearers would appear to require little argument – except, perhaps, with Jonathan Israel, whose conceptual scheme leads him to categorize Jacobinism as a "populist Counter-Enlightenment," and, exceeding any revisionist in antitotalitarian zeal, to label Robespierre modernity's first "fascist." For most of the rest of us, common sense would seem to indicate that we not withhold altogether the adjective "radical" from the First Republic. This is not to imply, of course, that there is any alternative scholarly consensus about the intellectual origins of Jacobinism. Those origins – in particular, its relations with either the Enlightenment or the prior history of republican ideas in France – remain one of the great unsolved mysteries in the historiography of the Revolution. But it can at least be suggested that Mark Hulliung's notion of Rousseau as having performed the first "autocritique" of the Enlightenment should not be disregarded, in calculating what Jacobinism owed to Citizen of Geneva.[27] As for the wider history of French republicanism, the closest thing we have to a synoptic survey of the field is Sonenscher's *Sans-Culottes*. The bulk of the book is devoted to reconstructing the genealogy of the idea, which Sonenscher traces back to currents of "neo-Cynicism," operating as a kind

---

[27] Mark Hulliung, *The Autocritique of Enlightenment: Rousseau and the Philosophes*, 2nd edition (New York: Routledge, 2017). For the wider contribution of Genevan "radicalism" to the age of revolutions, see Richard Whatmore, *Against War and Empire: Geneva, Britain, and France in the Eighteenth Century* (New Haven: Yale University Press, 2012).

of contraflow through the high Enlightenment. Only at the very end, in a chapter titled "Democracy and Terror," does Sonenscher briefly address the relation between the actual *sans-culottes* of the Year II and Robespierre and Saint-Just. There, it is Mably who is portrayed as the most relevant intellectual ancestor of the Jacobin leadership. But Mably was not alone in this regard: elsewhere, in a fundamental essay, Sonenscher has shown that he was one of the quartet of "levelers" cited by Babeuf at his trial (the others: Rousseau, Helvétius, and Diderot – Babeuf was not aware that the author of the *Code de la Nature* was instead Morelly), who shared overlapping beliefs linking radical republicanism to neo-Roman notions of an egalitarian "agrarian law."

What should we make of this pattern, the country appearing to cycle through in rapid succession, renewed efforts to realize each of the major reform movements to have emerged in the course of the Enlightenment? If nothing else, what the sequence suggests is the necessity of overturning – literally capsizing – what might be termed the "Israel thesis." Rather than "Radical Enlightenment" having "caused" the French Revolution, it instead looks as though the advent of the Revolution brought about a thoroughgoing *radicalization of the Enlightenment*. That it is, the fiscal collapse of Bourbon absolutism presented each of the three major reform tendencies of the Enlightenment with a second opportunity to achieve their goals in more advanced or developed – in a word, "radical" – forms. The result was that Montesquieuean ancient constitutionalism reached its final shape in the *Monarchien* plan for a "mixed government"; the principles and aspirations of the "moderate mainstream" of the Enlightenment were actualized, and then some, by the National Constituent Assembly; and the dreams of "classical republicans" such as Rousseau and Mably were surpassed by the awesome reality of the First Republic. Driving this process of radicalization forward, of course, was the appearance of a host of new political and class actors, prepared to seize the opportunities offered by the Revolution – the lawyers who swelled the ranks of the National Assembly, the peasants who lived out the Great Fear in the countryside, the *sans-culottes* crowds in Paris mobilized, in turn, by the Brissotins and the Jacobins. Given that, it is not surprising that with Thermidor, the pattern described here altered, even appearing to go into reverse in some respects – without, however, the Enlightenment ever ceasing to provide inspiration or models to the revolutionaries. Andrew Jainchill has made a convincing argument that the "republican center" that took over in 1795 created, in the Directory, a classically "mixed" or "balanced" constitution, faithful to the norms of

Pocock's "Atlantic republican tradition."[28] As for the Consulate and First Empire, an abundant literature has been devoted to their debt to the ideas and model of "enlightened despotism." There is no need to insist on the ways in which the two most significant and lasting domestic achievements of the Napoleonic regime, the Concordat and the Civil Code, conformed so exactly to the outlook of the Enlightenment's "moderate mainstream."

This is not to suggest that the dynamic of the Enlightenment's radicalization, in and through the Revolution, ever flagged. Paradoxically, or logically, this can be seen nowhere more clearly than in the realm of ideas themselves. The sheer scale of the ideological transformation wrought, not just by the French but by the Atlantic revolutions as a set, is still difficult to conceive today. In the space of some twenty-five years, virtually the entire inventory of modern political ideas suddenly emerged, one after another. The very notion of "revolution" itself, as the conscious and deliberate change of political regimes, now crystallized in its modern form, in France above all – with "conservatism" and "reaction" as its inevitable accompaniments, and "right" and "left" to define the political spectrum as a whole. It was the combined effects of the American and French revolutions that finally broke the millennial grip of monarchy over the Western mind: with a sole exception, every one of the new states launched in the Americas was a republic; the restoration of monarchy in France proved to be ephemeral. At the same time, the concept of "representative government," as the legitimate form of modern "democracy," suddenly took center stage throughout the Atlantic world. The first statement of modern political feminism was the work of a British radical, defending the French Revolution; resistance to the entrenchment of plantation slavery could henceforth call itself "abolitionism"; and "liberalism," understood as the vindication of the "natural rights" of individuals in the face of modernizing authoritarianism, was the gift of the Spanish resistance to Bonaparte. Meanwhile, not just "national sovereignty" but even "nationalism" itself now made their debuts, the latter shifting from Enlightenment patriotism to Romantic cultural nationalism in the course of the Atlantic upheavals. Last and not least, "socialism" and even "communism," the latter metamorphosing out of Jacobinism, took their first bows. By comparison with the Dutch Revolt and the English revolutions before it, and the "great unifications" of Italy, Japan, the United States, and Germany afterwards, this tremendous explosion of ideas – nearly every one of them

---

[28] Andrew Jainchill, *Reimagining Politics after the Terror: The Republican Origins of French Liberalism* (Ithaca, NY: Cornell University Press, 2008).

visibly the "radicalization" of an Enlightenment theme – is surely one of the most striking features of the Atlantic revolutions.

Entwinement

Among the ideas that assumed a definite shape in these years was that of "Enlightenment" itself – if not "invented" altogether, as Roger Chartier seemed to suggest, then certainly indelibly stamped by the Revolution. As it happens, the entwinement of Enlightenment and Revolution actually began long before 1789. As we have seen, in Dan Edelstein's view, a full history of the *idea* of the Enlightenment in France would have to return to the late seventeenth century, when the Quarrel of the Ancients and the Moderns provided the conditions of possibility for the periodizing impulse essential to it. This process of self-definition reached its early peak in the *Discours préliminaire* to the *Encyclopédie*, in which d'Alembert famously distinguished between the rigid *"esprit de système"* of their Cartesian predecessors and the more unrestrained *"esprit systématique"* of the *philosophes*. Not accidentally, however, it was at precisely this point that Darrin McMahon's "enemies of the Enlightenment" began to make their voices heard. For no sooner were the first volumes of the *Encyclopédie* in print, than critics began to warn, in increasingly alarmist tones, of the threat that the *philosophes* posed to altar and throne alike. A journalist such as Elie Cathérine Fréron was able to make an entire career out of vitriolic attacks on Voltaire. So it is scarcely surprising that, when the revolutionary assault on the Old Regime exceeded the direst predictions, the heirs of the original "enemies" swung into action, creating, in the course of the 1790s, a very durable myth about deliberate philosophic complicity in unleashing the furies of revolution. Of course, they were aided and abetted in these efforts by the first two revolutionary regimes themselves. The first *"grand homme"* installed in the *Panthéon*, the former royal church converted by the National Constituent Assembly to a *"temple de la Nation,"* was Mirabeau – for Jonathan Israel a fitting representative of "Radical Enlightenment." But the second, the first enduring inhabitant of the crypt, was the very emblem of the "moderate mainstream": Voltaire himself, who made a dramatic second and final re-entry into Paris in a lavishly orchestrated ceremony in July 1791. Three years later, the National Convention, negotiating the post-Thermidor political rapids, made a double maneuver, first replacing Mirabeau with Marat, followed by the reinternment of Rousseau, with pomp and festivities to rival those devoted to Voltaire.

Enlightenment and the French Revolution

That Voltaire and Rousseau, now contemplating each other across the crypt for all eternity, were mortal enemies during their lifetimes is a reminder of all the work left to be done, after the Revolution, in constructing the concept of "the Enlightenment" as a unitary intellectual movement.[29] Paradoxically, perhaps, French thinkers have never been at the forefront of these efforts – perpetually outdone by their opposite numbers on the other side of the Rhine. The most enduring pre-revolutionary capture of the concept was, of course, that of Kant, who in 1784 answered the question "What is enlightenment?" by defining it as "mankind's exit from self-incurred tutelage" and its motto as *"Sapere aude"* ("Dare to know").[30] Kant greeted the French Revolution with enthusiasm, then reacted to the Terror with the dismay common to observers of his generation. But by far the most searching and influential *philosophical* interpretation of the relation between the Enlightenment and the French Revolution came from his chief successor in the next generation. In the long chapter on *"Geist"* in *The Phenomenology of Spirit*, whose writing famously concluded in the wake of Napoleon's victory at Jena, Hegel charted the progress of "Spirit," from the initial rupture of Greek harmony represented by Sophocles' Antigone down to Kant's own ethical theory itself. The development of "self-alienated" Spirit reached its climax in the eighteenth century, with the great face-off between Christian religion and Enlightenment reason – literally a fight to the death, since the victory of the latter's leading principle, the "absolute freedom" of the individual, led inexorably to the Terror. Hegel interpreted the ethical systems of Kant and Fichte as attempts to overcome the searing contradiction between individual and collective autonomy made visible in the Revolution – before moving on to his even longer, and more controversial chapter, on religion, then ending the *Phenomenology* with a brief evocation of "absolute spirit" itself.

If any demonstration of the enduring power of Hegel's understanding of the relation between the Enlightenment and the Age of Revolutions were

---

[29] On the relations between the two in their lifetimes, see the late Robert Wokler, "The Enlightenment Hostilities of Voltaire and Rousseau," in Robert Wokler, *Rousseau, the Age of Enlightenment, and Their Legacies*, ed. Bryan Garsten (Princeton: Princeton University Press, 2012), 80–7; and for the twentieth-century prolongation of their war, by editorial proxy, see Wokler's unforgettable essay, "The Subtextual Reincarnation of Voltaire and Rousseau," *American Scholar* 67:2 (1998), 1–10.

[30] Immanuel Kant, "An Answer to the Question: What Is Enlightenment?," trans. James Schmidt, in James Schmidt, ed., *What Is Enlightenment? Eighteenth-Century Answers and Twentieth-Century Questions* (Berkeley: University of California Press, 1996), 58.

necessary, it has been supplied by Rebecca Comay's recent *Mourning Sickness: Hegel and the French Revolution*, a dazzling updating of the problematic for our own post-revolutionary epoch.[31] However, at just the moment that Comay was finishing her book, Hegel came under attack from an apparently impeccable source. In a series of lectures at the Collège de France in 2010, Vincenzo Ferrone, the leading Italian scholar of the Enlightenment of his generation, made one of the surprisingly rare attempts to survey the development of thinking about the subject across the two centuries since the Revolution. Two related obstacles, Ferrone argued, have prevented historians from approaching the Enlightenment on its own terms, as they might any other object of study. One has been the shadow cast on it by the French Revolution, the splicing of the two topics into one: "a dogma and the beating heart of European historical consciousness until now." The other has been the irresistible temptation to treat the Enlightenment as simultaneously a *philosophical* and a *historical* phenomenon. The chief culprit for both misunderstandings? Hegel, of course, whose *Phenomenology of Spirit* was the first in an unending line of what Ferrone dubs "centaurs" – monstrous blends of historical and philosophical analysis, obscuring any hope of seeing the Enlightenment *wie es eigentlich gewesen ist*. Joining Hegel in the dock are the likes of Marx and Nietzsche, Horkheimer and Adorno, Foucault, and so on. Happily, Ferrone concluded, historians in our time are at last severing the obfuscating bonds between the Enlightenment, the Revolution, and Philosophy – though he was compelled to admit, in an "Afterword" to the English translation of his lectures, that the field had now fallen under the baleful spell of yet another "centaur," in the guise of Jonathan Israel's conception of "Radical Enlightenment."

Should we endorse Ferrone's condemnation of Israel, together with the rest of the "centaurs," Hegel included? This chapter has presented an account of the relations between the Enlightenment and the French Revolution at odds, in many respects, with that of Israel. Rather than treat the Enlightenment as a kind of "unmoved mover" of the Revolution, it has tried to place both the intellectual movement and the political upheaval in a wider context, which highlights the slow transition to capitalism that unfolded across the early modern epoch, together with the international and interimperial conflicts that accompanied it. If anything, however, attention to this context serves to render the relations between the Enlightenment and the

[31] Rebecca Comay, *Mourning Sickness: Hegel and the French Revolution* (Stanford: Stanford University Press, 2011).

Revolution at least as necessary and intimate as they are in Israel's eyes. By 1806, the *philosophical* logic linking the one to the other was obvious to Hegel, whose own account, like that of Israel, treats *religious* belief as its pivot – a displacement that is perhaps constitutive of the very concept of "Enlightenment." By then, it was probably already too late to prevent Hegel from being succeeded by a long line of "centaurs." After all, if Hugo is to be believed, by the time of the July Revolution the word was already on the street: *"Je suis tombé par terre, c'est la faute à Voltaire, / Le nez dans le ruisseau, c'est la faute à Rousseau."*

3

Enlightenment and the Ibero-American Revolutions

BRIAN R. HAMNETT

Introduction

Did the Enlightenment lead to the political changes and revolutions across the Iberian monarchies during the 1810s and 1820s? Many commentators at the time, and after, assumed or argued that it did.[1]

Even so, we need to put the modes of thinking associated with the European Enlightenment into an Iberian and Ibero-American historical context. First and foremost, the cultural inheritance of the Iberian world should be taken into consideration. In the political context, this consisted of particular (and sometimes conflicting) sovereignties in composite monarchies characterized by corporate juridical structures. A range of traditions stemmed from the sixteenth-century humanists, such as Juan Luis Vives and Melchor Cano. In the Iberian world, Natural Law, deriving from St. Thomas Aquinas,

---

[1] See for these issues Daniel Mornet, *Les origines intellectuelles de la Révolution française, 1715–1787* (Paris: Armand Colin, 1933); Arthur P. Whitaker, *Latin America and the Enlightenment*, 2nd edition (Ithaca, NY: Cornell University Press, 1961 [1942]); Jean Sarrailh, *L'Espagne éclairée de la seconde moitié du XVIIIe siècle* (Paris: Klincksiek, 1954); R. J. Shafer, *The Economic Societies in the Spanish World (1763–1821)* (Syracuse, NY: University of Syracuse Press, 1958); John Tate Lanning, *The Eighteenth-Century Enlightenment in the University of San Carlos de Guatemala* (Ithaca, NY: Cornell University Press, 1958); A. Owen Aldridge, ed., *The Ibero-American Enlightenment* (Urbana: University of Illinois Press, 1971); William Joel Simon, *Scientific Expeditions in the Portuguese Overseas Territories (1783–1808)* (Lisbon: Instituto de Investigação Científica Tropical, 1983); Roger Chartier, *The Cultural Origins of the French Revolution* (Durham, NC: Duke University Press, 1991); Ana Cristina Araújo, *A cultura das Luzes em Portugal: Temas e problemas* (Lisbon: Livros Horizonte, 2003); Roberto Breña, *El primer liberalismo español y los procesos de emancipación en América: Una revisión historiográfica del liberalismo hispánico* (Mexico City: El Colegio de México, 2006); Federica Morelli, Clément Thibaud, and Geneviève Verdo, eds., *Les empires atlantiques entre Lumières et libéralisme (1763–1853)* (Rennes: Presses universitaires de Rennes, 2009); Brian Hamnett, *The Enlightenment in Iberia and Ibero-America* (Cardiff: University of Wales, 2018); E. Bradford Burns, "The Intellectual Agents of Change and the Independence of Brazil, 1724–1822," in A. J. R. Russell Wood, ed., *From Colony to Nation: Essays on the Independence of Brazil* (Baltimore, MD: Johns Hopkins University Press, 1975), 211–46.

was widely taught in colleges, seminaries, and universities. The neo-Thomism of the Dominican and Jesuit thinkers, Molina, Mariana, and Suárez, of the later sixteenth and early seventeenth century, still predominated in Hispanic political thinking well into the eighteenth century. Contractual theories of monarchy (*pactismo*), which examined the origin and nature of sovereignty, derived from that source. Furthermore, Natural Law had been updated in the works of Hugo Grotius, Samuel von Pufendorf, Christian Wolff, and Emer de Vattel, whose ideas of the autonomy of civil society and the independence of law from divine origins were entering Spanish and Spanish American colleges and universities in the second half of the eighteenth century. These varied traditions existed alongside the published codes of law, such as the *Nueva Recopilación* of 1567, which applied equally to Spain and the empire; the *Recopilación de las Leyes de los Reinos de Indias* of 1681; and the *Novísima Recopilación* of 1806. In this respect, we should view the ideas and practices advanced by the eighteenth-century Enlightenment and the constitutionalism and revolutionary movements of the 1810s and 1820s within the context of these antecedents.[2]

Beyond the debatable issue of intellectual influences, a range of alternative or complementary factors might also contribute to the causes of revolution – economic relations, social conditions, alienation of government from the governed, financial collapse, and the often bypassed but pervading impact of political breakdown? I prefer to put forward the view that revolutions, whether in France or the Hispanic monarchy, resulted from political breakdown. Accordingly, the rhetoric of liberation and equality, adopted from the Enlightenment, disguised the urgent intent of rebuilding the state and of asserting the rights of the state over competing bodies of authority. In such a way, revolutionary movements, whether in Europe or Ibero-America, made explicit the paradox within the Enlightenment between the reconstruction of institutions and the emancipation of peoples.[3]

---

[2] José Carlos Chiaramonte, "Fundamentos iusnaturalistas de los movimientos de independencia," in Marta Terán and José Antonio Serrano Ortega, eds., *Las guerras de independencia en la América española* (Zamora: El Colegio de Michoacán, 2002); Daniel Gutiérrez Ardila, *Un nuevo reino: Geografía política, pactismo, y diplomacia durante el Interregno en Nueva Granada (1808–1816)* (Bogotá: Universidad Externado, 2010), 81–110. These ideas fed into the Enlightenment but were challenged by several of its leading proponents, notably David Hume, who questioned the existence of Natural Law. See also O. Carlos Stoetzer, *The Scholastic Roots of Spanish American Independence* (New York: Fordham University Press, 1979).

[3] Timothy E. Anna, *Spain and the Loss of America* (Lincoln: University of Nebraska Press, 1983); Candelaria Saiz Pastor and Javier Vidal Olivares, *El fin del antiguo régimen (1808–1868)* (Madrid: Editorial Síntesis, 2001); Carlos Marichal, *Bankruptcy of Empire:*

The question of the popular response to critical thinking still remains unresolved. Did the spoken or written word contribute to the undermining of the existing order? The Enlightenment's dedication to scientific research and geographical exploration in the Ibero-American world does not suggest that this was an inevitable consequence of the dissemination of knowledge of the physical world. Bianca Premo's study attempts to move away from the intellectual history view of the Enlightenment with its roots in Europe, classically addressed in the works of Jonathan Israel, by focusing on a range of non-élite social and ethnic groups at the base of Spanish American society. Her innovation is to examine the challenge posed to authority by women, lower ethnic groups, and slaves, determined to improve their conditions and social standing through access to the law courts of the colonial legal system. They did so in the name of natural rights in opposition to "despotism" and tyrannical behavior. This was instinctive rather than as a result of a process of the filtering downward of ideas concurrent with their actions at the time. Since they assumed the language of natural rights, rather than espousing the Natural Law tradition taught in academic institutions, they represented, according to Premo, a spontaneous and popularly based Enlightenment from below. This Enlightenment was generated by the reality of a disadvantageous social situation and ethnic position. It germinated in Spanish America, given its specific socioethnic identities, rather than peninsular Spain. Since her focus is on areas not involved in the revolutionary mainsprings of the 1810s and 1820s, her study evades the central issue of this present chapter, which is the relationship between Enlightenment and Revolution. It does not discuss either the propensity of popular groups for revolutionary action or, conversely, their hostility or indifference toward it.[4]

Enlightened Absolutism

In the cases of the Austrian Habsburg monarchy, the Prussian Hohenzollern dynasty, the Romanov monarchy in the Russian Empire under Catherine II (1762–1796), the Hispanic and Portuguese monarchies, and several duchies, such as Tuscany, Enlightened ideas and policies were selectively put to the

---

Mexican Silver and the Wars between Spain, Great Britain and France, 1760–1810 (Cambridge: Cambridge University Press, 2007).

[4] Bianca Premo, *The Enlightenment on Trial: Ordinary Litigants and Colonialism in the Spanish Empire* (New York: Oxford University Press, 2017), 3, 10, 13, 15–16: "the Enlightenment was practised – not received in Spanish America but produced in it" (13).

service of government. This explains the term "Enlightened Absolutism," which originated in the Germanic territories and the Austrian Habsburg monarchy, to describe the imposition of reform from above for the mutual benefit of government and society, as perceived at the time by rulers and their ministers. Through the use of the extraparliamentary powers claimed by the monarch and exercised on his or her behalf by strong ministers, such as the Marquês de Pombal in Portugal between 1750 and 1777, attempts thereby were made to remove obstacles to renovation.[5]

The career of Gaspar Melchor de Jovellanos, the outstanding figure of the Spanish Enlightenment, shows the uneasy transition from reformer in an absolute monarchy to protagonist of a mild constitutional alternative in the radically altered political conditions of 1808–1810. Jovellanos was a political figure of note in the period from the 1770s until his death in 1811. Neither an absolutist nor a radical, he expressed a curious blend of traditionalism and liberalism. As a young administrator he had been overawed by the daring radicalism of Pablo de Olavide, chief administrator in Seville between 1767 and 1776, though not seduced by it. Subsequently, during the years 1778–1790 he became a protégé of Campomanes, President of the Council of Castile in Madrid, from 1766 until his fall in 1790.[6] Jovellanos became a member of the Supreme Central Junta after the collapse of the Bourbon dynasty in 1808. He was the leading proponent of a form of bicameral constitutionalism designed to provide a stabilizing way between disgraced absolutism and perilous revolutionism.[7] A mixture of Hispanic medieval study mingled with ideas taken from Montesquieu's *De l'esprit des lois* (1748) appeared to be reinforced with a perception of the (as yet unreformed)

---

[5] Kenneth Maxwell, *Pombal: Paradox of the Enlightenment* (Cambridge: Cambridge University Press 1995); Francisco Sánchez-Blanco, *El absolutismo y las Luces en el reinado de Carlos III* (Madrid: Marcial Pons, 2002).

[6] A younger son of Asturian gentry, Jovellanos' evident talents enabled him, through family connections and protectors, to attend the University of Alcalá de Henares, a focus of Enlightenment in Spain. In Madrid, he became an outstanding figure in the Royal Academies from the 1780s and Minister of Justice under Carlos IV in 1797–1798. Fernando Baras Escolá, *El reformismo político de Jovellanos (Nobleza y poder en la España del siglo XVIII)* (Zaragoza: Universidad de Zaragoza, 1993); José Miguel Caso González, *Jovellanos*, ed. María Teresa Caso (Madrid: Ariel Historia, 1998).

[7] Gaspar Melchor de Jovellanos, *Discurso leído por el autor en su recepción a la Real Academia de la Historia, sobre la necesidad de unir al estudio de la legislación el de nuestra historia y antigüedades* (1780), in *Biblioteca de Autores Españoles*, vol. XLVI, Part 1 (Madrid: Ediciones Atlas, 1963), 288–98; *Memoria en defensa de la Junta Central*, 2 vols., ed. José Miguel Caso González (Oviedo: Junta General del Principado de Asturias, 1992), vol. Apéndices, número XII, *Consulta sobre la convocación de las Cortes por estamentos* (Seville, 21 May 1809), 113–25.

"mixed constitution" of Great Britain.[8] These were presented as a potential model for Spain and the Indies. However, despite American interest in his ideas, particularly after his Report on Agrarian Reform in 1795, Jovellanos concerned himself primarily with Spain and not Spanish America – or the relationship between the two. Like other contemporaries, Jovellanos' central focus fell on the perennial question of why Spain had lost its past liberties and how to regain them in the present.[9]

Variations and Contradictions

We should be wary of attributing too much to the Enlightenment, viewing it as the sole (or even primary) determinant of the independence movements. John Leddy Phelan, for instance, has argued against Enlightenment influences in the rebellion of the *Comuneros* in New Granada (present-day Colombia) in 1781. Kenneth Maxwell has argued that the 1798 rebellion in Bahia was not motivated by Enlightenment ideas, but by local social and economic objectives. Furthermore, it is very doubtful that Enlightenment thinking motived or influenced the Túpac Amaru and Túpac Katari rebellions in Lower and Upper Peru in 1780–1783, which shook Hispanic rule to its foundations.[10]

Some European Enlightened writers, influential though they were in other respects, did not always find a favorable reception in the Americas. The reading of European writers, such as Cornelius de Pauw, William Robertson, and the Abbé Raynal, by American thinkers led to responses to their comments on the Americas and Americans. Not founded upon personal experience, such comments were regarded by American respondents as derogatory. Accordingly, they reassessed the Indigenous American past as

---

[8] See, for Montesquieu, J. W. F. Allison, *A Continental Distinction in the Common Law: A Historical and Comparative Perspective on English Public Law* (Oxford: Oxford University Press, 1996), 16–18, 46–7, 138–9.

[9] For Portuguese parallels, see Pedro Cardim, *Cortes e cultura política em Portugal no Antigo Regime* (Lisbon: Edições Cosmos, 1998); José Esteves Pereira, *O Pensamento político em Portugal no século XVIII: António Ribeiro dos Santos* (Lisbon: Imprensa Nacional – Casa de Moeda, 2005 [1983]).

[10] Kenneth Maxwell, *Conflict and Conspiracies: Brazil and Portugal, 1750–1808* (Cambridge: Cambridge University Press, 1973); John Leddy Phelan, *The People and the King: The Comunero Revolt in Colombia, 1781* (Madison, WI: University of Wisconsin Press, 1978); Sinclair Thomson, *We Alone Will Rule: Native Andean Politics in the Age of Insurgency* (Madison, WI: University of Wisconsin Press, 2002), 6–7. Isidro Vanegas, *La revolución neogranadina* (Bogotá: Ediciones Plural, 2013), 63, argues that none of the New Granada revolutionaries of 1808–1816 saw themselves as continuing from the rebellion of the *comuneros* of 1781, implying that they stood for different principles.

qualitatively equal to the European. The expelled Mexican Jesuit Francisco Javier Clavijero (1731–1787), whose *Storia antica del Messico* was published in Italy in 1781, became a leading figure portraying pre-Columbian America as comparable with the "Ancient World" in European historical perception. Such arguments emphasized the difference between the historical experience of Americans and that of their European counterparts. Clavijero's *History* became one of the founding works of Mexican historiography. Carlos María de Bustamante (1774–1848), a leading participant and propagandist of the Morelos phase of the Mexican independence movement, followed in this tradition by portraying the Aztec Empire as the precursor of the independent Mexican state.[11] In 1793, Manuel del Socorro Rodríguez, in New Granada, for his part, compared the pre-Columbian Chibcha civilization with the Middle East in the "Ancient World." Such arguments fed into an already existing examination (albeit often conducted in private company) of the position of the American territories within the Hispanic monarchy as a whole. This would have deep political implications as the Spanish monarchy disintegrated during the 1800s.[12]

Despite notable common features in the appeal for rationality and improvement, many variants emerged across Europe and the Americas. Frequent attention accorded to anti-clerical French *philosophes* in the historical literature has led to a mistaken assumption that this sentiment characterized Enlightenment as a whole. Many ecclesiastics, such as Bishop Baltasar Jaime Martínez Compañon (1737–1797) of Trujillo, Peru, on the contrary, played major roles in developing, extending, and implementing Enlightened projects.[13] Many ecclesiastics became protagonists of reforming ideas in church and state, such as the Mexican-born Benito Díaz de Gamarra, who gained his doctorate in law at the University of Pisa and was ordained at the Oratory of St. Philip Neri, in the Bajío woollen town of San Miguel el Grande, in 1767. He set about reforming his college curriculum on the lines of the European Enlightenment, dispensing with Aristotle in favor of Galileo,

---

[11] Carlos María de Bustamante, *Cuadro histórico de la revolución de la América mexicana* (Mexico City: Fondo de Cultura Económica, 1985 [1821–1827]); Elías Trabulse, "Clavigero. Historiador de la Ilustración mexicana," in Alfonso Martínez Rosales, ed., *Francisco Xavier Clavigero en la Ilustración mexicana, 1731–1787* (Mexico City: El Colegio de México, 1988), 41–57.

[12] Clément Thibaud, *Libérer le nouveau monde: La fondation des premières républiques hispaniques. Colombie et Venezuela (1780–1820)* (Paris: Éditions Les Perséides, 2017), 170–1. Rodríguez was chief editor of the official *Papel Periódico* (1791–1797) in Santa Fe de Bogotá.

[13] Emily Berquist, *The Bishop's Utopia: Imaging Improvement in Colonial Peru* (Philadelphia: University of Pennsylvania Press, 2014).

Copernicus, and Newton, which aroused the ire of traditionalists. The cleric, José Antonio Alzate y Ramírez (1737–1799), editor of literary periodicals in Mexico City, championed the natural sciences. Members of academic bodies, many of them ecclesiastical, advanced the new ideas, often in conflict with traditionalists. These bodies included the Academia de San Carlos in Mexico City and the University of San Marcos, the intellectual base of the imperial reformer, José Baquíjano y Carrillo (1751–1817), who met Jovellanos and Olavide in Seville in the 1770s. At the Real Convictorio de San Carlos in Lima, the rector, Toribio Rodríguez de Mendoza (1750–1825), championed the teaching of Spanish law from the Middle Ages onward, along with mathematics and physics, in face of traditionalist hostility. Many leading figures of the New Granada Independence movement had been educated at the Colegio de Nuestra Señora del Rosario in Santa Fe de Bogotá. The Universidad de Santo Tomás de Aquino played a comparable role in Quito. Leaders of the revolutionary movement of the 1810s in Buenos Aires, such as Juan José Castelli (1764–1812) and Mariano Moreno (1778–1811), had received their education at the University of Chuquisaca (now Sucre) in Upper Peru. These three institutions of higher learning were among the American bulwarks of Enlightenment.[14]

Carlos Herrejón Peredo argues that the priest Miguel Hidalgo (1753–1811), who led the first insurrectionary movement in New Spain in September 1810, designed to overthrow Spanish rule, was a product of the Mexican Enlightenment, and that from the start he believed in separation from the Hispanic monarchy. Hidalgo's circle of friends before the cataclysm of 1810 included New Spain's premier Enlightened figures, José Antonio Riaño, Intendant of Guanajuato, and Manuel Abad y Queipo, Bishop-elect of Michoacán. These two reformers became opponents of the revolution: Riaño was killed in the rebel siege of the Guanajuato Granary, and Abad issued the first excommunication of Hidalgo. Enlightenment in New Spain, then, did not lead inevitably or automatically into support for revolution. Instead, the outbreak of insurrection in 1810 divided its proponents into hostile camps.[15]

[14] David Brading, *Espiritualidad barroca, política eclesiástica y renovación filosófica: Juan Benito Díaz de Gamarra (1745–1783)* (Mexico City: Centro de Estudios de Historia de México, 1993); Clément Thibaud, *La Academia de Charcas y la Independencia de América (1776–1800)* (Sucre: Editorial Charcas, Fundación Cultural del Banco Central de Bolivia, Archivo y Biblioteca Nacionales, 2011). See Hamnett, *The Enlightenment in Iberia and Ibero-America*, 190–207, for the Peruvian Enlightenment.

[15] Carlos Herrejón Peredo, *Hidalgo, maestro, párroco e insurgente* (Zamora: El Colegio de Michoacán, 2014).

Royalist opponents of revolution, furthermore, included such Enlightened figures as the *oidor* of the Mexico City Audiencia, Ciriaco González Carvajal, who had been a reforming administrator in the Spanish Philippines, and Antonio Bergosa y Jordán, Bishop of Oaxaca, who had supervised the compilation of population statistics of his diocese in 1803–1805. Also in the category of *ilustrado* was the opponent of the South American revolutions, Viceroy Abascal of Peru (1806–1816), who had previously been president of the Audiencia of Guadalajara in New Spain. From this we can see, first, the extent of Enlightened practices among representatives of the Spanish colonial administration and episcopacy, and, second, the scale of opposition among such figures to the revolutionary and separatist movements of the 1810s. The range of opinion among representative figures of the Enlightenment highlights the profound division of allegiance at the time. Many found themselves caught in the middle, witnessing the destruction inflicted by revolutionary and counterrevolutionary movements alike.[16]

The Iberian Monarchies

Fundamentally, the Spanish and Portuguese empires subsisted through the maintenance of equilibrium between local interest groups and metropolitan objectives. In a sense, the Iberian powers had achieved such an equilibrium by default in the two centuries between c. 1550 and c. 1750. It had not necessarily been the policy objective to do so, but the combination of external pressures and the formation of internal networks of interest accounted for it. Imperial careers traversing all continents of the Hispanic and Lusitanian empires further bound these territories together and to the monarchs served. The Catholic Church, which sacralized the monarchies through symbolism and practice, provided a further centripetal agency.[17]

The influence and practical application of the Enlightenment in the Iberian world should be understood in relation to the problems of its time and as part of the proposed solutions to overriding issues, crises, and, ultimately, political collapse in 1808. Fissures appeared, as early as the 1760s and 1770s

---

[16] Hamnett, *The Enlightenment in Iberia and Ibero-America*, 150, 197, 303 n.18.

[17] Alejandro Cañeque, *The King's Living Image: The Culture and Politics of Viceregal Power in Colonial Mexico* (New York: Routledge, 2004); José M. Portillo Valdés, *Crisis atlántica: Autonomía e independencia en la crisis de la monarquía hispana* (Madrid: Marcial Pons, 2006), 16–21; Frances L. Ramos, *Identity, Ritual, and Power in Colonial Puebla* (Tucson: University of Arizona Press, 2012); Erik Lars Myrup, *Power and Corruption in the Early Modern Portuguese World* (Baton Rouge: Louisiana State University, 2015).

concerning what approach to adopt – shoring up or entirely removing existing institutions. In Spain, Pedro Rodríguez de Campomanes, José Moñino (Conde de Floridablanca), Jovellanos, and Francisco Saavedra, and Rodrigo de Souza Coutinho in the Portuguese monarchy, strove to bolster the *ancien régime* in state and church by a series of reforms designed to excise anomalies and increase the effectiveness of existing institutions. The Enlightenment, initially, was harnessed by the Spanish and Portuguese states to legitimize reform programs, which had profound effects on social and political structures. These were intended to tighten administrative and fiscal systems and bind imperial dominions more loosely together. This was Enlightenment minus liberty, representation, and devolution of power, expressed in authoritarian form. Its objective was that Spain and Portugal should retain (and even extend) control of their imperial territories, while fending off the rival powers, Great Britain and France. The extension of freer trade within the empire between 1765 and 1789, the extension of the Spanish Intendant system through the Americas and Philippines in the same period, and the establishment of new *consulados* in Manila (1769), Caracas and Guatemala (1793), Buenos Aires and Havana (1794), Cartagena, Santiago de Chile, Veracruz, and Guadalajara (1795) represented essential fundamental aspects of the reforms.[18] The Caroline reformers regarded the entire Hispanic monarchy as the "Nation," ruled under one system of government. Since no form of representative government existed in the peninsula no concession to American self-government was ever made.

Much of the history of the later seventeenth and eighteenth centuries deals with metropolitan efforts to recover control of the overseas territories. To do

---

[18] *Reglamento y aranceles reales para el Comercio Libre de España a Indias de 12 de octubre de 1778* (San Lorenzo el Real, 1778), applied to a range of Spanish ports beyond Cádiz and followed from the decrees of 16 October 1765, referring to the Spanish Caribbean, and 2 February 1778, extending the concession of freer trade within the empire to Buenos Aires and Montevideo, Valparaíso and Concepción in Chile, and Arica, Callao, and Guayaquil in Peru. The regulation henceforth included the kingdoms of Santa Fe (especially Cartagena) and Guatemala in these provisions, but excluded Venezuela in deference to the privileged, Basque-managed Caracas Company, and New Spain in deference to the interests of the Consulado of Mexico. They were not included until 1789. Javier Ortiz de la Tabla, *Memorias políticas y económicas del Consulado de Veracruz, 1796–1822* (Seville: Escuela de Estudios Hispano-Americanos, 1985); Gabriel B. Paquette, *Enlightenment, Governance, and Reform in Spain and Its Empire, 1759–1808* (Basingstoke: Ashgate, 2009); Gabriel B. Paquette, *Imperial Portugal in the Age of Atlantic Revolution: The Luso-Brazilian World, c. 1770–1850* (Cambridge: Cambridge University Press, 2013); Allan J. Kuethe and Kenneth J. Andrien, *The Spanish Atlantic World in the Eighteenth Century: War and the Bourbon Reforms, 1713–1796* (Cambridge: Cambridge University Press, 2014).

so, ministers in both monarchies would either have to enlist the support of local interest groups and work through them or else thoroughly subordinate them. Although the Portuguese monarchy appeared more willing to adopt the former policy, neither government succeeded entirely in pursuing either policy. The explanation lay in two overriding factors that would become evident during the later eighteenth and early nineteenth centuries: the growing determination of American poles of power and wealth to maintain and expand the positions they had already acquired within their home territories; and the inability of both metropoles to mobilize sufficient resources in order to assert effectively the plenitude of power which they claimed. As the course of events from the 1790s to the 1820s would demonstrate, it was the metropoles which collapsed.[19]

The Hispanic Enlightenment developed one characteristic aspect that distinguished it from other European Enlightenments. This was its attention to the historical experience of the Middle Ages. Elsewhere in Europe, neomedievalism would become associated in subsequent decades more with Romanticism than with Enlightenment. In Spain, however, this earlier preoccupation resulted in the need to elaborate a construction of ideas that could legitimately challenge the expansion of royal and ministerial power by the eighteenth-century Bourbon dynasty. The attention given to developing factual history provided this search for viable alternatives to renovated absolutism. In consequence, theories of the constitution became articulated, and were founded upon a reinterpretation of such medieval legal provisions as the Visigothic *Fuero Juzgo* and the Castilian *Siete Partidas* in response to the constitutional requirements of the early nineteenth century. Above all, it meant a reassessment of the function of the medieval *Cortes* of the distinct peninsular kingdoms and provinces in relation to royal authority. The resuscitation of the *Cortes* became an urgent matter after 1808 in the absence of the legitimate monarch who was held in captivity in France until 1814.[20]

---

[19] This is the argument in Brian R. Hamnett, *The End of Iberian Rule on the American Continent, 1770–1830* (Cambridge: Cambridge University Press, 2017).

[20] Francisco Martínez Marina, *Ensayo histórico-crítico sobre la antigua legislación y principales cuerpos legales de los reinos de León y Castilla: Especialmente sobre el Código de las Siete Partidas de D. Alfonso el Sabio*, 2 vols. (Madrid: Hija de J. Ibarra, 1808); Francisco Martínez Marina, *Teoría de las Cortes, o grandes juntas nacionales de León y Castilla* (Madrid: Imprenta de Fermín Villapando, 1813). A canon of San Isidro in Madrid, he was a protégé of Campomanes. Brian R. Hamnett, "The Medieval Roots of Spanish Constitutionalism," in Scott Eastman and Natalia Sobrevilla Perea, eds., *The Rise of Constitutional Government in the Iberian Atlantic World: The Impact of the Cádiz Constitutional of 1812* (Tuscaloosa: University of Alabama Press, 2015), 19–41.

The other side of the Enlightenment argued for demolition rather than preservation. This wing is what Jonathan Israel has described as the "Radical (or Democratic) Enlightenment." He views this direct connection between Radical Enlightenment and revolution as fundamental to the shaping of the modern world.[21] In Spain, Olavide's severe criticisms and mockery of the old regime, for which he was brought down by the Inquisition in 1776–1778, put him in this category. Valentín de Foronda (1751–1821), consul in Philadelphia from 1801 to 1810, and a political economist, became a radical liberal in the 1810s.[22] The political objectives of leading Spanish liberals, such as Manuel Josef Quintana, Agustín Argüelles, and the Conde de Toreno, included the demolition of the corporate inheritance of the old regime during the first Hispanic constitutional period of 1810–1814. Unicameralism and representation according to population would replace juridical structures and the *Cortes* of the medieval kingdoms. Radical though this was, the democratic intent of the liberal version of representative government remained a matter of doubt.[23]

Bourbon Spain experienced deep-rooted crisis during the 1790s, followed by political collapse in 1808. This crisis was not brought on by the example, imitation, or impact of the French Revolution, or by the Napoleonic intervention of 1808–1814, but by structural causes specific to Spain and its empire. Political collapse in metropolitan Spain, furthermore, profoundly affected the entire Hispanic monarchy. It was not preceded by widespread critique of monarchy and the old regime as such, as had been the case in later eighteenth-century France – at least, not until the period of Manuel de Godoy's supremacy at the court of Carlos IV between 1793 and 1808.[24]

The Portuguese monarchy, by contrast, did not experience any parallel crisis or breakdown, because the context and the issues continued to be

---

[21] Jonathan I. Israel, *Radical Enlightenment: Philosophy and the Making of Modernity, 1650–1750* (Oxford: Oxford University Press, 2001); Jonathan I. Israel, *Democratic Enlightenment: Philosophy, Revolution, and Human Rights, 1750–1790* (Oxford: Oxford University Press, 2012).

[22] Marcelin Défourneaux, *Pablo de Olavide, ou l'Afrancesado (1725–1803)* (Paris: Presse universitaire de France, 1959); Francisco Sánchez-Blanco, *Ilustración goyesca: La cultura en España en el reinado de Carlos IV (1788–1808)* (Madrid: Centro de Estudios Políticos y Constitucionales, 2007); Hamnett, *Enlightenment in Iberia and Ibero-America*, 100–3.

[23] Albert Dérozier, *Manuel Josef Quintana et la naissance du libéralisme en Espagne*, 2 vols. (Paris: Les Belles Lettres, 1968–1970).

[24] Carlos Corona Baratech, *Revolución y reacción en el reinado de Carlos IV* (Madrid: Ediciones Rialp, 1957); Pere Molas Ribalta, ed., *La España de Carlos IV* (Madrid: Tabapress, 1991); Emilio de la Parra López, *Manuel Godoy: La aventura del poder* (Barcelona: Tusquets, 2002).

substantially different to those operating in Spain. Unlike Spain, Portugal did not contend for a position on the European political stage with the other powers. Although beset like Bourbon Spain by constant financial pressures, Portugal did not face financial collapse under the strain of repeated warfare, as Spain did after 1795. The Portuguese government was not facing political disaster in the 1790s and 1800s, as was the Spanish government of Carlos IV through the incapacity of the king and open hostility at all levels to the supremacy of Godoy after 1793. On the contrary, competent ministers were able to guide the Lusitanian monarchy, with the full support of the prince regent, Dom João, through the difficulties of the Napoleonic Wars, French pressures, the deterioration of relations with Spain, and the reality of invasion in 1807–1808, and save the royal family and government by emigration to Brazil, with the support of the British. In such a way, Souza Coutinho preserved several of the policies of Pombal, Portugal's de facto Enlightened Despot of 1750–1777, without substantially altering the absolutist nature of Braganza government, while in Brazil after 1808. The devastation and impoverishment of metropolitan Portugal after the French invasions of 1807–1811, however, could not be prevented.[25]

Ilustrados and Iluminados at a Time of Multiple Identities

The study of population, environment, and natural resources led to examination of the place of humanity within these contexts, and hence, to the place of man in society. From this basis, scientific practices and philosophical ideas might be transferred to the social and political plane at a time of resentment at increasing metropolitan control and ministerial power. This issue lies at the heart of any assessment of the impact of the Enlightenment on subsequent political movements. In the Hispanic and Luso-Brazilian monarchies, *ilustrados* and *iluminados* gave considerable attention to medicine, natural history, geology, geography, physics, chemistry, biology, and botany. While such disciplines certainly exposed the extent of the material problems in both monarchies and induced a sense of backwardness in relation to more materially successful states at the time, such as Great Britain, France, the

---

[25] Ana Rosa Cloclet da Silva, *Inventando a Nação: Intelectuais ilustrados e estadistas luso-brasileiros na crise do Antigo Regime português, 1750–1822* (São Paulo: Editora Hucitec, 2006); Kirsten Schultz, "Royal Authority, Empire, and the Critique of Colonialism in Rio de Janeiro, 1808–1821," *Luso-Brazilian Review* 37:2 (2000), 7–31.

Netherlands, and certain parts of Germany, they did not lead inevitably in the direction of political revolution. The relation between scientific modes of thought and political consciousness remained ill-defined.[26]

Circumspection among scientific and political thinkers was required, however, in view of the pervading censorship by church and state, especially during the 1790s, when revolution in France and the French Caribbean was making imperial government fearful for its own position. The Quito medical reformer, Eugenio Espejo (1747–1795) was arrested three times, although exile in New Granada gave him the opportunity to meet Francisco Antonio Zea (1766–1822), who would become Bolívar's vice president of Colombia at the Congress of Angostura in 1819, and Antonio Nariño, before becoming a supporter of the Quito Junta for autonomy of 10 August 1810. The case of Nariño (1765–1823) in New Granada is illustrative. Born in the viceregal capital, Santa Fe de Bogotá, Nariño was the son of a Galician father who married into a leading city family. His father-in-law, Manuel Bernardo Álvarez, procurator of the Audiencia of Santa Fe, held a leading position in the colonial administration. Nariño became a city councillor aged twenty-four; however, notoriety overtook him in 1794, when he was indiscreet, or provocative, enough to translate the French revolutionary *Declaration of the Rights of Man and of the Citizen* (1789) into Spanish. The colonial administration took this as an assault on the legitimacy of its position. Nariño, who, it turned out, was an admirer of Raynal, Gaetano Filangieri, the Spanish political economist Bernardo Ward, and Foronda, was brought to trial for sedition. In his defense, he claimed not to be a revolutionary seeking to overthrow the Spanish colonial government and the existing social order, but, instead, holding to the Natural Law tradition. This was New Granada's *cause célèbre*. In an assault on one of the capital's leading families, the viceregal government deported him to Spain for imprisonment. The resourceful Nariño, however, managed to escape from Cádiz, fleeing to France and then

---

[26] Rosa Zeta Quinde, *El pensamiento ilustrado en el "Mercurio Peruano," 1791–1794* (Piura: Universidad de Piura, 2000); Renan Silva, *Los ilustrados de Nueva Granada, 1760–1808: Genealogía de una comunidad de interpretación* (Medellín: Banco de la República, Editorial Universitaria, 2002); Renan Silva, *La Ilustración en el virreinato de la Nueva Granada: Estudios de historia social* (Medellín: La Carreta Editoriales, 2005); Daniela Bleichmar, Paula de Visa, Kristin Huffine, and Kevin Sheehan, eds., *Science in the Spanish and Portuguese Empires, 1500–1800* (Stanford: Stanford University Press, 2009); Adam Warren, *Medicine and Politics in Colonial Peru: Population Growth and Bourbon Reforms* (Pittsburgh, PA: University of Pittsburgh Press, 2010); Thomas F. Glick, "Science and Independence in Latin America (with Special Reference to Nueva Granada)," *Hispanic American Historical Review* 71:2 (1991), 307–4.

England, where he presented himself as working for Hispanic American independence and standing for civil and commercial liberty.[27]

In New Granada, a remarkable transition took place among men of science, leading them first to reform, and then to revolution. Zea, for instance, became part of the Royal Botanical Expedition to New Granada, which José Clemente Mutis (1732–1808) had first brought there from Spain in 1783. Mutis disseminated knowledge of the ideas of Linnaeus, Copernicus, and Newton among Santa Fe notables. Francisco José Caldas (1768–1816), astronomer and writer, who met Alexander von Humboldt and Aimé Bonpland in Quito in 1802, had also been associated with the expedition. A leading participant in the revolutionary movement, he was executed by Spanish royalist forces on 29 October 1816.

The career of the aspiring revolutionary Francisco de Miranda (1750–1816), spanned both the "Age of Enlightenment" and the "Age of Revolutions." The son of a Canary Island merchant in Caracas and not a scion of the predominant planter class, the young Miranda rose to the rank of colonel in the Spanish Army during Spain's participation in the War of British–American Independence. Financial difficulties accounted for abrupt departure to the United States in 1783–1785, where he became a champion of Spanish American independence, viewing it as parallel to that of the thirteen British colonies in 1783. Miranda's historical significance remains uncertain. From the late 1770s until 1810, he spent virtually the entire time away from his homeland. Perhaps his greatest accomplishment lay in making the question of Spanish American independence a topic of discussion within governmental circles in the United States, Great Britain, and France. A number of historians have argued for Miranda's position as an *ilustrado*. Karen Racine describes him as "squarely in the centre of Enlightenment thought" with Hume and Raynal as his favorite authors.[28] John Lynch sees him as a deist, steeped in the ideas of the *philosophes*. John Maher describes him as "a cultured devotee of the Enlightenment who assembled one of the great private libraries of his time ... it is as a man of the Enlightenment that he

---

[27] Gabriel Torre Puga, *Opinión pública y censura en Nueva España: Indicios de un silencio imposible, 1767–1794* (Mexico City: El Colegio de México, 2010); Thibaud, *Libérer le nouveau monde*, 173, 178–80. Nariño had 25 difficult-to-obtain prohibited books in his library among the 1,617 books found by the criminal investigators in 1794. Vanegas, *La revolución neogranadina*, 50–8.
[28] Karen Racine, *Francisco de Miranda: A Transatlantic Life in the Age of Revolution* (Wilmington, DE: Scholarly Resources, 2003), 95, 98.

saw and presented himself and his project."[29] He had all thirty-six volumes of the *Encyclopédie* in his Grafton Street library in London, but which of them had he actually read? Jonathan Israel ranks him among the protagonists of Helvétius, Mably, Raynal, the encyclopedists, Beccaria, Filangieri, and Rousseau, and an enthusiast for radical ideas after 1783–1784: "the evidence plainly suggests it was radical literature that brought him to his militantly libertarian outlook."[30] Those eighteenth-century authors and ideas would have been widely discussed – rejected or accepted, digested or glossed over – in the circles frequented by Miranda during the three decades before 1810. He, however, was not the author of any book or paper associated with the Enlightenment. Was he, then, primarily a man of action? He was the champion of an idea of colonial liberation, but until 1810 remained continually frustrated from bringing this goal into effect.[31]

Miranda presented his first Project for Spanish-American Independence to the British Government in 1790, which provided for a constitutional monarchy under a nominal Inca, perhaps a throwback to the Túpac Amaru rebellion of 1780. There would be a senate of life-members. He expected the new system to be based on equality before the law and proposed the abolition of Indian tribute, although not of slavery, which at that time did not appear to have been an issue for him. State monopolies and the Inquisition would also be abolished. Much of this derived from the general Spanish American range of grievances. The fanciful promise of Inca-derived monarchy reappeared in his Project of 1801, in which the executive power would be entrusted to two Incas, one of whom would reside in the capital city and the other itinerant through the provinces. They would be elected by a "Colombian Council."[32]

We shall now turn to Juan Pablo Viscardo, whose ideas Miranda adopted. Born in Arequipa in 1748, Viscardo, who took his final vows as a Jesuit in

---

[29] William Spence Robertson, *The Life of Miranda*, 2 vols. (Chapel Hill: University of North Carolina Press, 1929); John Maher, ed., *Francisco de Miranda: Exile and Enlightenment* (London: Institute for the Study of the Americas, 2006), Introduction, 2–3; vol. II, 218–23.

[30] Israel, *Democratic Enlightenment*, 400–2, 517–19; John Lynch, "Francisco de Miranda: The London Years," in John Maher, ed., *Francisco de Miranda: Exile and Enlightenment* (London: Institute for the Study of the Americas, 2006), 22–53: 34–5.

[31] See Caracciolo Parra Pérez, *Miranda et la Révolution française* (Paris: J. Demoulin, 1925). It does not appear that, at least until 1810, Miranda envisaged anything other than complete independence of the entire Spanish Empire in the Americas as one, single state, possibly to be known as "Colombia."

[32] José Luis Salcedo-Bastardo, *Francisco de Miranda: América Espera* (Caracas: Biblioteca Ayacucho, 1982), doc. no. 100, 285–92, *Proyecto de gobierno provisorio*.

Cuzco in 1763, found himself expelled from Peru four years later. Aged only twenty-one, he arrived in Italy in April 1769. In 1781, Viscardo sought to enlist British support for the Túpac Amaru rebels in Peru and wrote to Charles James Fox, Whig foreign secretary from March to July 1782 to that effect. In London, he hoped to secure naval support for Spanish American independence. The signing of the Peace of Versailles in September 1783, however, restored peaceful relations between Britain and Spain, which lasted until 1796, when Spain realigned with revolutionary France. In 1784, Viscardo returned to Italy. Like Miranda, Viscardo spent decades in exile and came to know a range of personalities in power and with influence. Viscardo appears to have written his *Lettre aux espagnols américains* in the revolutionary Paris of 1792, though it was not published until 1796. He called for the complete independence of Spanish America and denounced what he described as the Spanish government's three centuries of rapacity, commercial monopoly, and despotism. These were standard charges at that time and would be repeated in Spanish America from 1808–1810 onward, as in Camilo Torres' *Memorial de agravios* of 1809 in New Granada. Viscardo's preference was for contemporary eighteenth-century writers and for Hispanic contractual ideas. His work certainly appealed to Miranda, who would borrow his ideas. Viscardo, however, did not leave a blueprint for government.[33]

Viscardo returned to London in January 1795 and died there in February 1798. He left his papers to Rufus King, the United States Minister in London, who, unable to read Spanish, passed them on to Miranda. The latter had the *Lettre* translated into English in 1799 with the aid of the US Embassy. He translated it into Spanish in the following year, and the British authorities disseminated it from Trinidad, which Britain had taken from Spain in 1797.

Miranda's second Project for Independence was presented to the British government in 1801. Significantly, he placed emphasis on the municipal councils, which would come to play such a major role in 1810 and thereafter, once the movement for home control of affairs had begun to take shape in Spanish South America. Equally significantly, in view of subsequent racial tensions, Miranda provided for one-third of the positions in these councils to be held by ethnic majorities, that is, by Indians and "people of color." It may have been the example of the successful establishment of federalism in the United States after 1787 that led Miranda to recommend the division of

---

[33] Miguel Batllori, S.I., *El Abate Viscardo: Historia y mito de la intervención de los jesuitas en la Independencia de Hispanoamérica* (Caracas: Instituto Panamericano de Geografía e Historia, 1953), 82, 87, 147, Apéndice.

powers for a federal state in Spanish America. Indirect elections to regional assemblies were designed to protect against demagogy. Free-black sons of free parents would be included in the franchise.[34] Unable to secure British assistance, Miranda returned in September 1805 to the United States, where, through Alexander Hamilton, he met former President John Adams in Washington in December 1805. From the United States, Miranda planned his arrival on the coast of Venezuela in 1806, using Viscardo's ideas in his Declaration of 10 January. Two attempts at landing at Puerto Cabello and Coro resulted in failure and escape to Trinidad. Local indifference and the general skepticism of the Venezuelan planter class, which had different ideas as to the future of the country to those of Miranda, helped to explain the debacle. Miranda had no base of support in Venezuela and was far better known in the various cities of Europe and the United States than in Spanish America. By late December 1807, Miranda was back in England. The reversal of alliances in the summer of 1808 diverted British attention from Spanish America to Spain, with the new Anglo-Spanish alliance making Miranda's continued presence in London an embarrassment to the British government. He continued to make useful contacts, however, namely with James Mill (1773–1836), a product of the Scottish Enlightenment, through whom he secured publication of Viscardo's *Lettre* and two collaborative articles of January 1809 in the *Edinburgh Review*, deploring the British alliance with Spain and underlining the beneficial consequences of Spanish-American independence for British commerce. With William Wilberforce (1759–1833), Miranda shared a hostility to the slave trade. In 1810, he presented him with two copies of the *Lettre*.[35]

Miranda returned to Venezuela a second time after the outbreak of revolution in Caracas, and he was elected, late in 1810, as one of the deputies for the province of Barcelona in the National Congress. This Congress met on 2 March 1811, and consisted of forty deputies from the seven provinces of the Captaincy General of Venezuela. Miranda favored an immediate declaration of independence from the Hispanic monarchy. This was read to Congress on 7 July. When, however, the first Venezuelan constitution was signed on 21 December, he disliked the division of executive power into a triumvirate, a reaction to absolute monarchy, considering such a move

[34] Salcedo-Bastardo, *Miranda*, no. 97, 263–71, *A los pueblos del continente colombiano*, London, 2 May 1801. This proclamation portrayed the imperial government as treacherous.
[35] Batllori, *Abate Viscardo*, 157, 301–3, for the text, *The Edinburgh Review*, vol. XIII, no. XXVI, art. 11, 277–311. Lynch, "Miranda."

unworkable given the circumstances of the day. The constitution showed the influence of the United States in its adoption of federalism. This was combined with the adoption of the French revolutionary declaration of the Rights of Man. Venezuela was to become a confederation of seven provinces. Although he suppressed opposition to independence in Valencia, Miranda was forced to capitulate to the royalist forces of Domingo de Monteverde on 25 July 1812, which brought down the First Venezuelan Republic. Bolívar's hostility to him facilitated royalist recapture of Miranda and his deportation to prison in Cádiz, where he died in 1816.[36]

Enlightenment and Liberalism

Within the Iberian world, the relationship of the overseas sectors of the Hispanic and Lusitanian monarchies to the metropolitan center in the peninsula would rise to the forefront of political issues during the 1810s and early 1820s. If the political transformation of Spain after 1808 implied the recovery of lost rights and the assertion of new ones, did these rights also extend to the overseas territories, and, if so, in what form were they to be legally expressed?

Much debate focused on the type of representation to be adopted. A solution was urgently required, so that some form of government could be put in place during the French occupation of most of the peninsula and the Hispanic monarchy thereby held together. What the position of the Spanish American territories should be in the new representative system remained a still unresolved question. The proportion of representation accorded to metropolitan Spain and Spanish America by the Cádiz system, whether in 1810–1814 or 1820–1823, was never resolved. That issue, combined with failure to take note of American demands for autonomy within the empire, decisively contributed to the collapse of Spanish rule in Mexico in 1821–1822.[37]

From the Cádiz Constitution of 1812, it was clear that Spanish liberal constitutionalists had departed from neither the exclusive establishment of the Catholic religion, retained in Article 12, nor from hereditary monarchy. At the same time, they saw peninsular liberalism in imperial terms. The

---

[36] Robertson, *Life of Miranda*, vol. II, 1–4, 109–17, 120, 137–40. The Congress, elected indirectly, would meet biannually. The provincial legislatures would elect the Senate in a bicameral system.

[37] Anna, *Spain and the Loss of America*, 258–65.

Enlightenment roots of this early Hispanic liberalism remained strong. Although different in historical context and objective from the measures taken during the eighteenth century by the absolute monarchs and their ministers, the reforms of the first constitutional period certainly had a Bourbon character. This was particularly evident in their unitarism, the concentration of representation and decision-making at the metropolitan center. Valencian and Catalan regionalists in the peninsula and autonomists in the Americas objected to the denial of representation in their own territories. Appeal to supposed medieval antecedents, moreover, enabled Spanish liberals in 1810–1814 and 1820–1823 to distance the "Spanish Revolution" from the violence of the French Revolution during the 1790s. The liberal cleric Joaquín Lorenzo Villanueva portrayed a Spanish constitutionalism deriving from the writings of Aquinas.[38]

Even so, counterrevolutionaries at the time and later continued to insist that the two revolutions were identical and equally destructive. Revolutionary doctrines aroused alarm in religious and traditionalist circles because they stated outright that sovereignty did not derive from God, but from below or from an abstract and terrestrial agglomeration described as the "people" or the "nation."[39]

Similarly, if Brazil under the Braganza absolute monarchy had been the political center of the Lusitanian world between 1808 and 1821, what was its position to be thereafter? The Portuguese Revolution of 1820 had led to the meeting of a *Cortes* in Lisbon and the temporary adoption of the Cádiz Constitution of 1812. Even though Brazilian deputies were summoned to the *Cortes*, Lisbon would remain, as Madrid likewise claimed to be during the second Spanish constitutional period, the political center of government and representation. The Lisbon liberals clearly intended to reduce the position of Portuguese America to a series of disjointed provinces directly subordinate to the metropolitan government. As a result, the previous status of Rio de Janeiro would be reduced from the capital city of a large American territory to the role of slaving port in the provinces. Such a prospect transformed the dominant planter and mercantile classes of Rio into revolutionaries opposed to liberal Portugal, determined, in alliance with the other southeastern elites of São Paulo and Minas Gerais, to reassert their political hegemony within

---

[38] Joaquín Lorenzo Villanueva, *Las angélicas fuentes o el tomista en las cortes* (Cádiz: Imprenta de la Junta de Provincia en la Casa de Misericordia, 1812).

[39] See Hamnett, *The Enlightenment in Iberia and Ibero-America*, Chapter 9, "The Counter-Enlightenment," 242–63, 322–7.

the Brazils. The language of liberation provided their rhetoric of rejection. Even so, this movement did not intend to restore monarchical absolution but to transform Brazil into a form of constitutional monarchy through which the propertied elites would govern the country in their own interests. Emperor Pedro I's rejection of the projected Brazilian constitution in 1823 and his grant of a more conservative form in 1824, modeled on Louis XVIII's *Charte Constitutionelle* of 1814, provoked widespread opposition. The military and naval struggle to put down the extended rebellion of the northeast in 1824, in some ways a replay of the Pernambuco Rebellion of 1817 but on a larger scale, showed imperial Brazil to be in no way immune from the violence in Spanish America. Even so, slaveholding Brazil had a moderated constitutional monarchy until 1831, when for the ten years of the Regency, Brazil became virtually a de facto decentralized republic.[40]

Revolutionary Aims and Limitations

Rejecting central control from Cádiz right from the start, Spanish American constitutionalists in Venezuela, New Granada, the Río de la Plata, and Chile sought to construct their own representative systems, drawing both from internal historical experience and from contemporaneous external influences as they saw fit for their purpose. The matter of constitutional and juridical reconstruction divided political thinking.

The debate moved beyond divine right, scholasticism, contractual theory (*pactismo*), and Natural Law, toward the direction of "sovereignty of the people" or "sovereignty of the nation." It would prove necessary to define what a "nation" was and who "the people" were. That, in turn, raised the question of the indivisibility or plurality of sovereignty, the latter as expressed in a federal state. The subject of sovereignty opened discussion of forms of representation – corporate or according to population, unicameral or bicameral – and from there to types of electoral system – indirect or direct, with or without literacy, property or income qualifications.

On principle, Spanish American revolutionaries rejected the monarchy and derided the past, upholding the ideas of natural rights, sovereignty of the nation or people, republicanism, representative government, political liberty,

---

[40] Nuno G. F. Monteiro, *Elites e poder: Entre o Antigo Regime e o liberalismo* (Lisbon: Imprensa de Ciências Sociais, 2003); Lúcia Maria Bastos Pereira das Neves, *Corundas e constitucionais: A cultura política da Independência (1820–1822)* (Rio de Janeiro: FAPERJ, 2003); Evaldo Cabral de Mello, *A outra independência: O federalismo pernabucano de 1817 a 1824* (São Paulo: Editora 34, 2004).

and citizenship. Declarations to this effect could be found in virtually all the constitutions which appeared in the years from 1811 to 1826. These principles were testimony to the impact of Enlightened thinking, mingled with Natural Law, *pactismo*, and neoscholasticism, during the movements of emancipation from Spanish rule. Here and there, ideas or institutions borrowed from the British North American and French revolutions could be discerned. They provided a spiritual or moral connection between those foreign revolutions and the movements in the Hispanic world. Interpretation of such principles, application, and purpose, however, depended upon circumstance, context, and willingness. In practice, the moral break with the colonial order did not necessarily mean the automatic abandonment of attitudes, practices, and customs that had prevailed for centuries. These included social and ethnic relations, working practices – including slavery where prevailing – and the two ever-altering balances between executive power and legality, and central government and region, province or locality.[41]

In 1808–1810, the issues of where sovereignty lay, who was to govern, what form of government there was to be, and how the administration of justice was to be provided – all issues undoubtedly discussed in private throughout the preceding twenty years at least – became paramount throughout the monarchies. They would take different forms across the diverse territories. Selective acquisitions from the newer traditions of the American and French revolutions would be grafted onto preexisting traditions and perspectives in Spanish America. These latter would be adopted insofar as they were perceived as having relevance in the Spanish American context or if they could be used as propaganda to counter the legitimism championed by royalists. Clément Thibaud points to many such examples on both accounts. Constitutional declarations deriving from the American Revolution appeared in New Granada alongside adoptions of the French revolutionary *Declaration of the Rights of Man and of the Citizen*, especially in the pristine years of the Colombian Revolution in 1811–1813. The revolutionary constitutions of 1791 and 1793 also appeared in this way. The Cartagena Revolution borrowed from the US Bill of Rights and the debates of Congress in 1787 for its own constitution in 1812.[42]

---

[41] Gutiérrez Ardila, *Un Nuevo Reino*, 239–339; Vanegas, *La revolución neogranadina*, 316–23, 411–18. In New Granada, an estimated fourteen constitutions were published between 1811 and 1816.
[42] Thibaud, *Libérer le nouveau monde*, 258–60, 265, 304–5.

Republicanism had been adopted by the United States after 1776 and in France after 1792. It was never adopted in constitutional Spain, at least not until the First and Second Republics established in 1873 and 1931, respectively. This was despite the second constitutional regime's belated deposition of Fernando VII in 1823. Metropolitan Portugal did not become a republic until 1910. The Spanish American movements took more readily to republicanism, even though in most cases it took time. Mexico, seceding from the metropolitan government in Madrid in 1821, experimented briefly with monarchy in 1822–1823 and again in 1862–1867. The royalist sector of Peru retained Bourbon allegiance until 1825. Brazil became a constitutional monarchy as the Brazilian Empire under the Braganza dynasty until 1889, when it finally adopted federalism under the 1891 constitution. The republican predilection in Hispanic America was not a servile imitation of either the United States or France but, rather, derived from home traditions and modes of thought.[43]

We should be clear what were the aims of the leaders of revolutionary movements. In the two very different contexts of New Granada and the Río de la Plata, for example, their aim was not to dismantle the Hispanic legal system, despite removal of the colonial political institutions after September 1810, but to codify the Fundamental Law derived from medieval Iberia and thereby revise the judicial system, usually following the models of Beccaria and the Italian Enlightenment. The basis, however, continued to be the older *ius gentium*, or Natural Law tradition with certain of Montesquieu's ideas included in the general body of thinking on the subject.[44]

Beneath the brandishing of new ideologies and experimentation with new institutional forms, the reality was that the revolutions were sustained by a very traditional body, the *cabildo*, the colonial municipal council. In those cases where revolutionary governments took power in Spanish South America, the transformation of the councils into elective *ayuntamientos constitucionales*, under the terms of the Cádiz Constitution of 1812 and the

---

[43] Josefina Z. Vázquez, ed., *El establecimiento del federalismo en México, 1821–1827* (Mexico City: El Colegio de México, 2003); Brian R. Hamnett, "Factores regionales en la desintegración del régimen colonial en la Nueva España: El federalismo de 1823–1824," in Inge Buisson, Günter Kahle et al., eds., *Problemas de la formación del Estado y de la nación en Hispanoamérica* (Bonn: Inter Nationes, 1984), 305–17.

[44] José Carlos Chiaramonte, "Gli Iluministi napolitani del Río de la Plata," *Rivista Storica Italiana* 76 (1964), 114–32, has drawn attention to the importance of the Italian Enlightenment in restructuring southern Spanish America. See also José Carlos Chiaramonte, "The 'Ancient Constitution' after Independence (1808–1852)," *Hispanic American Historical Review* 90:3 (2010), 455–89.

ensuing administrative reforms of 1813, did not apply.[45] It had been from the unreformed American *cabildos* that the autonomous juntas of 1809 in Quito and then Caracas, Buenos Aires, Santa Fe de Bogotá, and Santiago de Chile in 1810 had been set up. In most cases, these councils had been extended at the decisive moment to include representatives of the leading corporate bodies and notables, lay and ecclesiastical, of the capital cities, as a *cabildo abierto*. The passage of the *cabildo* through the juntas to the congresses of incipient sovereign states did not occur out of the blue. Royal attempts to cower and diminish the American *cabildos* during the later eighteenth century had not been entirely successful. With the decline of imperial government under Carlos IV, many had recovered the initiative as centers of opposition to absolutism. In the absence of the viceroy, the Buenos Aires *cabildo* had rallied the colonial militia in 1806 to oppose the British assault on the city, and in Venezuela, Miranda's Manifesto to the Peoples of Northern South America on 2 August in the same year had appealed to the *cabildos* as natural leaders of the revolutionary cause.[46] The revolution, then, would be led by a traditional institution deeply implanted at the core of the colonial system and, accordingly, expected to survive it. This had nothing to do with the Enlightenment – except insofar as the congresses which came later would be conceived as new phenomena (though representing men of the old order) and embellished with the radical ideologies of new departure.

Another well-rooted colonial institution also played a crucial role in the procedure of constructing the new states. This was the parish – presided over, understandably, by the parish priest. In the new electoral systems, the parish provided the electoral base level for the tier system of indirect elections to the *Cortes* in the constitutional Cádiz system of 1812. Most subsequent constitutions adopted similar tier systems, as did the Mexican Federal Constitution of 1824. At the heart of the electoral procedure was the *vecino*, the recognized male resident of the appropriate locality, as determined throughout the colonial era – solid, respectable, propertied, with income and education. The position of the *vecino*, then, was not diminished in favor of the "populace," but, on the contrary, enhanced both in the Cádiz

---

[45] *Constitución política de la Monarquía española, promulgada en Cádiz a 19 marzo de 1812* (Barcelona: Librería Nacional de Sauri, 1836), Articles 312–317.
[46] *Constitución política*, Articles 35–58, under the presidency of the civil authority (*jefe político* or *alcalde*) "con asistencia del cura párroco" (Article 46).

system and by the Spanish American revolutionary systems in their complementary search for stability and respectability.[47]

The fundamental division in the revolutionary movements of New Granada appeared early, namely, the opposition between centralism based in the former viceregal capital, Santa Fe de Bogotá, and the preference of the outlying provinces for some form of confederation. The former became quickly associated with Nariño, president of the State of Cundinamarca from 21 September 1811, and the latter with Camilo Torres (1766–1816), who would become president of the United Provinces of New Granada (15 November 1815–14 March 1816). Both men personified the linkage between the Enlightenment and the revolutionary movements in New Granada. Torres, a lawyer who came from a modest family of Popayán, was educated at the Nuestra Señora del Rosario College in Santa Fe and had been commissioned by the city council to draw up a "Memorial of Grievances" in 1809 for presentation to Spain's Supreme Central Junta. Because of its unequivocal indictment of colonial abuses, this document was never sent. Caught up in the savage repression of the constitutional movement in New Granada by the Spanish Expeditionary Army under Pablo Morillo, Torres was put before a firing squad in Bogotá on 5 October 1816. At the Bolivarian Revolutionaries' Constituent Congress of Cúcuta in 1821, Nariño was elected, against considerable opposition to his centralist views, vice president of the Republic of Colombia, under the presidency of Bolívar, also a centralist.[48]

At the start of the monarchy's crisis, few, beyond a small number of separatists, such as Simón Bolívar, envisaged a break with the Hispanic monarchy. On the contrary, they hoped to see a reforming congress reshaping the position of the American territories as equal parts within the monarchy and not as separate states. Similarly, they continued to view the Bourbon monarch, Fernando VII (although in captivity), as the focus of unity, his person and position sustained by the Church. American separatism finally triumphed when this vision was no longer viable. Even so, the American movements for separation from the Hispanic monarchy never implied separation from the Catholic Church also. On the contrary, Catholic identity and affiliation permeated them, no matter what historic

---

[47] Morelli, *Territorio o nación*, 97–9, 202–13, 216–23, referring to the "oligarchization" of the post-colonial regime (99).

[48] Thibaud, *Libérer le nouveau monde*, 343–6, 348–52; Vanegas, *La revolución neogranadina*, 19.

traditions or foreign ideological positions had been acquired during the revolutionary struggles.

Simón Bolívar (1783–1830), unlike most contemporaries, had been a separatist and republican from his first consciousness of the problems facing Spanish America. Greatly influenced by the ideas of the Enlightenment, his political proposals, nevertheless, stemmed from bitter experience of the failures in Venezuela in 1812–1817, followed by victories in 1819–1826 in New Granada, Quito, and Peru. They sought to construct systems of government able to respond to American realities. Bolívar's republicanism, however, stopped short of federalism. Perhaps reacting too strongly to the failure of the First and Second Venezuelan republics of 1810–1812 and 1813–1814, respectively, Bolívar remained a committed centralist for the remainder his life. The models he preferred for Spanish American government derived from images of the Roman Republic or the British form of "mixed monarchy," although with neither lords nor kings. Whether the latter derived from Montesquieu's portrayal or from his own observation in London is difficult to ascertain. The principle of effective executive plus representation of the landed and monied classes, rather than the reality of corruption seems to have been his goal. At all events, he rejected the US model as inappropriate for Spanish American societies.[49]

Conclusion

It is not that the Enlightenment as a body of ideas caused, or even ran into, revolutionary movements, but that the lives of significant individuals spanned both. Notable figures participated in both Enlightenment and revolution, seemingly thereby linking the two phenomena. Generational conflict between older Enlightenment figures and their younger exponents, disciples or opponents appeared strikingly during the Iberian and Ibero-American upheavals of the decades from the 1790s into the 1820s.

In such a way, two generations brought the ideas and methods developed during the period, roughly from 1760 through the 1810s, into the crisis years of 1808–1810, and the changed conditions of 1811–1826. They were not themselves principally responsible for the external conditions which altered the foundations of the Hispanic and Luso-Brazilian monarchies in the broader period from the time of Pombal to the death of Bolívar in 1830 and the fall of the Brazilian Emperor Pedro I in 1831. Yet they were

---

[49] John Lynch, *Simón Bolívar: A Life* (New Haven: Yale University Press, 2006).

not caught up in these events passively, but as creators of new dimensions and as active participants through intensely contested issues, and often bloody conflicts, in which many lost their lives. The modes of thought developed during the Enlightenment frequently shaped their perceptions, even though the savagery of revolutionary struggles conflicted sharply with the cosmopolitan and humanitarian foundations of Enlightenment thinking. Their visibility and vulnerability made them targets of rival revolutionary groups and, equally, of the pitiless counterrevolution imposed throughout the Hispanic monarchy after 1814 and again after 1823.

The territories of the Iberian monarchies in the Americas were not as isolated from European or North American currents as their rulers might have wished. Intellectual contacts came with trade, legal or illegal, especially across the Caribbean to the ports of Venezuela and New Granada, despite periodic attempts at censorship by political and ecclesiastical officials. Critical ideas and reforming objectives, not necessarily revolutionary in intent, complemented existing channels of opposition to renovated absolutism in both monarchies. While the writings associated with the Enlightenment certainly framed the worldview of individuals, revolutionary regimes tended to take what suited them from the Enlightenment, the North American or French revolutions for the purpose of defining their objectives, identifying their cause with broader international currents, and legitimizing their capture of power. Even so, many institutions, mentalities, and practices of the colonial era survived, usually in constitutional, republican, and federal mutations in the post-independence era.

Much revolved around the overriding question of what laws should apply in the separated territories of the Iberian empires in Europe and the Americas. In many respects, the historiography has given priority to politics and the economy, rather than the problem of the law. This is surprising given the importance of the law during the colonial era, especially in Hispanic America. Enlightenment thinking on the nature of the law crucially influenced the type of legal codes adopted in Spanish America, as they were formulated from the middle of the nineteenth century. Even so, existing legal traditions, deriving from colonial legal compilations remained in force in the interim, surviving the political upheavals. The process of updating colonial laws in accordance with contemporary circumstances, however, took a long time to complete. The essential problem remained one of ironing out the anomalies and contradictions resulting from a legal system reflecting the juridical structures of the *ancien régime* and the requirements of the post-1810s liberal constitutional republics and, in a number of cases, federal systems.

4
Cultural Practices and Revolutions, c. 1760–1825

NATHAN PERL-ROSENTHAL

> ... by repeating the same action, till it be grown habitual ... the performance will not depend on memory, or reflection ... but will be natural ... Thus, bowing to a gentleman when he salutes him, and looking in his face when he speaks to him, is by constant use as natural to a well-bred man, as breathing ...[1]

The eighteenth century was an Age of Reason and an Age of Habit. John Locke epitomized both of these sometimes contradictory tendencies. His contractual theory of government, set out in the famous *Two Treatises of Government* (pub. 1689), argued that the consent of rational actors was the font of political power. But in the influential educational treatise he published in 1693, *Some Thoughts Concerning Education*, he explained that one formed a child into a gentleman by having him do "the same action" over and over until it had become "as natural to [him] ... as breathing." Where Locke the political theorist valorized the free and rational choices of individuals, Locke the educator stressed how the human mind was shaped by habit. These contrasting visions of human nature – let us call them *homo politicus* and *homo habitus* – coexisted uneasily in the eighteenth century.

This chapter is about how *homo habitus* collided with *homo politicus* during the Age of Atlantic Revolutions, c. 1760–1825. Scholars have long been deeply interested in how the sedimented habits of eighteenth-century society contributed to, resisted, and shaped the revolutionary political ideas and practices of the late eighteenth century. In this chapter, I undertake a critical analysis of the main ways in which scholars have interpreted the relationship between eighteenth-century cultural practice and revolutionary politics. The chapter draws primarily on the historiographies of eighteenth-century culture and revolutionary politics in North America, Europe (especially France

---

[1] John Locke, "Some Thoughts Concerning Education," in John Locke, *The Works of John Locke*, 9 vols. (London: C. & J. Rivington, 1824), vol. VIII, 45–6.

and the Netherlands), and Latin America (with particular reference to Peru, the area I know best in that region). I am interested in the answers scholars have offered to a few key questions. To what extent did eighteenth-century cultural habits create or generate revolutionary politics? Did revolutionary politics reshape eighteenth-century cultural forms? And to what extent did eighteenth-century cultural practices change: were they elements of continuity or did they experience "revolutionary" changes of their own?

Some definitions are in order. This chapter is about cultural practices, not "culture" in general. Culture is potentially a total phenomenon, encompassing everything that exists in the human world: thoughts, acts, built spaces, etc. Cultural practice aims to define a narrower field of inquiry: practices are *how actors do things*. This distinguishes cultural practices both from things themselves – objects or buildings – and from ideas, beliefs, and drives that motivate action. Practice is the act of putting brush to canvas, not the finished picture. Practice is collecting and preparing food, not the hunger that drives one to do so.[2] By revolutionary politics, I mean to encompass a wide range of the distinctive ideas and institutions that typified late eighteenth- and early nineteenth-century politics. These include obvious elements, such as the idea of popular sovereignty, the practice of democratic elections, the creation of law-making assemblies, and the spread of elected executives. They also include forms of politics "from below" that, though not unique to that period, were important to how the revolutionary era unfolded: crowd actions, rumors and conspiracy-mongering, and other "weapons of the weak."

This chapter develops in four parts. The first section offers an anatomy of eighteenth-century cultural practice. It describes three broad types of practice – social arts, the arts of everyday life, and fine arts – and discusses the contours of each one and the varied social profiles of their practitioners. The second and third sections explore in detail the two most common scholarly paradigms for understanding the relationship between cultural practice and politics in the revolutionary era. I first examine the approach exemplified by Jürgen Habermas' "bourgeois public sphere" thesis, which

---

[2] An extended discussion is in Nathan Perl-Rosenthal, "Atlantic Cultures and the Age of Revolution," *William and Mary Quarterly* 74:4 (2017), 667–96: 679–81. On practice, see Roger Chartier, *On the Edge of the Cliff: History, Language, and Practices*, trans. Lydia G. Cochrane (Baltimore, MD: Johns Hopkins University Press, 1997); William H. Sewell, "The Concept(s) of Culture," in Lynn Hunt and Victoria E. Bonnell, eds., *Beyond the Cultural Turn* (Berkeley: University of California Press, 1999).

sees eighteenth-century cultural practices as engines for the creation of revolutionary political situations. I then consider a second paradigm, exemplified by studies of revolutionary-era fine art, that emphasizes how revolutionary politics affected or changed cultural practices. Both paradigms provide powerful ways of understanding how cultural practice shaped and was shaped by revolutionary politics on an Atlantic scale. But both approaches, I argue, subordinate *homo habitus* to *homo politicus*: the first, by positing a teleological relationship between eighteenth-century culture and revolutionary politics; the second, by making revolutionary politics the primary agent of historical change.

The final section of the chapter discusses two newer, emergent paradigms for thinking about the relationship between cultural practice and revolutionary politics. One paradigm argues that culture change is itself a form of revolution: it proposes that the transformation of cultural practices, leaving aside more conventional political change, is itself a revolutionary development. The other paradigm looks at cultural practices as a mold for revolutionary politics, focusing on how old regime practices acted as a container or medium for revolutionary political ideas and practices. Both of these paradigms place cultural practice at center stage. The culture change-as-revolution paradigm eclipses the traditional *homo politicus* altogether. The cultural practice-as-vehicle approach, which I favor in my own work, posits that revolutionary political ideas and actions initially had to be enacted through the medium of eighteenth-century culture. Each of these paradigms, by taking seriously the autonomy of eighteenth-century cultural practice and rejecting a straight-line link between eighteenth-century culture and revolutionary politics, offers in its own way a means to revisit the old question of culture and revolution from a new angle. They may even encourage us to redefine what we think was "revolutionary" about the Atlantic age of revolutions.

Eighteenth-Century Cultural Practice

Socioeconomic stratification exerted a shaping influence on eighteenth-century cultural practice.[3] There were significant and consequential differences in who performed certain practices, how they were learned, and the

---

[3] On the socioeconomic trend in the eighteenth century, see Isser Woloch and Gregory S. Brown, *Eighteenth-Century Europe: Tradition and Progress, 1715–1789*, 2nd edition (New York: W. W. Norton, 2012), Chapter 4.

aim or purpose of the practices. Using these characteristics as criteria, we can sketch a rough and ready typology of three main groups of cultural practice in the eighteenth century: social arts, fine arts, and arts of everyday life. This tripartite division makes visible similarities among clusters of related practices. It also allows us to outline the socioeconomic profiles of those who were associated with each type of practice and to assess the degree to which each type of practice was homogeneous around the Atlantic world.

The social arts have drawn a great deal of historians' attention over the past several decades. This grouping includes forms of face-to-face sociability, social or communicative writing – such as letters and diaries – and public speaking. All of these practices required multifaceted training to become proficient: a command of genre and the cultivation of a variety of embodied skills, from handwriting to carriage of the body. Success in the art of eighteenth-century conversation, as in the related art of social dance, was the product of long training. Indeed, the training required was specific enough that it was codified and recorded in innumerable manuals and instructional guides. But a hallmark of the social arts was that these competencies were *not* normally acquired from books or via formal instruction. One learned them through informal training and by emulation of family, friends, and mentors. Thus, for instance, while a young woman might learn the technical skill of literacy from a writing-master, she would learn how to compose letters from a parent or an older sibling.[4] Similarly, young men learned skill in oral presentation primarily through participation in school debates or debating societies, in which the mentoring and instruction was informal.[5]

Following in the footsteps of Habermas' influential work on the public sphere, scholars have usually associated these practices with notions of elite gentility and/or with the rising "middling sorts" of the eighteenth century. Yet we should not overstate the monopoly that elites held on the social arts. Face-to-face sociability and literary writing and reading were certainly among the archetypical arts of the salon and the coffeehouse, two spaces that sat at the conceptual center of Habermas' notion of the emergent bourgeois public

---

[4] See Dena Goodman, *Becoming a Woman in the Age of Letters* (Ithaca, NY: Cornell University Press, 2009); Eve Tavor Bannet, *Empire of Letters: Letter Manuals and Transatlantic Correspondence, 1688–1820* (Cambridge: Cambridge University Press, 2005); Konstantin Dierks, *In My Power: Letter Writing and Communications in Early America* (Philadelphia: University of Pennsylvania Press, 2009).

[5] See Wilbur Samuel Howell, *Eighteenth-Century British Logic and Rhetoric* (Princeton: Princeton University Press, 1971).

sphere.⁶ And it is certainly true that skill in the social arts was an important element of eighteenth-century elite self-fashioning. The ability to write well, to dance, to converse, and to speak aloud were markers of one's elite status and essential to the performance of that identity.⁷ But those farther down the social ladder were not cut off from the social arts. The sphere of letter-writing expanded considerably over the course of the later seventeenth and eighteenth centuries. Social dance, albeit not the highly choreographed variety that prevailed among the elites, was widely popular among all classes. And recent scholarship on coffeehouses has revealed how many grub-street hacks and other members of the literary lower orders sat in them, among the gentlemen.⁸

The social arts as a whole became quite homogeneous around the Atlantic world over the course of the eighteenth century. This resulted, in good measure, from the diffusion of practices from eighteenth-century cultural hegemons, notably France and England.⁹ Translations of French and English letter-writing manuals, for instance, spread very similar ways of writing missives across multiple countries and empires: one found the same set of genres, including business letters, letters of introduction, and varieties of phatic correspondence, in many different linguistic and cultural zones.¹⁰ Forms of face-to-face sociability converged as well. The growing use of the English word "club" – naturalized in French and other languages during the eighteenth century – suggests this process of cultural diffusion.¹¹ The *cercles*,

---

⁶ See Jürgen Habermas, *The Structural Transformation of the Public Sphere: An Inquiry into a Category of Bourgeois Society*, trans. Thomas Burger (Cambridge, MA: MIT Press, 1989).

⁷ For the classic discussion of elite self-fashioning, see Stephen Greenblatt, *Renaissance Self-Fashioning: From More to Shakespeare* (Chicago: University of Chicago Press, 1980). See also J. J. de Jong, *Met goed fatsoen: De elite in een Hollandse stad, Gouda 1700–1780* (Amsterdam: De Bataafsche Leeuw, 1985); Goodman, *Becoming a Woman*.

⁸ On the expansion of letter writing, see esp. Susan E. Whyman, *The Pen and the People: English Letter Writers, 1660–1800* (Oxford: Oxford University Press, 2009). On coffeehouse culture, see Brian Cowan, *The Social Life of Coffee: The Emergence of the British Coffeehouse* (New Haven: Yale University Press, 2005), Chapter 8.

⁹ On the immense cultural prestige of France, see Peter Burke, *The Fabrication of Louis XIV* (New Haven: Yale University Press, 1992); T. C. W. Blanning, *The Culture of Power and the Power of Culture: Old Regime Europe, 1660–1789* (Oxford: Oxford University Press, 2002).

¹⁰ See Bannet, *Empire of Letters*, as well as Whyman, *Pen and the People*; Willemijn Ruberg, *Conventionele correspondentie: Briefcultuur van de Nederlandse elite, 1770–1850* (Nijmegen: Vantilt, 2005); Nathan Perl-Rosenthal, "Corresponding Republics: Letter Writing and Patriot Organizing in the Atlantic Revolutions, circa 1760–1792," Ph.D. dissertation, Columbia University, 2011.

¹¹ See Micah Alpaugh, "The British Origins of the French Jacobins: Radical Sociability and the Development of Political Club Networks, 1787–1793," *European History Quarterly* 44:4 (2014), 593–619.

salons, and clubs of France and Britain, in turn, found a homologue in the Spanish-speaking world in the form of *tertulias* or conversation societies. But the spread was not simultaneous: while clubs and *salons* already had a significant presence in the Anglo-French world in the early eighteenth century, *tertulias* did not become common in the Spanish-speaking world until the latter half of the century.[12]

Some of the social arts did vary considerably from region to region. This was often the result of pre-existing elite cultures shaping the reception of the rapidly diffusing social arts of the eighteenth century. In Spanish America, for instance, the persistent social and political weight of the Catholic Church and its institutions – particularly educational institutions and communities of monks and nuns – directed some arriving cultural practices into these social spaces.[13] New England and Virginia both imbibed the practices of social dance and forms of salon life from Britain. But the different elite cultures in these two regions – with Virginia considerably less urban and with less social mobility – affected how social dance and salon life took shape in these regions.[14]

Cultures of everyday life form a second broad group of cultural practices. These practices were, broadly, the practices required to sustain one's own life, the lives of one's family and community, and (in some instances) to earn one's livelihood. The purpose of these practices was not primarily aesthetic or communicative; they were intended to ensure physical survival and health, as well as the reproduction of the family.[15] This category includes practices related to dressing and caring for one's own body, preparation and

---

[12] See Dena Goodman, *The Republic of Letters: A Cultural History of the French Enlightenment* (Ithaca, NY: Cornell University Press, 1994); Susan Branson, *These Fiery Frenchified Dames: Women and Political Culture in Early National Philadelphia* (Philadelphia: University of Pennsylvania Press, 2001); François-Xavier Guerra, *Modernidad e independencias: Ensayos sobre las revoluciones hispánicas* (Madrid: Editorial MAPFRE, 1992), 92–113; Neller Ramón Ochoa Hernández, "El refugio de vagos ilustrados: Discursividad y cultura popular en las pulperías venezolanas (1770–1830)," *Presente y Pasado. Revista de Historia* 18:36 (2013).

[13] On Latin American convents, see esp. Margaret Chowning, *Rebellious Nuns: The Troubled History of a Mexican Convent, 1752–1863* (Oxford: Oxford University Press, 2006); Kathryn Burns, *Colonial Habits: Convents and the Spiritual Economy of Cuzco, Peru* (Durham, NC: Duke University Press, 1999).

[14] Kate Van Winkle Keller, *Dance and Its Music in America, 1528–1789* (Hillsdale, NY: Pendragon Press, 2007); Kenneth Silverman, *A Cultural History of the American Revolution: Painting, Music, Literature, and the Theatre in the Colonies and the United States from the Treaty of Paris to the Inauguration of George Washington, 1763–1789* (New York: Columbia University Press, 1976).

[15] I draw part of this definition from Michel de Certeau, *L'invention du quotidien*, vol. 1: *Arts de faire* (Paris: Gallimard, 1990).

consumption of food, care and management of domestic animals (whether livestock or pets), care and governance of children and other dependents. But it also extends to many leisure activities, such as "visiting," popular festivals, and participation in confraternities and similar organizations. All groups and classes of society, naturally, participated in these practices – though not, as we will see, in the same way.

Practices of everyday life, in spite of their diversity, had in common that they were learned without the benefit of any prolonged instruction. Unlike the social arts, these practices were not generally recorded in manuals or handbooks. One did not learn them through either formal instruction by a master or an informal apprenticeship or mentoring by a family member. Proficiency in everyday practices developed almost exclusively through osmosis, as individuals watched their parents, siblings, and communities live their daily lives. The practices of everyday life were the marrow of social self-reproduction, the process by which societies and communities drew on a shared *habitus* to recreate the practices that reproduced their own image.[16]

Because they did not emerge out of purposeful training, the practices of everyday life differed quite significantly from region to region. This is perhaps most self-evident in the matter of dress: costume, even for elites, varied considerably from region to region in the eighteenth century. This variability was the basis for the very popular collections of regional costume and dress that were consistently produced in Europe throughout the eighteenth and nineteenth centuries.[17] How one ate was another point of difference: foodways in Mesoamerica and eastern North America, for instance, differed far more than the kind of letters that elites in the two regions wrote during the eighteenth century.[18] Practices of self-care and childcare were similarly variable, especially outside the population of elites. Even within individual European countries, such as France or Spain, the populations of different regions had strongly rooted local traditions that remained visibly distinct into the revolutionary era.[19]

---

[16] See Pierre Bourdieu, *Outline of a Theory of Practice* (Cambridge: Cambridge University Press, 1977).

[17] See, for instance, Jacques Grasset Saint-Sauveur, *Costumes Civils actuels de tous les Peuples connus*, 4 vols. (Paris: Pavard, 1784–1788).

[18] Rebecca Earle, *The Body of the Conquistador: Food, Race and the Colonial Experience in Spanish America, 1492–1700* (Cambridge: Cambridge University Press, 2012), Chapter 4; David Hackett Fischer, *Albion's Seed: Four British Folkways in America* (New York: Oxford University Press, 1989).

[19] On local variability in these two countries, see Regina Grafe, *Distant Tyranny: Markets, Power, and Backwardness in Spain, 1650–1800* (Princeton: Princeton University Press,

Everyday practices differed just as significantly – and perhaps even more profoundly – among members of distinct social groups within a single society. The gap between elites and nonelites, and between different racial groups, were particularly marked. Take cultures of food cultivation and preparation. In the Caribbean, African-descended populations frequently maintained significant elements of African foodways, while European-descended populations maintained their own traditional foodways. For instance, the French colony of Saint-Domingue, one of the most agriculturally productive pieces of land in the hemisphere, imported quantities of wheat to feed the appetites of its European settlers.[20] Among Native peoples of North America, tribes and nations in a single region frequently produced food in quite different ways, with distinct gendered divisions of labor.[21]

Fine arts form a third main type of cultural practice. This category includes the practices of the main plastic arts (painting, drawing, sculpture), as well as forms of artistic fabrication that were identified more as crafts than arts: weaving, embroidery, fine woodwork, and the like. Printers, whose guild-bound craft produced both images and texts, including engravings, newspapers, and books, fall within this category. In addition to practices that produced tangible products, the fine arts also encompassed the work of professional performing artists, for whom the artistic product was embodied in the action itself: those who engaged in professional music-making, dance, and the creation and performance of theater and opera. The category of fine arts could also extend to the work of professional writers engaged in the composition of fictional literary works. One could also include the practices of architecture, interior design, and garden planning.

These fine arts and craft practices were defined, in the first instance, by the centrality of the aesthetic quality or intention in their production. All of them were intended, at least in good part, to create something beautiful or to elicit an aesthetic appreciation. In some cases, they were creating a beautiful object without any necessary practical function (such as a painting or sculpture – though they could be used for decor). In other cases, the intention was to

---

2012); Marc Bloch, *French Rural History: An Essay on Its Basic Characteristics*, trans. Janet Sondheimer (London: Routledge Kegan Paul, 1966).

[20] See, for example, Bertie Mandelblatt, "How Feeding Slaves Shaped the French Atlantic: Mercantilism and the Crisis of Food Provisioning in the Franco-Caribbean during the Seventeenth and Eighteenth Centuries," in Sophus A. Reinert and Pernille Røge, eds., *The Political Economy of Empire in the Early Modern World* (London: Palgrave Macmillan, 2013), 192–220: 192.

[21] Elizabeth A. Fenn, *Encounters at the Heart of the World: A History of the Mandan People* (New York: Hill & Wang, 2014), 229–43.

create ephemeral beauty (dance, theater, opera). In yet others, the goal was to create a functional object that was also aesthetically pleasing (anything from an artisanal or handmade object to a book to a building). But for all of these practices, the aesthetic result was not merely incidental, but a central part of the purpose for which the object or performance was being created.

Fine arts practices were distinguished as well by the specialized training they demanded and by the low social status that persistently attached to their practitioners. Individuals usually became proficient in fine arts practice through a long apprenticeship with an acknowledged master.[22] The position of the trainee during this process was distinctly subordinate, socially and often legally, to that of the master. Aspiring plastic artists, for instance, would typically get their start in the workshop of a master. This artisanal model contributed to the cementing of the relatively low social status of fine arts practitioners across the board. As a rule, the plastic arts were considered to occupy a place adjacent to, if not actually within, the category of artisanal work: painters, except for the most elite, were grouped with artisans in social classifications.[23] The story was similar with printers. Musicians, including many composers, were treated as low-status performers.[24] And thespians and other stage performers were often considered downright disreputable.[25]

The social arts practiced by the elites incorporated some fine arts practices. Social dance and music-making, for instance, were essential components of elite self-fashioning around the Atlantic world. Elite girls and women in the eighteenth century were expected to have some command of fine arts such as drawing and needlepoint. These practices were taught to young elite men and women in a manner that lay somewhere between the formal apprenticeship model of the fine arts and the informal training that prevailed for other social arts. Elite families, for instance, frequently employed professional dancing masters and musicians to instruct their children. Yet even when

---

[22] Jane Kamensky, *A Revolution in Color: The World of John Singleton Copley* (New York: W. W. Norton, 2016); Warren Roberts, *Jacques-Louis David and Jean-Louis Prieur, Revolutionary Artists: The Public, the Populace, and Images of the French Revolution* (Albany: State University of New York Press, 2000).

[23] See John Brewer, *The Pleasures of the Imagination: English Culture in the Eighteenth Century* (London: HarperCollins, 1997), Chapter 7. The elite group were increasingly seen as "learned men," but it was always necessary to defend this status: see Harrison C. White and Cynthia A. White, *Canvases and Careers: Institutional Change in the French Painting World* (New York: Wiley, 1965), Chapter 1.

[24] Christoph Wolff, *Johann Sebastian Bach: The Learned Musician*, updated edition (New York: W. W. Norton, 2013), Chapters 1–2.

[25] On theater, see, among others, Rahul Markovits, *Civiliser l'Europe: Politiques du théâtre français au XVIIIe siècle* (Paris: Fayard, 2014); Silverman, *Cultural History*.

they learned these fine arts practices from professionals, members of the elite remained resolute amateurs. This amateur status, in turn, allowed them to evade the low social status that marked fine arts practice.

Fine arts practices exhibited a striking homogeneity across the eighteenth-century Atlantic. Rococo and Baroque styles in painting, which gave way to neoclassicism in the latter part of the century, were Atlantic-wide phenomena, visible in the Americas and Europe alike.[26] The widespread presence of Georgian buildings across the British imperial world, with their red brick or stone bodies, minimally ornamented facades, and whitewashed window frames, is another measure of this cultural homogeneity.[27] These similarities in the practices of fine art across the Atlantic were the product of the influence that centers of cultural authority, particularly France and Italy, exerted on fine arts practitioners. French art, in particular, enjoyed a widespread prestige that made its influence visible even in places that had little or no direct communication with France itself. Even colonial painters and musicians, who might never see Italy or France, typically trained with a master whose cultural genealogy could be quickly traced back to one of these European artistic metropoles.[28] The long training that was required to become proficient in the fine arts reinforced this tendency toward emulation of European models.

Cultural Practices Causing Revolutions

Did cultural practices cause revolutions? The idea that eighteenth-century culture played some role in catalyzing the century's revolutions has been floating around since the 1790s. Both revolutionaries and counter-revolutionaries during the French Revolution asserted that the writers and *salonistes* of the French enlightenment had prepared the way for a political revolution.[29] During the past fifty years, versions of this argument have

---

[26] On the ubiquity of this style, see Gauvin A. Bailey, *The Andean Hybrid Baroque: Convergent Cultures in the Churches of Colonial Peru* (Notre Dame, IN: University of Notre Dame Press, 2010); Gauvin A. Bailey, *Baroque and Rococo* (London: Phaidon, 2012); Viccy Coltman, *Fabricating the Antique: Neoclassicism in Britain, 1760–1800* (Chicago: University of Chicago Press, 2006).

[27] G. A. Bremner, *Architecture and Urbanism in the British Empire* (Oxford: Oxford University Press, 2016).

[28] Kamensky, *A Revolution in Color*, Chapter 7. Indigenous artists in colonial Peru also drew on European printed matter: José de Mesa and Teresa Gisbert, *Historia de la pintura cuzqueña*, 2 vols. (Lima: Fundación A. N. Wiese, Banco Wiese, 1982); Bailey, *Andean Hybrid Baroque*.

[29] See Daniel Mornet, *Les origines intellectuelles de la Révolution française, 1715–1787* (Paris: Armand Colin, 1933).

become a part of the scholarly consensus about the origins of each of the revolutions around the Atlantic world. Some scholars have focused on forms of eighteenth-century elite culture, especially the social arts; others have stressed the role played by ordinary people and the practices of everyday life. Both approaches see revolutionary politics as emerging in good measure out of pre-revolutionary cultural practice with a "democratic" bent. These interpretations have been generative and have considerable explanatory power. They have allowed us to see culture and cultural practices as causes of revolutionary change in ways that previous generations did not.[30] Yet the very causal connections that this scholarship posits between culture and revolution also has a significant downside: it runs the risk of telescoping eighteenth-century cultural practice into a mere precursor or embryonic form of revolutionary politics.

One body of scholarship has argued that the pre-revolutionary sociable practices of the elite evolved more or less directly into revolutionary politics. This scholarship rests on an interpretation of eighteenth-century cultural practice that had become "democratized" well before the revolutionary era.[31] Historians have exhaustively documented the role that the relatively egalitarian structures of clubs and societies played in early revolutionary organizing in the French and American revolutions.[32] Similar arguments have been made about the role of Masonic lodges, with their ideal of brotherly camaraderie, in the coming of the Haitian Revolution.[33] Reading societies (*tertulias*) undergirded liberal reform movements and early republican politics across Latin America.[34] And in the Dutch Republic, relatively

---

[30] Twentieth-century Marxist historians held that revolutions had primarily economic and social causes, see Albert Mathiez, *La Révolution française* (Paris: Armand Colin, 1951); Georges Lefebvre, *La Révolution française* (Paris: Presses universitaires de France, 1930); J. Franklin Jameson, *The American Revolution Considered as a Social Movement* (Princeton: Princeton University Press, 1973).

[31] In the American context, the most forceful exponent of this view has been Gordon S. Wood, *The Radicalism of the American Revolution* (New York: Knopf, 1992).

[32] There is an enormous literature on this subject, but see esp. Michael L. Kennedy, *The Jacobin Clubs in the French Revolution: The First Years* (Princeton: Princeton University Press, 1982); David Ammerman, *In the Common Cause: American Response to the Coercive Acts of 1774* (Charlottesville: University of Virginia Press, 1974); Pauline Maier, *From Resistance to Revolution: Colonial Radicals and the Development of American Opposition to Britain, 1765–1776* (New York: Knopf, 1972).

[33] See John Garrigus, "A Secret Brotherhood? The Question of Black Freemasonry before and after the Haitian Revolution," *Atlantic Studies* 16:3 (2019), 321–40; Sudhir Hazareesingh, *Black Spartacus: The Epic Life of Toussaint Louverture* (New York: Farrar, Straus & Giroux, 2020), 157–8.

[34] See Horacio Villanueva Urteaga, *Gamarra y la iniciación republicana en el Cuzco* (Lima: Fondo del Libro del Banco de los Andes, 1981); Carlos Altamirano and Jorge Myers,

egalitarian civic militia organizations acted as one of the main engines of resistance to the Stadholderate during the 1780s.³⁵ Elite women played a key role in many of these types of sociability and have thus found a significant place in this historiography. This includes important work on Massachusetts and Philadelphia in the 1760s and 1770s; on the "republican court" of the early national United States; and on women in the French and Latin American revolutions, including Jeanne-Marie Roland in France and Micaela Bastidas in Peru.³⁶

Print culture has played a particularly important part in this story of culture causing revolution. The most prominent advocate of print culture's causal power in revolution has been Robert Darnton, who has spent much of his career arguing that the market in "forbidden" books in old regime France created the conditions for the outbreak of revolution.³⁷ Somewhat similar arguments have been made about the newspaper and pamphlet culture of the British North American colonies, claiming that these media did not merely act as tools of communication, but in fact helped to create a discursive space for the emergence of revolutionary politics.³⁸ Similarly, a number of scholars have argued that eighteenth-century Hispanic enlightenment print cultures, by opening up space for critical analysis of politics and

---

Historia de los intelectuales en América Latina (Buenos Aires: Katz, 2008), Part II; Norberto Galasso, *La Revolución de Mayo: El pueblo quiere saber de qué se trató* (Buenos Aires: Ediciones del Pensamiento Nacional, 1994), Chapter 1.

[35] Simon Schama, *Patriots and Liberators: Revolution in the Netherlands, 1780–1813* (New York: Knopf, 1977), 83–98; H. T. Colenbrander, *De patriottentijd: Hoofdzakelijk naar buitenlandsche bescheiden*, 3 vols. ('s-Gravenhage: Nijhoff, 1897), vol. 1, 256–80; C. H. E. Wit, *De Nederlandse revolutie van de achttiende eeuw 1780–1787: Oligarchie en proletariaat* (Oirsbeek: J. J. Lindelauf, 1974).

[36] See, for example, David S. Shields and Fredrika J. Teute, "The Republican Court and the Historiography of a Woman's Domain in the Public Sphere," *Journal of the Early Republic* 35:2 (2015), 169–84; Edith B. Gelles, *Abigail Adams: A Writing Life* (New York: Routledge, 2002); Sian Reynolds, *Marriage and Revolution: Monsieur and Madame Roland* (New York: Oxford University Press, 2012); Francisco A. Loayza, *Mártires y heroínas: Documentos inéditos del año de 1780 a 1782* (Lima: D. Miranda, 1945).

[37] See esp. Robert Darnton, *The Forbidden Best-Sellers of Pre-Revolutionary France* (New York: W. W. Norton, 1995); Roger Chartier, *The Cultural Origins of the French Revolution*, trans. Lydia G. Cochrane (Durham, NC: Duke University Press, 1991), Chapter 4, which also briefly (87–9) considers how revolution constructed enlightenment. For a different account, see Sarah Maza, *Private Lives and Public Affairs: The Causes Célèbres of Prerevolutionary France* (Berkeley: University of California Press, 1995).

[38] Latently present in Bernard Bailyn's *The Ideological Origins of the American Revolution* (Cambridge, MA: Belknap Press of Harvard University Press, 1967), it was fully articulated in Michael Warner, *The Letters of the Republic: Publication and the Public Sphere in Eighteenth-Century America* (Cambridge, MA: Harvard University Press, 1992), and subsequent scholarship on the public sphere.

manners, laid the groundwork for reform and independence movements in Latin America during the early nineteenth century.³⁹

Seeing the social arts as generators of revolutionary politics could in theory facilitate scholarship that covers multiple revolutions, though this potential has not yet been fully realized. The Atlantic revolutions have long drawn the attention of comparativists. The most influential comparative studies, however, were completed before the social and cultural turns took hold. The similarities among social arts across the regions of the Atlantic world could provide a basis for new comparative analyses of the revolutions that account for the causal force of cultural practices.⁴⁰ A few recent studies have begun to explore these interpretive and explanatory possibilities. Already in *Empires of the Atlantic World*, fifteen years ago, J. H. Elliott mulled over the idea that differences in pre-revolutionary print and sociable cultures in North and South America could help to explain some of the differences that arose between revolutions in the two regions. Janet Polasky's recent *Revolutions Without Borders*, while focusing on how various media acted as connectors among revolutions, also reflects on the ways in which different pre-revolutionary cultural practices influenced the divergent courses of the era's revolutions.⁴¹

In parallel with scholarship on the social arts and revolution, a sizeable literature has developed arguing that everyday cultures of the eighteenth century were major causes of revolution. The oldest scholarship in this vein, which dates to before the cultural turn, looked at how the subsistence practices of ordinary people drove them into revolution. This scholarship is indebted to E. P. Thompson's pioneering work on the "moral economy" of

---

³⁹ Guerra, *Modernidad e independencias*, Chapter 8; Noemí Goldman, "La ciudad letrada, 1776–1820," in Raúl O. Fradkin, ed., *Historia de la provincia de Buenos Aires*, vol. II: *De la Conquista a la crisis de 1820* (Buenos Aires: UNIPE, 2012). For a less sanguine view, see Angel Rama, *The Lettered City*, trans. John Charles Chasteen (Durham, NC: Duke University Press, 1996).

⁴⁰ A fuller version of this argument is given in Perl-Rosenthal, "Atlantic Cultures and the Age of Revolution." See R. R. Palmer, *The Age of the Democratic Revolution: A Political History of Europe and America, 1760–1800*, 2 vols. (Princeton: Princeton University Press, 1959–1964); Theda Skocpol, *States and Social Revolutions: A Comparative Analysis of France, Russia, and China* (Cambridge: Cambridge University Press, 1979); Charles Tilly, *From Mobilization to Revolution* (New York: Random House, 1978); Crane Brinton, *The Anatomy of Revolution* (New York: W. W. Norton, 1938); Wim Klooster, *Revolutions in the Atlantic World: A Comparative History* (New York: New York University Press, 2009).

⁴¹ J. H. Elliott, *Empires of the Atlantic World: Britain and Spain in America, 1492–1830* (New Haven: Yale University Press, 2006); Janet L. Polasky, *Revolutions without Borders: The Call to Liberty in the Atlantic World* (New Haven: Yale University Press, 2015).

the eighteenth-century lower orders.⁴² The sometimes-violent resistance of Bostonians to economic competition from British soldiers, for instance, was a spark for the Boston Massacre of 1770. And subsistence struggles propelled ongoing resistance to British imperial policy in New York, Charleston, Philadelphia, and elsewhere in the 1770s.⁴³ In similar fashion, the artisans and fishwives of Paris, when they confronted urban manufacturers and the royal family itself over shortages of basic necessities in 1789, acted on well-established cultural patterns that authorized them to appeal to the powers-that-be for aid in times of need.⁴⁴

Over the past generation, scholars have found causal explanations for revolution in a growing number of everyday practices, many of which were linked to particular social or racial groups. T. H. Breen's *The Marketplace of Revolution* argued that British consumer culture in North America provided American creoles with a common experience and a vocabulary of "choice" that they redeployed in the service of revolutionary change.⁴⁵ Interest in the revolutionary potential of everyday cultures has also been a common thread among scholars of the African diaspora. Carolyn Fick and others have argued that practices around communal prayer, marketing, and other forms of sociability were instrumental in the early organizing of the enslaved population in revolutionary Saint-Domingue/Haiti.⁴⁶ Similar everyday practices – praying together, eating together, working together – were at the heart of organized revolts by the enslaved in the late eighteenth- and early nineteenth-century United States and Caribbean.⁴⁷ The practices of daily life

---

⁴² E. P. Thompson, "The Moral Economy of the English Crowd in the Eighteenth Century," *Past and Present* 50 (1971), 76–136.

⁴³ Gary B. Nash, *The Urban Crucible: Social Change, Political Consciousness, and the Origins of the American Revolution* (Cambridge, MA: Harvard University Press, 1981); Lee R. Boyer, "Lobster Backs, Liberty Boys, and Laborers in the Streets: New York's Golden Hill and Nassau Street Riots," *New York Historical Society Quarterly* 57:4 (1973), 281–308; Eric Hinderaker, *Boston's Massacre* (Cambridge, MA: Belknap Press of Harvard University Press, 2017).

⁴⁴ See esp. David Garrioch, *The Making of Revolutionary Paris* (Berkeley: University of California Press, 2002).

⁴⁵ See T. H. Breen, *The Marketplace of Revolution: How Consumer Politics Shaped American Independence* (New York: Oxford University Press, 2004); T. H. Breen "'Baubles of Britain': The American and Consumer Revolutions of the Eighteenth Century," *Past and Present* 119 (1988), 73–104.

⁴⁶ See Carolyn E. Fick, *The Making of Haiti: The Saint Domingue Revolution from Below* (Knoxville: University of Tennessee Press, 1990); C. L. R. James, *The Black Jacobins: Toussaint L'Ouverture and the San Domingo Revolution*, 2nd edition (New York: Vintage, 1963).

⁴⁷ See, for example, Vincent Brown, *Tacky's Revolt: The Story of an Atlantic Slave War* (Cambridge, MA: Belknap Press of Harvard University Press, 2020); Shauna J.

were also crucial to the interactions between settlers and Natives in North America that contributed to the coming of revolutions and the shaping of republican polities in the 1770s and after.[48]

Because everyday practices differed significantly from region to region, and even within regions, many of these interpretations of revolution have a localist slant. Take the case of religious practices, an important factor in many of the era's revolutionary moments. These varied widely from region to region. There was the large divide between Protestant-majority and Catholic-majority societies. Within each Christian confessional "bucket" the differences were considerable: the bottom-up Calvinist-tinged communities of New England were religiously quite distinct from the top-down Anglicanism of Virginia and the British Caribbean, and both differed from the communalist ethos of the Moravian and Mennonite denominations. These differences, in turn, have led scholars to offer contrasting "Virginian" and "New England" accounts of how religious practices shaped revolutionary politics in those regions.[49]

Whether focused on the social arts or on everyday practices, however, interpretations that view culture-as-cause of revolutionary politics paradoxically run a significant risk of subordinating culture to politics, *homo habitus* to *homo politicus*. As Habermas did in his influential account, scholars working within this paradigm have tended to cast eighteenth-century culture as a nascent form of the revolutionary politics that emerged out of it. They have read eighteenth-century salons and coffeehouses as spaces of reasoned debate, the forerunners of republican deliberation. Putative changes in the culture of deference become annunciatory of democratic upsurge later in the century. Eighteenth-century religious practices are scrutinized for hints of proto- or pre-revolutionary behaviors. The result is that eighteenth-century cultural practice as a whole is telescoped into a form of revolutionary politics *avant la lettre*.

Sweeney, "Market Marronage: Fugitive Women and the Internal Marketing System in Jamaica, 1781–1834," *William and Mary Quarterly* 76:2 (2019), 197–222; Julius C. Scott, *The Common Wind: Afro-American Currents in the Age of the Haitian Revolution* (New York: Verso, 2018); Douglas R. Egerton, *Gabriel's Rebellion: The Virginia Slave Conspiracies of 1800 and 1802* (Chapel Hill: University of North Carolina Press, 1993).

[48] Colin G. Calloway, *The American Revolution in Indian Country: Crisis and Diversity in Native American Communities* (New York: Cambridge University Press, 1995); Richard White, *The Middle Ground: Indians, Empires, and Republics in the Great Lakes Region, 1650–1815* (New York: Cambridge University Press, 1991).

[49] See Rhys Isaac, *The Transformation of Virginia, 1740–1790* (Chapel Hill: University of North Carolina Press, 1982); Nathan O. Hatch, *The Sacred Cause of Liberty: Republican Thought and the Millennium in Revolutionary New England* (New Haven: Yale University Press, 1977).

Revolutions Changing Cultural Practices

The other dominant paradigm for thinking about the relationship between cultural practices and revolution has been the idea that political change led to changes in cultural practices. This paradigm, too, developed along with the revolutionary era itself. Many revolutionaries saw themselves as engaged in a struggle to change existing cultural practices as well as political ideas and forms. And both revolutionaries and counter-revolutionaries, though of course for different reasons, were eager to claim that the era's revolutions were indeed transforming the cultural sphere.

The fine arts offer a stark view of the sharp transformations that cultural practice could undergo at the hands of revolutionary politics. One element was the rapid and powerful imposition of revolutionary ideas on the arts. The revolutionary festivals planned and organized by the painter Jacques-Louis David during the first decade of the French Revolution, for instance, embodied the appropriation of the arts to revolutionary ends.[50] In the 1820s, artists in Latin America, including in the Andes and northern South America, turned to political and "revolutionary" subjects that they had not treated before.[51] Sculptures of republican leaders and allegories became commonplace, replacing images of absolute monarchs. Even the artisans who made dinnerware were affected: the era saw an explosion of ceramics bearing patriotic and revolutionary slogans and symbols.[52]

The era's revolutions also put their stamp on the fine arts by reshaping the trajectories of individual artists – and indeed entire art forms. As artists who had been patronized by old regime courts fell into disfavor or fled, others took their place. They brought new styles to prominence. Here again, David is the paradigmatic case: though his influence was already rising before the French Revolution, it gained a major boost from his closeness to its leaders.[53] The revolutionary era effected ruptures in the performing arts. In a number of revolutionary jurisdictions, such as France and the United States, theater was explicitly banned for some part of the peak period of revolutionary

---

[50] David Lloyd Dowd, *Pageant-Master of the Republic: Jacques-Louis David and the French Revolution* (Freeport, NY: Books for Libraries Press, [1948] 1969).
[51] See the case of Tadeo Escalante discussed in Jorge A. Flores Ochoa, Elizabeth Kuon Arce, and Roberto Samanez Argumedo, *Pintura mural en el sur andino* (Lima: Banco de Crédito del Perú, 1993); Ananda Cohen Suarez, *Heaven, Hell, and Everything in Between: Murals of the Colonial Andes* (Austin: University of Texas Press, 2016).
[52] See Breen, *Marketplace of Revolution*, Part II; J. F. F. Fleury-Husson, *Histoire des faïences patriotiques sous la révolution* (Paris: E. Dentu, 1867).
[53] Roberts, *Jacques-Louis David and Jean-Louis Prieur*.

activity. When it returned, public performances of theater designed to promote revolutionary ideas became common.[54] The fine arts were pressed, however incompletely, into the service of the revolutionary political agenda.

Revolutionary politics had a tangible impact on the social arts as well. The paradigmatic illustration of this impact is the imposition of new forms of speech and address during the French revolutionary era. Beginning in 1791 in France, and spreading over the course of the decade to countries that came under French domination ("sister republics"), republican governments strongly encouraged the use of informal modes of address. This practice was intended to reflect republican values and to foster a sense of equality among fellow citizens, while breaking decisively with the hierarchical order of the old regime.[55] Such forms of address were not seen as mere niceties. Formal, even baroque, modes of address had been an essential part of the old regime social order, intended to materialize and perform the proper hierarchy among the king's subjects. As such, the informal "tu" was intended to mark and sharpen a highly visible (or rather, audible) break in the social order.[56]

The reshaping of cultural practice around new political ideals took place in many other realms of the social arts beyond face-to-face sociability. In the early United States, for instance, a number of "dancing assemblies" made efforts to democratize social dance. They randomized or otherwise altered the selection of partners, which had traditionally been done in strict order of social precedence, in order to better reflect the young country's democratic principles.[57] The revolutionary era brought about similar shifts in formal rhetoric and public speaking. The polished and stylish rhetorical mode fashionable in the seventeenth and earlier eighteenth centuries gave way

---

[54] See, for example, Heather S. Nathans, *Early American Theatre from the Revolution to Thomas Jefferson: Into the Hands of the People* (Cambridge: Cambridge University Press, 2003), Chapter 2.

[55] See Alphonse Aulard, "Le tutoiement pendant la Révolution," in *Études et leçons sur la Révolution française* (Cambridge: Cambridge University Press, 2011 [1902]); Philippe Wolff, "Le tu révolutionnaire," *Annales historiques de la Révolution française* 62 (279) (1990), 89–94.

[56] On the crucial importance of forms of address, see in particular Giora Sternberg, "Epistolary Ceremonial: Corresponding Status at the Time of Louis XIV," *Past and Present* 204 (2009), 33–88.

[57] Nathan Perl-Rosenthal and Victoria Geduld, "The Power of a Minuet: Social Dance and Political Order in Eighteenth-Century America," unpublished paper presented at Draper Graduate Student Conference on Early American Studies, Storrs, Connecticut, 18–20 September 2008.

during the revolutionary era to more "republican" models of formal speech, which were aimed at larger and socially broader audiences.[58]

Yet for every area of the fine arts and social arts that bent in response to political change, there were many others that did not. I have argued elsewhere that eighteenth-century epistolary genres remained remarkably stable across the revolutionary divide: patriots adapted existing epistolary forms to new purposes, albeit with some difficulty, rather than radically changing them.[59] It was not until the 1810s, at the earliest, that the literary conventions and physical form of correspondence began to experience an Atlantic-wide transformation.[60] Similar continuities marked the fine arts. Though many printmakers and painters shifted their subject matter in response to the political winds, stylistic changes were much slower in coming. The revolutionary era may have accelerated the transition from Rococo to neoclassical styles, but the shift in style was neither abrupt nor tied to specific political moments. Indeed, given the long and arduous training required of visual artists, such abrupt stylistic shifts are hardly possible.[61] Professional music-making told much the same story: revolutionary politics may have accelerated processes of stylistic change, but it was hardly the cause of them.[62]

Even when governments mandated changes in the social arts, the changes were not always durable. Encouraged by the French government, the "tu républicain" became all but universal in public written communication. But the shift proved to be short-lived. By the time the Directory took power in 1795, the French government at all levels was again encouraging the use of the formal "vous." Before long, it had returned with a vengeance. During the first French Empire, the government – and society at large – did not merely return to the use of "vous," but actually mandated a revival of the most hierarchical forms of address of the old regime, including carefully graded honorifics for different forms of nobility. The reversion to "vous," which remains very much in use to this day, strongly suggests that the public

---

[58] See Sandra M. Gustafson, *Eloquence Is Power: Oratory and Performance in Early America* (Chapel Hill: University of North Carolina Press, 2000).
[59] Perl-Rosenthal, "Atlantic Cultures and the Age of Revolution"; Perl-Rosenthal, "Corresponding Republics"; Nathan Perl-Rosenthal, "Private Letters and Public Diplomacy: The Adams Network and the Quasi-war, 1797–1798," *Journal of the Early Republic* 31:2 (2011), 283–311.
[60] See the useful discussion in Anthony Howe and Madeleine Callaghan, eds., *Romanticism and the Letter* (London: Palgrave Macmillan, 2020), Chapter 1.
[61] See Robert Rosenblum, *Transformations in Late Eighteenth Century Art* (Princeton: Princeton University Press, 1967), on the persistence of neoclassicism.
[62] See Charles Rosen, *The Classical Style: Haydn, Mozart, Beethoven* (London: Faber, 1971).

never fully embraced the "tu républicain." The impact of revolutionary politics on this part of the social arts, at least, was more modest than might appear at first glance.

The cultural practices of everyday life, finally, showed a high degree of continuity from the pre- to the post-revolutionary eras. One of the key findings of social historians of the late eighteenth and early nineteenth centuries has been that the lifeways of ordinary people and communities did not change abruptly with the political winds. Indeed, in many instances changes in the practices of everyday life did not take root until deep into the nineteenth century. Eugen Weber's *Peasants into Frenchmen* showed, among other things, that the state modernization that followed the French Revolution did not reach its tentacles into much of rural France until well after the 1830s. Scholars working on Latin American peasants and the American South, similarly, have emphasized the ways in which the populations of these post-revolutionary states only slowly adopted new ways of living. Much of the day-to-day life of these communities – including the economic foundation of an agrarian economy and the use of bound labor – remained unchanged for decades after the revolutions erupted.[63]

Some areas of everyday life did undergo noticeable changes, but these proved to be ephemeral. In revolutionary France, for instance, the early republican government mandated the metric system for weights and measures and reconceived the calendar. This system was then extended, in some fashion, to much of the rest of Europe. But while the metric system survived and spread – a rare success – the calendar revisions were scrapped in the early nineteenth century.[64] Another area of everyday practice in which there were radical but usually not very durable changes was costume. In France, the United States, and parts of urban Latin America, political cockades and more "republican" garb spread widely, driven by a combination of individual choice and public pressure. Both men and women adopted distinctively "republican" hairstyles.[65] In France, some officials during the Directory were

---

[63] See, for example, Sinclair Thomson, *We Alone Will Rule: Native Andean Politics in the Age of Insurgency* (Madison: University of Wisconsin Press, 2002); Eugen Weber, *Peasants into Frenchmen: The Modernization of Rural France, 1870–1914* (Stanford: Stanford University Press, 1976); Maurice Agulhon, *Le Cercle dans la France bourgeoise: 1810–1848: Étude d'une mutation de sociabilité* (Paris: Armand Colin, 1977).

[64] Matthew John Shaw, *Time and the French Revolution: The Republican Calendar, 1789–year XIV* (Woodbridge: Boydell Press for the Royal Historical Society, 2011).

[65] See Elizabeth Amann, *Dandyism in the Age of Revolution* (Chicago: University of Chicago Press, 2015).

mandated to wear classically inspired costumes.[66] Yet many of these innovations, including both those which were more "bottom up" (such as hairstyles) and those which were more "top down" (such as the costumes of the Directory), disappeared in relatively short order. Even when the result was not a mere reversion to pre-revolutionary styles, the shaping force that revolutionary politics exerted on these types of everyday practice was at best ambiguous and often ephemeral.

The paradigm of revolutionary politics transforming cultural practice, like its mirror twin the culture-as-cause paradigm, provides an important perspective on the culture–revolution nexus. The paradigm's great advantage is that it focuses our attention on how political events and ideas changed *homo habitus*. It shows us that even eighteenth-century cultural practices that had become as "natural ... as breathing," from modes of dress to ways of speaking, bent or shifted in response to the massive political upheaval of the period. Yet this approach, too, has significant blind spots. One problem is that only weak evidence links persistent changes in cultural practice directly to the influence of revolutionary politics. It can be difficult to distinguish the influence of revolutionary politics from shifts in cultural practice that were already underway before the revolutionary period, or changes propelled by factors internal to the practices themselves. A second and more profound problem with this paradigm is that it risks prioritizing politics over culture, *homo politicus* over *homo habitus*, because it views cultural practices as the recipients of changes emerging from the domain of politics. It fails, in its own way, to reckon with the autonomy and quiddity of culture.

Two New Paradigms

During the past decade, there has been movement toward developing two other approaches to thinking about the relationship between *homo politicus* and *homo habitus*. Neither one, at present, is as widely employed as the first two paradigms. Both offer alternatives to the dominant paradigms that tend to swallow up *homo habitus* in *homo politicus*. One of these newer approaches is a notion of culture change *as* revolution. This approach, best represented by the recent work of Colin Jones, Dror Wahrman, and Leora Auslander, argues that we should see changes in cultural practices as constituting a

---

[66] See Thierry Lemoine, ed., *Au temps des merveilleuses: La société parisienne sous le Directoire et le Consulat: 9 mars–12 juin 2005*, Musée Carnavalet-Histoire de Paris (Paris: Paris Musées, 2005).

revolution in their own right. In a powerfully argued edited volume on the *Age of Cultural Revolutions*, Jones and Wahrman assert that the real revolution of the late eighteenth and early nineteenth centuries was a shift in culture, not changes in high politics or the social order. They argue convincingly, based on recent decades of scholarship, that there were deep continuities in social, economic, and even political structures around the Atlantic world. What changed dramatically was culture, a category that for them encompasses not only practices but also ideologies and "languages."[67] Wahrman offers an example of this rereading with an article on the fluidity of gender identity in the revolutionary era. He argues that there was a significant shift in how individuals perceived their identities, their "mental maps" of their selves, during the late eighteenth century.[68] Jones has also carried on this work, particularly in his remarkable recent history of the "smile revolution" in eighteenth-century France, which tells of the rise and fall of depictions of the smile in pre- and early-revolutionary France.[69]

Where Wahrman and Jones focused their argument on the social arts, Leora Auslander, in her *Cultural Revolutions*, has extended a similar approach to everyday practices. Auslander structured her project around a meta-analysis of existing scholarship on three revolutions (seventeenth-century England, United States, France). She observes that the vast majority of cultural historical scholarship on these three revolutions has examined what she calls the "mobilization of culture" in the service of revolutionary politics (the second dominant approach discussed above), but that relatively little has looked at "cultural revolution itself."[70] Auslander's proposal is that we should look at how the everyday practices of daily life themselves – particularly in interaction with material culture, such as the use of furniture and forms of dress or consumption – created distinctive and "revolutionary" ideas of selfhood and interdependence. These new selves might or might not lead as well to new "conceptions of political representation."[71] Auslander's account, like that of Wahrman and Jones, has a strong gendered dimension. And like their project, it explores the revolutionary processes of cultural

---

[67] Colin Jones and Dror Wahrman, eds., *The Age of Cultural Revolutions: Britain and France, 1750–1820* (Berkeley: University of California Press, 2002), 1–3, 13.
[68] Ibid., 280.
[69] Colin Jones, *The Smile Revolution in Eighteenth Century Paris* (Oxford: Oxford University Press, 2014).
[70] Leora Auslander, *Cultural Revolutions: Everyday Life and Politics in Britain, North America, and France* (Berkeley: University of California Press, 2009), 1.
[71] Ibid., 11.

change somewhat decoupled from the changes in high politics that were unfolding in the later eighteenth century.

Embracing the culture-change-as-revolution paradigm that these scholars have sketched opens up new perspectives for the field of revolutionary studies. Their approach inverts the field's traditional polarity: instead of telescoping *homo habitus* into *homo politicus*, as both of the dominant paradigms do, these scholars focus exclusively on the transformation of *homo habitus*. Their claim, as I take it, is not merely that we should pay more attention to cultural changes during the revolutionary era. Their proposal is much bolder: they want to revisit the very definition of revolution in the "age of revolution." Perhaps, they suggest, we should think about the age of Atlantic revolutions as defined by transformations of culture rather than the political and socioeconomic transformations that have long been its landmarks. Taken to its logical conclusion, this approach might entail a radical reworking of our map of the revolutionary world. It would no longer be self-evident that France or North America was the center of revolutionary change in this period. We would have to consider the possibility, for instance, that the most cutting-edge cultural transformations were happening elsewhere in the revolutionary world – such as West Africa or Latin America.[72]

In my own recent and forthcoming work, I have been developing a fourth way of thinking about the nexus between revolution and cultural practices: cultural practices acted as containers or vehicles for new political ideas and practices. This approach focuses on examining the mutual influences that pre-revolutionary cultural practices and revolutionary politics had on each other. In making this argument, I am pursuing leads from Lynn Hunt's ground-breaking cultural histories of the French Revolution. In *Politics, Culture, and Class in the French Revolution*, Hunt offered a pioneering account of "political culture," a political agenda or argument expressed through cultural forms. She extended this analysis in subsequent work, including the brilliant and controversial *Family Romance of the French Revolution*. Scholars of the revolutionary era have wholeheartedly embraced the final synthesis of this work, the idea of political culture. What has been lost along the way, in my view, is how Hunt arrived at this point. Her work treats politics and culture as distinct domains: interdependent and mutually

---

[72] On African and Latin American "modernities," see José M. Portillo Valdés, *Crisis atlántica: Autonomía e independencia en la crisis de la monarquía hispana* (Madrid: Marcial Pons, 2006); Bronwen Everill, *Not Made by Slaves: Ethical Capitalism in the Age of Abolition* (Cambridge, MA: Harvard University Press, 2020).

influencing, to be sure, but each with its own distinct features and dynamics of change over time. This delicate and bi-directional dance between cultural forms and political ideas, so central to Hunt's work, is worth recovering.[73]

Making a case for cultural practice-as-vehicle requires three argumentative moves. The first is to recognize that old regime cultural practices did not have an *ipso facto* pre-revolutionary character. Scholars' wide acceptance of the culture-as-cause paradigm has made it into an article of faith that many of the eighteenth-century social arts did have a proto-revolutionary character. As I have suggested above, I am skeptical about this claim, which tends to telescope all manner of social arts into embryonic forms of revolutionary politics. But even if this claim does hold for the social arts, it does not extend to other types of practice. Most of the eighteenth-century fine arts, for instance, were clearly not proto-revolutionary. Eighteenth-century academic painters and sculptors, to say nothing of fabric and ceramic craftspeople, followed aesthetic paths shaped by their customers and communities of practitioners, and did not show any telos toward political revolution. By the same token, there is little reason to see a proto-revolutionary image in most eighteenth-century practices of everyday life. How people found and prepared food, cared for their bodies and the bodies of others, and entertained themselves changed in the eighteenth century, but not in any single direction. These practices also differed substantially from place to place and group to group.

The varied cultural practices of the eighteenth century became the vehicles for the enactment of revolutionary ideas and politics toward the end of the century. Every act of revolutionary politics, every gesture, had perforce to take place through existing cultural forms. When patriot leaders wrote pamphlets to the public, or private letters to one another, they drew on familiar literary and epistolary genres. Each revolutionary print, no matter how radical and acerbic, came from a plate made by printmakers who had

---

[73] See Lynn A. Hunt, *Politics, Culture, and Class in the French Revolution* (Berkeley: University of California Press, 1984), 12–14; Lynn A. Hunt, *The New Cultural History* (Berkeley: University of California Press, 1989), Introduction; Lynn A. Hunt, *The Family Romance of the French Revolution* (Berkeley: University of California Press, 1992). For more extended critiques of the political culture paradigm, see Perl-Rosenthal, "Atlantic Cultures and the Age of Revolution"; Nathan Perl-Rosenthal, "The Culture of Democracy," *Dissent* 65:2 (2018), 176–80. My approach is also influenced by Paul Friedland, *Political Actors: Representative Bodies and Theatricality in the Age of the French Revolution* (Ithaca, NY: Cornell University Press, 2002), esp. Part II; David Waldstreicher, *In the Midst of Perpetual Fetes: The Making of American Nationalism, 1776–1820* (Chapel Hill: University of North Carolina Press, 1997).

honed their craft over many years. Every cockade and Phrygian cap worn as a symbol of revolutionary allegiance had to first be made (and often sold) by hands experienced in fabric craft. The process of fitting revolutionary politics into these old regime practices was always complex and not consistently successful. In a recent article, I contrasted the epistolary strategies used by Bostonian patriots and St. Dominguan revolutionaries in the 1770s and 1790s, respectively. Both groups tried to repurpose old regime epistolary forms in order to advance revolutionary agendas. But where Toussaint Louverture deftly reworked the conventions of letters to bring ex-slaves and white potential allies together, the Bostonians struggled to escape the restraints of decorum that eighteenth-century letter-writing practice imposed on their political projects.[74]

Many of these cultural practices – especially the social arts as practiced by elites – were just as widely spread in countries that were bastions of counter-revolutionary activity (such as Britain and the Habsburg empire) as they were in those countries bathed in political revolution, such as France. Social dance, rhetoric, the arts of letter-writing: these were an integral part of eighteenth-century culture in the anti-revolutionary corners of the Atlantic world. In those regions, cultural practices could simply continue as before, without becoming a vehicle for any particular political agenda. Social dance and fine arts practices in Britain and the Habsburg lands, for instance, underwent relatively few of the sharp changes they experienced during this period in the early United States or Latin America. But some eighteenth-century cultural practices in these regions were enlisted for political purposes: as vehicles for *counter*-revolutionary ideas and politics. In turn-of-the-century Vienna, for instance, imperial officials leaned on the brilliant music scene to produce compositions that would shore up the authority and stability of the regime. In other German-speaking lands, an anti-revolutionary nationalist ideology began to grow in literary and philosophical circles.[75]

As individuals who were engaged in new forms of politics (whether revolutionary or counter-revolutionary) re-deployed old regime cultural practices to achieve new kinds of political goals, the cultural practices they used gradually experienced a transformation. The cultural containers were

---

[74] Perl-Rosenthal, "Atlantic Cultures and the Age of Revolution," 684–94. See also the discussion of epistolary practices in the Dutch patriot movement of the 1780s, which I argue complicated efforts to bridge the divide between elite and non-elite patriot groups, in Perl-Rosenthal, "Corresponding Republics," Chapter 4.

[75] On music, see David Wyn Jones, *The Symphony in Beethoven's Vienna* (Cambridge: Cambridge University Press, 2006), 90–4.

gradually reshaped by their new political contents. This process has some resemblance to the second dominant paradigm discussed above, the idea of revolution reshaping culture. But where the dominant paradigm focuses on short-term cultural changes, such as the institution of "tu" or changes in dress, I argue that we should look to longer-term shifts. Fundamental changes in any domain of cultural practice need a considerable amount of time to develop and take root. Epistolary forms did change in ways that were consonant with revolutionary politics: the polished style of the eighteenth century gave way to looser and more affective modes of writing. But the transition took decades, not weeks or months. Cities eventually became more democratic spaces for leisure and commerce, but it was not until the early nineteenth century that this change took hold.[76] All in all, as I argue in my current work, the impact of revolutionary politics on cultural practices occurred on the scale of generations, with the most significant and durable changes coming only with the slow, inexorable passage from one generation to the next.[77]

Like the culture-change-as-revolution approach advanced by Wahrman, Jones, and Auslander, the culture-as-container approach I propose leads naturally to questions regarding what exactly was revolutionary about the revolutionary era. A culture-as-container approach regards cultural practices as neither a primary cause of revolutionary politics nor as passive objects to be transformed by political forces. Instead, it looks at cultural practices as existing in dynamic contact with revolutionary politics: cultural practices provided a necessary vehicle for revolutionary politics, but in the process, they also shaped, promoted, and constrained patriots' ability to realize their political agenda. Recognizing the deep imbrication of revolutionary politics with old regime culture, in other words, is not a complicated way of saying that revolutions were not "revolutionary." It is an invitation to change the questions we ask about the revolutionary past. Instead of rating revolutions by their supposed revolutionary-ness, we can ask how resourceful patriots in every revolution dealt with the universal problem of fitting together deeply engrained cultural practices with new political agendas. And it can help to continue the ongoing rethinking that has increasingly re-imagined counter-revolutionary politics as an integral part of the revolutionary age.

★ ★ ★

[76] See, for example, Dell Upton, *Another City: Urban Life and Urban Spaces in the New American Republic* (New Haven: Yale University Press, 2008).

[77] This is a central theme of my current book project, *The Age of Revolutions and the Generations Who Made It* (New York: Basic Books, 2024).

The end of the age of Atlantic revolutions, usually dated to the mid-1820s, came nearly a century and a half after Locke wrote his influential twin treatises on education and government. For Locke, writing at the start of the politically stable eighteenth century, there was no obvious conflict between the genteel *homo habitus* and the social contract-making *homo politicus*. The era of revolutions that swept across Europe, the Americas, and West Africa in the late eighteenth and early nineteenth centuries set *homo habitus* against *homo politicus* in ways that Locke had never imagined. To some extent, scholars have shown, it was eighteenth-century culture itself that spurred the development of revolutionary politics. But just as important as these causal relationships were the multiplying tensions that arose as old habits and new politics collided. The cultural practices of the old regime had taken shape in societies that were by and large monarchical in their politics, and which were growing increasingly stratified socioeconomically. The revolutionary era abruptly injected democratic, republican, and, in some instances, egalitarian projects into the center of Atlantic-wide political discourse. Revolutionaries swept away some of the practices of the old regime, demanding the abolition of formal modes of address or shutting theaters and concert halls. Far more often, however, revolutionaries adopted the eighteenth-century cultural practices they knew so well in order to enact their new political projects. They made commercial letters into vehicles for organizing rebellion, made social dance a container for egalitarian principles, turned the act of dressing into a display of political loyalty, and much more. We need to know more about the revolutionary era merger of *homo politicus* with *homo habitus*: its successes, its failures, and, above all, the ways in which this encounter transformed both the political and the cultural.

PART II

★

THE BRITISH COLONIES

5

The Revolution in British America: General Overview

MARK PETERSON

The challenge of writing the history of the American Revolution begins with definitions and boundaries. The problem even vexed its participants. In 1815, John Adams asked Thomas Jefferson, "What do we mean by the Revolution? The war? That was no part of the Revolution; it was only an effect and consequence of it. The Revolution was in the minds of the people, and this was effected, from 1760 to 1775." By contrast, consider Benjamin Rush's January 1787 remarks:

> There is nothing more common than to confound the terms of *the American Revolution* with those of *the late American war*. The American war is over; but this is far from being the case with the American revolution. On the contrary, nothing but the first act of the great drama is closed. It remains yet to establish and perfect our new forms of government, and to prepare the principles, morals, and manners of our citizens for these forms of government.[1]

John Adams' view was understandable for a Bostonian. New England's break with Britain was complete by 1775, even if other colonies lagged behind. Benjamin Rush's view from Philadelphia that much of the Revolution was still to come was equally plausible. America's republican governments were then in crisis, and constitutional reform seemed a distant hope. Curiously, both Adams and Rush all but excluded the period from 1775 to 1783 most commonly associated with the American Revolution. Despite their disagreement on chronology, they shared the conviction that the Revolution was primarily a transformation in popular conceptions of government among enfranchised citizens.

---

[1] The Adams and Rush quotations are from Bernard Bailyn, *The Ideological Origins of the American Revolution* (Cambridge, MA: Belknap Press of Harvard University Press, 1967), 1, 230.

Today, few would be satisfied with such narrow definitions. Surely the Revolution did involve the war by which these colonies achieved independence. But Adams and Rush were right to think that cannot be all. What *would* be a satisfactory twenty-first century answer to this vexing problem?

The era of US independence now stands midway between the first continuous European contact with the North American continent, the early sixteenth-century Spanish entradas into Florida and Mexico, and our present moment. The revolt of the thirteen colonies marks the midpoint in a half millennium's extraordinary transformation of North America. Five centuries ago, the region occupied today by the contiguous United States – the land stretching from the Atlantic to the Pacific, north of the Rio Grande and south of the Great Lakes – had the lowest ratio of human population to natural resources of any major portion of our planet.[2] Spanish conquistadors focused their colonizing efforts on more attractive locations, excited by the immediate riches in silver and gold to be found in more populous lands: Mexico, not Florida. In more northerly parts of America, Indigenous populations were sparse and precious export commodities were scarce. Colonization here was slow and haphazard. But after two centuries of these halting projects, the most successful North American colonizers, England and France, grew increasingly aware of the wealth that awaited the empire capable of exploiting the productive capacities of this temperate and fertile continent.[3]

The first half of the eighteenth century saw explosive growth in British America's settler population, European and African, free and enslaved. An equally rapid expansion of its material prosperity provided free British Americans with an extraordinarily high standard of living. Imperial officials began to realize that the state and the people who controlled and developed North America could not help but grow rich – by European standards of wealth.[4] A twenty-first century understanding of the American Revolution

---

[2] Other regions with sparse populations in 1500, such as Australia, Siberia, or the Southern Cone of South America, had far less fertile land and/or far more forbidding climates – and consequently much lower carrying capacities for human population than eastern North America. For illustrations, see the *World Population History* website, https://worldpopulationhistory.org/map/1502/mercator/1/0/25. See also the *Worldmapper* website, https://worldmapper.org/maps/population-year-1500/?sf_action=get_data&sf_data=results&_sft_product_cat=population&sf_paged=2.

[3] See J. H. Elliott, *Empires of the Atlantic World: Britain and Spain in America, 1492–1830* (New Haven: Yale University Press, 2007).

[4] Peter H. Lindert and Jeffrey G. Williamson, *Unequal Gains: American Growth and Inequality since 1700* (Princeton: Princeton University Press, 2016); John McCusker and Russell Menard, *The Economy of British America, 1607–1789* (Chapel Hill: University of

needs to explain the ensuing conflict over who would gain this prize, under what terms, and who would be excluded. It also needs to reckon with the benefits and costs of this contest, including its assumptions about the relationships between population, land, and wealth, for the world we live in today.

Thus configured, the American Revolution stands at the center, both temporally and conceptually, of the transformation of North America, the most dramatic reconfiguration of human populations and their influence on the planet in the past half-millennium. The first two centuries of European colonization generated an overall *decline* in North America's human population. The unsteady influx of colonists from 1500 to 1700 failed to make up for losses from disease, warfare, and social dislocation suffered by Indigenous populations.[5]

In 1700, the inhabitants of eastern North America, Indigenous and colonist, within the territory that became the United States in 1783, barely registered on a world population scale. The region, larger in area than Western Europe, held perhaps half a million people out of a global population of 610 million – less than one-tenth of 1 percent of the world's total.[6]

By 1900, the United States, now spanning the continent, had become one of the largest and most rapidly growing national population centers in the world. A more than fiftyfold growth over two centuries had made it home to 5 percent of the world's population. It was already the world's largest and most dynamic economy.[7]

Today, the US population, at 4.15 percent of the world's total, is relatively smaller than it was in 1900, but the US GDP stands at 20 percent of global

---

North Carolina Press, 2014 [1985]). The indigenous peoples of North America were (already) quite rich before permanent European contact – not by measurements such as GDP or wealth in monetary units, but as occupants of land suited to supporting plentiful human subsistence with relatively little effort; see Edmund S. Morgan, *American Slavery, American Freedom* (New York: W. W. Norton, 1975), 44–70.

[5] D. H. Ubelaker, "Population Size, Contact to Nadir," in D. H. Ubelaker et al., eds., *Handbook of North American Indians*, vol. III: *Environment, Origins, and Population* (Washington, DC: US Government Printing Office, 2007), 694–701.

[6] US territory in 1783 was 888,000 square miles. France, Germany, Spain, the Netherlands, Belgium, Italy, Switzerland, Denmark, and the UK comprise 852,000 square miles. In 1700, Western Europe had 13 percent of the world's population. Historical estimates of global population are drawn from *World Population History*, https://worldpopulationhistory.org; *Our World in Data*, https://ourworldindata.org/world-population-growth.

[7] As nation-states, only China and Russia were larger than the United States in population in 1900. The British Raj in India was much more populous as well, but the United States had long since surpassed the United Kingdom proper in population.

production. American households consume 32 percent of the world's purchased goods, nearly three times higher than the next closest nation (China, with 18.5 percent of global population, "underconsumes" at 12 percent of the world's total). Although China surpassed the United States in 2011 in aggregate national energy consumption, on a per capita basis the United States still consumes three times as much energy as China. The United States accounts for 37 percent of the world's military spending, more than the next nine nations combined, which collectively have ten times the US population.[8] If we frame the American Revolution in this five-century transformation, and understand it as the critical set of conflicts that determined the future disposition of the North American continent, accelerated its demographic and economic growth, and established its forms of government, then we can see it clearly as the turning point in this world-historical development.

At the revolution's beginning, c. 1754, the resources of North America lay mainly in the hands of Indigenous people, distributed across hundreds of polities, while three European empires held footholds of varying size and strength, mainly on the continent's edges. At its end, c. 1814, a single confederated nation, created out of wars fought to control America's resources, and led by the children of empire, was positioned to take the whole for itself. The transformation included a new form of government and political economy which concentrated power in the hands of American citizens under a constitution designed to promote endless economic growth. The revolution's outcome set a path for the continent's future and projected an implicit vision of a new form of global empire.

How Did All This Happen?

The driving force behind these transformative conflicts lay in the extraordinary demographic and economic expansion of colonial British America in the eighteenth century. This was an intricate, varied, and interconnected process of growth, which generated striking differences in demography, political economy, and aspirations for territorial expansion across the colonies. These differences created complex challenges for colonial governance that lay at the heart of Britain's imperial crisis.

In 1700, after a century of colonization, colonial British America could claim a population of about 250,000, hugging the Atlantic coast in a broken

---

[8] For global production, spending, and consumption figures, see *The Global Economy*, www.theglobaleconomy.com/rankings/household_consumption_dollars.

string of settlements stretching from New England to South Carolina. The British West Indies added 150,000 more settlers, bringing the colonial total to roughly 400,000, barely 6 percent of the 6.2 million residents of England, Wales, and Scotland. Scattered as they were across some two dozen colonies, the crown's overseas subjects merited little consideration in the constitutional settlements spurred by Britain's "Glorious Revolution" at the end of the seventeenth century.

Each region of British America, including the West Indies, experienced rapid growth over the next seventy-five years, generating a population boom at rates seldom seen in human history.[9] By the eve of US independence, the colonial population had seen an eightfold increase, from 400,000 to 3.3 million people, growing from 6 percent to approach half the size (44 percent) of Britain's homeland population. But the manner in which each colonial region's population grew differed widely one from another, as did their economies. A survey of these regional differences, focusing on population, political economy, and territorial expansion, provides a first critical insight into the origins and configuration of the American Revolution.[10]

The population of the British West Indies more than tripled between 1700 and 1775, but at that rate it was the *slowest* growing region of British America. Its European population, nearly all from the British Isles, barely grew at all, from 32,000 to 45,000. It was the African population that tripled, to nearly 450,000, an enslaved population that outnumbered its masters by ten to one. To reach a labor force of this size, British slave traders shipped more than a million captive Africans to the islands through the century. The sugar plantations that generated the islands' notorious wealth had work regimes so severe and death rates so high that natural increase among slaves was impossible. But they made the West Indian planter class among the richest individuals in the world. Consequently, the West Indies was the only colonial region well-represented in Parliament. Over 10 percent of the House of Commons members came from families that resided or owned property in the islands. While the West Indies

---

[9] The Indigenous American population rebounded after the disasters of the seventeenth century, but not at the phenomenal growth rates of the eighteenth-century settler colonial population.

[10] Population estimates in the following paragraphs are drawn from McCusker and Menard, *The Economy of British America*; US Census Bureau, *Historical Statistics of the United States, Colonial Times to 1970*, Chapter Z, Colonial and Pre-Federal Statistics, www2.census.gov/library/publications/1975/compendia/hist_stats_colonial-1970/hist_stats_colonial-1970p2-chZ.pdf, 10 August 2021. For immigration estimates, see Bernard Bailyn, *The Peopling of British North America: An Introduction* (New York: Random House, 1986).

created more commercial wealth for the empire than any other region, its demographic growth generated little expansion in land acquisition: Britain gained small amounts of Caribbean territory during the imperial wars of the eighteenth century, but West Indian economies grew by the intensification of slave labor rather than territorial expansion.[11]

New England stood at the opposite end of the spectrum of colonial regions. In Massachusetts, Connecticut, Rhode Island, and New Hampshire, the population grew far faster than in the West Indies, from roughly 100,000 in 1700 to 700,000 in the 1770s. None of this sevenfold growth stemmed from immigration. Instead, New England's demographic growth depended on the extraordinary fertility of the region's families. Its English population doubled every twenty-five years, spreading northward into Maine, New Hampshire, and the future Vermont. Slavery played little part in this demographic explosion. The 15,000 enslaved people in New England in 1770 constituted about 2 percent of the region's population. However, the region's economy was tightly linked to the West Indies' slave plantations. From its earliest days, New England's merchants shipped the region's humble products – fish, timber, meat, grain – to supply Caribbean sugar plantations. They carried the islands' sugar to London to gain the credits necessary to supply New England colonists with imported consumer goods.[12]

Between these two extremes, in both geography and political economy, lay the Chesapeake colonies of Maryland and Virginia, dedicated to growing tobacco for export to Europe on a model similar to sugar in the Caribbean, though not as lucrative. Through the seventeenth century, most of the labor in Chesapeake tobacco production was performed by white indentured servants. The African enslaved population in 1700 was, at 20,000, about one-fifth of the region's 90,000 colonists. The eighteenth century saw enormous growth in both the slave and free populations, with the slave population growing much faster. By 1770, Virginia and Maryland had 257,000 enslaved Africans, a more than twelvefold increase. Slaves were now nearly

---

[11] Trevor Burnard, *Planters, Merchants, and Slaves: Plantation Society in British America* (Chicago: University of Chicago Press, 2015); Trevor Burnard, *Jamaica in the Age of Revolution* (Philadelphia: University of Pennsylvania Press, 2020); McCusker and Menard, *The Economy of British America*, 144–68; Michael Craton, "Reluctant Creoles: The Planters' World in the British West Indies," in Bernard Bailyn and Philip D. Morgan, eds., *Strangers within the Realm: Cultural Margins of the First British Empire* (Chapel Hill: North Carolina University Press, 1991), 315–62.

[12] Bernard Bailyn, *The New England Merchants in the Seventeenth Century* (Cambridge, MA: Harvard University Press, 1955); McCusker and Menard, *The Economy of British America*, 91–116.

two-fifths of the Chesapeake population, a percentage midway between New England and the West Indies.

Unlike New England, Chesapeake's white population grew by continued immigration as well as natural increase. Unlike the West Indies, the Chesapeake's enslaved population reproduced itself as well as growing through continued importation. The Chesapeake did have large slaveholding plantations, but most of its slaveowners were small farmers who owned one or two slaves, and there were ten times as many white colonists in Chesapeake as there were in the West Indies. Unlike the West Indies, Virginia's growth as a slave society involved enormous expansion across space. The immense land claims granted to Virginia in its colonial charter, together with tobacco's tendency to exhaust the soil, generated intense land hunger among Chesapeake planters at every level.[13]

The remaining major regions, the Middle Colonies – New York, New Jersey, Pennsylvania, and belatedly Delaware – and the Lower South – the Carolinas and Georgia – developed later than the first three regions. In demographic and economic terms, they bridged the gaps between their neighboring regions, while sharing in their dramatic growth. New York and Pennsylvania resembled New England, though with a far more diverse group of European migrants comprising their white population. These included New York's earlier Dutch colonists along with large migrations in the eighteenth century from Germany and Scotland. As a result, this region's population grew the most dramatically of all, from roughly 50,000 in 1700 to 600,000 by 1770. Of this total, about 6 percent were enslaved Africans, much more like New England than the Chesapeake.

Like New England, Middle Colony merchants shipped agricultural products to the West Indies, implicating this region in the slave economy far beyond its small enslaved population. Unlike New England but like Virginia, New York and Pennsylvania both received extensive land claims in their charters. Despite their rapid population growth, they had come nowhere near to colonizing all this land, still possessed by Indigenous Indians. Growing numbers of migrants in the decades before US independence moved to this region seeking opportunity.[14]

---

[13] Allan Kulikoff, *Tobacco and Slaves: The Development of Southern Cultures in the Chesapeake, 1680–1800* (Chapel Hill: University of North Carolina Press, 1986); McCusker and Menard, *The Economy of British America*, 117–43.

[14] Aaron Fogleman, *Hopeful Journeys: German Immigration, Settlement, and Political Culture in Colonial America, 1717–1775* (Philadelphia: University of Pennsylvania Press, 2014); McCusker and Menard, *The Economy of British America*, 189–208.

The Lower South colonies – North Carolina, South Carolina, and Georgia – were the last to develop, with Georgia founded in the 1730s. Of the continental colonies, these, especially South Carolina and Georgia, most resembled the West Indian economic and demographic model. Early in the eighteenth century, Carolina planters substituted rice for sugar as a commodity that rewarded intensive investment in slave-labor plantations. The settler population of this region was tiny in 1700, at perhaps 15,000. By 1770, it had grown to 350,000, still the least populous region. Its enslaved African population, at 160,000, was 45 percent of the total, seemingly close to Chesapeake levels. But this was mainly due to North Carolina's demographic similarity to Virginia. (Except for its later development and more diverse economy, North Carolina resembled the Chesapeake as much as the Lower South.) In the Carolina and Georgia sea islands, the intensive rice plantation regions approached Caribbean enslavement levels at 90 percent of the population. South Carolina overall had a 61 percent enslaved population (slavery was less prevalent in its backcountry region), the only continental colony with a slave majority. To generate these numbers, the Lower South led the continental colonies in African slave importations. The intensity of plantation agriculture there discouraged European immigration to this region. Although Georgia had extensive claims to western lands, almost as large as Virginia's, it lacked a substantial white population capable of exploiting this territory. Georgia's population in 1770 was only 23,000, nearly half of these enslaved.[15]

The differences among these colonial regions manifested themselves in the varied characters and expectations of colonists. Indeed, when delegates from the continental colonies first met in the Congress of 1774, they famously remarked on the foreignness of one another's manners.[16] Yet some of the interests shared across regions helped to generate coalitions among the colonies, shifting and unstable as they were. Slavery marks the regional division most commonly noted and heavily analyzed by scholars. Our knowledge of future conflicts encourages a focus on the distinction between the two northerly regions where slaves were less than 10 percent of the population (and where gradual abolition would occur after independence),

---

[15] Russell R. Menard, "Slave Demography in the Lowcountry, 1670–1740: From Frontier Society to Plantation Regime," *South Carolina Historical Magazine* 101:3 (2000), 190–213; S. Max Edelson, *Plantation Enterprise in Colonial South Carolina* (Cambridge, MA: Harvard University Press, 2011); McCusker and Menard, *The Economy of British America*, 169–88.

[16] Jack N. Rakove, *The Beginnings of National Politics: An Interpretive History of the Continental Congress* (New York: Knopf, 1979), 43–5.

and the three southerly regions with enslaved populations of 40 percent or more. But the three intensive slave regions were actually divided between those deeply invested in the continued importation of enslaved Africans – the West Indies and the Lower South – and the Chesapeake, where the slave population's natural increase and a declining tobacco industry made transatlantic slave imports seem unnecessary in the later eighteenth century.[17]

The divide over slavery coincides with another, more subtle break. The three intensive slave regions sent the vast majority of their exports (nearly 85 percent) directly to Britain, where they boosted the domestic economy and contributed mightily to the royal treasury. By contrast, the two northern regions sent only 20 percent of their exports directly to Britain. Instead, their agricultural products, timber, and fish went to sustain the plantation colonies. The merchants of Boston, New York, and Philadelphia traded widely across the Atlantic world, earning credits that helped to make the free white populations of the northern colonies into a booming consumer market for British manufactures, on a much larger scale than the plantation colonies.[18]

But the plantation vs. nonplantation colonies were not the only interest-based coalitions across the regions. In terms of demographic growth, the Chesapeake actually resembled New England and the Middle Colonies much more than the West Indies or Lower South, as places experiencing rapid natural increase. However, New England differed from the Middle Colonies and the Chesapeake in its lack of European immigration and its limited geographical access to trans-Appalachian lands coveted by migrants swarming to the backcountry. In that sense, the Chesapeake colonies shared with the Middle Colonies a keen interest in westward expansion for their growing white population, potentially leaving the era of African slave importation behind.[19]

In short, the rapid growth of the populations and economies of all regions of colonial British America, together with the dramatic varieties across its

---

[17] David Eltis and David Richardson, *Atlas of the Transatlantic Slave Trade* (New Haven: Yale University Press, 2010), 208; Peter H. Wood, "The Changing Population of the Colonial South: An Overview by Race and Region, 1685–1790," in Gregory A. Waselkov, Peter H. Wood, and M. Thomas Hatley, eds., *Powhatan's Mantle: Indians in the Colonial Southeast* (Lincoln: University of Nebraska Press, 1989), 57–132; Woody Holton, *Forced Founders: Indians, Debtors, Slaves, and the Making of the American Revolution in Virginia* (Chapel Hill: University of North Carolina Press, 1999), 66–73.

[18] McCusker and Menard, *The Economy of British America*, 108, 130, 160, 174, 199; T. H. Breen, *Marketplace of Revolution: How Consumer Politics Shaped the American Revolution* (New York: Oxford University Press, 2005).

[19] Bernard Bailyn, *Voyagers to the West: A Passage in the Peopling of America on the Eve of the Revolution* (New York: Knopf, 1986), 204–39, maps on 209, 347.

regions, generated a complex and often conflicting array of colonial interests and expectations. These pressures shaped the first phase of the revolutionary transformation, the Seven Years' War in its American theater.

Phase One: The Seven Years' War in America

By mid-century, the rapid but uneven growth of colonial populations was creating a noticeable geographical bulge in a settlement pattern that otherwise remained close to the Atlantic littoral. In western Pennsylvania, Maryland, and Virginia, through gaps in the Appalachian barrier close to the headwaters of the Ohio River, the colonial population pushed into Indian territory, encroaching on land that was also claimed by France. It is no coincidence that Benjamin Franklin's prescient *Observations Concerning the Increase of Mankind*, which predicted North America's demographic expansion, was first published in 1755 as an appendix to William Clarke's *Observations on . . . the French with regard to their Encroachments on the British Colonies of North America*. Although the global war that began in the 1750s had roots in European balance-of-power politics, its eruption in North America in 1754 was generated by British settler expansion into the Ohio country and French and Indian military efforts to keep them out.[20]

The military conflict began in western Pennsylvania but shifted northward over time. After a disastrous start, Britain began investing heavily in the troops and materiel necessary to counter the strength of France's military and their Indian allies. The war moved toward the eastern Great Lakes and the St. Lawrence Valley, where France had the most to defend and where its armies could be resupplied from overseas. As a consequence, the military victories Britain eventually achieved, notably Wolfe's defeat of Montcalm at Quebec in 1759, as well as the ghastly ethnic cleansing campaign against the "French neutrals" in Nova Scotia, involved far more participation from northern colonial troops, especially New Englanders, than from the southern continental colonies. From 40 to 60 percent of military-age men in Massachusetts and Connecticut fought for the king. More than half of the provincial soldiers in the war came from those two colonies. Soldiers from the northern colonies predominated even when the war, in its late phase,

---

[20] Eric Hinderaker and Peter Mancall, *At the Edge of Empire: The Backcountry in British North America* (Baltimore, MD: Johns Hopkins University Press, 2003), 73–97; Fred Anderson, *Crucible of War: The Seven Years' War and the Fate of Empire in British North America, 1754–1766* (New York: Knopf, 2000).

moved into the Caribbean, and troops from New England and New York supported Britain's siege of Havana in 1762.[21]

The Peace Treaty of 1763 confirmed France's withdrawal from North America and restored Havana to Spain in return for ceding East and West Florida to Britain. With Louisiana ceded to Spain as well, French America was reduced to its Caribbean plantations, but without continental colonies to supply them. Britain's plantation colonies of Jamaica and South Carolina had participated in their own self-defense (aided by British regulars) against threats largely of their own making – Tacky's Revolt, the 1760 slave uprising in Jamaica, and the Cherokee War of 1759–1761 on Carolina's western frontier. By contrast, the colonies from Virginia northward, and especially New England, took pride in contributing not only to their own defense, but to the military ventures that defeated the "Gallic foe" and expanded Britain's domain, including all of France's continental possessions east of the Mississippi and four new ceded islands in the Caribbean.[22]

From an imperial viewpoint, these immense gains presented immense burdens as well. The debt generated by the war is well known. At £132 million in 1763, it was far beyond any amount Britain had ever experienced: annual interest payments on the debt alone were almost as large as Britain's entire budget had been in 1754. British homeland tax rates were at record highs. Equally challenging were the new costs of governing the extensive territories in America, an inland empire several times larger than the Atlantic coastal colonies.[23]

On the other side of the globe, a new model for Britain's exploitation of colonial possessions emerged when military victories by East India Company forces, including the defeat of the nawab of Bengal at the Battle of Plassey, transformed this immensely wealthy region into a tributary state. In 1765, the Mughal emperor granted the *diwani*, Bengal's annual land revenues, to the East India Company. With this shift from a trading enterprise to

---

[21] Anderson, *Crucible of War*, offers the most thorough account of the war's progress. On New England soldiers in the siege of Havana, see Elena Schneider, *The Occupation of Havana: War, Trade, and Slavery in the Atlantic World* (Chapel Hill: University of North Carolina Press, 2018), 128; Thomas Agostini, "The Provincials Will Work Like Giants: British Imperialism, American Colonial Troops, and Trans-Atlantic Labor Economics during the Seven Years' War," *Early American Studies* 15:1 (2017), 64–98.

[22] On the Cherokee War, see Anderson, *Crucible of War*, 457–71, and on the Treaty of Paris, Anderson, *Crucible of War*, 503–6. On Tacky's Revolt, see Vincent Brown, *Tacky's Revolt: The Story of an Atlantic Slave War* (Cambridge, MA: Harvard University Press, 2020); Burnard, *Jamaica in the Age of Revolution*, 103–30.

[23] John Brewer, *The Sinews of Power: War, Money, and the English State, 1688–1783* (New York: Knopf, 1988).

territorial sovereignty in India, for the first time, Britain possessed something to what Spain had acquired when conquistadors plundered the Mexica empire in 1519: a ready-made source of vast wealth, acquired by military conquest of a large, rich, and densely populated country.[24]

For two centuries, patriotic Britons had generated ideological propaganda to distinguish England's overseas empire – supposedly Protestant, commercial, maritime, and free – from its opposite, Spain's Catholic, extractive, land-based, and authoritarian colonial rule. Now Britain possessed an empire that included colonies of both kinds, not to mention large numbers of Hindus, Muslims, and native American "infidels" who fell outside the bounds of the Eurocentric Christian binary. That Parliament and the ministers of a newly crowned young king would seek a systematic reordering of this sprawling and motley empire should come as no surprise.[25]

Recognizing the empire's complexity, Whitehall and Parliamentary leaders shunned the idea that a single uniform policy could suit all the colonies. Yet the various reforms they propounded starting in 1763 shared the unifying assumption that imperial sovereignty was singular, and belonged to the "king-in-parliament" enshrined by the Glorious Revolution, the Acts of Union, and eighteenth-century political development in Great Britain. The colonies lay outside this zone of sovereign self-government, and were necessarily subordinate to metropolitan Britain's colonial governing structure, which combined Parliamentary legislation and crown administration to make its determinations.[26]

The newly acquired colonial territories required the greatest amount of active attention. Urgent decisions had to be made: how would they be governed? How would land be distributed? What religious establishment or forms of toleration would be created? What degree of military force would be needed to keep the peace? Notably, the peoples of these new

---

[24] P. J. Marshall, *The Making and Unmaking of Empires: Britain, India, and America, c. 1750–1783* (Oxford: Oxford University Press, 2005), 119–57; William Dalrymple, *The Anarchy: The East India Company, Corporate Violence, and the Pillage of an Empire* (New York: Bloomsbury, 2019).

[25] David Armitage, *The Ideological Origins of the British Empire* (Cambridge: Cambridge University Press, 2000), 170–98.

[26] In the Stamp Act (1765) and the subsequent Declaratory Act (1766), Parliament asserted its sovereign power over the subordinate colonies, but assigned different levels of taxation to different colonies, with the wealthier West Indies given higher tax rates than the North American colonies; Edmund S. Morgan and Helen M. Morgan, *The Stamp Act Crisis: Prologue to Revolution* (Chapel Hill: University of North Carolina Press, 2011 [1955]); Andrew O'Shaughnessy, "The Stamp Act Crisis in the British Caribbean," *William and Mary Quarterly* 51:2 (1994), 203–26.

acquisitions did not fall easily under the "Protestant, commercial, maritime, and free" rubric that had characterized the "old empire." As a result, the new imperial measures favored colonial governments of a more authoritarian character. They featured rule by appointed governors, often military men; they lacked representative assemblies, only to be gained at the governor's discretion; and they allowed for the toleration of Catholics, Hindus, and Muslims as well as non-English legal regimes.[27]

Although this may not have been intentional, the post-1763 measures seemed to favor the authoritarian and extractive end of the British colonial spectrum. Clearly, the wealth of a Bengal or the profits of a Jamaica could generate the specie needed to pay the costs of empire in an age of global military competition. By comparison, the new measures portrayed the older continental colonies – the most Protestant, commercial, maritime, and free – as the problem children of the empire. Within the new constellation of British colonies, Bengal and New France were fine as they were, while Massachusetts and Virginia needed to be brought to heel.[28]

The empire's rulers faced implicit questions of value: what were colonies supposed to be? What were they for? The extant colonies, old and new, offered a wide range of answers. Were colonies extensions of the home country, spreading the virtues of British liberty beyond the confines of the small home islands, and providing opportunities for Britons to exploit new territories? The colonies from New England to the Chesapeake offered variations on this model, depending on one's vision of Britain's true nature, from the more republican and egalitarian Massachusetts to the more aristocratic and stratified Virginia. Or were colonies to be forever subordinated dependencies whose value lay in the generation of wealth for the home islands, regardless of who labored in the plantations and whether their societies bore any resemblance to that of Britain? Their value was measured by profit figures on an imperial balance sheet, a positive balance of trade that brought more wealth into His Majesty's Treasury and the purses of his subjects in Great Britain.

Britain's answers to these questions were shaped by the pressing demands of the financial quandary created by the Seven Years' War. Expensive "hybrid

---

[27] The Royal Proclamation of 1763 began this process, which would then be modified by Parliament in future legislation, see https://avalon.law.yale.edu/18th_century/proc1763.asp.

[28] For an example of this argument, see Stephen Hopkins, "An Essay on the Trade of the Northern Colonies," *Providence Gazette*, 14 January 1764.

warfare"[29] across vast oceans and on distant continents was the cost of winning and preserving new colonies. Therefore, balance sheet values would shape imperial reforms. Their implementation broke the empire apart along the fault lines created by the colonies' varied forms of demographic growth, economic development, and political culture.

Phase Two: The Colonial Rebellion

The first to feel the pinch of Britain's reforms were the Indian nations of the trans-Appalachian West. Even before the Treaty of Paris ended the Seven Years' War in 1763, Britain's military leaders had begun to scale back gifts of trade goods to their Indian allies, wrongly believing that France's withdrawal would mean Indian subordination to British rule without the need for expensive gifts. Pontiac's War was a response to this retrenchment, as well as to white settler encroachment on Indian lands. It demonstrated an emerging belief among Indigenous nations that pan-Indian resistance could repel Anglo-American power on the continent. The first fruit of British victory over France in America was violent opposition from unconquered Indigenous allies who objected to being treated like conquered children.[30]

Across the settler colonies, new British measures for the collection of revenue and land administration precipitated similar reactions. Beginning in 1763 with the Sugar Act, followed quickly with the Currency Act (1764), the Stamp Act and the Quartering Act (1765), Parliament began to bring the colonies under a tax and regulatory regime similar to the home island. Revenues raised in the colonies would be spent in the colonies to manage the heightened costs of empire, including the permanent maintenance of regular troops there. At the same time, the crown began a new land management regime with the Royal Proclamation of 1763. Generated by alarm over Pontiac's War and the potential cost of military conflict across Britain's new land claims, the Proclamation barred settlers and land speculators from taking up trans-Appalachian land for the indefinite future. It also organized new governments, without constituent assemblies, for Quebec, the Floridas, and the Ceded Islands. And it transformed the acquisition of

---

[29] Linda Colley, *The Gun, the Ship, and the Pen: Warfare, Constitutions, and the Making of the Modern World* (New York: W. W. Norton, 2021).

[30] Eric Hinderaker, *Elusive Empires: Constructing Colonialism in the Ohio Valley, 1673–1800* (New York: Cambridge University Press, 1997), 146–50; Gregory Evans Dowd, *War Under Heaven: Pontiac, the Indian Nations, and the British Empire* (Baltimore, MD: Johns Hopkins University Press, 2002).

The Revolution in British America: General Overview

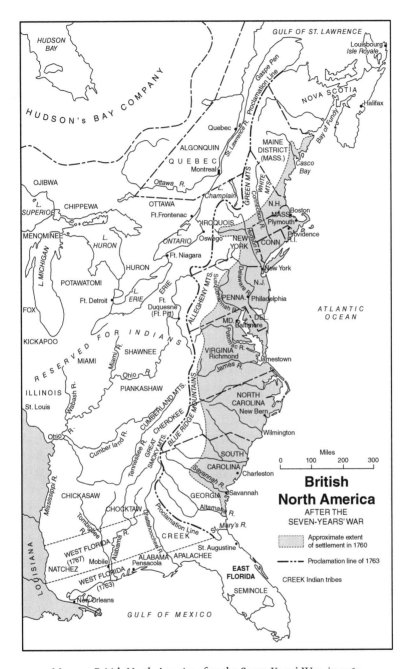

Map 5.1 British North America after the Seven Years' War, in 1763.

land from Indians into a diplomatic process, requiring negotiations between crown or colony officials and Indian nations, rather than private purchase, for all future Indian land cessions.[31]

These multifaceted land, revenue, and regulatory measures, each responding to a different long-standing issue in colonial governance, affected the colonial regions in varied ways. The Proclamation's restriction on westward expansion was a contentious issue for Virginia planters, but meant little to New England merchants. The Sugar Act's reduced duties on imported sugar and enhancement of the customs service, intended to minimize smuggling and raise revenue, irritated merchants in Boston, New York, and Philadelphia who dealt with customs officials, but benefited West Indian planters. Yet over the course of the next decade, the collective force of these measures generated episodes of resistance that coalesced into an oppositional movement of varying strength across the British colonial world.[32]

Resistance emerged most quickly and persistently in New England. This region had the strongest commitment to republican forms of self-government, going back to its roots as a puritan refuge from the heavy hand of England's episcopacy. By the eighteenth century, New Englanders had embraced the ideology of Britain's empire – Protestant, commercial, maritime, and free – demonstrated by their contributions to Britain's military ventures (which New England clergy supported as a Protestant crusade against "popery"). With their vigorous Protestant establishment and vibrant overseas trading economy, New Englanders imagined themselves as equal partners with the homeland in Britain's empire. Yet the post-war reforms hit New England hard – the war's end meant a retraction of military spending that had buoyed the region. Parliament's new direct taxation and heightened enforcement damaged the region's commercial economy in the midst of a post-war recession.[33]

Critically, Parliament's novel demands for revenue from colonial subjects not directly represented in that body, bypassing the region's own venerable assemblies, triggered New Englanders' ideological convictions dating back to England's civil wars of the 1640s. Although New Englanders had minimal

---

[31] Colin G. Calloway, *The Scratch of Pen: 1763 and the Transformation of North America* (New York: Oxford University Press, 2006); Peter D. G. Thomas, *British Politics and the Stamp Act Crisis: The First Phase of the American Revolution, 1763–1767* (Oxford: Oxford University Press, 1975).

[32] Pauline Maier, *From Resistance to Revolution: Colonial Radicals and the Development of American Opposition to Britain, 1765–1776* (New York: Knopf, 1972).

[33] Morgan and Morgan, *The Stamp Act Crisis*; Marc Egnal, *A Mighty Empire: The Origins of the American Revolution* (Ithaca, NY: Cornell University Press, 1988), 126–39.

expectations for the trans-Appalachian West, other elements of the Proclamation of 1763 aroused their fears. Toleration for Roman Catholics in Quebec and the creation of new colonial governments without representative assemblies resurrected the specter of James II's Dominion of New England. In 1689, New England had risen in rebellion to overthrow the Dominion's authoritarian government and defend their charter liberties. The combined effect of Britain's post-1763 reforms seemed threateningly familiar, and their persistence over the next decade convinced many New Englanders that the empire was determined to punish its most loyal but least directly remunerative colonies. Parliament's response to Bostonians' violent opposition to the 1773 Tea Act was the last straw. By closing the port of Boston, remodeling Massachusetts' government along authoritarian lines, undermining its judicial autonomy, and strengthening the military's law enforcement powers, Parliament pushed the region into a second armed rebellion against imperial authority.[34]

By contrast, New England's trading partners in the West Indies had little to fear from imperial reforms. Britain's restrictions on continental land acquisition affected them not at all, while the Ceded Islands offered new opportunities to replicate the plantation complex. With long experience as rulers of an oppressed laboring population, they had no objection to the authoritarian governments that Britain imposed on the former French and Spanish colonies. Although the islands' legislators grumbled over new commercial taxes and regulations, these measures strengthened a system of which they were the chief beneficiaries. Unlike New England, West Indian planters craved the protection of royal military forces, and were more than content with a closed mercantilist trade system. Thanks to their immense wealth, the planter elite had strong representation in Parliament. There was nothing in their history or their aspirations for the future that pushed the planter class toward violent resistance.[35]

Virginia, then, was critical, the oldest continental colony and the largest in area, population, and wealth. Virginia's white population, like New England's, was primarily English in its origins. Virginia, too, had an ancient heritage of self-rule, not on the egalitarian model of New England but as a dominant and self-confident plantation oligarchy accustomed to having its

---

[34] Bailyn, *Ideological Origins of the American Revolution*; Katherine Carté, *Religion and the American Revolution: An Imperial History* (Chapel Hill: University of North Carolina Press, 2021); Benjamin Labaree, *The Boston Tea Party* (New York: Oxford University Press, 1964).

[35] Burnard, *Jamaica in the Age of Revolution*; O'Shaughnessy, *An Empire Divided*.

way. Virginia possessed the only college in the southern colonies, founded by the Glorious Revolution monarchs, William and Mary, where the sons of planters were schooled in the empire's Whig traditions. Most significantly, Virginia possessed immense trans-Appalachian land claims and an economy based on agricultural expansion.[36]

In summer 1774, shortly after the Coercive Acts punishing Massachusetts for the destruction of East India Company tea, Parliament passed the Quebec Act. The expanded province of Quebec now included the entire region north of the Ohio River and west to the Mississippi, territory long claimed by Virginia, whose landowners and speculators had imagined it as the source of their future prosperity. As a result, Virginians forged a volatile compromise between the republican ideals of radical Whigs and the imperial ambitions of creole elites. Virginia's support for Massachusetts at the First Continental Congress in the fall of 1774, endorsing the cause of Boston as the "cause of all America," turned a localized rebellion into a continental revolution. Between them, New England and Virginia had well over a third of the free white population of British North America. Collectively they would supply the majority of soldiers for the Continental Army, formed when Virginia's George Washington took command of the New England militia who had repelled the British incursion on Lexington and Concord in April 1775.[37]

Britain failed to suppress the rebellion where it was hottest, in New England. Under Washington's command, the Continental Army's siege of Boston held. Crown forces evacuated Boston in March 1776 and retreated to Nova Scotia. In the face of New England's indomitable resistance, British strategy turned to finding weak spots in the coalition of colonies just then forming a union, hoping to isolate New England's rebels from the rest. In the summer of 1776, Britain's massive expeditionary force easily captured New York City and the surrounding area. But the following year's poorly coordinated campaign from Canada through the Hudson Valley ended in General Burgoyne's ignominious surrender at Saratoga.[38]

---

[36] Holton, *Forced Founders*; T. H. Breen, *Tobacco Culture: The Mentality of the Great Tidewater Planters on the Eve of Revolution* (Princeton: Princeton University Press, 1985); Richard R. Beeman, *The Varieties of Political Experience in Eighteenth-Century America* (Philadelphia: University of Pennsylvania Press, 2004), 31–68.

[37] Colin G. Calloway, *The Indian World of George Washington: The First President, the First Americans, and the Birth of the Nation* (New York: Oxford University Press, 2018); Holton, *Forced Founders*.

[38] For useful summaries and bibliographies of the war for independence, see Edward G. Gray and Jane Kamensky, eds., *The Oxford Handbook of the American Revolution* (New York: Oxford University Press, 2012); for a single narrative account, see Robert Middlekauff, *The Glorious Cause: The American Revolution, 1763–1789* (New York:

This failure to isolate New England led British forces to shift southward, attempting to break the Lower South away from the Confederation. For these slave societies, as for Virginia, rebellion was a bet on the future of western development. But it was a riskier bet for the Lower South, given their greater fears of slave insurrection and the limited capability of their smaller white populations for western expansion. The brutal warfare in the deep south, including considerable Patriot–Loyalist violence, devastated the region's economy and slave system. British regulars readily captured territory but could not pacify the region's internecine conflicts.

Britain also cultivated alliances with trans-Appalachian Indians, whose military power prevented rebel forces from conquering the western backcountry. But this effort, too, failed to weaken the confederation of coastal colonies. To the contrary, Britain's wide-ranging Indian alliances enhanced sentiments that Indians stood as impediments to the colonists' destiny.[39]

The relative success of the Continental Army in the northern fighting of 1775–1777, especially the victory at Saratoga, convinced France to ally itself with the American confederation. The French alliance transformed the war. French naval power and military strength, drawn from a population triple that of Britain, threatened British possessions in India, West Africa, the Mediterranean, and the Caribbean, as well as the potential invasion of the British homeland. The need to defend its global empire vastly increased Britain's military expenses and distracted its focus from the American rebellion. After a two-year campaign through the Lower South failed to pacify the region, General Cornwallis retreated to coastal Virginia to resupply his army. Admiral George Rodney's decision to defend Jamaica with the British fleet rather than pursue Comte de Grasse's French fleet northward led to Cornwallis' entrapment and surrender at Yorktown in October 1781. British political support for the war collapsed and peace negotiations began. The war's end reflected its origins, as Britain chose to defend the more remunerative parts of the empire at the expense of the rebellious continental colonies.[40]

Oxford University Press, 1982); see also Stephen Conway, *The War of American Independence, 1775–1783* (New York: St. Martin's Press, 1995).

[39] Sylvia Frey, *Water from the Rock: Black Resistance in a Revolutionary Age* (Princeton: Princeton University Press, 1991); Calloway, *American Revolution in Indian Country*, 272–301.

[40] O'Shaughnessy, *Empire Divided*, 213–37; Conway, *War of American Independence*, 133–60.

Phase Three: The American Settlement

The peace treaty of 1783 granted the new United States far more territory than its military efforts had won. It awarded the trans-Appalachian west, south of the Great Lakes and north of Florida, to the United States, despite Indians' continuing control of this immense region. Britain retained its Canadian possessions, and the treaty returned Florida and the Gulf Coast to Spain. During the treaty negotiations, other options were on the table, including continued British possession of the territory north of the Ohio, or a pan-Indian national territory under Spain's protection. Had the treaty confined the United States to the coastal regions actually held by the thirteen states, with a strong British or Spanish presence defending trans-Appalachian Indian sovereignty, the Articles of Confederation might have sufficed as a frame of government for the United States. The bulk of the confederation's governance would have been conducted by the states, with relatively little for a national government to do. But the western claims presented the United States with the same governance challenges that Britain, with its consolidated power, had failed to solve after 1763, and that the Confederation Congress was ill-equipped to manage.[41]

The war had devastating consequences for the North American economy, but not for its population growth. Trade embargoes and war's destruction caused an extended downturn in the formerly thriving colonial economy on a scale not seen again until the Great Depression of the 1930s. Yet despite the depression and the war's dampening of immigration, settler populations continued their rapid increase. The first US census of 1790 recorded nearly 4 million residents, another doubling from the end of the Seven Years' War, with half under age 16 – a very young American population.[42] The west was seen by most Americans, Thomas Jefferson not least among them, as a future home for this booming population and a solution to the nation's economic woes. Jefferson and others in the Confederation Congress engineered compromises among most states with western land claims to cede them to the

---

[41] Richard B. Morris, *The Peacemakers: The Great Powers and American Independence* (New York: Harper & Row, 1965); Peter S. Onuf, *The Origins of the Federal Republic: Jurisdictional Controversies in the United States, 1775–1787* (Philadelphia: University of Pennsylvania Press, 1983); Max Edling, *Perfecting the Union: National and State Authority in the US Constitution* (New York: Oxford University Press, 2021).

[42] Allan Kulikoff, "'Such Things Ought Not to Be': The American Revolution and the First National Great Depression," in Andrew Shankman, ed., *The World of the Revolutionary American Republic* (New York: Routledge, 2014), 134–64.

national government. They also enacted ordinances that sketched out plans for future land sales, the making of territories, and eventually new states.[43]

Although the Confederation Congress succeeded in making these plans, it lacked the powers and the practical force necessary to turn the plans into action. It had no executive branch, no judicial power over individuals, no national court system with jurisdiction over the territories, and no national taxation powers. Its use of military force was confined to defensive warfare, and its actual armed forces consisted of about 250 troops. Thus, Congress in the mid-1780s could not restrain the thousands of white settlers flocking westward or manage the conflicts with powerful Indian confederacies caused by the migrants. The west descended into chaos and violence. Britain retained its control of forts in the Northwest Territory to supply Indian allies, and Spanish Florida's boundary with the US southwest remained indeterminate – further signs of America's limited power to realize its territorial claims.[44]

The west was not the only challenge faced by Congress. Managing the war debt and generating a reliable national revenue to serve the government's limited purposes constituted another cluster of significant problems. But these could have been solved by giving Congress the power to collect customs duties, without other dramatic revisions to the Articles. More troublesome was the challenge of conducting international diplomacy (including westward expansion) as a loose confederation of states with opposing internal interests. Political independence had not solved the old question of what continued expansion should mean. Would the United States create colonies, even temporary ones, in their own western territories, and on what model? The Northwest Ordinance of 1787 articulated a vision of gradual egalitarian expansion that was essentially a more republican version of Britain's older imperial ideology. But the Carolinas and Georgia promoted an expansion of the West Indian model, where a small white elite would profit from slave labor in newly settled western territories. Fierce divisions over diplomacy during the confederation era were driven by conflict between these visions. New York lawyer John Jay's negotiations for a

---

[43] Georgia and the Carolinas refused to cede their western claims, but all the states from Virginia northward did so; see Onuf, *Origins of the Federal Republic*. On Jefferson and spatial expansion, see Drew R. McCoy, *The Elusive Republic: Political Economy in Jeffersonian America* (Chapel Hill: University of North Carolina Press, 1980).

[44] Calloway, *The Indian World of George Washington*, 294–9; Andrew Cayton, *The Frontier Republic: Ideology and Politics in the Ohio Country, 1780–1825* (Kent, OH: Kent State University Press, 1986).

commercial treaty with Spain foundered on its agreement to postpone US navigation of the Mississippi through the port of New Orleans for twenty years – a fatal impediment to westward expansion from the viewpoint of the southern states that rejected the treaty.[45]

Virginians led the way out of the stalemate, and toward rapid western expansion, by organizing 1787's constitutional convention and presenting a radical plan for a wholly new form of national government. Drafted by James Madison, one among many Virginians with frustrated interests in western land speculation, the Virginia Plan proposed a representative national government, elected by and with direct power over individual citizens. It called for a forceful executive branch, a national judiciary, and the ability to tax and to organize peacetime armies for use in the territories – all powers the confederation congress lacked. Fierce objections were raised by what are commonly called the "small states," essentially the coastal states lacking western land claims. They feared a future in which large states, potentially immense in both area and population, would dominate a representative republic. The fundamental assumption, widely held even in the most urbanized regions like New England, was that the United States would remain agrarian for the imaginable future. Wealth and power in a representative republic would therefore concentrate in the biggest states with the most people.[46] The key determinant for realizing this vision of a continuously expanding agrarian nation was the power to acquire Indian-owned territory and turn it into commodified real estate. The Virginia Plan, when added to the confederation's land ordinances, would provide exactly that.[47]

The Convention delegates altered Madison's plan considerably through compromises needed to gain majority consent. Further amendments generated during the state ratification debates also modified the Virginia Plan. Vestiges of the Articles were retained in the equality of states in the Senate, and in the need for supermajorities in the Senate's ratification of treaties. In this sense, the new Constitution still retained elements of a treaty alliance, a "peace pact" among the states. Protections for slaveowners' human property

---

[45] McCoy, *Elusive Republic*, 123–4; Rakove, *Beginnings of National Politics*, 349–50.
[46] In the 1790 US census, 94.3 percent of the population lived in rural communities, defined as places with fewer than 2,500 people. There were thirty-one "urban" places, of which nineteen were in New England; only seven were south of the Mason–Dixon line.
[47] Accounts of the Philadelphia Constitutional Convention of 1787 are legion; recent entries include Richard Beeman, *Plain Honest Men: The Making of the American Constitution* (New York: Random House, 2009); Michael Klarman, *The Framers' Coup: The Making of the United States Constitution* (New York: Oxford University Press, 2016).

were added in the form of the "three-fifths" clause that enumerated slaves for purposes of representation and taxation, as well as in the Fugitive Slave clause and the twenty-year prohibition on Congress abolishing the slave trade. The Bill of Rights, demanded by opponents of the Constitution in the ratification debates and passed by Congress in its first session, guaranteed traditional English liberties (cast in more universal language) against the national government's enhanced powers. But the Bill of Rights did not apply to the states, who exercised their own internal policing powers (for example, religious establishments) regardless of limitations on the national government. Consequently, if the general tenor of the new Constitution endorsed a vision of continued expansion on the model of the northern colonies, an extension of British society on a republican and egalitarian model, it nonetheless carved out space for protecting the existence and expansion of slave-based extractive societies.[48]

The result was a very strange nation-state, something new under the sun. What was *not* distinctive about the United States was its federated nature, which was not uncommon in the western past going back to the Greeks, and practiced among Indigenous Americans across the hemisphere. Rather, its peculiarity lay in the odd bifurcation of the United States into two separate constitutional zones. One was the thirteen founding states, whose citizens (but not slaves) enjoyed the full benefits of the Constitution's powers and protections; the other consisted of national territories, where most autonomous Indian nations then lived. US citizens who moved to the territories, under terms controlled by the national government, temporarily relinquished their rights and lived under an appointive government, without representation in Congress, much like those that Britain had erected over the territories acquired in the Seven Years' War. *Temporarily* is the key word. In the plan for perpetual expansion, the national government would arrange Indian land cessions or Indian removal through diplomacy, violence, or both. This would make way for white settler populations who would gradually gain assembly rights, eventually statehood, and full membership in the national confederation – nearly complete equality with the founding states.

---

[48] See Pauline Maier, *Ratification: The People Debate the Constitution, 1787–1788* (New York: Simon & Schuster, 2010). On the Bill of Rights, see Jack N. Rakove, *Original Meanings: Politics and Ideas in the Making of the Constitution* (New York: Knopf, 1996), 288–338. On slavery and the Constitution, recent debates are summarized in David Waldstreicher, *Slavery's Constitution: From Revolution to Ratification* (New York: Hill & Wang, 2009); Sean Wilentz, *No Property in Man: Slavery and Anti-slavery at the Nation's Founding* (Cambridge, MA: Harvard University Press, 2018).

Nearly, because one essential difference remained. The original thirteen states retained control over any state lands yet to be occupied by white settlers, whereas in any new states formed out of the national domain (such as the Northwest Territory), the national government would control the process of gaining land cessions and overseeing land sales and distribution. In short, what the 1783 Treaty of Paris projected and the 1787 Constitution consolidated was a two-zone expansionist machine, an ongoing engine of colonization and incorporation of territory into the home country with no obvious limits – this was the *Novus Ordo Seclorum*.[49]

From the time the first national government under the Constitution met in 1789, the use of military force to defeat Indian resistance became one of its principal functions. The process began in the Northwest Territory. The earlier renunciation by the states of their claims to this region, together with the Northwest Ordinance, confirmed it as national territory where the federal government had a free hand to act. Under British rule, the king's troops had been the colonizers' enemy, restraining their movement into Indian country. But under the Constitution's structure it was clear that state militias were expected to do the work of defending the extant states against potential foreign attacks, while the national army, paid for by national taxation, would be used to subdue Indian resistance in national territory. National soldiers would be no threat to citizens in the states, but would serve as the means to advance their interests at the expense of noncitizens in the territories.[50]

This process moved more slowly in the southwest because North Carolina and Georgia were reluctant to cede their western claims to the United States. These Lower South states, skeptical of the national government, still hoped to capitalize on western land for themselves despite the Constitution's prohibitions. For these states, the Constitution was understood as something of a bargain. Georgia ratified quickly to gain the protection of national forces in an imminent war with the Creek Indians for which it was unprepared. North Carolina's 1788 convention rejected the Constitution. The transactional question underlying this skepticism was whether slave societies would be acceptable as future states in the union.[51]

---

[49] Onuf, *Origins of the Federal Republic*, 21–46; see also Peter S. Onuf, *Statehood and Union: A History of the Northwest Ordinance* (Notre Dame, IN: University of Notre Dame Press, 2019).

[50] Edling, *Perfecting the Union*, 75–104; Gregory Ablavsky, *Federal Ground: Governing Property and Violence in the First U.S. Territories* (New York: Oxford University Press, 2021).

[51] Maier, *Ratification*, 122–4; Calloway, *Indian World of George Washington*, 350–1.

By the 1810s, the combination of military force and settler population growth across the trans-Appalachian West coerced land cessions from the region's Indians, but also completed the exclusion of British and Spanish claims to this territory. The War of 1812, the Treaty of Ghent that ended it, and the Adams–Onis Treaty of 1819 confirmed US control over the entirety of the continent east of the Mississippi and south of the Great Lakes. But it was the Louisiana Purchase of 1803 and its incorporation into the national project that marked the conclusion of the revolutionary transformation of America.

There was nothing inevitable about the incorporation of the trans-Mississippi west into the United States. The 1783 Paris Treaty confirmed Spain's control of this region, allowing Spain to expand its North American colonization, while connecting Florida to its western possessions and placing the entire coast of the Gulf of Mexico under Spanish control. However, the French Revolution and Napoleon's subsequent military conquests weakened Spain's imperial hold and led to Louisiana's transfer to France in 1800. Napoleon's interest was fed by the prospect of suppressing Haiti's revolution, restoring slavery in the French Caribbean, and using Louisiana to support Saint-Domingue much as Britain's continental colonies had done for Jamaica. But the failure of Napoleon's Haitian campaign created the necessary conditions for Jefferson's diplomats to purchase the immense Louisiana region, no longer needed by France, rather than the narrow privileges to navigate the Mississippi they were seeking.

The future of the trans-Mississippi West was determined not by this 1803 purchase of pre-emption rights, but in the political process developed by Congress for Louisiana's incorporation into the nation. The Constitution and Northwest Ordinance provided clear guidance on settler expansion and state-making within the territory granted to the United States in 1783. This process was rooted in the innovative methods for constitution-making developed at the state and national level from 1776 to 1787, which emphasized the right of self-determination (for white colonizers, not Indians). But the Constitution was, and remains, silent on whether the United States can acquire additional territory, by conquest or purchase, beyond its 1783 limits, and, if so, on the terms by which such territory might be incorporated in the bifurcated national domain. Would any such territory be under the same rules for expansion and potential statehood that governed the national territories? Could it be admitted directly to the union as a state by a simple act of Congress? This resembled the problem that had plagued and ultimately fractured the British empire after 1763, when new territorial conquests with radically differing populations and characteristics were treated differently from the older colonies.

Many American leaders, including President Jefferson himself, recognized the problem. The most populous part of Louisiana, around New Orleans, consisted of French and Spanish colonists and their enslaved African laborers. These non-British colonists had no tradition of republican self-government. They now "belonged" to the United States through no choice of their own. How should they be incorporated in the union? In private correspondence, Jefferson argued that if the nation incorporated alien lands whose peoples had "different circumstances, prejudices, and habits," it would significantly alter its constitution by redefining the component parts of the body politic. Jefferson recommended, again in private, that a Constitutional Amendment be required for any future state to be admitted to the union out of previously foreign territory. The logic of American constitutionalism demanded a high level of consensus – two-thirds majorities in both houses of Congress, and ratification by three-fourths of the states – if such momentous amendments to the union's character were contemplated.[52]

Numerous members of Congress, predominantly from northern states, unwittingly shared Jefferson's view. In 1811, when Congress debated the admission of the State of Louisiana, they proposed an Amendment as the only constitutionally justifiable method. But they were voted down, and Louisiana was admitted by simple majority votes in the House and Senate. Jefferson remained silent in support of his party's and region's interests.

This vote was the most consequential alteration to the US Constitution before the Civil War. Every new state admitted to the union would gain Congressional representation proportional to its free population, plus three-fifths of its enslaved population, plus two senators, and proportionate electoral votes for the presidency. By making the admission of acquired foreign territory to statehood possible through simple majorities in Congress, this new process provided political factions in Congress, already forming around divisions over slavery, the incentive to pursue territorial conquest and state-making as standard methods to enhance their power, subdue their opponents, and oppress minority interests. Rather than competing for support among the citizens of a relatively fixed national order, American political

---

[52] Thomas Jefferson to John Breckinridge, 12 August 1803; Thomas Jefferson to Levi Lincoln, 30 August 1803; Thomas Jefferson to Wilson Cary Nicholas, 7 September 1803, in *Founders Online*, National Archives, https://founders.archives.gov/documents/Jefferson/01-41-02-0139; https://founders.archives.gov/documents/Jefferson/01-41-02-0225; https://founders.archives.gov/documents/Jefferson/01-41-02-0255.

parties could, and did, succeed by making territorial expansion a normal part of politics, winning elections by expanding the nation to gain more seats for their cause. No nation on earth had ever functioned in this way before.[53]

The implementation of the Louisiana Purchase completed the revolutionary transformation of America by enshrining unlimited territorial expansion for the exclusive benefit of white Americans as the prize at the center of national politics. This process defined the American answer to the question Britain faced in 1763 about what kinds of colonies they wanted to promote, what values their imperial project should embody. In the particular answer that Louisiana offered, there lay not only an opening but a mechanism for the territorial expansion of the slave society model far beyond the dreams of planters in 1763 or 1783.

The immense liberatory effect, both actual and potential, of the revolt against British rule by the thirteen colonies is not to be denied. The rejection of monarchy and aristocracy, the promotion of equality before the law for all citizens, and the development of representative government answerable to its constituents were all enormous advances in the direction of democracy, and have had substantial influence within and beyond the United States. Equally influential has been the American development of methods for generating constitutional frameworks of self-government distinct from the actions of sitting legislatures or rulers. The American rejection of Old World forms of hierarchy, class, religious establishments, restrictions on mobility and economic opportunity – these have inspired people around the world to seek similar freedoms for themselves. Many Americans initially excluded from the benefits of citizenship have used the rhetoric of liberty and equality enunciated in the nation's founding documents to seek their own emancipation and empowerment, generating social transformations in the process.[54]

At the same time, the founding era's exclusions were a feature, not a bug, in the regime constructed by the victors in the contest for control of North America's future. These victors promoted a vision of political economy based on the exploitation of North America's resources, for the benefit of some and at the expense of others not yet or never to be included in the privileges of US citizenship. Thomas Jefferson and Alexander Hamilton are often depicted

---

[53] Adam Dahl, *Empire of the People: Settler Colonialism and the Foundations of Modern Democratic Thought* (Lawrence: University of Kansas Press, 2018).

[54] Classic statements of this argument include Bailyn, *Ideological Origins of the American Revolution*, 230–360; Gordon S. Wood, *The Radicalism of the American Revolution* (New York: Knopf, 1992); Jonathan Israel, *The Expanding Blaze: How the American Revolution Ignited the World, 1775–1848* (Princeton: Princeton University Press, 2017).

as polar opposites in their competing visions for America's future political economy, leaders of the competing political parties that grew around them. Jefferson imagined America as an egalitarian utopia of yeomen farmers, but dependent on debased laborers in foreign countries to supply Americans with manufactures and to consume America's produce. Hamilton favored the growth of domestic manufacturing to promote American economic independence, unconcerned about the potential for profound domestic inequality it would generate. However, despite their bitter political conflicts, both implicitly agreed on the necessity of an oppressed Caliban, somewhere, who would hew the wood and draw the water to make Prospero's miracles of abundance possible for enfranchised American citizens.

The result has been an American society capable of being as divided between the haves and have nots as its Old World predecessors, but far more dynamic, devoted to human mobility in pursuit of perpetual growth. It has made the United States a marvel of modern history, whether measured by territorial expansion, population growth, GDP, or levels of wealth – a dynamo of agricultural and industrial production in the nineteenth century, the avatar of consumer society in the twentieth century. But with human-generated climate change and global inequality looming as the crises of the twenty-first century, it makes little difference which current party or policy best captures the founders' intentions, if all the leading actors in those eighteenth-century arguments shared the same assumptions about limitless resources and infinite growth that are at the root of today's existential problems. It is time for that American Revolution to be over and the search for new directions to begin.

6

The Myth of "Salutary Neglect": Empire and Revolution in the Long Eighteenth Century

HOLLY BREWER

On 22 March 1775, during a debate in Parliament over whether to repeal the 1774 Coercive Acts that would ultimately precipitate the American Revolution, Edmund Burke, agent for the colony of New York, Whig politician, and later conservative icon, spoke passionately about the importance of such repeal in words that now appear in every US history textbook and help to frame current understandings of the role of the British empire in North America and of the origins of the American Revolution: "I know that the colonies in general owe little or nothing to any care of ours, and that they are not squeezed into this happy form by the constraints of watchful and suspicious government, but that, through a wise and salutary neglect, a generous nature has been suffered to take her own way to perfection."[1] According to Burke, England's "salutary neglect" had nurtured freedoms, both politically and economically, such that the colonies, like a human child of a "generous nature," had somehow made their own way "to perfection." While Burke acknowledged that dissenting religious thought and some understanding of English political disputes in the seventeenth century (to which questions of taxation had also been central) had nurtured America's political development, Burke saw America's independent character as emerging naturally, as a result of neglect. Much of the historiography

---

[1] Edmund Burke, *Works* (London: Holdsworth & Ball, 1834), vol. 1, 186. Burke was clearly fascinated with a state of nature, and early in his life certainly idealized it, writing in 1756 in his "Vindication of Natural Society" that "All empires have been cemented in blood": Edmund Burke, *Works* (London: F. C. & J. Rivington, 1815), vol. 1, 17. Though he did not believe that "natural liberty" existed anywhere "free from the mixture of political adulterations" (1:35), yet he argued then that societies closer to the state of nature suffered less from injustice and massive wars that killed by the thousands.

concurs: America, left in the state of nature, partly because of the frontier situation and Britain's failure to exert real authority, developed her own liberties, almost inevitably. The shift in policy after 1763, which ended "salutary neglect" and enforced new taxes, upset the colonists and fed their fears about losing their freedoms. These fears, and misunderstandings, and the shift in policy led step by step to revolution.

The words "salutary neglect," however, have borne too much weight, leading to profound misconceptions. Burke's speech idealized American freedoms in pursuit of his own ideals and goals in British politics and also policies toward Ireland. While Burke had given deep thought to the American situation as editor of his uncle's history of the British empire and indeed in his role as Member of Parliament, Burke's views were profoundly shaped by Britain's own political situation. Burke, a member of the opposition Whig party that was struggling to reform rotten boroughs in England and political corruption in Ireland, was partly using America's history and character as a foil, as a state of nature with which to influence Britain's own politics. Why should this Member of Parliament, who had never visited America's shores or been himself a member of the Board of Trade, be our authority, defining for us the political economy of early America? While brilliant in his own way, no doubt, this defender of American liberties (who is oddly enough still immortalized in the old Whig dining room in Parliament as simply a supporter of the American Revolution) had his own agenda, one that profoundly shaped his speeches about colonial American history.

In this chapter I want to challenge Burke's myth of salutary neglect on many levels, beginning by exploring how it came to occupy its current, dominant status. The levers of imperial control were powerful throughout the colonial period; colonial political systems did not develop "in a state of nature"; the tendrils of legal control were invidious and far-reaching; and force – the power of empire – was never far away. British navies, in particular, supplemented by occasional armies and colonial militias under the command of the governor, along with all the mechanisms of legal control – sheriffs and executions, heads on stakes at the public crossroads – lurked always on the horizon, ready to intervene if necessary, at least in the public imagination. My chapter is a call to think deeply about the power of empire – in ways we historians have not done for a long time – during the colonial period. In doing so we will not only develop a richer understanding of what broke down between 1763 and 1776, but also of what came before. Salutary neglect it was not.

Origins of the Idea of Salutary Neglect

Historians began to use the term to describe the role of the British empire in the years before the revolutionary tensions more than 150 years ago, during the Civil War, and it slowly seeped into broader interpretations. They used it to emphasize American exceptionalism, often tied to explanations about the growth of both capitalism and democracy in early America, as did James Russell Lowell in 1890. Burke, he wrote, stated that a chief cause of the colonies' marvelous growth, both political and economic, was that "'through a wise and salutary neglect, a generous nature has been suffered to take her own way to perfection.' But by that 'wise and salutary neglect' he meant freedom from the petty and short-sighted meddlesomeness of a paternal government; he meant being left to follow untrammeled the instincts of our genius under the guidance of our energy. The same causes have gone on ever since working the same marvels."[2] By the early twentieth century it was often used only to describe one era of relatively lax enforcement: in 1922 William Guitteau described it being the appropriate phrase only during the "years from 1715–1740 … under Walpole, during which Period the colonies were improving their opportunities to developing along their own lines."[3]

When the phrase was first developed it also began to be readily applied to the United States' own role vis-à-vis its territories and colonies, and especially to its role in South America, as in a 1902 article in the *American Historical Review*. Charles Francis Adams (grandson and great-grandson of John Quincy and John Adams) argued there that the United States should endeavor to treat those of "inferior races" as though they were capable of self-government, and follow the same policy of "salutary neglect" that Britain had used with regard to its colonies before the revolution. It was a big if, however, as Adams then argued that many "inferior races" such as those who lived in Haiti, were not yet capable.[4] It is as though the theory of a beneficent empire that governed with a light hand was being used to justify the entire concept of empire. It is therefore important not to separate out the development of the historiography from that actual history and from arguments

---

[2] James Russell Lowell, *The Writings of James Russell Lowell: Literary and Political Addresses* (New York: Houghton, Mifflin, 1890), 203.
[3] William Backus Guitteau, *Government and Politics in the United States* (New York: Houghton Mifflin, 1922), 78.
[4] Charles Francis Adams, "An Undeveloped Function," *American Historical Review* 7:1 (1902), 203–2, 226–9.

about American (and British) exceptionalism. Only when Britain shifted policies, and became too interventionist, it must be understood, was its presence unwelcome and revolution a necessity that sought merely to restore the older order.

During the Cold War, however, it began to appear everywhere in the historiography in a way that made the revolution merely a footnote to an already achieved system of governance liberties, and economic growth. It did so at the same time as scholars began to reject the ideal of a powerful empire in which a mercantilist (as opposed to a capitalist) system operated. James Henretta's 1972 book seemed to provide an explanation for the concept by then so widely used. It had the title *Salutary Neglect: Imperial Administration under the Duke of Newcastle*. Henretta is often now cited as the go-to reference. Ironically, however, Henretta's analysis does not show such neglect, or at least not in the deeper sense. He argued that imperial policies were often poorly enforced and weakly administered due to corruption at home. But those imperial policies were still pervasive. Recent scholarship still largely relies upon the term but has become more subtle: Gautham Rao, for example, in his book on customs houses, argues that salutary neglect represented the "deterioration of the rule of imperial law," and that the customs officials in the colonies only "selectively enforce[d] the navigation laws." Eliga Gould follows Henretta to argue that the Whig ministries during the reigns of George I and George II (1715–1760) generally encouraged lax enforcement, so beyond merely Robert Walpole's administration as prime minister (1721–1742).[5] James Seelye and Shawn Selby describe it as "the term given to the period in American history when the British government unofficially reduced its involvement in and oversight of, the American colonies."[6] Meanwhile, Henretta, my now retired colleague, in response to reading earlier versions of this chapter, has written a brief entry on "Salutary Neglect" for the *Encyclopedia of Virginia*, which does a good job of narrowing its meaning to selective enforcement of imperial policies.[7] And yet in the

---

[5] Gautham Rao, *National Duties: Custom Houses and the Making of the American State* (Chicago: University of Chicago Press, 2016), 33–4; Eliga H. Gould, *The Persistence of Empire: British Political Culture in the Age of the American Revolution* (Chapel Hill: University of North Carolina Press, 2011), 16.

[6] James E. Seelye, Jr. and Shawn Selby, *Shaping North America: From Exploration to the American Revolution* (New York: ABC-CLIO, 2018), vol. 1, 855.

[7] James A. Henretta, *Salutary Neglect* (Princeton: Princeton University Press, 1972); James A. Henretta, "Salutary Neglect," *Encyclopedia of Virginia*, https://encyclopediavirginia.org/entries/salutary-neglect.

broader scholarship, the term is an anchor which means an era of non-enforcement, a meaning embedded in the term "neglect."

It is rare to see a strong statement challenging the concept, as that by Jonathan Eacott in his book on the British empire in India and how their policies there impacted the Americas: "When it came to the Atlantic colonists trading with Asia, the British government did not practice Salutary Neglect."[8] It is far more common to see the term used as it is in textbooks, and implicitly in the way most courses on the American Revolution begin in 1763, with the end of the Seven Years' War and the end of Salutary Neglect. That beginning is profoundly misleading. While 1763 did mark a shift in policy, and an era of greater parliamentary intervention in new taxes imposed on the colonists themselves, it was an incremental change rather than a dispositive one. Many earlier taxes had been imposed on (and collected from) colonists and had regulated their trade and their laws. Acknowledging such a reality allows for a more nuanced understanding of the origins of the American Revolution, one that places it much more deeply in the context of struggles over broader rights.

A disclaimer is in order: English authorities did not exercise strict and terrible control over the colonies during the whole of the colonial period. Of course not. But the levers of control were all the more powerful for the ways they permeated the system, legally and culturally. Power was negotiated on many levels and in many forms, and renegotiated as well at many points, with the outbreak of wars, on the accession of new kings, in the midst of new commercial developments and trading relationships. The power of empire enabled and undergirded the growth of slavery; navies and armies enabled control not only of forts but also of water routes. Controlling slaves on plantations depended upon the threat of force, always present; should slaves rise up, imperial governments could send troops. One study of early Barbados, for example, acknowledges that "the island's slave plantation system could not survive outside the protective umbrella of the metropolis, so they [the Barbadian elite] accepted imperial rule in exchange for protection."[9]

---

[8] Jonathan Eacott, *Selling Empire: India in the Making of Britain and America* (Chapel Hill: University of North Carolina Press, 2016), 120.

[9] Gary Puckrein, *Little England: Plantation Society and Anglo-Barbadian Politics, 1627–1700* (New York: New York University Press, 1984).

Military and Legal Support for Colonies and Corporations

What is almost as fascinating about the growth of the British empire during the long eighteenth century from 1660 to 1776 is that political power was often embedded in semi-commercial enterprises, from the Royal African Company to the East India Company and the South Sea Company. Such monopoly companies had the power to govern at the same time as they were to some extent separate; yet they were never wholly so. The proprietary colonies and companies shared this mixed commercial and political identity. As other scholars have recently emphasized, this was mercantilism, and not free trade, even if that rhetoric sometimes emerged. The state provided protected platforms for trade and set norms that benefited crown revenue.[10]

Even "free traders" in the slave trade who emerged within the shadow of the Royal African Company after 1712 in particular, plied their trade with the protection of empire, including that of the company. Protection of privileged trade routes was what the war on pirates that consumed the decade after the Peace of Utrecht in 1713 was all about. It is no accident that African slaves often appear in the narratives about pirate escapades, or that some of the biggest captures and executions – including the massive trial and execution of the crew of the "Dread Pyrate" Roberts – occurred off the coast of Africa. His 264 surviving crew members were tried by the Royal African Company at their main fort (Cape Coast Castle) in 1722; Roberts and his crew had been raiding ships involved in the slave trade. Wars were fought between empires over control of trade routes and of land forts that helped to enable those routes, not only in Africa and India but throughout the mainland colonies and the Caribbean. The British population willingly agreed to have themselves taxed to provide the huge navies that enabled the suppression of piracy and control over trade routes – in exchange for dramatic profits that buoyed businessmen and created, in John Brewer's words, a nation of shopkeepers. The navies were the sinews of power of the British empire.[11]

---

[10] Philip J. Stern, *The Company-State: Corporate Sovereignty and the Early Modern Foundations of the British Empire in India* (Oxford: Oxford University Press, 2011); Steve Pincus, "Rethinking Mercantilism: Political Economy, the British Empire, and the Atlantic World in the Seventeenth and Eighteenth Centuries," *William and Mary Quarterly* 69:1 (2012), 3–34; Nuala Zahedieh, "Making Mercantilism Work: London Merchants and Atlantic Trade in the Seventeenth Century," *Transactions of the Royal Historical Society* 9 (1999), 143–58.

[11] In 1722, 264 pirates (Roberts' crew – he was killed in the battle) were tried at Cape Coast Castle, the headquarters of the Royal African Company; 54 were executed immediately. On Roberts, see, for example, Jennifer G. Marx, "The Golden Age of

The British navy was powerful earlier as well. During the extended period of war between England and France and Spain from 1689 to 1713, for example (even despite the brief periods of peace), all trade between Virginia and England depended on naval convoys. Without them trade stopped. The records of the Board of Trade are replete with requests for the convoys to arrive, and to arrive more regularly. For a colony that produced primarily a staple crop that they could not eat, war without convoys meant poverty and starvation.[12] Indeed, during these decades of limited trade, Virginians turned forcefully to the production of cotton and began weaving their own clothes. The threat to the king's custom duties (which in Virginia were mainly on the production of tobacco) was so great that Edward Randolph, the Surveyor General of Customs in the American Colonies, thought England should take urgent action to prevent the growing of cotton and manufacture of cloth. In 1694, he reported that:

> Want of ships & an extreame scarcity of English Goods putts the people generally upon planting Cotton. Which thrives in all places: with great successe. I find it a growing Evill & will in a little tyme be followed by all. & tobacco left off wholy in 6 or 7 yeares unlesse the Inhabitants can be plentifully supplyed with goods at cheap Rates. I heare many say that they intend to leave off planting tobacco and emply their servatns upon making linnen & woolen Cloath. Coll. Custis makes 500 yards of woollen yearely in his house more than he has occasion to spend. Which he sells to his Neighbors.[13]

Piracy," in David Cordingly, ed., *Pirates: Terror on the High Seas from the Caribbean to the South China Sea* (East Bridgewater, MA: World Publications Group, 2007), 100–23: 123; John Brewer, *The Sinews of Power: War, Money, and the English State* (New York: Knopf, 1989), xviii: "Judged by the criteria of the ability to take pounds out of people's pockets and to put soldiers in the field and sailors on the high seas, Britain was one of Europe's most powerful states, one which had acquired prodigious powers over its subject"; on shopkeepers, see 184–6.

[12] The records of the convoy system exist throughout the records at the British National Archives for Virginia and undoubtedly other colonies; reading through these records reveals how crucial this system was. See, for example, CO 5/1309, items A7–A8, which contain an urgent request for a convoy to accompany more than 100 waiting ships (1697). Also see items A12–A14, about squadron protection for Virginia trade. Very little secondary literature on it exists, and the analysis is thin. See Arthur Pierce Middleton, "The Chesapeake Convoy System, 1662–1763," *William and Mary Quarterly* 3:2 (1946), 182–207; Douglas Bradburn, "The Visible Fist: The Chesapeake Tobacco Trade in War and the Purpose of Empire, 1690-1715," *William and Mary Quarterly* 68:3 (2011): 361–86.

[13] Edward Randolph, *Letters and Official Papers*, ed. Alfred S. Goodrick, 7:430–431, 14 March 1692 (1692/3).

Randolph's concerns led the English Parliament to pass the "Woolens Act" of 1699, which explicitly restricted the ability of colonists to manufacture and to export cloth, especially wool, but also linen and cotton. In the decades that followed, royal governors were ordered to report on (and suppress) all such attempts. Thus, after Lord Cornbury, Royal Governor of New York reported to the Board of Trade (the main British oversight body over the colonies) in 1708 that "The Manufactures settled here in this Province are Linnen and Woollen; they make very good Linnen for common use, and I don't doubt but in time they will improve that considerably; as for the woollen I think they have brought that too great perfection already." The Board of Trade responded to him and to other governors that they should take all legal means to prevent sales of these products, even in local shops.[14]

These comments about cloth manufacture raise fundamental questions about economic regulation in England's colonies in the Americas and especially staple-crop production, questions that have often been answered with economic explanations that avoid the political. Indeed, the production of particular staple crops is often seen as a natural development, part of the mercantilist system to be sure, but still somehow just what people wanted to do. But the elaborate state incentives mattered. Growing certain crops, and not others, producing certain goods, but not others; such were the restraints of not merely a mercantilist state, but of a particular set of negotiated policies that benefited some in the empire but not others. Tobacco and sugar in particular, perhaps partly by historical chance, were "enumerated" crops that after 1660 raised direct and substantial revenue for the English crown, via excise taxes that were increasingly rigorously collected at British ports.[15]

Customs controls in the colonies – while not perfectly enforced – were also often onerous and rigorous, depending on the colony and the values at stake. Policies could easily shift and change the course of enforcement. This is more than just a question of mercantilist policy – it is about both ideologies and interest, and who was in power. In other words, the empire's political economy was an octopus, with multiple arms and tentacles, squeezing itself into small spaces at the same time as it ignored other nooks and crannies. It is

---

[14] George Louis Beers, *Commercial Policy of England toward the American Colonies* (New York: Columbia College, 1893), 78.

[15] Peter Linebaugh, *The London Hanged: Crime and Civil Society in the Eighteenth Century* (London: Allen Lane, 1991). Linebaugh has many examples of sailors and longshoremen being sentenced to hang for stealing tobacco from barrels (and thus avoiding the excise). The excise at some points represented twelve times the actual cost of tobacco in Virginia, a simply immense tax.

not that the empire created all trade, that innovation and risk were unimportant; it is that the empire in many ways regulated and enabled certain possibilities. Thus, the long-standing trade with Portugal, for wine, for example, was shaped by treaties and agreements which created tariffs that made French wine more expensive and Portuguese wine much cheaper, especially after the Glorious Revolution and increasing conflict with France. French claret became the drink used to deny the legitimacy of the Glorious Revolution and toast the "king over the water"; port became the drink of good Whigs.[16]

What was distinctive about the English empire, especially after 1689 and the fall of James II, was that it was not as absolutist as the French and Spanish (though even in those empires control was never absolute) as Henry Kamen has shown.[17] Yet it is important, even crucial, to acknowledge that bureaucratically the control over empire fell not to Parliament, but to the monarchy. The colonies belonged to the king or queen. It was his or her Privy Council, his or her Board of Trade, who had to approve colonial laws, which had oversight over colonial court decisions, which set and enforced trade policies and sent navies and convoys and troops. The sovereign also benefited substantially from incomes from the colonies that increased his or her authority. In 1688, James II was earning so much money in excise taxes on New World products that he could pay for an army of 40,000 without calling Parliament. While those taxes had to be reauthorized by Parliament at the accession of each new monarch, they routinely were.[18]

The Limits of "Free Trade"

It is in this context that we should think about Walpole's encouragement of freer trade in some items (such as rice from Carolina) and his encouragement of elected assemblies which framed Burke's thinking about "salutary neglect." Walpole, that first Whig prime minister, sought public approval for policies, particularly for the City of London and from colonists when he could. But he was not thereby willing to lessen the power of the Navigation

---

[16] See, for example, Charles Ludington, *The Politics of Wine in Britain: A New Cultural History* (New York: Palgrave Macmillan, 2013), e.g., 115. David Hancock, *Oceans of Wine* (New Haven: Yale University Press, 2009), emphasizes British trade connections with the Portuguese, but does not really investigate the politics behind the failure to tax madeira even as French wines were heavily taxed.

[17] Henry Kamen, *Empire: How Spain Became a World Power, 1492–1763* (New York: HarperCollins, 2004).

[18] Stephen S. Webb, *Lord Churchill's Coup* (New York: Random House, 1997).

Acts. Far from it: under his leadership Parliament created new regulations. So, in 1733, he sought to shift the collection of tobacco taxes in London from the venue of customs (which was riddled with smuggling) toward the excise collectors (where it could be more rigorously controlled). After this policy shift, those taxes were still enforced, which, though collected in London, significantly reduced the price at which planters in Virginia and Maryland could sell their tobacco. He approved the Carolina planters' proposal to sell rice directly to Europe only because there was not already a high tax on it; such an exemption was only for rice, which was the only good such ships could carry, and it was still taxed. He wrote the words that George I spoke on that occasion in 1721: "by a due consideration of this matter the produce of these duties, compared with the infinite advantages that will accrue to the kingdom by their being taken off, will be found so inconsiderable." By encouraging local assemblies, he was not weakening imperial power. It was during his tenure that many new imperial taxes and regulations were passed by Parliament, including the 1733 Molasses Act that would be the basis for the later 1764 Sugar Act.[19] He was thereby encouraging representative government (in the form of local assemblies and also Parliament), but he was not making the colonies less dependent. He was encouraging Parliament to assert its privileges to regulate taxes in the empire while arguably slightly weakening the king's power over them. During his term as prime minister, some regulations and duties (which did not directly relate to imperial finance) were reduced or even ignored, while other economic regulations were being rigorously enforced.[20]

While the ligaments of legal control were complex and negotiated, they were also omnipresent. Those in power in the colonies – not simply governors, but the many appointed officials, including councilors (who composed the upper house in most colonies), judges, customs collectors and naval inspectors, militia colonels, surveyors, sheriffs, and hangmen – all held their

---

[19] J. M. Robertson, *Bolingbroke and Walpole* (London: Fisher Unwin 1919), 85, 107, 136; Paul Langford, *The Excise Crisis: Society and Politics in the Age of Walpole* (Oxford: Clarendon, 1975); Julian Hoppit, *Britain's Political Economies* (Cambridge: Cambridge University Press, 2017), 118, 302.

[20] Long ago Charles Andrews also denied that Burke's concept of salutary neglect was an apt one. However, he saw imperial control as more economic than political. I here emphasize both, and think that they were intertwined. Andrews wrote "Under this somewhat rough and ready method of treatment, which was not at all what Burke called it, 'salutary neglect,' but rather the mercantilist's idea of how a mother country should guide her colonies, the English colonies in America became self-reliant, self-governing, and self-supporting groups." Charles Andrews, *The Colonial Background of the American Revolution* (New Haven: Yale University Press, 1924), vol. IV, 74–5.

The Myth Of "Salutary Neglect"

authority by appointments, by patronage. Even the rules about who could vote or hold office, issues we think of as exemplifying local control, were often set by imperial regulations. While this was a corrupt system, as Lewis Namier argued (a point emphasized by Henretta as well), such systems of patronage were still powerful. Henretta argues that the corruption weakened the ability to implement oversight, especially when it meant that the Board of Trade approved agents who remained in England, and appointed deputies to act in their stead. Still, patronage gave leverage to those in control of empire, to bring varying policies into practical effect, policies that sometimes fit not only with their interests, but with their ideals.[21]

Consider, for example, two seventeenth-century episodes which will help make sense of the eighteenth century. In 1652, as Virginia burgesses with Governor Berkeley's prompting denied the validity of the Commonwealth and threatened to execute anyone who even spoke about the trial and beheading of Charles I, they were met with the reality of Cromwell's troops, some 1,000-strong. The Virginia forces assembled to fight them quickly surrendered. The Commonwealth troops came with a commission to reconstitute authority in Virginia: the new government was to be based on the burgesses, which were in turn to elect their own council and governor, who were to serve at their pleasure. More importantly, all of those who voted were required to swear allegiance to the new commonwealth. What had been punishable by death became in the passing of a week the keys to power. During the decade between 1651 and 1659, those in power in Virginia had Puritan sympathies: the burgesses chose as their governor in 1653 Mr. Richard Bennett – an outspoken Puritan who had fled Virginia earlier when the royalist Governor Berkeley prosecuted dissenters from the Church of England. During this decade, Virginia executed its only witch and passed laws – nearly all of which were systematically repealed in 1660 (as they were in England) – that went in a direction sympathetic to the legal reforms sought by many under Cromwell and in New England. Only with the Restoration was hereditary slavery formally legalized in Virginia (in 1662), alongside hereditary monarchy. At the same time, the rules about who could vote were transformed, a powerful council and royal governor were restored, and the balance of power in the colony shifted substantially.[22]

---

[21] Lewis Namier, *The Structure of Politics at the Accession of George III* (London: Springer, 1957); Henretta, *Salutary Neglect*, Introduction.

[22] Thomas J. Wertenbaker, *Virginia under the Stuarts 1607–1688* (Princeton: Princeton University Press, 1914), esp. 99–103; William Waller Hening, ed., *The Statutes at Large:*

The second such episode occurred throughout the colonies in the years surrounding the Glorious Revolution in England. Charles II and James II had gotten rid of the charters of five of the Northern colonies (they strongly disliked those in New England, especially, suspecting them of too much religious radicalism, of sheltering regicides, etc.). They substituted a Dominion of New England, which abolished elections (in Massachusetts Bay before that time they had even elected their governor annually), and vested authority in a royal governor and council. Though undoubtedly unpopular, none dared to protest these reforms too openly – the colonies were simply too weak and dependent. Only when news of the Glorious Revolution – and the flight of James II – filtered into the colonies did many colonists rise up in rebellion against their colonial governors and overthrow them. But the colonists were then left without proper governments. It was into that vacuum of power that the Salem Witch trials emerged, spiraling quickly out of control under the aegis of a court of Oyer and Terminer with doubtful legal authority, while Massachusetts Bay officials lobbied desperately in England for the restoration of their former charter or something that looked like it.[23] They received – under William and Mary, who in many ways supported elected government – a new charter that allowed them to elect both upper and lower houses, but with a royal governor, not the elected governor they had before 1685. Only the arrival of that royal governor stopped the witch hunts. The point is not that this is the only explanation for witchcraft. The point is legal power emanated from England not only in terms of legitimacy, but in terms of its potential force. Without that sanction, even in Massachusetts Bay, famous for its town meetings and elected government, anxiety reigned and all authority was questionable.

Similar episodes in response to the Glorious Revolution can be traced throughout the colonies, from Leisler's Rebellion in New York to the radical

---

Being a Collection of All the Laws of Virginia, from the First Session of the Legislature, in the Year 1619. Published Pursuant to an Act of the General Assembly of Virginia, Passed on the Fifth Day of February One Thousand Eight Hundred and Eight, 3 vols. (Philadelphia: Thomas DeSilver, 1823), vol. I and esp. vol. II, which begins with the repeal of most laws of the commonwealth period. On witchcraft in Virginia, see Mechal Sobel, *The World They Made Together: Black and White Values in Eighteenth-Century Virginia* (Princeton: Princeton University Press, 1987). On restoration and slavery, see Holly Brewer, "Slavery, Sovereinty, and 'Inheritable Blood': Reconsidering John Locke and the Origins of American Slavery," *American Historical Review* 122:4 (2017), 1038–78.

[23] "Massachusetts' Agent [Elisha Cooke] Describes Events in London, 16 October 1690," in Michael G. Hall, Lawrence H. Leder, and Michael G. Kammen, *The Glorious Revolution in America: Documents on the Colonial Crisis of 1689* (New York: W. W. Norton, 1972), 69–75.

uprising in Maryland (which resulted in the Calverts losing their proprietary government, though not their revenues), and Parson Waugh's revolt in Virginia. While in many colonies, including Jamaica, Barbados, and Virginia, the older authorities kept nominal control and acted quickly to restore order by shifting their allegiance officially to their new monarchs, the situation was profoundly unstable as everyone held their breaths to see how the shape of government in the colonies would change. In many colonies those changes were profound but unstable.

Glorious Revolution, Political Reforms, and the (Still) Limited Power of Elected Assemblies in the Eighteenth Century

The settlements that emerged in the wake of the Glorious Revolution throughout the British empire in North America were in many ways the forms that many governments would keep until the Revolution, and in some cases long afterwards. The point is that the British king (especially) was not bound to abide by any particular formulation. And the king could regulate and oversee laws in all colonies, since he and his Privy Council and Board of Trade were silent partners in legislation, overturning what they did not like. While Parliament could pressure the king in all of this, as they did William III in 1696, in the face of strong evidence from colonies like Virginia that James II's cronies were still in place and oozing corruption from the body politic, Parliament had only moral leverage. That leverage was stronger under Walpole than in other eras, and over time the governments set in place in the 1690s developed the force of habit. But the king still had the ability – certainly with Parliament's consent – to overturn those governments, which is precisely what happened with the Coercive Acts, and why they held such threat. It made colonists in many regions remember what had happened under James II, remember their dependency – explicitly so. Indeed, the form of the new government imposed on Massachusetts in 1774 was almost identical to that imposed by James II in 1684: a royal governor and council, and suspension of town authority as well as trial by jury in many cases. It must have seemed eerily familiar and also real. These acts built upon George III's alliance – since his accession to the throne in 1760 – with Tories who explicitly did not care about sovereignty vested in the people (or consider that important). Thus, while Walpolean policies had encouraged the growth of the lower houses of assembly in the colonies, George III's ministers were quite pointedly restraining those assemblies. That was the underlying issue behind the opposition to Parliamentary taxation in the 1760s; the colonists were not represented, and the limited powers that they had gradually accrued over the course of the eighteenth century were being undermined.

The key word here is *limited* powers of the colonial assemblies. Most colonies' charters allowed the election of colonial assemblies that were supposed to approve local taxes, and could as well (with the assent of the appointed upper houses and governors) pass other laws. Such laws (and taxes) also had to be approved in England by oversight bodies, which included the Board of Trade, the Privy Council, and the king himself. Judges, too, held their seats at the pleasure of royal governors, and many positions of local governance were appointed. In Massachusetts in the 1760s, for example, more than 700 local officials were appointed at the pleasure of the crown, and could be dismissed at will.[24]

Rather than solely emphasizing the singular (and somewhat democratic) element of colonial governance, it is perhaps more accurate to say that the assemblies exercised somewhat of a check on the governors' and councils' sometimes arbitrary power, as well as that of the empire. Despite the increasing power of the elected assemblies during the eighteenth century, they still had limited powers, and could be called and dismissed at the pleasure of royal governors.[25] Royal governors and councils had considerable – if negotiated – power over the shaping of laws, which in turn helped to shape those who had authority, and what kind of authority. Imperial authorities also shaped institutions like the postal service, which helped to speed business and news and regulated commerce by limiting the printing of paper money.

In addition to approving laws, English courts also provided checks on colonial laws and policies. It is increasingly clear that we should see the empire as more like the federal system that came after the revolution, except that the federal part of it was mostly appointed and/or hereditary. Recent studies, such as Mary Sarah Bilder's *Transatlantic Constitution* and Daniel Hulsebosch's *Constituting Empire*, show beautifully how the Privy Council served as a court (comparable to the later US Supreme Court) that reviewed cases and set precedents that in turn shaped local decisions in Rhode Island and New York. Bilder has created a database of some of these appeals.[26]

---

[24] Richard L. Bushman, *King and People in Provincial Massachusetts* (Williamsburg, VA: Institute of Early American History and Culture, 1985), Chapter 2.

[25] See, for example, Jack P. Greene, *The Quest for Power: The Lower Houses of Assembly in the Southern Royal Colonies, 1689–1776* (Chapel Hill: University of North Carolina Press, 1963).

Likewise my own work shows how English legal institutions and courts and precedents influenced colonial laws and court decisions that impacted peoples' lives on a regular basis. Colonial court cases could also be appealed directly to English common law and Chancery courts.[27] Many of the key court decisions of the Privy Council related to trade and the ability to regulate the terms of exchange, contracts, and debts.

It is only when one sees empire on these many levels, in the way it helped to regulate and enforce so many kinds of relationship, not only of trade and commercial organization but also of personal authority, that its real power lies exposed. Consider only Virginia's 1705 law about who could testify in a court of law, which built on the English Test Acts of 1673. This law, which would later become the basic law that would prevent slaves from testifying against their masters, was in 1705 framed to fit with the earlier English law. It excluded not only people of non-Christian background, but also "recusant Catholics" (who refused to conform to the Church of England) and Jews.[28] Not to be able to testify is to be denied a crucial right, one we value greatly now but that also mattered then. How does one conduct business? Prosecute debts? Accuse an assaulter?

It is easy to ignore the struggle over the shape of the law – including the common law over these two centuries if we believe people like Burke, who notoriously saw the common law as unchanging. But it was changing, in sometimes profound ways, as part of these struggles over justice and authority, struggles that were negotiated within and throughout empire as different groups with different ideologies took control. It is a complex story, but an

---

[26] See https://amesfoundation.law.harvard.edu/ColonialAppeals.

[27] Mary Sarah Bilder, *The Transatlantic Constitution: Colonial Legal Culture and the Empire* (Cambridge, MA: Harvard University Press, 2004); Daniel J. Hulsebosch, *Constituting Empire: New York and the Transformation of Constitutionalism in the Atlantic World, 1664–1830* (Chapel Hill: University of North Carolina Press, 2006); Holly Brewer, *By Birth or Consent: Children, Law, and the Anglo-American Revolution in Authority* (Chapel Hill: University of North Carolina Press, 2005). Colonists used English legal guides routinely as the basis of legal interpretation. Colonists also appealed cases directly to common law and equity courts, often using a legal fiction that the case originated in London, which became the catch-all jurisdiction. One such example is the 1677 case of *Butts* v. *Penny*. For more on the impact of the high courts of common law on slavery in the empire, see Holly Brewer, "Creating a Common Law of Slavery," Yale Law School, 2014, https://papers.ssrn.com/sol3/papers.cfm?abstract_id=3828635.

[28] Hening, *Statutes at Large*, vol. III, 276–8, Chapter XIX, Session XXXI (October 1705): "That popish recusants convict, negroes, mulattoes and Indian servants, and others, not being christians, shall be deemed and taken to be persons incapable in law, to be witnesses in any cases whatsoever."

important one. "English liberties" were not enshrined in English law in 1607 nor yet fully in 1776, but certain of them had gained broader adherence and application.[29]

Putting the empire back in has many effects on how we think about the coming of the American Revolution. We can see, aside from anything else, much better how the colonists were already paying taxes without consent – but they were relatively silent taxes, going directly to the crown, and collected in England. We can understand both the growth in the power of the houses of assembly – and the undercutting of it by the Coercive Acts in 1774 – as growing out of contests over political ideology and who was in power (and the degree of their power) in England.[30] We can understand on a much deeper level why English policies toward the colonies were so inconsistent between 1763 and 1776, swaying back and forth between Whigs and Tories as they too struggled for power in England itself in that crucial decade. We can understand that the threat that many colonists felt to their "liberties" was much more real than we usually give them credit for. But most of all we can begin to understand just how momentous that revolution was – the decision and the action – even though some people stumbled into it.

The crucial role of negotiation (and misunderstanding) in the coming of the revolution is clear in Alexis de Tocqueville's interview in 1831 with Charles Carroll, aged 95, the last surviving signer of the Declaration of Independence. Carroll then owned more than 13,000 acres and 300 slaves, regretted the loss of "our aristocratic institutions" and the growth in power of "the mob" in the wake of the revolution. Tocqueville reported that "Everything in his conversation breathed the tone and ideas of the English aristocracy." He remarked to Carroll that he sounded like an English aristocrat in his disapproval of all the legal changes that had come in the wake of the American Revolution. He then asked the question that any good historian would ask ... if you did not believe in the principles of the Declaration of

---

[29] David Lieberman, *The Province of Legislation Determined* (Cambridge: Cambridge University Press, 1989); Brewer, *By Birth or Consent*; J. C. D. Clark, *The Language of Liberty 1660–1832: Political Discourse and Social Dynamics in the Anglo-American World* (Cambridge: Cambridge University Press, 1994); Caroline Robbins, *The Eighteenth-Century Commonwealthman: Studies in the Transmission, Development and Circumstance of English Liberal Thought from the Restoration of Charles II until the War with the Thirteen Colonies* (New York: Atheneum, 1968); Bernard Bailyn, *The Ideological Origins of the American Revolution* (Cambridge, MA: Belknap Press of Harvard University Press, 1971).

[30] John Brewer, *Party Ideology and Popular Politics at the Accesssion of George III* (Cambridge: Cambridge University Press, 1976).

The Myth Of "Salutary Neglect"

Independence, why did you sign it? Carroll's answer was that he thought that the king and Parliament would back down, would "make up with us" just as they had in the previous decade.[31] He did not expect revolution.

Carroll was obviously not representative of all those who signed the Declaration, or even of all the "great proprietors" who owned plantations in the South (as Tocqueville put it), but his response helps to illuminate an underlying theme of this chapter. The growth of English liberties in America was not a natural consequence of the frontier emerging somehow seamlessly from a state of nature. The political, legal, and economic situations in the colonies were constantly negotiated in a struggle for power that was occurring not only on the level of empire but in England itself. "Salutary neglect" was largely a myth. Certainly the word "neglect" is a misleading one, implying a complete absence of metropolitan power, and the phrase sets up a dichotomy that leads toward fundamental misrepresentations about the character of the British empire in the Americas and indeed around the world. To the degree that such "salutary neglect" existed (that Walpole allowed smuggling, for example), it was part of this negotiation and struggle over the meaning and terms of power. While some could escape the power of empire in the short term, it was constantly tugging at their sleeves. One could take up land in the "wilderness," for example (assuming one was not killed by the natives upon whom one was encroaching), but the only way one owned it was by getting a legal title – and that demanded negotiation with all the ligaments of colonial authority, from surveyor and courts to secretary of the colony. How one could develop it, and what one could grow, how one could pass it on, were often regulated by laws that might emerge in the colonies but were subject to royal veto. Other regulations were imposed directly by imperial authorities.

All of this brings us back to Edmund Burke the Whig (as he was in 1775). He wanted to see liberties as flourishing naturally in the New World, fostered only by neglect. In fact, the growth of the institutional structures that supported "English liberties" and representative government was part of this broad negotiation over power in which he was intimately involved in Ireland. American colonies became his state of nature whose very existence was a weapon with which to circumscribe the power of George III in England. Just so, such principles had served the same purpose earlier for

---

[31] I discuss Tocqueville's interview in Holly Brewer, "Tocqueville as Historian of the Struggle between Democracy and Aristocracy in America," *Tocqueville Review* 27:2 (2006), 381–402: 395.

John Locke when he wrote his *Two Treatises of Government*, and, as I have argued elsewhere, when he and others who had helped William and Mary in the Dutch Republic to plan revolution sought to reform those colonies in its wake, when they were appointed to the Board of Trade by William III. While they did push through some reforms, their efforts at reform were cut short by the early death of William III from a hunting accident. Who was in power in England mattered for the shape of empire.[32]

The fierce jockeying for power under George III, who sought to grasp some of the tattered mantle of divine right that his Stuart forebears had once claimed, helps to explain the disjointed and ineffective bungling that characterized the decade before 1775. Earlier in his speech quoted above Burke acknowledged that Parliament's "frequent changes" in policy over the preceding decade had led the colonists to a state of "continual agitation." Every supposed remedy given by Parliament had led to "an heightening of the distemper."[33] This inconsistent policy lost George both his legitimacy and finally his colonies. The degree of incompetence and mismanagement (by General Gage, for example) would be amusing had it not had such consequences. But Gage's actions (and his failure to act, exemplified by his lenience in not arresting conspirators) can only be understood in this broader context, of a two-century-long struggle over power and principles in England and its empire, a struggle that shaped in different ways England's two seventeenth-century revolutions, and that contributed heavily to America's own.

---

[32] Holly Brewer, "Slavery, Sovereignty, and 'Inheritable Blood': Reconsidering John Locke and the Origins of American Slavery," *American Historical Review* 122:4 (2017): 1038–78.

[33] Burke, *Works*, vol. 1, 181–2, same speech, during debates over Coercive Acts, in opposition.

7
The British Atlantic on the Eve of American Independence

PATRICK GRIFFIN

Ordering the land is easy. Terrestrial space lends itself to borders. Rivers and mountains are natural boundaries that can be repurposed as lines to separate one group from another. Lines drawn on maps also can inscribe workable boundaries. Though more permeable than natural barriers, they can be manned, defended, and policed. Holding the line at either natural or man-made borders on the land depends on resources and will. Maps sustain and presuppose at least an illusion of control and boundedness, and, in some cases, an actual mastery.[1]

Ordering the sea can be as difficult as plowing it. Simón Bolívar used this image again and again, purportedly too as his dying words, to describe the difficulties of governing a post-revolutionary society. But his notion of plowing the sea speaks to the challenges of bringing sovereign order to it. It does not lend itself to lines. It is featureless. And it must be shared. International law and admiralty law, of course, recognize this reality. So, too, do charts. Charts, commonly regarded as the maps of the sea, do not function as maps at all. They are tied to winds that criss-cross and to routes that intersect, where ships are likely to track given what nature allows.

The crisis that would eventuate in the American Revolution began as Britain tried to do the impossible: to plow the sea by trying to map sovereignty onto an oceanic system. This did not mean that British officials attempted to plant their flag on an ocean, even if, as Benjamin Franklin conceded in 1766 when questioned by British Members of Parliament, the sea was theirs.[2] Moreover, this does not mean that they tried to change in some fundamental way how admiralty or maritime law functioned. Rather,

---

[1] On maps, see Max Edelson, *The New Map of Empire: How Britain Imagined America before Independence* (Cambridge, MA: Harvard University Press, 2017).

[2] Franklin quoted in Eliga Gould, *Among the Powers of the Earth: The American Revolution and the Making of a New World Empire* (Cambridge, MA: Harvard University Press, 2012), 82.

they faced the urgent need to bring control to a watery space, not to contain the ocean or halt the proverbial tides but to manage the implications of all the traffic that moved upon it. The British in the 1760s and 1770s needed to harness the promise of an ocean and manage how it was exploited and to contest the ability of their subjects in America from being able to do so. They were not alone in aspiring to plow the Atlantic. But they had the belief that they could, and this led to resistance in the provinces, those places across the ocean.

This chapter will explore how the transformation of the Atlantic system during the late seventeenth and early eighteenth centuries created "a British Atlantic world." It will do so from a comparative perspective; for that is the only way to properly appreciate the process and the crisis that followed. The British Atlantic experience represented a variation on a common European imperial theme. For the British case, what had been semi-autonomous sets of colonies in the Caribbean and on the eastern seaboard of North America through the integration of the Atlantic were drawn into a British economic and cultural orbit. The movement of unprecedented numbers of men and women from the Old World to the New, a steady flow of British manufactured goods in the same direction, and the spread of British ideas about self, society, and government to the colonies transformed colonies and metropole and bound them together as never before. The end result was that by time of the Seven Years' War what had been English colonies in America had become British provinces. The change would affect how men and women in British North America defined themselves and conceived of their relationship to the metropole. British Americans had become adaptable peoples; they also felt a simultaneous attraction to and repulsion from the center, much like members of the Irish Ascendancy and Scottish lowlanders.

From the center, things appeared more complex. For integration was tied into European power politics, and the systemization of the Atlantic led to confusing imperial entanglements that had to be sorted out. In the years before the American Revolution, the British hoped to do just that, to try to fix the Atlantic, a task that other powers conceded could not be accomplished. With changes to the Atlantic, with the space becoming a system, they had to figure out both how to profit from the system and how to police it. That meant they had to conceive of empire anew. What follows is a discussion of those changes and then how the British in the years after the Seven Years' War faced the same sort of challenges that other European powers confronted as all hoped to impose sovereignty onto a dynamically changing system. The British just happened to come the closest to pulling off the impossible. They did so through reform. In an increasingly competitive world, they had to try to manage the ocean and harness what had become its defining features: its unruliness and the entanglements and connections that had emerged over the preceding century. From this perspective, the crisis leading to the American Revolution revolved around the implications of ordering space in new ways and trying to bring rule to unruliness, to untangle entanglements, and to disconnect the connections that made the Atlantic system as dynamic as it was. All of this, of course, touched off a provincial response.

This "provincial dilemma" not only entailed a reconsideration of belonging within empire; it also necessitated British provincials in America to reconsider their status within their home societies. Atlantic integration depended on the exploitation of the enslaved and the appropriation of more land that had been held by Natives. Through systemic changes, therefore, British North American elites also had to devise new justifications for the mastery of their own provincial societies. Thus, the new imperial dilemma would also exacerbate tensions within British American provinces. The chapter will culminate with an examination of how, with the crises set off by the Stamp Act and the Townshend Duties, "the British Atlantic world" was poised to explode.[3]

Entanglement

Entanglement, alas, has become an all-too-trendy term, one almost as ubiquitous as "Atlantic" or "the global." Like the related idea of "connected history," it speaks in almost platitudinous fashion to how all history is truly transnational and how events, processes, and the peoples that negotiate both are shaped by the things that happen in many places. It suggests just how messy and complex things can be once we understand nation as an historical construct and see that global processes determined much of the local. In fact, it puts a label on what most good historians intuitively do. Yet the eighteenth-century Atlantic was one place-in-time when and where the term fits. Peoples, lines of trade, intellectual currents, and imperial aspirations were all knotted and tangled in ways that presented unprecedented opportunities for some and almost insuperable challenges for others.[4]

---

[3] For a fuller consideration of the themes raised in this chapter, see Patrick Griffin, *The Age of Atlantic Revolution: The Fall and Rise of a Connected World* (New Haven: Yale University Press, 2023).

[4] See Eliga H. Gould, "Entangled Histories, Entangled Worlds: The English-Speaking Atlantic as a Spanish Periphery," *American Historical Review* 112:3 (2007), 764–86. Also see Jorge Cañizares-Esguerra, "Entangled Histories: Borderland Historiographies in

We know part of this story well. In the eighteenth century, the accelerated movement of people, goods, and ideas transformed the Atlantic, changing it from something we could call a world into something resembling a system. We use the word "network" to explain what happened, and this notion, which can be likened to intersecting or radiating lines on a chart, gets at what was occurring in the system in the years before the Seven Years' War. At the most basic level, ships came and went with greater frequency. In their hulls were transported the produce cultivated in the New World destined for the Old, and the goods made in Europe bound for the Americas. Migrants also came and went. Also generally moving in this westerly direction were the ideas that people used to rationalize the transformations in production, consumption, and interactions that were increasingly defining the lives of all peoples who lived on or near the Atlantic. And with time, as the century progressed, the reach of the Atlantic extended further and further into the North American continent, just as it captured the imagination of more and more people further east in Europe.[5]

We also recognize the drivers of change. Free migrants from places like Ireland and Germany peopled North America, soon followed by Scots, as part of a massive shift in population westward. Here they displaced growing numbers of Native Americans, and with this exchange, a land-rich New World began to function as a safety valve for a labor-saturated Old World.[6] These people represented a broader transformation that defined the period and place. With the eighteenth century, for the British world in particular, systemic dynamics began to reach further and further from the center. The people who would now move came from the margins of the system. An English Atlantic was becoming a British Atlantic. With the

---

New Clothes?," *American Historical Review* 112:3 (2007), 787–99; Jorge Cañizares-Esguerra, ed., "Introduction," *Entangled Empires: The Anglo-Iberian Atlantic, 1500–1830* (Philadelphia: University of Pennsylvania Press, 2018). On how the idea of "connected history" works, though without an in-depth discussion, read the series of essays by Sanjay Subrahmanyan, *Explorations in Connected History: From the Tagus to the Ganges* (New Delhi: Oxford University Press, 2005).

[5] Nicholas P. Canny and Philip D. Morgan, "Introduction," in *Oxford Handbook of the Atlantic World, c. 1450–c. 1850* (Oxford: Oxford University Press, 2011), 1–17; Ian K. Steele, *The English Atlantic, 1675–1740: An Exploration of Communication and Community* (New York: Oxford University Press, 1986).

[6] Bernard Bailyn, *The Peopling of British North America: An Introduction* (New York: Vintage, 1988). On movement as the chief driver of change, see Patrick Griffin, "Mobility and the Movement of Peoples," in Carla Pestana, Paul Mapp, and Eliga Gould, eds., *Cambridge History of America and the World* (New York: Cambridge University Press, 2022), 115–202.

movement of people, the space began to work in systemic fashion. More central to systematization, slave labor, premised on the coerced movement of millions of Africans from the Old to the New World, sustained the developing whole. Slavery drove the system, with addictive substantives like sugar, coffee, and tobacco underscoring inhuman suffering and generating massive wealth. The plantations on which slaves toiled and sugar was grown propelled integration within the system and the development of metropolitan economies.[7] Consolidation of the Atlantic, then, stemmed from free and unfree movement, the labor it provided, and what it produced. Think here of the growth of South Carolina as a slave society dependent on rice production and the increasingly large migrant population in fertile backcountry regions of Pennsylvania and Virginia, and how both yoked the peripheries to the center in more thoroughgoing ways.[8]

The changes transformed scale and the nature of space. At its most basic, the ocean became less like a barrier and more of a highway. The movement of goods, of course, served as the most visible expression of development.[9] Markets grew, the world heaved to supply and demand, speculation increased, and new wealth was generated. The flow of goods and peoples across the ocean, then, bound the Atlantic together more tightly than before, generating as it did new wants and needs.[10] The British, of course, were not the only ones to enter this brave new world. The French, with the development of sugar production in places like Saint-Domingue, the Portuguese with Brazilian gold mining and coffee and sugar, and the Spanish with the growth of chattel slavery and increased agricultural production were experiencing the same sort of system-wide changes, including the movement of free and unfree people.

The changes had dramatic implications for colonists in America and the nature of their societies. Before the eighteenth century, diverse colonies had become stable through conquest of Natives on the littoral. They were defined by a persistent localism, by the distinctive nature of their origins, and by

---

[7] Trevor Burnard and John Garrigus, *The Plantation Machine: Atlantic Capitalism in French Saint-Domingue and British Jamaica* (Philadelphia: University of Pennsylvania Press, 2016).
[8] Ira Berlin, *Many Thousands Gone: The First Two Centuries of Slavery in North America* (Cambridge, MA: Harvard University Press, 1998).
[9] On this dynamic, see T. H. Breen, *The Marketplace of Revolution: How Consumer Politics Shaped American Independence* (New York: Oxford University Press, 2004); Bailyn, *The Peopling of British North America*.
[10] Joseph C. Miller, ed., *The Princeton Companion to Atlantic History* (Princeton: Princeton University Press, 2015).

English custom and culture.[11] And they were bound to the center as spokes on a wheel. These settlements proved as diverse as they were simple. There was trade within the cisatlantic world, but most tended to be relatively homogeneous and isolated settlements that were taking on the rudiments of societies. The changes to the Atlantic bound each to the center as never before. Moreover, ties to places in the cisatlantic, especially the Caribbean, became much more robust. Cities like Philadelphia became entrepôts within the broader Atlantic, sites that tied Atlantic commerce to the productivity of frontier regions that were peopled by new migrants streaming across the sea. The city, in fact, bound farms down the Great Wagon Road as far south as North Carolina to ports throughout the Atlantic. Migrants ventured down the road to new settlements; the produce they produced moved up it, destined to fill the hulls of ships owned by hyper-connected Quaker merchants. Charleston developed as a city within a broader slave society binding West Africa and the Caribbean to plantations and to the metropole. Boston became, as one scholar argues, a city-state bound to the Atlantic economy. As its trade developed, its hinterland grew accordingly. It had started that way. The changes to the Atlantic, to which it contributed, accelerated development in this direction.[12]

What we might not have appreciated is how knotted this space became with integration. The same ties binding South America to Spain, Brazil to Portugal, Saint-Domingue and New France to France, and the British Caribbean and North American mainland to Britain and Ireland twisted around each other. Though in a remarkably short period of time English, French, Spanish, and Portuguese societies in the Americas were tied more closely to the metropole by economic and cultural links, they were bound together as well by licit and illicit trade.[13] French trade with the rest of the world increased by more than four times, and with its colonial holdings,

---

[11] See Lockridge's new introduction in Kenneth A. Lockridge, *A New England Town: The First Hundred Years* (New York: W. W. Norton, 1985).

[12] April Lee Hatfield, *Atlantic Virginia: Intercolonial Relations in the Seventeenth Century* (Philadelphia: University of Pennsylvania Press, 2007); Mark Peterson, *The City-State of Boston: The Rise and Fall of an Atlantic Power* (Princeton: Princeton University Press, 2019); Frederick Tolles, *Meeting House and Counting House: The Quaker Merchants of Colonial Philadelphia, 1682–1763* (New York: W. W. Norton, 1948); Dylan Leblanc, "The Empire in Chains: Government Men and the Atlantic Slave Trade, 1670–1770," Ph.D. dissertation, University of Notre Dame, 2019.

[13] Even Prussia was tied more securely to the New World. Images of the monarch appeared on enameled snuff boxes, filled with tobacco from America traded by other nations. See Christopher M. Clark, *Iron Kingdom: The Rise and Downfall of Prussia, 1600–1947* (Cambridge, MA: Harvard University Press, 2006).

tenfold, over the course of the century. Much of this growth, we know, was based on trade with and for other Europeans that flouted laws. In the French case, smuggling demonstrated how the new system that was emerging was outstripping political controls put in place in the previous century to ensure colonies served metropoles. But the French were, in fact lagging behind. The Dutch and the British proved stealthier and more adept at the circumvention of laws.[14] The most prominent smuggling arrangement was called the "Dutch trade," the illicit movement of goods between the Dutch and Danish ports in the Caribbean, Cap Français and Port-au-Prince in Saint-Domingue, and places in British North America, such as the city that specialized in such traffic: New York.[15] The French, in fact, needed Anglo-Americans, who provided a great deal of the timber products that went into building sugar mills in Saint-Domingue. This clandestine trade, illicit as well, proved vital to France's sugar and Atlantic maritime industry, which was the most dynamic sector of the whole French economy.[16]

All were tied together, particularly as smuggling became the chief economic activity for some regions. Even runaway slaves participated in these economies.[17] Gold from mines in Brazil, for instance, proved critical to Britain's ability to wage war in the eighteenth century.[18] The porousness of the vast Spanish empire, spanning two continents, made it difficult to police, and in some regions – such as the Spanish Main and the east coast of Central America – smuggling became a way of life. It was to these places that the finished goods of the British and Dutch came, while what was locally produced left. So enmeshed with others was the Spanish New World economy that one scholar claims they became the very model of the "entanglements" that made this world go round. Even traditional enemies like the British used Spanish smugglers as go-betweens with the even more hated French. And, as we know, hyper-connected Irish traders in the British

---

[14] Michael Kwass, "The Global Underground: Smuggling, Rebellion, and the Origins of the French Revolution," in Suzanne Desan, Lynn Hunt, and William Max Nelson, eds., *The French Revolution in Global Perspective* (Ithaca, NY: Cornell University Press, 2013).
[15] Thomas M. Truxes, *Defying Empire: Trading with the Enemy in Colonial New York* (New Haven: Yale University Press, 2008), 51.
[16] Kenneth Banks, *Chasing Empire across the Sea: Communications and the State in the French Atlantic, 1713–1763* (Montreal: McGill-Queen's University Press, 2002).
[17] Jeremy Adelman, *Sovereignty and Revolution in the Iberian Atlantic* (Princeton: Princeton University Press, 2006), 21; Colin Jones, *The Great Nation: France from Louis XV to Napoleon 1715–99* (New York: Columbia University Press, 2002), 345, 361–2.
[18] D. W. Jones, *War and Economy in the Age of William III and Marlborough* (Oxford: Oxford University Press, 1988).

Isles, the Caribbean, and North Atlantic ports used their ability to move between French and British worlds to deliver the goods of all to all.[19]

The growth of smuggling demonstrated the convoluted ways this Atlantic system was developing. Spanish silver mined in South America was the currency of choice for merchants from Asia who sold their tea to factors from the East India Company, who then shipped it to warehouses in England, from whence middlemen sent it to America, where it was sweetened with sugar produced by enslaved persons from Africa in the Caribbean. If they could get their hands on cheaper tea, North American colonists would trade with the French and the Dutch, who used their own permeable networks.[20] Throughout the Atlantic, actors crossed theoretically sovereign boundaries with abandon, and much of the economic vitality and cultural energy of the Atlantic was sustained through such crossings. Entrepôts in both the Old and New Worlds depended on the autonomy to cross boundaries.[21] Even Bostonians, the people we would consider the most isolated in America, depended on Latin America for precious metal to mint coins. They needed European markets to sell their cod. They specialized in salvaging Spanish wrecks. And individuals like Thomas and John Amory and John Hancock depended on smuggled sugar products to distill rum.[22]

Nowhere were these growing entanglements more complex than with the slave trade. The first few decades of the eighteenth century witnessed all sorts of traders, acting almost as independent free agents, vying with one another to bring humans across the ocean. The British would play a prominent role in this burgeoning arena of free and unregulated trade. In fact, it was unregulatable. With the end of the Royal African Company's monopoly on the slave trade, all sorts of men now attempted to enrich themselves. And

---

[19] Wim Klooster, *Revolutions in the Atlantic World: A Comparative History* (New York: New York University Press, 2009), 122; Gould, "Entangled Histories"; Edwin Williamson, *Penguin History of Latin America* (London: Allen Lane, 1992), 106, 184. On the Irish, see Truxes, *Defying Empire*.

[20] On this, see Jane Merritt, *The Trouble with Tea: The Politics of Consumption in the Eighteenth-Century Global Economy* (Baltimore, MD: Johns Hopkins University Press, 2017), 4–5, 29, 52–3.

[21] On these themes for the French, see Kwass, "The Global Underground"; Lynn Hunt, "The Global Financial Origins of 1789," in Suzanne Desan, Lynn Hunt, and William Max Nelson, eds., *The French Revolution in Global Perspective* (Ithaca, NY: Cornell University Press, 2013), 15–44.

[22] Peterson, *The City-State of Boston*. Also see Jack Greene, *Pursuits of Happiness: The Social Development of Early Modern British Colonies and the Formation of American Culture* (Chapel Hill: University of North Carolina Press, 1988).

those who could ship the enslaved in the most cost-effective way could supply all empires, whether licitly or illicitly. The places that such trade occurred typified the changing Atlantic, as they were dominated by African creoles who worked with traders from any number of nations speaking any number of languages.[23] Moreover, after the War of the Spanish Succession the British were granted what was called the "asiento," or the monopoly in shipping enslaved persons from West Africa to Spanish America. This, if anything, increased smuggling and international tensions. It also hastened the development of the plantation economy of Cuba when it, too, began producing sugar and relying solely on African labor to do so.[24] From slaving factories in West Africa, British and Dutch merchants supplied the plantations of all imperial powers in the New World.[25]

Exchange and Change

What had been discrete Atlantic worlds were now intersecting as never before, and integration led to all sorts of Atlantic entanglements and parallels. The period created "a shared world of experience and taste" for many throughout the Atlantic.[26] Merchants, of course, specialized in trade from one metropole to its colonies; but the most adept also mastered trade in persons and in goods between imperial worlds. This Atlantic traffic could be considered a pure, undiluted form of capitalism. Though facilitated by the state, states did not have the capacity to regulate. Laws, of course, had been established earlier on to stop such interactions, but officials, who could be bribed, ignored them. Some elites in the center had a stake in boundary-crossing, as wealth was increasingly tied to the fortunes of colonies that could no longer be kept within prescribed bounds. And so, officials bowed to riches and, by knowingly looking the other way and encouraging corruption, they greased the

---

[23] For this dynamic, see LeBlanc, "The Empire in Chains." On creoles, and their outsized role, see Berlin, *Many Thousands Gone*.

[24] Williamson, *Penguin History of Latin America*, 142.

[25] On smuggling and British connivance, see Edmund Morgan and Helen S. Morgan, *The Stamp Act Crisis: Prologue to Revolution* (Chapel Hill: University of North Carolina Press, 1962).

[26] Zara Anishanslin, *Portrait of a Woman in Silk: Hidden Histories of the British Atlantic World* (New Haven: Yale University Press, 2016), 10; T. H. Breen, "Baubles of Britain: The American and Consumer Revolutions of the Eighteenth Century," *Past and Present* 119 (1988), 73. Also see Janet Polasky, *Revolution without Borders: The Call to Liberty in the Atlantic World* (New Haven: Yale University Press, 2015).

wheels of untrammeled exchange that was remaking the Atlantic. The British were just one group to do so.[27]

The same goes for the developing provincial elite, or creoles, who were growing wealthy through entangled trade of all sorts, even if officials worried that the developing system was becoming uncontrollable by the center. This, too, represents the great story of the age, as those born into colonies now considered themselves provincials of broader worlds tied to the center. Think here of the planters in Barbados or Jamaica. Many had secured enough wealth to build townhouses in London and to enjoy the best of all worlds, as Voltaire's Candide would have said. They, like other colonial elites, had a commitment to ruling their own societies and becoming lords of all they surveyed. They also yearned to have standing in the center. We have long called this crisis over how a creole elite struggled to define itself a "provincial dilemma," one made manifest in intellectual life and in even the ways they posed for portraits. Painters like John Singleton Copley, the Boston-born son of Irish immigrants who was also a product and agent of a changing Atlantic, was able through his work to capture this dilemma on canvas and to provide a creole elite with the ability to demonstrate their status in the periphery and in the center. They surrounded themselves with the goods of empire, those status symbols that came from the British center that could demonstrate to all that they dominated their own local societies. Copley, unsurprisingly, painted portraits of the Amory brothers and of John Hancock, urbane men of trade and proud Britons.[28] These merchants had become both "Citizens of the World" and enthusiastic British subjects. So had planters in the South and in the Caribbean. The same, it goes without saying, applies to the wealthy and connected in Philadelphia and New York.[29]

The implications of all of this change proved as varied as change itself. Let us start with subtle effects. The newly entangled space rested on oppression and opportunism, both of which challenged older ways of knowing and understanding. At their most radical, the ideas that traveled through the

---

[27] Vincent Brown, "The Eighteenth Century: Growth, Crisis, and Revolution," in Joseph C. Miller, ed., *The Princeton Companion to Atlantic History* (Princeton: Princeton University Press, 2015), 36–45.

[28] Jane Kamensky, *A Revolution in Color: The World of John Singleton Copley* (New York: W. W. Norton, 2016). On the dilemma of provincials, see Bernard Bailyn and John Clive, "England's Cultural Provinces: Scotland and America," *William and Mary Quarterly*, 3rd ser., 11:2 (1954), 200–13; Patrick Griffin, "The Birth, Death, and Resurrection of the Provincial Dilemma," *History Compass* 9 (2011), 134–46.

[29] David Hancock, *Citizens of the World: London Merchants and the Integration of the British Atlantic Community* (New York: Cambridge University Press, 1997); Gould, *Among the Powers of the Earth*, 87, 90.

space and attempted to rationalize it questioned older notions about social organization and political organization. Church hierarchies and older assumptions about politics and what made a person a person now came under scrutiny as a vibrant press allowed for dissemination of ideas that had arisen in tandem with the entangled Atlantic. Developments as diverse as the Great Awakening in the British North American colonies and the rise of Enlightenment sensibilities in France, Rome, Portugal, and Spain, which challenged clerical establishments, all spoke to how the transformation of the Atlantic from a world into a system encouraged a democratizing impulse. The Great Awakening, in fact, can be considered a British Atlantic variation on the common theme. The Irish and the Scots, we have learned, embraced ideas about social improvement or university learning to negotiate a changing world. Men and women from American provincial societies flocked to hear New Lights lionize the breaking down of old boundaries, both territorial and ecclesiastical, and to tell all that redemption was an individual struggle. Itinerant preachers were not so much reacting to wrenching change as the epitome of it. These men were, in fact, the greatest exports from Britain that were yoking Old World to New World as never before.[30]

Such notions also spoke to the ways that contexts were shifting. New vistas were opening for untold numbers of persons, new possibilities were emerging, just as new inhuman institutions were taking shape to provide labor and claim land. In a world of free agents, often exploiting one another, the idea of the individual had great purchase, as did new notions of human difference and race to justify such exploitation. The same held for the autonomy of travel, which freed people from older obligations to the land and to institutions like the Church. The economy, politics, and society became, as trite as it sounds, questions to be addressed, and the answers to them could no longer be assumed. Each nation had a different term for what could be regarded as a process, sensibility, movement, or transnational spirit. Enlightenment thought and religious revival, though opposed in articulation, stemmed from many of the same international opportunities and

---

[30] On this, see Franco Venturi, *The End of the Old Regime in Europe 1776–1789* (Princeton: Princeton University Press, 1991). On the Awakening as an Atlantic event, see Frank Lambert, *Pedlar in Divinity: George Whitefield and the Transatlantic Revivals* (Princeton: Princeton University Press, 1993); Timothy Hall, *Contested Boundaries: Itinerancy and the Reshaping of the Colonial American Religious World* (Durham, NC: Duke University Press, 1994). For the Scots and the Irish and integration, see James Livesey, *Civil Society and Empire: Ireland and Scotland in the Eighteenth-Century Atlantic World* (New Haven: Yale University Press, 2009).

constraints.³¹ They were addressing the same implications presented by entanglements.

The movement of ideas made for criss-crossing streams of information, enabled by a vibrant print culture. What made its way to print justified, rationalized, and allowed what was happening. Print carried new philosophical theories that could be consumed throughout the entangled Atlantic; it also carried news of what goods could be purchased at trading centers and what itinerant preachers were coming to town. It also conveyed a great many debates, some of which touched on the ways that people were trying to come to terms with the dynamic changes increasingly defining their lives. Benjamin Franklin's preoccupation with both "liberal" ideals and with the circulation of money and "currency" throughout the Atlantic system stemmed from his access to print in his brother's newspaper shop and then his realization that print, with his ownership of the *Pennsylvania Gazette*, made this world go round every bit as much as trade. Not coincidentally, he saw to it that George Whitefield's visits were publicized in his paper, just as he published essays arguing that paper currency would entice even more migrants to Philadelphia. He suggested that Americans needed to embrace the burgeoning system's imperatives.³²

Some implications of the entangled systematization of space were more easily discernible than shifting ideas. The nature of warfare in the eighteenth century, for instance, reflected Atlantic-wide changes. Throughout much of the early part of the century, European nations and their respective colonies were engaged in a succession of wars over European dynastic rivalries, and, as such, conflict centered on Europe. But as the century wore on, and as the Atlantic grew into an integrated system, warfare increasingly began to include the Americas, and beginning with the War of Spanish Succession, further exacerbated rivalries over America. For dynastic considerations now had Atlantic implications, and what happened across an unregulated space complicated power relations for Europe. Most simply, the acceleration of capital investment in land, goods, and labor provided the state with the fiscal capacity to engage in far-off wars.³³ The state could, of course, always raise taxes and levy war. Now it could do so in ways previously unimaginable. Its

---

[31] John Robertson, *The Enlightenment: A Very Short Introduction* (Oxford: Oxford University Press, 2015).

[32] Carla Mulford, *Benjamin Franklin and the Ends of Empire* (New York: Oxford University Press, 2018).

[33] John Brewer, *Sinews of Power: War, Money, and the English State* (Cambridge, MA: Harvard University Press, 1990); Banks, *Chasing Empire*.

reach now could extend around the world, and, unsurprisingly, the conflicts in which states became involved grew over the eighteenth century. They became longer in duration; they involved more people; their intensity increased; and they could extend beyond Europe, including even flashpoints in provincial regions where imperial lines crossed or butted up against one another. Think here of South Carolina, with the Spanish to the south, or New England, with the French just to the north. All European powers played this game, as survival in an anarchic and increasingly competitive world dictated as much. As one scholar argues, the Atlantic had become "an increasingly explosive, violent, and profitable knot."[34]

The Atlantic was shifting power from the East to the West. The economy of the British metropole, for example, was growing dependent on its colonists as both producers and, most especially, as consumers. The importance of colonies was just as pronounced for the French, not merely because of trade, but because of international struggles over power. The French had, up to this point in the eighteenth century, focused their energies on the Continent. The succession of wars that increasingly involved holdings across the Atlantic in America reoriented strategy toward extra-European regions. For the French, the pull west proved to be inexorable. Though the state had not tapped into new wealth as fully as it would have liked, mercantile interests were growing more and more wealthy in the unregulated Atlantic. The British had willy-nilly encouraged its people to compete relentlessly in the world, all the while winking and nodding as mercantilist trading rules were flouted. Quite quickly, the old rules of Continental focus and rivalry seemed to have been compromised, requiring new spending on troops and navies with an eye toward the Atlantic.[35]

The Unstable Stasis of the Atlantic System

The system, therefore, proved to be as unstable as it was dynamic. It captured the energies of people, often in the most coercive ways, and transformed such energy into further integration and into wealth. States had visions of regulating their own imperial claims, to make straight the tangles of integration and so rationalize the great levels of development that defined the space. But the bumptiousness of that development, as well as the

---

[34] Adelman, *Sovereignty and Revolution*, 17.
[35] On this, see Bailey Stone, *The Genesis of the French Revolution: A Global-Historical Interpretation* (New York: Cambridge University Press, 1994).

ways so many claims intersected and clashed, made such pretensions impossible to act upon, especially as states did not have the capacity or the reach to remake the Atlantic as they saw fit. The system, to use a scientific metaphor, had reached an unstable stasis. And because the future of all of the Atlantic empires now rested in this space, the tangles were sure to ensnare. Certainly, one of the greatest figures of the Enlightenment saw things this way. Adam Smith foresaw an Atlantic in which states would try to control persons and markets to increase power for the struggles they faced in Europe. The "jealousy of trade," as Smith put it, would lead to more frequent and more intensive conflicts.[36]

All played out in the epic conflict of the period, the Seven Years' War. Fittingly, the war began on the furthest verge of this changing world, the Ohio Country, where British provincial speculators and traders bet that those same settlers that hastened systemic integration would soon be streaming, and it would soon engulf the integrated whole. Names are telling. Americans called it, of course, "the French and Indian War." Ultimately, they saw it through the prism of immediate threats to their lives, liberty, and property. Europeans used the more sanitized term "the Seven Years' War," referring to the formal declaration of war in 1756 and its end through treaty in 1763. Whatever the name, it grew, at least in part, out of the changes wrought in the Atlantic that defined the eighteenth century. And it, too, just like ideas and the bodies and goods moving across the ocean would also serve as midwife to further systemic development. In other words, it arose from the world it had a hand in creating and sustaining.[37] As armies grew, as economies became more dependent on their colonies with increased demand enveloping Atlantic societies, as the slave-based plantations became the engine room of capital development, as more and more men and women were displaced and encouraged to venture overseas by the new systemic imperatives, competitive stakes were heightened as never before. The so-called militarized capitalism that was driving and defining the Atlantic dictated that here an epic story of eighteenth-century development would

---

[36] On this, see Robertson, *The Enlightenment*, 71, 78.
[37] Fred Anderson, *The Crucible of War: The Seven Years' War and the Fate of Empire in British North America, 1754–1766* (New York: Knopf, 2000); Patrick Griffin, *The Townshend Moment: The Making of Empire and Revolution in the Eighteenth Century* (New Haven: Yale University Press, 2017). For a discussion of names, and the Atlantic dynamics driving the War, see Patrick Griffin, "'The War with Many Names': The Seven Years' War, the French and Indian War, and the Origins of Revolution in America," *Desperta Ferro Historia Moderna* 43 (2018). Banks, *Chasing Empire*, also takes this tack.

play out.[38] The British, of course, the eventual victors, met new systemic demands most effectively.[39]

Much of this was lost on the people of British North America. They considered themselves proud Britons with the victory over France in a global war that was fought for dominance of an Atlantic system. They saw themselves as participants in a great drama of empire, and now a constituent part of the greatest empire the world had ever seen. Creole elites had for some time tried to style themselves like men and women from the metropole, wearing and consuming what the center regarded as fashionable and what made them, in their eyes anyway, the equals of those in England. A war, which had centered on America, heightened this sensibility. These provincials also believed that they were subjects of the greatest of all kings and legatees of an exceptional British history of freedom. They had acquired a conscious sense that they, too, had a role to play in a future of liberty that was unfolding. Unlike, say, planters in the Caribbean who had to attach themselves to empire because of fear of those who toiled in their midst, those in North America, on the face of it, saw their attachment as motivated by love and common interest.[40]

For those in the peripheries of the British Atlantic and those at the center, the period after the war created a profound sense of urgency, just as it became in the minds of all a "moment." It was clear that history presented all Britons, those in Britain and those in America, with a turning point. The question was how they would respond to its challenges and opportunities. And this gets us to the crisis that stemmed from trying to plow the seas and that would eventuate in revolution in America. In the immediate aftermath of the Seven Years' War, with a sense that stakes in the Atlantic had grown higher still, a series of British ministries tried to reform the entangled space to control it. Though officials debated over the proper measures to employ, all believed that the period necessitated a plan to reform what they regarded as a ramshackle empire that might not be up to the task. Some measures spoke directly to the issue of control of watery space. As early as 1758, one British official argued that foreign "usurpations" of land claimed by Britain in

---

[38] Brown, "Eighteenth Century."
[39] Brendan Simms, *Three Victories and a Defeat: The Rise and Fall of the First British Empire* (New York: Basic Books, 2008).
[40] Breen, *Marketplace of Revolution*; Brendan McConville, *The King's Three Faces: The Rise and Fall of Royal America, 1688–1776* (Chapel Hill: University of North Carolina Press, 2007); Andrew O'Shaughnessy, *An Empire Divided: The American Revolution and the British Caribbean* (Philadelphia: University of Pennsylvania Press, 2000).

America could no longer be tolerated. America had become too important to the British economy, and entanglements could bring further war. As Eliga Gould argues, the British embarked on a mission "to strengthen their maritime empire in America," hoping to turn "this entangled commerce to their own advantage."[41] Indeed, the first post-war Act passed for colonies by Parliament – the Customs Enforcement Act – targeted trading abuses and was meant to benefit British customs revenue by empowering naval officers to act as customs officials. The measure recognized the severity of the problem, one that had grown through wartime smuggling.[42]

The famous litany of Acts that we know led to revolution in America stemmed from this impulse. The Sugar Act, for instance, was enacted to enforce old laws on the book that would crack down on that chief manifestation of Atlantic entanglement: smuggling. Sugar, its by-products like molasses, wine, indigo, and coffee were all targeted, and the Act was designed "as an attack on entrenched abuses."[43] In fact, the period and problems posed by integration ushered in an earnest debate about how to manage the Atlantic and the competition it fostered, generating the first tangible and the most comprehensive attempts to map sovereignty onto the Atlantic. Such a program was clearly manifest with the Stamp Act. Passed to raise money to keep troops on North American soil, as most assumed it would just be a matter of time until France sought to win back what it had lost, the Stamp Act reflected the ways that sovereignty in the Atlantic mattered more than ever before. Parliament enacted the measure assuming that sovereignty quite naturally had to extend outward and that it was the only institution capable of reforming empire, and it targeted those provincials who had benefited from Atlantic consolidation. Other measures passed from this point forward pointed to the same set of assumptions. The idea of the Townshend Duties was premised, in part, on shoring up those offices which oversaw trade and regulated it. They were designed to police illicit traffic by establishing new offices for collection and enforcement.[44] These acts, then, are best construed as reform measures designed to domesticate the Atlantic.

The other way the Atlantic was rationalized was through a clear sense of sovereignty and authority. This also was the general thrust of the Townshend Duties. The center, nearly all of these acts announced, but most especially the Townshend Acts, would now disentangle imperial relations and map sovereignty onto what had been an ungovernable space. The British

[41] Gould, *Among the Powers of the Earth*, 83, 86, 91.   [42] Truxes, *Defying Empire*, 226.
[43] Truxes, *Defying Empire*, 189.   [44] Griffin, *The Townshend Moment*.

were not creating something *ex nihilo*. A proper relationship between the metropole and provinces could be found in the works of Roman historians. By using this older blueprint, one to which all Europeans subscribed, officials were tapping into a rich vein of ideas about imperial governance. To those officials who promoted measures like the Townshend Duties, it was self-evident that the colonies in America had to be treated like Roman provinces. They also believed that subordinating colonies, not bringing them in on an equal footing with even a kingdom like Ireland, would prove the only means of ensuring that virtue flourished for the whole. The Atlantic had to be integrated politically just as it had been consolidated through economic and cultural networks, and the provinces in North America had to effectively be made part of the state.

This does not mean that the British wanted to revert to what we could call simple mercantilist models of political economy. Officials wanted to harness Atlantic potential, not stem it. So, while the urgency of the moment impelled officials to design acts to curtail provincial wealth generation, it also pushed them to come up with newer ways of addressing the possibilities of the moment. The Free Port Act of 1766, for instance, which was part of a broader vision for the Atlantic, created a number of free trading centers in the Caribbean that could skirt the rules imposed by the Navigation Acts, allowing, for instance, the exportation of enslaved persons to other European powers. While North America would be policed to ensure that the center benefited from foreign trade, some islands in the Caribbean would be freed up to trade across imperial lines.[45]

The British were not alone. All powers attempted to reform to manage the watery space. The French tried, even though they had lost the war, focusing their efforts on Saint-Domingue, hoping it would enrich the center. Still holding the most profitable plot of land in the world, French officials enacted reforms that increased the autonomy and wealth of planters there and merchants at home. These measures served everyone's purposes, except for perhaps the state's treasuries, and, of course, the enslaved. Loss, however, had shrunken empire, or at least grand pretensions of a vast Atlantic empire, even as Saint-Domingue was generating more and more wealth. Reform, therefore, though efficacious, proved to be more modest than the British

---

[45] Gregory E. O'Malley, *Final Passages: The Intercolonial Slave Trade of British America, 1619–1807* (Chapel Hill; University of North Carolina Press, 2014); Frances Armytage, *The Free Port System in the British West Indies* (London: Longmans Green, 1953).

version. The Spanish case was a bit more puzzling. On paper, the administrative divisions into audiencias and viceroyalties suggested both an understanding of the importance of centralized authority and the wherewithal to see it through. Overlapping jurisdictions also provided stability for Spanish America. They also created challenges. The extent of Spanish holdings and the sophistication of creole societies in America would make centralization a far more challenging task than it was for the British. Spanish officials hoped to enact robust reform measures. Famously, reform initiatives would set-off revolts in the Andes and in New Granada, both of which demonstrated the tangled nature of any reform program. Comprehensive packages tended to reveal provincial tensions and, if pressed too vigorously, could set them off. In the face of such challenges, officials in the center suppressed what revolts against authority they could, as in New Granada, or acquiesced where they could not extend their power fully, as in the Andes. Ultimately, officials sponsored a free trade system within the empire, empowering provincial elites and dramatically cutting back on the power of metropolitan merchant cliques in some key cities. The move rationalized what could be imagined in light of the power of the Spanish state, or lack thereof, and the need to hold onto empire in the face of growing geopolitical tensions. The same went for the Portuguese. Reform measures, which could not be carried out fully, increased the autonomy of creoles.[46]

Of all the European powers, therefore, the victors of the war were able to follow through most comprehensively on a package of robust reform measures. And they did so tenaciously. If one initiative failed, another was devised quickly. The reasons are simple. The British had the most to defend and the most now to lose. All powers tried. But only Britain had the capacity to implement and articulate a broad and ambitious package. Their task was simplified by the fact that their holdings were not as extensive or as well-developed as other European powers, most especially Spain. The British did what they did because the stakes had become so high, certainly in the minds of officials, and the need to raise revenue so pressing in the wake of the war. And because they had the power to believe they could. The costs of victory

[46] Gabriel Paquette, *Enlightenment, Governance, and Reform in Spain and Its Empire, 1759–1808* (New York: Palgrave Macmillan, 2008); Gabriel Paquette, *Imperial Portugal in the Age of Atlantic Revolutions: The Luso-Brazilian World, c. 1770–1850* (Cambridge: Cambridge University Press, 2013); Kenneth Maxwell, *Conflicts and Conspiracies: Brazil and Portugal, 1750–1808* (New York: Routledge, 2004); Michael Kwass, *Privilege and the Politics of Taxation in Eighteenth-Century France: Liberté, Égalité, Fiscalité* (New York: Cambridge University Press, 2000).

and the capacity of the state separated the British from the rest. Holding onto what had been won meant the provinces would have to be subordinated.[47]

The Desire for Continued Autonomy

We know the rest of the story well. Resistance was intense and was premised upon certain ideas that underscored Britishness itself. Smuggling became a patriotic virtue, especially for those merchants who had benefited from the unregulated Atlantic. Americans felt justified in pushing back, as the ideas they espoused, such as consent and individual rights, represented the very ideals that metropolitans hailed as distinctively British, ideals that had been vindicated at the time of the Glorious Revolution. Indeed, integration of the space had heightened American attraction to them.[48] Moreover, with each passing crisis, it seemed the lid was coming off American society. By anyone's measure, American society was becoming politicized, as common men and women began also to see their plight as part of the broader struggle with Parliament. Home rule, then, could not be disentangled from rule at home, and creoles in all Atlantic societies, but most urgently British North America had to weigh their confidence against their anxiety as they tried to figure how they would manage forces from below. These dilemmas confronted creole elites with all sorts of devilish choices to make. Such was the crisis unleashed by British attempts at reforming empire in the wake of the war.[49] This was their true "provincial dilemma," one much more vexing than the simple tug-of-war over identity with which we usually associate the term.

But instead of seeing this as a story of a provincial people maturing, or of the appeal and logic of a set of ideals that justified the liberty they enjoyed, or of socioeconomic strife in towns and cities in the wake of the war, we would be wise to see the response of Americans as a creole *cri de coeur* to continue to enjoy the autonomy that entanglements conferred and that both enriched and guaranteed their status in society. Creoles in British North America, as

---

[47] For a good look at British reform, see Jack Greene, *Evaluating Empire and Confronting Colonialism in Eighteenth-Century Britain* (New York: Cambridge University Press, 2013).
[48] Gould, *Among the Powers*; Bernard Bailyn, *The Ideological Origins of the American Revolution* (Cambridge, MA: Belknap Press of Harvard University Press, 1967).
[49] For a comparative look at confidence and anxiety in this age, see Burnard and Garrigus, *The Plantation Machine*. On the bumptiousness of these years, and how the crisis of authority destabilized American communities, see Alan Taylor, *American Revolutions: A Continental History* (New York: W. W. Norton, 2017); T. H. Breen, *The Will of the People: The Revolutionary Birth of America* (Cambridge, MA: Harvard University Press, 2019).

provincials, were necessarily a people of paradox: anti-imperial when it came to the metropole and imperial when it came to dominance at home. This paradox, the manifestation of Atlantic systematization, formed the horns of their dilemma.[50]

The response of British American creoles in the wake of the Stamp Act and the Townshend Duties speak to these tangled dilemmas. Merchants wanted the wealth that the new system offered, but they also relished the autonomy that had gone hand-in-hand with it. Freedom permitted the flouting of laws. Freedom from metropolitan consideration also made them masters of all they surveyed. They could treat subject people as they saw fit, both those that toiled around them and the Natives who inhabited the frontiers. New measures passed by Parliament to regulate the Atlantic and to begin establishing new political arrangements with the colonies, as the Townshend Duties were designed to do, threatened both freedoms: one to trade with autonomy; the other to police their own societies as they saw fit. What the British were intending to do would undo, in their minds, all that the Atlantic had promised. And so, they resisted.[51]

The problem the British confronted was not simply pushback from provincials. All centers experienced resistance, and most acquiesced in light of it. In fact, the failure of Spanish and Portuguese officials to make good on reform measures they hoped to impose in light of provincial griping led to a veritable golden age of creole autonomy. No, for the British failure stemmed from their inability to control creoles as they tried to manage the Atlantic. All of their strategic aims, and this followed in one ministry after another, and all of the different tactics they used – from taxation to the creation of revenue boards – were premised on regulating and simplifying and so benefiting from an entangled space. Without the ability, despite pretensions to the contrary, to establish effective measures to control creole populations, to stop smuggling, and to regulate trade, they had no hope of success.[52] Moreover, the ways that provincials had been able to exploit entanglements ensured that reeling them in, so to speak, even if they declared their allegiance to the crown, would involve some sort of coercion. The ocean was so big, and the British craft of state so small.

---

[50] I refer to this as their "provincial dilemmas" in *The Townshend Moment*. Joshua Simon sees it as the ideology of what he calls "Creole Revolution." See Joshua Simon, *The Ideology of Creole Revolution: Imperialism and Independence in American and Latin American Political Thought* (Cambridge: Cambridge University Press, 2017).

[51] Griffin, *The Townshend Moment*.

[52] See Patrick Griffin, *America's Revolution* (New York: Oxford University Press, 2012).

Something else was at work as well. Because this system was so imbricated, any call for reform would be sure to create crisis in places throughout. American creoles clearly sensed the implications of reform measures in just this way. Such is evident when it came to how they articulated fears of slave rebellions. Far from being paranoid or panicked by what the British were up to, and so simply projecting fears about home rule onto rule at home, creole elites were giving voice to the thoroughly networked nature of their world and what British overtures could do to destabilize what was in place. Enslaved persons, they knew, were deeply affected by what went on in the network. The enslaved knew of rebellions elsewhere, and they knew how the system enriched their masters. More to the point, slaves made the Atlantic the entangled, enriching space it had become. The same went for Native Americans. When the men who signed the Declaration of Independence in Philadelphia spoke of George III whipping up Natives in an anti-colonial frenzy, they knew what they were talking about. The whole network was based on the exploitation of lands and the removal of the Indigenous from their land. In other words, once entanglements were being untangled, the fallout would be immeasurable and severely so. The stakes had become high, not only for European powers but for all complicit in creating the sustaining the system.

In light of British failure to plow the proverbial sea, American pretensions to independence would seem self-evident. And this is something that Edmund Burke seemed to sense. It is one reason why he would suggest that Britain should admit the difficulty of reforming the Atlantic and grant Americans the autonomy they had enjoyed before the war.[53] But it was too late. The crises that gripped the colonies with reform measures drove some essential points home for American creoles about how their societies had changed with integration and what a future within the empire would mean for their prosperity and their security. With independence, elites could control their own societies, which British reform measures had disrupted. Elites could also continue to take advantage of what the entangled Atlantic had to offer without paying any sort of real price. And, as they weighed their provincial dilemmas, as all creoles throughout the Atlantic would whenever push came to shove, they believed that they could control those below and on the margins whose exploitation drove the consolidation of the Atlantic. By attempting to do what was impossible, ironically, the British had done what the poet Keats would lament in his epitaph. They had writ their name in America in water.

---

[53] Richard Bourke, *Empire and Revolution: The Political Life of Edmund Burke* (Princeton: Princeton University Press, 2015).

8

Cities and Citizenship in Revolution

JESSICA CHOPPIN RONEY

The Search for Citizenship

A potent metaphor for the transformations wrought by the American Revolution was that it turned *subjects* into *citizens*. Subjecthood derived from the feudal past and referred to the "natural" personal ties of allegiance and obligation owed utterly and in perpetuity by a subject to their lord. Subjecthood assumed and operated in a hierarchical world with different rights and obligations adhering to individuals based upon their rank. Citizenship, as it came to be understood and used in the late eighteenth century, derived not from personal bonds of allegiance to an individual lord, but from a consensual relationship to a defined community: the "state" or the "nation" (themselves concepts still in flux). Deeply influenced by contract theory, this notion of citizenship rested upon consent, a territorially defined community of allegiance (which unlike subjecthood could be vacated), and the uniform, equal rights and obligations of all members.

Citizenship was born in cities. Indeed, the very word *citizen* originally meant an inhabitant of a city. It was in cities that notions of a spatially specific community of allegiance, a concept of uniform rights and obligations, and a severance of personal obligations to a lord first emerged. The history and example of cities – classical, historic, and contemporary – stretching back to Rome, the city-states of the Italian Renaissance, and the distinctive status granted to towns and cities in the British Isles, furnished the raw materials to expand the concept gradually in the eighteenth century. In the medieval period, urban citizenship had assumed distinct characteristics when it became clear that in order to flourish as centers of manufacturing and commerce, cities and towns required exemptions from feudal obligations to local lords. Municipal charters, granted by the monarch, created urban corporations or (in Scotland) burghs whose primary function was to regulate and support the local economy freed from vassalage to the local aristocracy. All the major cities of the British Isles, including London, Bristol,

Liverpool, Cardiff, Dublin, Edinburgh, and Glasgow, and about 300 British towns (around one-third of all market towns), had charters. Freeman status, though not equally open to all, conferred the right to trade in the city, and expanded participation in policymaking beyond noblemen, usually to wealthier merchants and craftsmen. Incorporated cities potentially posed a challenge to the prerogatives of the monarch, causing Charles II and James II each to restrict municipal corporations' autonomy in the seventeenth century. For all the economic advantages of incorporation, however, charters did not provide a basis for clear local government, and by the late seventeenth century they were ill-suited to meet the governance needs of most British cities. Indeed, after 1700 few English or Welsh towns sought corporate charters, and citizens invested their time in advocating for reforms to their existing corporations or forming civic associations to work around them altogether. Nevertheless, this model of incorporated towns was the template policymakers and colonists alike carried with them as they envisioned urban citizenship in North America.[1]

Cities and towns loomed large in colonial projectors' visions of American settlement. Cities inculcated virtue, education, politeness – in a word, urbanity. Moreover, projectors and colonists anticipated their importance in the local economy. The Virginia Company (1607) and the Massachusetts Bay Company (1630) alike sought from the beginning to cluster their colonists in urban settlements, though with radically differing levels of success. Proprietary projectors, from the Earl of Carlisle with his plans for Barbados (1628) to Lord Shaftesbury in his plans for Carolina (1680) to William Penn with his obsessively planned capital for Pennsylvania (1682), emphasized the importance of cities to their colonial projects. Almost all the provincial capitals and large towns of British America were seaports (Williamsburg, Virginia, and Spanish Town, Jamaica were the exceptions).[2]

---

[1] Rosemary Sweet, *The English Town, 1680–1840: Government, Society and Culture* (Harlow: Pearson, 1999); Joanna Innes and Nicholas Rogers, "Politics and Government," in Peter Clark, ed., *The Cambridge Urban History of Britain* (Cambridge: Cambridge University Press, 2008), 529–74; Hendrik Hartog, *Public Property and Private Power: The Corporation of the City of New York in American Law, 1730–1870* (Ithaca, NY: Cornell University Press, 1983); Jon C. Teaford, *The Municipal Revolution in America: Origins of Modern Urban Government, 1650–1825* (Chicago: University of Chicago Press, 1975); T. M. Devine, "Scotland," in Peter Clark, ed., *The Cambridge Urban History of Britain* (Cambridge: Cambridge University Press, 2008), 151–64; Paul D. Halliday, *Dismembering the Body Politic: Partisan Politics in England's Towns, 1650–1730* (Cambridge: Cambridge University Press, 1998).

[2] Paul Musselwhite, *Urban Dreams, Rural Commonwealth: The Rise of Plantation Society in the Chesapeake* (Chicago: University of Chicago Press, 2019); Emma Hart, *Building Charleston: Town and Society in the Eighteenth-Century British Atlantic World* (Charlottesville: University of Virginia Press, 2010); Jessica Choppin Roney, *Governed*

Unhindered by an existing urban footprint or ancient guild restrictions, colonial cities could fully orient their geography toward and embrace their function as commercial entrepôts. British restrictions on American banking, a contracted currency supply, and metropolitan control of the trade in enumerated American commodities, including tobacco, sugar, and furs, impeded colonial economic development generally and tended to dampen urban financial sectors. Conversely, these very same policies transformed Atlantic-facing British ports like Glasgow, Liverpool, and Bristol into major cities and dominant forces in shaping the flow of goods, services, and money in the British Atlantic. The merchants of Boston and Newport availed themselves of the same economic opportunities, engaging vigorously in the carrying trade to and from the Caribbean. The final major trade fueling the Atlantic economy, the African slave trade, injected both labor and capital into provincial economies, encouraging horizontal and vertical linkages, sophisticated financial products, and, in the very bodies of enslaved people, providing repositories for capital and credit. The transatlantic and intra-continental transshipment of enslaved people ensured the growth and importance of cities in all the plantation colonies outside the Chesapeake, particularly Charleston, South Carolina, Kingston, Jamaica, and Bridgetown, Barbados, while fueling the long-distance trading activities of merchants from Newport, Rhode Island to Bristol, England, and becoming major economic engines in both those cities as well as in many other port towns. Grain-, fish-, and provisions-exporting cities like Philadelphia, New York, Boston, and Norfolk dealt in commodities not enumerated by the Navigation Acts and found a stable market among the plantation colonies of the Caribbean. Colonial manufacturing, apart from trades related to building houses or building and supplying ships, often suffered from competition with British goods, yet through the eighteenth century, colonial cities became major centers of production, consumption, and distribution. Finally, the economy of Halifax, Nova Scotia, founded in 1749 as an administrative and naval outpost, revolved around supplying and serving the garrison. Whatever the orientation toward the Atlantic economy, within each city the diversity of activities in urban marketplaces allowed a range of actors, including women, free blacks, and enslaved people, to participate. By the period of the American Revolution, British Atlantic cities were growing, multifaceted, commercial communities with thriving service sectors and brisk rental and real estate

by a Spirit of Opposition: The Origins of American Political Practice in Colonial Philadelphia (Baltimore, MD: Johns Hopkins University Press, 2014).

markets. Philadelphia, with nearly 27,000 residents, led the way, followed by New York, Boston, Kingston, Charleston, Newport, and Norfolk, Virginia.[3]

For all their economic importance, the status of urban citizens themselves remained a fraught issue through the colonial period. While central planners celebrated the allegedly civilizing influence of cities, metropolitan officials as well as provincial agricultural elites looked askance at the economic and political power of urban merchants and unruly urban residents. Chesapeake planters, aided by a landscape criss-crossed by bays, rivers, and inlets, resisted centralization either at Jamestown or, despite metropolitan pressure after Bacon's Rebellion, anywhere else. In the early eighteenth century, Maryland's governor attempted to create a powerful commercial class through a tightly constricted corporate charter for the new city of Annapolis only to be thwarted by a suspicious planter-dominated legislature. In Virginia, when Norfolk emerged as a mercantile hub exporting timber, tar, and tobacco, planters bestowed upon it municipal incorporation, not as a way of ensuring its independence, but as a way of subordinating it to the House of Burgesses and limiting its power. Jamaican planters, meanwhile, maintained their provincial capital at land-locked Spanish Town rather than at the port city of Kingston specifically to constrain the influence of the urban merchants in the latter. The middling artisans and traders of Charleston pushed with increasing insistence for incorporation by the middle of the eighteenth century, but were met with implacable resistance by rice and indigo planters. Agricultural elites in the plantation colonies thus proved to be united and successful in limiting the independent political clout of cities and their citizens, even as the economic functions of cities were central in all but the Chesapeake.[4]

---

[3] Jacob M. Price, "Economic Function and Growth of American Port Towns in the Eighteenth Century," *Perspectives in American History* 8 (1974), 123–86; Stephen J. Hornsby, *British Atlantic, American Frontier: Spaces of Power in Early Modern British America* (Hanover, NH: University Press of New England, 2005); Mark A. Peterson, *The City-State of Boston: The Rise and Fall of an Atlantic Power, 1630–1865* (Princeton: Princeton University Press, 2019); Mark A. Peterson, "The War in the Cities," in Jane Kamensky and Edward G. Gray, eds., *The Oxford Handbook of the American Revolution* (Oxford: Oxford University Press, 2012), 194–210; Gregory E. O'Malley, *Final Passages: The Intercolonial Slave Trade of British America, 1619–1807* (Chapel Hill: University of North Carolina Press, 2014); Trevor Burnard, "Towns in Plantation Societies in Eighteenth-Century America," *Early American Studies* 15:4 (2017), 835–59; Hart, *Building Charleston*; Robert Olwell, *Masters, Slaves, and Subjects: The Culture of Power in the South Carolina Low Country, 1740–1790* (Ithaca, NY: Cornell University Press, 1998); Gary B. Nash, *The Urban Crucible: Social Change, Political Consciousness, and the Origins of the American Revolution* (Cambridge, MA: Harvard University Press, 1979).

[4] Paul Musselwhite, "Annapolis Aflame: Richard Clarke's Conspiracy and the Imperial Urban Vision in Maryland, 1704–8," *William and Mary Quarterly* 71:3 (2014), 361–400; Trevor Burnard, "'The Grand Mart of the Island': The Economic Function of Kingston,

The pattern of hedging urban power proved to be remarkably similar in the largest city in British America. Philadelphians pursued a charter for the same reason feudal towns had originally sought them: to limit the power of the local lord, in this case William Penn. This protection achieved, the Philadelphia Corporation lacked financial resources and therefore the ability to intervene robustly in local matters beyond the regulation of its urban marketplace. The Pennsylvania Assembly, on the one hand, and eventually local voluntary associations, on the other, assumed control of many local services, leaving the corporation relatively anemic. Within a generation the membership of the municipal corporation skewed Anglican and Presbyterian, and in politics sided with the proprietary Penn family, diverging sharply from the Pennsylvania Assembly which was firmly Quaker and opposed to proprietary power. Under these circumstances, the assembly had no reason to encourage any concentration of political power in Philadelphia. The province's largest and most important city thus found incorporation insufficient to advance much political autonomy. As the growing city became ever more ethnically and religiously diverse, and less like the Quaker oligarchy that wielded outsized power in the assembly, the formal political power of Philadelphians, who were dramatically under-represented in the legislature, diminished. In the mid-Atlantic, the region that embraced municipal incorporation more than any other in British North America, with eleven of the total fifteen incorporated municipalities, the institution did little to endow townspeople with substantial political power, either internally within their communities, or as constituencies within their colonies.[5]

New York City stood in singular contrast to Philadelphia and all the other incorporated towns. The Corporation of the City of New York featured broad inclusion for residents and enjoyed substantial property which enabled it to intervene decisively in local affairs. The corporation leveraged the income generated from those properties and rentals of corporation property (such as wharves) to shape both public and private development (requiring grantees to pave streets adjacent to corporation wharves, for example). The Corporation of New York was the most active, powerful, participatory, and

---

Jamaica in the Mid-Eighteenth Century," in Kathleen E. A. Monteith and Glen Richards, eds., *Jamaica in Slavery and Freedom: History, Heritage and Culture* (Kingston: University of the West Indies Press, 2002), 225–41; Hart, *Building Charleston*.

[5] Pennsylvania had four municipal corporations (Philadelphia, Chester, Bristol, and Lancaster); New Jersey had four (Perth Amboy, New Brunswick, Burlington, and Elizabeth); New York had two (New York City and Albany); and Delaware had one (Wilmington). Teaford, *Municipal Revolution in America*, 119–20. On Philadelphia, see Roney, *Governed by a Spirit of Opposition*.

wealthiest of the American municipal corporations, and it carved out space for itself against the prerogative of the New York Assembly, though it remained dependent upon both the legislature and the crown, from which its charter derived, for its governance functions.[6]

Where other British colonies were organized around county- or parish-level government, New England focused on town and city government, but without municipal corporations. In Massachusetts, planners rejected feudal-style incorporation serving commercial interests. The towns themselves emerged originally as religious communities, with full political rights extended to all men who were full members of the Church, though by the end of the seventeenth century they also had to meet certain property requirements. The governing town meeting that emerged was predicated upon unanimity and homogeneity (ethnic, occupational, and religious), rather than proto-democratic principles. Moreover, because the towns lacked charters, the Massachusetts legislature retained the power to intervene in all matters, including affairs of local governance and the very boundaries and make-up of the town. New England towns, then, remained subordinate to their legislatures.[7]

Here the exception was Boston, which, like New York, largely avoided domination by rural interests. Boston, in common with New England towns, lacked municipal incorporation, but in this case because its citizens rejected it. Though Bostonians debated incorporation numerous times, ultimately they feared incorporation would inhibit business (since only freemen could operate in the city) and constrain participation to the wealthy, an inferior system they believed to the existing town meeting. As a result, Boston never had a public marketplace, normally a space under corporate or some form of local government, until merchant and human trafficker Peter Faneuil donated one in 1740, eliciting concern even at this degree of commercial centralization. Because Boston was not incorporated it never enjoyed formal independence from the provincial government, yet because the city's economy relied on the transatlantic carrying trade, it was never beholden to its hinterland for a saleable commodity or cowed by powerful agricultural elites. Instead, the sociopolitico-economic interests of the colony congregated so powerfully in the city that one historian has called Boston a "city-state" that entirely dominated not just Massachusetts but all of New England. Boston

---

[6] Hartog, *Public Property and Private Power*.
[7] Michael Zuckerman, *Peaceable Kingdoms: New England Towns in the Eighteenth Century*, (New York: Alfred A. Knopf, 1970); Teaford, *Municipal Revolution in America*.

may not have chosen the benefit of a municipal charter, but ultimately it hardly needed the protections such an instrument would have provided.[8]

By 1763, cities had emerged as distinctive political spaces. In the feudal past, corporate citizenship had endowed city residents with powers and qualities distinct from subjecthood. In the application of that model to overwhelmingly rural, agricultural North America, however, landed elites successfully constrained the use or meaning of formal civic personhood everywhere but New York City. Most British American towns and cities lacked power or autonomy from their local legislatures, and to the extent that municipal corporations did exercise independence, they came to be accused of being feudal throw-backs, out of step with the increasingly anti-hierarchical tenor of burgeoning American resistance.

The Expansion of Citizenship and the Question of Self-Rule

American cities had long created space for citizens to participate actively in or comment upon politics. Home to dense clusters of taverns, coffee shops, mercantile exchanges, wharves, churches, and public spaces "out-of-doors," cities facilitated what Jürgen Habermas has called "the public sphere," a space for political discussion, opinion formation, and debate. Here, in these mostly male-dominated spaces, men of all walks of life could hear about or weigh in on current events. Elite sociability at tea tables, balls, and in private salons provided a separate mixed-gender vector for conversation and critique. Meanwhile, the crowded, fluid, and contested nature of urban streets, marketplaces, theaters, sporting venues, and public festive events carved out spaces for marginalized actors, including women, free blacks, and enslaved people, to express their views on and even shape policy. By 1775, thirty-seven newspapers, concentrated in port towns and provincial capitals from Kingston to Boston, helped to disseminate urban news and opinion among distant cities and into the countryside.[9]

Cities, moreover, fostered voluntary associations, many of which performed vital civic functions in their respective cities. Philadelphia, British America's largest city, had also its most developed voluntary associational culture by virtue of the weakness of its municipal corporation and the intense

---

[8] Peterson, *City-State of Boston*.
[9] Jürgen Habermas, *The Structural Transformation of the Public Sphere*, trans. Thomas Burger (Cambridge, MA: MIT Press, 1991).

need for fire protection, poor relief, and even military protection. Through organizations that ranged from the social to the intellectual to the quasi-governmental to the extra-legal, Philadelphia men of all social classes fostered a civic culture that was at once broadly participatory, inviting men not only to comment but to act on matters of public policy, yet at the same time sharply exclusive, gathering together only the like-minded and in no way answering to the general public. On the eve of the revolution between one-fifth and one-half of adult white men in Philadelphia belonged to a voluntary association, including libraries, fire companies, a hospital association, ethnic societies, insurance and poor relief societies, and even militias. In other cities citizens likewise embraced voluntary associations. In New York, as many as one-quarter of adult men participated in a voluntary association, in organizations similar to the range in Philadelphia but also including a chamber of commerce and the Society for Reformation of Manners and the Suppression of Vice. In Charleston, lacking municipal government, an array of town commissions provided a space for middling citizens to regulate the city's public spaces and wharves. In Boston, fire companies formed under the supervision of the town selectmen, while an active club scene addressed needs ranging from ethnic sociability to "the encouraging of trade and commerce." In all these cases, voluntary associations and local governmental commissions drew men into active performances of their citizenship.[10]

Before 1775, then, North American cities, incorporated or not, boasted a well-established infrastructure of urban civic activism that vested the concept *citizenship* with qualities not of special, feudal-era rights pertaining specifically to urban freemen, but with a set of community-oriented behaviors, commitments, and duties. The noteworthy citizen improved and defended his community (and specifically it was *his* community; a full citizen in British America was figured to be free, male, and white). Importantly, this construction moved citizenship from being a status derived from place, to the performance of a set of actions. It decoupled *citizenship* from cities altogether. This evolution had deep roots in political philosophy, stretching back to the Italian Renaissance and seventeenth-century English political theorists, conceiving full political participation as being rooted in property ownership and

---

[10] Roney, *Governed by a Spirit of Opposition*; Hart, *Building Charleston*; Teaford, *Municipal Revolution in America*; Benjamin L. Carp, "The Fire of Liberty: Firefighters, Urban Voluntary Culture, and the Revolutionary Movement," *William and Mary Quarterly* 58 (2001), 781–818.

defense of the community through the local militia. As urban residents embraced civic activism to protect their towns from fire or to build hospitals, they participated in rather than precipitated this move to imagine citizenship as no longer being tied to tightly circumscribed locality, but as a set of principles governing political behavior and relationships – citizenship as generalizable process rather than particular civic identity.[11]

At least two consequences followed. The first was to tie the concept of citizenship more tightly than ever to adult, white manhood. Where single, property-owning women had been able to purchase freewoman status in municipal corporations, acquiring a degree of participatory citizenship, this newer concept of citizenship as the performance of duties, especially military protection, and which imagined women as incapable of performing such duties, foreclosed their active citizenship. Women's political personhood was subsumed under that of the male head of her household, usually her father or her husband, and single women remained in a kind of limbo where they held property rights but not political rights. In this sense, the expansion of citizenship beyond place to the performance of acts constituted simultaneously the constraint of citizenship, denying female, urban residents access that some of them had once enjoyed and foreclosing that particular route for women and other marginalized people to make future political claims.[12]

The second consequence was to undercut entirely the premises that had made corporate citizenship useful or powerful as a way to protect urban communities from domination by rural interests, even in the fifteen towns that held such formal protections. As the colonies entered a period of escalating tensions with Britain over the allocation of political power, the citizens of British American cities had their own grievances and interests, based not only on their political relationship with the British Empire but also with their own respective provincial authorities – especially colonial assemblies and governors. In some cases, citizens decried their legislatures in terms resonant with those used in protest of crown and Parliament. In the midst of debates about self-rule and *imperium in imperio* (government within another government), most towns and cities (Boston may have been the major exception) had few resources to enforce their own claims to local rule,

---

[11] Roney, *Governed by a Spirit of Opposition*; James Livesey, *Civil Society and Empire: Ireland and Scotland in the Eighteenth-Century Atlantic World* (New Haven: Yale University Press, 2009).

[12] Karin Wulf, *Not All Wives: Women of Colonial Philadelphia* (Ithaca, NY: Cornell University Press, 2000).

or to resist provincial assemblies controlled by rural voters and agricultural elites. Here it is worth pausing to reflect that in most North American colonies the urban population comprised no more than 5–10 percent of the free population, though these percentages were considerably higher in the Caribbean. The problem James Madison would later identify in framing the federal Constitution pertained here as well: how to protect a minority from a majority. Leading into the revolution, urban citizens had few tools at their disposal to realize municipal autonomy.

Internally, cities were riven by their own class, occupational, religious, ethnic, and racial divides. As long as cities prospered, and as long as that prosperity was reasonably equitably shared (among free people, anyway), as was true for the first decades of the eighteenth century, urban unrest remained attenuated. But as economic downturns hit, and as wealth came to be concentrated in fewer hands in the largest seaports by the middle of the eighteenth century, social pressures became more volatile. The depression that followed the Seven Years' War affected Boston, New York, and Philadelphia badly, fracturing the inhabitants of those cities along socioeconomic lines. Urban crowds could and frequently did assert their own opinions on public affairs, not through electoral politics or voluntary associations, but through collective, usually spontaneous, angry popular actions. Through crowd actions, laboring and marginalized people of both sexes who were denied formal participation, vented their outrage upon targets deemed to have violated the public good or collective norms. Though popular unrest was by no means confined to urban areas – the period before the revolution saw agrarian uprisings in many places – its association with city streets, wharves, and public places was nonetheless strong in the minds of elites and confirmed their worst fears of dangerously disorderly cities to be kept on short tether.[13]

Entering the revolutionary period, American cities posed a challenge to the social and cultural order of both their own provinces and Britain's. Many provincial elites worried about the economic power and separate interests of urban merchants; they worried about urban disease, poverty, and dangerous

---

[13] Nash, *Urban Crucible*; Pauline Maier, "Popular Uprisings and Civil Authority in Eighteenth-Century America," *William and Mary Quarterly* 27:1 (1970), 4–35; Benjamin L. Carp, *Rebels Rising: Cities and the American Revolution* (Oxford: Oxford University Press, 2007). On rural uprising, see, for example, Rachel Klein, "Frontier Planters and the American Revolution: The South Carolina Backcountry, 1775–1782," in Ronald Hoffman, Thad Tate, and Peter Albert, eds., *Uncivil War: The Southern Backcountry during the American Revolution* (Charlottesville: University of Virginia Press, 1985), 37–69; A. Roger Ekirch, "Whig Authority and Public Order in Backcountry North Carolina, 1776–1783," in Ronald Hoffman, Thad Tate, and Peter Albert, eds., *Uncivil War: The Southern Backcountry during the American Revolution* (Charlottesville: University of Virginia Press, 1985), 99–124.

social fluidity; and they decried the luxury, vice, and consumerism of cities, even as they too participated eagerly in the acquisition of European goods and fashions flowing through American ports. Meanwhile, cities operated as intense sites of creolization that might simultaneously concern metropolitan officials. Like the colonies of which they were a part, cities blended ideas, goods, and rituals of social performance imported from England with beliefs, practices, and political necessities particular to their own circumstances, labor arrangements, economies, and geographies. In every region apart from the Chesapeake and Nova Scotia, cities acted as the fulcrum points of empire. They organized and transported the resources of their hinterlands (whether geographically adjacent as in most places, or far-flung, as in the case of Boston), and served as emporia for the sale, marketing, and instruction in European imports and fashions. Thus, while they were by no means unique in forging particular American creole identities, cities were intense and contested sites where beliefs, social and political practices, and local institutions had the potential to challenge the designs of centralizing metropolitan authorities. In so doing, citizens both aligned with but simultaneously concerned their rural neighbors.[14]

Even as their own particular internal, provincial, and imperial power struggles unfolded, citizens were by nature of their geography and circumstances at the vanguard of revolutionary politics. The communications and shipping points of the Atlantic economy, port cities were the first to hear news of metropolitan policies, receive unwanted stamped paper or taxed tea, and, ultimately, to face British troops. To remain quietly on the side-lines was not an option for most citizens: not in the earliest days of protest and still less once war broke out. Nonetheless, the frequently unruly political agitation and radical rhetoric coming out of cities concerned landed elites who were by no means moved to expand urban political autonomy.

The taxation policies Britain pursued in the 1760s and 1770s, and the non-importation resistance crafted by the colonists to combat them, both disproportionately affected urban merchants and citizens. The Stamp Act of 1765 taxed the legal paperwork and newspapers at the heart of commercial life in every city from Boston to Bridgetown. Protest raged from St. Kitts to New Hampshire and popular actions in Boston, Newport, New York, and Charleston took destructive turns against the homes and private property of prominent stamp tax promoters. Similar destruction in Philadelphia was only averted when one crowd advancing on two stamp supporters' homes was met by another crowd

---

[14] Livesey, *Civil Society and Empire*.

standing guard over them – the latter motivated by direct loyalty to Benjamin Franklin whose home was one of the two threatened. These protests echoed previous crowd actions, and though many elites also rejected the Stamp Act, many were also shocked and concerned by the violence, lack of deference, and disorder of the urban response to it. Americans vowed to stop consuming British goods in protest, led by merchants who, however, were ultimately unenthusiastic promoters of this particular strategy which affected their livelihoods more directly than any other group.

After the repeal of the Stamp Act, British officials moved in 1767 to what they thought would be more politically acceptable external taxes on a few goods. Yet the Townshend Duties provoked new rounds of protest against taxation without consent. Violent street protest played little role this time. Instead, large cities and small towns lined up to publish in newspapers long lists of specific goods they would no longer import from Britain. Merchants joined the cause most reluctantly, uneasily eying their counterparts in rival cities and fearing lest their competitors abandon nonimportation agreements first and get a jump on resupplying coveted British goods. Urban merchants thus came under deep suspicion and hundreds of local committees formed to police their activities and enforce compliance with nonimportation agreements. Rituals of public humiliation and shaming and widely published subscription lists operated to coerce offenders and at the same time to bind together the nonconsuming public. The policing of one another's, and particularly merchants', behavior, and the need to attract diverse constituencies to the cause, including women, added to the sense of social upheaval, with traditional leaders and elites suddenly subject to scrutiny and raucous critique from their neighbors. Meanwhile, nonimportation served to help agricultural elites, particularly southern planters, who used the moment to help dig themselves out of debt. As their fortunes improved, those of merchants became more precarious. In short, though the nonimportation movement played out across the eastern seaboard, its effects were felt perhaps most dramatically, and often with the most social and economic upheaval and direct cost, in urban settings. By 1770, with the duties on all goods but tea rescinded, the nonimportation movement petered out. Many blamed merchants, who were concentrated in cities, for the lack of vigor and virtue in continuing to promote the cause.[15]

---

[15] T. H. Breen, *The Marketplace of the Revolution: How Consumer Politics Shaped American Independence* (Oxford: Oxford University Press, 2004).

The final round of urban revolutionary activism began explosively with the vehement rejection of the 1773 Tea Act. One after the other, American ports refused entry to the ships carrying the taxed tea, with the exception of Boston. There the tea was landed with the intent to sell, and a violent crowd action – by no means spontaneous or riotous, but deliberately planned and elite-led – dumped the tea in Boston Harbor. The so-called Intolerable Acts, designed to punish Boston for the destruction of the tea, galvanized the other colonies. Alarmed at still more taxation without consent and with the authoritarian cast of the Intolerable Acts, twelve colonies sent delegates to the First Continental Congress in Philadelphia in 1774. There they agreed to comprehensive nonimportation and nonconsumption of tea and all British goods. If colonial demands had not been met after a year, the Continental Association would move as well to non-exportation of key American commodities. Well aware of the disappointing results of depending on merchants or voluntary acquiescence in 1765 and 1767, organizers created the Continental Association, a network of committees elected by local committees to enforce the commercial boycott. These committees changed the political landscape of North America, knitting distant communities together in a single endeavor and empowering local committees to intervene intimately in people's everyday choices and activities. Committees and accompanying radical political organizing flourished in mainland British cities with the exception of the military garrison outpost of Halifax.[16]

The protests and organizing that mounted after 1774 were significant in cities for two major reasons. First, they spurred the political mobilization of ordinary people, asking them to participate and comment upon imperial policy, and to police their neighbors. Because most large cities had long histories of well-developed civic organization that had called upon and expanded men's political engagement and capacities, in most places this mobilization did not emerge entirely out of nowhere, but built upon existing social and civic infrastructure. At the same time, the protests occurred within a long-building context of increasing poverty and the concentration of wealth in the large seaports. The protests and organizing in 1774–1775 and beyond entailed unexpected challenges to the existing sociopolitical structure and brought about a radicalism particularly concentrated in urban areas. Second, the protests and organizations to enforce them added a new behavior, even a litmus test, for performing citizenship, whether in or out of cities. To defend

---

[16] Breen, *Marketplace of Revolution*.

the community by late winter 1774 meant to drink coffee or herbal concoctions, to wear homespun, to promote local manufactures, to pillory backsliders, and to drill with the local militia. Men who failed to perform these acts, or who publicly refused or argued against them, lost their claims to citizenship, to full political participation, and instead stood attainted as "traitors." Urban dwellers played a prominent role in crafting this new language for performing citizenship, and often it manifested in ways that assaulted old assumptions about propriety, deference, or hierarchy. In this language of citizenship, elite merchants might be traitors and humble shoemakers patriots.

While cities were central to organizing the response to British taxation, and while their residents occupied the front lines in writing a new script for revolutionary citizenship, urban municipalities themselves held little sway in the political fight. The vast majority of the formal protest, local enforcement, and inter-colonial collaboration occurred either at the level of provincial legislatures or newly created local committees. Provincial revolutionaries treated cities as units within and subservient to the larger polity, not as distinct entities with their own interests. Pennsylvania proved a rare exception, expanding the number of seats in the assembly in spring 1776 more fairly to represent Philadelphia and the western counties, but this move was a rearguard attempt by conservatives to mollify protest. Pennsylvania radicals who celebrated more representation for Philadelphia did so not out of concern for Philadelphia autonomy or to amplify the voice for its distinct needs, but because they hoped to pack the assembly with more radical delegates. At another extreme, Norfolk, Virginia, found itself violently suppressed by its provincial authorities, despite long, active engagement in anti-imperial protests. In fall 1775, Norfolk's municipal corporation failed to eject Governor Dunmore's ship from its harbor after he fled there. The Virginia militia marched on Norfolk in December 1775, occupied it, and used a skirmish with Dunmore's naval forces on 1 January 1776 as an excuse to set the town on fire. Virginia revolutionaries would blame Dunmore for the fire and characterize Norfolk (inaccurately) as a Loyalist enclave, but however they spun the event, they subdued the city and its merchants, and rendered them entirely subservient to the planter-dominated province.[17]

Cities were, as many historians have argued, crucibles of revolution, but such studies have focused on cities as spaces rather than as polities, and

---

[17] Paul Musselwhite, "'This Infant Borough': The Corporate Political Identity of Eighteenth-Century Norfolk," *Early American Studies* 15:4 (2017), 801–34.

concentrated on how people occupied and used those spaces toward revolutionary protest and ferment. They have failed to consider how cities as discrete political communities, commercially oriented minorities in overwhelmingly rural and agricultural societies, participated in or were affected by discussions about self-rule. One historian has gone so far as to argue that "Political activity in the cities helped lead the colonists to independence, but in the process, the cities rendered themselves obsolete." As protest moved to war, "city-dwellers now became minority populations within the larger movement."[18] In reality, cities as distinctive polities were always obsolete or grossly inadequate. In the few cases where they had their own unique municipal corporate structures, cities hobbled along with feudal-era forms that provided weak local governance and scant protection from rural elites. Likewise city-dwellers were always minorities – and were treated like it. The historical evolution of the concept of *citizenship* and the performances of citizenship particular to the revolutionary protest against British taxation owed much to how urban men and women had fashioned it. But the politics of the revolution had little to do with cities or their particular orientations or needs.

Republicanizing Cities

In the course of the war, the suspicion of cities as places and urban dwellers in particular only amplified. The British occupied all of the major seaports for significant periods of time: Boston (1775–1776); New York City (1776–1783); Newport (1776–1779); Philadelphia (1777–1778); Savannah (1778–1782); and Charleston (1780–1782). In each case, citizens had to decide whether to remain behind and protect their homes or flee. To stay or to go, both when the British entered, and again when they retreated, might be taken as a sign of political support for one side or the other, potentially with lasting consequences. British troops wrought much destruction on public and private property while they occupied the cities. The State House in Philadelphia (today known as Independence Hall), for example, was unusable because the British had used its yard as an open pit for garbage, dead horses, and dead men. When American forces retook the cities, often those citizens who had remained behind faced a reckoning for their own behavior as well as blame for the vandalism of the troops. In Philadelphia, urban crowds took to

---

[18] Carp, *Rebels Rising*, 213.

lampooning elites who had frolicked and socialized with the British officers. On one occasion they dressed a lower-status, possibly African American woman in a gown and wig and paraded her through the streets as an indictment of the extravagance and duplicity of all the wealthy families who had remained behind, and particularly the infidelity of elite women.[19]

Tellingly, the British capture of the cities had not been determinative in the war effort. In taking the cities, the British did not subdue the countryside, even (and perhaps particularly) around New York, the city it held by far the longest. Rebels, including the fledgling government in Philadelphia, simply melted into the hinterlands and continued to wage the war from there. Moreover, the British were unable to hold any of the cities apart from New York for long. Massachusetts put up fierce resistance and bottled up the troops so effectively in Boston that less than a year after war broke out at the battles of Lexington and Concord the British evacuated. The British held Philadelphia for less than a year, and evacuated it without a fight because the city held so little strategic value, and the entry of France into the war in 1779 necessitated realigning its forces and military strategy. Newport in turn had to be abandoned when the French fleet arrived in fall 1779.

The British held onto the plantation colony cities of Savannah and Charleston and the Loyalist stronghold New York until the end of the war, but in each case these cities came to be isolated beachheads. The capture of Savannah and Charleston had been part of a grand Southern Strategy to retake what British planners hoped was a more Loyalist-leaning plantation South, but the arrival of the British into economies that relied upon racialized, dehumanized forced labor ignited a bitter three-way war between Americans, British, and enslaved (now, in some cases, formerly enslaved) African Americans. The ferocity of the resulting civil war in the Carolinas, and the prevalence of the endemic diseases malaria and yellow fever, bedeviled the easy conquest the British had assumed, and despite promising inroads in 1780, by summer 1781, the British had become bottled in Charleston and Savannah with little control beyond. Escaped formerly enslaved people fled to British lines, swelling the cities with refugees. In 1782, with armed conflict over but the formal peace treaty still to come, the British voluntarily evacuated both cities, taking tens of thousands of African

---

[19] Donald F. Johnson, "Ambiguous Allegiances: Urban Loyalties during the American Revolution," *Journal of American History* 104 (2017), 610–31; Benjamin H. Irvin, "The Streets of Philadelphia: Crowds, Congress, and the Political Culture of Revolution, 1774–1783," *Pennsylvania Magazine of History and Biography* 129:1 (2005), 7–44.

Americans with them as "contraband." New York City, conquered in 1776 by the largest expeditionary force the British had ever assembled, remained the only part of the rebellious colonies still under British control. Loyalists, who had flocked to New York from the region and from the other colonies, held out the hope that the British would retain the city and use it toward some reconciliation or even reconquest of North America. Their hopes were dashed when on 25 November 1783, in accordance with the Treaty of Paris the British formally ceded control of the city to George Washington and the Continental Army, and sailed for Halifax, the military garrison now converted into the headquarters of a massive refugee camp for tens of thousands of displaced Loyalists and freed people whom the British refused to abandon.[20]

The revolutionary cities were now cities of the new republic, but what that would mean in light of a long history of political marginalization, amidst a crippling post-war depression, the closure of trade with the British Empire, cities in need of rebuilding, and suspicion at the motives of many townspeople was by no means certain. Cities, at the forefront of commercial boycotts before the war and already painfully divided by socioeconomic class, were now beset by food and fuel shortages, sky-rocketing prices, and hyper-inflation. Meanwhile, British imports began to flood the market, undercutting local manufactures and deepening the painful economic woes of cities that had few resources to aid those who had fallen on hard times.

The tensions boiled over early in Philadelphia in the infamous Fort Wilson incident. In the aftermath of the British evacuation of the city, impoverished and hungry crowds had tried to enforce price controls, excoriating what they saw as price-gougers who made a profit off their pain. The crowds invoked ancient ideas of a moral economy in which the government has a duty to intervene to ensure access to basic goods like food. Many elites in Philadelphia, however, disagreed. Opponents to price controls often subscribed to the new economic theories of supply and demand recently articulated by Adam Smith; many were themselves war profiteers; and some were tainted by having remained in Philadelphia and comported themselves a little too amicably with the officers during the British occupation. Matters came to a head in October 1779 when a crowd decided to seize James Wilson, signer of the Declaration of Independence and future drafter of the Constitution, to answer for war profiteering and his friendship with

---

[20] Sylvia Frey, *Water from the Rock: Black Resistance in a Revolutionary Age* (Princeton: Princeton University Press, 1991).

suspected Loyalists. Wilson and about twenty friends withdrew into his house which came under attack by the crowd. Each side fired on the other, and the fight was only broken up after the Light Horse cavalry arrived, but not before five men had been killed and seventeen more wounded. This kind of urban disorder, now directed not against British oppressors but at the very men who led the Revolution, shocked and discomfited Patriot leaders. The cities needed to be controlled.[21]

Now old city charters and even the premise of local rule came furiously under attack. Critics argued that municipal corporations were aristocratic and monopolistic feudal-era relics with no place in a republic. As we have seen, the origins of municipal corporations indeed lay in the feudal past and bestowed special privileges on those people who qualified as citizens – a special status attained usually through purchase, inheritance, or, in the case of women, through marriage. Republican theorists charged that by granting particular rights and powers to some, corporations (municipal or otherwise) abridged the rights of everyone else, and indeed of the virtuous whole community. Moreover, with their privileges, corporations were empowered to pursue their own interests to the exclusion and at the expense of the overall public good. As a form of municipal government, old city charters were not only anachronistic in the new era but, some argued, actively pernicious.[22]

Republican political theory vacillated over the legitimacy and authority of local governments below the level of the province. Even as they emphasized the importance of consent and self-determination, revolutionaries claimed to represent a unitary public, and, indeed, argued that the public could only be unitary. Any diversion or disagreement signified not a healthy range of opinion, but that some people or groups were prioritizing their own selfish interests above those of the whole. The earliest iterations of American republicanism allowed no space for diverse constituencies with different needs or perspectives, and the problem of protecting minorities from majorities – or sometimes majorities from minorities – did not yet register as a pressing concern.[23]

---

[21] Eric Foner, *Tom Paine and Revolutionary America* (London: Oxford University Press, 1976).

[22] Oscar Handlin and Mary F. Handlin, "Origins of the American Business Corporation," *Journal of Economic History* 5 (1945), 1–23; Pauline Maier, "The Revolutionary Origins of the American Corporation," *William and Mary Quarterly*, 3rd series, 50 (1993), 51–84.

[23] John L. Brooke. "Consent, Civil Society, and the Public Sphere in the Age of Revolution and the Early American Republic," in Jeffrey L. Pasley et al., eds., *Beyond the Founders: New Approaches to the Political History of the Early Republic* (Chapel Hill: University of North Carolina Press, 2004), 207–50.

The idea that American cities might need separate accommodations or tailored institutions flew in the face of unitary republican political theory. One of the critical steps on the way to declaring independence had been the Continental Congress' invitation in May 1776 to the colonies to write new state constitutions since their royal charters were no longer valid. Through the 1770s, 1780s, and 1790s, the states wrote a flurry of constitutions, incrementally adding innovations like separate constitutional conventions and ratification by the people. In all these cases, the polity was imagined at the scale of the state, and the mechanisms of power were thought rightly to rest at that level. Intermediary bodies, whether municipal or county governments, must be strictly subordinated to the state lest they counteract the good of the whole. Thus, even as states tussled back and forth with the national government about the allocation of power between them, and even as states staked their case in part on the importance of local governance that would be sensitive to conditions within their local communities, they staunchly resisted similar arguments inside their states that might enlarge municipal autonomy. Instead, states reincorporated cities (or incorporated them for the first time) with charters that firmly established the primacy of the state legislatures: Charleston in 1783 (and at the same time the legislature changed its name from Charles Town to Charleston); Newport in 1784; Norfolk in 1787; Philadelphia in 1789; and, finally, Boston in 1822.

New York City was the exception. New York State's 1777 constitution explicitly protected the New York City Corporation. Given that the city was at that time controlled by the British Army, this measure had little practical effect, but the precedent set in the 1777 constitution endured and was reaffirmed in 1821 when New York drafted its next constitution. After the war, with New York's population and economy rapidly rebounding, the state and the city worked in tandem, with corporation officials downplaying rather than enforcing their autonomy and thereby avoiding a power struggle between state and municipal officials. In this case, the city corporation's deep history of legal, political, and especially economic strength made it a useful institution for rebuilding after the war and contributed to its perpetuation. Meanwhile, the shrewd willingness of corporation officers voluntarily to work hand-in-glove with state authorities prevented the latter from attempting to enforce direct supervision.[24]

---

[24] Hartog, *Public Property and Private Power*.

As a final coda to how a new nation of citizens viewed the real and appropriate political place of cities, consider the new federal capital. Article I, Section 8, mandated that Congress would "exercise exclusive Legislation in all Cases whatsoever, over such District (not exceeding ten Miles square) as may, by Cession of particular States, and the Acceptance of Congress, become the Seat of the Government of the United States."[25] The framers insisted that the capital be under the direct control of Congress because they understood that, with the modest exception of New York City, all American towns and cities were politically subservient to their states. To place the national government in one or another city, then, might give that state undue power. Despite agitation to attract the national capital to an existing city, particularly New York or Philadelphia which had both served before in that capacity, the framers ultimately chose to construct a new city. The District of Columbia (DC) was founded in 1796, carved out of land ceded by both Maryland and Virginia (though the latter rescinded its land later in the nineteenth century). It remained for decades, as Charles Dickens scornfully termed it in an 1842 visit, a "City of Magnificent Intentions," a swampy, dilapidated little town.[26]

The capital city of a republic founded upon the principles of consent and equal representation had for its own part neither. Citizens of DC could not vote for local representatives, had no representation in Congress, and could not vote for president, even though they paid federal taxes. Not until 1973 did DC receive self-rule, though with restrictions and with continued Congressional oversight over both its laws and budget. DC residents can now vote for president (since 1961), but at the time of writing still pay federal taxes without any voting congressional representation. This lack of municipal autonomy or extension of basic political rights to its citizens may seem anomalous in the twenty-first century, but in fact originated out of the particular late eighteenth-century political circumstances when the District was founded. Powerful rural interests had long harbored deep suspicions of American cities, acted to counteract urban political autonomy, and, in most cases, used the upheaval of the American Revolution to enhance rather than reexamine that asymmetry. In the nation's capital, the divorce between cities and citizenship became complete.

[25] "The Constitution of the United States," 1787, America's Founding Documents, National Archives, accessed 4 July 2020, www.archives.gov/founding-docs/constitution-transcript.
[26] Keith Melder, *City of Magnificent Intentions: A History of Washington, District of Columbia*, 2nd edition (Washington, DC: Intac, 1997).

9

The Other British Colonies

TREVOR BURNARD

During the eighteenth century, Britain, even more than other European seaborne empires, built a vast and increasingly integrated overseas empire, largely located in the Americas. The Seven Years' War established the British Empire as global and highly successful, meaning that the pre-Seven Years' War conception of a commercial empire whose benefit to Britain was trade and a place of settlement for Britain's excess population was altered to consider Britain's enhanced geopolitical position as a major world power. In 1763, the future looked rosy, and Britain embarked upon policies of establishing an imperial system which would place colonial possessions more firmly than before under metropolitan control. That effort at systematic rationalization of colonial governance proved, as we know, disastrous, resulting in the American Revolution and a permanent division from 1783 in the British American empire, with thirteen of Britain's twenty-seven colonies in the Americas declaring independence. A slight majority of Britain's colonies extant in 1776 remained within the British Empire, including some of Britain's wealthiest and most promising colonies. In the French Revolutionary and Napoleonic wars, Britain added to these possessions through major acquisitions of territory in the Caribbean and by establishing new colonies in regions of the world as different as Africa and Australasia. The end of the American Revolution signaled a new period in the history of the British Empire, but it was far from a period in which the empire's geographic center moved decisively to the East from the West. The British colonies in the Atlantic world that either remained or were acquired during the Age of Atlantic Revolutions were vital parts of a changing geopolitical and economic order in which Britain solidified its global dominance in the period economic historians have termed the Great Divergence (when the West overtook the East in economic power). The Atlantic colonies that Britain retained during the Age of Revolutions helped to undergird these global transformations, by providing wealth and power to Britain in a period when the Industrial Revolution was making it unprecedently rich.[1]

The title of this chapter, however, betrays a lingering notion that somehow the British colonies in the Americas which remained in the empire following the Treaty of Paris in 1783 were diminished parts of a less dominant British empire and that they were side players to the main events. These events were the drama of an American Revolution and the creation of a powerful new nation, the United States of America, and the French Revolutionary and Napoleonic wars, which were mainly focused on conflicts over control of Europe with secondary battles over dominance by European empires in India. This chapter challenges this notion that somehow the "other" British colonies were of secondary importance in the Atlantic revolutions. It will argue that the British West Indies and Canada were central to the Atlantic revolutions from the period of the Seven Years' War until the end of slavery in the British West Indies in 1834. It will explore the dynamism of these colonies in the mid-eighteenth century and argue that economically most colonies survived the American Revolution largely intact and with the promise of a considerable future ahead of them. Expansion in the British Atlantic after 1783 showed how valuable West Indian colonies continued to be to British geopolitical and economic policies, and how Canada was rapidly becoming a set of colonies that were developing into vibrant settler societies. Yet for the former set of colonies, the future was compromised by the fact that their social structure and economic profitability was based almost entirely on the continuation of both the Atlantic slave trade and slavery. These institutions, however, were increasingly problematic in the age of the Atlantic revolutions as ideological conflicts over human rights and democratic principles led many Britons to question the morality of having an empire founded largely upon slavery. The sudden explosion of abolitionist sympathy from 1788 made the "other" British colonies the object of fierce debate, in which the themes and ideologies of the Atlantic revolutions were played out in dramatic fashion. The "other" British colonies were not incidental to the Atlantic revolutions. They were fundamental to understanding the character and the achievement of social, political, and economic change in the Atlantic world from 1763 to 1834.

---

[1] For how a new kind of British empire emerged during the Age of Revolutions, which continued into the nineteenth century, see James Belich, *Replenishing the Earth: The Settler Revolution and the Rise of the Anglo-World 1783–1939* (Oxford: Oxford University Press, 2009).

From the Seven Years' War to the American Revolution

As the Age of Atlantic Revolutions dawned during the reshaping of European empires that occurred during the Seven Years' War, few people involved with the expansion of imperial Britain would have considered their possessions in the Caribbean, Ireland, Canada, and India as "other" and as somewhat inferior and unimportant compared with the Thirteen Colonies that later became the United States of America in 1788. Indeed, it was more the opposite case – one reason why the British governments in the 1760s and 1770s made such catastrophic policy mistakes in relation to British North America is that they were paying more attention to other parts of the empire rather than to the Thirteen Colonies, which had been allowed to have a considerable amount of local autonomy and largely left alone. Before the Seven Years' War, the empire was not especially centralized, if compared, say, with the Spanish empire. As Patrick Griffin argues, "the empire resembled a rabbit warren of differing arrangements passed under different monarchs all for different reasons to address different problems."[2]

The two most important parts of empire c. 1760 were Ireland – which was both a kingdom and a colony and which is not part of this chapter – and the West Indies. The British Caribbean was central to the dominant British visions of empire in the protean period between the end of the Glorious Revolution and the start of the Seven Years' War. British statesmen in the age of Robert Walpole thought that maximizing labor productivity, as with slavery, and producing goods, such as sugar, at the lowest possible cost for the benefit of a growing consumer class was central to any imperial policy. Thus, the British West Indies occupied more attention and received more favorable treatment than did the northern colonies, while advancing the Atlantic slave trade was a key commercial aim. The plantation system was at the center of imperial thought and practice, and until the 1760s virtually no one doubted its utility to the British nation. British statesmen listened to absentee planters from the Caribbean, such as the fabulously wealthy William Beckford, William Pitt's close friend and a radical lord mayor of London as well as the greatest slaveowner in the empire, in ways that they

---

[2] Patrick Griffin, *The Townshend Moment: The Making of Empire and Revolution in the Eighteenth Century* (New Haven: Yale University Press, 2017), 25.

never did to the relatively parvenu representatives of colonies in British North America.³

If we take a less American-centric view of the American Revolution than is normal, then we can see the age of the Atlantic revolutions in the British empire as starting outside the Thirteen Colonies, in the years of imperial triumph between 1759 and 1762, rather than the customary date of 1763. In these years, Britain acquired a global empire that seemed to betoken lasting geopolitical and economic dominance for the small European island. The major events of this period happened outside the Thirteen Colonies, and the great imperial heroes, like General James Wolfe and Robert Clive of India, made their reputation in this new empire. Britain acquired Quebec, meaning that it now had massive holdings north and west of its existing American possessions. It also achieved a dominance it had never had in Bengal with the acquisition of the *Diwani*, or rights to tribute in that rich province. Indeed, James Vaughn argues that the second British empire began on 12 August 1765 when the extractive riches of India fell into Britain's grip.⁴ And perhaps the most remarkable triumph of the Seven Years' War came in the Caribbean in 1762 when imperial and American troops besieged and took the seemingly impregnable citadel of Havana in Cuba, creating unprecedented tremors throughout the Spanish empire, as the Spanish realized that their American possessions were suddenly vulnerable.⁵ It was in the "other colonies" where the empire that was to come in the nineteenth century evolved – one divided between settler societies, like Australia and Canada and to an extent Ireland and South Africa, and extractive societies, such as the new colonies of the British West Indies in the southern Caribbean taken in the first years of the nineteenth century as well as the colonies in Asia and Africa.⁶

Another, more ominous event, at least for white settlers, occurred in May 1760 in Jamaica, which signaled a different start to the Age of Revolutions than what we customarily associate with settler protests about taxation without representation beginning around 1765. Enslaved men, probably

---

³ Perry Gauci, *William Beckford: First Prime Minister of the London Empire* (New Haven: Yale University Press, 2013).
⁴ James Vaughn, *The Politics of Empire at the Accession of George III: The East India Company and the Crisis and Transformation of Britain's Imperial State* (New Haven: Yale University Press, 2019), 1.
⁵ Elena Schneider, *The Occupation of Havana: War, Trade, and Slavery in the Atlantic World* (Williamsburg, VA: Omohundro Institute of Early American History and Culture; Chapel Hill: University of North Carolina Press, 2018).
⁶ C. A. Bayly, *Imperial Meridian: The British Empire and the World, 1780–1830* (London: Longman, 1989).

under the leadership of Wager or Apongo, a military chieftain from Dahomey who had become enslaved in western Jamaica, cultivated in secret an island-wide conspiracy to overthrow settler government and institute an African-style system of rule, similar, probably, to that practiced by Maroon communities in the Jamaican interior. The conspiracy exploded into rebellion by accident when Tacky, more than likely a lieutenant of Wager in northern Jamaica, started a rebellion earlier than Wager intended. One result of this premature start to rebellion was that we have always named the revolt after Tacky, rather than Apongo. The rebellion soon became a massive island-wide war, which in its seriousness as a challenge to white rule was unprecedented in the British empire before the Sepoy rebellion in India in 1857. The enslaved rebels were overcome through the determined actions of a skilled governor, Sir Henry Moore; the fortuitous presence of many regular sailors and soldiers in Jamaica serving during the Seven Years' War; and the help given to the white military by Maroons, who fulfilled in 1760 their part of a bargain they had entered into in 1739 to support white rule in return for the imperial government's recognition of their autonomy.[7]

Tacky's Revolt showed in a startling manner that enslaved people were dangerous opponents who would fight for their freedom if given the chance. The revolt was thus an important foreshadowing of the much greater Haitian Revolution of 1791–1804, even to the extent of being a rebellion happening in wartime when white society was under stress from the threat of foreign invasion. The lessons that Jamaicans, and planters throughout the West Indies, learned from Tacky's Revolt, however, were very different from the lessons of the Haitian Revolution, mainly because the revolt was put down, albeit with difficulty, rather than being successful. What slaveowners learned from Tacky was that a slave revolt could be overcome if Whites were ever vigilant about policing enslaved behavior; if Whites were united around notions of white supremacy, in which all Blacks, both free and enslaved, were put in inferior positions to Whites; and, most importantly, that any sign of rebellion from enslaved people was dealt with through maximum force and gruesome acts of retribution. If enslaved people were rigorously controlled and kept in a state of perpetual fear, then the highly profitable system of the British West Indies – then entering a period of peak prosperity until 1776 through which planters became easily the richest group

---

[7] Vincent Brown, *Tacky's Revolt: The Story of an Atlantic Slave War* (Cambridge, MA: Harvard University Press, 2020).

within the British empire – could be preserved from any further shock like the slave war of 1760.[8]

If race was one dividing line within the "other colonies" of British America in the years between the Seven Years' War and the American Revolution, then religion was another. The new acquisitions taken from France in the settlement of 1763 were religiously diverse with large populations of Catholics in Quebec and Grenada complicating an empire in the Atlantic which was previously almost completely Protestant, except in Ireland. The terms on which the new Atlantic colonies were to be established were strongly assimilationist in tone. Catholics were promised freedom of worship, but it was also made clear that the influence of the papacy was not welcome. Where there were Protestant settlers involved, as in Grenada, opposition to any encouragement of Catholics was fierce. They argued that the very survival of the colony depended on "the support of the Protestant religion, and the driving from the councils and offices of the nation, all enemies of that persuasion." Protestant planters withheld taxes, resulting in a virtual paralysis of government, a paralysis that won widespread sympathy in Britain and North America.[9] In Quebec, assimilation proceeded more slowly, mainly because British settlement in the colony was limited before the nineteenth century. But some accommodation had to be made with the huge French Catholic majority. By 1774, the British government was convinced that this mainly French colony could not stay within the empire if the mass of its population felt their religion and the legal basis of their society were under threat. The result was the Quebec Act of 1774, in which the right of French colonists to practice their Catholic religion was recognized while the colony was denied its own assembly for the moment. The Act aroused great opposition in both the Thirteen Colonies and in Britain, suggesting that popery and despotism were taking root in the empire.[10] But the larger significance of the Quebec Act was to show that Britain could create viable imperial policies that satisfied settler populations even while it was alienating its largest settler population, in the Thirteen Colonies.

---

[8] Trevor Burnard, *Jamaica in the Age of Revolution* (Philadelphia: University of Pennsylvania Press, 2020).
[9] Andrew Jackson O'Shaughnessy, *An Empire Divided: The American Revolution and the British Caribbean* (Philadelphia: University of Pennsylvania, 2000), 124–6; Hannah Weiss Muller, *Subjects and Sovereign: Bonds of Belonging in the Eighteenth-Century British Empire* (Oxford: Oxford University Press, 2017).
[10] Philip Lawson, *The Imperial Challenge: Quebec and Britain in the Age of the American Revolution* (Montreal and Kingston: McGill and Queen's University Press, 1990).

As Andrew O'Shaughnessy has argued in a penetrating essay on British imperial policy and the American Revolution, British policy in the empire was not, as Americans sometimes imagined, *sui generis* in relation to North America. Rather, Britain embarked upon a series of parallel initiatives throughout the British empire in the 1760s which were intended to solidify support for the empire. The only place where their policies did not work was in the Thirteen Colonies. In the "other colonies," empire was strengthened among settler populations in this period and loyalty to Britain was enhanced, even in Ireland, where Catholic unrest was moderated by Protestant enthusiasm for greater imperial participation, including service in the armed forces. O'Shaughnessy notes that the common themes in imperial policy included concerted attempts "to reform the empire, increase revenues, regulate trade, improve defenses, and strengthen metropolitan control," all reflected in a rising number of imperial officials. He notes that Britain was hardly alone in wanting to reform the empire – France and Spain did so at the same time.[11] Between the 1720s and the 1760s, the growing power of the British state and its fiscal–military system created an ever more tightly integrated empire in terms of migration; the imperial economy, social, religious, and political cultures; and Anglicization. Thus, as John Murrin argues, the American Revolution was a countercyclical event – a crisis of imperial *integration* that the British state could not handle.[12] Or, more precisely, they could not handle it in respect to the Thirteen Colonies. Everywhere else in the empire, integration proceeded quite well. Thus, it is misleading to see the period before the American Revolution as a crisis. For everywhere except the Thirteen Colonies, imperial policies in the 1760s proved to be an opportunity for imperial growth and economic prosperity. Considering the "other colonies" in this period encourages us to realize that, as O'Shaughnessy comments, "those who argue today that the best policy would have been to continue past practices and maintain the status quo ignore the extent to which the problems posed by the aftermath of the Seven Years' War, required solutions that could only be effectively coordinated by a central government," including securing Caribbean islands from enslaved revolt, managing religion in Canada, overseeing the treatment of Indigenes in

---

[11] Andrew Jackson O'Shaughnessy, "British Imperial Policy and the American Revolution," in Elaine Chalus and Perry Gauci, eds., *Revisiting the Polite and Commercial People* (Oxford: Oxford University Press, 2019), 191–2.

[12] John M. Murrin, *Rethinking America: From Empire to Republic* (New York: Oxford University Press, 2018), 162–3.

North America and India, and ensuring that the costs of empire did not outmatch the resources of the home country.[13]

The War of American Independence

In general, British settlers outside the Thirteen Colonies, including Protestants in Ireland, were relatively happy with the direction of imperial politics in the years immediately before American independence. American revolutionaries had some support in Canada, Ireland, and in the British West Indies, but not enough to lead anyone in these colonies to seriously contemplate joining in rebellion. Advocates of rebellion in the Thirteen Colonies never tried to include West Indians in their plans – West Indians were not invited, for example, to participate in the Continental Congress and thus did not join in the radicalizing process that happened when politicians from different colonies came together for the first time. Americans often had a very low opinion of West Indians whom they thought had undue influence in Britain and whose preening power they resented. James Otis, for example, the John the Baptist of the Boston revolutionary movement, fulminated in 1764 that the Caribbean colonies were a "compound mongrel mixture of *English, Indian* and *Negro*," as opposed to New Englanders who were "freeborn *British white* subjects, whose loyalty has never yet been suspected." Otis believed, in arguments that foreshadowed those of the early abolitionist, Granville Sharp, a few years later, that West Indian planters, accustomed to being slaveowners, would, "for a little present gain," make other Americans "worse than enslaved people if possible," worse than the Africans whose treatment Otis deplored.[14]

In 1774, the Jamaica Assembly sent a message of support to the Continental Congress. It lamented, using the customary rhetoric of political helplessness that it had used in petitions to the crown since the 1720s, that their colony was so "weak and feeble" that they could not "now intend, or ever could have intended, resistance to Great Britain." In other words, they offered Americans only moral rather than actual support. The Continental Congress replied with withering scorn. They sent a message to Jamaica that gave them "the warmest gratitude for your pathetic mediation on our behalf with the Crown." American Patriots never made any attempt to either

---

[13] O'Shaughnessy, "British Imperial Policy," 205.
[14] Burnard, *Jamaica in the Age of Revolution*, 204–5, 207.

recruit West Indians to their cause or left it open, as they did with Canada, for West Indians to join with them in rebellion, or to become additional states in the United States after independence. By the early 1770s, a gap had opened between the Thirteen Colonies and the West Indies that never closed. White settlers in the British Caribbean were instinctively Loyalist, believing that they could defend their most critical imperial interests through the representations of well-connected West Indians living in Britain. Moreover, Britain tended to reward the West Indies because they were convinced that the islands were central to imperial geopolitics and because their economic contributions to Britain were too great to ignore.

The one event that might have led West Indians to throw in their lot with American revolutionaries was the decision by Lord Mansfield in the *Somerset* case of 1772 to stop a Virginia planter resident in Britain from sending his enslaved man to Jamaica. *Somerset* was a galvanizing event that convinced southern and West Indian slaveowners that Britain was prepared to compromise colonial liberties. Alan Taylor has noted that it created a storm of controversy in Virginia, intensifying opposition to British taxation policies in the colony at a moment when, unlike much of the British Caribbean, Virginia was in the economic doldrums.[15] *Somerset* was an event that convinced southerners and West Indian planters that Britain was prepared to compromise colonial liberties, one of the most important of such liberties being the right to absolute control over property, included property in humans. But the outrage over *Somerset* was not enough to unite Virginians, South Carolinians, Georgians, and West Indians together, and it did not transform the conflict with Britain in the 1770s from an arcane battle over taxation and representation to one over the more substantial issues of the preservation of slavery in plantation societies. One reason why *Somerset* did not unite the plantation colonies as one against perceived British tyranny was that Lord Mansfield had been very careful to circumscribe his decision so that its implications were never realized until the 1780s with the birth of a popular abolitionist movement in Britain. Thus, *Somerset* was an abstraction rather than a practical issue in British American plantation societies. It was not followed by any legislation that curtailed planters' rights. All it did was limit the power of slaveowners in Britain to sell their enslaved property. And it was decided at a period of peak

---

[15] Alan Taylor, *The Internal Enemy: Slavery and War in Virginia, 1772–1832* (New York: W. W. Norton, 2013), 3–4.

prosperity in the Caribbean, and not long before Britain had decided, in *Campbell* v. *Hall*, to settle the constitutional issue that most vexed West Indian settlers, which was the extent to which the king's prerogative prevailed over planter pretensions to local autonomy.

Americans were more interested in provoking rebellion in Canada. They thought that Anglo-Canadians were as disposed to rebellion as they were, having heard that their northern compatriots were as offended by British authoritarianism and as susceptible to republicanism as themselves. There was some incipient support for American rebels. After the battles of Concord and Lexington in 1775, Anglo-Canadian Patriots in Montreal poured black paint over a bust of George III, topped it with a bishop's miter, and hung a sign on it calling George III "the Pope of Canada or the English Fool." It encouraged the Continental Army to invade Canada under the command of Benedict Arnold and Richard Montgomery. It was a disastrous failure, with the Americans soon beaten back to their colonies in disgrace – in ways like the more concerted campaign to conquer Canada in the war of 1812. Quebec's defenders, unlike 1759, had won against outside attackers, securing the province in the British empire, with General Guy Carleton the hero. Carleton then launched a counter-offensive in New York in 1776, inflicting a major defeat on Patriots at Lake Champlain before retreating to Canada in winter. This retreat when he had Americans at his mercy was severely criticized in Britain, temporarily derailing Carleton's previously stellar career, although he returned to favor in 1783 as commander-in-chief of British forces in North America. Conceivably, if Carleton had continued his attacks on American troops, parts of New York – a center of Loyalism – might have become incorporated into Canada.

Loyalism

Revolutionary enthusiasm throughout the British empire as war started was more muted than is commonly believed – we need to include as Loyalists most Whites in the British West Indies and Canada, as well as Irish Protestants and probably a large majority of Britons. And while enslaved people and Native Americans tended to see the American Revolution as a battle between two equally disliked groups, more of them helped the British than assisted American revolutionaries. Even in the Thirteen Colonies, the number of Loyalists was large, especially if we add to the relatively few people who actively espoused Loyalist ideas the majority of the population who wanted to stay neutral in the conflict and who tended to continue to have sympathies for the king and empire well after 1776.[16] There were many people who were outraged by the American revolt and believed it should be suppressed and the political doctrines of the American Patriots should be revealed to be pernicious. Support for the revolution fell dramatically throughout the "other colonies" after France and Spain entered the war on the American side after 1778. As Stephen Conway argues, American Patriots came to be seen in Britain after the American Revolution became a global war less as fellow-countrymen, fighting erroneously against their mother country, than as foreigners, determined to undermine British liberty and authority.[17]

P. J. Marshall describes very well the Loyalist position, which was held not just in the Thirteen Colonies, where active Loyalists were relatively numerous, especially in highly divided and politically polarized colonies such as New York and North Carolina, but in the "other colonies" where the default position was Loyalism. He notes that "loyalists rejected American independence since they did not believe that Americans were a separate people," but were "communities within the empire with rights and privileges of their own derived from the British constitution." They accepted the right of the British parliament to tax the colonies and believed that what Bostonians had done in the 1773 Tea Party had gone beyond the boundaries of legitimate dissent into outright and disloyal rebellion. Many Loyalists, especially those of higher social status, feared that the wild ideas of liberty thrown about by revolutionaries would have a levelling tendency and by promoting lawless anarchy were harming an empire that they saw as the entity assuring Britons abroad of the benefits of the peerless British constitution.[18]

Simon Taylor of Jamaica (1740–1813) is an example of a man of loyalist principles. A fabulously wealthy planter, who died a millionaire, he was a fervent patriot and loyal subject who could see nothing positive in the coming of the American Revolution. He saw it as "truly alarming," and highly threatening to his own and Jamaican prosperity. Initially, he had some sympathy for the American cause. Conflict between Britain and America, he thought, might have some beneficial results, lancing a boil between two recalcitrant sides, so that "good might come out of evil." Events in Boston in

---

[16] Ruma Chopra, *Choosing Sides: Loyalists in Revolutionary America* (Lanham, MD: Rowman & Littlefield, 2013).

[17] Stephen Conway, "From Fellow-Nationals to Foreigners: British Perceptions of the Americans Circa 1739–1783," *William and Mary Quarterly*, 3rd series, 59 (2002), 65–100.

[18] P. J. Marshall, *Remaking the British Atlantic: The United States and the British Empire after American Independence* (Oxford: Oxford University Press, 2012), 68–9.

1774 turned him firmly against American Patriots. He wrote to a friend in that year that he supported the Coercive Acts because "after what the Americans have done Britain cannot give up the point [as] it would only be making them more arrogant than they are at present and I look upon them as dogs that will bark but dare not stand when opposed [and are] loud in mouth but slow to action."

Taylor remained loyal to Britain throughout the war, as abolition transformed the Jamaican political landscape after 1788 and as the Haitian Revolution exploded in the 1790s. All three events, especially the latter two, disturbed him greatly. Jamaica's plight in the early 1780s, when hurricanes struck the island; when French invasion seemed imminent as Jamaica was dragged into the maelstrom of the American conflict; and when plantation profits plummeted and enslaved people faced starvation as a result of supplies from North America drying up; made him grumble that he might leave Jamaica "to go to some other Government where we might be able to make a shift to live, and not be held in Egyptian bondage." Abolitionism he thought to be lunacy, led by "that Madman Wilberforce," whose power to influence Britons toward an animosity to the slave interest which Taylor thought a bulwark of the national interest amazed him. The arrival of the French Revolution and what he saw as the ultimate disaster of slave revolt in Saint-Domingue made him fear for the future. His self-image as a fervent and conservative British patriot contributing to British wealth and influence through his activities as a wealthy planter and colonial politician made him not only opposed to the excesses, as he saw them, of the French Revolution in the 1790s, but to the dreadful republicanism of the newly established United States. What he saw in the United States was the "cant of philosophy, liberty and equality," ideas he considered "the most pernicious vermin that were ever created." American ideology was intended "to overcome all established government and in order to establish in their room murder, anarchy and confusion."[19]

For men such as Taylor, and for many other conservatives in the "other colonies," bewildered at the changes initiated during the Age of Revolutions, all of which seemed to undermine hierarchy and support insubordination and alarming doctrines such as republicanism and even Black equality, there seemed no safe space to go to. Abolitionist Britain had betrayed him and fellow patriotic slaveowners. He could not go to the United States as that

---

[19] Christer Petley, *White Fury: A Jamaican Slaveholder and the Age of Revolution* (Oxford: Oxford University Press, 2018).

would mean that he would have "to learn the new philosophy of rights of Men." He was protected from any real harm by his massive wealth, but in the latter half of his life he saw personal fulfillment matched by dismay at the public events unfolding around him. His money could not protect him, he believed, from the ravages of a revolutionary world and from the betrayal of his reflexive loyalty to monarch, Church, the Tory Party, and to a hierarchical order in which slavery sustained an agreeable culture of deference.[20]

Loyalists in the Thirteen Colonies who shared Taylor's opinions were unable to fulminate in private, but were forced to move as a result of American independence. The Loyalist diaspora was large – about 80,000 people, including not just Loyalists but also thousands of their slaves – was dispersed around the British empire, including Britain itself. About 8,000 Whites and 5,000 Blacks went to Britain, where they found themselves ignored and shunned as embarrassing reminders of Britain's loss in America. Most Loyalists stayed within the empire, taking up incentives of land and supplies. Over half went to Canada, while about 6,000 from the American South went to Jamaica and the Bahamas, taking their enslaved property with them. As Maya Jasanoff contends, "loyalists landed in every corner of the British Empire" so that by the time of the French Revolution, "the map of the loyalist diaspora looked much like the map of the empire as a whole."[21]

One special group of Loyalists was African Americans. They were people who saw the American Revolutionary War as a way to gain their freedom – they were far from being the conservative defenders of the old order, such as Simon Taylor. Thousands fled plantations to join the British Army, which in response was forced to adopt a liberationist role being the de facto guarantor of escaped Blacks' freedom. David George was one of the 20,000 Blacks who soldiered for the British, escaping slavery on 30 January 1779 to serve in the British Army, where he was also an active and much-beloved preacher to black communities and soldiers, He and his family were among 1,500 free Blacks who were evacuated from Charleston in November 1782, headed for Nova Scotia. He established a Baptist congregation in Shelburne, living in a "smart hut" with a quarter acre of land attached. Shelburne, however, was no paradise. George discovered "the White people were against me." The pressure of living as a free Black in British North America proved to be

---

[20] Burnard, *Jamaica in the Age of Revolution*, 194–8.
[21] Maya Jasanoff, *Liberty's Exiles: American Loyalists in the Revolutionary World* (New York: Alfred A. Knopf, 2011), 10.

intolerable by the 1790s, so he moved with hundreds of other free Blacks from Nova Scotia and 300 or so destitute Blacks in Britain to Sierra Leone. He died in Freetown, Sierra Leone, in 1810, after years of preaching to a loyal flock.[22]

Where Loyalists were most important was in British North America, in the five provinces that came to make up Canada in the nineteenth century. The loss of the Thirteen Colonies made areas on the northern fringe of empire important places for the Loyalist diaspora of the 1780s. Canada received a sudden influx of new inhabitants from the United States – the great majority of the 80,000 Loyalists who left the United States, including more ordinary people than the Whites who went to Britain and fewer slaveowners than went to the West Indies and the Bahamas. Many left because they rightfully feared discrimination in the new republic due to their enthusiasm for the unwritten British constitution, British concepts of liberty, and the benefits of being White people in a British empire that was favorable to settler values and interests. But in most respects, the Loyalists heading to Canada were not dissimilar to the Americans who remained in the United States. They harbored republican ideas and were as keen on political autonomy as were colonial Americans. It appears that few Loyalists carried much ideological baggage with them into exile. Many were attracted by what seemed to be Canadian largesse. Taxes (ironically, given the causes of the American Revolution) were lower than in the United States. Merchants could trade with places like the British West Indies from which Americans were nominally and sometimes practically excluded in the 1780s. Most Loyalists remained instinctively Americans and their societies were more American than British in the late eighteenth century, despite fervent efforts by ruling elites to make Canada anglicized and thus different from both French Canada and the United States. The ruling elite did have the state-supported Church of England in the non-French parts of the colony as a bulwark of society, but Canada, in its ethnic diversity, religious pluralism, and determination for self-government, stayed part of a wider British Atlantic world in which the United States was central, even if not politically part of the British empire. It was probably not until the war of 1812 that American identity was replaced firmly by an attachment to Britain in Canada. As Alan Taylor notes, that Anglo-American war – a final manifestation of the revolutionary struggles of the 1770s but with a different result than in the

---

[22] David's career can be traced in Jasanoff, *Liberty's Exiles*.

1780s – was "a civil war between kindred peoples, recently and incompletely separated by the American Revolution."[23]

The Caribbean and the French Revolution

The American Revolutionary War was a significant event in the changing relationship between West Indian planters and the metropole, as Eric Williams stressed long ago.[24] But the French Revolution and its transatlantic consequences were more significant than what followed the American Revolution. Until the 1790s, planters and merchants in the British West Indies were reasonably in control of the political process in their islands – they ran the colonial state so that it complemented the imperial state in ways that made their interests, and especially their concerns over security, of paramount importance. At the beginning of the 1790s, the future looked rosy for White West Indians. They had overcome the economic dip of the early 1780s, when French invasion threatened, supplies from America had dried up, and the Atlantic slave trade was in trouble. By the late 1780s, plantation productivity was at or above the level it had been in the early 1770s. Planters prospered. They were confident that they could overcome the sudden challenge of abolitionism, which, as they saw it, had exploded out of nowhere in the late 1780s and which they considered was a phenomenon that would be soon put down.

The start of the Haitian Revolution in 1791 as a by-product of the French revolutions, which quickly transformed debates over liberty and equality into a war over slavery, and the advent of world war in the Caribbean, as French, Spanish, and British troops competed for dominance in a sector of the world now seen as very valuable, changed irrevocably West Indian planters' feelings that they were in control of events. What comes out extremely clearly in writings of the period from prominent planters like Simon Taylor is that they felt bewildered and confused by the rapid changes to the old order that came about as revolution swamped the Caribbean in the 1790s. The Haitian Revolution, it is true, did lead to a short-term financial bonanza as the Saint-Domingue economy imploded and the British West Indies made bumper profits. Simon Taylor made the extraordinary sum of £56,000 in the

---

[23] Alan Taylor, "The Wart of 1812 and the Struggle for a Continent," in Andrew Shankman, ed., *The World of the Revolutionary American Republic: Land, Labor, and the Conflict for a Continent* (New York: Routledge, 2014), 259.

[24] Eric Williams, *Capitalism and Slavery* (Chapel Hill: University of North Carolina Press, 1944).

out of the ordinary year of 1792. But revolution and war forced West Indian planters to embrace the principles of loyal and patriotic counter-revolution and necessitated compromising on their previously strong demands for colonial autonomy on the North American model. White West Indians were forced, as Christer Petley argues, "to accept their deepening military dependence on Britain while trying to defend a slave system that appeared to be increasingly prone to revolutionary upheaval." It meant that "by 1807, these planters were left with little choice other than to accept a resounding political defeat, when Parliament abolished the slave trade."[25]

Warning signs were developing for West Indian planters before the challenge of the French Revolution. The image of the planter deteriorated after the American Revolution. Planters were increasingly excoriated in Britain's popular press as cruel despots, addicted to "venery" with black women and demonstrating in their "orientalist" behavior similar to that of nabobs in the East India Company disturbing signs that they had deviated appreciably from proper British decorum.[26] But their power over running things in the colonies was still strong before the mid-1790s. White West Indians had a long tradition of colonial rebelliousness and their threats to resist metropolitan demands still had some force in the early 1790s. If Britain had ended the slave trade in this period, it may have encountered violent and potentially successful opposition from West Indian planters.

This possibility of successful violent resistance to imperial decrees ended just a few years later. On the face of it, the British West Indies prospered and expanded during the transatlantic French revolutionary period. Not only did it get an economic windfall by replacing Saint-Domingue as the principal provider of sugar to Europe, the seemingly inexorable march of abolitionism as seen in 1788 was halted due to parliamentary fears that allowing any reform movements to develop would expose Britain to the revolutionary impulses that were tearing apart France. Moreover, Britain fought the French in the Caribbean, and while it failed to take over Saint-Domingue/Haiti from enslaved rebels, it successfully conquered other islands and part of Guiana, establishing a new beachhead for plantation agriculture in the southern Caribbean. In addition, British merchants, including slave traders, penetrated Spanish American markets more effectively than ever before.

---

[25] Christer Petley, "Slaveholders and Revolution: The Jamaican Planter Class, British Imperial Politics, and the Ending of the Slave Trade, 1775–1807," *Slavery & Abolition* 39 (2018), 53–79: 55.

[26] Trevor Burnard, "Powerless Masters: The Curious Decline of Jamaican Sugar Planters in the Foundational Period of British Abolition," *Slavery & Abolition* 32 (2011), 185–98.

But the short-term gains planters and merchants achieved in the early 1790s were more than outweighed by the long-term consequences of the radicalization of the French Revolution as manifested in Saint-Domingue and the outbreak of war between Britain and France. These wars were enormously expensive, costing £20 million between 1793 and 1798, and led to the deaths of over 40,000 British servicemen, mostly from tropical disease. As Petley argues, "this augmented the abolitionist image of the West Indies as a place of cruelty with revivified visions of a torrid war zone, characterized by pestilence and death."[27] And, while abolitionism was seemingly halted in the 1790s, it really was a reform movement gathering storm, as was to be proven in the following decade. It attracted attention not just from the public but from statesmen such as the prime minister, William Pitt, who feared that slave unrest was inevitable if the West Indies continued to import large numbers of "unacculturated" Africans to work on plantations. West Indian planters to an extent countered these fears by lobbying successfully Parliament and local legislatures to adopt policies of amelioration, in which the conditions of slavery would be made supposedly less harsh while the institution was continued and strengthened.

Planters hoped that through amelioration emancipation could be endlessly delayed. But the adoption of amelioration as a slave-owning strategy showed planter weakness insofar as they had admitted for the first time that they needed to be responsive to metropolitan criticisms of slavery and could not treat their enslaved property as they pleased. Evidence presented to Parliament about the horrors of the slave trade and about the brutality of slavery in the Caribbean was widely distributed within abolitionist networks and highlighted to a hostile British public just how vicious and deadly was the system of West Indian plantation agriculture. It seemed a system that was bound to result in disaster and slave rebellion, just as was the case in Saint-Domingue. As Claudius Fergus argues, "by the turn of the century, the Haitian Revolution and its sister revolts in the eastern Caribbean had opened the eyes of architects of imperialism to the real cost of racial slavery and brought to a head the debate on prosperity versus security."[28] William Wilberforce, the leading representative of the abolitionist movement in the British Parliament, made the link between abolition and security clear. He

---

[27] Petley, "Slaveholders and Revolution," 68.
[28] Claudius Fergus, "'Dread of Insurrection': Abolitionism, Security, and Labor in Britain's West Indian Colonies, 1760–1823," *William and Mary Quarterly*, 3rd series, 66 (2009), 757–80: 764.

took the arguments that were made by pro-slavery writers who advocated for amelioration rather than emancipation and turned them on their head. Wilberforce argued that an imperial policy that continued to import Africans through the slave trade imperiled the safety of the islands as it ensured that slave revolts would inevitably occur, meaning that "rivers of blood would flow." If people wanted to keep their property in the West Indies safe, then parliament "should abolish the importation of slaves, as the first step towards the salvation of these islands."

Britain expanded its possessions in the British West Indies during the French revolutionary and Napoleonic wars, taking territory from France, Spain, and the Netherlands. This imperial expansion means that we cannot say that the end of the American Revolution saw a diminishment of Britain's interests in the Atlantic world. But it was a different Atlantic world from that which had existed in the first half of the eighteenth century, where power had to be negotiated carefully between a relatively weak imperial state and powerful local elites. By the end of the eighteenth century, the imperial state, greatly expanded through a decade of constant global warfare, was much stronger than before and the power of colonial elites, especially in the Caribbean, was much weaker. Britain demanded – and got – more say in how the new British colonies created through imperial expansion were to be run than they had done in the past and more than in Canada, where settlers demanded that they retained a certain degree of autonomy and where they were not constrained in such demands by living among enslaved people. No newly conquered territory, for example, was granted a legislative assembly and the economic ambitions of white settlers were frustrated by legislation that limited their access to land and labor.

The greater control Britain exercised over its Caribbean colonies made it easier to implement the abolition of the slave trade in 1807. Local politicians failed to produce the sustained and effective opposition to metropolitan interference in their affairs. Petley concludes that it was the French and Haitian revolutions "that provided the political context in which abolitionists could outmaneuver these slaveholders."[29] Abolitionists had successfully convinced British leaders that it was abolition, and not the slaveholders, that could better uphold British liberty and keep these colonies secure.

Abolitionists were helped in their campaigns for the abolition of the slave trade (1807) and the abolition of slavery (1833) by the actions of enslaved

---

[29] Petley, "Slaveholders and Revolution," 71.

people. From the 1790s onwards, enslaved people showed that they were unhappy with their condition and that they wanted freedom immediately through a series of revolts which, though not successful, destabilized the plantation system and illustrated to a metropolitan public how far slave-owners were from being the humane masters they pretended to be. The year 1795 was crucial, with a war against the Maroons in Jamaica, insurgency by so-called "Black Caribs" in St. Vincent and, most dangerously for British imperialists, an enormous servile revolt in Grenada that involved free Blacks and enslaved people. This rebellion was, like the war in Haiti, very complex, with enslaved people being both rebels and serving as soldiers in the British Army. The rebellion lasted for 18 months and cost the lives of 7,000 enslaved people as well as causing perhaps £5 million in damages to the previously thriving Grenadian plantation system. Indeed, the 1795–1796 slave rebellion in Grenada led by Julian Fedon, a free man of color, was far more destructive for slaveholders than the better-known slave revolts in Barbados in 1816 and in Demerara in 1823. It was far more costly in terms of lives lost than the much more famous Jamaican Baptist War of 1831 – a revolt customarily thought to have accelerated the movement toward immediate emancipation. It is also the revolt that was closest in time to the Haitian Revolution and the one most heavily influenced in ideology and by the extent of violence in that revolution and the French Revolution.

A Settler Society in the North

The result of the American Revolution was ambivalent for Canada. For many Britons, the imperial crisis had produced a growing sense that the Hanoverian regime had allowed its subjects too much political liberty. The lesson they learned from their defeat was that firmer control over colonial places was necessary. This authoritarianism was pronounced in Upper Canada, Bengal, and Ireland, where an imperial revolution of government was promoted in which popular sovereignty was disdained, where there was a renewed emphasis on subordination and civil obedience, and a marked reluctance to tamper with any aspect of Britain's constitution.[30]

The most important consequence of the American Revolution in Canada was a rapid increase in population. Both the French and British populations grew appreciably from the late eighteenth century, the former by natural

---

[30] Eliga H. Gould, *The Persistence of Empire: British Political Culture in the Age of the American Revolution* (Chapel Hill: University of North Carolina Press, 2000), 182.

increase and the latter by both natural increase and extensive migration from Britain. In 1775, there were 125,000 Europeans in Canada, 90,000 of whom were French Catholics in Quebec. By 1806, there were 460,000 Europeans in Canada, of whom 250,000 were mostly French Catholics in Lower Canada, while 70,000 were Protestant Britons and Americans in Upper Canada, with a further 65,000 mostly Protestants (including thousands of free Blacks in Nova Scotia) in the three maritime provinces on the Atlantic Ocean. Population increase exploded after 1815. In the next 30 years, 730,000 British migrants arrived in Canada, of whom two-thirds came after 1830. It was a population heavily weighted toward the Celtic areas of Britain. Over half of migrants after 1830 came from Ireland, especially from Ulster, and a disproportionate number of migrants came from Scotland. The diverse nature of the British diaspora into Canada made it clear that nineteenth-century British North America was not simply a primitive and colder reproduction of England. The population was British in its attachments, but tended to reject the deferential social practices of Britain and the authoritarian preferences of imperial rulers in favor of informality and democracy.

In 1837, a rebellion occurred in Lower Canada. The province was suffering from a severe economic downturn and French *habitants* became agitated. In November of that year, a few thousand French *patriotes* rose in revolt in the countryside near Montreal. The revolt was quickly crushed by British troops, with twelve rebels executed and fifty-eight transported to Australia. The result of the rebellion, however, was a rethinking of the relationship between Upper and Lower Canada (established in the 1791 Constitution Act and united together in 1841) in which Britain and the Canadas were pushed toward a new imperial structure that resembled a partnership of separate states.[31] What the development of Canada into a largely self-governing federation by 1867 shows is that, as P. J. Marshall suggests, "the pre-revolutionary British Atlantic world was able to survive the upheavals of war and American independence." The worlds of the United States and that of Canada were connected together in numerous social and economic ways and "where political developments had put obstacles in the way of continuing communication, they were being circumvented."[32]

Canada and the United States formed an Atlantic version of an Anglophone world, even if there were many people, including French Americans and Native

---

[31] Michel Ducharme, *The Idea of Liberty in Canada during the Age of Atlantic Revolutions, 1776–1838* (Montreal: McGill-Queen's University Press, 2014).

[32] Marshall, *Remaking the British Atlantic*, 313.

Americans (who are treated elsewhere in these volumes), who resisted incorporation into Canada and assimilation into the dominant Anglo-Canadian culture. Canada was an important node in what James Belich has depicted as a "settler revolution" in which people in the "Anglo-world" shared common attitudes to things and thoughts. Some of these thoughts included a belief in white supremacy, the superiority of British values over all other values, a commitment to egalitarian politics and social customs, and an exclusionary approach to the place of nonwhite races within the Canadian polity. As Belich argues, although the "Anglophones were never again to share a single state," they remained "a transcontinental, transnational entity" in which transfers between the United States and Canada were constant and significant.[33] As Marshall concludes, "common transatlantic values survived the sundering of imperial links," including, importantly, a devotion to the common law and to Protestant principles.[34]

Conclusion: The Centrality of Empire

The trajectories of the West Indian and the Canadian colonies of Britain veered in separate directions in the nineteenth century. The white settlers of the West Indies had a diminished role within empire compared with their dominant role in the mid-eighteenth century, and while free people of color became participants in the political process and the formerly enslaved benefited from freedom, meaning that the social and political structures in the Caribbean became more complex, the societies in which these groups competed were diminished ones that were increasingly seen as imperial "problems" rather than as beneficial to Britain's wealth and power. In Canada, by contrast, white settler populations prospered, making British North America a stunning imperial success story, as important to the British empire as India and more important than any other settler society established after the end of the American Revolution.

What unites the histories of the "other colonies" during the Age of Revolutions is that they stayed within and helped indisputably to shape the growth and development of the British empire in the nineteenth century. The loss of the Thirteen Colonies did not stop, though it did divert into new directions, Britain's surge to unprecedented imperial expansion after 1783. The Age of Revolutions remained the age of empire with imperialism as least as important as revolutionary ideology in shaping the zeitgeist and the global geopolitical reality of the period.

---

[33] Belich, *Replenishing the Earth*, 49, 56.   [34] Marshall, *Remaking the Atlantic*, 314.

10

The Participation of France and Spain

GONZALO M. QUINTERO SARAVIA

Introduction

Traditionally the American Revolution has been studied as an exceptional case within the narrow margins of the British Thirteen North American colonies. However, during the past decades a more nuanced and enlarged picture has emerged in which the European empires in North America are not considered and much less studied as separate entities but, as Eliga H. Gould has suggested, as "part of the same hemispheric system or community."[1]

The origins of the American Revolutionary War can be traced back to the various consequences of the Seven Years' War (1754–1763).[2] At the continental level, the disappearance of France and Spain from eastern North America left the colonists somewhat less dependent on Britain for protection and gave London the opportunity "to bring our Old Colonies into order," assisted by the presence of a unprecedently large body of royal troops.[3] In the Americas and the Caribbean, the humiliating defeats suffered by Spain would serve as a wake-up call and lead to a profound reorganization of its empire. Internationally, both France and Spain considered that the peace treaties of 1763 had dangerously altered the international balance of power in favor of

---

[1] Eliga H. Gould, "Entangled Histories, Entangled Worlds: The English-Speaking Atlantic as a Spanish Periphery," *American Historical Review* 112:3 (2007), 764–86: 765.

[2] For the Seven Years' War and its consequences, see Fred Anderson, *Crucible of War: The Seven Years' War and the Fate of Empire in British North America, 1754–1766* (London: Faber & Faber, 2001); Stephen Conway, "Blue Water Policy: La Royal Navy et la politique étrangère britannique de 1763 à 1778," in Olivier Chaline, Philippe Bonnichon, and Charles-Philippe de Vergennes, eds., *Les marines de la guerre de l'Indépendance américaine (1763–1783)*, vol. 1: *L'instrument naval* (Paris: Presses de l'université Paris-Sorbonne, 2013), 27–38: 28–32.

[3] Lord Bute's words quoted by Thomas C. Barrow, "A Project for Imperial Reform: Hints Respecting the Settlement for Our American Provinces, 1763," *William and Mary Quarterly* 24:1 (1967), 108–26: 109.

Britain, and redressing this situation would become their main objective in the following decades.

Revolt: April 1775–July 1776

Since the conflict in the Thirteen Colonies offered a perfect opportunity to weaken the British empire, Paris and Madrid adopted what the French finance minister Turgot described as "a temporizing policy ... giving the Americans hope but taking care not to provoke the British," which translated into secret support for the American rebels with cash and supplies in order to prevent any reconciliation.[4]

Popular uprisings and revolts against taxation were a recurrent feature within empires during the eighteenth century, so when the "shot heard round the world" was fired in Lexington and Concord on 19 April 1775, few living outside the British North American colonies paid much attention. Among these few were a small group of Dutch, French, and Spanish merchants who had commercial ties with the Thirteen Colonies and were willing to enter the lucrative although dangerous business of supplying the American rebels.

As early as August 1774, American ships were carrying gunpowder from Amsterdam to Nantucket, and in March of the following year Isaac van Dam, a New Yorker of Dutch descent, became Virginia's agent on the Dutch Caribbean island of St. Eustatius, a place that would become a major market for military supplies for the Americans.

On 15 February 1775, the Spanish merchant Diego Gardoqui wrote to Jeremiah Lee, the wealthiest merchant in Massachusetts with whom he had collaborated for twelve years in the cod-fish exporting industry, about his efforts to procure "300 muskets & bayonets, and about double the number of pair of pistols."[5] Between 1777 and 1783, the firm Gardoqui & Sons would ship arms and materiel to the amount of 549,948 pesos (about 2 million livres tournoises).

Although shipments of French gunpowder crossed the Atlantic through various channels during 1775 and the firm Penet & Pliarne from Nantes contracted with the Continental Congress in January 1776, it would not be

---

[4] Richard Warner Van Alstyne, *Empire and Independence: The International History of the American Revolution* (New York: John Wiley, 1965), 92.

[5] José Gardoqui to Jeremiah Lee, Bilbao, 15 February 1775, in *Naval Documents of the American Revolution* (Washington, DC: Government Printing Office, 1964–2014), vol. 1, 401.

until the involvement of playwright and spy Pierre-Augustin Caron de Beaumarchais that the French and Spanish governments started to become seriously involved in supporting the American rebels.[6]

From June 1775, Beaumarchais insisted that in order to keep the Americans fighting it would be necessary to supply them with large quantities of materiel. In order to do so, he offered his services through a dummy mercantile firm called Roderique Hortalez et Cie. The company was created with an initial capital of 1 million livres tournoises secretly delivered by the French treasury, and shortly afterwards matched by another million from the Spanish. The idea was that Roderique Hortalez et Cie. would send military materiel in return for tobacco that would be sold in France, and the profits reinvested in the company. On 24 January 1777, the first shipment arrived in Portsmouth, New Hampshire. By the end of 1777, twelve ships chartered by Beaumarchais had crossed the Atlantic, and during the operations of Roderique Hortalez and Cie. more than 5 million livres tournoises-worth of supplies were delivered to the American rebels. Beaumarchais' initial success stirred other Frenchmen to follow his lead, such as Dr. Jacques Barbeu-Dubourg and the wealthy merchant Jacques-Donatien Le Ray de Chaumont. In Nantes alone, for example, shipments to North America doubled from 1776 to 1777.[7]

Besides merchants and/or smugglers, France and Spain made extensive use of secret agents and spies. Well before any unrest broke out in the Americas, both countries had sent agents to both sides of the Atlantic. Between 1764 and 1770 alone, at least four French agents were sent to England on reconnaissance missions to identify possible landing sites for an eventual invasion. During the mid-1750s, two Spanish naval officers, Jorge Juan and Antonio de Ulloa, had collected British industrial military secrets in London.

As early as 1764, France sent François de Sarrebourse de Pontleroy de Beaulieu to Philadelphia, who was followed a couple of years later by Baron de Kalb, and Julien Alexandre Achard de Bonvouloir in September 1775. Spain was also active establishing a network of "observers" directed from New Orleans and Havana. Spanish authorities attached so much importance to the task of gathering reliable intelligence about their eventual enemy that,

---

[6] Claude Van Tyne, "French Aid before the Alliance of 1778," *American Historical Review* 31:1 (1925), 20–40: 20; "Diary of Richard Smith," [Philadelphia], 9 January 1776, in *Naval Documents*, vol. 3, 693.

[7] Gaston Martin, "Commercial Relations between Nantes and the American Colonies," *Journal of Economic and Business History* 4 (1932), 812–29: 822–7.

a few years later, in 1782, in the North American theater of operations alone, they spent 400,000 pesos on "secret commissions."[8]

Revolution: July 1776–July 1778

Besides claiming for the United States "to assume among the powers of the earth, the separate and equal station," *The unanimous Declaration of the thirteen united States of America* was also "a necessary step for the securing of foreign aid in the ongoing war effort."[9] In its last paragraph, it states that among the consequences of independence "they have full Power to levy War, conclude Peace, contract Alliances, establish Commerce, and to do all other Acts and Things which Independent States may of right do." That this was one of the main points at stake was also clear to the delegates present in Philadelphia at that time, both those in favor such as Richard Henry Lee from Virginia and those against like John Dickinson from Pennsylvania.[10] As Thomas Paine wrote in his *Common Sense*, published anonymously on 10 January 1776, "an open and determined declaration for independence" was necessary because "it is unreasonable to suppose, that France or Spain will give us any kind of assistance, if we mean only to make use of that assistance for the purpose of repairing the breach, and strengthening the connection between Britain and America."[11]

Now it was the turn of American diplomats to cross the Atlantic. Silas Deane had already been sent to France as a secret envoy, and in September 1776 Congress appointed him official commissioner along with Benjamin Franklin and Arthur Lee. This was America's first diplomatic mission and almost immediately obtained a grant of 2 million livres tournoises, plus another contract of 2 million livres-worth of American tobacco. However, this initial success made the commissioners overconfident, which created not a few problems for the French government who tried to keep its assistance as secret as possible. Deane created additional problems while hiring foreign officers for the Continental Army, two of whom would be instrumental in

---

[8] Remittance of 400,000 pesos to Bernardo de Gálvez for secret commissions, Juan Ignacio de Urriza to José de Gálvez, letter no. 896, Havana, 19 January 1782, Archivo General de Indias, Santo Domingo, 1659.
[9] David Armitage, *The Declaration of Independence: A Global History* (Cambridge, MA: Harvard University Press, 2007), 10.
[10] Gary Wills, *Inventing America: Jefferson's Declaration of Independence* (New York: Vintage, 1979), 325.
[11] Thomas Paine, *Common Sense; Addressed to the Inhabitants of America, on the Following Interesting Subjects* (Philadelphia, PA: R. Bell, 1776).

advancing the American cause: the "Baron" de Kalb and the Marquis de Lafayette. The outrageous demands from others like Charles Jean Baptiste Tronson du Coudray would lead Congress to recall Deane.[12]

A potentially serious crisis broke out in August 1777, when the American privateer Captain Gustavus Conyngham arrived in Dunkirk to sell his prizes and the American diplomatic envoy, William Carmichael, did not follow his instructions to order Conyngham to return to America but instead suggested to him that he continue his privateering activities. Immediately the British ambassador to Versailles threatened war unless all American ships were expelled from French ports. The French government had no alternative but to comply. For months to come, this episode left much ill-will between the American diplomats and the French ministry of foreign affairs. To make matters worse, the relationship among the American commissioners deteriorated, and the American mission to France was on the verge of bankruptcy. Since it was not in the interests of France to leave the Americans stranded, in November 1777, the Count de Vergennes, minister of foreign affairs, earmarked an additional 3 million livres for the American cause, which he believed would be enough to keep them fighting until France was ready to declare war on Britain.

France had been preparing for revenge against Britain almost since the day after its humiliating defeat in the Seven Years' War. As stated earlier, France wanted to return to the previous international balance of power, and to achieve this objective it worked hard both in the diplomatic and the military fields. French international efforts were helped by the increasing British isolation in Europe, which had started in 1762 when Britain's subsidy to Prussia was not renewed. It had grown when it was unable to pull Austria from its alliance with France, and was completed by its failure to attract Russia despite the signature of a commercial treaty in 1766.[13] French military preparations concentrated on its navy. The navy not only implemented an

---

[12] Classic studies on the American diplomacy during the Revolution include Samuel Flagg Bemis, *The Diplomacy of the American Revolution* (New York: Appleton-Century, 1935); Richard B. Morris, *The Peacemakers: The Great Powers and American Independence* (New York: Harper & Row, 1965); Lawrence S. Kaplan, *Colonies into Nation: American Diplomacy, 1763–1801* (New York: Macmillan, 1972); Jonathan R. Dull, *A Diplomatic History of the American Revolution* (New Haven: Yale University Press, 1985). Also see Robert W. Smith, *Keeping the Republic: Ideology and Early American Diplomacy* (DeKalb: Northern Illinois University Press, 2004); Eliga H. Gould, *Among the Powers of the Earth: The American Revolution and the Making of a New World Empire* (Cambridge, MA: Harvard University Press, 2012); Robert W. Smith, *Amid a Warring World: American Foreign Relations, 1775–1815* (Washington, DC: Potomac, 2012).

[13] Dull, *Diplomatic History*, 26–32.

aggressive program of shipbuilding, but also closed the gap between the total number of ships listed and those fit for service. The shipyards were filled with all kinds of materiel, and, perhaps more importantly, the naval administration was completely reformed.[14] But despite impressive results, by 1775 the French navy had only 59 ships of the Line (three-deckers with at least 90 guns) against the British 117.[15] Clearly not enough for the French to confront the Royal Navy on their own.

The American victories at Saratoga (19 September and 7 October 1777) are often considered as a turning point in securing a stronger French commitment to the rebels' cause. But although Saratoga proved the resolution of the rebels to wage war to gain independence, and showed their capacity to successfully confront large British detachments, their previous defeat at Brandywine (11 September 1777) and at Germantown (4 October 1777) also highlighted that the Continental Army could not defeat the main British Army without foreign military assistance. The French had already decided and had been preparing to enter the war against Britain, and the news about Saratoga provided the perfect justification or excuse for doing so.[16]

On the diplomatic front, the air started to clear between the American envoys and the French ministers by late 1777, enabling the signature on 6 February 1778 of three agreements: the Treaty of Amity and Commerce, the Treaty of Alliance, and a separate and secret clause related to the future inclusion of Spain into the other two.

On the advice of his fellow commissioners, Arthur Lee went to Spain. The timing could not have been worse. Since October 1776, Spain and Portugal had been fighting for Colonia del Sacramento in the Río de la Plata. Since the Spanish government was extremely anxious not to provoke a British intervention in favor of its Portuguese ally, they gave Lee an extremely cold reception. He was not even authorized to reach the capital but instead directed to Burgos. When by May, it was clear that no concrete results would be achieved, a tired and disgusted Lee left Spain for Berlin.[17] The crisis

---

[14] Jonathan R. Dull, *The French Navy and American Independence: A Study of Arms and Diplomacy, 1774–1787* (Princeton: Princeton University Press, 1975), 11, 14.

[15] The number of ships varies according to different authors, mainly due to the different sources used and the distinction made or not between total ships and those that were serviceable.

[16] Dull, *French Navy*, 89–94; Dull, *Diplomatic History*, 89–92; Larrie D. Ferreiro, *Brothers at Arms: American Independence and the Men of France and Spain Who Saved It* (New York: Knopf, 2016), 96.

[17] Paul H. Giddens, "Arthur Lee, First United States Envoy to Spain," *Virginia Magazine of History and Biography* 40:1 (1932), 3–13: 13.

with Portugal officially ended on 11 March of the following year when the Treaty of El Pardo was signed, leaving the Spanish government free to weigh which policy would better serve the national interest.

At this time Spain believed the best option was to prolong the war as much as possible in order to wear down both opponents, which would not only strengthen its relative power but hopefully resolve once and for all what had long been thorns in Spain's flesh: the British presence in Gibraltar, Minorca, the coast of Campeche (Mexico), Florida, and Honduras. At the same time, the Spanish government considered the independence of the United States to be a by-product of the war that could set a dangerous example for the Spanish possessions in the Americas. Confronted with the option of sharing North America with the British empire or with the new and small republic which had an extremely weak central government, established by the Articles of Confederation, Spain chose the latter. In this context, it is not surprising that the Spanish government never considered the United States an ally. For Spain, the American Revolutionary War was just another imperial war between France and Spain against Britain. Spain's delaying tactic was summed up by Count de Floridablanca, the Spanish secretary of state, who declared that Spain should "prepare for the war, as it is inevitable, but do everything to prevent it."[18]

Transatlantic War: July 1778–June 1779

Although the signature of the Treaty of Alliance between France and the United States of North America was an implicit declaration of war on Great Britain by France, it took several months before hostilities started. France needed time both to ensure the arrival in America of Admiral d'Estaing's fleet and not to appear as the aggressor. That was particularly important for several reasons. First, the preamble of the Treaty of Alliance stated that it would enter into force "in case Great Britain ... should break the Peace with France, either by direct hostilities, or by hindering her commerce and navigation." Second, to prevent Britain from asking for Dutch help; and, third, to be able to exchange Austria's nonintervention in this new war, despite the existing Franco-Austrian defensive alliance, for France's abstention in Austria's dispute over Bavaria with Prussia.

---

[18] Miguel Avilés Fernández, *Carlos III y el fin del antiguo régimen* (Madrid: EDAF, 1982), 73.

Figure 10.1 Cartoon printed in Amsterdam, c. 1781. A Frenchman, a Spaniard, and a Dutchman celebrate their triumph milking the cow of British commerce, while John Bull (Britain) kneels in prayer and the British lion howls in pain because his paw had been hurt by a broken teapot. In the background is the surrender of Yorktown, represented by four Englishmen approaching an Indian king on his throne (America) surrounded by Justice, Mars (war), and Hercules (fortitude). Courtesy of Library of Congress.

France's proclaimed main objective in the war – to secure the United States' independence directly – served its own geopolitical interest to weaken the British empire, restore France to its pre-1763 position in European politics, and reinforce its alliance with Spain. Other important French war aims were to secure the rights over the Newfoundland fisheries and full sovereignty over the islands of St. Pierre and Miquelon, since the expert fishermen trained in these waters were among the best sailors the French Navy could recruit. France also considered it essential to regain Senegal in order to be able to develop its own slave trade. And, last but not least, France aimed to end the prohibition on fortifying Dunkirk, which had been stipulated in the Treaty of Utrecht, since it was considered an affront to France's honor.[19]

---

[19] Henri Doniol, *Histoire de la participation de la France à l'établissement des États-Unis d'Amérique: Correspondance diplomatique et documents* (Paris: Imprimerie nationale, 1886–1892), vol. II, 781–8.

The Participation of France and Spain

The first shots of the war between France and Britain were fired on 17 June 1778, when British ships opened fire on a French frigate off the coast of England, officially starting the war.[20] Little over a month later, on 27 July and also in English Channel's waters, two large fleets engaged in the inconclusive first Battle of Ushant.

In order to prevent the full use of British naval power, France needed a quick and decisive victory. To achieve that, a force of twelve ships-of-the-line and four frigates under Admiral Count d'Estaing was dispatched to America. His instructions were to "perform a courageous act," but the details were left to d'Estaing to decide. After consulting with Conrad Gérard de Rayneval, France's first minister to the United States who was on board the admiral's flagship on his way to America, d'Estaing decided to head for the mouth of the Delaware to confront the British squadron commanded by Admiral Richard Howe, but when the French forces arrived on 7 July, the British had already evacuated Philadelphia and Admiral Howe's ships had sailed to New York. Eager to take advantage of his superior numbers, d'Estaing immediately sailed for New York, but once there he was informed that the entrance was possibly too shallow for his ships. Being deprived of the chance to confront Admiral Howe, d'Estaing sailed to Rhode Island where American forces under General Sullivan were to join in the assault against Newport. Coordination between American and French forces proved to be difficult, and the delay in starting the attack allowed the British squadron under Admiral Howe to arrive at Newport on 9 August 1778. The appearance of Howe's thirteen ships-of-the-line and seven frigates forced d'Estaing to exit Newport harbor for the open sea to confront the British, but the chase had to be abandoned because of a strong storm that severely damaged several of the French ships. After returning to Newport for several days, d'Estaing had no choice but to leave for Boston for repairs. The departure of the French squadron infuriated the American troops who accused the French of having abandoned them. The ill-will between the new allies increased in Boston, when a mob of angry Patriots wounded a couple of French officers, one of

---

[20] For the naval operations during the war, see Dull, *French Navy*; Chaline, Bonnichon, and Vergennes, *Les marines de la guerre*, vol. I; Olivier Chaline, Philippe Bonnichon, and Charles-Philippe de Vergennes, eds., *Les marines de la guerre de l'Indépendance américaine (1763–1783)*, vol. II: *L'operationnel naval* (Paris: Presses de l'université Paris-Sorbonne, 2018); Olivier Chaline, Philippe Bonnichon, and Charles-Philippe de Vergennes, eds., *La France et l'Indépendance américaine* (Paris: Presses de l'université Paris-Sorbonne, 2008). Also see the study of the Spanish Navy by Agustín Guimerá and Olivier Chaline, eds., *La Real Armada: La Marine des Bourbons d'Espagne au XVIIIe siècle* (Paris: Presses de l'université Paris-Sorbonne, 2018).

whom died shortly afterwards. This episode was a violent reminder of how difficult it was for the Americans to overcome the Francophobia into which they had been raised during decades of imperial rivalry between France and Britain. Even though the potentially extremely negative consequences of the Boston incident were overcome by the joint efforts of George Washington and Admiral d'Estaing, it would take some time and the concurrence of other prominent actors for the Franco-American alliance to work.

Conrad Gérard de Rayneval presented his credentials to the US Congress as French minister on 6 August 1778. A seasoned diplomat with an unusually good command of the English language, Gérard had been Vergennes' right hand in the negotiations with the American representatives in Paris. His instructions insisted that the "first and most essential" of his duties was to prevent the United States from concluding a separate peace with Britain.[21] But to achieve it he first needed to overcome an important cultural barrier. As a professional diplomat he was used to dealing with governments and their representatives, but in North America he would confront a particularly complicated power structure. At his arrival, Congress was extremely divided into two main factions. The eastern faction was suspicious of the conservative influence of France on its own radical view of the American Revolution, and the southern faction was more socially conservative and pragmatic in its political aims and thus more favorable toward the alliance with France.

Only a week after Gérard's arrival in Philadelphia, Silas Deane, the former American representative in Paris who had sailed with him from France, had his first hearing before Congress to face Arthur Lee's accusations about his private commercial dealings while in France. The bitter confrontation between personalities and political factions quickly evolved into one with serious political implications for the future of the Franco-American alliance. Despite his instructions not to become involved, Gérard was forced or decided to throw his diplomatic weight around and to spend a substantial part of his financial resources in favor of those in Congress he believed to be closest to France's interests. The Deane–Lee dispute would drag on for several months, leaving behind some relevant political casualties. Thomas Paine was dismissed from his post as secretary of the Committee of Foreign Affairs but was later hired by Gérard as a propagandist. Henry Laurens resigned the presidency of Congress and John Jay, a strong defender of Deane, was elected in his place. In the end, Silas Deane's public career was

---

[21] See Gérard's instructions in Doniol, *Histoire de la participation*, vol. III, 153–7.

over while the pro-French faction in Congress succeeded in imposing its views.[22]

The other threat to French interests that Gérard had to deal with was the Carlisle Commission. In March 1778, the British Parliament decided to send a final peace offer to the American revolutionaries. Named after its president, Frederick Howard, 5th Earl of Carlisle, the commissioners were prepared to concede many of the American demands with two exceptions: independence and Parliament's sovereignty. The Commission's arrival in Philadelphia on 6 June 1778 exacerbated tensions in Congress.[23] Gérard worked behind closed doors with Henry Laurens (who was still president of Congress) to help him present a public image of a unified Congress.[24] The success of Gérard in fulfilling his instructions was made official by a resolution adopted by Congress on 24 January 1779 stating that "neither France or these United States may of right, so these United States will not conclude either truce or peace with the common enemy, without the formal consent of their ally first obtained."[25]

The other Frenchman who had already been deeply involved in the American Revolution was the Marquis de Lafayette. After his arrival in the United States in June 1777, Lafayette had won the trust of George Washington, fought in several battles, commanded American troops, and had even been wounded fighting for the American cause. After the retreat of the French fleet from Newport, Lafayette used his influence with the American high command to try to appease the increasing anti-French sentiment among the American troops. By the end of 1778, he decided to return to France in order to push for a stronger commitment from his country. He arrived in Paris in February 1779, and after a saving-face house arrest – he had left for America without leave – he was received as a hero by the French public. During the next year he would use his celebrity status to advocate for increasing the pressure on Britain, volunteering for the planned invasion of the British Isles, and later working with Benjamin Franklin to overcome the French government's doubts about the convenience of sending a French army corps to fight in America.[26]

---

[22] Charles J. Stillé, "Silas Deane, Diplomatist of the Revolution," *Pennsylvania Magazine of History and Biography* 18:3 (1894), 273–92: 289–90.
[23] Alan Taylor, *American Revolutions: A Continental History, 1750–1804* (New York: W. W. Norton, 2016), 189.
[24] Doniol, *Histoire de la participation*, vol. III, 400–2.
[25] Congress, resolution of 14 January 1779, in Worthington C. Ford et al., eds., *Journals of the Continental Congress, 1774–1789* (Washington, DC: US Government Printing Office, 1904–1937), vol. XIII, 61–3.
[26] For a recent biography of Lafayette, see Laura Auricchio, *The Marquis: Lafayette Reconsidered* (New York: Alfred A. Knopf, 2014). On the role of Benjamin Franklin as

The fiascos of Newport and New York were only the first in a series of setbacks suffered by the American and French forces between July 1778 and June 1779. A squadron detached from d'Estaing's forces was unable to coordinate with American forces and failed to retake Savannah, after which three ships-of-the-line were sent to Martinique but were taken by surprise by a much larger British force under Admiral Hyde Parker (18 December 1779).

In India, the British took advantage of the French declaration of war to expel them from the region. As soon as the news of the declaration arrived, the Governor General of Bengal, Warren Hastings, rushed to seize Chandernagore and ordered the British troops in Madras to attack Pondicherry, which they conquered in October 1778. In March of the following year, Mahé, the last French settlement in India, also fell, and the British dominion of the region was secured with the arrival of the squadron under Admiral Edward Hughes.[27]

Only in the Caribbean did the French achieve some minor successes. The British island of Dominica was taken by surprise by an attack from French Martinique in September 1778. After being forced to withdraw from Newport, on 4 November, Admiral Count d'Estaing departed for the Caribbean. The same day, Commodore William Hotham's squadron left New York for the West Indies to reinforce Admiral Samuel Barrington, who after Hotham's arrival seized the French island of St. Lucia on 13–14 December. The following day, the British fleet was attacked by d'Estaing but had to withdraw. After the arrival of more British naval reinforcements in January, both navies spent the first half of 1779 watching each other. In June, d'Estaing took advantage of the return to Europe of some of the British ships to attack and conquer St. Vincent and Grenada. After an indecisive action fought near Grenada on 6 July, both navies abandoned Caribbean waters before the arrival of the peak of the hurricane season in September. Such an accumulation of setbacks increasingly convinced the French government that it was possible to defeat Britain only if Spain entered the war.

The news about the signature of the treaties between France and United States, and those about France's entry in the war without previous proper consultations were not well received by the Spanish government. On 4 April,

---

diplomat, see Jonathan R. Dull, "Benjamin Franklin and the Nature of American Diplomacy," *International History Review* 5:3 (1983), 346–63.

[27] Philippe Haudrère, "La Révolution de l'Inde n'aura pas lieu: Les Français dans l'Océan Indien durant la guerre de l'Indépendance américaine," in Olivier Chaline, Philippe Bonnichon, and Charles-Philippe de Vergennes, eds., *La France et l'Indépendance américaine* (Paris: Presses de l'université Paris-Sorbonne, 2008), 153–68.

two months before the first shots of the war were fired, the Spanish chargé d'affaires in London, Francisco Antonio Escarano, had a meeting with a representative from the British government who insisted on its goodwill toward Spain. The Count de Floridablanca instructed Escarano to explore the possibility of a Spanish mediation between France and Britain, but only if he was certain that the proposal would be well-received. While these contacts were taking place, Floridablanca tried to keep his distance from both contenders. The idea behind the mediation was to allow Spain to remain neutral in the conflict. According to Floridablanca, neutrality better served Spain's national interests than any other outcome, even Britain's defeat by France, either by France alone or with Spanish help, since this victory could come at the price of Spanish foreign policy becoming subservient to that of France. Keeping Spain's independence from France while eroding Britain's position acquired after 1763 was an extremely difficult if not impossible balance to maintain for long. Nevertheless, in the short run, the mediation proposal succeeded in buying much-needed time to ensure the safe arrival at the Iberian Peninsula of both the treasure ships from Peru, and a fleet returning from Buenos Aires after the end of the conflict with Portugal over Colonia del Sacramento.

On 29 May 1778, Floridablanca sent the Marquis de Almodóvar, the Spanish ambassador to London, Spain's conditions for her mediation proposal. A mediation that not only did not include any guarantee for the recognition of the United States' independence but also disregarded them as a party in the following negotiations.[28] By the end of September, Spain officially requested both France and Britain to declare if they were willing to accept the Spanish mediation. The response from the French foreign minister was positive but it took over a month for him to send France's specific demands.

The British government, however, was not pleased with the request since it could be interpreted that Spain was suggesting an arbitration instead of a mediation, but on 14 November 1778, Lord Grantham, British ambassador to Madrid, delivered a note to Floridablanca accepting Spain's mediation. His only demand was a very significant one: all French forces had to be withdrawn from America before the eventual mediation.[29] Since Floridablanca

[28] Floridablanca to Almodóvar, Madrid, 29 May 1778, Archivo Histórico Nacional (henceforth AHN), Estado 4268.
[29] Floridablanca to Lord Grantham, note, El Escorial, 14 November 1778, AHN, Estado 4.199.

wanted to be able to blame the British government for Spain entering the war he decided to send a last proposal which included a truce without the evacuation of British-occupied territory in North America. By this time Floridablanca was deep into the negotiations of a treaty of alliance with France – the Treaty of Aranjuez, signed on 12 April 1779 – and discussing both the objectives and the joint plan of action for the imminent war. On 3 April 1779, he issued an ultimatum to Britain with a series of demands, including this time the de facto recognition of American independence. The ultimatum was officially rejected by the British government on 4 May, and a few days later Floridablanca issued orders to the Spanish fleet under Admiral Luis de Córdoba to ready its departure to join the French for a joint attack on the British Isles. On 1 June, a message from King George III was read in Parliament asking for additional resources "in this critical juncture." During the debate in the days that followed, it became clear that war with Spain was imminent.[30] On 26 June, a royal decree was published ordering the cessation all communications with subjects of the British monarch, not exactly a formal declaration of war but for everyone it was evident that from that moment on Spain and Britain were at war.

Floridablanca's delaying tactics were crucial to ensure Spain's war readiness. The army had been reformed, fortresses in Spanish America rebuilt, the navy modernized, and its units increased. Between 1774 and 1784, the docks of the Spanish empire built thirty-eight large war vessels (ships-of-the-line and frigates), while during the same period Britain built fifty-three and France forty-five.[31]

Global War: June 1779–September 1783

The official entry of Spain into the war not only tipped the balance of the conflict, giving France and Spain numerical superiority both at land and sea, but also profoundly changed the general strategy of the war. The combined Bourbon navy in 1779 had 121 ships-of-the-line compared with 90 for Britain,

---

[30] T. C. Hansard, ed., *The Parliamentary History of England from the Earliest Period to the Year 1803* (London: Hansard, 1814), vol. xx, 828–54.

[31] For the data on the Spanish navy, see José Ignacio González-Aller Hierro, "Relación de buques de la Armada española en los siglos XVIII, XIX y XX," in Enrique Manera Regueyra, ed., *El buque en la Armada española* (Madrid: Sílex, 1999), 454–97: 455–63. For Britain, see N. A. M. Rodger, *The Command of the Ocean: A Naval History of Britain 1649–1815* (London: Allen Lane, 2004), 608. For France, Chaline, Bonnichon, and Vergennes, *Les marines de la guerre*, vol. 1, 9.

117 compared with 95 in 1780, and 124 compared with 94 in 1781.[32] This clear superiority opened up new theaters in this now truly global war, spreading British resources thin. Britain would be forced to abandon a purely American perspective of the conflict and adopt a more global view of the war in which it had to relinquish the freedom to choose when and where to strike and instead assume a defensive position, which prevented concentration of its forces against the North American rebels. Britain's situation would be further complicated by its increasing international isolation, especially through the Russian initiative of a "League of Armed Neutrality" against the British threats to attack any vessel carrying arms or supplies to its enemies. During the following years, the Russian Armed Neutrality Declaration of 10 March 1780 would be signed by most European countries (Denmark, 9 July 1780; Sweden, 1 August 1780; Prussia, 8 May 1781; Austria, 9 October 1781; Portugal, 13 July 1782; and the Two Sicilies, 10 February 1783).[33] The British were not the only ones who had to change their strategy; the French also had to modify theirs since the Spanish government succeeded in imposing its own priorities regarding the use of the combined forces, making the French "hostage" to Spain's war aims.[34] This was translated at the operational level by the auxiliary role that the French forces would assume in the American theater. French land forces would serve under George Washington's command and French naval forces would "act as auxiliaries" of the Spanish.[35] For the American revolutionaries, as Richard Morris has stated, "France had in effect modified her alliance with America, and changed and enlarged the purposes of the war without America's consent and even without her knowledge."[36]

---

[32] David French, *The British Way in Warfare, 1688–2000* (London: Unwin Hyman, 1990), 76.

[33] Isabel de Madariaga, *Britain, Russia, and the Armed Neutrality of 1780: Sir James Harris' Mission to St. Petersburg during the American Revolution* (New Haven: Yale University Press, 1962).

[34] John Reeve, "British Naval Strategy: War on a Global Scale," in Donald Stoker, Kenneth J. Hagan, and Michael T. McMaster, eds., *Strategy in the American War of Independence: A Global Approach* (New York: Routledge, 2010), 73–99: 86; Rodger, *Command of the Ocean*, 136.

[35] Quote from the letter from the Marquis de Castries (French Minister for the Navy) to Admiral de Grasse, Brest, 17 March 1781, Archives nationales, Marine B⁴ 216, ff. 199r.–200v., in Olivier Chaline, "Le comte de Grasse à la tête de son armée navale," in Olivier Chaline, Philippe Bonnichon, and Charles-Philippe de Vergennes, eds., *Les marines de la guerre de l'Indépendance américaine (1763–1783)*, vol. 1: *L'instrument naval* (Paris: Presses de l'université Paris-Sorbonne, 2013), 295–311: 297, 310–11.

[36] Morris, *The Peacemakers*, 15–16.

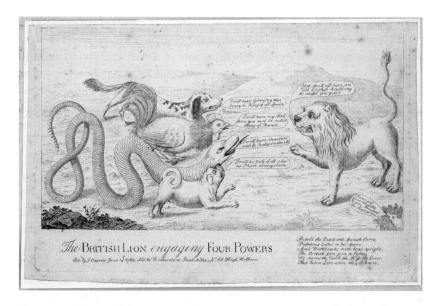

Figure 10.2 The British lion engaging four powers, 1782. Courtesy of Library of Congress.

Although Spain entered the war as an ally of France and not of the United States, informal diplomatic contacts were established on both sides of the Atlantic. In early 1778, Spain sent an unofficial envoy to the United States. Juan de Miralles, a merchant from Havana, arrived in June in Philadelphia, where he established a close relationship both with Robert Morris, one of the main financiers of the revolution, and George Washington. Miralles would die in April 1780 while visiting Washington's headquarters in Morristown, New Jersey. In September 1779, John Jay was appointed minister to Spain, where he met the same cold reception as his predecessor, Arthur Lee. Jay's mission was self-defeating from the start. On the one hand, his instructions from Congress were utterly unrealistic: he was to obtain financial aid, the signature on a commercial agreement, and the recognition of the United States as a nation. On the other hand, his insistence on being recognized as the official representative of his country, his lack of knowledge of the Spanish language, and his self-righteousness completely alienated him from Spanish political circles. In the end, Jay left Madrid after what has been called "thirty murderous months on the periphery of the Spanish court" having achieved little, if anything at all, and taking with him a strong contempt for Spain that would have deep consequences for future bilateral relations.[37]

The first Franco-Spanish joint action against the British was an attack on the British Isles. After much discussion, the two countries agreed on an assault on the Isle of Wight and later on Portsmouth, with the intention not of conquering territory but of creating a financial panic which would force the British government to sue for peace.[38] In the end, the attempt to "take the war against Carthage to Carthage itself" with a combined Franco-Spanish fleet of eighty-two ships-of-the-line was not successful.[39] Delays in the rendezvous of the two forces, an outbreak of scurvy, lack of coordination between the two fleets, and a constant change of plans forced the abandonment of the project in September 1779, which nevertheless succeeded in preventing the British Home Fleet from leaving English waters. The English Channel would remain a much contested area for the rest of the war, and although the British would twice defeat the French in the second and third battles of Ushant (12 December 1781 and 20–21 April 1782) they were forced to keep an important part of their naval forces there, thus preventing their use in other theaters of operations.

Gibraltar had been a major concern in Spain's foreign policy since its occupation by British and Dutch forces in 1704 during the War of the Spanish Succession, and the recovery of this territory would be a priority for generations to come. The Treaty of Aranjuez clearly stated Gibraltar as Spain's main objective for entering the war against Britain. As early as June 1779, Spanish forces started to build up a blockade in order to force Gibraltar to surrender due to starvation, but the small size of the Spanish fleet enforcing it allowed for the arrival of two relief convoys, the first under Admiral George Rodney in January 1780, and a second under Admiral George Darby in April of the following year.

By early 1782, after more than two and a half years of blockade and siege it became clear that a new strategy was needed. This time the main thrust would come from the sea through the use of supposedly indestructible floating batteries. For what is now known as the "Grand Assault" against

---

[37] John P. Kaminski, "Honor and Interest: John Jay's Diplomacy during the Confederation," *New York History* 83:3 (2002): 293–327. The quote is from Stacy Schiff, *A Great Improvisation: Franklin, France, and the Birth of America* (New York: Henry Holt, 2005), 254.

[38] John Brewer, *The Sinews of Power: War, Money and the English State, 1688–1783* (Cambridge, MA: Harvard University Press, 1988), 191.

[39] Floridablanca to Vergennes, El Pardo, 13 January 1779, AHN, Estado, 4.199.

Gibraltar it was decided that French forces would not only join the Spanish, but that a French general would be given the supreme command of the operation: the duc de Crillon, an experienced soldier who had just succeeded in conquering the island of Minorca in the Mediterranean for Spain (February 1782). After much preparation, the assault was launched on 13 September 1782. The participation of 35,000 men, forty-seven ships-of-the-line, and ten floating batteries, against a British garrison of 7,500 men, makes Gibraltar's "Grand Assault" the largest battle of the American Revolutionary War by far. The newly designed floating batteries resisted even the red-hot shots from the British guns, but the inaction of the Spanish ships under the command of Admiral Luis de Córdova left them unsupplied and at the mercy of the defenders' concentrated fire. The result was a complete failure. Although the blockade continued, the British garrison was resupplied and reinforced on 18 October and Gibraltar saw no major action for the rest of the war.

In North America, the first action was that of the governor of Spanish Louisiana, Bernardo de Gálvez, who in September 1779 attacked Fort Manchac on the left bank of the Mississippi. After a quick victory, he marched to Baton Rouge, which surrendered on 16 October. These Spanish victories succeeded in dispersing British forces that could otherwise have united against Spain or the American rebels. They also relieved pressure from the British against Georgia and South Carolina and made it impossible for the two British armies operating in the North and South to unite. It additionally ensured that Spanish aid to the revolutionaries would safely reach Washington's Continental Army.[40]

Mobile was the next Spanish target, where Governor Gálvez arrived on 27 February, at the head of 1,300 Spanish soldiers. The only hope for the small British garrison of Fort Charlotte at Mobile was to receive reinforcements from Pensacola, but they arrived a day after Mobile had surrendered. John Adams, about to leave Paris, wrote to the Count of Vergennes, that "the advantages which Spain has gained in West Florida ... show that the English are on the losing hand in this quarter."[41] After recovering from their initial surprise, the British responded by trying to regain control of the Mississippi with attacks against San Luis de Ilinueses, modern St. Louis, Missouri, in May 1780, and Mobile in early 1781. Both were unsuccessful.

[40] Gonzalo M. Quintero Saravia, *Bernardo de Gálvez: Spanish Hero of the American Revolution* (Chapel Hill: University of North Carolina Press, 2018), 146–61.
[41] John Adams to the Count de Vergennes, Paris, 13 July 1780, in Francis Wharton, ed., *Revolutionary Diplomatic Correspondence of the United States*, 6 vols. (Washington, DC: Government Printing Office, 1889), vol. III, 849.

The main objective in this theater of operations was Pensacola, but its defenses and the size of its British garrison demanded a much larger force than the one that Governor Gálvez had under his direct command.[42] In order to get reinforcements, Gálvez left New Orleans for Havana. Despite the arrival of a large Spanish fleet under Admiral José Solano, the troops on board were in such a parlous state that several months were needed to restore their health. Finally, on 16 October 1780, almost 4,000 men set sail from Havana for Pensacola. Just two days later, a nearly week-long hurricane sank several ships, damaged the rest, and scattered all off course. The expedition had to return to Havana where Gálvez had to fight for his command against the senior military officers there who demanded his dismissal.

After several months of negotiations, they agreed to a plan, not to attack Pensacola but to reinforce the defenses of the already conquered territories against an imminent British counterattack that was expected. On 28 February 1781, five warships, twenty-seven transports, and more than 1,500 soldiers set sail from Havana, but Gálvez did not even pretend to go to Mobile or New Orleans, heading instead directly for Pensacola. The Spanish forces were clearly insufficient for a successful siege, but Gálvez was betting that once the siege started the military commanders in Havana would have no choice but to send him reinforcements. This time the voyage was uneventful, and, on 9 March, the Spanish ships sighted the island of Santa Rosa, at the entrance of Pensacola Bay. The main challenge for entering Pensacola Bay was the shallow water over a sandbank that connected Santa Rosa Island to the mainland. After an unsuccessful attempt to enter the bay, the navy commander of the Spanish squadron refused to continue. Since Gálvez had no direct authority over the navy squadron, he resorted to challenging the navy. He went aboard the *Galveston*, a brig that had been seized from the British and that was under Gálvez's direct authority as governor, and gave orders to proceed. When the *Galveston* crossed unharmed inside the bay, the navy officers had no choice but to follow.

Between 22 March and 19 April, reinforcements arrived from Mobile, New Orleans, and Havana, raising the total number of Spanish troops, which also included some French naval officers and sailors who volunteered for the attack on land, to almost 7,500 men. At 9:30 on the morning of 8 May, a Spanish shot directly impacted the British magazine producing a large

---

[42] Quintero, *Bernardo de Gálvez*, 180–244.

explosion that destroyed most of the Queen's Redoubt. Spanish troops were quickly assembled for the assault, but before the order was given a white flag was hoisted. After short negotiations, the British garrison in Pensacola surrendered not only the city but the whole of British Florida as well.

The news of the Spanish–French victory at Pensacola went uncelebrated by the American revolutionaries for several reasons. The main one was that the terms of the British capitulation stated that its soldiers were to be returned to British territory on the sole condition of not bearing arms against Spain or France in the present war, which left them free to fight against the American rebels. Second, at this juncture the Americans preferred that Spain continue the war in Florida in order to prevent the concentration of British forces against them. Furthermore, with the conquest of Pensacola, Spain had acquired West Florida from the British, thereby blocking the Americans' access to the Caribbean. The American rebels were not fighting the British only for their enemy's territories to be seized by another European colonial power.

After the successful cooperation between the French and Spanish navies and taking full advantage of having at their disposal the only shipyard in the Caribbean in Havana, Spain assumed responsibility for the defense of the entire Caribbean, including all French possessions there, thus allowing the French fleet under Count de Grasse to confront the British fleet under Rear Admiral Thomas Graves at the Battle of the Chesapeake (5 September 1781) which would facilitate General Washington's victory at Yorktown.

Fighting also took place in Central America, where the Spaniards had to face what Andrew O'Shaughnessy has described as "a ludicrously ambitious series of campaigns."[43] In late 1779, a British expedition from Jamaica under the command of Commodore John Luttrell, instead of reinforcing Belize as originally planned, decided to attack San Fernando de Omoa, in modern Honduras. The Spanish garrison in Omoa capitulated on 20 October 1779. The British occupation of the place was short-lived, since less than a week later a Spanish relief force arrived in Omoa and recovered the fort for Spain.

In 1780, the British decided to strike more ambitiously. This time the objective was to seize the San Juan River and its source, Lake Nicaragua, thereby dividing the north and south dominions of Spanish America. On March 1780, 400 British soldiers and 600 Miskito Indians entered the San Juan River and attacked the Inmaculada fort, which fell after a month-long siege. The extremely insalubrious conditions of the place caused the British

---

[43] Andrew Jackson O'Shaughnessy, *An Empire Divided: The American Revolution and the British Caribbean* (Philadelphia: University of Pennsylvania Press, 2000), 189.

garrison to abandon it by the end of July. Shortly afterwards it was reoccupied by Spanish forces.

On 17 March 1782, Spanish forces under the command of Matías de Gálvez, Bernardo's father and at the time Captain General of Guatemala, defeated the British garrison on the Island of Roatán. Returning to the mainland, the Spanish forces captured the British forts of Criba y Quepriva in Honduras. The defeat of the French fleet under Admiral de Grasse at the Battle of the Saintes in April 1782 allowed Archibald Campbell, governor of Jamaica, to send an expedition that reconquered both forts in August.

While the Spanish forces had been actively fighting the British along the Mississippi, in the Floridas, and Central America, the French soldiers sent to North America would not engage the enemy until autumn 1781. The idea of sending a French expeditionary force to join the fight of the Continental Army was first presented by Luzerne to Washington in September 1779, but, in the end the Americans were only informed, not consulted nor was permission requested, notwithstanding French and American concerns related to the way French soldiers would be received by the local population. On 11 July 1780, the French fleet under Chevalier de Ternay arrived at Newport carrying 5,000 French soldiers commanded by the Count de Rochambeau. These men were supposed to be the first division of a total French expeditionary force of 15,000, but after several delays due to the British blockade of the port of Brest, Paris decided that it would be less expensive to support the Continental Army financially rather than to send the additional 10,000 soldiers. The first meeting between Rochambeau and Washington took place on 22 September, where both commanders decided that the primary objective should be New York and that the 30,000 soldiers needed would comprise half from America and half from France.

As the months passed without any action from the French troops, Rochambeau yielded to the pressure from the Americans and Lafayette to send a French detachment to the Chesapeake. But after an exchange of fire with a slightly numerically superior British squadron on 16 March 1781, the French returned to Newport. This failed attempt to support the American military operation in Virginia raised discontent against the French. This sentiment was encouraged by the British through the publication of an intercepted letter written by Washington in which he slightly criticized the French.[44]

---

[44] Washington to Lund Washington, New Windsor, 28 March 1781, in John C. Fitzpatrick, ed., *The Writings of George Washington from the Original Manuscript Sources, 1745–1799* (Washington, DC: US Government Printing Office, 1931–1944), vol. XXI, 385–6.

On 22 and 23 May 1781, another conference took place between Washington and Rochambeau at Wethersfield, Connecticut, where after much discussion Rochambeau acceded to Washington's plan to attack New York. On 10 June, the French expeditionary force left Newport and marched to White Plains, New York, where they met with the Continental Army on 5 July. The combined force of 10,000 men, half American and half French, spent the following days exploring the terrain and waiting for reinforcements to arrive. As days turned into weeks, and despite Washington's pleas to the governors of the nearby states and to Congress, the prospects of a successful attack against New York were dimming fast. The final blow to the Franco-American plans against New York came on 11 August when 3,000 Hessian mercenaries arrived, increasing the total British garrison to 11,000 men. At this crossroads, news from the French fleet under Admiral Count de Grasse arrived. Rochambeau and de Grasse agreed that the only realistic option was to direct their efforts against the Chesapeake. On 14 August, Washington finally accepted the change of objective, and preparations began to move south.

The more than 350-mile march of the combined American and French forces was further complicated by the need for secrecy in order to keep the British garrison at New York convinced of an imminent attack against them. The Franco-American forces left their encampments on 19 August, and arrived at Philadelphia on 30 August. At this juncture, some of the men of the Continental Army refused to continue unless they were paid on the spot with "real" money instead of the much-depreciated Continental paper currency. With the revolutionary coffers empty, the Americans turned to Rochambeau who advanced 26,000 hard dollars which he had just received from Count de Grasse.

While on their way to Yorktown, news arrived of the battle between Admiral de Grasse's fleet against the British fleet of Admiral Thomas Graves at the Chesapeake on 5 September. Although the battle was tactically inconclusive, the withdrawal of the British Navy from the mouth of the Chesapeake Bay precluded the possibility of resupply or reinforcement.

The march continued, and on 28 September, more than 16,000 men under the command of General Washington surrounded Yorktown: around 9,000 Americans (5,500 Continental Army soldiers and 3,000 militiamen from Virginia) and 7,000 Frenchmen (4,000 soldiers commanded by Rochambeau plus 3,000 landed from Count de Grasse's fleet), against General Charles Cornwallis' 8,000 soldiers and sailors manning Yorktown's defenses. On 6 October, the heavy shelling began, and on the night of 14

Figure 10.3 The capture of Yorktown, 1781. Bridgeman Images.

October, two columns (one French and one American) charged against two redoubts. After a short fight, both positions were taken, and the fate of Yorktown was sealed. The British surrendered four days later.[45] Militarily, the British defeat at Yorktown was severe although not decisive, but it had one major political consequence: parliamentary support for pursuing the war in North America came to an end. By March 1782, Prime Minister Lord North resigned, and the new government under the Marquess of Rockingham soon began peace negotiations. Although the Franco-American victory at Yorktown was the last major military operation in North America, ending the narrative of the revolutionary war in most of the traditional American historiography,[46] much was still at stake in other regions.

The Caribbean had seen action prior to Spain's entry in the war, but now it would become the major theater of operations.[47] Even before June 1779,

---

[45] For the campaign and the siege of Yorktown, see John D. Grainger, *The Battle of Yorktown, 1781: A Reassessment* (Rochester, NY: Boydell, 2005).

[46] James Breck Perkins, *France in the American Revolution* (Boston: Houghton Mifflin, 1911); William Stinchcombe, *The American Revolution and the French Alliance* (New York: Syracuse University Press, 1969); Robert Middlekauff, *The Glorious Cause: The American Revolution, 1763–1789* (New York: Oxford University Press, 1982); Ward Christopher, *The War of the Revolution* (New York: Skyhorse, 2011); Stephen Conway, "Yorktown, The Peace and Why the British Failed," in Clifford J. Rogers, Ty Seidule, and Samuel Watson, eds., *The West Point History of the American Revolution* (New York: Simon & Schuster, 2017), 177–220.

[47] O'Shaughnessy, *An Empire Divided*, xii.

d'Estaing's fleet had spent more time in Caribbean waters than in North American ones, and the two French fleets sent in 1780 and 1781 had the Caribbean as their destination. The preeminence of the Caribbean was reinforced by the Spanish navy. In August 1780, Admiral José Solano arrived in Havana with twelve ships-of-the-line and 12,000 men to strengthen the already important allied naval presence in these waters.

The naval operations in the Caribbean during 1780 were but a prelude to a major Franco-Spanish offensive. In January, a fleet comprising sixteen ships-of-the-line under Admiral Count de Guichen left France and upon his arrival at Martinique was joined by the seven ships-of-the-line under the Count de Grasse. Between 7 April and 19 May, the French force and a British fleet under Admiral George Rodney fought on three occasions but in none of them was either side able to claim victory. The other major development in 1780 took place near the Azores – far away from the Caribbean but closely linked to the region – where on 9 August, a British convoy of sixty-three merchant ships carrying reinforcements and supplies for the British Caribbean, was intercepted and almost completely captured by a joint Franco-Spanish fleet under the command of Admiral Luis de Córdova. The last event in 1780 that profoundly impacted the war in the Caribbean took place on 20 December, when Britain declared war on the Netherlands, making their Caribbean territories the objective of the following British campaign.

In early 1781, Admiral George Rodney commanded the capture of St. Eustatius, a territory used by the American revolutionaries since the beginning of the war to provide them with military supplies. More occupied in securing the plunder of the commercially rich island than continuing the fight, Rodney spent some precious time in St. Eustatius allowing the French fleet of Admiral de Grasse to overpower a British squadron under the command of Rodney's second, Samuel Hood, near Martinique. After a series of operations in which both fleets unsuccessfully tried to outmaneuver the other, Rodney decided to return to Britain before the start of the hurricane season, leaving behind half of his force under Hood. De Grasse seized the opportunity to send a squadron to capture Tobago and, more importantly, to sail to North America, making possible the decisive Franco-American victory at Yorktown. De Grasse returned to the Caribbean in November 1781, closely followed by Hood, allowing the French governor of Martinique to recapture the former Dutch enclaves of St. Martin, Saba, and even St. Eustatius. But de Grasse's main reason for returning to Caribbean waters was to join the Spanish land and naval forces that were concentrating in Saint-Domingue for the attack against Jamaica.

Jamaica was by far the richest of all British possessions overseas. In 1774, the aggregate value of Jamaica's plantations was calculated to be over £20 million and the revenue obtained by Britain from the Caribbean was double that from all the North American colonies.[48] It was no surprise, then, that for the British government the defense of Jamaica was second only to that of the British Isles.[49]

While waiting for the arrival of the French and Spanish fleets, de Grasse twice attempted to attack St. Lucia and later directed his force toward St. Kitts, which was conquered in February 1782 after strong resistance. When the complex preparations for the joint Franco-Spanish expedition against Jamaica kept delaying the date of the departure, in the meantime, Spain launched a small operation against the island of New Providence, in the Bahamas, which was conquered in May 1782. What appeared to be an irresistible wave of allied victories was then halted by Admiral Rodney, who in the Battle of the Saintes (12 April 1782) completely defeated de Grasse, redeeming his much tarnished reputation after his conduct in St. Eustatius and ending any chance of a Franco-Spanish invasion of Jamaica.

By the end of 1780 the French had been forced out of Asia, but late that year the entry of the Dutch Republic in the war and the arrival of a new navy minister in France, the Marquis de Castries, who had been working at the Compagnie des Indes between 1764 and 1768, resulted in new attention being given to the region. A French squadron under Pierre André de Suffren was able to conquer Trincomalee, Ceylon (29 August), a former Dutch settlement seized by the British just six months before. Another squadron arrived in March 1783 and succeeded in lifting the British siege against Cuddalore.[50]

As mentioned above, the most important consequence of the Battle of Yorktown was a political change in Britain. In March 1782, the Tory prime minister, Lord North, was replaced by the Whig, the Marquis of Rockingham, who presided over the government for just a few months before his death on 1 July. His successor, the Earl of Shelburne, exercised direct control over the peace negotiations with the Americans, to whom he

---

[48] T. G. Burnard, "'Prodigious Riches': The Wealth of Jamaica before the American Revolution," *Economic History Review* 54:3 (2001), 506–24: 512.

[49] O'Shaughnessy, *An Empire Divided*, 208–9; David Syrett, *The Royal Navy in American Waters, 1775–1783* (Aldershot: Scholar Press, 1989), 121; John A. Tylley, *The British Navy and the American Revolution* (Columbia, SC: University of South Carolina Press, 1987), 170.

[50] For the French military actions in India, see Haudrère, "La Révolution de l'Inde n'aura pas lieu."

offered extremely favorable terms in order to sign a separate peace agreement as soon as possible, thereby freeing up British troops in North America and possibly using them in the Caribbean against France and Spain.[51] A preliminary agreement was reached on 30 November, which, in order to respect the letter of the terms of the Franco-American Alliance would not come into effect until France and Britain had also reached theirs. Despite this violation of the spirit of Article 8 of the 1778 Franco-American Treaty of Alliance, the French government decided to overlook it since the French Treasury was exhausted and it served French interests to increase the pressure on Spain to agree to the end of the war.[52] The negotiations were extremely complex since accommodating the different interests of the contenders was far from easy, especially those of Spain whose government was fixed on recovering Gibraltar which British public opinion was completely against. In the end, it would be Spain's ambassador to Versailles, the Count of Aranda, who circumventing his own instructions reluctantly agreed to renounce Gibraltar in exchange for keeping Minorca and the two Floridas.[53] The hostilities ended on 20 January 1783 with the signature of an armistice and preliminary peace agreements between the British and the United States, France, and Spain, and on behalf of the Netherlands. The war officially ended with four separate peace treaties: between the United States and Britain signed in Paris; France and Britain at Versailles; Spain and Britain, also at Versailles (all three signed on 3 September 1783); and Britain and the Netherlands on 20 May 1784.[54] Britain, the apparent loser, would not only remain by far the main trading partner of the new republic, but the loss of its North American colonies would be the trigger for important reforms in its administration, treasury, and navy, and would mark the beginning of a

---

[51] Dull, *Diplomatic History*, 145.

[52] "Treaty of Alliance Between the United States and France," 6 February 1778, https://avalon.law.yale.edu/18th_century/fr1788-2.asp.

[53] Dull, *Diplomatic History*, 157–8; Jonathan R. Dull, "Vergennes, Rayneval and the Diplomacy of Trust," in Ronald Hoffman and Peter J. Albert, eds., *Peace and the Peacemakers: The Treaty of 1783* (Charlottesville: University of Virginia Press, 1986), 113–29: 126–8; Thomas E. Chávez, *Spain and the Independence of the United States: An Intrinsic Gift* (Albuquerque: University of New Mexico Press, 2002), 211–12.

[54] On the peace treaties, see Lawrence S. Kaplan, "The Treaty of Paris, 1783: A Historiographical Challenge," *International History Review* 5:3 (1983), 431–42; Prosser Gifford, ed., *The Treaty of Paris (1783) in a Changing States System* (Washington, DC: Woodrow Wilson International Center for Scholars, 1985); Hoffman and Albert, *Peace and the Peacemakers*; J. R. Dull, "France and the American Revolution Seen as Tragedy," in Ronald Hoffman and Peter J. Albert, eds., *Diplomacy and Revolution: The Franco–American Alliance of 1778* (Charlottesville: University of Virginia Press, 1981), 80–7.

second British empire concentrated in the East, abandoning the idea of British settlement or territorial control overseas for an expansion of trade tightly controlled by the metropolis.[55] Since the American Revolution started when the colonists clamored for recognition of their rights as Englishmen, Britain's subsequent imperial forays were marked by hierarchy, difference, and executive fiat. For France, victory at war would come at such a high cost that King Louis XVI had no other option but to convene the Estates-General in 1789, which would be the beginning of the end for France's *ancien régime*.[56] As for Spain, although unable to reincorporate Gibraltar, the 1780s would mark the zenith of its empire, when a decades-long process of reforms would be delivering results. It would, however, be a relatively short-lived apogee. Less than three decades later, and mainly as a direct consequence of the Napoleonic invasion of the Iberian Peninsula, its more than 300-year-old empire would start to crumble.[57]

---

[55] For the historiographical debate about the first and second British empires, see C. A. Bayly, "The Second British Empire," in Robin W. Winks, ed., *The Oxford History of the British Empire*, vol. v: *Historiography* (Oxford: Oxford University Press, 1999), 54–72.

[56] For the consequences of the peace treaty for France, see Dull, "France and the American Revolution." Recent studies offering a more complex interpretation include Jean-Pierre Poussou, "Les conséquences financières et économiques de la guerre d'Indépendance américaine pour les royaumes de France et de Grande-Bretagne," in Olivier Chaline, Philippe Bonnichon, and Charles-Philippe de Vergennes, eds., *La France et l'Indépendance américaine* (Paris: Presses de l'université Paris-Sorbonne, 2008), 203–20; T. J. A. Le Goff, "Le financement de la participation française à la guerre d'Indépendance et ses conséquences: L'État et la conjoncture financière des années 1780," in Olivier Chaline, Philippe Bonnichon, and Charles-Philippe de Vergennes, eds., *Les marines de la guerre de l'Indépendance américaine (1763–1783)*, vol. 1: *L'instrument naval* (Paris: Presses de l'université Paris-Sorbonne, 2013), 335–64.

[57] Despite the interpretations of traditional national histories placing the origins of the Latin American independence well before 1808, and the efforts to construct a large scheme of Atlantic revolutions that swept the ocean from the United States to France and back again to the Americas, the last twenty years have seen the emergence of a broad historiographical consensus that the process, or processes, of Latin American independence was mainly triggered by the Napoleonic invasion. On the evolution of the historiography on this subject, see François-Xavier Guerra, "Lógicas y ritmos de las revoluciones hispánicas," in François-Xavier Guerra, ed., *Las revoluciones hispánicas: Independencias americanas y el liberalismo español* (Madrid: Editorial Complutense, 1995), 13–46; Gabriel B. Paquette, "The Dissolution of the Spanish Atlantic Monarchy," *Historical Journal* 52:1 (2009): 175–212.

11

Britain, Ireland, and the American Revolution, c. 1763–1785

STEPHEN CONWAY

Britain and Ireland played a part in Robert Palmer's *Age of the Democratic Revolution*. Each had a chapter devoted to it in his seminal study, alongside others that covered developments in North America, France, the Swiss cantons, the Dutch Republic, Poland, Germany, Italy, and the Habsburg lands. Palmer presented his revolutionary era as one that owed much to the example of the American Revolution. He saw that era as characterized, above all, by the burgeoning of democratic sentiment in all manner of diverse settings, often inspired by events in North America. Palmer's bold picture of a revolutionary age continues to influence some accounts of the last third of the eighteenth century. In many ways, however, historians have challenged both its details and its overall argument.[1]

Modern scholarship tends to stress the importance of the Seven Years' War and its outcome as the spur to change across the globe (not just in Palmer's primarily Atlantic world).[2] Both the victors and the vanquished – especially the British, French, and Spanish, but also the Prussians and Austrians – faced new fiscal challenges in the aftermath of the war that encouraged them to pursue more interventionist policies that caused dissatisfaction, both at home and in their dependent territories. That view would suggest that the American Revolution, rather than being the "cause" of change elsewhere, was just one symptom of wider shifts initiated by the

---

[1] For an important recent collection of essays on democracy in this period, see Joanna Innes and Mark Philp, eds., *Reimagining Democracy in the Age of Revolutions: America, France, Britain, Ireland, 1750–1850* (Oxford: Oxford University Press, 2013).

[2] On the Seven Years' War and its consequences, see, for example, Fred Anderson, *Crucible of War: The Seven Years' War and the Fate of Empire in British North America, 1754–1766* (New York: Knopf, 2000); Franz A. J. Szabo, *The Seven Years' War in Europe, 1756–1763* (London: Routledge, 2008); Daniel A. Baugh, *The Global Seven Years' War, 1754–1763: Britain and France in a Great Power Contest* (Abingdon: Pearson, 2011); Hamish Scott, "The Seven Years' War and Europe's Ancien Régime," *War in History* 18 (2011), 419–55.

Seven Years' War – shifts that themselves influenced the calls for political overhaul in many places. Many historians now also see the political developments of the period as more connected with the recovery of lost or threatened rights than with the assertion of a new desire for "democracy" in any way that we would recognize it today. In many places, the events associated with Palmer's "democratic revolution" began as a conservative reaction to the reforming endeavors of rulers, not as a grassroots desire to extend popular participation. That was clearly the case in North America, where the constitutional crises of the 1760s and early 1770s saw the colonies as the defenders of the status quo against the initiatives of the British state.

This chapter considers first Ireland, where, on the face of it, change was dramatic; until quite recently, historians wrote of an Irish Revolution that accompanied or followed on from the revolution in North America. We then move on to look at Britain. In each case, we reflect on the importance of longer-term tensions lurking beneath the surface. We also assess the role of the Seven Years' War as a catalyst for reform endeavors in both Ireland and Britain. The chapter evaluates the impact on both Ireland and Britain of the American Revolution and particularly its war. We will see that the course of the conflict not only played a crucial role in the fortunes of the reformers; military failure provided the spur to proposals for change. While the chapter acknowledges anticipations of later democratic programs, it also recognizes that most of the popular reforming efforts in the period usually derived from a desire to turn the clock back rather than usher in a new democratic era.

Ireland

When members of eighteenth-century Ireland's Protestant ruling class mused about the nature of their country, they imagined it as an ancient kingdom, connected with Britain by a common monarch, but otherwise as self-governing.[3] It certainly possessed institutions that provided the basis for

---

[3] See Jacqueline Hill, *From Patriots to Unionists: Dublin Civic Politics and Irish Protestant Patriotism, 1660–1840* (Oxford: Clarendon, 1997), 142. For an account that makes comparisons with the American colonies, see J. L. McCracken, "Protestant Ascendancy and the Rise of Colonial Nationalism, 1714–1760," in T. W. Moody and W. E. Vaughan, eds., *A New History of Ireland*, vol. IV: *Eighteenth-Century Ireland, 1691–1800* (Oxford: Clarendon, 1986), Chapter 5. For useful works on Ireland in this period, some of which offer a rather different interpretation from the one advanced here, see R. B. McDowell, *Ireland in the Age of Imperialism and Revolution, 1760–1801* (Oxford: Clarendon, 1979); Neil Longley York, "The Impact of the American Revolution on Ireland," in H. T. Dickinson, ed., *Britain and the American Revolution* (Harlow: Longman, 1998), Chapter 8; David Dickson, *New Foundations: Ireland, 1660–1800*, rev. edition (Dublin: Irish Academic Press,

Map 11.1 The British Isles, 1775.

2000), Chapter 5; Martyn J. Powell, *Britain and Ireland in the Eighteenth-Century Crisis of Empire* (Basingstoke: Palgrave Macmillan, 2003); Ian McBride, *Eighteenth-Century Ireland: The Isle of Slaves* (Dublin: Gill Books, 2009), Part IV; S. J. Connolly, *Divided Kingdom: Ireland, 1630–1800* (Oxford: Oxford University Press, 2008), Chapter 10; S. J. Connolly, "The Limits of Democracy: Ireland, 1778–1848," in Joanna Innes and Mark Philp, eds., *Reimagining Democracy in the Age of Revolutions: America, France, Britain, Ireland, 1750–1850* (Oxford: Oxford University Press, 2013), 174–88.

theoretical autonomy. Ireland had its own bi-cameral parliament at Dublin, with a House of Lords made up of hereditary peers and a House of Commons elected by Protestant landholders and borough property owners. The kingdom had its own courts, which used common law as the basis for adjudication and judgment. It also had its own established church – the Church of Ireland. Yet all of these institutions derived from English originals. The Dublin legislature not only replicated the structure of the Westminster Parliament; it used the same procedures. Irish common law, by the eighteenth century, was barely distinguishable from English common law; Irish courts stopped using ancient Irish Brehon law in the seventeenth century.[4] And the Church of Ireland, despite its pretentions to separateness, was in reality an extension of the Church of England, with the same Protestant Episcopalian doctrines and structures. Subservience to England was most emphatically symbolized, however, by the operation of Poynings' Law (1494), which subjected all legislation introduced into and passed by the Dublin parliament to the approval of the English Privy Council.[5]

Ireland's Protestant elite needed the British connection to sustain their power in an island in which they formed a small minority (80 percent of Ireland's population was Catholic; and even amongst the Protestants, Presbyterian dissenters outnumbered members of the Church of Ireland, who in theory were alone eligible to hold public office). At the same time, however, Ireland's Protestant ruling class resented any interference from London in their management and control of their country. Periodic heavy-handed interventions from across the Irish Sea provoked determined resistance and assertions of Ireland's rights as a separate jurisdiction. In 1698, William Molyneux, the scholarly MP for Dublin University, argued the case for the Irish parliament's supremacy (and denied that Westminster's past encroachments established precedent for that legislature's claims to superiority). In one revealing passage, Molyneaux explicitly compared the Dublin parliament not with Westminster but with the Polish *Seym* – another institution convinced of its status and determinedly resistant to any attempts to undermine its privileges. Molyneaux, in other words, presented the Irish legislature as part of a European system of local representative institutions,

---

[4] For the export of English institutions to Ireland, see Nicholas Canny, *Making Ireland British, 1580–1650* (Oxford: Oxford University Press, 2001).

[5] For the Irish old order, see Eoin Magennis, *The Irish Political System, 1740–1765: The Golden Age of the Undertakers* (Dublin: Four Courts Press, 2000); and, more generally, Toby Barnard, *The Kingdom of Ireland, 1641–1760* (Basingstoke: Palgrave Macmillan, 2004).

offering an alternative to the English comparison.[6] When Westminster passed the Irish Declaratory Act in 1720, asserting its ability to exercise its legislative supremacy over the Dublin legislature, Ireland's Protestants reacted bitterly. Two years later, when an English manufacturer received a patent from the British government to mint copper coinage for use in Ireland, the Irish parliament protested vehemently to the king. In 1753, the English Privy Council's amendment of a money bill passed by the Dublin House of Commons provoked another crisis, which again brought into sharp relief the competing claims of British political management and Irish legislative autonomy.

The Seven Years' War, or rather its outcome, intensified the tension, moving it up to a new and more dangerous level. The war was brilliantly successful for the British state, leading to an expansion of empire in North America, the West Indies, West Africa, and (not long afterwards) in India, where the British East India Company became a major territorial power. But this great imperial expansion came at an enormous financial cost – the near doubling of the national debt – and was greeted with anxiety as well as celebration by the British ruling elite. Had the British empire, now (contemporary British commentators believed) the largest empire the world had seen since the days of Ancient Rome, over-expanded? Classically educated politicians were acutely aware that the Roman empire had unraveled by its many enemies picking away at its peripheries. Would the extended British empire face the same fate, this time at the hands of the defeated Bourbon powers, France and Spain? The response to these anxieties was a drive in governing circles to bind the empire more tightly together by asserting greater authority from the center and keeping on hand larger military forces than usually was the case in peacetime.

Ireland, though not part of the imperial expansion, was affected by the new tendency to increased interference from the metropolitan center and by the London government's commitment to maintaining a larger peacetime army. Irish lord lieutenants, hitherto absentees for most of their period of office, who delegated day-to-day authority to local "undertakers," recruited from amongst the Irish Protestant elite, now became resident. They, rather than the undertakers, now sought to control the Irish parliament, using their appointed secretaries (usually not Irishmen) as parliamentary managers. Just as importantly, Lord Townshend, the first resident lord lieutenant,

---

[6] William Doyle, "The Union in European Context," *Transactions of the Royal Historical Society*, 6th series, 10 (2000), 167–80: 170.

negotiated a deal with the Irish Protestant elite to increase Ireland's contribution to the costs of maintaining an expanded empire. In return for their paying for a larger army in Ireland (15,000 men rather than 12,000), the lifetime of Irish parliaments would be limited to 8 years, allowing more frequent general elections.[7] The package advanced the Irish Patriot cause in two ways. First, it brought into focus the role of Ireland as subservient to British interests, as the augmented army paid for by Irish taxpayers would be used in wartime just as the smaller one had been before – as a mobile reserve to be deployed elsewhere, not as a force to defend Ireland's Protestant minority from the Catholic majority.[8] Second, the deal enhanced the status and accountability of the Irish parliament, enabling it to act as a more effective defender of Irish Protestant interests.

The recurring American crises in the period 1764–1775 caused by Westminster's attempts to tax the American colonies played a comparatively small role in stimulating Irish resistance. True, Irish Protestant commentators drew parallels, when it suited them, with their opposition to British interference in the government of Ireland and the Americans' opposition to the claims of the British Parliament to intervene in their internal affairs. A particular moment of anxiety was when, in order to sweeten the bitter pill of repeal of the American Stamp Act, the Westminster Parliament passed an American Declaratory Act in 1766. Modeled closely on the earlier Irish Declaratory Act, the 1766 legislation asserted the right of the British Parliament to legislate for the American colonies "in all cases whatsoever." The wording was deliberately ambiguous on the matter of taxation; Lord Rockingham's government had sought to reassure opponents of repeal of the Stamp Act without provoking the Americans by refusing to clarify whether taxation of the colonies was included in Westminster's claims. That ambiguity led to great unease across the Irish Sea, where the passage of the American Declaratory Act, which seemed so similar to the Irish Declaratory Act, caused much speculation that Ireland, as well as America, might now be subject to taxation levied by the British legislature.[9] When British taxes did not materialize, however, that anxiety dissipated. Most of

---

[7] See Martyn J. Powell, "The Reform of the Undertaker System: Anglo-Irish Politics, 1750–1767," *Irish Historical Studies* 31 (1998), 19–36; Thomas Bartlett, "The Augmentation of the Army in Ireland, 1767–1769," *English Historical Review* 96 (1981), 540–59.
[8] See Charles Ivar McGrath, *Ireland and Empire, 1692–1770* (London: Pickering & Chatto, 2012), esp. Chapter 6.
[9] York, "Impact of the American Revolution on Ireland," 211.

the time, in fact, Irish Protestant commentators preferred to emphasize not their similarities to the colonies across the Atlantic, but their differences. The favored image remained, as it had been since Molyneux's day, Ireland as a separate kingdom, with an ancient constitution designed to preserve its rights.

The outbreak of fighting between the colonists and the British Army in 1775 provided fresh opportunities for pressing Ireland's case. The war divided Irish opinion. Amongst the Protestant population, the Presbyterians, especially those in Ulster, showed much sympathy for their co-religionists across the Atlantic. Members of the Church of Ireland were more inclined to support the government, which secured the Dublin parliament's permission to deploy a significant portion of the Irish garrison against the rebels in North America. Catholic Ireland seems to have been no less divided. Ballads and poetry of the time suggest a strong sense of delight at British difficulties in suppressing the insurrection in the colonies.[10] But schadenfreude (pleasure at the discomfort of the enemy), was not the only reaction amongst Catholics. Irish Catholic elites recognized an opening. They believed that a conspicuous display of loyalty would secure a softening of the penal laws directed against Catholic landownership and worship. That display was not just rhetorical; members of the residual Catholic gentry used their influence to help the British Army find recruits. Irish Catholics played a bigger part in filling the British regiments than they had ever done before.

Catholic recruitment on this scale could not have happened if there had not been changes in the attitude of the British political elite. Leading politicians in London began to view Catholicism as less of a threat than in the past. In part, the roots of this reappraisal lay back in the Seven Years' War, when any lingering hope of a restoration of the Catholic Stuart dynasty to the British and Irish thrones finally disappeared. British victory changed the dynamics of European politics. In 1766, on the death of the Stuart claimant James III (also known as the Old Pretender), even the Pope gave up on the exiled dynasty and recognized the Hanoverians as legitimate monarchs. The acquisition of new Catholic populations in Canada and the West Indies may also have softened attitudes to Catholicism amongst the British political elite, which was obliged to find acceptable ways of governing the crown's new subjects. The Quebec Act of 1774, which made major concessions to the French Canadian Catholic majority, established a

---

[10] See Vincent Morley, *Irish Opinion and the American Revolution, 1760–1783* (Cambridge: Cambridge University Press, 2002), esp. Chapters 2–4.

precedent for more limited concessions to Ireland's Catholic population.[11] But the deterioration of relations with the old (and very Protestant) British colonies in the 1760s and early 1770s probably played a bigger part in encouraging more positive views of Catholicism. As the British state found itself grappling with problems posed by Congregationalist Protestants in New England, Catholics appeared less of a threat to the constitution and more as a conservative prop that might help to see off the radical Protestant challenge. The willingness of Catholic elites to facilitate the enlisting of much-needed recruits for the army therefore reinforced the emerging British government view that Catholics should be seen as potential friends rather than established enemies. The need for recruits became especially pressing when the war in America broadened to become a global conflict with the intervention of first France in 1778 and then Spain in 1779. The British state responded by sponsoring legislation to ease restrictions on Catholic landownership and worship, expecting in return a redoubling of the efforts of the Catholic elite to find more men for the army.[12]

The British government's courting of Irish Catholics no doubt intensified Irish Protestants' desire to assert their right to rule over their own kingdom without interference from London. The coming of the war with France and then Spain provided the Protestants with a great opportunity, just as the earlier outbreak of fighting with the colonies had given the Catholic elite the chance to press for concessions. In the case of the Protestants, the decisive factor was the threat of invasion by the Bourbon powers. Ever since the Reformation, Protestants on both sides of the Irish Sea had viewed Ireland as vulnerable in the event of a conflict with a great Catholic power, for the obvious reason that the great bulk of its population was, and remained, resolutely Catholic. Protestants responded to this latest threat by forming paramilitary volunteer units, ostensibly to defend their communities if the enemy landed, but also to overawe their Catholic neighbors. Given that a significant portion of the regular army garrison had been sent to North America, the volunteers seemed to have had a military justification for their actions, and at first the lord lieutenant and other members of the Irish government looked on them benignly. In August 1778, Sir Richard Heron, the chief secretary, told the sovereign (or mayor) of Belfast that the lord

---

[11] See Jacqueline Hill, "Religious Toleration and the Relaxation of the Penal Laws: An Imperial Perspective, 1763–1780," *Archivum Hibernicum* 44 (1989), 98–109.

[12] R. Kent Donovan, "The Military Origins of the Roman Catholic Relief Programme of 1778," *Historical Journal* 28 (1985), 79–102.

lieutenant "very much approves of the Spirit of the Inhabitants . . . who have formed themselves, into Companies for the Defence of the Town."[13] It soon became evident, however, that the volunteers had a political more than a military function.

The American war highlighted the role of the British state in imposing economic restrictions on Ireland's overseas trade, particularly with the colonies across the Atlantic. With very few exceptions, Irish goods destined for North America had to go through a British port, where they would pay British customs duties, increasing their cost to the colonial consumer. Irish mercantile interests had long wished to see this imposition removed. The war made matters much worse. The government introduced an embargo on the export of provisions, a major part of Ireland's overseas trade, which hit merchants and farmers badly. The logic of the embargo was clear enough; foodstuffs should be prevented from reaching the enemy and remain available to supply the British armed forces operating in the rebel colonies. But the way in which it was imposed, by the fiat of the lord lieutenant, acting on instructions from London, provided another reminder of Ireland's subservience to British interests. Even government supporters in the Dublin parliament believed that some relief was imperative. Under pressure from many avenues, the British government decided that it needed to do something to placate the Irish. In the spring of 1778, on the eve of formal war with France, the Westminster Parliament offered major concessions on Irish admission to British colonial trade.

Within a short time, however, these concessions were watered down in the face of a fierce backlash from British merchants and manufacturers who feared Irish competition in colonial markets. The London government's retreat enraged Irish Protestants. They instituted boycotts of British goods (much as the Americans had done in response to British taxes in the 1760s and 1770s). More worryingly, from the point of view of the governments in Dublin and London, some of the volunteer units began to flex their muscles. In October 1779, volunteers lined the streets as the Dublin parliament met. William Brownlow, an opposition MP and a volunteer officer himself in County Armagh, wrote with much satisfaction that this military display would "be the cause of some reflection on the other side of the water."[14] The next month, the Dublin volunteers assembled on College Green and

---

[13] Public Record Office of Northern Ireland, Belfast, Downshire Papers, D 607/B/29.

[14] Historical Manuscripts Commission, *Twelfth Report, Appendix Part x, Charlemont Manuscripts*, i (London: HMSO, 1891), 359.

decorated the statue of William III with slogans proclaiming "Free Trade or else." When 900 of the volunteers demonstrated their ability to fire their muskets in the disciplined manner of parade-ground drill, the significance of the gesture was not lost on ministers in London. In December, the British government offered again the trading concessions that they had agreed before their retreat in 1778.

Lord North, the British prime minister, had been persuaded to move by the fear that Ireland was going the same way as America. If he hoped that his commercial sops had bought off the Irish Protestants, he was much mistaken. Emboldened by their success, the volunteers and the opposition in the Dublin parliament sought changes to the political relationship with Britain that would safeguard the trade settlement. Legislative independence now became the declared objective of the more radical volunteer units. With the volunteers poised menacingly in the background, opposition MPs, for their part, sought to secure an amendment to Poynings' Law and introduce their own Irish Mutiny bill, which would have given the Dublin parliament, rather than Westminster, control over the regular army in Ireland.

In the short term, the government saw off these challenges, and for a while the lord lieutenant and his chief secretary restored their authority. In 1780 and 1781, the volunteers, though still in being, seemed to lose political momentum. In Ireland, as in England, 1780 saw a conservative reaction, as those with a stake in the existing system rallied to its defense. In the Irish case, anxiety about the revolutionary potential of the volunteers no doubt played a part. Lord George Germain, the secretary of state for the colonies, hoped that the volunteers' actions on College Green ("this State of Anarchy and Confusion," as he described it) would "rouse the men of sense and property" to come to the aid of the government. His wish may well have been fulfilled.[15] When the Rathfriland volunteers criticized the Irish parliament for agreeing to a perpetual rather than annual Mutiny Act, Lord Glenawly took back the muskets that he had provided to the corps.[16]

The reformers' time came, however, when the war in America effectively ended at Yorktown. News of this major British defeat encouraged the opposition MP Henry Grattan to propose a motion in the Dublin parliament in February 1782 declaring Irish legislative independence. Grattan's motion

---

[15] National Library of Ireland, Dublin, Heron Papers, MS 13052, Germain to the Earl of Buckinghamshire, 20 November 1779.
[16] Stephen Conway, *The British Isles and the War of American Independence* (Oxford: Oxford University Press, 2000), 214.

did not pass, but the new government in London, led by the Marquis of Rockingham, gave the Irish opposition what they had been seeking. Rockingham's party had supported Irish demands while in opposition at Westminster, and had close links with the opposition in the Dublin parliament. Rockingham, using the same persuasive powers that he had deployed to secure repeal of the Stamp Act in 1766, eventually won over a majority at Westminster to accept repeal of the Irish Declaratory Act in May 1782. In the following year, his successor, Lord Shelburne, secured the passage of a Renunciation Act, by which the British Parliament formally disavowed any intention to legislate for Ireland.

The constitutional crisis of 1778–1782 brought forth discussion in Irish radical circles about the need for changes within Ireland itself. To some, the obstructiveness of government-supporting MPs in the Dublin parliament during the course of the crisis pointed to the unrepresentative nature of the Irish legislature; too many legislators had been under executive influence and were therefore unresponsive to the wishes of the electorate. Volunteering, furthermore, politicized many middling class Protestant Irishmen, making them reluctant to return to their former political deference after they had taken part in debating, writing petitions and addresses, and even electing their own officers.[17] In June 1782, a convention of volunteers at Dungannon, with delegates from more than 300 corps in attendance, voted in favor of proposals for more equal representation in the Irish parliament. The following year, another volunteer convention at Dungannon, echoing demands then current in England, called for annual parliaments, secret ballots, the abolition of rotten boroughs, redistribution of seats to counties and populous towns, and extension of the franchise. These demands were subsequently scaled back (annual parliaments, secret ballots, and the abolition of rotten boroughs were dropped) at the Grand National Convention that met at Dublin in November 1783. But, even in this modified form, the proposals were decisively rejected by the Irish parliament. Over the next two years, the reformers made little headway. Divided between moderates and radicals, they struggled to become a cohesive force. Conservative interests, furthermore, rallied to defend the existing dispensation and became increasingly confident that they had seen off the threat posed by the volunteers. The impetus for reform petered out.

---

[17] Ian McBride, *Scripture Politics: Ulster Presbyterians and Irish Radicalism in the Late Eighteenth Century* (Oxford: Clarendon, 1998), 10, 124–33.

How, then, are we to interpret Ireland's part in Palmer's "Age of the Democratic Revolution"? The aftermath of the American war certainly saw pressure for greater popular involvement in Irish politics. The volunteers themselves, or at least some of their units in Ulster, embodied democratic principles – they elected their officers, in much the same way as New England militia companies did. The proposals of the Dungannon Convention in 1782 and 1783 pointed the way to the program of the British Chartists in the nineteenth century. But we should be careful not to exaggerate the importance of these "democratic" demands in the great turmoil in Irish political life in the period 1778–1785. By far the largest concern of Irish Protestants was to change the political relationship with Britain. Historians are now inclined to downplay the significance of the changes of 1782–1783. British governments, they tell us, soon recovered the initiative and reasserted their control.[18] But, from our current perspective, the important point is that, in seeking to reclaim their autonomy, Ireland's Protestants were looking backwards not forwards. Most of them were not interested in a democratic transformation of Ireland. Their ambition was simply to rule Ireland – or see it ruled by their own political elite – without interference from London. The British government's embroilment in the American war, especially when it broadened to become a global conflict from 1778, provided an opportunity for the redress of long-standing Irish Protestant grievances. The First Newry Volunteers summed up their objective very clearly when they were formed in September 1778: their aim was to defend their country from foreign and domestic enemies, "to resist Usurpation and maintain the Constitution."[19] Though their methods were very different, they were the heirs of a tradition stretching back at least to Molyneux's claims of Irish legislative autonomy at the end of the seventeenth century.

Britain

Historians used to assume that the preliminaries of the American Revolution had a profound effect on the emergence of the reform movement in Britain. Perhaps influenced by Palmer's thesis, they depicted an eastward movement

---

[18] See, for example, R. F. Foster, *Modern Ireland, 1600–1972* (London: Allen Lane, 1988), 251; James Kelly, *Prelude to Union: Anglo-Irish Politics in the 1780s* (Cork: Cork University Press, 1992), 1.

[19] Public Record Office of Northern Ireland, T 3202/1A, Minute-book of the First Newry Volunteers, original agreement and association, 22 September 1778.

of ideas across the Atlantic, from the colonies to Britain. American claims to exemption from parliamentary taxation rested on the argument that the colonies were not represented at Westminster. George Grenville, the prime minister who introduced the notorious Stamp Act in 1765, responded by claiming that the colonies were indeed represented, not actually in the sense that they had MPs sitting for American constituencies, but "virtually" because there were British MPs who knew American circumstances and could speak for the colonies. Once the issue of the nature of representation was raised, older studies suggest, it stimulated a lively debate in Britain itself about whether Parliament was truly representative of the commons of the realm. In this interpretation, American resistance appeared as the spur to the development of more democratic ideas in Britain.[20] But this perspective underplays the complexity of the process of the movement of ideas. The Americans themselves based their resistance on their English political heritage, citing the English constitution (including Magna Carta and the Bill of Rights) as their protection; they were defending, as they saw it, their rights as Britons or even as English people. Even during the debates of the 1760s and 1770s, the movement of ideas was not unidirectional. Colonial newspapers followed closely the career of John Wilkes, the English libertarian, whose challenge to what he and his supporters saw as the authoritarian tendencies of the British government encouraged the Americans to see themselves as involved in the same struggle.[21]

Another approach, much favored by past generations of historians, is to stress the significant changes taking place in the British economy and British society in the course of the eighteenth century. As Britain's economy became more commercialized and overseas trade became more important, the prosperous middling sort, particularly in the urban centers, became more numerous and more critical of a political system that excluded them.[22] This structural argument, though attractive in many ways, and relevant to the final campaigns for parliamentary reform leading up to the passage of the Great Reform Act of 1832, is less than convincing when applied to the era of the American Revolution. Not the least of the difficulties is the relative

[20] See, for example, John Cannon, *Parliamentary Reform, 1640–1832* (Cambridge: Cambridge University Press, 1972), 53, 60, 67, 96. See also John Brewer, *Party Ideology and Popular Politics at the Accession of George III* (Cambridge: Cambridge University Press, 1976), Chapter 10.

[21] P. D. G. Thomas, *John Wilkes: A Friend to Liberty* (Oxford: Clarendon, 1996), Chapter 10.

[22] For a controversial dismissal of such a view, see J. C. D. Clark, *English Society, 1688–1832: Ideology, Social Structure, and Political Practice during the Ancien Regime* (Cambridge: Cambridge University Press, 1985).

silence of many of the new urban centers in the reform campaigns of the 1760s–1780s. As we will see, though London played a prominent role, the counties led the way. At least some new urban centers, such as Birmingham, seem to have found ways to secure informal or indirect representation of their interests under the unreformed system, and therefore had no strong incentive to press for change.[23] Historians of eighteenth-century Britain, furthermore, tend now to focus more on the survival and continued vitality of aristocratic and landed power than on the inexorable rise of the middle class.[24]

Recent scholarship prefers to lay emphasis not on socioeconomic structural shifts or the influence of American revolutionary ideology, but on the impact of the changes wrought by the Seven Years' War in the genesis of the reform movement in Britain. As noted earlier, that conflict effectively ended the threat of a restoration of the Catholic house of Stuart. French defeat in the war dealt a mortal blow to Jacobitism, the movement to restore the Stuarts. In 1766, as we have seen, even the Pope acknowledged George III as the legitimate monarch. With the threat to the Protestant regal succession removed, those critical of the existing system felt freer to propose alternatives; earlier inhibitions caused by the need for Protestant solidarity in the face of the danger of a Catholic restoration no longer operated.[25] Dissenters pressed for changes in the religious aspects of the constitution, especially the repeal of the seventeenth-century Test and Corporation Acts, which limited public office-holding to Anglicans. In the political sphere, proposals emerged for reform of the representation. Shorter parliaments and action against bribery at elections, together with secret ballots and a redistribution of parliamentary seats, became the hobbyhorses of a small body of metropolitan radicals. For the most part, however, we can see a similar emphasis as in the religious sphere on restoring old rights. The Society of the Bill of Rights, set up in 1769, as its name suggests, invoked the Bill of Rights of 1689 and saw itself as defending English liberties against the authoritarian tendencies

---

[23] See *History of Parliament: The House of Commons, 1754–1790*, ed. John Brooke and Sir Lewis Namier, 3 vols. (London: HMSO, 1964), vol. 1, 8. See also Paul Langford, "Property and 'Virtual Representation' in Eighteenth-Century England," *Historical Journal* 31 (1988), 83–115.

[24] See, for example, John Cannon, *Aristocratic Century: The Peerage of Eighteenth-Century England* (Cambridge: Cambridge University Press, 1984); J. V. Beckett, *The Aristocracy in England, 1660–1914* (Oxford: Blackwell, 1986). Paul Langford, *Public Life and the Propertied Englishman, 1689–1798* (Oxford: Clarendon, 1991), sees a fusion of landed and commercial and aristocratic and middle class in a new propertied alliance.

[25] See Stephen Conway, *War, State, and Society in Mid-Eighteenth-Century Britain and Ireland* (Oxford: Oxford University Press, 2006), Chapter 7.

of post-war British governments. Those authoritarian tendencies perhaps owed something to the growth of empire following the Seven Years' War and the need, as many leading British politicians and administrators saw it, to exercise greater central control over such diverse and expanded dominions. Though John Wilkes was to propose a parliamentary motion calling for a more equal representation of the people in 1776, his reputation was made in his much earlier libertarian stand against the use of general warrants to prosecute those involved in the publication of material offensive to the government.

It was not until the crisis years of the American war and its aftermath that anything we could identify as a movement for parliamentary reform emerged in Britain. The stimulus, if we are to take seriously the testimony of contemporaries, was not emerging American ideas of democracy, but military and financial failure. The colonists, despite the breezy confidence of some government supporters in 1775, proved impossible to subdue. In 1777, the Americans compelled the surrender of a British field army at Saratoga, in upper New York. Saratoga encouraged the French government to accelerate its plans to intervene in the war. From 1778, Britain faced an increasing array of foreign enemies. Invasion of the home islands became a real possibility when a Franco-Spanish fleet secured control of the Channel in the summer of 1779. Meanwhile, increased taxes, a mounting national debt, trade dislocation, economic depression, and a fall in land values combined to persuade even conservative squires in the counties that all was not well. Associations of the disgruntled began to emerge in the English counties and some of the boroughs, calling for change.[26]

Members of the associations believed that the root cause of the malady was the unrepresentative nature of the House of Commons. Rather than reflecting public opinion, it had become a rubber stamp for ministerial decisions. The seeming toothless-ness of the Commons was the cause of widespread lamentation. The associations assumed that this state of affairs had arisen because the government had diverted much of its increased wartime tax income into sinecures and pensions designed to win over MPs to support whatever the ministry wanted. An unrepresentative Commons, instead of acting as a much-needed check on the power of government, was

---

[26] For two older studies, see Herbert Butterfield, *George III, Lord North, and the People, 1779–1780* (London: G. Bell & Sons, 1949); Ian R. Christie, *Wilkes, Wyvill, and Reform, 1760–1785* (London: Macmillan, 1962). For a more recent examination, see Conway, *British Isles and the War of American Independence*, Chapter 6.

allowing ministers to commit blunder after blunder in the running of the war as well as creating an unsupportable national debt.

Unity over the nature of the problem was not matched by unity over the nature of the solution. Some associations favored changes to the way Parliament was elected. In February 1780, Nottingham's Committee of Association called for manhood suffrage in the counties and boroughs, equal-sized constituencies, secret ballots, and annual parliaments. In April, a Society for Constitutional Information, formed in London, demanded manhood suffrage. The following month, a subcommittee of the Westminster Committee of Association presented the case for equal electoral districts, annual parliaments, secret ballots, universal male suffrage, payment of MPs, and the abolition of the property qualification of MPs – in other words, a complete anticipation of the demands of the Chartists nearly sixty years later. But these views remained on the radical fringe; they were not representative of mainstream reforming opinion. Most associations were much more cautious than Nottingham or Westminster. The Yorkshire Association, the first to be formed (in December 1779), probably the most numerous in membership, and arguably the most important, limited its proposals to shorter parliaments and the creation of 100 constituencies.[27] The new seats, we might note, were to be in the counties, not the boroughs. The aim of the Yorkshire reformers was a restoration of the influence of independent country gentlemen in Parliament. Such MPs, the Yorkshire Association believed, would be unlikely to be won over by government bribes; to qualify for their seat they had to meet a property threshold, which, in theory at least, shut out those without substantial private means. As urban radicals pressed for the accommodation of "new" interests in the boroughs and even the abolition of the property qualification for MPs, the Yorkshire reformers sought to reinforce the influence of the landed interest and to use the property qualification as a safeguard against the government using financial inducements to win over parliamentarians.

Pressure for reform of representation failed to gain traction in the course of 1780. Divisions over the best remedy were only part of the problem. More important was the caution induced by the rioting in London and many other places sparked by the government's concessions to Catholics. London's Gordon Riots caused a tremor of anxiety amongst property owners, which reduced the appetite for change in the political system. Still more important,

---

[27] See Ian R. Christie, "The Yorkshire Association, 1780–1784: A Study in Political Organization," *Historical Journal* 3 (1960), 144–61.

perhaps, was an improvement in British military prospects in the war. The Yorkshire Association had been formed at the nadir of British fortunes, after control of the Channel had been lost and invasion appeared distinctly likely. In the early autumn of 1780, by contrast, news arrived of the British capture of Charleston, South Carolina. The recovery of the southern rebel colonies now seemed eminently possible. Military failure and humiliation had been replaced by military success and renewed confidence. For the reformers, the moment had passed.

Final British defeat in America, however, brought ideas of political reform back onto the political agenda. As so often, military failure encouraged much soul-searching. Established institutions were examined afresh, and Parliament, widely seen as the principal cause of the catastrophe, faced new calls for radical overhaul. Indeed, for a brief period, reform was even considered seriously by Parliament itself. William Pitt, first as a supporter of Lord Shelburne's government and then as prime minister, introduced a series of reform proposals to the House of Commons. All of them secured a respectable level of support from MPs, but none was successful. Pitt's first effort, in May 1782, met opposition from MPs who argued that it was distraction from the continuing conflict with the Bourbon powers and the Dutch (who had been added to the list of Britain's enemies at the end of 1780). Even so, it failed by only twenty votes. The closeness of the result encouraged extra-parliamentary supporters of reform, who organized a petitioning campaign. Pitt's next attempt, almost exactly a year later, proved unfortunate. He was by this time in opposition and could not expect the support of government-supporting MPs. His proposal was defeated by 243 votes to 149. Pitt's last effort, in April 1785, might have been expected to be more fruitful as he was the prime minister. As it turned out, he did only marginally better than in 1783. Despite the endeavors of his extra-parliamentary supporters to inspire another petitioning campaign, enthusiasm for change was much less evident in 1785 than in earlier years. As in Ireland, the appetite for parliamentary reform seems to have diminished as the crisis of the war and its aftermath became a memory rather than a current experience.

Notable in all these reforming initiatives is the spur provided not by American ideological example but by failures in the American war. The ebbs and flows of the military situation exerted a profound influence on the state of the reform movement. Whether the cause of reform owed as much to other external developments is less clear. While the British reform movement was certainly not hermetically sealed from outside influences, it reacted more to developments in Ireland than to political inspiration provided by the new United States. British reformers invoked the success of the Irish in securing first commercial concessions and then legislative independence, not the flowering of democratic sentiments in the United States. For the most part, however, they drew on British or English political traditions, just as the Irish Protestants drew on their own traditions, or perhaps myths, of legislative independence. The British reformers sought to restore a representative Parliament, which they hoped would act as a proper check on government. They looked back nostalgically, in other words, to a largely imagined time when Parliament was more independent of government and better able to hold it to account.

A still more substantial challenge to the Palmer thesis is apparent in the British case. Many of those involved in the calls for reform at the end of 1779 and early 1780 were not interested in any changes to the representative system that we might regard as "democratic." We have seen that the squires of the Yorkshire Association recommended more frequent elections and the creation of 100 new county seats. They did not seek an extension of the franchise, or even greater representation for the growing boroughs. Their aim was not to open up the system and bring in more participants, but to keep it in the hands of people like themselves. True, the counties usually had bigger electorates than the boroughs. But with the continuation of open voting (the Yorkshire Association rejected secret ballots) the county electorate remained very exposed to landlord pressure. The Yorkshire reformers looked to bolster aristocratic and gentry influence and exclude those they thought might be most susceptible to government money – MPs of limited means. Their program, in other words, could be interpreted as the antithesis of democracy as we would understand it.

We should also note that many of those who joined the county associations would not even sign up to this very limited and essentially conservative program. They clamored not for parliamentary reform but for what contemporaries called "economical reform" (a saving of public money). Part of the inspiration for economical reform was undoubtedly wartime taxation and a desire to exert greater control over state expenditure. But concern over high levels of taxation was based on more than just the usual reluctance to bear heavier burdens. It was linked to a more fundamental anxiety about the role of Parliament. Wartime expenditure had not been adequately checked, advocates of economical reform argued, because the government had used some of its increased tax revenue to buy support for its measures in Parliament. The House of Commons, economical reformers believed, had lost, or was rapidly losing, its ability to hold the government to account; far too many MPs were now financially beholden to ministers and therefore very unlikely to do anything to jeopardize their income.

The principal targets of the economical reformers were therefore MPs who were in receipt of money from government, known in the language of the time as "placemen" or "pensioners." "The Civil List," a prominent member of the Yorkshire Association argued, "is certainly the Banefull Source from which all Corruption Springs."[28] Parliamentary supporters of economical reform included the main opposition parties. In April 1780, the Commons supported a motion proposed by John Dunning, a Shelburnite MP, declaring that the "influence of the crown [or executive] has increased, is increasing, and ought to be diminished." Thereafter the economical reform movement faced the same problems as the parliamentary reform movement; the government's position was bolstered by the Gordon Riots and news of the fall of Charleston. Bills to prohibit government contractors from sitting in the House of Commons and from revenue officers voting in parliamentary elections, proposed by opposition MPs, both failed. But Lord North's attempt to kick the issue into the long grass, where it could be quietly forgotten, backfired spectacularly. In March 1780, he proposed a royal commission to examine the public accounts. To almost everyone's surprise, the commissioners took their role seriously. Rather than bury the matter until the political temperature had cooled (surely North's intention), they came out with a series of reports that provided the opposition with further ammunition.

The opposition's opportunity to put their remedies into practice came when the war in America effectively ended at Yorktown. Though North's government limped on for some months, everyone knew that it was finished, its authority broken by military failure across the Atlantic. The new ministry, headed by Rockingham, was acutely aware of public expectations and determined not to disappoint them. There was no outright prohibition on MPs receiving salaries or sinecures from government, but places were abolished, including the now unnecessary secretaryship of state for the American colonies, and money was saved in the process. Edmund Burke's Civil List Act of 1782 cut 134 named offices. Rockingham's successor, Shelburne, cut another 144. Pitt, who became Prime Minister in December 1783, carried on the process of retrenchment. In the revenue services alone,

---

[28] North Yorkshire Record Office, Northallerton, Wyvill MSS, ZFW 7/2/4/33, Stephen Croft to the Revd. Christopher Wyvill, 20 December 1779.

some 440 places disappeared between 1784 and 1793. True, all post-war eighteenth-century governments had followed a similar path. Faced with an increased national debt and levels of taxation that MPs were reluctant to sustain, they had cut spending by reducing the size of the army, navy, and revenue services after every major international conflict. But the economical reforms of the Rockingham and Shelburne ministries were at least as much ideologically as financially driven. Burke, like the associations that supported economical reform, envisaged a program of parliamentary purification, not just a money-saving exercise.

Economical reform, some historians argue, pointed the way to the future. We might see it as the start of a long drawn-out process that transformed the nature of government in nineteenth-century Britain. The old order, based on patronage and corruption, gave way to the new, founded on merit, probity, and cheap government.[29] But its backward-looking aspects are surely more noteworthy. Economical reform was in many ways a reaffirmation of the traditional remedies proposed by earlier generations of "country" politicians, who had sought to secure the independence of Parliament from the executive or crown. The division between "court" (government and its servants) and "country" (those suspicious of executive power and its tendency, if unchecked, to expand) predated the emergence of the more familiar Whig and Tory parties in the late seventeenth century. Attitudes that we can associate with country-minded politicians, furthermore, continued to be influential during the age of intense party conflict in the early eighteenth century, sometimes cutting across party allegiances and uniting otherwise hostile backbench MPs in a country alliance.[30] The country platform of legislative independence from the executive found expression in the clause in the Act of Settlement of 1701 that stated "That no Person who has an Office or Place of Profit under the King or receives a Pension from the Crown shall be capable of serving as a Member of the House of Commons."[31] But this proved to be no more than a temporary triumph;

---

[29] See, esp. Philip Harling and Peter Mandler, "From 'Fiscal–Military' State to Laissez-Faire State," *Journal of British Studies* 32 (1993), 44–70; Philip Harling, *The Waning of "Old Corruption": The Politics of Economical Reform in Britain, 1779–1846* (Oxford: Clarendon, 1996).

[30] See, for example, Geoffrey Holmes, *British Politics in the Age of Anne*, rev. edition (London: Hambledon, 1987), Chapter 4. See also Julian Hoppit's comments on the existence of a "country persuasion" rather than party around 1700, in Julian Hoppit, *A Land of Liberty? England, 1689–1727* (Oxford: Oxford University Press, 2000), 159.

[31] W. S. Costin and J. Steven Watson, *The Law and Workings of the Constitution: Documents, 1660–1914*, 2 vols. (London: Adam & Charles Black, 1961), vol. 1, 95.

the high-water mark of country achievement. Later governments circumvented this prohibition, leading country MPs to propose repeated place bills, designed to return to the principle stated with such clarity in 1701. Eighty years later, the economical reform movement aimed at the same objective – a purification of the House of Commons and a restoration of its historic role as an independent check on the executive.[32] Once again, then, we can see that reform in the era of the American Revolution was more about a restoration of a lost past than the creation of a new (and democratic) future.

Conclusions

What emerges from this chapter is the relatively limited impact of external ideological influences. British reformers cited Irish example not in order to put Irish ideas into practice in a different setting, but as evidence of what a mobilized extra-parliamentary reform movement could achieve. Neither British nor Irish reformers seem to have drawn inspiration from the democratic ideas that are often associated with the American Revolution. Perhaps this should not surprise us: the revolution began as a conservative defense of the status quo and its eventual democratic achievements were localized, usually temporary, and often a by-product of the break with Britain, not its cause. Even if we are surprised, and expected to see American ideological influence, we have to accept that there is not a great deal of evidence that political developments in the colonies and then the United States were in the forefront of the minds of either British or Irish reformers. If there was a movement of ideas across the Atlantic in the 1760s and 1770s, it was multidirectional; Americans were at least as influenced by the British as vice versa. The American development that did have a profound impact on the fortunes of British and Irish reform was the fluctuating and ultimately unsuccessful course of the War of Independence. When British arms struggled and then eventually were defeated, reform became much more popular; when, as in 1780, the war seemed to be turning in Britain's favor, the pressure for change slackened. Ministerial and parliamentary failures in the running of the war, more than American revolutionary ideas, seem to have been the spur to calls for a different form of government.

This chapter has also sought to sound a note of caution against too ready an assumption that the most important features of a period are those that

---

[32] For a pithy summary, see the entry on "Court and Country Party," in John Cannon, ed., *The Oxford Companion to British History* (Oxford: Oxford University Press, 2002).

seem to point to later developments. No form of historical study is perhaps more prone to a tendency to whiggish teleology (identifying an end and reading backwards from there) than accounts of the emergence and growth of the parliamentary reform movement in Britain and Ireland. To avoid slipping into thinking that the only features of our period that are important are those that led ultimately to the Great Reform Act of 1832 is no easy task. Despite the challenges, we should approach this subject by trying to establish the priorities of the time and not magnify the significance of what seems to represent the future. In the period covered in this chapter at least, what we might see as forward-looking democratic impulses were less popular than backward-looking (and undemocratic) remedies for present discontents. Most Irish participants in reforming efforts sought to recover the independence of the Dublin parliament rather than transform the workings of the representative system within Ireland. They hoped to restore a legislative autonomy that Irish Protestants had been striving to achieve, or assert, since at least the end of the seventeenth century. In Britain, we can see an interesting foreshadowing of the democratic program of the nineteenth-century Chartists in the proposals of some of the urban associations during the crisis years of the American war. Most parliamentary reformers in this period, however, were much more cautious, and those connected with the Yorkshire Association looked to solutions that would have reinforced the hold of the landed interest and were far from democratic in any way that we would recognize now. More importantly, what seems to have been the most widespread movement for change at this time was for economical not parliamentary reform. Economical reform, though in some respects pointing the way to a new and very different system of government that operated from the middle of the nineteenth century, was essentially a refurbishment of the old country platform of legislative independence and parliamentary purification. As with so many reforming endeavors, it sought to recover a better yesterday rather than establish a new and more democratic tomorrow.

12

A Contest of Wills: The Spectrum and Experience of Political Violence in the American Revolution

WAYNE E. LEE

Violence used to pursue a political outcome is primarily a contest of wills. One side pushes, the other pushes back, in the reciprocal escalation identified in Carl von Clausewitz's opening philosophical speculation on the nature of war. This inherent logic, however, applies not just to war, but to political violence more generally. Actors in the drama of what became the American Revolution used a wide spectrum of types or forms of violence, of which the *war* for independence was only a part – however critical. Their choices about *how* to use violence reflected both the level of escalation in the contest and their cultural notions about the meaning and limits associated with various types of violence. And because in the real world there is no such thing as two singular opposed wills, but instead a vast shifting audience of more or less interested parties, violence is intended not only to diminish the enemy's will, it is also supposed to mobilize more will for one's own side from the as yet uncommitted.

Will is something that must be cultivated, nurtured, and, at times, desperately appealed to – exemplified by Thomas Paine's *cri de cœur*, "these are the times that try men's souls." Appealing to will in this way demands a strategic narrative: A claim that "we are winning/can win"; "we are fighting for your interests"; "they are corrupt/evil/ungodly"; "we represent your values and beliefs," and so on. Violence is just a piece of that broader strategic narrative. Violence has an instrumental function, in that it has material results of death, harm, or destruction, nominally designed to build up will on one side and diminish it on the other, but its use must in part match the claims of the strategic narrative, in its effects *and* in its manner.[1]

---

[1] Strategic narrative concept from Emile Simpson, *War from the Ground Up: Twenty-First Century Combat as Politics* (Oxford: Oxford University Press, 2012).

In mid-eighteenth-century European culture, the outlines of the right manner of violence were clear in word and spirit, if not often in deed. Public protest, riots, and warfare each had certain protocols. Generally, they shared the requirement that violence be preceded by claims and complaints, and that the actual violence be conducted within certain bounds. The "rules" of riot were mostly unspoken, slowly evolving, and frequently contested (particularly on a class basis). On the other hand, the expected behaviors in war, known broadly as the laws and customs of war, were more clearly articulated and even written down, but they were also the ones least likely to be fully obeyed.

Political violence was further modulated and shaped by the identity of the opponent, especially by the prospect of a future post-conflict relationship with them as fellow subjects or citizens. This vision did not typically include Indians or slaves, and so violence against them took more extreme forms. On the other hand, the American Revolution was a civil war, and violence *within* the "white" population was aggravated by a sense of betrayal. Each side claimed the other was a traitor – an ideological stance whipped up over the long process of mutually escalating will mobilization.[2]

Taken together, these cultural and strategic forces shaping violence – restraining it or aggravating it – produced highly idiosyncratic results in any given locale or time. It did so because violence is always about more than just the contest of wills. Other variables impinged: existing local animosities, recent events, ethnic or class divides, distance from British or American regular forces, the presence of slaves, the proximity of Indians, and more.

I have thus far insisted that political violence exists on a spectrum and therefore shares certain inherent logics. At the same time, as behavior moved along the spectrum, observers and participants imputed different meanings to what they saw and did. The categories mattered. To be *at war* differed from being in the midst of a riotous protest. The American Revolution and the accompanying war included a wide set of categories of political violence, all of which occurred within the same overall clash of wills. And in most cases, those categories were also *stages*. They defined the progression of events created by the escalatory contest of wills. I have divided these

---

[2] Wayne E. Lee, *Barbarians and Brothers: Anglo-American Warfare, 1500–1865* (New York: Oxford University Press, 2011). This problem is also at the core of T. Cole Jones, *Captives of Liberty: Prisoners of War and the Politics of Vengeance in the American Revolution* (Philadelphia: University of Pennsylvania Press, 2019).

categories of political violence into three groups: intimidative and catalytic; regular and logistical; and retaliatory. I will define each in turn.

Intimidative and Catalytic Violence

In the British colonies in North America, from the mid-1760s through the early 1770s, those Americans resisting increased British government engagement in colonial affairs felt driven to more extreme measures (although not in any linear sense). The terms of the dispute in ideological, economic, and political terms shifted at times, and interest in them varied from place to place and over time. For the most part, the precise terms need not detain us here, having been dealt with by Patrick Griffin, Chapter 7, above. Suffice it to say, that the mid-1760s had seen the beginning of a contest of wills over the appropriate form of imperial governance. That contest had included various forms of protest violence (generally intended to both communicate grievance and intimidate key actors) and repressive state responses, but it was not until the very end of 1773 and then throughout 1774 that violence began to catalyze further violence, in a series of escalating steps, until the contest shifted into "regular" militarized violence.

The key event proved to be the Boston Tea Party on 16 December 1773. The event itself, a clandestine, semi-festive destruction of property – in this case tea – at the center of the ongoing dispute over taxation and governance, was carefully structured by its participants to continue the dialogue and to prove political will. It simply said Boston would not back down. Among the other colonies, support for this new radical step was not initially universal. Some observers believed it crossed certain lines; it was clear to all, for example, that there was a substantial difference between forcing the cargo back out to sea and actually destroying it.[3] At any rate, news of the destruction had reached all the American colonies by January 1774, leading others to copy the Bostonians, and over the course of 1774 tea was turned away in Philadelphia, New York City, and Portsmouth, was burned wherever found in various inland towns, or ended up in the harbor in Boston (again), New York City, Annapolis, and Greenwich, New Jersey.[4]

---

[3] Harlow Unger, *American Tempest: How the Boston Tea Party Sparked a Revolution* (Cambridge, MA: Da Capo Press, 2011), 173; Benjamin Woods Labaree, *The Boston Tea Party* (New York: Oxford University Press, 1964), 146–7.

[4] Labaree, *Boston Tea Party*, 153–69; Unger, *American Tempest*, 174–5.

How long and how far this sense of unity over the Tea Act would have carried the disgruntled colonists' will to resist must remain a mystery. The British government's response, however, quickly stoked American will to another level. In a series of legislative moves, quickly condemned by the colonists as the "Intolerable Acts," Parliament punished Boston and the entire colony of Massachusetts. The separate Acts first closed the port of Boston and then voided the colonial charter, substituting royal appointees for virtually all executive offices. Other Acts protected accused officials from local prosecution and appeared to threaten the quartering of troops in private homes.[5] In May 1774, the governor general, Lieutenant General Thomas Gage, arrived in Boston with four regiments, bringing the army back from the colonial periphery to the center.[6]

Suppressing domestic disorder was very much a part of the role of the army, despite England's well-developed dislike of a standing force. The state, if pressed, had few other mechanisms on which to fall back.[7] Officials in London, including Gage himself, were persuaded that a show of force in Boston would bring the situation back into line. Gage suggested to King George that the protestors would "be Lyons, whilst we are Lambs[,] but if we take the resolute part they will undoubtedly prove very meek," and he further suggested that "the four Regiments ... if sent to Boston are sufficient to prevent any disturbance."[8] In this they underestimated the deeply rooted colonial will to resist.

The Intolerable Acts fell on fertile soil – the colonists had long been cultivating resentment combined with resistance. But the Acts also crucially created a new level of intercolonial unity – although not among those in the Caribbean or Canada. Although the Acts specifically targeted Boston, the intellectual work had already been done that led many colonists elsewhere to see the Acts as evidence of a larger problem of British corruption. More specifically to our purposes here, the Acts catalyzed a more unified colonial willingness to use violence, or to prepare for violence, especially in its armed

---

[5] Robert Middlekauff, *The Glorious Cause: The American Revolution, 1763–1789* (New York: Oxford University Press, 1982), 229–31.

[6] Richard Archer, *As If an Enemy's Country: The British Occupation of Boston and the Origins of Revolution* (New York: Oxford University Press, 2010), 91–104.

[7] John Shy, *Toward Lexington: The Role of the British Army and the Coming of the American Revolution* (Princeton: Princeton University Press, 1965), 394–5. For the army's role in domestic disorder, see Richard Vogler, *Reading the Riot Act: The Magistracy, the Police, and the Army in Civil Disorder* (Bristol, PA: Open University Press, 1991); Tony Hayter, *The Army and the Crowd in Mid-Georgian London* (London: Macmillan, 1978).

[8] King George to Lord North, 4 February 1774, in John Fortescue, ed., *The Correspondence of King George the Third*, 6 vols. (London: Macmillan, 1928), vol. III, 59.

form. Where very often the protests and riots of the preceding decade, up to and including the Tea Party itself, had followed the customs of protest violence and had avoided weapons, especially firearms, colonial responses to the ministry's crackdown in 1774 escalated substantially. Pauline Maier pointed out that this escalation occurred in part because the ministry's fundamental authority, to include that of the king himself, was now being questioned. Earlier protests had sought to *limit* British authority, but "by 1775, the validity of that authority as a whole was contested."[9]

As the colonists groped toward armed resistance, and as each side accused the other of arming or preparing to arm, the Whigs recognized that will needed shape. Will might provide the spirit, but the flesh would be the institutions and bureaucracies of rule, as well as the tools of war. Mobilization is always about men, money, and will. In the case of the American Revolution, will came first, governing institutions came next. The Intolerable Acts provoked the meeting of the First Continental Congress beginning in September 1774, and that meeting is justly celebrated as a key step on the road to revolution and a unified government. It is important to remember, however, that it was essentially just a debating society. It was *not* an effective legislative or governing body. In normal times, governance proceeded through local courts, town councils, and a few royal officials, all nominally backed by the power of the militia and ultimately by the regular army. Over the course of 1774 and 1775, even well before the "first shot" in April 1775, the rebels moved to seize or create the instruments of governance.

Doing so often required intimidative violence to cow opponents, a form of political violence carefully honed since 1765. Increasingly, however, it also required usurping the institutions of governance. Virginia's House of Burgesses continued to meet in May 1774 despite being officially dissolved; in June, Westborough, Massachusetts, acquired cannon and other arms; in August, Worcester, Massachusetts, using intimidative violence, met and rejected British authority over their governance, and laid out the logic for independence; Whigs took over the Berkshire court in August, and other towns in Massachusetts soon followed suit.[10] Some of the biggest crowds coalesced in efforts to intimidate and drive out officials recently appointed to civil office through the Intolerable Acts. One such appointee fled Taunton in

---

[9] Pauline Maier, *From Resistance to Revolution* (New York: Alfred A. Knopf, 1972), 245.

[10] Ray Raphael, *The First American Revolution: Before Lexington and Concord* (New York: New Press, distributed by W. W. Norton, 2002), 61–6, 68, and passim chronicles these and other early moves in Massachusetts. Also T. H. Breen, *American Insurgents, American Patriots: The Revolution of the People* (New York: Hill & Wang, 2010), 84–98.

Figure 12.1 The Somerville powder house, from where British troops stole 250 barrels of gunpowder in 1774, setting off the "Powder Alarm," due to which many rural residents went to Boston to fight. Alamy.

August 1774, and his house was threatened by "about five hundred persons assembled, many of them Freeholders and some of them Officers in the Militia ... they had then no Fire-arms, but generally had clubs."[11] Incidents like this proliferated all over Massachusetts, some more violent, including tarring and feathering, a horrific form of intimidative violence that is not to be dismissed as cartoonish. Taken together they so thoroughly ended royal rule in Massachusetts outside Boston that historian Ray Raphael has called the mid- to late-1774 period the "First American Revolution."

[11] Quoted in Raphael, *First American Revolution*, 69.

Escalating the contest of wills, the British felt compelled to react, leading to the so-called "Powder Alarm," on 1 September 1774. British forces in Boston launched a successful surprise raid to seize the gunpowder in the central magazine about 6 miles northwest of Boston. As word spread, however, the "powder alarm" – the story that the British were on the march, were taking provincial arms, that people had been killed, and all the rest of the flotsam of the rumor mill – led militia contingents to turn out all over Massachusetts and even Connecticut. Thousands of armed men took to the roads, and even once assured that no war was underway, thousands more continued to assemble to attack and intimidate alleged Tories.[12] The powder alarm, coming as it did mere days before the first sitting of the First Continental Congress, was yet another key catalytic step, as now the inhabitants and the army were confronting each other about the control of arms and powder. It threatened a "category" jump in political violence from protest to war. T. H. Breen argues that the radical turn taken by the First Continental Congress in mid-September was driven by the radicalism in Massachusetts and the power demonstrated by the thousands of men who had turned out in arms in response to the Powder Alarm.[13] Thus energized, the Congress resolved on 27 September to prohibit imports from Great Britain. Gage, overturning his own earlier advice, sent for reinforcements.

The First Continental Congress' nonimportation resolution led naturally and immediately to new mechanisms for assuming control of local government – and of arms.[14] Nonimportation was an old tactic, but this time around, an intercolonial congress promulgated a "Continental Association" or pact, that encouraged counties, towns, and cities to elect committees – building on the old Committees of Correspondence, but now generally called Committees of Safety – "whose business it shall be attentively to observe the conduct of all persons" regarding the association, and if an apparent violator be accused to the "satisfaction of a majority of any such committee," they shall publicize their name "to the end, that all such foes to the rights of British-America may be publicly known, and universally contemned."[15] T. H. Breen's description of this process and its significance is hard to improve:

---

[12] David H. Fischer, *Paul Revere's Ride* (New York: Oxford University Press, 1994), 44–50; Breen, *American Insurgents*, 134–49.

[13] Breen, *American Insurgents*, 152; David Ammerman, *In the Common Cause: American Response to the Coercive Acts of 1774* (Charlottesville: University of Virginia Press, 1974), 73–6.

[14] The fully fledged "Continental Association" was not signed until 20 October.

[15] See Ammerman, *In the Common Cause*, 85. The Association text is found in Library of Congress, *Journals of the Continental Congress, 1774–1789* (Washington, DC: Government Printing Office, 1904–1937), vol. 1, 75–81, quote on 79.

In communities throughout America the committees determined the progress of revolution. They quickly seized the political initiative, and before those who harbored doubts about the wisdom or legality of taking up arms against the king could organize effective countermeasures, they found themselves marginalized by extralegal bodies fully prepared to intimidate, even terrorize those who dared to criticize the American cause.[16]

Intimidative violence was thus a central tactic; Loyalists or "nonassociators" found themselves confronting the prospect or reality of violence.[17] Under the terms of the association, the committees became ruling tribunals; they decided who the enemy was and roused popular enforcement of their writ by co-opting the colonial militia system. The militia was a natural mechanism for spreading the committee's rule, in part simply because it was a long-extant channel of communication to the white male public via an established hierarchical authority.[18]

Asserting control over fiscal and military institutions also took place at the provincial level. In October, General Gage tried to cancel the meeting of the Massachusetts General Court, but they met anyway, reconstituting themselves as a Provincial Congress. The congress quickly identified key arms purchases, and reached out to the existing network of tax collectors (sheriffs, constables, and so on) to "recommend" that they continue collecting taxes, but now to redirect them to the congress' newly appointed receiver-general of revenues.[19] On 23 November, Massachusetts also authorized the creation of 12,000 "minutemen," selected from the general militia. That same month, a provincial congress in Connecticut authorized a similar body of minutemen. In December, Maryland's Provincial Convention recommended that its county committees collect funds to buy arms.[20] Also in December, Whigs in New Hampshire seized the British fort in Portsmouth Harbor, taking the powder and cannon there – narrowly avoiding British reinforcements intended to prevent just such a move.[21] Throughout New England, the shadow government was rapidly becoming the de facto government.

---

[16] Breen, *American Insurgents*, 162.
[17] Holger Hoock, *Scars of Independence: America's Violent Birth* (New York: Crown, 2017), 31–6, recounts some examples of the committees both restraining and encouraging violence, but emphasizes violence; Ammerman, *In the Common Cause*, 122, emphasizes the committees' efforts at restraint.
[18] Ammerman, *In the Common Cause*, 103–24, documents the spread of the committees and their general functioning.
[19] Raphael, *First American Revolution*, 160–1; Ammerman, *In the Common Cause*, 141–2, documents the full range of military preparations by the Massachusetts Provincial Congress prior to April 1775.
[20] Ammerman, *In the Common Cause*, 123.   [21] Maier, *Resistance to Revolution*, 244.

News of the Continental Congress and the nonimportation association reached London in December. The ministry chose to escalate, and it sent Gage more troops and more decisive orders. Crucially, those orders included a clause that was becoming common currency as each side escalated the stakes: "Force should be repelled by Force." Violence in self-defense was always deemed justifiable – it was probably the most fundamental of the "laws of war." Gage was further advised to cease being timid in the face of such undisciplined rabble, and specifically to use the army to arrest key leaders of the resistance. Those orders arrived in April, and Gage, already eager for permission, leapt at the opportunity.[22] Britain's army *marched* first; whether they *fired* first at Lexington is less relevant.

The contest of wills now shifted decisively into the mental framework of war. Prepared by the Powder Alarm in September, and forewarned about British intentions in April, the militias of towns all over Massachusetts rapidly converged on Concord. They saw themselves as "repelling force with force," and they harassed the British column all the way back to Boston, and then settled in to besiege the city. Wartime violence had its own rules and a different set of meanings. And unlike many riots, revolts, and even rebellions in contemporary Europe, this revolt (it was not yet a revolution) jumped more or less straight from the "riot-protest" violence paradigm, to a conventional symmetrical war paradigm. American institutional preparations and long-germinating resentment meant that the *scale* of the American response – in numbers, in organization, and in equipment – rapidly forced the British to treat them as an equal combatant – exactly what the ministry had convinced itself that the Americans were *not*. It had persistently assumed the Americans were a "rude Rabble without plan," apt to disperse at the first show of force.[23]

The events of that day, both in reality and as rumored, also foreshadowed several key aspects of violence in the war to come.[24] First, the fighting constituted a narrative that both sides would use to justify themselves: the Americans were fighting in self-defense (said the Whigs) and the Americans were rebels against their lawful king (said the British and Loyalists). Second, during the fighting, the other side had clearly demonstrated its fundamental inhumanity (both sides accused the other of various atrocities, including the

---

[22] Ammerman, *In the Common Cause*, 134–7.
[23] Instructions to Gage, quoted in Ammerman, *In the Common Cause*, 135.
[24] The events at Lexington and Concord are narrated in great detail in Fischer, *Paul Revere's Ride*.

Figure 12.2 Retreat of British troops from Concord, 1775. Alamy.

rumor that the colonists had scalped a British soldier).[25] Ultimately for the British, Lexington and Concord was a double failure. They had escalated violence to crush resistance, but the march to Concord not only failed in its tactical objective of arresting key leaders, it also inflamed resistance at a strategic level.

Networks of committees and newspapers rapidly spread the news of Concord around the mainland colonies, and over the next two to three months there ensued quite a number of copycat munitions raids, by both sides. The royal governor of Virginia spirited away some of the powder from the central magazine on 20/21 April[26]; the Whigs seized the magazine in Baltimore on 25 April; most famously, Ethan Allen and Benedict Arnold seized the artillery at Fort Ticonderoga on 10 May. The next day, Georgia's

---

[25] See, for example, the *Resolution of the Massachusetts Congress, 5 May 1775* (Salem: E. Russell, 1775); and the Circular Letter to the Committee of South Carolina, 30 June 1775, in *Colonial Records of North Carolina*, vol. x, 51; Fischer, *Paul Revere's Ride*, 273; Wayne E. Lee, *Crowds and Soldiers in Revolutionary North Carolina: The Culture of Violence in Riot and War* (Gainesville: University Press of Florida, 2001), 140–1.

[26] Michael A. McDonnell, *The Politics of War: Race, Class and Conflict in Revolutionary Virginia* (Chapel Hill: University of North Carolina Press, 2007), 49–50.

Whigs took the magazine in Savannah, and the Virginia Whigs took over the one in Williamsburg on 5 June.

In addition to these efforts to seize the physical means of violence, the fighting at Concord inspired a broader wave of Whig efforts to further consolidate their hold on the means of rule. Most notably, the Second Continental Congress convened in early May, and it adopted the army outside Boston as its own "Continental army" on 14 June. Over the next month, in addition to borrowing money to buy military supplies, the congress drafted the "Declaration of the Causes and Necessity for Taking up Arms." Armed violence demanded this kind of rhetorical positioning, and the drafters pointedly returned to the self-defense argument: "against violence actually offered, we have taken up arms." Furthermore, the drafters were careful to shape their words to fit the *nature* of the violence to which they were responding, and that they were enacting. In the final draft British soldiers did not "attack," they "assaulted"; the British did not "kill," they "murdered"; meanwhile, the word for the Americans involved was changed from "men," to "a soldiery."[27] The Whigs thus sought to seize the initiative in the competition of strategic narratives that paralleled the forceful competition of the armies, *and* in the competition between the shadow governments versus the royal governments. The success of Whig organizing was made most visible in the flight of royal governors, usually to a ship in the harbor. But each of the thirteen rebelling colonies experienced a roughly similar story of Whig intimidation of comparatively disorganized Loyalists, including defeating several nascent loyalist militias.[28]

The reciprocal escalation inherent to a conflict of wills continued apace. Many of these moves by the individual colonies led to a British reaction, and British reaction led to further Whig radicalization, and so on. Initially, it took time for news to travel to London, and more time again for orders and reinforcements to be gathered and dispatched. Gage, and other royal governors on the continent, also made their own unilateral decisions, and, taken

---

[27] Lee, *Crowds and Soldiers*, 141. The various drafts reflecting these word changes are in Library of Congress, *Journals of the Continental Congress*, vol. II, 128–57, see esp. 135, 139.

[28] Jim Piecuch, *Three Peoples, One King: Loyalists, Indians, and Slaves in the Revolutionary South, 1775–1782* (Columbia: University of South Carolina Press, 2008), 36–92; McDonnell, *Politics of War*, 43–139; John E. Selby, *The Revolution in Virginia, 1775–1783* (Williamsburg, VA: Colonial Williamsburg Foundation, 1988), 41–79; Hoock, *Scars*, 23–51; Gregory T. Knouff, *The Soldiers' Revolution: Pennsylvanians in Arms and the Forging of Early American Identity* (University Park: Pennsylvania State University Press, 2004), 197–207; Lee, *Crowds and Soldiers*, 139–58.

as a whole, the first series of British responses to the fighting at Concord and the siege of Boston rapidly made things worse. British choices in these early months significantly bolstered the American will to resist and broadened the war beyond Massachusetts.[29] Some of these early moves have not received the attention they deserve, in part because Lexington and Concord has been rightly seen as the central, paradigm-shifting catalyst. Even so, the push for full independence was not yet unanimous, especially across regional, ethnic, and economic interest lines. Initial British military violence, however, almost seemed *designed* to instill unity and escalate rebel will. In mid-June, Gage's forces in Boston lashed out at their besiegers in the Battle of Bunker Hill. The colonial forces retreated, but they exacted a terrible toll, and the experience encouraged Americans to believe that they could defeat the regular British Army. More damaging were rumors (generally unsubstantiated) in mid-summer 1775 that British governors were encouraging slaves and Indians to join them against the colonists.[30] In Virginia, Michael McDonnell has shown how the very early slave uprisings there (as early as April 1775) were key in creating a gentry–populace unity behind the Whig effort to assert rule. White Virginian fears were then cemented when the royal governor of Virginia, Lord Dunmore, made such a slave rebellion official British policy with his proclamation on 7 November 1775. In it, he promised that slaves joining British forces would be granted freedom.[31] In October 1775, British forces burned Falmouth (now Portland, Maine), bolstering Whig claims of self-defense. British forces repeated the crime at Norfolk in January 1776.[32] The British did all this while also expanding the war to the other colonies, especially the Carolinas, by promising troops to support Loyalist risings in North and South Carolina (all of which were defeated). And to pile calamity upon calamity for the British strategic narrative, the Cherokees actually did raid the southern frontier in the summer of 1776, leading North Carolinian Thomas Jones to hope that no "Tory will ever after this open his mouth in favour of the British Government which of all Governments on Earth I believe at this time it is the most Tyrannical and bloody."[33]

---

[29] Generally, see Middlekauff, *Glorious Cause*, 315–16.
[30] Lee, *Crowds and Soldiers*, 142–3; Piecuch, *Three Peoples, One King*, 63–81. British officials recognized the perils of calling on Indian allies, whom they initially aimed to keep loyal, but quiet. Arming slaves had more support, including from colonial governors, who should have understood the likely backlash. See Piecuch, *Three Peoples, One King*, 34–5, 39, 40–1.
[31] McDonnell, *Politics of War*, 49, 138.
[32] Both incidents are related in Hoock, *Scars*, 85–126.
[33] Thomas Jones to James Iredell, 23 July 1776, in *Papers of James Iredell*, vol. 1, 415–16.

In the end, mutually escalating intimidative violence – by both sides – nominally intended to undermine the will of their opponents, had become catalytic violence transforming resistance and protest into war. Intimidative violence had begun in the 1760s firmly within a paradigm of controlled crowd action designed to transmit grievances to authority *without* stirring up excessive state repression.[34] As both sides refused to back down from the contest of wills, the violence escalated, and then became catalytic when each side made moves with logistical and institutional implications. Seizing the tools of war invoked new fears and signaled escalation beyond the bounds of protest and communication. Furthermore, throughout the slowly escalating crisis from 1765 to 1775, both sides struggled to win the support of the populace through competing strategic narratives – they repeatedly framed themselves as the *right actor* in the crisis. The ultimate expression of this from the American side would be the Declaration of Independence itself. Aside from its high ideals about the equality of men, it is primarily a list of grievances. Intriguingly, of the twenty-seven enumerated complaints, nine are specifically about the use of violence (and many of the more "political" grievances simply repeat each other). This framing would be key as the crisis transformed into war, because war demanded the mobilization of men, money, and, again, will. It remained to be seen how long each side could sustain that will.

Regular and Logistical Violence

The colonists' transition from resistance to war preceded their final declaration of independence by over a year. Nevertheless, the logics of open war asserted themselves immediately, blended with what eighteenth-century military men *thought* war should look like. This was not just George Washington's desire for a "respectable army" – as real as that was.[35] There was a wide-ranging, broadly held belief that wars were only truly won through decisive clashes – not through a guerrilla war aimed at national will or endurance. This set of beliefs then defined how will, men, and money

---

[34] Key studies are Pauline Maier, "Popular Uprisings and Civil Authority in Eighteenth-Century America," *William and Mary Quarterly* 27 (1970), 3–35; William Pencak, Matthew Dennis, and Simon P. Newman, eds., *Riot and Revelry in Early America* (University Park: Pennsylvania State University Press, 2002); Thomas P. Slaughter, "Crowds in Eighteenth-Century America: Reflections and New Directions," *Pennsylvania Magazine of History and Biography* 115 (1991), 3–34.

[35] Don Higginbotham, *George Washington and the American Military Tradition* (Athens, GA: University of Georgia Press, 1985).

were mobilized and directed. Although Americans believed themselves better prepared to fight in the North American environment than their British counterparts, there was no initial intent to fight a guerrilla war: the militia were to stand toe-to-toe against the redcoats and slug it out.[36] This attitude toward the decisiveness of conventional combat was distinctly more overt and influential at the beginning of the war, but it arguably held on to the end, and it was this attitude which lent Yorktown its decisiveness in the minds of the British political public. Historian James Whitman has referred to this belief as a *jus victoriae*: war was a dispute-resolution tool in which victory was a verdict with legal meaning. In his formulation, they thought of war as:

> a legitimate means of settling disputes and resolving legal questions through violence. Under this alternative view, the law of war, instead of focusing on the *jus ad bellum* and the *jus in bello*, concerned itself with what I call the *jus victoriae*, the law of victory. The *jus victoriae* assumed that war was not a last resort used in self-defense and comparably dire circumstances, but a kind of acceptable legal procedure.[37]

This cultural vision of war's function shaped early strategies by channeling the contest of wills into the contest of regular armies striving for overt battlefield victory. On assuming command in October 1775, British general William Howe hoped for a "decisive Action, than which nothing is more to be desired or sought for by us as the most effectual means to terminate this expensive War."[38] Washington shared this impulse, from his first temptation to assault the British lines outside Boston, through to his successes at Trenton and Princeton, and beyond.[39] Structural realities, however, quickly impinged on this cultural desire. After some initial victories (or near victories) at Concord, Boston, Ticonderoga, and Charles Town, and against Loyalist forces in North and South Carolina, the rebels' financial weakness, combined with the British ability to move forces by sea, led *not* to a decisive battle, but to a form of positional warfare, in which both sides avoided the

---

[36] The guerrilla war option was barely discussed at the outset of the war, and was then explicitly rejected by Washington and the Continental leadership. John Shy, "American Strategy: Charles Lee and the Radical Alternative," in John Shy, ed., *A People Numerous and Armed* (Oxford: Oxford University Press, 1976), 133–62.

[37] James Q. Whitman, *The Verdict of Battle: The Law of Victory and the Making of Modern War* (Cambridge, MA: Harvard University Press, 2012), 10.

[38] Quoted in Ira D. Gruber, "British Strategy: The Theory and Practice of Eighteenth-Century Warfare," in Don Higginbotham, ed., *Reconsiderations on the Revolutionary War* (Westport, CT: Greenwood, 1978), 14–31: 24.

[39] Edward G. Lengel, *General George Washington: A Military Life* (New York: Random House, 2005), 365–67.

extreme risks of battle, but tried instead to tempt the other to gamble recklessly.[40] The political value of controlling cities acted as the planetary masses around which this risk aversion–gamble dynamic orbited. The British mounted a massive amphibious operation to take New York City that forced Washington to gamble in defending it. It was very nearly fatal for the American cause. The British repeated the process with a carefully planned, amphibiously supported move against the rebel capital at Philadelphia the next year, forcing Washington again to gamble at the Battle of Brandywine. Thereafter, Washington mostly avoided gambling, choosing to attack sections of the British Army, but not any one whole field force – at least until the final gamble at Yorktown. To be sure, in many ways the right victory in either positional warfare or in an open battle *could* have decisive political consequences, because of how it affected the will of combatants to join in or go on.

The American victory at Saratoga in 1777 had precisely this effect on will. In that campaign, British general John Burgoyne gambled with a risky thrust down the Hudson Valley that the Americans and the regional geography turned into a positional fight. Unable to overcome prepared American positions and floundering in an insoluble logistical environment, Burgoyne had to surrender or starve. Saratoga's decisiveness, however, derived from its effect on *will*, not from the number of men killed or prisoners taken. Not only did it convince the French to intervene, but it also led the British ministry to seriously reconsider the war's goals. Parliament voided the Tea Act and the Massachusetts Government Act (which had given the royal governor vast powers), and Lord North authorized the so-called Carlisle Commission to negotiate with the Continental Congress. That commission essentially offered a commonwealth-like status, to include granting the right of taxation to the colonial assemblies, dramatically reversing a decade of British government resistance to such ideas.[41] That the Americans were beyond such persuasion by this point reflected how war has its own logics and momentum. The commitments and costs of war had pushed the rebels beyond accepting a return to the conditions they had demanded while still mere protestors.

---

[40] Assessments of American and British strategy, see Donald Stoker, Kenneth J. Hagan, and Michael T. McMaster, eds., *Strategy in the American War of Independence: A Global Approach* (London: Routledge, 2010); Lengel, *General George Washington*; Gruber, "British Strategy."

[41] John Ferling, *Almost a Miracle: The American Victory in the War of Independence* (Oxford: Oxford University Press, 2007), 263–5.

In many ways the strategy for both sides changed after the French entered the war, but for now let us turn to the violence of this "regular" war of armies. Within that paradigm, contemporaries expected certain rules and limits to be observed. To be sure, they equally expected to be disappointed in that regard, but the so-called customs and usages of war persistently structured and shaped the violence of the regular war. Those customs and usages were intended first and foremost to contain the violence of war to the actions of armies in direct conflict. They theoretically protected noncombatants from armed violence; they regulated the appropriation and/or permanent transfer of movable and real property; they set boundaries around the killing of one's enemy (not as or after he surrenders, not while a prisoner, and so on); and, perhaps most reliably, they created an "etiquette of belligerence" that allowed room for negotiation, prisoner exchanges, safe surrenders of fortifications, and so on.[42] All of these customs, increasingly codified in quasi-legal texts, protected both sides, especially officers in uniform, from anarchic violence.

For its part, Washington's Continental army adhered relatively well to those customs, in no small part because doing so enhanced the rebellion's international standing, while also burnishing the honor of its officers. Most examinations of the army's behavior agree that the Continental army rarely engaged in "wanton violence against civilians, such as rape or murder," and that Continental troops accepted quarter, protected prisoners, and within the economic constraints of the weak central government, provided for prisoners in confinement until they were exchanged.[43] These conventions were particularly critical and successful insofar as they enhanced communication between the two regular armies. War's escalatory logic, in which not only

---

[42] The "etiquette" phrase is from Geoffrey Parker, "Early Modern Europe," in Michael Howard, George J. Andreopoulos, and Mark R. Shulman, eds., *The Laws of War: Constraints on Warfare in the Western World* (New Haven: Yale University Press, 1994), 40–58: 42. See Eliga H. Gould, "Zones of Law, Zones of Violence: The Legal Geography of the British Atlantic, circa 1772," *William and Mary Quarterly*, 3rd series, 60:3 (2003), 471–510: 477, for the widespread acceptance of these European notions of just war.

[43] Martin and Lender, *A Respectable Army*, 129–30 (quote). Also Lee, *Barbarians and Brothers*; Armstrong Starkey, "Paoli to Stony Point: Military Ethics and Weaponry During the American Revolution," *Journal of Military History* 58 (1994), 7–27; Daniel Krebs, *A Generous and Merciful Enemy: Life for German Prisoners of War during the American Revolution* (Norman: University of Oklahoma Press, 2013), 84–91, 118–20, and passim; Charles H. Metzger, *The Prisoner in the American Revolution* (Chicago: Loyola University Press, 1971), esp. 151–62; Ken Miller, *Dangerous Guests: Enemy Captives and Revolutionary Communities during the War for Independence* (Ithaca, NY: Cornell University Press, 2014).

did one side seek to outfight the other, but both sides also increasingly emotionally invested in retaliation, were more or less contained by these conventions. Retaliation was a formal threat built into the system; it was designed to force the other side to amend its behavior, or suffer in kind. There were a number of highly volatile incidents on both sides that could easily have led to an escalation of violence, particularly in regard to the treatment of prisoners. The conventions that encouraged and protected inter-army communication, however, helped to prevent such escalation.[44]

One problem that remained central, however, and which seemed particularly insoluble with respect to the treatment of prisoners, was the status of the war as a "rebellion." The normal customs and usages of international war suggested that prisoners be exchanged via formal "cartels" in which equal numbers of men could be returned to their respective armies. To British authorities, however, setting up such a cartel meant acknowledging the legitimacy of the American revolutionary government. Some informal cartels proceeded regardless, but many Americans were held in confinement for long periods of time. The ensuing violence visited on the bodies of men held overlong in poor conditions resulted in part simply from an unfamiliarity with the problems and logistics of long-term mass confinement. The British partial solution of using the hulks of ships, anchored in the harbor, was particularly notorious, but even when held ashore, American prisoners suffered in ways disproportionate to the British government's capacity to care for them.[45] American leaders in turn, as T. Cole Jones has suggested, increasingly shifted toward official retaliation in their treatment of prisoners, and often overruled Washington while refusing exchanges and breaking surrender agreements.[46]

The place of a rebellion within the conventions governing war was also central to the British Army's use of violence in other circumstances that otherwise should have been contained or constrained by the laws of war.

---

[44] Washington regularly communicated with British commanders about the treatment of prisoners and the role of retaliation. George Washington, *The Papers of George Washington: Revolutionary War Series*, 23 vols., ed. Dorothy Twohig (Charlottesville: University of Virginia Press, 1985–), vol. I, 289–90, 301–2, 326–7; vol. VI, 76; vol. VIII, 58–61, 91–4, 137–8, 453, 498, 522–3, vol. IX, 228–30, 496; Library of Congress, *Journals of the Continental Congress*, vol. VII, 16, 135; Abstracts of debates in Continental Congress, 20 February 1777, *State Records of North Carolina*, vol. 11, 381–2; *Pennsylvania Gazette*, 28 January 1778. See also Metzger, *Prisoner in the American Revolution*, 154–8, 160, 162.

[45] Edwin G. Burrows, *Forgotten Patriots: The Untold Story of American Prisoners during the Revolutionary War* (New York: Basic Books, 2008). See also the comparison in David H. Fischer, *Washington's Crossing* (New York: Oxford University Press, 2004), 378–9.

[46] Jones, *Captives of Liberty*.

A Contest of Wills

Figure 12.3 A prison hulk. Alamy.

British officers saw the colonists as unnatural rebels abandoning their rightful king. By long tradition, one upheld even in the emergent codification of the laws of war, rebels merited no mercy.[47] As a result, even though the most senior British commanders recognized the strategic value of *persuasion* – of building loyalism through containing violence, paying for supplies, and encouraging a return to obedience – many of the officers operating independently in the field often acted in the "fire and sword" tradition of suppressing rebellions ruthlessly. Even within the open war between the regular armies, the British willingness to abandon the usual customs and usages of war was readily apparent, and has been documented by Stephen Conway, Armstrong Starkey, and Holger Hoock. The grossest examples were those in which British regular troops bayonetted surrendering Americans, seemingly on orders at Paoli (1777), "Baylor's Massacre" (1778), and at Waxhaws (1780), but also more occasionally in the midst of other battles, even under the eyes of George Washington.[48] On other occasions, British officers' worst instincts were barely avoided: upon seeing American prisoners marching out of the

---

[47] Lee, *Barbarians and Brothers*, 20–2, 58, 61, 71, 91, 175.
[48] Stephen Conway, "'The Great Mischief Complain'd Of:' Reflections on the Misconduct of British Soldiers in the Revolutionary War," *William and Mary Quarterly* 3rd series, 47 (1990), 370–90; Hoock, *Scars*, 243–74; Todd W. Braisted, *Grand Forage 1778: The Battleground around New York City* (Yardley, PA: Westholme, 2016), 99–112; Starkey, "Paoli to Stony Point"; Jim Piecuch, *The Blood Be upon Your Head: Tarleton, Buford and*

surrendered Ft. Washington in November 1776, for example, one officer exclaimed "What! Taking prisoners! Kill them, kill every man of them." Fortunately, the order was ignored or countermanded in that instance.[49]

These battlefield "massacres" were accompanied by deliberate campaigns of destruction.[50] In addition to the early war burning of Falmouth and Norfolk discussed earlier, Major General William Tryon launched a whole series of indiscriminately destructive raids in New York and Connecticut, the latter seemingly contradicting commander-in-chief General Henry Clinton's intention that Tryon restrict himself to military targets.[51] In 1779, Tryon's forces landed at Norwalk and proceeded to sack and burn the town. The official report to Congress claimed that eighty homes, eighty-seven barns, seventeen shops, four mills, and two churches had been destroyed.[52] Tryon's raids involved a substantial force under British central command, but even areas free from the movements of large forces could be subject to this kind of devastation. Jean Lee's study of Charles County, Maryland, found that every year until 1783 saw small numbers of boat-based raiders landing from Chesapeake Bay, destroying towns, warehouses, and plantations, up to and including sacking and burning Benedict in 1783, *after* news of the peace treaty had reached Maryland.[53] Operations in the southern backcountry notoriously included some mid-level officers destroying property with only the weakest of efforts to determine if it belonged to an actual rebel or not.[54] Possibly the worst destruction from deliberate devastation occurred in Virginia in 1781 when General Charles Earl Cornwallis adopted destruction as official army policy, something he had avoided during the earlier phases of his campaign in the Carolinas. County magistrates in the area compiled claims for damages, and the residents of St. Bride's Parish in Norfolk County, for example, claimed to suffer £39,543 in damage to buildings, livestock, household goods, plantation tools, grain, forage, and even tobacco. Thomas

---

the Myth of Massacre (Lugoff, SC: Southern Campaigns of the American Revolution Press, 2010).
[49] Quoted in Ferling, *Almost a Miracle*, 153.
[50] For the British wrestling with what level of violence to employ, in addition to Conway (cited above), see Burrows, *Forgotten Patriots*, 142–8.
[51] Paul David Nelson, *William Tryon and the Course of Empire: A Life in British Imperial Service* (Chapel Hill: University of North Carolina Press, 1990), 150–1, 157, 163–70.
[52] Dorothy Denneen Volo and James M. Volo, *Daily Life during the American Revolution* (Westport, CT: Greenwood, 2003), 221–2.
[53] Lee, *Price of Nationhood*, 144.
[54] Sylvia R. Frey, *Water from the Rock: Black Resistance in a Revolutionary Age* (Princeton: Princeton University Press, 1991), 116, 129–30.

Jefferson, then governor of Virginia, estimated the damage from the six-month campaign at £3 million.[55]

In theory such fire and sword campaigns were intended to quench will through punitive terror. Overwhelmed by violence, the Americans would give up. The British lacked sufficient forces, however, to apply it thoroughly enough to succeed. Instead, throughout the war, this kind of fire and sword violence bolstered American propaganda efforts. This is the central paradox of violence used to oppress a population: rather than suppress will, it may stir it up. This is especially so when the policy is inconsistently applied. Vacillation between a policy of violent suppression and one of pacification and of encouraging a return to good governance created the space for the victims to turn their anger into action. Holger Hoock identified a key moment from early in the war when American successes at Trenton and Princeton in late 1776 pushed British lines back toward New York City. This recapture of territory recently occupied by the British Army allowed for the "discovery" of many instances of abuse and violence against the local population, including accusations of rape. Congress saw the opportunity to enhance their strategic narrative, and it created a committee of investigation to gather evidence of British misconduct. The eventual report was circulated in the newspapers to an already anxious population.[56] This nervousness about British Army conduct was only enhanced by the arrival of German mercenaries. Although the Hessians had first arrived in North America in May 1776, they had initially been deployed to Canada, and only arrived in the main theater of war accompanying the fleet attacking New York City.

This kind of propaganda effort helped to sustain American will, but in terms of the population's experience of bodily violence, such deliberately destructive military operations or killings of prisoners were relatively rare. More persistent and pervasive, however, was the violence inherent to eighteenth-century logistics, especially in a sparsely settled countryside.[57] Armies in this period represented a concentration of people and animals exceeding that of most cities, and, like cities, they required food to be brought to them in order to survive. Cities had the advantage of an

---

[55] Frey, *Water from the Rock*, 210–11; John R. Maass, *The Road to Yorktown: Jefferson, Lafayette, and the British Invasion of Virginia* (Charleston, SC: History Press, 2015).

[56] The report is in Library of Congress, *Journals of the Continental Congress*, vol. VII, 276–9, vol. 8, 565; Hoock, *Scars*, 156–76.

[57] What follows on logistics first appeared in Wayne E. Lee, "The Civilian Experience of War during the American Revolution," in David S. Heidler and Jean T. Heidler, eds., *Daily Lives of Civilians in Wartime Early America: From the Colonial Era to the Civil War* (Westport, CT: Greenwood, 2007), 31–70.

infrastructure and a market system to transport that food. Armies had to invent their own and the demand could be extreme. Washington estimated that an army of 15,000 men required 100,000 barrels of flour and 20 million pounds of meat in one year.[58] In contrast to that demand, the Commissary General Joseph Trumbull estimated that Philadelphia, sitting at the center of America's largest flour production industry, could supply only 20,000 barrels of flour – one-fifth of the necessary total.[59] To meet demand the American main army hoped to draw supplies from areas distant from their main activities and unthreatened by the British. Commissary agents traveled the countryside with wagons and small parties of soldiers purchasing flour and beef, and then transporting it to supply depots, and from there to the army. An army on the march hoped for supplies coming from those depots, but would also simultaneously send out advance parties to communities in their line of movement, encouraging them to gather together foodstuffs for easy purchase. When desperate, which was often, the army simply sent out parties from its own ranks into the immediately surrounding countryside, and they proceeded from house to house buying food to take back to camp.

Crucially, all these methods of supply hinged upon money. American troops were less and less able to pay for the supplies they requisitioned, and even when they had cash, inflation had reduced its value to a point where farmers were unwilling to part with their produce. Some farmers simply carted their goods to the better paying British. When the system broke down, and frequently the independent militia forces simply had no system at all, the only recourse was to *impress* food and property from the surrounding area. Both Washington and Congress tried hard to avoid impressment, but by 1780 it had become standard. Conditions in the South were worse, in part because of more dispersed settlement and less developed transportation infrastructure, but also because of deliberate British devastation. When General Nathanael Greene took command of the southern army, some estimates suggest that as much as 50 percent of his army's food came through impressment.[60]

When so many soldiers are tasked with getting that much of their food through less than formal means, it becomes very difficult to control their interactions with civilians. It was already a fine line between foraging and plundering, and soldiers going to individual homes in order to secure food

---

[58] Higginbotham, *War of American Independence*, 304.
[59] Volo and Volo, *Daily Life*, 178.
[60] E. Wayne Carp, *To Starve the Army at Pleasure: Continental Army Administration and American Political Culture, 1775–1783* (Chapel Hill: University of North Carolina Press, 1984), 98.

A Contest of Wills

could easily cross over that line. From a civilian perspective, part of the problem with this process was its random quality. One never knew how ill- or well-treated one would be by a party of foragers, nor how often one's house might be subject to the experience. Furthermore, there were whole classes of armed men, popularly referred to as "banditti," who made little pretense at distinguishing between "supply" and "plunder." Thus, the unsuspecting civilian might encounter Private Joseph Martin, who on his own personal foraging expedition in 1777, found himself among a flock of "geese, turkeys, ducks, and barn-door fowls," and who recalled that he could "have taken as many as I pleased, but I took up one only."[61] Or, that same civilian might experience the type of plunderer who had little or no connection to an army at all, like the virtually unrestrained whaleboat plunderers who raided from Connecticut across the sound into Long Island. Andrew Miller in Long Island, for example, answered the pounding at his door, and immediately was struck with the breech of a musket, which broke the bone over his eye, "tore his eye all to pieses, [and] broke his cheek bone." The raiders plundered his house and left him for dead.[62] Some areas between the armies, perhaps most famously Westchester County, New York, were nearly constantly subjected to both official and unofficial foraging by both sides.[63]

Much of the foraging in Westchester and around the continent, was delegated to the militias. Unfortunately, this put the *most* problematic aspect of military–civilian interactions into the hands of the institution *least* capable of controlling it. For a whole set of structural reasons, including short tours, entrepreneurial volunteerism, fragmented unit recruitment, rapid officer turnover, and weak support services, militia units were the most likely to either feel *forced* into plundering (by hunger), or to *have chosen* plundering as part of a desire to retaliate.[64] In many ways retaliation constituted a completely separate form or phase of political violence, and it was by far the worst.

---

[61] James Kirby Martin, ed., *Ordinary Courage: The Revolutionary War Adventures of Joseph Plumb Martin*, 2nd edition (New York: Brandywine Press, 1999), 60.
[62] Harry M. Ward, *Between the Lines: Banditti of the American Revolution* (Westport, CT: Praeger, 2002), 39.
[63] Wayne K. Bodle, *The Valley Forge Winter: Civilians and Soldiers in War* (University Park: Pennsylvania State University Press, 2002); Hoock, *Scars*, 127–50; Adrian C. Leiby, *The Revolutionary War in the Hackensack Valley: The New Jersey Dutch and the Neutral Ground, 1775–1783* (New Brunswick, NJ: Rutgers University Press, 1962); Francis S. Fox, *Sweet Land of Liberty: The Ordeal of the American Revolution in Northampton County, Pennsylvania* (University Park: Pennsylvania State University Press, 2000); Ward, *Between the Lines*.
[64] Lee, *Crowds and Soldiers*, Chapter 7; Wayne E. Lee, "Restraint and Retaliation: The North Carolina Militias and the Backcountry War of 1780–1782," in John Resch and Walter Sargent, eds., *War and Society in the American Revolution* (DeKalb: Northern Illinois University Press, 2007), 163–90.

The Militias' War and Retaliatory Violence

Militias around the colonies, both Patriot and Loyalist, operated both in conjunction with and independently of the regular troops. The violence they enacted when associated with regular forces for the most part fits into the previous category of "regular and logistical" violence. When operating on their own, however, the militias were far more prone to the pitfalls associated with retaliation. As discussed previously, perhaps the most crucial function of the formal conventions of eighteenth-century war was to allow for communication between the armies. Commanders, informed of one outrage or another, could threaten retaliation as a way of trying to reform the enemy's behavior. By and large, the regular armies of the two sides thereby avoided retaliation in practice – however frequently they might threaten it. Independently operating militias frequently resorted to it.

This willingness to employ retaliatory violence arose from several factors. Militia forces were far more likely to know their counterparts on the opposite side, to have and to hold grudges, to know where to find enemy-associated families, to hear familiar names linked with violent acts, and so on. Militias also might coalesce as a "volunteer" unit with idiosyncratic or even entrepreneurial goals only tangentially related to the nominal war effort. Indeed, some units were raised specifically to retaliate for one action or another by the enemy, while others may have simply sought profit from the chaos. And all of these conditions worsened as the war dragged on. Sometimes militia violence began to lose the clarity of its political function. "Will" was still at issue, meaning both sides sought to enspirit supporters and cow enemies, but they now often sought or cultivated will by a retaliatory intent – not merely escalatory. Violence was framed not as a contest of sides, but as an act of justice through self-redress.

There are many regional examples from which one could choose, but most of these kinds of back-and-forth retaliatory relationships emerged in regions near, but usually out of the immediate reach of, British forces. For example, the long British occupation of New York City created several zones of intense retaliatory violence, partly instigated by logistical violence designed to supply the British occupation forces, but over time deteriorating into localized retaliatory violence. Westchester County and the lower Hudson valley, parts of Connecticut, and the whole ring of New Jersey that surrounded New York City, all experienced this phenomenon.[65] The

---

[65] Ward, *Between the Lines*; Leiby, *War in Hackensack*; Sung Bok Kim, "The Limits of Politicization in the American Revolution: The Experience of Westchester County,

foraging around Philadelphia in 1777 had some similar consequences, but the British evacuation in 1778 brought relief, and the peripheral retaliatory violence died down somewhat. Most notoriously, when the British shifted their war effort to the southern colonies, their strategy was partly premised on relying more heavily on Loyalist support.[66] British garrisons in Savannah and Charles Town, plus their campaigns striking north into North Carolina, created peripheral zones of contesting militias.

This is not to say all militia activity was anarchic violence. In many ways the officers and men of most of these organizations strove to make their violence have meaning beyond simply gratifying some emotional or material need. Their efforts at control often failed, in part because the right of retaliation was seen as legitimate, in part because the authority of officers in these units was transitory, and in part because neither the British nor the rebelling states were very successful at meeting the militias' logistical needs. Foraging easily became plundering; plundering drifted into violence; violence by one side demanded retaliation by the other. Throw into this dynamic the occasional "fire and sword" raids by British regular forces, and populations on the periphery of the British Army found many reasons to desire retaliation.[67]

* * * * * *

This chapter has focused on the role of will in an essentially binary contest: between the British authorities who expected obedience and the colonists who became rebels and ultimately sought independence. As with most civil wars, there were other parties, some of them armed, some of them not, some of them invested in the struggle, and some of them not, who also wielded or experienced political violence. Among other things, white women were subjected to sexual and other forms of violence as proxies for their

---

New York," *Journal of American History* 80 (1993), 868–89; Judith L. Van Buskirk, *Generous Enemies: Patriots and Loyalists in Revolutionary New York* (Philadelphia: University of Pennsylvania Press, 2002).

[66] See Ricardo A. Herrera, "The King's Friends: Loyalists in British Strategy," in Donald Stoker, Kenneth J. Hagan, and Michael T. McMaster, eds., *Strategy in the American War of Independence: A Global Approach* (London: Routledge, 2010), 100–19.

[67] Ronald Hoffman, "The 'Disaffected' in the Revolutionary South," in Alfred F. Young, ed., *The American Revolution* (DeKalb: Northern Illinois University Press, 1976), 273–316; John S. Pancake, *This Destructive War: The British Campaign in the Carolinas 1780–82* (Birmingham: University of Alabama Press, 1985); Ronald Hoffman, Thad W. Tate, and Peter J. Albert, eds., *An Uncivil War: The Southern Backcountry during the American Revolution* (Charlottesville: University of Virginia Press, 1985).

husbands, as participants in the fight, or to ensure their submission within the patriarchal system that the revolution might have seemed to threaten.[68] A similar dynamic, far more overtly violent, affected the enslaved population. From the moment that Governor Dunmore promised freedom to escaping slaves, the planters' fears of revolt led them to wield savage preemptive violence, sometimes founded on the flimsiest of rumors. For the enslaved men and women themselves, the war offered glimmers of another life, and some who made it to British lines were able to find freedom in Nova Scotia, England, or even Sierra Leone. For those left behind, the planters' sense of the necessity of reasserting control must have led to savage violence in the short term (mostly unrecorded), and we know it led to new systematic forms of slave labor "management" violence in the ensuing decades.[69] Better documented is the very different wartime violence waged between the Patriots and Native Americans, whether or not the Indians had actively allied with the British. There were countless small-scale raids on the frontier, and there were a number of large-scale campaigns both by and against various groups of Native Americans. Those contests witnessed most of the categories of violence thus far discussed: regular and logistical, and retaliatory, to which was added intercultural and racialized violence, with a consequent almost habitual application of much more frightful forms of violence.[70]

The end of the American War of Independence did not see the end of political violence. Efforts, often violent, to reassert control over women, slaves, and Native Americans continued after the war, and disputes over the treaty with Britain persisted through the war of 1812.[71] Perhaps the most outstanding issue with respect to public political violence was the future of relations with the Native Americans. In a very real sense, the "regular war" was concluded with a style of treaty then customary among early modern states. The treaty defined what state would own what, where the new boundaries were, how commercial debts would be honored, and how

---

[68] Sharon Block, *Rape and Sexual Power in Early America* (Chapel Hill: University of North Carolina Press, 2006).

[69] The original work on this subject is Benjamin Quarles, *The Negro in the American Revolution* (Chapel Hill: University of North Carolina Press, 1961). See also Ira Berlin, "The Revolution in Black Life," in Alfred F. Young, ed., *The American Revolution* (DeKalb: Northern Illinois University Press, 1976), 349–82; Frey, *Water from the Rock*.

[70] Colin G. Calloway, *The American Revolution in Indian Country: Crisis and Diversity in Native American Communities* (Cambridge: Cambridge University Press, 1995).

[71] A full discussion of post-war violence against Loyalists, slaves, women, and Indians would require a separate essay.

property or prisoners would be returned or restored. Crucially, however, it made no mention whatsoever of the Indian peoples living in the lands ceded by the British crown. In that way, although the treaty may have helped to contain violence against former Loyalists, it likely fostered the eruption of further violence in the trans-Appalachian west. Settlers fought Indians and vice versa on a familial scale; scratch militia and small war parties tracked and killed each other on a regional scale; and, occasionally, fully organized regular forces clashed with confederations of Indian nations. All of it was "political violence" in that it sought to control territory or assert political sovereignty. These assorted conflicts, ultimately decided more by the demographic weight of the settler population than by violence itself, would continue to the dawn of the twentieth century. In all cases, the white population asserted the right to use violence in support of a civic order they believed to have been forged in the crucible of the American Revolution.[72] That civic order seemingly required the displacement or deracination of Native Americans.

[72] Colin G. Calloway, *The Victory with No Name: The Native American Defeat of the First American Army* (New York: Oxford University Press, 2015); Rob Harper, *Unsettling the West: Violence and State Building in the Ohio Valley* (Philadelphia: University of Pennsylvania Press, 2018); Kathleen DuVal, *Independence Lost: Lives on the Edge of the American Revolution* (New York: Random House, 2016).

13

Recovering Loyalism: Opposition to the American Revolution as a Good Idea

LIAM RIORDAN

The view that the American Revolution initiated the Age of Atlantic Revolutions can truncate the manner in which Loyalists, loyalism, and their transnationalism are understood. The standard conceptualization assumes that Patriots and their social movement were the important agents of change and the essential historical subjects that need to be explained. This approach generally operates within parameters fashioned by Patriots and the national priorities that their success advanced. Recovering loyalism as a potent subject in its own right offers several valuable correctives. Loyalists can enrich our sense of thriving transnational connections prior to the era of modern nation-states and contributes to an Atlantic analytical perspective and a deeper assessment of emergent globalization. Because historians generally empathize with their subject, close consideration of Loyalists can also help to balance the one-sidedness of revolutionary interpretation. Evaluating loyalism as a "good idea" is not a call to validate its political program; indeed, loyalism's lack of a singular agenda contributed to its defeat. Loyalists were not a unified group, and to suggest so can reinscribe a static caricature that clouds understanding of why large numbers of people opposed the rebellion that created the United States. Rather than relitigate the American Revolution, this chapter simply contends that we can learn a great deal by recognizing Loyalists and loyalism as reasonable positions in the late eighteenth century.[1]

English-speaking colonists from Nova Scotia to Jamaica (as well as Britons in the home islands) shared a general sense of loyalism as Britishness, but the crucial catalyst of anti-Loyalist violence gave diverse "American" Loyalists in the thirteen rebellious colonies distinctive coherence in a punishing period of

---

[1] For imperial and loyalist persistence, see Jeremy Adelman, "An Age of Imperial Revolutions," *American Historical Review* 113 (2008), 318–40; Eric Nelson, *The Royalist Revolution: Monarchy and the American Founding* (Cambridge, MA: Harvard University Press, 2014).

civil war.² Placing these Loyalists at the center of historical analysis elevates coercion, physical violence, and the duress of wartime mobilization as essential dimensions of revolutionary change. Attention to the social conditions of everyday life in colonial North America also demands an awareness of Indigenous and enslaved people as critical actors in the composition of loyalism. As historian Jane Kamensky has suggested in her compelling portrayal of the painter John Singleton Copley, who never returned to the United States after the war, we need to recover the American Revolution in color rather than render it in black and white drained of the messiness of lived experience.³ Emphasizing that Patriot and Loyalist sensibilities took shape in relationship to one another and changed over time is a useful initial corrective to help to restore process as critical to historical interpretation.

Those who opposed Patriot rebellion in colonial North America understood their position to be based on lawfulness, a clear sense of historical precedent, and the application of Enlightenment reason to their circumstances.⁴ No more self-interested than Patriots, Loyalists considered remaining within the British empire to be the best route to life, liberty, and the pursuit of happiness. Along with the benefits of English law and balanced government were the self-evident rewards of British commercial, martial, and Protestant ascendancy that seemed to be durable certainties. By contrast, the rebels were irrational law breakers whose hyperbole made a mockery of common sense and who risked plunging colonial society into anarchy. No reasonable person could take seriously the claim that tyrannical British governance aimed to enslave colonists.

A broad comparison of the US, Haitian, and Latin American independence movements suggests that the first of these was more oligarchic and lacked an equivalent commitment to attacking slavery and to including Indians within the post-colonial nation. Patriots mobilized as a distinctly settler colonial movement that embraced disturbing popular attitudes like a desire for access to Indigenous land unencumbered by imperial restraint and an embrace of chattel slavery as essential to a dynamic economy.⁵ Such dark Patriot impulses along with a

---

² Brad A. Jones, *Resisting Independence: Popular Loyalism in the Revolutionary British Atlantic* (Ithaca, NY: Cornell University Press, 2021).
³ Jane Kamensky, *A Revolution in Color: The World of John Singleton Copley* (New York: W. W. Norton, 2016).
⁴ On loyalists (like patriots) as Whigs and Lockeans, see Janice Potter, *The Liberty We Seek: Loyalist Ideology in Colonial New York and Massachusetts* (Cambridge, MA: Harvard University Press, 1983), esp. 84–106.
⁵ For a comparative starting point, see "AHR Forum: Revolutions in the Americas," *American Historical Review* 105 (2000), 92–152. On the centrality of violence for Patriot

willingness to deploy popular violence are foundational to US political culture and make the recovery of Loyalists as something other than villains, cowards, or fools essential to achieve a less partisan view of a significant turning point in world history whose implications remain polarizing. Loyalists were diverse, reasonable, and possessed valid motives for their opposition to rebellion. In short, there were good reasons to oppose the American Revolution even though they are usually obfuscated by the teleological conceptualization of it as the opening event of the Age of Atlantic Revolutions.

Revolutionary Origins: Partisan Chronology and Geography

How best to answer the basic question of the extent of popular support in the thirteen mainland colonies for and against the American Revolution is no simple task. A leading synthesis estimates the political allegiance of those in the colonies that rebelled to have been 20 percent Loyalist, 40 percent Patriot, and 40 percent disaffected to either side.[6] The large group of non-partisans – those who hoped to weather the crisis without getting involved – is especially important and must have been considerably more than 40 percent of the population in the decade before 1775 as the resistance movement built to the breaking point of war. While fully committed rebels probably did not constitute a majority of the total population at any time until the war was over, British officials clearly underestimated the breadth and depth of Patriot mobilization. Moreover, Loyalists contributed to key flaws in British decision-making. Loyalists overestimated their own strength and ability to act, and they consistently called for more severe repression of rebels and a more destructive war that intensified its brutality. Loyalist actions unquestionably fueled polarization, which is significant because they were a more important presence in every region of what would become the United States than is usually recognized.

To offer a static measure of partisan allegiance does a mis-service to the dynamic interaction of chronology and geography as lodestars of historical analysis, key factors that are often selectively presented in a lopsided Patriot

---

mobilization and its institutionalization in the early republic, see Robert G. Parkinson, *The Common Cause: Creating Race and Nation in the American Revolution* (Chapel Hill: University of North Carolina Press, 2016); Eliga H. Gould, *Among the Powers of the Earth: The American Revolution and the Making of a New World Empire* (Cambridge, MA: Harvard University Press, 2012).

[6] Alan Taylor, *American Revolutions: A Continental History, 1750–1804* (New York: W. W. Norton, 2016), 211–13.

narrative of the American Revolution. That bias is especially clear when considering its origins. The well-rehearsed Patriot chronology of the coming of the American Revolution centers on burdensome imperial taxation and three waves of colonial protest in response to the Stamp Act in 1765, the Townshend Act crisis of 1767–1770, and the Tea Act of 1773, the last of which triggered punishments for Boston and Massachusetts that led directly to the start of the war in April 1775. This prioritization of the external revolution that pit all (more accurately, many) colonists against the empire has served Patriots well by focusing attention on their success in forging principled and restrained unity against a "foreign" enemy.[7]

A Loyalist narrative, not surprisingly, emphasizes alternative aspects of imperial–colonial relations and of late-colonial society that are less flattering to the rebels and their national legacy. For example, the Royal Proclamation of 1763 and the Quebec Act of 1774 also fueled major colonial grievances because they attempted to craft a more stable place for Indigenous groups and French-speaking Catholics within the empire.[8] Imperial projection of power across vast spaces entangled human diversity and governance, and the Patriot alternative to these two reforms championed a narrower view of who merited rights and citizenship. For most Loyalists, rebels dangerously fused populist appeals with exclusivist claims to legitimate violence.

New England, of course, stood at the vanguard of the American Revolution and Patriots were over-represented there. Yet the early spark of rebellion there also meant that New England produced searing examples of loyalism that can be traced back as far as the attacks on colonial officials (almost all of them born in the colonies) and their property in the anti-Stamp Act protests of 1765. The anger that fueled such stark violence must have been triggered by something in addition to the formal politics of empire, as has long been noted in neo-progressive interpretations of radical Patriot impulses.[9] Yet the implications of serious social conflict in late-colonial society for the meaning of loyalism has proved to be elusive.

---

[7] Note the continuity from Edmund S. Morgan, *The Birth of the Republic 1763–89*, 4th edition (Chicago: University of Chicago Press, 2013 [1956]) to Pauline Maier, *From Resistance to Revolution: Colonial Radicals and the Development of American Opposition to Britain, 1765–1776* (New York: W. W. Norton, 1991 [1972]); T. H. Breen, *American Insurgents, American Patriots* (New York: Hill & Wang, 2010).

[8] Colin G. Calloway, *The Scratch of a Pen: 1763 and the Transformation of North America* (New York: Oxford University Press, 2006); Philip Lawson, *Imperial Challenge: Quebec and Britain in the Age of the American Revolution* (Montreal and Kingston: McGill-Queen's University Press, 1989).

[9] Gary B. Nash, *The Urban Crucible: The Northern Seaports and the Origins of the American Revolution*, abridged edition (Cambridge, MA: Harvard University Press, 1986 [1979]).

Historians of the revolution usually stress the symbolic nature of threatened violence and that Patriot elites recoiled from the more extreme actions by those beneath them, yet it is crucial to recognize that the threat and use of violence pushed rebellion forward and limited public expressions of loyalty. From Deborah Franklin's fear that rioters would destroy her Philadelphia house in order to remove the stamp collector whom she sheltered in August 1765 to the "cruel torture" of John Malcolm in Boston in 1774, whose five-hour tar-and-feathering caused "flesh [to] come ... off his back in Stakes," the decade after 1765 accustomed colonists to violence as a tool of social change.[10]

Peter Oliver, a leading figure in colonial Massachusetts and an early target of mob attacks, crafted a classic Loyalist account about the abusive rebels. Like almost all Loyalists, he saw the origins of the rebellion in a self-serving campaign by a handful of power-seeking leaders who drew others to their cause through shockingly effective propaganda. Loyalists could not countenance that rebels drew upon valid or broadly based popular support. Oliver repeatedly decried how a handful of "abandoned Demagogues" misled a contented populace to set "the Wheel of Enthusiasm" in motion.[11]

Just as Patriot leaders are generally presumed to have represented the rebel rank-and-file, so too the views of a leader like Oliver resonated among those who agreed that a place within the empire brought too many benefits to be jettisoned. Oliver's tone is extreme and cutting, but no more so than leading rebel provocateurs and apologists. Indeed, we should have some sympathy for Oliver's vitriol as a response to the lawless abuse that he, his family, and friends repeatedly suffered. A chilling example occurred at his brother's burial in Boston in March 1774 where "a large Mob attended, & huzzaed at the intombing." Oliver so feared for his own safety that he did not visit his dying brother or attend his burial as "never did Cannibals thirst stronger for human Blood ... Humanity seemed to be abhorrent to their Nature."[12]

Bostonian Daniel Leonard, whose pseudonymous newspaper articles were among the boldest public expressions of loyalism just prior to the start of war, emphasized the illegality of rebel claims to authority. As he noted about

---

[10] Deborah to Benjamin Franklin, 22 September 1765, Benjamin Larrabee, ed., *The Papers of Benjamin Franklin* (New Haven: Yale University Press, 1968), vol. XII, 270–4; Ann[e] Hulton, 31 January 1774, *Letters of a Loyalist Lady* (New York: Arno Press, 1971), 71.

[11] Peter Oliver, *Peter Oliver's Origin and Progress of the American Rebellion*, ed. Douglass Adair and John A. Schutz (Stanford: Stanford University Press, 1961 [1781]), 145.

[12] Oliver, *Origin and Progress*, 112.

the growing persecution, "it is chiefly owing to these committees, that so many respectable persons have been abused, and forced to sign recantations and resignations" and to "have been obliged to quit their houses, families, and businesses, and fly to the army for protection." He beseeched his readers, "My countrymen, I beg you to pause and reflect ... have not these people, that are thus insulted, as good a right to think and act for themselves?"[13] Leonard would only last in Massachusetts as long as the British Army was there to protect him. Like Oliver, who wrote his long-unpublished account of the origins of the rebellion from safety in England, both fled rebel terror in New England in March 1776 along with 1,100 other Loyalists evacuated from Boston. The ability to migrate within the empire, often with military and government support, undercut Loyalist strength even before independence was declared.

The multiple episodes of censorship and violence that punished New York City printer James Rivington offers a searing example of a targeted Loyalist spokesman. A broad campaign was waged against him by multiple committees of safety in New Jersey, and he was denounced even in a Boston newspaper. It is instructive to note how often rebel vigilantes traveled to neighboring communities to act. When Rivington learned that a New Jersey mob had hung him in effigy in early April 1775, he responded by printing an image of his own metaphorical execution and defiantly announced his commitment to the liberty of the press. He insisted that he published items from all parties, but when "he ventured to publish sentiments which were opposed to the dangerous views and designs of certain demagogues, he found himself held up as an enemy to this country." Rivington further explained that his "Bacchanalian" foes were fueled by "New England Rum" and made "liberty the prostituted pretense of their illiberal persecution." Rather than be "governed by a few factious individuals," he preferred "the good old laws and constitution, under which we have so long been a happy people."[14]

The symbolic attacks on Rivington changed to direct violence the following month when a mob destroyed his print shop. Although New York's Provincial Congress called for him not to be further molested in June 1775, Rivington would be attacked again in November, and his press carried away to Connecticut. At this point he fled to British protection, returning to New York City in 1777 when it was in safe British hands.

[13] Leonard as *Massachusettensis*, 2 January 1775, quoted in Potter, *Liberty We Seek*, 31.
[14] *New York Gazetteer*, 20 April 1775.

Figure 13.1 New York printer James Rivington publicized his own symbolic execution by a New Jersey mob in his *New York Gazetteer*, 20 April 1775. Courtesy of the *Journal of the American Revolution*.

When the rebels regained power at the end of 1783, mobs again closed his press, even though there were some indications that he may have been a double agent, who provided key information about the British naval deployment that led to the rebel victory at Yorktown. The evidence about the possibility that he supported both sides during the war remains murky, but it is clear that Rivington suffered grave consequences for his failure to comply with rebel demands that preceded and outlasted the war.[15]

---

[15] The most sustained recent attention is by Todd Andrlik, "James Rivington: King's Printer and Patriot Spy?," *Journal of the American Revolution* 1 (2013), https://allthingsliberty.com/2014/03/james-rivington-kings-printer-patriot-spy/#_edn6. Also

The Pennsylvania political leader Joseph Galloway highlights Loyalist advocacy of the benefits of empire. He and his mentor Benjamin Franklin had led efforts to end the Penn family's proprietorship by making Pennsylvania a royal colony in the 1760s. As a delegate to the Continental Congress, Galloway championed reconciliation and acknowledged that the British constitution did not have appropriate safeguards for colonial liberties within the empire. His "Plan of Union" to modernize colonial–imperial relations lost in Congress by a vote of six to five with one colony undecided in late 1774, a critical juncture where resistance might have been channeled into reform were it not for rash New England provocateurs. Even at the end of June 1776 several colonial delegations did not support withdrawing from the empire, and the initial versions of the Declaration of Independence did not claim to be a unanimous decision until New York joined the rest on 9 July. Galloway would be among the most active Loyalists anywhere, restored to leadership when the British controlled Philadelphia during the war, and then as an exile in England.[16]

While pre-war violence could plausibly be blamed on occasional and supposedly leaderless mobs going too far, as John Adams argued in his successful defense of British troops at their trial for the still wrongly titled Boston Massacre, the Continental Congress legitimated and systematized surveillance and punishment through the association it called for in late 1774. It sanctioned local committees of safety throughout the colonies to enforce boycotts, limit political discourse, and ostracize and even punish those who violated its terms. Local committees, usually in coordination with the militia, claimed to act on behalf of the whole community. Historian T. H. Breen has called attention to the insurgency from 1774 to 1776 as essential for the coming of the revolution. For him, the association provided a structure for local enforcement that contained its excesses within an emergent republican framework of governance, but to Loyalists these were menacing outrages carried out by thugs.[17]

The seizure of political control by extra-legal bodies that claimed to be provincial governments built on the mobilization begun by local committees

---

see Jones, *Resisting Independence*, 108–17, 127–33, 148–53, 200–3; Ruma Chopra, *Unnatural Rebellion: Loyalists in New York City during the Revolution* (Charlottesville: University of Virginia Press, 2011), 221–2.

[16] John Ferling, *The Loyalist Mind: Joseph Galloway and the American Revolution* (University Park: Pennsylvania State University, 1977). On the divided nature of colonial opinion throughout 1774, see Mary Beth Norton, *1774: The Long Year of Revolution* (New York: Knopf, 2020), on Galloway's plan, 195–9.

[17] Breen, *American Insurgents*, 160–84.

and acted on independence prior to its assertion by the Continental Congress. This transition, so thoroughly examined from a Patriot perspective, was an enormous setback for Loyalists, who badly misjudged the stability of the colonial status quo. Not a single colonial governor, save for John Trumbull of Connecticut, would continue as a state governor; all others were forced from office by 1776. The expulsion of top government officials was crucial to the expansion of the conflict beyond New England. Without a functioning colonial government to structure their mobilization, Loyalists were imperiled even before the war arrived in most areas.

A central exhibit in recovering Loyalists as reasonable actors is to reconsider the Declaration of Independence as a showcase of rebel hyperbole. Trumpeting that "all men were created equal" was false and even grotesque when penned by a slaveowner like Thomas Jefferson. The point-by-point exegesis of the Declaration by the most famous Loyalist Thomas Hutchinson, the multi-generational son of Massachusetts and its last civilian governor, helpfully grounds the document in its initial moment of circulation. While Hutchinson did poke at the hypocrisy of rebel slaveowners and the Declaration's absurd claims of equality, the now famous preamble was not its most important passage at the time. Hutchinson's critique focused on the meat of the Declaration, its catalogue of the king's supposed abuses that were "alledged to be the evidence of injuries and usurpations" that justified lawful rebellion. To Hutchinson, the list actually demonstrated "the criminality of this Revolt." Its many "false and frivolous" grievances simply rationalized the long-denied, but now openly declared, goal to achieve self-serving independence beyond the bounds of empire.[18]

Hutchinson had been attacked and vilified so badly that he went into self-imposed exile in England in 1774. Dying there before the end of the war, he never returned to his "country" of Massachusetts. His assessment in 1776 was that "discerning men" in the colonies like himself, having witnessed and experienced widespread abuse due to their loyalism, "concealed their sentiments, because under the present free government in America, no man may, by writing or speaking, contradict any part of this Declaration, without being deemed an enemy to his country, and exposed to the rage and fury of the populace." The hypocrisy of rebel propaganda was clear. Worse yet, to disagree with its baseless assertions in public (and, increasingly, even to do so in private) meant running the real risk of personal attack. What

---

[18] Thomas Hutchinson, *Strictures upon the Declaration of the Congress at Philadelphia* (London, 1776), 10 [3].

particularly galled Hutchinson, and what lay at the center of most Loyalists' understanding of the rebellion, was that the vast majority of colonists were "loyal subjects, [who] have been deluded, and by degrees induced to rebel against the best of Princes, and the mildest of Governments."[19] Worse would come, however, as the legitimation of violence dramatically expanded with the descent into war.

Loyalism and War

Although difficult to avoid, it is anachronistic to characterize individuals in the thirteen colonies that would successfully rebel as "Loyalist" or "Patriot" prior to a breaking point that intensified from 1774 to 1776. For many, likely a strong majority of colonists, a decisive, though not necessarily permanent, moment of commitment came later still, only when the war arrived on their doorstep and its political and social polarization could no longer be avoided. As the military historian John Shy has valuably noted, the "great middle group of Americans" began the war as "potentially loyal subjects of the Crown" and "ended [it] as knowing, skeptical, wary citizens of the United States." His key insight frames the war as a transformational "political education conducted by military means" for the "apathetic majority."[20] Most people, then as now, went about their everyday lives without much interest in the increasingly angry tone of public life. Those who accepted the status quo, perhaps wanting to see it reformed but certainly not overthrown, surely represented a large majority of the total colonial population. In order to change this, Patriots needed to mobilize ordinary colonists and did so through wild claims about British tyranny, intimations of a more just future polity, and dedicated coercion that intensified as resistance turned to war.

The standard narrative about the revolution, of course a Patriot one, lingers on its origins in New England and the heady earliest days of the war from Lexington and Concord to Bunker Hill, yet for all intents and purposes the active war ended there with the major British evacuation of Boston in March 1776 – before the colonies' decisive break in formal politics in July. The trajectory from New England origins to continental unity expressed in the Declaration of Independence is misleading for a number

---

[19] Liam Riordan, "A Loyalist Who Loved His Country Too Much: Thomas Hutchinson, Historian of Colonial Massachusetts," *New England Quarterly* 90 (2017), 344–84. Hutchinson, *Strictures*, 8, 32.

[20] John Shy, *A People Numerous and Armed: Reflections on the Military Struggle for American Independence*, rev. edition (Ann Arbor: University of Michigan Press, 1990 [1976]), 235, 236.

of reasons, most importantly because it elides the cauldron of war as essential to the American Revolution and its national progeny.

British assessments of the allegiance of colonists dictated the fundamental course of the war. When New England seemed too lawless to control without excessive force, the next move was to isolate it from all of the other more loyal colonies. The next main theater of the war opened in the mid-Atlantic with devastating defeats for the rebels around New York City in August and September 1776. The large mid-Atlantic, from Rhode Island to Maryland in its most expansive bounds, held strong potential for loyalism due to its high rates of immigration, strong ethnic and religious diversity, and its general economic prosperity – all of which led colonists in the region to doubt the prudence of rebellion. Moreover, the Covenant Chain alliance with the Haudenosaunee (Iroquois or Six Nations), and the Kanyen'kehaka (Mohawk) nation in particular, added an influential military ally from Indian country against the rebels. New York City would remain the British military headquarters for the remainder of the war, and British martial prowess in the region was also displayed by holding Philadelphia in 1777 and 1778 and Newport from 1776 to 1779.[21]

The southern colonies had the largest potential Loyalist population, and, not coincidentally, the south would be the longest and most intense military theater of the war. Loyalism here hinged on its composition as a coastal slave society in the process of expanding into Indian country as swiftly as possible. As early as the famous proclamation of Virginia's royal governor in November 1775 that offered freedom to rebel-owned slaves who rallied to the Loyalist cause, it was clear that the war in the south would profoundly intertwine with slavery. Enslaved people represented a decisive strategic resource that could advance British victory, but this also fueled rebel fear of the British as slave liberators and pushed many disaffected slave masters to join the rebellion. Dunmore's Proclamation, and a similar policy announced by General Henry Clinton later in the war,

---

[21] On loyalist cities, see Judith L. Van Buskirk, *Generous Enemies: Patriots and Loyalists in Revolutionary New York* (Philadelphia: University of Pennsylvania Press, 2002); Donald F. Johnson, *Occupied America: British Military Rule and the Experience of Revolution* (Philadelphia: University of Pennsylvania Press, 2020); Christopher Sparshott, "Loyalist Refugee Camp: A Reinterpretation of Occupied New York, 1776–83," in Rebecca Brannon and Joseph S. Moore, eds., *The Consequences of Loyalism: Essays in Honor of Robert M. Calhoon* (Columbia: University of South Carolina Press, 2019), 61–74; Aaron Sullivan, *The Disaffected: Britain's Occupation of Philadelphia during the American Revolution* (Philadelphia: University of Pennsylvania Press, 2019).

exemplify loyalism as a rare opportunity for enslaved people to escape the systematic violence of slavery with the support of a powerful institution. Loyalism among enslaved people was fundamentally tied to the exigencies of war.[22] A second key feature of southern colonies that opened space for loyalism to flower was the hostility of backcountry settlers toward coastal elites, which had informed varied western Regulation movements prior to the revolutionary war. Here, too, the mobilization of Loyalists was imperiled by racial factors. When the Cherokee took up arms against rebels in 1776, few colonists on the frontier rallied to a Loyalist standard associated with Native Americans.[23]

From a Loyalist perspective, Georgia is an important colony to highlight: James Wright had been its effective royal governor since 1760, it was the only colony to use tax stamps in 1765, and it had no delegate at the Continental Congress until July 1775. It would also be the sole rebellious colony restored to civil government under British authority during the war. Yet even here the rebel recourse to violence forced Governor Wright to flee to the protection of a British naval vessel in February 1776.

Scholars of loyalism have long foregrounded the American Revolution as a civil war, and recent studies without an explicit Loyalist framework are also increasingly grappling with the centrality of violence in creating the United States. Historian Michael A. McDonnell urges that the war and its cruel incoherence become more central to future assessments of the revolution.[24] Attention to wartime loyalism highlights how the precarious position that war thrust upon all people was especially perilous for Loyalists. When British generals seemed to turn the other cheek and not crush the rebellion, most famously by allowing Washington's forces to retreat from New York City in 1776, Loyalists were incensed. What ensued was a "nightmare world" for Loyalists – too British for the rebels and too American for the British.[25] As the internecine civil war drove ever more punishing polarization, Loyalists were increasingly vilified and abused.

---

[22] Sylvia R. Frey, *Water from the Rock: Black Resistance in a Revolutionary Age* (Princeton: Princeton University Press, 1991).
[23] On the cross-racial Loyalist coalition, see Jim Piecuch, *Three Peoples, One King: Loyalists, Indians, and Slaves in the Revolutionary South, 1775–1782* (Columbia: University of South Carolina Press, 2008).
[24] Michael A. McDonnell, "War Stories: Remembering and Forgetting the American Revolution," in Patrick Spero and Michael Zuckerman, eds., *The American Revolution Reborn* (Philadelphia: University of Pennsylvania Press, 2016), 9–28.
[25] Piers Mackesy, *The War for America, 1775–1783* (Lincoln: University of Nebraska Press, 1993 [1964]), 511.

Internationalizing and Personalizing Civil War: Indigenous, Settler, and Black Loyalism

The War of American Independence involved colonies and empires, Indigenous nations and confederacies, and enslaved people from the African diaspora and their descendants. Recovering loyalism in the multinational context of these entangled polities benefits from close attention to individuals' wartime experiences. Interspersing top-down military and international relations perspectives with the personal trajectories of Loyalists from distinct corners of colonial society demonstrates the causal manner in which the war fueled loyalism. Representative figures that follow include a female Mohawk (Kanyen'kehaka) diplomat, a white soldier from Georgia, and an enslaved person from North Carolina. Comparison of their circumstances advances a fuller recovery of loyalism.

Although the rebels and the British both initially sought Native American neutrality in the war, the integral interaction of Indians with colonial society meant that most Indigenous groups east of the Mississippi were drawn into the conflict where their interests were very much at stake. These groups took varied positions vis-à-vis the rebellion and often differed within tribes and confederacies where generational divisions often separated militant young warriors and older chiefs who favored neutrality. Yet, when forced to commit to one side or the other, most collective Indigenous groups favored British success. It must further be emphasized that the foreign policy of autonomous Native nations overwhelmingly viewed loyalism as an alliance with the British as opposed to dependence upon them.

The degree of strategic self-interest in arriving at such a commitment should not exclude Indians from the fold of loyalism any more than it should for enslaved people or those of European descent. Political allegiance for individuals and groups arises from a complex mixture of self-understanding, ideals, and situational circumstances. To categorize nonwhite motivations as totally determined by self-interest would deny them human agency in a manner that betrays a fundamental ethical responsibility of historians. It is also clear, however, that enslaved people of African descent within colonial society and Indigenous people in Indian country had different structural relationships with colonial and British power, and this shaped their distinctive commitments to loyalism as a good idea.

Spurred by calls from northern First Nations to ally together against the rebels, a divided Cherokee nation inaugurated the earliest large-scale Indigenous attack against the rebels in July 1776. In part, because the

British siege of Charleston had failed in June, rebels from Georgia, the Carolinas, and Virginia mobilized in the west. When warriors proved elusive, noncombatants were attacked and tribal property and food resources were destroyed on a large scale. Some Cherokee entered a peace treaty with southern states in 1777, though supporters of Dragging Canoe remained mobilized and allied with white Loyalists to conduct antirebel attacks as late as 1782. The early Cherokee mobilization heightened rebel solidarity against a "savage" alliance of British and Indians, a hostility that persisted to the forced deportation of the 1830s and beyond.[26]

Similar forces emerged in the northwestern borderlands, where the most ardent Indian Loyalists were among the Mohawk nation of the Haudenosaunee, especially following the leadership of individuals like Joseph Brant (Thayendanegea) and his sister Mary Brant (Koñwatsi'tsiaiéñni). Their Loyalist commitments expand our understanding of the variegated tapestry of loyalism informed by the complex engagement of many Indigenous people with colonial society.[27] Sir William Johnson, the northern superintendent of Indian affairs and the common law husband of Mary Brant, had been a powerful figure across the northwest since the 1750s. His death in 1774 further destabilized a region on the brink of civil war, and in 1775 and 1776 hundreds of his supporters, including his son Sir John Johnson, fled to Quebec, and they provided significant Loyalist military service, often in close partnership with Indian allies.

The allegiance of Native Americans in the northwest became critical during the pivotal event in the mid-Atlantic theater of the war, the Saratoga campaign of summer and fall 1777, which sought to unite British forces from Quebec to New York City and to isolate rebellious New England. Mary Brant had long been a key diplomatic figure in the region, and the war revived her prominence as a key negotiator in the large New York–Iroquoia–Quebec borderland from 1777 into the 1790s. She provided crucial military intelligence to allied British, Indigenous, and settler Loyalist

---

[26] Colin G. Calloway, *The American Revolution in Indian Country: Crisis and Diversity in Native American Communities* (New York: Cambridge University Press, 1995), 182–212; Peter H. Wood, "George Washington, Dragging Canoe, and Southeastern Indian Resistance," in Tamara Harvey and Greg O'Brien, eds., *George Washington's South* (Gainesville: University Press of Florida, 2004), 259–77; Piecuch, *Three Peoples, One King*, 36–91. For a rich assessment of interdependence in the Gulf Coast, see Kathleen DuVal, *Independence Lost: Lives on the Edge of the American Revolution* (New York: Random House, 2015).

[27] Susan M. Hill, *The Clay We Are Made of: Haudenosaunee Land Tenure on the Grand River* (Winnipeg: University of Manitoba Press, 2017), esp. 155–162, examines Joseph Brant's contested legacy and stresses that he was neither a Kanyen'kehaka political leader nor a war chief.

forces that advanced from the west under Brigadier General Barry St. Leger in summer 1777 as part of the large campaign to cut off New England. Her warning of an attack coming from Mohawk Valley rebel militia and Patriot-allied Oneida led to the infamous Battle of Oriskany in August that had Haudenosaunee warriors on both sides of the bloody encounter. Direct violence among the Six Nations warriors at Oriskany challenged the Confederacy's long-standing peace protocols and remains a controversial and tragic memory in Haudenosaunee communities today.[28] When British General John Burgoyne surrendered after the battles of Saratoga two months later, a crucial phase of major British offensive actions in the mid-Atlantic ended.

While the Haudenosaunee and the Cherokee suffered internal divisions and major losses, considerable elements of both sustained military operations throughout the war. Mary Brant was forced from her home at Canajoharie on the Mohawk River by the threat of personal violence from both rebels and Oneidas. From this point on she performed critical diplomatic work to renew and maintain a Six Nations alliance with the British. She spoke at key Haudenosaunee council meetings, and operated from strategic British military bases, first at Fort Niagara and then at Carleton Island, where she linked Indigenous warriors from many nations and the British.

Wartime correspondence among British leaders repeatedly mention Mary Brant as an essential figure. An influential leader of a society of matrons among the Haudenosaunee, she was also related by marriage to many of the Loyalist and British Indian officials in the region like Sir John Johnson and Guy Johnson, whose influence, in turn, was enhanced by their relationship with her. Brant's symbiotic commitments as a Mohawk and as a Loyalist are on full display in a letter that she wrote to British Indian agent Daniel Claus (the husband of her stepdaughter), who then transmitted the information to Governor General Frederick Haldimand. Mary Brant had heard that her brother Joseph had been treated badly by British officers at Fort Niagara, and she warned that this was precisely what the rebel general and Indian official Peter Schuyler had said would occur if the Iroquois allied with the British. She insightfully explained, "the whole Matter is, that the Officers at Niagara are so haughty & proud, not knowing or considering that the Kings

---

[28] Barbara Graymont, *The Iroquois in the American Revolution* (Syracuse, NY: Syracuse University Press, 1972); Karim M. Tiro, *The People of the Standing Stone: The Oneida Nation from the Revolution through the Era of Removal* (Amherst: University of Massachusetts Press, 2011).

Interest is so nearly connected with that of the Indians."[29] The ardent Mohawk loyalism of Mary and Joseph Brant arose from multiple causes. Their immediate strategic assessment of the conflict was grounded in their multicultural experiences from being born in the Ohio Country to their lives at the edge of and within colonial society in the Mohawk Valley. Their intimate personal relationships with colonists and their active Anglicanism did not negate their Haudenosaunee values, nor did it for generations of their Mohawk ancestors and descendents with similarly entangled British ties.

Wartime exigencies fostered unexpected cooperation among those opposed to the rebels. Loyalist militias in the northwest often united colonists and Indigenous people to contest the balance of power all along the uncertain edges of New York and Pennsylvania. A fragile working relationship between Joseph Brant and father and son Walter and John Butler, who led the Loyalist militia known as Butler's Rangers, spearheaded repeated attacks on rebel communities. Their success triggered the Sullivan Expedition in summer 1779, the largest offensive of the war into Indian country by the Continental Army. In spite of its brutal destruction of Iroquois towns, fields, and noncombatants, the Haudenosaunee were not vanquished. Brant and related Loyalist groups continued their borderland attacks on rebel outposts from 1780 to 1782 as substantial Loyalist military capacity survived the ravages of the Sullivan Expedition.[30] These endeavors were embedded in continuous conflict over the Ohio Country from the mid-1750s to at least 1815. Although individual leaders and circumstances changed, after 1763 the Ohio Country beyond New York, Pennsylvania, and Virginia witnessed nearly continuous conflicts in which British imperial success consistently appeared better than a victory by settlers to most Indigenous nations and individuals.[31]

The British debacle at Saratoga in 1777, which had precipitated Mary Brant's movement west, also led directly to France's formal announcement

---

[29] Mary Brant to Daniel Claus, 12 April 1781, reprinted in Lois M. Huey and Bonnie Pulis, *Molly Brant: A Legacy of Her Own* (Youngstown, NY: Old Fort Niagara Association, 1997), 108.

[30] Joseph R. Fischer, *A Well-Executed Failure: The Sullivan Campaign against the Iroquois* (Columbia: University of South Carolina Press, 2007).

[31] On Indigenous persistence, see Susan Sleeper-Smith, *Indigenous Prosperity and American Conquest: Indian Women of the Ohio River Valley, 1690–1792* (Chapel Hill: University of North Carolina Press, 2018). For contrasting views of Indigenous–imperial alliances, compare Wayne E. Lee, *Barbarians and Brothers: Anglo-American Warfare, 1500–1865* (New York: Oxford University Press, 2011), esp. Chapter 8, with the revisionist assessment in Gregory Evans Dowd, "Indigenous Peoples without the Republic," *Journal of American History* 104 (2017), 19–41.

as a US ally in February 1778. This transformed the war with major consequences for Loyalists. The Patriot alliance with the Catholic absolutist state in 1778 opened rebels to an avalanche of criticism. The arch-conservative minister Jonathan Odell, a Loyalist refugee from New Jersey now in New York City, seized upon the Franco-American pact in his most effective satirical poem, *The American Times*:

> Now, now erect the rich triumphal gate;
> The French alliance comes in solemn state:
> Hail to the master-piece of madness, hail;
> The head of glory with a serpent's tail!
> This seals, America, thy wretched doom;
> Here, Liberty, survey thy destin'd tomb;
> Behold the temple of tyrannic sway
> Is now complete – ye deep-ton'd organs play;
> Proclaim thro' all the land that Louis rules –
> Worship your faint, ye giddy-headed fools.[32]

Cooperating with Britain's long-standing foe confirmed what Loyalists already knew – that rebel hypocrites would do anything to advance their own self-interest. Like so much that comes to light with sustained attention to the war, the Patriot alliance with the paragon of the *ancien régime* marked their fundamental failure to align actions and ideals.

The expansion of the civil war into a continental and transatlantic conflict involving the superpowers of the era profoundly reoriented the war. Britain made new diplomatic overtures to the rebels, but when the Continental Congress rejected the generous terms of the Carlisle Peace Commission in 1778, open to a wide range of concessions short of complete independence, the possibility of a negotiated settlement vanished. The new British commander-in-chief Henry Clinton was instructed to initiate a southern campaign, the largest British offensive of the war, but it would be conducted with reduced European forces, some redeployed to the more valuable West Indies, others called back for home defense. While 65 percent of British land forces were deployed in North America at the start of 1778, by September 1780 that presence had fallen to just 29 percent.[33] Loyalists now needed to play a far more prominent martial role. Altogether some fifty Loyalist corps and another

---

[32] Jonathan Odell, *The American Times* (London, 1780), lines 183–192.
[33] Stephen Conway, "Britain and the Revolutionary Crisis, 1763–1791," in P. J. Marshall, ed., *The Oxford History of the British Empire: The Eighteenth Century* (Oxford: Oxford University Press, 1998), 325–46: 341.

312 commissioned companies of militia and voluntary troops would be raised with over 10,000 Loyalists in the Provincial Line in 1780–1781.[34]

The southern campaign was an effective new British strategy, and the classic study by Piers Mackesy argues that it had real potential to succeed. Similarly, US military historians James Kirby Martin and Mark Lender note that 1780 was the nadir of the war for Continental forces.[35] The expectation of strong settler, enslaved, and Indigenous mobilization against the rebels was central to the southern strategy of the British. This "Americanization" of the war fueled the signature feature of this theater, fratricidal violence that was not so much an American vs. British conflict as a punishing internal civil war. Assigning blame to who levied the initial or the most atrocious violence cannot be resolved in the dark downward cycle of retaliation. Detailed studies of southern Loyalists at war, however, find that the "extreme" and "relentless cruelty" of the rebels exceeded that of the British, and most agree that the worst abuses were perpetrated by militia forces, rather than regular army ones, on both sides.[36]

William Martin Johnston, a young man whose father was a colonial official, slaveowner, and merchant, had fled Savannah with Governor Wright in February 1776. Like most ardent male Loyalists, he was forced from home early in the war and experienced remarkable mobility as a soldier. Even in 1776, wartime chaos had forced Johnston from his native Georgia to Massachusetts, Nova Scotia, and New York City.[37] He served in the force that liberated Savannah in late December 1778 and fought throughout the southern campaign from East Florida to Virginia. His war was marked by atrocious violence. After a much younger brother was hanged

---

[34] W. O. Raymond, "Loyalists in Arms," *New Brunswick Historical Society Collections* 5 (1904), 189–223: 190.

[35] Mackesy, *War for America*, 256, 511–13; James Kirby Martin and Mark Lender, *"A Respectable Army": The Military Origins of the Republic, 1763–89*, 3rd edition (Chichester: Wiley, 2015), 157–64. For a less sanguine view of British potential, see Shy, *A People Numerous*, 231–3, esp. n. 35.

[36] Piecuch, *Three Peoples, One King*, 6–7, 11–12, 141 (quotation), 334 (quotation). Also see Carole W. Troxler, "Before and after Ramsour's Mill: Cornwallis' Complaints and Historical Memory of Southern Backcountry Loyalists," in Brannon and Moore, *The Consequences of Loyalism*, 75–88; Wayne E. Lee, *Crowds and Soldiers in Revolutionary North Carolina: The Culture of Violence in Riot and War* (Gainesville: University Press of Florida, 2001).

[37] Johnston's experiences can be reconstructed from his Loyalist Claims Commission application AO13/36/96-98 and through his wife's memoir, written in 1836, Elizabeth Lichtenstein Johnston, *Recollections of a Georgia Loyalist*, ed. Arthur Wentworth Eaton (Spartanburg, SC: Reprint Company, 1972 [1901]).

by rebels, Johnston gathered a group of "bad-looking men" to exert revenge and returned from that vendetta with a bloody sword and used pistols, as his grandson later recalled. On another occasion, he beat a traumatized soldier in his own unit to make him continue fighting rather than flee at the bloody Battle of Eutaw Springs. Although Johnston suffered from a "nervous complaint" brought on by the trauma of war, he received promotions and seems to have thrived in harrowing circumstances.[38] The war likely provided opportunities that would have eluded Johnston in civilian life. Prior to the war, when he trained in medicine under Benjamin Rush in Philadelphia, he gambled, drank excessively, and attacked a night watchman. His father repeatedly admonished him to change his ways in order to "wipe off the stain your former conduct had fix'd on your character."[39]

The late colonial world was also turned upside down for North Carolina Loyalist Thomas Peters. As an enslaved person, his close parallels with Johnston can easily be overlooked, but both began their long military service at the very start of the war. When North Carolina Loyalists were routed at Moore's Creek Bridge in February 1776, some 20 miles upriver from Peters' home in Wilmington, all seemed in disarray. The next month Peters seized the opportunity to liberate himself when he was among the loyal refugees who fled to British naval vessels anchored off Cape Fear. The forty to fifty Blacks who sought freedom with the British seem to have inspired Henry Clinton to form the Black Pioneers, the best-known black unit in the British forces, and the only corps composed of people of African descent to be added to the provincial establishment.[40] The Black Pioneers were charged (like other pioneer units) with building fortifications, supplying wood and provisions, and additional tasks to sustain the fighting force. Their sustained military service, including high mortality rates, commends us to understand them as Loyalists and soldiers. Indeed, the muster records for the Black Pioneers in which Peters served for the duration of the war were kept by the same official who also did so for Johnston's New York Volunteers.[41]

---

[38] Johnston, *Recollections*, 25–33, 64–5.

[39] Lewis Johnston to William Martin Johnston, 20 August 1774, Elizabeth Lichtenstein Johnston Papers, microfilm reel 10362, Public Archives of Nova Scotia. This letter is not among those republished in her *Recollections*.

[40] Clinton to Howe, 20 April 1776, quoted in Todd W. Braisted, "The Black Pioneers and Others: The Military Role of Black Loyalists in the American War for Independence," in John W. Pulis, ed., *Moving On: Black Loyalists in the Afro-Atlantic World* (New York: Garland, 1999), 11.

[41] On Afro-British military service, see Philip D. Morgan and Andrew Jackson O'Shaughnessy, "Arming Slaves in the American Revolution," in Christopher Leslie Brown and Philip D. Morgan, eds., *Arming Slaves: From Classical Times to the Modern Age*

General Clinton, like Governor Dunmore, understood that people enslaved by the enemy could play a critical role in defeating the rebellion. Clinton's formation orders for the Black Pioneers made plain that he considered its members to be able to honor their oath of enlistment. Moreover, he stressed that "at the extirpation of the present Rebellion th[ey] shall be intitled (as far as depends upon me) to their freedome." He also directed the unit's white officers to "treat these people with tenderness & humanity."[42] A large muster for the Black Pioneers, while serving in Newport, Rhode Island, in April 1777, reveals that sixty-six of its ninety-one members had been recruited prior to July 1776.[43] This strategic alliance served the interests of both the British and enslaved people, and the militarization of southern Loyalists began at the very onset of war, even though the south would not become its principal theater until the very end of 1778.

Although British prospects brightened with the southern campaign, Loyalist enthusiasm at the start of the war, parallel to the better-known *rage militaire* among rebels in 1775, had been squandered. Loyalists had learned painful lessons about the limits of British support, and those who joined the British Army or served in Loyalist militias generally had few other options as the war went on. Overall, the failure to effectively integrate colonists into the British Army at the onset of the war was "the heart of the loyalist problem."[44]

The shortcomings of the restored civil government in wartime Georgia suggests that the barrier to return to some antebellum status quo may have been insurmountable, largely because of conflict between Loyalist officials and British military ones. Governor Wright felt that "the Generals &c. have always Set their faces against this Province" and that only royal insistence led to the restoration of civil authority, "which the military cannot bear." Meanwhile, the British military commander at Savannah responded in kind that Wright and his council were "the most Absurd of all."[45] The dilemma

---

(New Haven: Yale University Press, 2006). Loyalist musters are in the extensive Ward Chipman Papers, see n. 43.

[42] The formation orders and oath are both reprinted at www.royalprovincial.com/military/rhist/blkpion/blklist.htm.

[43] Black Pioneers muster, 4 April 1777, Muster Master General's Office, Loyalist Muster, 1776–1785, Ward Chipman Papers, M.G. 23, D 1, Series 1, vol. 25, 88–89A [?], Library and Archives Canada, http://heritage.canadiana.ca/view/oocihm.lac_reel_c9818/439?r=0&s=5.

[44] Paul H. Smith, *Loyalists and Redcoats: A Study in British Revolutionary Policy* (Chapel Hill: University of North Carolina Press, 1964), 9.

[45] Quoted in Kenneth Coleman, "Restored Colonial Georgia, 1779–1782," *Georgia Historical Quarterly* 40 (1965), 12–13.

fully on display in Georgia arose from mutual suspicion between Loyalist and British leaders. While Loyalists had a strong Anglo-American sense of their world, their colonial commitments could place them almost as much at odds with Britons as with Patriots.

Loyalist Diaspora

Prioritizing the wartime experiences of Loyalists brought three individuals to our attention. Mary Brant, William Johnston, and Thomas Peters hailed from distinct corners of colonial society, and all exerted themselves effectively as Loyalists at war. After the British defeat, each joined the Loyalist diaspora and lived the rest of their lives outside the United States. Wartime circumstances forged commonalities among them, but their paths diverged when martial mobilization passed. Brant received lavish compensation for her wartime service. In addition to a substantial award from the Loyalist Claims Commission, Quebec Governor Frederick Haldimand recognized her value with an annual pension of £100, which continued her favored status by the previous governor, Guy Carleton. Both felt that Indigenous people merited compensation for "their steady attachment to the King's Service and the Interests of Government Ruined by the Rebels." Haldimand also had a house built for her in Cataraqui (later Kingston, Ontario), where she would be reunited with her pre-war Anglican minister, John Stuart, who collaborated with Joseph Brant on a Mohawk translation of the gospel of St. Mark, published in 1787. Two of her daughters would marry colonial officials, following the path of their boundary-crossing mother's accommodation with colonization and empire. Loyalist Indians, like all Loyalists, were shocked and embittered at their abandonment by the British in the peace treaty that ended the war. Nevertheless, Joseph Brant forged a lasting relationship between the Haudenosaunee and the British shaped by "a Permanent, Brotherly Love, and Amity," as he stated in 1783.[46] First Nation allies were crucial to the Loyalist coalition.

Unlike the well-placed Brants, William Johnston suffered sharp decline after the war. Lacking a purposeful role as a Loyalist officer whose violence was sanctioned by war, he returned to self-destructive excess. He spent considerable time away from his family, supposedly pursuing medical training in Britain like his father, but amassing debts in England that

---

[46] Huey and Pulis, *Molly Brant*, 75–81; Hill, *Clay We Are Made of*, 128, 127 (quotations).

ultimately led him to Jamaica. Although none of the Loyalist trio highlighted here had long lives, Johnston was the youngest when he died at age fifty-three in 1807 in Jamaica, where he held minor offices as a poorhouse and plantation physician, posts secured through the patronage of Governor Alured Clarke, under whom Johnston had served during the war.

Thomas Peters had used the war to change his legal status from enslaved to free, and his Loyalist military service included other profound changes. The famous "Book of Negroes" that recorded the vital statistics of formerly enslaved people being evacuated from British New York City in November 1783 allows for a basic reconstruction of his household when the family moved to Nova Scotia. It records him as from Wilmington, North Carolina, and his wife, Sally Peters, and her twelve-year-old daughter, Clara, both also identified as part of the Black Pioneers, had formerly been enslaved in South Carolina. An infant John, less than two years old and "born within the lines," completed the household.[47] Their family was a wartime creation of people brought together from different colonies, and their post-war trajectory would continue to be shaped by dramatic and transformative mobility.

Historian R. R. Palmer's pioneering assessment of the Age of Democratic Revolutions noted that by the close of the War of American Independence at least 60,000 colonists had fled to live in other corners of the British Atlantic, a remarkable displacement that far exceeded the ratio of refugees from revolutionary France.[48] This seems less exceptional, however, when we consider that Loyalists were an unusual sort of refugees. Rather than stateless people, their migration was aided by a powerful empire embarrassed by its military failure. Palmer concluded that the dramatic size of the Loyalist exodus indicated the radical qualities of the American Revolution that initiated the Atlantic Revolutionary Age that followed. Loyalists do advance our perception of a radical (and abusive) rebel movement, but to primarily cast Loyalists as a foil to explain Patriots fails to assess opposition to the American Revolution as a historical subject in its own right.

The detailed documentation for those who fled rebel-controlled states yields a critical insight that is too frequently overlooked. Loyalists

---

[47] The "Book of Negroes" is available in several formats. For the British copy, see www.novascotia.ca/nsarm/virtual/africanns/BN.asp. The US one is reprinted in Graham Russell Hodges, *The Black Loyalist Directory: African Americans in Exile after the American Revolution* (New York: Garland, 1996). The Peters family name is spelled "Potters" in both versions.

[48] R. R. Palmer, *The Age of the Democratic Revolution: A Political History of Europe and America, 1760–1800* (Princeton: Princeton University Press, 2014 [1959–1964]), 141.

represented the full socioeconomic spectrum of colonial society. Historian Wallace Brown established this based on an assessment of nearly 3,000 individuals who applied to the British government to be compensated for their financial losses due to loyalism. Applicants to the Loyalist Claims Commission (LCC) needed bureaucratic skill and persistence, and the process had an internal bias in favor of those with substantial wealth, since success required documentation of property losses. Given those barriers it is remarkable that so many applicants were common farmers requesting restitution for very modest losses, men like Zebedee Linnekin who applied from St. Andrews, New Brunswick, for the value of 25 acres that he had been forced to abandon in sparsely settled Maine.[49]

While LCC claimants represented the full occupational and socioeconomic range of colonists, this group also deviated from colonial society's overall demographic profile in telling ways. Religious and ethnic outsiders to the colonial order are over-represented among those who filed claims, as are recent immigrants. Among religious minorities several pacifist groups like Moravians, Mennonites, and Quakers were (and are) often considered Loyalists. While there were Patriot and Loyalist individuals from these religious communities, for the most part they pursued a neutral position that was usually considered illegitimate by the belligerents on either side. The over-representation of "conscious minorities" among rank-and-file loyalists reflects that they feared American abuse of power more than they feared British tyranny.[50] As the Boston Congregational minister and ardent Loyalist Mather Byles pungently expressed: "which is better, to be ruled by one tyrant three thousand miles away, or by three thousand tyrants not a mile away?"[51]

Equally significant, the LCC cohort was over-represented among those who fled large urban centers and the sea coast. Because every major coastal city from Boston to Savannah was at one time controlled by the British military, the dependence of loyalism on military support is hard to overstate.

---

[49] Wallace Brown, *The King's Friends: The Composition and Motives of the American Loyalist Claimants* (Providence, RI: Brown University Press, 1965), and extended by Christopher F. Minty, "Reexamining Loyalist Identity during the American Revolution," in Brannon and Moore, *The Consequences of Loyalism*, 33–47. Peter Wilson Coldham provides concise individual summaries of LCC applicants in *American Migrations 1765–1799* (Baltimore, MD: Genealogical Publishing Co., 2000), 147–8 (Linnekin).

[50] William H. Nelson, *The American Tory* (London: Oxford University Press, 1961), 91.

[51] Quoted in Wallace Brown, *The Good Americans: The Loyalists in the American Revolution* (New York: Morrow, 1969), 74.

As the main British headquarters in the rebellious colonies from September 1776 to November 1783, New York City was the most important refugee center and the largest evacuation site. Georgia, New York, and South Carolina had far and away the highest percentage of LCC applicants relative to their total populations, surely because the British military held their colonial capitals at the end of the war and evacuated loyal subjects.[52] Had the war ended with the British still in control of Boston, Newport, or Philadelphia, those places and their hinterlands would be even more visible as Loyalist strongholds. Military support was essential for loyalism to surface due to the rebels' punitive commitment to violence.

The richest scholarship about Loyalists has examined their Atlantic and even global trajectories as post-war refugees. Maya Jasanoff's *Liberty's Exiles* evocatively views Loyalists as the vanguard of nineteenth-century British imperialism with Janus-faced impulses of both benevolence and coercion. Focusing primarily upon those who fled the new United States in 1783, she explores the simultaneously inclusive and exclusive goals of British imperial governance.[53] Whereas Patriots have dominated scholarly attention as harbingers of the nation-state, Jasanoff portrays loyalists as bellwethers of global British imperialism.

The leading destination for Loyalist refugees was British North America. At a minimum some 36,000 Whites, 3,000 recently free Blacks, and 2,000 Indigenous people moved north to the Canadian Maritimes and Quebec, amounting to at least two-thirds of all Loyalist departures from the new United States.[54] Most went to Nova Scotia, which prompted the creation of New Brunswick as an explicitly Loyalist colony in 1784. The demographic impact of Loyalists in Quebec was far more modest and occurred over a longer period stretching into the 1790s. Yet, here too, the Loyalist presence spurred significant changes in governance with the creation of Upper and Lower Canada in 1791. Loyalist refugees included some conservative Tories, for whom the lesson of the rebellion was that the empire should limit seditious

---

[52] Brown, *King's Friends*, 253.
[53] Maya Jasanoff, *Liberty's Exiles: American Loyalists in the Revolutionary World* (New York: Alfred A. Knopf, 2011). She makes sharper analytical points in Maya Jasanoff, "The Other Side of Revolution: Loyalists in the British Empire," *William and Mary Quarterly* 65 (2008), 205–32.
[54] For Loyalist migration figures, see Jasanoff, *Liberty's Exiles*, 351–8. My estimate for migration to British North America is higher, as explained in Jerry Bannister and Liam Riordan, "Loyalism and the British Atlantic, 1660–1840," in Jerry Bannister and Liam Riordan, eds., *Loyal Atlantic: Remaking the British Atlantic in the Revolutionary Era* (Toronto: University of Toronto Press, 2012), 19–20.

popular assemblies, but most Loyalists strove to ensure that colonial assemblies remained (or became) viable institutions to protect their rights.[55]

Most Indigenous Loyalists operated beyond the direct oversight of colonial governments. Nearly 2,000 Haudenosaunee and related Indigenous Loyalists settled to the west of Fort Niagara on the Grand River, between Lake Erie and Lake Ontario, in 1783 and 1784. From Grand River, Joseph Brant worked to build a new confederacy of Iroquois and western Indians to oppose US expansion into the Ohio Country. This included wide-ranging diplomatic efforts at Indian conferences, at the US capital, and a second mission to London in 1786 that yielded major battlefield victories in the early 1790s. While the massive grant on the Grand River of some 2,000,000 acres by Governor Haldimand was contested and shrank over time, Grand River remains the largest First Nation reserve in Canada today.[56]

The most closely studied and best remembered loyal refugees are the 8,000–10,000 Black Loyalists.[57] Almost all of these free people of African descent went to London (around 5,000) or Nova Scotia (around 3,000). They still faced discrimination and even re-enslavement, which, once again, led to bold action by Thomas Peters.[58] He repeatedly petitioned provincial authorities in Nova Scotia and New Brunswick to fulfill the terms of the imperial government's loyalist settlement. When this failed, he secured power of attorney from over 200 Black families and traveled to London, where he appealed to the British government for Black Loyalists to be "useful Subjects to his Majesty ... wherever the Wisdom of Government may think proper to provide for them as free Subjects of the British Empire." His remarkable efforts secured support for an exodus to Sierra Leone in 1792 of some 1,200 Black "Nova Scotians," as they and their descendants would be called, where they founded a colony committed to anti-slavery,

---

[55] Compare the top-down imperial assessment of C. A. Bayly, *Imperial Meridian: The British Empire and the World, 1780–1830* (London: Longman, 1989) with more locally informed ones by David Bell, *Loyalist Rebellion in New Brunswick: A Defining Conflict for Canada's Political Culture* (Halifax: Formac, 2014); Elizabeth Mancke, David Bent, and Mark J. McLaughlin, "'Their Unalienable Right and Privilege': New Brunswick's Challenge to the Militarization of the British Empire, 1807–1814," *Acadiensis* 46:1 (2017), 49–72; Jones, *Resisting Independence*.

[56] Hill, *The Clay We Are Made of*, esp. Chapter 4.

[57] James W. St. G. Walker, *The Black Loyalists: The Search for a Promised Land in Nova Scotia and Sierra Leone 1783–1870* (Toronto: University of Toronto Press, 1992 [1976]); Cassandra Pybus, *Epic Journeys of Freedom: Runaway Slaves of the American Revolution and Their Global Quest for Liberty* (Boston, MA: Beacon Press, 2006).

[58] Carole Troxler, "Re-enslavement of Mary Postall in South Carolina, East Florida, and Nova Scotia," *Acadiensis* 37 (2008), 70–85.

British liberty, and evangelical Christianity. Writing to officials in London after arriving in West Africa, Peters expressed "a Grateful sense of His Majesty's goodness in removing us" and promised to always follow the king's "Religion and Laws, and [to] endeavor to instruct our children in the same."[59] Such ardent transatlantic Afro-British loyalism was probably the least anticipated consequence of how the War of American Independence transformed the British empire and its subjects.

The creation of Sierra Leone may represent loyalism at its most hopeful, but that highlight must be balanced against the post-war migration of White Loyalists, with at least 17,500 human beings as their enslaved property, overwhelmingly to the British West Indies. This forced migration of enslaved people owned by Loyalists was roughly double the size of the free Black Loyalist exodus.[60] Loyalists and their diaspora challenge pat understandings of the Age of Atlantic Revolutions in varied ways that force us to grapple with the profound contradictions of an era in which slavery and liberty as well as English, British, American, natural, Christian, and commercial rights were contested and interconnected with one another.

The portrait of the Loyalist Claims Commissioner John Eardley-Wilmot by Benjamin West, the Pennsylvania-born history painter to the king, provides a fitting close to this recovery of loyalism as a good idea (Figure 13.2). The allegorical painting in its background shows diverse Loyalists being shielded by Britannia and boldly presents a heroic British self-understanding of the empire and its benevolent embrace of defeated Loyalists. Here Britannia welcomes Loyalists of all sorts from royal officials and common farmers to widows, orphans, people of African descent, and, at its very center, a Native American man who shelters wartime victims as he reaches out to Britain. As the historian Maya Jasanoff observes of this and a related engraving, "it is hard to imagine a more straightforward image of an inclusive British Empire that had managed to mint moral capital out of its wartime defeat."[61]

---

[59] For Peters' petitions from Britain (1790) and Sierra Leone (1792), see CO217/63/f58–59 and CO267/9a-b, both available at www.flickr.com/photos/52115725@No3/4946082782/in/photostream/.

[60] See Jennifer K. Snyder, "Revolutionary Repercussions: Loyalist Slaves in St. Augustine and Beyond," in Bannister and Riordan, *Loyal Atlantic: Remaking the British Atlantic in the Revolutionary Era*; Carole Watterson Troxler, "Uses of the Bahamas by Southern Loyalist Exiles," in Bannister and Riordan, eds., *Loyal Atlantic: Remaking the British Atlantic in the Revolutionary Era*, 165–207.

[61] Jasanoff, "Other Side of Revolution," 218.

Figure 13.2 Portrait of Loyalist Claims Commissioner John Eardley-Wilmot by Benjamin West. Getty Images.

Loyalism, of course, had multiple motivations and resonances, and included a dark side that contributed to imperial exclusion and expansion in the nineteenth century. For many, a Loyalist commitment simply reflected standing pat with the status quo that rebellion threatened in unpredictable ways, but as the war unfolded, to be a Loyalist was an increasingly high-risk act. The broad coalition of Loyalists proved difficult to sustain in the face of a more homogeneous Patriot movement that demonstrated remarkable persistence in the face of adversity. In the end, diversity proved to be a loyalist liability, especially when its inclusion of racial outsiders spurred many neutral and undecided colonists to embrace rebellion. The military success of the rebellion and ongoing US claims to offer an ideal model of post-colonial transition have masked alternative conceptions of society and human relations in which imperial hierarchy tolerated capacious subjecthood.[62]

---

[62] On cross-racial imperial alliances beyond Anglo-America, see Marcela Echeverri, *Indian and Slave Royalists in the Age of Revolution: Reform, Revolution, and Royalism in the Northern Andes, 1780–1825* (Cambridge: Cambridge University Press, 2016).

Transnational Loyalists and Distorted National Legacies

Recovering loyalism in full color remains difficult because of how history as a professional practice remains centered upon explaining and validating the nation. Not surprisingly, the three national traditions for whom loyalism in the American Revolution is most relevant have done more to distort than to clarify our understanding of loyalism. In Canada, Loyalists came to be celebrated in the late nineteenth century as the best and brightest founders of the English-speaking nation. While this inaccurate claim was always contested, distaste for its elitist and ethno-nationalist celebration stimulated a sharp rejection of the "Loyalist Myth" a century later that still makes the subject unappealing for many historians working within a Canadian national framework.[63] In the United States a derogatory caricature of Loyalists lingers – they were supposedly aristocrats whose self-interest as colonial beneficiaries so marred their political vision as to be tinctured by cowardice.[64] Meanwhile, the ascent of a powerful Whig political tradition and its academic proponents in Great Britain also found no meaningful place in their past for shrill and provincial Loyalists, nor for the policies of King George III and his allies.[65] This distorted trio of Anglo-national perspectives overlap in telling ways. Loyalists are celebrated as loyal elites in Canada and dismissed for the same reason in the United States, while British and American assessments generally share the certainty that Loyalists were on the wrong side of history.

Loyalism's diverse coalition was a liability at the time, and it remains an interpretive obstacle today. Even White Loyalists ranged from high church conservatives, fairly labeled as Tories, to many others deeply committed to representative government, usefully conceptualized as loyal Whigs.[66] Many of the latter would challenge post-war imperial reforms that aimed to limit

---

[63] Norman Knowles, *Inventing the Loyalists: The Ontario Loyalist Tradition and the Creation of Usable Pasts* (Toronto: University of Toronto Press, 1997); Janet Ajzenstat and Peter J. Smith, eds., *Canada's Origins: Liberal, Tory, or Republican?* (Ottawa: Carleton University Press, 1995).

[64] Specialized studies transcend this limitation, yet a powerful Patriot lens about the era persists, see, for example, Bernard Bailyn's properly celebrated *The Ordeal of Thomas Hutchinson* (Cambridge, MA: Harvard University Press, 1974), esp. 403–8.

[65] For a revisionary challenge to Whig disdain, see Andrew Jackson O'Shaughnessy, *The Men Who Lost America: British Leadership, the American Revolution, and the Fate of the Empire* (New Haven: Yale University Press, 2013).

[66] L. F. S. Upton, *The Loyal Whig: William Smith of New York and Quebec* (Toronto: University of Toronto Press, 1969).

self-representation in Upper Canada, New Brunswick, and the Bahamas, where Loyalists were especially influential. Black Nova Scotians in Sierra Leone gave voice to an especially radical loyalism, such as when 132 Afro-British colonists signed a petition to make fellow Black Loyalist Thomas Peters their governor in 1792.[67] On Grand River, Indigenous loyalism as alliance (rather than subordination) continued through the war of 1812 and even to the present.[68] We still need to assess varied dimensions of loyalism in relationship to one another in order to more fully assess its meanings and legacies.

Recovering the manifest diversity of loyalism can help to overcome a simplistic good vs. bad dualism that still frames too many assessments of the American Revolution. The tendency to stress Loyalist flaws and shortcomings along with a corollary confidence about Patriot virtues and achievements remains potent. Deeper engagement with the full scope of Loyalist responses to rebellion has gained impetus as contemporary globalization increasingly encourages transnational frameworks for studying the past. Loyalists were transnational figures in a colonial world that was American and British, as well as Indigenous, African, and imperial. This complexity has proved difficult to see, since Loyalists lacked a post-war national vessel for historians to use to champion their multidimensional perspectives, perhaps suggesting why biography has been such a strong vein in loyalist scholarship. Loyalism was a reasonable alternative to rebellion, but the recovery of loyalism still requires greater attention to colonial circumstances, the contingencies of war, and the fundamental place of violence in creating the Age of Atlantic Revolutions.

---

[67] Walker, *Black Loyalists*, 149–51, 159–263. Pybus narrates this well in *Epic Journeys*, but views Black Loyalists as motivated by "the animating principles of the revolution," 205.

[68] On deep Haudenosaunee continuities, see Hill, *The Clay We Are Made of*.

14

White Women and the American Revolution

AMI PFLUGRAD-JACKISCH

The era of the American Revolution is an extremely important period in the history of women and gender in early America. During these decades the intertwining forces of Atlantic trade, Enlightenment political theory, religious revival, and the circumstances of the war redefined women's relationships to the market, the state, and the family. Specifically, the war politicized and transformed the household into a site of political activism for women in ways previously unknown in the British American colonies, creating new roles for American women both inside and outside the household.

Perhaps more importantly, this era also provides a crucial bridge between colonial notions regarding the "true nature" of women and nineteenth-century perspectives about gender and race that shaped American ideas about women's proper role in society and political culture for decades to come. At the turn of the eighteenth century, colonists still viewed white women as irrational, disorderly, and lustful beings who needed proper discipline from their husbands and fathers to check their naturally unruly behavior. By the second decade of the nineteenth century, however, Americans regarded white women as the new republic's moral compass and a critical moral counterweight to men's baser appetites and rash political and economic behavior. This dramatic change in the standing of white women in American society laid the foundation for women's accepted public roles and their political struggles into the early twentieth century.

Eighteenth-Century Women and Atlantic Trade

At the beginning of the eighteenth century, trade between Great Britain and the British North American colonies flourished. Transatlantic shipping tripled during these years, providing colonists with access to a wide range of British manufactured goods. As a result of this economic growth, colonists experienced a marked growth in population and improvements in their health and standards of living. At the same time, American colonists participated in this trade by exporting staple crops like tobacco, rice, wheat, and indigo, and they benefited from the expansion in shipbuilding and adjacent industries like rope-making. Between 1720 and 1770, per capita colonial exports from Britain increased by 50 percent.[1] Furthermore, the greater availability of transferable instruments of credit such as notes, bonds, and bills of exchange fostered overseas trade by making it easier for merchants, planters, and middling and ordinary people to purchase goods on credit. The combination of these factors generated a consumer revolution and an increase in colonial prosperity that allowed all but the poorest white Americans to buy manufactured goods.

This expansion in trade greatly affected the lives of American women from diverse economic backgrounds in different, but equally, important ways. Increasing choice and opportunities for consumer goods raised the standard of living for white women and created new distinctions in status. Wealthy and middling white women bought tea services, luxury fabrics, and food, and they had greater variety and selection in styles, colors, and patterns of cloth, ribbon, gloves, lace, carpets, and other furnishings than previous generations. The availability of ready-made cloth, sugar and other food stuffs, soap, candles, tools, kitchenware, and herbal remedies made ordinary women's lives easier as well, and men and women of all different socioeconomic levels enjoyed tea.[2] Trade networks and the consumption of goods reached well beyond port cities into nearly all moderately rural areas and small-town centers. Manufactured goods even made their way into backcountry areas in western Virginia and North Carolina where the poorest colonists acquired consumer merchandise from small stores, peddlers, or at auctions.[3]

As much as women enjoyed these new consumer goods, unless they were spinsters or widows, legally they only "possessed" these goods and did not own them. Under the common law doctrine of coverture, married women could not own property. In British American colonies, a married woman's legal identity was subsumed under her husband's and she had no legal will other than his, nor could she make contracts without her husband's consent.[4] Although coverture laws existed throughout the colonial era, local courts did not always enforce or uniformly apply them. The 1760 publication and

---

[1] Alan Taylor, *American Revolutions: A Continental History, 1750–1804* (New York: W. W. Norton, 2016), 25.

[2] T. H. Breen, *The Marketplace of Revolution: How Consumer Politics Shaped American Independence* (New York: Oxford University Press, 2004).

[3] Ann Smart Martin, *Buying into a World of Goods: Early Consumers in Backcountry Virginia* (Baltimore, MD: Johns Hopkins University Press, 2008).

[4] Marylynn Salmon, *Women and the Law of Property in Early America* (Chapel Hill: University of North Carolina Press, 1986), 14–15.

widespread usage of William Blackstone's *Commentaries on the Laws of England*, however, prompted the standardization and enforcement of coverture laws. This had the effect of making married women's ability to own property separately from their husbands more difficult.[5]

Nevertheless, the growing market economy made women in British colonial America part of a larger commercial network of exchange and credit as both purchasers and sellers of goods. While the majority of women in the eighteenth century continued to live in poor to middling farm households, women increasingly made up an important part of the population in rapidly growing port cities and commercial centers like New York, Philadelphia, Boston, Newport, Williamsburg, and Charleston. There, white women commonly ran taverns, inns, specialty shops, and general stores. At least ninety women kept shops between 1740 and 1776 in Boston, and in colonial seaports like New York and Philadelphia a substantial number of married women operated as "she-merchants" or "she-traders."[6]

Other women, like Eliza Lucas Pinckney of South Carolina, were female planters and entrepreneurs. Pinckney managed her father's and later her own properties in the South Carolina Lowcountry and helped to make indigo a cornerstone of South Carolina's economy. She aggressively commanded the enslaved people on her three plantations and ably conducted the international business aspects of her commodities production. She even read law in her free time and wrote wills for some of her poorer neighbors.[7] Similarly, in Virginia, Frances Bland Randolph Tucker managed three plantations after the death of her first husband. After her remarriage to St. George Tucker in 1778, she served as his partner in managing their five estates and held key roles of responsibility beyond the household, such as collecting rents and debts, communicating with merchants, keeping on top of the price of tobacco, and managing her overseers and enslaved laborers.[8]

---

[5] Holly Brewer, "The Transformation of Domestic Law," in Michael Grossberg and Christopher Tomlins, eds., *The Cambridge History of Law in America*, vol. 1 (Cambridge: Cambridge University Press, 2008), 297–302, 316–18.

[6] Patricia Cleary, *Elizabeth Murray: A Woman's Pursuit of Independence in Eighteenth-Century America* (Amherst: University of Massachusetts Press, 2000), 46; Ellen Hartigan-O'Connor, *The Ties That Buy: Women and Commerce in Revolutionary America* (Philadelphia: University of Pennsylvania Press, 2011); Karin Wulf, *Not All Wives: Women of Colonial Philadelphia* (Philadelphia: University of Pennsylvania Press, 2011); Sara T. Damiano, *To Her Credit: Women, Finance, and the Law in Eighteenth-Century New England Cities* (Baltimore: Johns Hopkins University Press, 2021).

[7] Lorri Glover, *Eliza Lucas Pinckney: An Independent Woman in the Age of Revolution* (New Haven: Yale University Press, 2020).

[8] Philip Hamilton, *The Making and Unmaking of a Revolutionary Family: The Tuckers of Virginia, 1752–1830* (Charlottesville: University of Virginia Press, 2003), 48–67.

Although Pinckney and Tucker were in many ways exceptional women, both exemplified the women's connections to the Atlantic economy and the important roles they played in managing their households. Both English and French visitors to the eighteenth-century South noted the industriousness of American plantation mistresses. One Frenchman who visited Virginia commented that while the men drank and chewed tobacco their wives not only managed the responsibilities of their households, but did so well. Englishman Joseph Hadfield was astounded at the demanding nature of southern women's responsibilities, which largely included supervising enslaved household laborers. "All was method and regularity," Hadfield observed, "and I must say that no women are better wives or managers."[9]

Undoubtedly women needed to be extraordinarily well organized. Despite their ability to buy ready-made cloth and some foodstuffs that made life easier, the list of household responsibilities for planters and rural women remained long. Without the help of automated technology women routinely completed the arduous tasks of laundering clothes, food preparation, clothing production, cultivating the family's vegetable garden, caring for livestock and other animals, food preservation and storage, and nursing sick family members. For childbearing women, all of these tasks occurred in concert with the rhythms of pregnancy, childbirth, breast feeding, and child rearing. Urban and elite women with servants or enslaved people had some advantage in this regard, as they enjoyed access to a wider variety of ready-made consumer goods and supervised some of these domestic tasks rather than having to do them themselves.

Although new ideas about cleanliness, etiquette, self-presentation, and entertaining created an added set of pressures and expectations for many American women in the eighteenth century, the revolution in consumer goods positioned white women as key players in the creation of culture and status. In determining the proper use of goods, women shaped ideas about etiquette and new forms of sociability that had important implications for how colonial Americans defined class status, racial categories, femininity, and what constituted "civilization."[10] More importantly, as consumer goods

---

[9] Jean-François Clermont-Crèvecœur, *The American Campaigns of Rochambeau's Army, 1780, 1781, 1782, 1783*, 2 vols., trans. and ed. Howard C. Rice, Jr. and Anne S. K. Brown (Princeton: Princeton University Press, 1972), vol. 1, 66; Joseph Hadfield, *An Englishman in America 1785*, ed. Douglas S. Robertson (Toronto: Hunter-Rose, 1933), 8.

[10] Sophie White, *Wild Frenchmen and Frenchified Indians: Material Culture and Race in Colonial Louisiana* (Philadelphia: University of Pennsylvania Press, 2012); Kathleen M. Brown, *Foul Bodies: Cleanliness in Early America* (New Haven: Yale University Press,

became the centerpiece of growing tensions between American colonies and England, the household itself became politicized and women's cultural and economic authority in this area positioned them as actors in the politics of the revolution.

Women on the Eve of the Revolution and the Politicization of the Household

In the decades prior to 1776, Enlightenment political theory and the religious upheaval of the First Great Awakening ran on parallel tracks in revolutionary America, which laid the ideological foundation for the desacralization of the monarchy and broke down traditional social hierarchies. Both movements stressed the importance of the individual under the law and in the eyes of God. For women, the recognition of the value of each individual was important in establishing women as political actors during this period. While these ideas did not translate into social or political equality for women, they helped to promote the idea that women were naturally virtuous in both the political and religious sense, advanced women's individual political agency, and elevated their status within the household as complementary partners. Additionally, women gained greater choice in marriage partners and new ideas regarding consent and marriage opened the door for less restrictive divorce laws after the war.

Beginning in the 1730s and 1740s and lasting through the 1770s, waves of evangelical religious revivals, which historians collectively call the first "Great Awakening," spread across the colonies. This new form of Protestantism stressed the need for personal conversion or "new birth" and placed enormous weight on an individual's decision to accept salvation. Although Puritans and other Anglicans also highlighted the need for personal conversion over the course of one's lifetime, evangelical Christians sought a sudden, emotionally experienced conversion that they likened to a thunderclap. During religious revival meetings, evangelical sects like the Baptists, Presbyterians, and Methodists challenged not only the authority of the established Anglican Church, but also the underpinnings of secular authority generally. Eschewing traditional social order and worship styles, women spoke with authority about their spiritual awakenings at public meetings and revivals where preachers emphasized the leveling power of the Holy

---

2009); Breen, *Marketplace of Revolution*; Richard L. Bushman, *The Refinement of America: Persons, Houses, Cities* (New York: Vintage, 1992).

Spirit. Some women even held positions of authority as lay exhorters. Although the Great Awakening did not destroy social distinctions inside or outside the Church, it did weaken traditional social hierarchies and laid the foundation for the subsequent decline in patriarchal and governmental authority connected to the revolution.[11]

Thus, by emphasizing the importance of the individual and softening traditional social and political hierarchies, the dual forces of political Enlightenment and evangelical revival set the stage for the radicalism of the American Revolution that would play out in response to new British economic policies. As key consumers in the colonial economy, women were primed to play a central role in the coming political crisis.

British victory in the Seven Years' War had effectively pushed the French out of North America and greatly expanded British landholdings. The long conflict, however, had left the British government with an enormous debt. Many political leaders in England believed that American colonists ought to pay their fair share of the war's expenses, arguing that that American colonists had benefited most from British gains in North America. Consequently, Treasury officials and Parliament devised a new plan to raise the revenue needed to pay off Britain's rapidly expanding national debt. Beginning in 1763, the government implemented a new series of laws and policies for the purpose of collecting revenue from the colonies.

At the time the British government implemented their new economic plan, American women played a central role in household decisions about the purchase of British manufactured goods and in managing their family's resources. The flourishing of transatlantic trade and corresponding consumer revolution spurred social and economic changes that placed women at the intersection of the household's three functions: reproduction, production, and consumption. Thus, as the guardians of household resources and the buyers and sellers of foodstuffs, clothes, tableware, and other manufactured goods, women necessarily became part of the political debates over taxation.[12]

---

[11] Gary Nash, *The Unknown American Revolution: The Unruly Birth of Democracy and the Struggle to Create America* (New York: Penguin, 2005); Thomas S. Kidd, ed., *The Great Awakening: A Brief History with Documents* (Boston, MA: Bedford/St. Martin's Press, 2008); Gordon S. Wood, "Religion and the American Revolution," in Harry Stout and D. G. Hart, eds., *New Directions in American Religious History* (New York: Oxford University Press, 1997). See also Thomas S. Kidd, *The Great Awakening: The Roots of Evangelical Christianity in Colonial America* (New Haven: Yale University Press, 2007).

[12] Breen, *Marketplace of Revolution*, 230.

The Stamp Act of 1765 in particular sparked widespread protest from both American men and women. The Act levied taxes on a wide range of documents, commissions, licenses, contracts, newspapers, and even playing cards. As a result, the Act affected the everyday lives of a variety of colonists from all parts of colonial society, angering lawyers, printers, merchants, dockworkers, *and* female consumers. The new taxes also came at the same time as the colonies were experiencing a post-war economic downturn and households needed to make careful choices about how they managed their expenses.

Women based their objection to the Stamp Act, however, on more than just household economics. Some women cited philosophical and political reasons for their decision to participate in the protests. Like men, women understood that part of the reason the Stamp Act had so angered American colonists was that its passage struck at the heart of colonial government autonomy. These women rejected the British government's belief that it had the sovereign right to tax American colonists "in all cases whatsoever" and they worried that the government had become corrupted and abused its authority. For example, at a meeting in the home of Ephraim Brown in Providence, Rhode Island, the "Daughters of Liberty" unanimously resolved that the Stamp Act was unconstitutional and that they would purchase no more British manufactured goods until it was repealed.[13]

Thus, beginning with the Stamp Act, women were thrust into the political debates over British economic policy. Moreover, male advocates of boycotts and nonconsumption pacts came to realize that they could not be successful without the support of white women.[14] Initially, women's participation in political protests was largely limited to consumer boycotts, the rejection of British manufactured goods, and the conscious creation of homemade goods. These efforts took place mainly in private homes. Overwhelmingly, it was men who took part in public political demonstrations and in more violent actions that involved the destruction of property, physically threatening customs officials and tax collectors, and burning or beheading British officials in effigy. However, this would later change as political protests against British economic policies intensified on the eve of the revolution.

The passage of the Townshend Acts of 1767, subsequent events like the Boston Massacre in 1770, and the passage of the Tea and Coercive Acts in 1773 and 1774, respectively, sparked further and more fervent protests,

---

[13] Ibid., 232.   [14] Ibid., 230; Taylor, *American Revolutions*, 111.

boycotts, and violence. As a result, women, too, became increasingly vocal in their opposition to British policy, and in some instances moved their protests out of the home and into the streets or other public spaces. In 1770, John Adams noted in his diary that a "vast number of men and women" followed the coffin of young political martyr Christopher Seider through streets of Boston in an elaborate procession past Liberty Tree.[15] Women also assisted men who ritually shamed boycott breakers and Loyalists. In 1772, Loyalist Peter Oliver derided a Boston woman who threw pillows out of her window to a passing mob to provide the feathers for a tarring and feathering that was in progress below.[16] On occasion, women also organized their own public protests. For example, in 1774 women in Wilmington, North Carolina, publicly burned tea in a solemn street procession.[17]

Generally, though, women's public political acts consisted of support for boycotts and displays of domestic manufacture like spinning bees, where women gathered to make homespun cloth, eschewing British manufactured goods. Women also signed their names to nonimportation and nonconsumption agreements, and composed agreements of their own. In 1770, nearly 300 women in Boston signed an agreement alongside local merchants to abstain from tea. Another 100 women wrote and signed their own boycott agreement.[18] Women in Virginia and South Carolina wore homespun clothes to public events to show support for colonial boycotts.[19] Perhaps most famously, in 1774, fifty-one women in Edenton, North Carolina, wrote a declaration that resolved to stop buying English imports in opposition to the Tea Act. The women's meeting was lampooned in the 1775 British cartoon, "A Society of Patriotic Ladies at Edenton in North Carolina." Although British and American supporters of the crown ridiculed them and described them as masculine, the attention that their declaration received made clear that women's political protests carried cultural weight and posed a threat to the opposition.

---

[15] Alfred F. Young, "'Persons of Consequence': The Women of Boston and the Making of the American Revolution, 1765–1776," in *Liberty Tree: Ordinary People and the American Revolution* (New York: New York University Press, 2006), 100–43: 118–19.

[16] Taylor, *American Revolutions*, 111; Linda K. Kerber, "'History Can Do It No Justice': Women and the Reinterpretation of the American Revolution," in *Toward an Intellectual History of Women: Essays by Linda K Kerber* (Chapel Hill: University of North Carolina Press, 1997), 79–80.

[17] Cynthia A. Kierner, *Beyond the Household: Women's Place in the Early South, 1700–1835* (Ithaca, NY: Cornell University Press, 1998), 81.

[18] Carol Berkin, *Revolutionary Mothers: Women in the Struggle for America's Independence* (New York: Vintage, 2005), 15.

[19] Kierner, *Beyond the Household*, 73–5.

Figure 14.1 A Society of Patriotic Ladies, at Edenton, North Carolina, 1775. Courtesy of Library of Congress.

Women also expressed their political awareness, ideology, and patriotism privately in letters and by writing patriotic poems, essays, and plays that were often published in newspapers. In 1772, Mercy Otis Warren anonymously published her satiric play, *The Adulateur*, that critiqued Tories and in particular Massachusetts' Royal Governor Thomas Hutchinson. Women's diaries and letters included commentary on political events, pamphlets, and congressional resolutions.[20] Women also politicized their social lives by shunning neighbors who held opposing political views and by choosing to forgo fashionable elaborate dresses and hairstyles such as the "high roll" associated with self-indulgent Toryism. Instead, they wore homespun and sported flat-headed hairstyles that signaled their support for the Patriot cause.[21]

On the eve of the revolution, women politicized their everyday lives and choices in meaningful ways. Their participation in boycotts and protests gave depth to Patriot claims that they spoke on behalf of the entire community. Not all American men supported the idea of women's participation in political protests, and some continued to be skeptical about women's ability to make sacrifices for the good of both family and colony. These men, however, increasingly faded into the background of colonial society as the war began and women's political efforts solidified emerging ideals about women's sound moral judgment and fortitude, imbuing women with a new moral authority.

Choosing Sides

Although the colonies did not declare formal independence from Britain until the summer of 1776, military engagements between British soldiers and colonial militias began in 1775 at Lexington and Concord in Massachusetts and in Great Bridge, Virginia near Norfolk. Moreover, in the fall of 1774, the First Continental Congress adopted the Articles of Association, which instituted a boycott of all British goods throughout the colonies effective 1 December 1774. Colonial legislatures also formally expelled British merchants from the colonies, effectively ending all trade with Britain. Thus, even before war officially began, the time to choose sides – Loyalist or Patriot – could no longer be avoided, and continued economic engagement with Britain was a sure sign of loyalty to the crown.

For female merchants whose livelihood depended on access to British manufactured goods and credit, negotiating consumer boycotts became tricky. Many merchants chose to leave the colonies and relocate to Britain,

---

[20] Joan R. Gundersen, *To Be Useful to the World: Women in Revolutionary America, 1740–1790* (Chapel Hill: University of North Carolina Press, 2006), 176.

[21] Kate Haulman, *The Politics of Fashion in Eighteenth-Century America* (Chapel Hill: University of North Carolina Press, 2011), 165.

Canada, or the British West Indies. Milliner Jane Rathell of Williamsburg, Virginia, for example, found that after her British supplier John Norton and Company could no longer provide her with goods, she was unable to maintain her business and she decided to return to England. Wealthier Loyalist shopkeepers like Elizabeth Murray decided to stay in America to protect their property. Still others, like Philadelphia apothecary Elizabeth Weed, who supported the Patriots, switched to suppliers in Germany for her medicinal cure ingredients and she continued her business throughout the war.[22]

The politicization of everyday activities made women's routine domestic responsibilities, like food preparation, caring for the sick, the production of clothing, and consumer purchases, statements of political allegiance and women themselves political actors. Patriot officials often viewed women's hospitality, feeding, housing, and nursing of British soldiers as an extension of their political will, and sometimes charged them with aiding and abetting the enemy.[23] The types of treasonous acts with which these women were charged were consistent with their perceived roles in society such as food preparation and caring for the sick. For example, in Philadelphia, Patriot authorities convicted Susannah Longacre and Rachel Hamer of giving aid to the enemy after they gave food to British soldiers who came to their homes looking for supplies.[24] In Virginia, Mary Willing Byrd's neighbors suspected her of loyalism after she nursed and fed an injured British soldier. Although these women may have been acting on behalf of their political loyalties, it also seems clear that some women "aided" soldiers out of extreme fear or in order to protect themselves from further harm.

During the war, women who supported the Patriot cause continued to exhibit support for the Americans by soliciting goods from Patriot

---

[22] Kaylan M. Stevenson, "'Until Liberty of Importation Is Allowed': Milliners and Mantuamakers in the Chesapeake on the Eve of the Revolution," in Barbara B. Oberg, ed., *Women in the American Revolution: Gender, Politics, and the Domestic World* (Charlottesville: University of Virginia Press, 2019), 39–59: 52–3; Cleary, *Elizabeth Murray*; Susan Hanket Brandt, "Marketing Medicine: Apothecary Elizabeth Weed's Economic Independence during the American Revolution," in Barbara B. Oberg, ed., *Women in the American Revolution: Gender, Politics, and the Domestic World* (Charlottesville: University of Virginia Press, 2019), 60–79: 68–9.

[23] G. S. Rowe, "*Femes Covert* and Criminal Prosecution in Eighteenth-Century Pennsylvania," *American Journal of Legal History* 32:2 (1988), 138–56: 150.

[24] Rowe, "*Femes Covert* and Criminal Prosecution," 151. Also see Kacy Tillman, "Women Left Behind: Female Loyalism, Coverture, and Grace Growden Galloway's Empire of Self," in Mary Balkun and Susan Imbaratto, eds., *Women and the Formation of Empire* (New York: Palgrave, 2016).

Figure 14.2 Nancy Hart defending her home against British soldiers. Many women experienced trauma on the home front during the revolutionary war. Getty Images.

merchants, choosing homespun clothes, participating in spinning bees, and making clothes and blankets for soldiers. Women also endorsed the Patriot cause by wearing special ribbons. For example, in the Carolinas women wore green feathers to champion American General Nathanael Greene.[25] In addition, women raised funds for troops. Esther De Berdt Reed's 1780 broadside "Sentiments of an American Woman" inspired women to form the Ladies Association of Philadelphia (LAP), which raised money for soldiers in the Continental Army. Published in the *Pennsylvania Gazette*, Reed's tract encouraged women to stand firm in support of the republic with "courage" and "constancy," renouncing with the highest pleasure "vain ornaments."[26]

In response, women throughout Pennsylvania, New Jersey, and Maryland created local chapters of the LAP. Going door-to-door to request donations, LAP women raised $300,000 and contributed over 2,000 shirts for soldiers. The LAP also inspired women in other states, who consequently procured additional clothes and blankets for the Continental Army.[27] The wives of

---

[25] Kierner, *Beyond the Household*, 96.
[26] Berkin, *Revolutionary Mothers*, 44–7; Jacqueline Beatty, "Ladies Association of Philadelphia," *Encyclopedia of Greater Philadelphia*, Library Company of Philadelphia, http://philadelphiaencyclopedia.org/archive/ladies-association-of-philadelphia.
[27] Berkin, *Revolutionary Mothers*, 44–6; Beatty, "Ladies Association of Philadelphia."

prominent political and military figures like Martha Washington and Martha Jefferson also worked to aid American soldiers during the war. Jefferson published an appeal in the *Virginia Gazette* that encouraged Virginia's women to join their sisters in other states and successfully raised supplies and funds for the Continental Army.[28]

Women who publicly acknowledged their loyalty to the Crown, however, often faced severe consequences in the form of frightening and violent encounters with Continental soldiers and local officials. Massachusetts Loyalist Christian Barnes was greatly alarmed when the local Committee of Safety appeared at her house to harass her after she provided British military officers with food. The Committee's members threatened to destroy her home if her family ever "aided" the enemy again. Barnes again faced danger when a man supporting the Patriots came to her door and demanded that she serve him dinner. He insulted and abused her and told her he would blow her brains out if she did not provide him with a horse.[29]

Women declared their loyalism in a number of different ways, first and foremost by openly declaring their political allegiance to the crown. Other women chose more unassuming ways to assert their political views, such as refusing to place a candle in their window to show their support for the British.[30] Grace Growden Galloway of Philadelphia was less subtle in her approach. A staunch and vocal Loyalist, she chose to stay in her home after Patriots forced her Loyalist husband to leave the city. In June 1778, members of the local Committee of Safety informed Galloway that they were confiscating her house as a result of her support for the British. Galloway attempted every legal means to keep her home, ultimately she was unsuccessful. In August, the local confiscation committee arrived to take possession of the house. After she refused to open her door, a group of Patriot men violently forced their way inside her home and literally wrenched Galloway out of her house as she clung resolutely to the doorframe.[31]

As military and political lines began to take shape in the early phase of the revolution, American women often expressed their political loyalties in everyday activities that were specific to women's socially accepted roles. In addition, women stepped out into new public roles to solicit funding and

---

[28] Jon Kukla, *Mr. Jefferson's Women* (New York: Vintage, 2008), 77–8.
[29] Cleary, *Elizabeth Murray*, 173–4.   [30] Kierner, *Beyond the Household*, 96.
[31] Judith Van Buskirk, "They Didn't Join the Band: Disaffected Women in Revolutionary Philadelphia," *Pennsylvania History: A Journal of Mid-Atlantic Studies* 62:3 (1995), 306–29: 320.

other support for American troops. Women's newly politicized household responsibilities, such as food preparation, clothing choice, and family spending and consumption brought them into public conflict with friends, neighbors, and soldiers, at which time they demonstrated their capacity for political action and allegiance even in the face of great danger.

On the Homefront

Although Native American women and some white women on the periphery of British North American population centers had experienced the brutality and displacement of military conflict during the Seven Years' War, it was not until the outbreak of hostilities between the British and Americans beginning in 1775 that most white women experienced the profound traumas, shortages, and violence of war. After the battles at Lexington and Concord, Boston merchant Elizabeth Murray noted with alarm the long train of fearful women who fled ahead of soldiers with crying children in their arms.[32] Eliza Lucas Pinckney's experiences during the war also highlight the danger and dislocation that women faced when soldiers came through their region. British forces expelled Pinckney from her South Carolina home and confiscated her property. To her mortification she became a refugee without "a place to lay my head." Soldiers carried off her cattle and cut down her timber. A lifelong slaveholder, she was shocked to see the people she enslaved flee to join the British.[33] As troops from both sides moved through residential areas, they foraged for supplies, burned crops, stole and destroyed tools, animals, and food. Many women whose homes were in their path experienced the near-total destruction of their property. A few like Catherine Schuyler took matters into their own hands. Rather than see the British use her wheat to feed enemy troops, she tossed flaming torches into her fields as they arrived at her farm.[34]

Worse still, troops also occupied women's homes as they moved from battle to battle. Soldiers expected women to "host" them, to provide them with food, and to wash their laundry. Both British and American troops occupied Mary Willing Byrd's Virginia plantation multiple times as they moved through her neighborhood. The British completely destroyed her crops, killed her livestock, damaged large parts of her property, and took her tools, kitchen equipment, and farming implements with them. In addition,

---

[32] Cleary, *Elizabeth Murray*, 172.   [33] Glover, *Eliza Lucas Pinckney*, 192.
[34] Berkin, *Revolutionary Mothers*, 41.

forty-nine of her enslaved laborers freed themselves upon the arrival of British troops. Yet, with few other options, Byrd and her four teenage daughters nursed, fed, and entertained both the British and American troops in these terrifying encounters.[35]

Undoubtedly Mary Willing Byrd feared for the safety of her daughters in the presence of so many soldiers. When Byrd first heard that British soldiers were heading in the direction of her plantation, she frantically loaded her daughters into her carriage and sent them away from the house, but their enslaved driver, seeing his own opportunity to secure his freedom, abandoned the girls on the road. Rape was a disturbingly common experience for women on the homefront. Newspapers and military reports carried graphic details of soldiers raping young girls and gang rapes. British officer Lord Rawdon callously remarked that "A girl cannot step in to the bushes to pluck a rose without running the most imminent risk of being ravished, and they are so little accustomed to these vigorous methods that they don't bear them with proper resignation."[36]

The war and its deprivations affected life in all thirteen states, and fighting took place in most parts of the country and in major population centers. As men left home for military service or took on other war-related activities, many women assumed men's duties while also maintaining their regular domestic responsibilities. Some women became heads of households and fully took over running farms and shops. They negotiated the sale of crops, purchased farm equipment, and paid laborers or managed, bought, and sold enslaved people. By the end of the war, as one New Hampshire wife's letter noted, for many families "the" farm became "our" farm.[37]

Cut off from trade, women and families faced severe food shortages and high prices during the war. Confident in their abilities to evaluate the fair price of consumer goods, women created their own moral economy in towns across the new republic and actively confronted those whom they believed to be hoarding foodstuffs in order to drive up prices. Facing shortages in everyday necessities like sugar and coffee, in more than thirty recorded instances crowds of women confronted shopkeepers and merchants and meted out their own justice to those whom they believed were price

---

[35] Ami Pflugrad-Jackisch, "'What Am I But an American': Mary Willing Byrd and Westover Plantation during the American Revolution," in Barbara B. Oberg, ed., *Women in the American Revolution: Gender, Politics, and the Domestic World* (Charlottesville: University of Virginia Press, 2019), 171–91.
[36] Berkin, *Revolutionary Mothers*, 39–41.
[37] Quoted in Berkin, *Revolutionary Mothers*, 33.

gouging. Abigail Adams recorded one of these incidents in a letter to her husband. She relayed that around 100 women assembled at the warehouse of a "stingy merchant," who had reportedly been withholding coffee in his store and then selling it for a high price. The women demanded access to the coffee. When the merchant refused, they seized him by his neck and tossed him in a cart. The women then confiscated his keys, took the coffee, and left. According to Adams, "A large concourse of Men stood amazd silent Spectators of the whole transaction."[38] Throughout the war confrontations like the one Adams described took place in New York, Pennsylvania, Rhode Island, Connecticut, Maryland, and Virginia. Despite mixed reactions to these crowds of women no one argued that women overstepped their proper social roles when they challenged hoarding merchants.[39]

Thousands of poor white women also followed both the British and Continental armies as cooks, washerwomen, seamstresses, nurses, scavengers, and sexual partners. Many of the women became "camp followers" in order to be close to their sons or husbands, but others simply had no other place to go. Some women moved with their husbands onto the battlefield, carrying buckets of water. "Molly Pitcher" evolved as a term used to describe these women, the most famous of whom was Mary Ludwig Hays who took over loading her husband's gun after he had been wounded at the Battle of Monmouth in 1778.[40]

More rarely, women disguised themselves as male soldiers and enlisted in the army. Anna Marie Lane and Margaret Corbin enlisted as men in order to stay near their husbands. During the war, Corbin was injured after taking her husband's place at his cannon, and in 1779 she became the first American woman to receive a disability pension for military service.[41] Deborah Sampson Gannett (more commonly referred to as Deborah Sampson) also famously collected a military bounty and masqueraded as soldier Robert Shurtleff in the Continental Army for seventeen months before her true identity became known. According to the men in her unit, Sampson fought bravely beside them in battle. Her true identity was revealed only after she became ill and a doctor removed her clothing for treatment. Upon

---

[38] Abigail Adams to John Adams, 30 July 1777, *Founders Online*, National Archives, https://founders.archives.gov/documents/Adams/04-02-02-0235.

[39] Barbara Clark Smith, "Food Rioters and the American Revolution," *William and Mary Quarterly* 51:1 (1994), 3–38.

[40] Berkin, *Revolutionary Mothers*, 51; Holly A. Mayer, *Belonging to the Army: Camp Followers and Community during the American Revolution* (Columbia: University of South Carolina Press, 1996).

[41] Berkin, *Revolutionary Mothers*, 60.

discovering that she was a woman, the army granted Sampson an honorable discharge. After the war, Sampson married Benjamin Gannett, Jr. and had three children. Later in life, she went on a popular speaking tour to talk about her experience in the military. She petitioned Congress for a veteran's pension, which she received only after she secured the support of several Massachusetts congressmen and Paul Revere. Interestingly, in 1836, her husband Benjamin Gannett posthumously received a veteran's pension from Congress as a widower of the revolutionary war. He is the only man to ever have done so.[42]

At least one other woman successfully fought as a male soldier without detection during the revolution. Sally St. Clair disguised herself as a man and fought for the Patriots in Savannah, Georgia, but her true sex was not discovered until after she died in combat. Not all women who attempted to enlist as male soldiers were able to conceal their sex. At least two other women were jailed for attempting to join the army.[43] Women's motivations for enlisting in the military remain unclear. However, historians have suggested that it was some combination of patriotism, securing the hefty military bounty, and – for those who were married – their desire to stay with their husbands.

The war dramatically affected all American women. During these years, women demonstrated their capacity for courage, political reasoning, and loyalty. They stepped into roles they did not usually perform, and worked to establish their own freedom in the face of great danger. Collectively this helped to change American political culture and the way the Americans perceived women's "proper" role in society.

New Republican Government and Women's Citizenship

By the 1780s, Americans acknowledged white women's moral and intellectual capabilities, and rejected the idea that women were morally or mentally inferior to men. The spread of evangelical and Enlightenment ideas that stressed the importance of the individual and the politicization of the household economy before the revolution laid the foundation for this transformation. The war itself, however, provided concrete examples of women's

---

[42] Alfred F. Young, *Masquerade: The Life and Times of Deborah Sampson, Continental Soldier* (New York: Vintage, 2004).
[43] Berkin, *Revolutionary Mothers*, 60–1.

fortitude, piety, ethical judgment, and patriotism that cemented these notions firmly within early American politics and culture.[44] Moreover, although there were few tangible changes in women's legal status in the new republic, in the decades after the revolution, Americans understood women to be political beings who made political choices and exercised political judgment. In short, they recognized that women's thoughts and actions affected the country's economic and political culture in important ways that colonial Americans had not.[45]

After the colonies declared their independence from Britain, each of the new states devised a republican constitution. The idea of volitional allegiance was at the heart of the new legal code. Under a republican government, loyalty to the state was the voluntary act of individuals. Thus, citizens asserted that they had willingly chosen to give their allegiance to the United States. To make this choice, citizens – both male and female – were assumed to have some degree of free political will.[46] Particularly during the war years, it was not at all difficult for Americans to believe that women chose to give their allegiance to America or Britain, as they saw evidence of women's political judgments and allegiance in their daily lives. In general, men and women both deemed women to be citizens of the new republican state.

Although women considered themselves to be citizens and rights-bearing individuals, most women, regardless of their knowledge of currents events and political culture, did not imagine themselves as officeholders – or even as voters (although a small percentage of women did believe they should be able to vote). Instead, they believed their role as wives, mothers, and daughters was to influence men's political decisions and to offer sound moral judgment on such matters rather than to participate directly.[47] In the post-revolutionary era, Americans weighed the idea of equal rights for all

---

[44] Ibid., 151–2.
[45] Rosemarie Zagarri, "Women and Party Conflict in the Early Republic," in Jeffery Pasley, Andrew Robertson, and David Waldstreicher, eds., *Beyond the Founders: New Approaches to the Political History of the Early American Republic* (Chapel Hill: University of North Carolina Press, 2004), 109.
[46] James H. Kettner, *The Development of American Citizenship, 1608–1870* (Chapel Hill: University of North Carolina Press, 1978), 207, 269–74; Linda Kerber, *Women of the Republic: Intellect and Ideology in Revolutionary America* (Chapel Hill: University of North Carolina Press, 1980), 121; Joan R. Gundersen, "Independence, Citizenship, and the American Revolution," *Journal of Women in Culture and Society* 13:1 (1987), 59–77: 60–8; Joan Hoff, *Law, Gender, and Injustice: A Legal History of U.S. Women* (New York: New York University Press, 1991), 80.
[47] Rosemarie Zagarri, *Revolutionary Backlash: Women and Politics in the Early American Republic* (Philadelphia: University of Pennsylvania Press, 2007), 38–9; Berkin, *Revolutionary Mothers*, 158–9.

individuals in a republican state against their perceived need to maintain existing gender and racial hierarchies that subordinated women to men and Blacks to whites. For the sake of social order, many argued, wives ought to submit themselves to the rule of their husbands as men submitted themselves to the rule of law – contractually and with their consent. Most Americans believed that women willingly relinquished legal equality upon marriage to maintain social stability.

Writers, cultural commentators, and political leaders of the day drew on two different natural rights ideologies for men and women, one Lockean and the other Scottish. Scottish Enlightenment philosophy advanced that society was inherently unequal and hierarchical, but each individual occupied an important place in that order and carried rights and responsibilities for their station. Using these ideas, early Americans stressed women's duties and obligations to the state, rather than emphasizing ideas about liberty and choice that Lockean ideas conveyed to men. For women, moral obligation and the preservation of social harmony took precedence over the individual autonomy that men enjoyed. Thus, American women and men had separate and distinct rights, not equal rights.[48] In conjunction with newly solidified cultural ideals about women's moral authority and integrity, the notion of distinct rights for women reinforced the idea that their political role was to influence the men, rather than directly participating in politics as a voter or officeholder.

Another important transition in the relationship of men and women to the republican state was the creation of "independent" status for property-owning white men. Under British rule all women as well as men were considered to be dependants of the king. The framers of new state governments, however, created two different categories of citizenship: dependent and independent. Independence was based on property ownership.[49] In theory, property ownership (not gender) determined whether or not a citizen was entitled to full political participation as voters or officeholders. In practice, however, all married white women, whom the laws of coverture prevented from being property owners, automatically fell into the dependent category. This further bolstered the acceptance of different political obligations for female citizens. Despite the recognition of women's individual

---

[48] Rosemarie Zagarri, "The Rights of Man and Woman in Post-Revolutionary America," *William and Mary Quarterly* 55:2 (1998), 203–30.
[49] Hoff, *Law, Gender, and Injustice*, 80; Gundersen, "Independence, Citizenship, and the American Revolution," 60.

political agency during the war, all state legislatures adopted coverture into their new legal codes nearly unchanged and unchallenged.[50]

This left a gray area where unmarried property-owning women were concerned, who technically qualified as independent under republican state law. Although support for unmarried women's suffrage in revolutionary America was limited, it did exist. In 1778, propertied Virginia widow Hannah Corbin complained to her brother Richard Henry Lee that widows who met the property qualifications ought to be able to vote.[51] Despite Corbin's sentiments, by the 1780s, nearly all state laws explicitly stated that only free or white "male" property owners were eligible to vote.

There was one exception: New Jersey. The 1776 New Jersey state constitution stated that all "inhabitants" who met the property qualification could vote. The state's property-owning women (who were by default unmarried) utilized their right to vote in local, state, and federal elections until 1807. That women exercised their right to vote further advanced the belief that at least part of the female population hoped to participate in politics via suffrage. Upon hearing that women had voted in New Jersey, Abigail Adams wrote to her sister that she too would certainly exercise her right to vote if Massachusetts permitted it. The propriety of women's suffrage, however, became a contentious topic of debate. In 1791, after women's votes in Elizabeth, New Jersey, nearly cost a Democratic-Republican candidate the election, some people worried that women's suffrage had degraded the political process, masculinized women, and undermined male authority. By the early 1800s, newspapers began publishing frequent editorials in opposition to women voting. Eventually, in 1807 the New Jersey legislature passed a new law that disenfranchised women.[52]

Additionally, women continued to communicate directly with the government by petitioning state legislatures and Congress. Although some women had petitioned colonial governments, after the revolution women used petitions much more consistently to request economic relief or a change in the law. Women's petition requests commonly included debt relief or

---

[50] Marylynn Salmon, *Women and the Law of Property in Early America* (Chapel Hill: University of North Carolina Press, 1986), 14–15; Kerber, *Women of the Republic*, 119–36; Hoff, *Law, Gender, and Injustice*, 90; Gundersen, "Independence, Citizenship, and the American Revolution," 68; Kierner, *Beyond the Household*, 197–8.

[51] Richard Henry Lee to Hannah Lee Corbin, 17 March 1778, in James Curtis Ballagh, ed., *The Letters of Richard Henry Lee*, vol. 1 (New York: Macmillan, 1911), 392–3.

[52] Zagarri, *Revolutionary Backlash*, 30–6.

recovery, military pensions, separate estates, and property and inheritance disputes.[53]

Increasingly, the idea that a woman's political role in the new republic ought to consist of influencing her husband, brothers, sons, and fathers overshadowed any lingering ideas about women's direct participation in government. The combination of recognizing white women's moral authority, distinct political obligations, and intellectual abilities led to an important shift in women's familial and political position as educators. Americans believed that the success of a republic – where people formed the reservoir of power – depended upon the moral rectitude, education, and patriotism of its citizens who could resist demagogues and corruption. In the new nation, white women took on the important role of cultivating virtuous, morally upright citizens.

This new civic role for women elevated the importance of motherhood to new heights. At the same time, however, it diminished women's roles in the public sphere and removed them from the possibility of direct political participation, leaving single and childless women with seemingly no political connection to the state at all.[54] Moreover, the ideal of "republican motherhood" was not attainable for all women. Poor white women who could not afford to stay at home and educate their children took to peddling goods, and worked as maids, servants, and laundresses to help support themselves and their families.

Greater access to education was one of the ways that women's lives changed the most after the American Revolution. As republican mothers rearing the next generation of citizens, it was essential for women to be well-educated. In 1787, John Poor opened the Philadelphia Young Ladies' Academy and across the nation Americans established many other ladies' academies to train young women in government, moral philosophy, and political theory. The course of study in many places was the same as the boys' curriculum and included history, geography, mathematics, composition, and rhetoric in addition to government.

---

[53] Cynthia Kierner, *Southern Women in Revolution, 1776–1800* (Columbia: University of South Carolina Press, 1998), 231–2.

[54] See Mary Beth Norton, "The Evolution of White Women's Experience in Early America," *American Historical Review* 89:3 (1984), 593–619; Mary Beth Norton, *Liberty's Daughters: The Revolutionary Experience of American Women, 1750–1800* (Ithaca, NY: Cornell University Press, 1980); Kerber, *Women of the Republic*; Ruth H. Bloch, "The Gendered Meanings of Virtue," *Signs* 13:1 (1987), 37–58; Gundersen, *To Be Useful to the World*; Kierner, *Beyond the Household*.

Although some critics warned that women's education would create "masculine" women who were unattractive in their appearance and would neglect their household duties, the majority of Americans agreed that women's education was crucial to republican government.[55] Intellectual Judith Sargent Murray of Massachusetts was a vocal advocate for women's equality and championed women's education as a key component in the success of the nation. Having faced substantial financial difficulties after the death of her first husband, Murray argued that women needed education in order to support their families or themselves if unmarried.[56]

As the market economy in the United States began to take shape, new possibilities for women's investments also developed. Elite women with financial resources invested money in bonds, stocks, and securities to generate additional income. In particular, women across the country purchased stock in insurance companies and invested in joint-stock ventures and transportation companies. Between 1790 and 1812, the highest rate of women's investment in stock and bank bonds occurred in Maryland, Pennsylvania, Massachusetts, and New York. Between 1812 and 1822, 25 percent of stockowners in the Philadelphia bank were women.[57]

A large portion of the women who made these types of investment were unmarried young women or widows. But married women like Abigail Adams, who managed her family's finances and investments while her husband John was away, made savvy economic decisions about where to invest the couple's money. Abigail favored investment in federal bonds rather than land. She insisted that bonds were "much more productive" than investment in land. She set aside money that she had earned via her investments and called it "my own pocket money" or the "money which I call mine," although under coverture her husband legally owned it all and could withdraw it from her at any time. After the war, women also continued to manage farms and plantations, and to own businesses. In 1790, over 25 percent of female heads of households ran boarding houses, inns, shops, and other businesses.[58]

---

[55] Berkin, *Revolutionary Mothers*, 153–5.
[56] Sheila L. Skemp, *First Lady of Letters: Judith Sargent Murray and the Struggle for Female Independence* (Philadelphia: University of Pennsylvania Press, 2013).
[57] Robert E. Wright, *Hamilton Unbound: Finance and the Creation of the American Republic* (Westport, CT: Greenwood Press, 2002), 174, 180–4.
[58] Woody Holton, "Abigail Adams, Bond Speculator," *William and Mary Quarterly* 64:4 (2007), 821–38: 827, 829. Also see Woody Holton, *Abigail Adams: A Life* (New York: Free Press, 2009); Francis White, *The Philadelphia City Directory* (Philadelphia: Young,

White Women and Partisan Politics

Women remained interested in and knowledgeable about political events and debates in the new republic, sometimes claiming partisan political identities. After attending the debates over the ratification of the constitution in Virginia, Alexander White reported on women's attendance to his mother-in-law: "We have a gay circle of Ladies to hear the debates and have the pleasure of believing them all Federalists."[59] The persistence of party conflict provided a new context for understanding women's role in political culture. Political partisans believed women's approbation helped to broaden their party's appeal and widen popular support. Women's methods for political expression, though, were in keeping with their wartime activities. During the 1792 election cycle, women wore tricolored cockades for the Republicans and black badges for Federalists, and sixteen young women in white dresses participated in a Republican Party parade, processing behind men while playing musical instruments. In private letters women argued over the Jay Treaty, Jefferson's election in 1800, and the 1807 Embargo.[60] Although the moral sanctioning of partisan activities by women carved out a political role for them in the new nation, at the same time it enhanced the idea that women inhabited a moral sphere that was different from the rough and tumble world of men. Increasingly, this put women in a position outside politics as peacemakers and moral counterweights to men's overheated political arguing.[61]

Similarly, some women hosted American-style "salons" in private homes in Philadelphia and Washington to discuss events and politics with other women and sometimes men. Whereas men gathered in coffeehouses, taverns, and other public spaces to discuss political affairs, elite women created spaces in their homes where they could informally engage in politics. Unlike French or English salons that rejected political discussion in favor of literature and other intellectual pursuits, American salons gathered explicitly for the purpose of developing women's political ideas and networks. The women who participated in these discussions ultimately sought to influence male officeholders and voters. This new framework valorized women's

---

Stewart & McCulloch, 1785); Clement Biddle, *The Philadelphia City Directory* (Philadelphia: James & Johnson, 1791).
[59] Alexander White to Mary Wood, 10–11 June 1788, in John P. Kaminski et al., *Documentary History of the Ratification of the Constitution*, vol. x: *Virginia* (Madison: Wisconsin Historical Society Press, 1993), 1591–2.
[60] Zagarri, "Women and Party Conflict in the Early Republic," 110–18.
[61] Zagarri, "Women and Party Conflict in the Early Republic," 117–19.

moral influence on men and helped to lay the groundwork for the division between a masculine public sphere and a feminine private one that would become a way of life in the nineteenth century.[62]

Legacy of the Revolution for Women

Slowly over the course of the early republic, Americans began to redefine white women's perceived capacity for political thought and participation. In 1805, the Massachusetts Supreme Court case *Martin v. Massachusetts* captured the contours of the debate over women's citizenship in the new nation. In the case, plaintiff James Martin sued the Commonwealth of Massachusetts to reclaim property that Patriot officials had confiscated from his Loyalist parents during the revolution after they fled the United States and resettled in England. His mother, Anna Martin, had originally brought the property into their marriage and she bequeathed it to her son after her husband's death. At issue was whether or not – as a married woman – Anna Martin had willingly left Massachusetts with her husband during the war, or if she had no other choice but to follow her husband to England and leave the property behind.[63]

Attorneys for James Martin argued that Anna could not have said no to her husband. As a woman under coverture she had no choice but to abandon the land to confiscation because married women were not capable of choosing a separate political allegiance for themselves. Furthermore, they argued, Anna could never have been a citizen of Massachusetts because married women had no "political relation to the state more than an alien."[64] The Commonwealth's attorneys fervently countered the plaintiff's claims and asserted that all women were citizens of the state and entitled to the rights that citizenship conveyed. They maintained that Anna, politicized by the revolution, competently made the choice to give her political loyalty to Britain. Consequently, they claimed, her land was subject to the state's Loyalist confiscation law. Stunningly, the court ruled in favor of James Martin, stating that as a married woman Anna had no political will of her

---

[62] Susan Branson, *These Fiery Frenchified Dames: Women and Political Culture in Early National Philadelphia* (Philadelphia: University of Pennsylvania Press, 2001); Catherine Allgor, *Parlor Politics: In Which the Ladies of Washington Help Build a City and Government* (Charlottesville: University of Virginia Press, 2000); Kierner, *Beyond the Household*, 26.

[63] Linda K. Kerber, "The Paradox of Women's Citizenship in the Early Republic: The Case of Martin vs. Massachusetts, 1805," *American Historical Review* 97:2 (1992), 349–78.

[64] Attorney James Blake, as quoted in Kerber, "The Paradox of Women's Citizenship," 369.

own. When she left American soil, the justices stated, she was under the total control and direction of her husband and therefore was incapable of being disloyal to the state.[65]

The ruling *Martin v. Massachusetts* marks a turning point in American opinions about the political capacity of women. Beginning in the 1760s, white women's political activism and agency grew and developed as a result of Enlightenment theory, religious revival, and the politicization of the household economy. Revolutionary fervor created new political spaces for women as they engaged in political protests and boycotts. The circumstances of the war further refined Americans' perceptions of women's fortitude, political allegiance, piety, and self-direction during the war. Collectively these factors combined to create a new foundation for white women's participation in republican political culture as the guardians of moral and political virtue. These new notions of women's political connection to the state through moral authority and motherhood, however, created increasingly separate political spaces for women and men.

Despite the development of women's political agency during the revolution, by the early 1800s many Americans began to look to the patriarchal family to restore order and social authority. Men abandoned the idea that women could be competent political actors and instead promoted a specifically masculine ideal of citizenship. State legislators and jurists began to reflect on the legal system that their father's generation had created in the throes of war and they revised their ideas about women's citizenship, inheritance, and allegiance to the state. This refashioning slowly chipped away at any possible claims women had to economic independence or direct political participation. Women's biology, they argued, made them inadequate for governing. By the 1820s, women's duties as wives and mothers alone mediated their political connection to the state, while the characteristics of the ideal American citizen became inherently white and male.[66]

---

[65] Kerber, "The Paradox of Women's Citizenship," 355–78.
[66] Kierner, *Beyond the Household*, 102–3; Hoff, *Law, Gender, and Injustice*, 80–1; Zagarri, *Revolutionary Backlash*, 165–70, 176; Kerber, "History Can Do It No Justice"; Bloch, "The Gendered Meanings of Virtue," 46, 53–8; Gundersen, "Independence, Citizenship, and the American Revolution," 59–77.

15
Blacks in the British Colonies

JAMES SIDBURY

Sometime in 1760 or 1761 a young man was enslaved in West Africa and sold into the Atlantic. On arriving in northern Virginia, he was purchased by a man named Daniel Tebbs. In 1763, George Washington, having just returned to Mt. Vernon from the Seven Years' War with a newly won reputation for military leadership, bought the young man from the estate of Tebbs. At some point during the ensuing two decades the enslaved man stopped going by his now lost birth name and became Harry Washington.

The new name – at least the new surname – probably was not claimed immediately. The future first president purchased Harry to partially fulfill the labor draft he owed as an investor in the Dismal Swamp Company, which sought to drain the enormous wetland on the border of Virginia and North Carolina and turn it into valuable farm land. Within a few years George had reclaimed Harry from the company and put him to work in the house and stables at Mt. Vernon. Harry Washington ran away at least once prior to the American Revolution, and then escaped Mt. Vernon for good in July 1776 when he ran to a British ship cruising the Potomac. He went to New York City, where he joined the force sent to occupy South Carolina in 1780. There he served as an officer with the Black Pioneers. He returned to New York City with the British Army when it withdrew from Charleston, and he was evacuated to Nova Scotia with 3,000 other Black Loyalists in 1783. Despite becoming a landowner in Nova Scotia, he grew dissatisfied and moved to Sierra Leone as one of the founding settlers of Britain's West African colony.[1]

Harry Washington's life offers a vivid personification of different ways to understand the place of African and African-descended people in the

---

[1] Cassandra Pybus, "Washington's Revolution (Harry That Is, not George)," *Atlantic Studies* 3 (2006), 183–99; Douglas R. Egerton, *Death or Liberty: African Americans and Revolutionary America* (New York: Oxford University Press, 2009), 194–221.

revolutionary movements that roiled the English-speaking Atlantic from 1775 to 1838. Atlantic revolutions challenged monarchy and some other forms of inherited privilege, and in doing so they helped to stimulate the first politically effective challenges to the racial slavery that had built American empires and continued to enrich many Europeans. Many scholars focus on the failures of the Atlantic revolutionary movement, seen as a whole, to challenge inherited racial privilege. That a black man who had been owned by and claimed the surname of the father of the new American republic fought with the British for his liberty while his master was fighting for that of the new nation underscores both the promise of revolutionary change in the eighteenth-century Atlantic and one of the tragic ways that revolutionary change fell short. Harry Washington continued struggling for freedom and equality for as long as he appears in the documentary record. He won important battles, escaping slavery at Mt. Vernon, and then acquiring property and the material trappings of personal independence in both Nova Scotia and Freetown. But notwithstanding those victories, the pernicious power of white racism undermined his efforts to live the life he envisioned. In short, Harry Washington's life can be seen to embody both the promise and the failures of the Age of Revolutions.

His story also offers an entry point to a different, complementary narrative about Blacks in the English-speaking world during the Age of Revolutions, one that is equally present in his biography. The barriers and openings created for Harry Washington (and by extension for Africans and African Americans in British America) by Atlantic revolutions and his responses are important, but too narrow a focus on them comes at a cost. By foregrounding white racism and progressive white-dominated political movements that sought to counter some of the effects of that racism, enslaved and free Black people can be too easily reduced to victims of the forces arrayed against them. Washington's story illustrates that Blacks, while victimized, were much more than passive victims. His struggles to escape slavery, to fight against those who had enslaved him, and then to continue to fight against his erstwhile allies for his own vision of true equality in Sierra Leone underscore the efforts of Africans and people of African descent to define the parameters of liberty in the Age of Revolutions. Both of these stories are important.

Before the Revolutions

To explore how African and African-descended people responded to the Age of Revolutions requires a bit of background. The eighteenth century witnessed a massive expansion of slavery in British America. In 1700, Barbados and four other small islands in the Lesser Antilles were well-established slave societies, home to overwhelming black and enslaved majorities forced to labor in sugar cane plantations. Maryland and Virginia were just completing long and gradual transitions from their reliance on bound labor forces that combined indentured Englishmen and enslaved Africans to bound labor forces that were overwhelmingly black and enslaved, though neither tobacco colony's population as a whole would ever approach a black and enslaved majority. Enslaved people played important roles in England's other American colonies, and most of their economies were increasingly reliant on trade with Britain's plantation colonies, but the institution of slavery did not dominate them. By mid-century things looked different, largely because of developments in Jamaica and the Carolina Lowcountry. England's colonies in the Chesapeake and the Lesser Antilles had cemented their status as slave societies, though they had followed different paths. Natural reproduction fueled the explosive growth of slavery in the Chesapeake, while the Caribbean islands relied on steady importations of enslaved Africans to maintain their bound labor forces. The steady supply of African captives that these islands needed was secured through British merchants' increasing domination of the Atlantic slave trade.[2]

That domination also contributed to the emergence of the two new slave societies that reshaped British America. Jamaica got off to a hesitant start when England conquered it as part of Cromwell's "Western Design," but when it turned to sugar in the late seventeenth century, it did so with a vengeance. By the 1720s it had surpassed Barbados to become Britain's biggest sugar producer; by the 1750s, it began equaling and then surpassing the total sugar production of Barbados and all of Britain's Lesser Antillean islands combined. Jamaica achieved this remarkable growth on the ravaged backs of enslaved Africans. On the mainland, something analogous occurred in South Carolina. Following the discovery that rice could serve as a staple crop for the Lowcountry, white Carolinians began enthusiastically purchasing African captives and forcing them to grow rice in malarial swamps. By

---

[2] Richard Dunn, *Sugar and Slaves: The Rise of the Planter Class in the English West Indies, 1624–1713* (Chapel Hill: University of North Carolina Press, 1972); Ira Berlin, *Many Thousands Gone: The First Two Centuries of Slavery in North America* (Cambridge, MA: Harvard University Press, 1998), 109–76; Edward B. Rugemer, *Slave Law and the Politics of Resistance in the Early Atlantic World* (Cambridge, MA: Harvard University Press, 2018), 11–34, 75–170; David Eltis and David Richardson, *Atlas of the Transatlantic Slave Trade* (New Haven: Yale University Press, 2010), 21–36 (esp. tables 13 and 14 on 26–7 and table 18 on 32).

1710, South Carolina had a black majority, and it continued to develop into the British North American society that was most dependent upon and committed to chattel slavery. Kingston and Charles Town became key points of entry for British slavers, and a steady flow of captive Africans was forced onto Carolinian and Jamaican plantations throughout the first decades of the eighteenth century. Georgia would follow South Carolina's lead during the second half of the century. With two solid anchors – one in North America and one in the Caribbean – African slavery became increasingly central to Britain's American colonies.[3]

As English colonists increased their investment in enslaved workers, they began forcing them to work more intensely. In the Caribbean this entailed efforts to organize gang labor and the supervisory staff overseeing it, to standardize accounting practices, and to diversify agricultural production into subsistence and secondary cash crops to ensure that the enslaved were forced to work during rare slack periods in sugar's agricultural calendar. In the Lowcountry, rice planters made slaves build dams and sluices in order to claim as much land as possible for rice production, and they turned to indigo as a second staple whose land and labor needs dovetailed conveniently with those of rice. Like their counterparts to the south, Chesapeake planters also forced more labor from the enslaved, developing new crops and diversifying in other ways, while refining accounting practices in order to organize enslaved labor more efficiently. The process of diversification was more complicated than this brief account suggests: Lorena Walsh has traced myriad regional variations in the Chesapeake, and Justin Roberts has shown that different strategies were followed in Jamaica and the Lesser Antilles. But regional variations aside, the big story is the same. Across British plantation America the eighteenth century was a time when slaveowners developed new managerial techniques to increase the productivity of their enslaved labor forces. Violent coercion based on physical brutality formed the foundation of those managerial innovations. During the decades that preceded the American Revolution, chattel slavery expanded geographically, economically, and culturally within British America, and enslaved Africans and people of African descent bore much of the brunt of Britain's rise to supremacy within the Atlantic world.[4]

---

[3] Rugemer, *Slave Law and the Politics of Resistance*, 75–170; David Eltis, "New Estimates of Exports from Barbados and Jamaica, 1665–1701," *William and Mary Quarterly* 52 (1995), 631–48.

[4] Philip D. Morgan, *Slave Counterpoint: Black Culture in the Eighteenth-Century Chesapeake and Lowcountry* (Chapel Hill: University of North Carolina Press, 1998), 179–87; S. Max

The enslaved fought against masters' efforts to force them to work longer and harder. Throughout the Americas that struggle involved day-to-day battles over the terms of labor. Historians have documented the strategies that the enslaved used – from feigning illness to sabotaging equipment to the ever-present threat of running away. These efforts surely hindered masters' efforts to extract more labor from slaves' bodies, but the enslaved could not halt, much less reverse, the trend toward greater productivity. Masters' use of the whip and other even more brutal forms of corporal punishment, which they combined with different kinds of positive incentives, produced many of the results they sought. On a few occasions the persistent low-level conflict escalated into open rebellion. Needless to say, rebellions were forbiddingly difficult to organize and forbiddingly dangerous to execute. But the violence and degradation visited upon the enslaved made them an ever-present threat and an occasional reality.[5]

Two bloody rebellions that occurred in British America in the decades before the Thirteen Colonies initiated the Age of Atlantic Revolutions ensured that the threat posed by slave resistance remained present for Anglo-Americans. On 9 September 1739, approximately sixty men, most probably recent arrivals from Angola, rose up along the Stono River outside Charles Town. They killed about twenty white Carolinians before marching toward promised sanctuary in Spanish St. Augustine. The Stono Rebellion was small by comparison with slave uprisings in the Caribbean and Brazil, but it forced white Carolinians to confront the threat posed by a slave majority. South Carolina virtually halted slave importations for more than a decade and sought to implement new controls on the enslaved. Twenty years later a much larger uprising threatened to wipe out the plantation regime of Jamaica. In 1760, in the midst of the Seven Years' War, more than 1,000 enslaved Jamaicans – probably many more than 1,000 – rose up and attacked their masters over the course of roughly 12 months. Regional uprisings encompassed both the eastern and western halves of the island and killed approximately sixty white Jamaicans. White Jamaicans responded

---

Edelson, *Plantation Enterprise in Colonial South Carolina* (Cambridge, MA: Harvard University Press, 2006), 92–125; Lorena S. Walsh, *Motives of Honor, Pleasure, and Profit: Plantation Management in the Colonial Chesapeake, 1607–1763* (Chapel Hill: University of North Carolina Press, 2010), 394–623; Justin Roberts, *Slavery and the Enlightenment in the British Atlantic, 1750–1807* (Cambridge: Cambridge University Press, 2013), 26–237.

[5] Morgan, *Slave Counterpoint*, esp. 1–23, 146–203, 300–437, 463–76; Berlin, *Many Thousands Gone*, 109–76; Trevor Burnard and John Garrigus, *The Plantation Machine: Atlantic Capitalism in French Saint-Domingue and British Jamaica* (Philadelphia: University of Pennsylvania Press, 2016), 101–36.

by doubling down on their militarized strategies for controlling the enslaved majority. Tacky's Revolt, as this linked series of uprisings came to be called, dwarfed the Stono Rebellion in size, but both events reminded Anglo-Americans that the enslaved did not willingly continue to labor on plantations for the benefit of others. The striking expansion of slavery throughout British America and the commitment of the enslaved to resist set the stage for Blacks' engagement with revolutionary upheaval during the Age of Atlantic Revolutions.[6]

From Dunmore in Virginia to Dessalines in Gonaïves

On 7 November 1775, John Murray, the Earl of Dunmore and the Royal Governor of Virginia responded to white Virginians' growing resistance to royal authority by proclaiming martial law and declaring "all indentured Servants, Negroes, and others, (appertaining to Rebels,) free" if they would "join his MAJESTY'S Troops" in "reducing this Colony to a proper Sense of their Duty, to his MAJESTY'S Crown and Dignity."[7] Dunmore's Proclamation did not appear out of thin air. For much of the decade of contention that followed the passage of the Stamp Act, Blacks had been discussing the possible implications of a conflict between their colonial masters, on the one hand, and the royal government, on the other. They had speculated that the king might in fact side with the enslaved against those who were defying royal authority, sometimes suggesting that his willingness to do so lay at the heart of their masters' desire for independence. These discussions fit into a century-old pattern of enslaved people throughout the Atlantic suggesting that European monarchs favored emancipation.[8] Dunmore's Proclamation was, however, more than a rumor. It gave official form to what had previously been unsubstantiated talk, and in doing so it helped to bring to the fore a tension that persisted throughout much of the Age of Revolutions. White Virginians quickly defeated Dunmore and his

---

[6] Vincent Brown, *Tacky's Revolt: The Story of an Atlantic Slave War* (Cambridge, MA: Harvard University Press, 2020); Peter Wood, *Black Majority: Negroes in Colonial South Carolina from 1670 through the Stono Rebellion* (New York: Norton, 1974), 308–26; John K. Thornton, "African Dimensions of the Stono Rebellion," *American Historical Review* 96 (1991), 1101–13.

[7] See www.encyclopediavirginia.org/Lord_Dunmore_s_Proclamation_1775.

[8] Wim Klooster, "Slave Revolts, Royal Justice, and a Ubiquitous Rumor in the Age of Revolutions," *William and Mary Quarterly* 71 (2014), 401–24.

"Ethiopian Regiment," but British raiders on the Chesapeake and elsewhere continued to offer freedom to enslaved Virginians willing to fight against white masters who professed to support human liberty. Harry Washington escaped from Mt. Vernon with the help of some of those raiders.

Between Dunmore's Proclamation in 1775 and a very different proclamation – the Haitian Declaration of Independence that Jean-Jacques Dessalines issued in the city of Gonaïves in 1804 – Blacks throughout Anglophone America negotiated a confusing and rapidly changing reality. From 1775 to 1783, Blacks living in the Thirteen Colonies faced the disruptions of war and the halting, occasional and inconsistent efforts of the two warring sides to win their allegiance. During the years immediately following the Treaty of Paris, Black Americans tried in various ways to hold the new nation to its professed creed of human equality.

The revolutionary war offered Blacks in North America many potential opportunities, but none that were reliable, so it is unsurprising that different people living in different places pursued different strategies. Mapping those strategies sheds light on what the ambiguities of the Age of Revolutions meant for enslaved and free Blacks living in the new republic. Most of the leaders of the struggle for American independence would have preferred to have ignored questions of Black freedom and to have left Black people on the side-lines, but Dunmore's Proclamation eliminated any chance of that happening. In its wake, and in the wake of analogous decisions on the ground by different British military commanders, approximately 20,000 enslaved Black people ran to British armies over the course of the war. The willingness of so many to risk brutal punishment for the uncertain possibilities represented by vague promises of freedom from the world's greatest slaving power is impressive, and it undoubtedly created anxiety on the part of American slaveholders. The chief significance of slaves who ran to the British does not, however, lie in the direct threat their resistance posed to American slavery. The 10,000 Black Virginians who escaped bondage over the course of the war comprised barely 5 percent of those held in bondage in the Commonwealth at the beginning of the revolution. By the time of the first Federal Census – less than a decade after the signing of the Treaty of Paris, the total number of enslaved people in the state had not simply recovered, it had grown by more than 100,000. This happened despite the fact that Virginia prohibited the Atlantic trade during those years. The story varied from state to state and from locality to locality – the opportunity to escape to British armies was not evenly distributed across North America. But local and regional variations aside, escaping to the British did not fundamentally undermine the institution of slavery anywhere in the fledgling nation.[9]

The opportunity to run to the British did, however, create an almost unprecedented opportunity for some slave communities. It is a commonplace in the scholarly literature that the normative runaway was an individual young man. That was true for many reasons, including the fact that it was easier for a single Black person to pass unnoticed when traveling than for a group and that women found it more difficult to travel unnoticed than men. Those who ran to the British during the war did not fit this pattern. Historian Cassandra Pybus' analysis of Black Virginians who ran to the British "points to a series of premeditated and well-organized escapes by interconnected family groups."[10] Others ran with friends – Harry Washington was accompanied by two other members of the Mt. Vernon slave community. The presence of British armies on American soil during the American Revolution – or of ships raiding coastal communities – created a chance for Black communities to escape from slavery together and thus to shed the shackles of slavery without having to give up the communal ties that made their lives under slavery bearable. This was an opportunity that would be replicated in Virginia during the war of 1812 and throughout the South during the Civil War, and in each case, tracing those who escaped in groups offers an unusual and rich picture of the communal aspirations of the enslaved.[11] The American Revolution did not offer a large percentage of enslaved Blacks the chance to pursue these aspirations, but it created conditions in which roughly 20,000 people of African descent were able to do so, of whom roughly 8,000–10,000 succeeded in leaving the United States, many of them with kin and neighbors, to live the rest of their lives as free people.

Black allegiance to the British crown can be partially explained in straightforward practical terms tied to this unusual opportunity, terms which become clear when compared with what Patriot forces offered to the

---

[9] Sylvia Frey, *Water from the Rock: Black Resistance in a Revolutionary Age* (Princeton: Princeton University Press, 1991); Benjamin Quarles, *The Negro in the American Revolution* (Chapel Hill: University of North Carolina Press, 1961).

[10] Cassandra Pybus, "Jefferson's Faulty Math: The Question of Slave Defections in the American Revolution," *William and Mary Quarterly* 62 (2005), 243–64 (quotation on 252). For a graphic visualization of one of these interconnected family groups, see www.blackloyalist.info/person/display/1513.

[11] James Sidbury, *Ploughshares into Swords: Race, Rebellion, and Identity in Gabriel's Virginia, 1730–1810* (Cambridge: Cambridge University Press, 1997), 26–7, 32–3; Alan Taylor, *The Internal Enemy: Slavery and War in Virginia, 1772–1832* (New York: Norton, 2013), 245–74.

enslaved during the war. Much attention has been lavished on the proposal of John Laurens, son of Charleston's leading slave trader, to offer emancipation to enslaved Carolinians in order to recruit them to meet South Carolina's quota in the Continental Army. But the proposal went nowhere, and though Henry Laurens gestured in support of his beloved son's emancipation plan, he showed his true colors after joining the American delegation just as it was completing the negotiation of the Treaty of Paris. Arriving at the last minute, he managed to insert a clause prohibiting British commanders from "carrying away any Negroes ... of the American inhabitants" when they withdrew from their final posts in the newly-independent nation.[12] Of the thirteen original states in the American union, only Rhode Island offered anything approximating John Laurens' plan. Two regiments of enslaved Rhode Island men were enlisted with the promise that those who survived would receive freedom after the war. But even in this case, members of the Rhode Island regiments expected to return home to find their wives and children still in bondage. Some argue that the skill and valor of these Black Rhode Island soldiers helped to turn George Washington against slavery and thus partially explain his decision to manumit his slaves upon his death, so their significance should not be discounted. But they stand as a stark exception to the ways the rest of the new states handled the possibility of enlisting enslaved soldiers, and thus their experience highlights the appeal that the crown's greater openness to offering freedom for service had for Blacks in North America.

Free Blacks living north of the plantation belt, where slavery existed but was economically marginal, engaged actively with the apparent promise of equality in the ideology that fueled the independence movement. Crispus Attucks famously joined the Boston toughs harassing British troops quartered in the city and was killed in the Boston Massacre. Prince Hall, who later founded the African Masonic movement in the United States, joined the Continental Army and encouraged other Blacks to follow suit. Phillis Wheatley of Massachusetts, America's first famous Black poet, wrote an ode to "His Excellency General George Washington." Free Black engagement with the independence movement would transition first into a struggle for the end of slavery and then for greater equality during the era of the Early Republic.[13]

---

[12] See www.ourdocuments.gov/doc.php?flash=true&doc=6&page=transcript.
[13] Manisha Sinha, *The Slave's Cause: A History of Abolition* (New Haven: Yale University Press, 2017), 34–96.

Figure 15.1 Four Continental Army soldiers at the siege of Yorktown, 1781. The soldier on the left served in the First Rhode Island Regiment. Watercolor by French soldier Jean Baptiste Antoine de Verger. Alamy.

The African-descended people who won freedom by fighting with the British during the revolution scattered in different directions as free people after the war. The two largest groups, comprising a majority of the total, went either to Great Britain or, like Harry Washington, to Nova Scotia. Members of both groups struggled to build economically secure lives as free people in the face of structural inequality and white racism. Almost 500 of the "Black poor" from London and well over 1,000 of the Black Loyalists who originally settled in Nova Scotia became disillusioned with their new homes and set out as pioneering settlers of Sierra Leone, Great Britain's West African settler colony. Harry Washington was one of them. A much smaller number of Black Loyalists went to the Caribbean, where they founded the first Baptist churches in both the Bahamas and Jamaica, exerting a cultural influence that greatly exceeded their numerical importance. The formerly enslaved people who fled American masters to support the British war effort did not find easy lives or escape the stifling racism present throughout the Anglophone world. Harry Washington disappears from the record after being banished from Freetown following an 1800 settler rebellion against company rule in Freetown. But the Black Loyalists did escape slavery, and many, like Washington, spent the rest of their lives fighting for the respect and levels of equality that the American republic denied most Black people.[14]

The American Revolutionary War played out very differently for African and African-descended people living in the British West Indies. Historian Andrew O'Shaughnessy discerns an uptick in relatively small-scale incidents of collective resistance during the decade preceding the Declaration of Independence and he sees murky ties linking those incidents to increasing divisions within Britain's empire. A major slave conspiracy developed in Hanover Parish, on the northwest corner of Jamaica in 1776, and though some white Jamaicans warned that the conspirators had taken inspiration from natural rights arguments circulating among their masters, the trial depositions point to a different connection to the revolution. Enslaved conspirators planned the uprising to coincide with the scheduled redeployment of British troops from the island to the rebellious mainland. The revolution did not inspire the Hanover plotters, but it did create conditions they thought favorable to their plans. The plot was discovered before it was put into execution, and notwithstanding a great deal of planter anxiety – or perhaps because of heightened surveillance associated with that anxiety – the Hanover Parish Conspiracy was not followed by other uprisings during the revolutionary war.[15]

Instead, the revolutionary war years were a starving time for Black people living in the British Caribbean. The sugar islands had grown dependent on foodstuffs from the mainland – that demand had helped to fuel economic development throughout Anglo-America – so when Parliament cut off trade with the rebellious provinces in 1775, it initiated a period of horrific suffering among Blacks on the islands. Without access to North American grain and fish that masters had purchased to feed the enslaved, the price of foodstuffs throughout the Caribbean skyrocketed. Starvation followed among enslaved populations that were already overworked and underfed. Man-made hardships were exacerbated by a series of natural disasters, including six major hurricanes between 1780 and 1786. The break in trade hit the small islands of the Lesser Antilles the hardest, because they were most committed to sugar

[14] Maya Jasanoff, *Liberty's Exiles: American Loyalists in the Revolutionary World* (New York: Random House, 2011), 48–52, 173–5, 229–32, 265–309; Pybus, "Washington's Revolution"; James Sidbury, *Becoming African in America: Race and Nation in the Early Black Atlantic* (New York: Oxford University Press, 2007), 91–156.

[15] Andrew Jackson O'Shaughnessy, *An Empire Divided: The American Revolution and the British Caribbean* (Philadelphia: University of Pennsylvania Press, 2000), 146–54; Richard B. Sheridan, "The Jamaican Slave Insurrection Scare of 1776 and the American Revolution," *Journal of Negro History* 61 (1976), 290–308.

monoculture and thus most reliant on imported food, but Jamaica suffered most from the hurricanes. It is impossible to make a meaningful allocation of the degree to which the trade embargo that resulted from the American Revolution as compared with the damage done by storms exacerbated the already endemic subsistence crisis that afflicted Blacks in the Caribbean, but scholars estimate that roughly 15,000 enslaved people living in the British Caribbean died of starvation or of diseases associated with malnutrition between 1776 and 1786. It was, however, the war-related break in the Atlantic slave trade which kept white West Indians from replacing those who died with newly purchased Africans. This affected sugar production, which made it worthy of white planters' attention. Otherwise, the hardships of the 1770s and 1780s might have been difficult to distinguish from the demographic disaster that was the norm on sugar islands. Nonetheless, those who survived the disruptions associated with war and hurricanes must have suffered terribly.[16] The years of the American Revolution were, in short, a starving time for Blacks in the British Caribbean, and things remained difficult for several years following the Treaty of Paris.

Blacks living in different sections of the new United States faced quite diverse circumstances during the first decades following independence. Those living north of the Mason–Dixon Line engaged with the implicit promises of a government founded on natural rights, and they helped to win victories that put the North on the road to emancipation. A remarkable generation of African American men assumed leadership positions in Black communities stretching up the Atlantic seaboard from Philadelphia to Boston and allied with white antislavery activists to push their states to outlaw slavery. Black freedom came gradually to the North, beginning with the partially effective prohibition of slavery in Vermont's 1777 constitution and the landmark passage of Pennsylvania's gradual emancipation act in 1780 – the first legislatively enacted abolition Act in the Americas. By 1804, all northern states had either declared slavery illegal or passed free womb laws that guaranteed freedom to any child born to an enslaved mother. Such children remained bound to their mothers' owners for terms that ranged from eighteen to twenty-five years.

Post-nati laws, as they are sometimes called, worked more quickly than originally intended for two reasons. They first benefited enslaved

---

[16] Richard B. Sheridan, "The Crisis of Slave Subsistence in the British West Indies during and after the American Revolution," *William and Mary Quarterly* 3rd series, 33 (1976), 615–41; Trevor Burnard, *Jamaica in the Age of Revolution* (Philadelphia: University of Pennsylvania Press, 2020), 206. I thank Trevor Burnard for allowing me to read and cite his manuscript prior to publication.

northerners. Once the laws passed, and slavery was perceived to be on the wane, it became more difficult for masters to force the enslaved to continue working. Masters frequently struck deals in which they granted freedom sooner than the law mandated if the person bound to labor agreed not to run away for a specified number of years. As a result, slavery began to die out more quickly than anticipated in much of the North. The arrival of emancipation laws was not, however, an unalloyed boon for enslaved northerners. Gradual emancipation laws created loopholes through which unscrupulous northern slaveowners sold people who were due to gain their freedom into perpetual bondage in states to the south. Because such sales were illegal, they are difficult to track, but scholars have shown that they were depressingly common.

The decades following the American Revolution transformed the slave-owning societies north of the Mason–Dixon Line into free societies, but they did so with more ambiguous effects on Black northerners than might be apparent. On the one hand, slavery died a more rapid death than the operation of gradual emancipation laws would have indicated. Vibrant free Black communities emerged in the urban North – in Philadelphia, New York City, and Boston, but also in smaller urban centers like Albany, Hartford, New Haven, New London, Newport, Pittsburgh, and Providence. Like other contemporary Americans, Black northerners engaged in a flurry of institution-building, founding churches and social organizations that joined the struggle against slavery, and engaged in communal self-help while seeking to defend and extend the rights accorded to free Black people in their states and localities. Many of these institutions, including most prominently the African Methodist Episcopal Church and the African Masonic movement (later Prince Hall Masonic movement), declared in their names a commitment to a transformative African identity through which they asserted collective standing as a people who were determined to fight for racial equality within both the new nation and the world of nation-states. In many ways, the first decades following independence were a hopeful time for Black northerners. The very real successes won by those who rallied behind Richard Allen, James Forten, Prince Hall, and Paul Cuffe should not obscure, however, the lost stories of the many Black northerners whose promise of freedom was stolen and who found themselves sold into perpetual bondage in the plantation South.[17]

---

[17] James Oliver Horton and Lois E. Horton, *In Hope of Liberty: Culture, Community and Protest among Northern Free Blacks, 1700–1860* (New York: Oxford University Press, 1997), 125–55; Sinha, *The Slave's Cause*, 130–59; Sidbury, *Becoming African in America*;

Developments in the post-revolutionary South were, in many ways, the mirror image of those in the North. Legislators in some states responded to antislavery sentiment associated with the revolution by passing laws liberalizing manumission and offering minimal and virtually impossible to enforce protections to the enslaved. But those benefits paled in comparison with the ways that the post-revolutionary South redoubled its commitment to slavery as an institution and to racism as a prop for that institution. If the revolution put the North on the road to emancipation and fostered the emergence of vibrant and activist – if embattled – urban free Black communities, it pointed the South toward an expansionist future which would spread slavery across millions of acres of land that would be taken from Native peoples and incorporated into the plantation complex. Blacks, like Natives, would fight these processes and bear unconscionable burdens for white southerners' successes.[18]

The most important products of white southern antislavery sentiment following the revolutionary war were liberalized manumission laws in Upper Southern states and associated increased rates of manumission that created substantial free Black populations. Manumission did undermine slavery in Delaware, where roughly 70 percent of Blacks were enslaved at the time of the first federal census, but barely 40 percent remained enslaved in 1810. It constituted a challenge to the institution in Maryland, where almost a quarter of the Black population was free in 1810. But Virginia established a firewall by tightening of the law regulating manumission in 1806, and any hope that white southerners would voluntarily turn away from the peculiar institution proved illusory. Fearful that free people of African descent might create a breach in the racial order, laws and extra-legal practices sought to convert them into what historian Ira Berlin famously described as slaves without masters.[19]

Three related developments ensured that slavery would tighten its hold in the South, and that deeply rooted black communities in the Chesapeake and Carolinas would suffer the consequences. First, land-hungry white settlers

---

Shane White, *Somewhat More Independent: The End of Slavery in New York City, 1770–1810* (Athens, GA: University of Georgia Press, 1991), 114–49, 185–206.

[18] Walter Johnson, *River of Dark Dreams: Slavery and Empire in the Cotton Kingdom* (Cambridge, MA: Harvard University Press, 2013); Adam Rothman, *Slave Country: American Expansion and the Origins of the Deep South* (Cambridge, MA: Harvard University Press, 2005); Claudio Saunt, *Unworthy Republic: The Dispossession of Native Americans and the Road to Indian Territory* (New York: Norton, 2020), 231–302.

[19] Ira Berlin, *Slaves without Masters: The Free Negro in the Antebellum South* (New York: Random House, 1981).

systematically dispossessed Native peoples of the land that would become the states of Kentucky, Tennessee, Alabama, Mississippi, Louisiana, Missouri, Arkansas, and Texas. Second, the invention of the cotton gin made the production of short-staple cotton economically practical, ensuring that much of that land would attract planters seeking to supply the burgeoning textile industry with the raw material that it needed. Third, the federal government closed the Atlantic slave trade in 1808, ensuring that the resulting demand for enslaved laborers would be met by forcibly disrupting existing American slave communities through an interstate slave trade.

Black Southerners responded to these changes in several ways. Benjamin Banneker, the remarkable Black autodidact from Maryland, wrote a powerful letter to Thomas Jefferson seeking to shame him into honoring the antislavery implications of his professed beliefs. Recalling the time when Jefferson "clearly saw into the injustice of a State of Slavery," and trusting that the author of the Declaration would "readily embrace every opportunity to eradicate the train of absurd and false ideas and oppinions which" blighted black lives, Banneker expressed confidence that "you need neither the direction of myself or others" to know how "to proceed herein."[20] Jefferson's failure to answer the letter was only one indication that Banneker's professed confidence was misplaced. Others protested through actions rather than letters. During the 1790s a steady stream of reported slave conspiracies appeared in letters and newspapers. It is often difficult to determine how much of what found its way into reports reflects insurrectionary activity by the enslaved, and how much reflects white anxiety with partial roots in the massive rebellion that broke out on the northern plain of Saint-Domingue and initiated what would become the Haitian Revolution.

That difficulty does not pertain to the largest and most important of that decade's slave conspiracies. In the summer of 1800, many enslaved people living in or near Richmond, Virginia, and led by a blacksmith named Gabriel planned to rise up, take the city, and hold Governor James Monroe hostage to abolition. Witnesses at the trials of alleged conspirators revealed that Gabriel and his lieutenants mixed appeals couched in scriptural language with assertions of hostility toward their enslavers and claims to inclusion within the circle of natural-rights-bearing people. Gabriel's Conspiracy was betrayed before it could be put into effect, but it reveals the refusal of enslaved Virginians to accept white efforts to exclude them from the

---

[20] See https://founders.archives.gov/documents/Jefferson/01-22-02-0049.

promises of revolutionary equality. That was most vividly illustrated when one conspirator declared on the gallows that he had nothing more to say in his own defense than "what General Washington would ... had he been taken by the British and put to trial": he had "adventured [his] life ... to obtain the liberty of [his] countrymen, and ... [was] a willing sacrifice in their cause."[21] Neither Gabriel's followers nor the other enslaved southerners who sought to obtain liberty for their countrymen succeeded, but their efforts reveal both a sharp awareness of the hypocrisy of their master's claims to be liberty-loving republicans, and a growing sense of their shared collective identity – their links to fellow "countrymen."[22]

Gabriel's Conspiracy was formed at a moment when the stability that helped to fuel that sense of collective identity was being subjected to a new kind of pressure. Most Black Virginians could trace their families' histories in Virginia back several generations, which meant they had forged communities with those they had grown up working and playing with. Slave families were always subject to vagaries they could not control, but while inheritance, sale, and the ongoing opening of new tobacco quarters forced many to make painful and unwanted moves away from their loved ones, they did not generally have to move beyond the reach of their kin and communities. As white settlers took the land of Cherokees, Shawnees, and other Native peoples in present-day Kentucky and Tennessee, new land became available, and increasing numbers of easterners moved west to claim it. Many of those easterners took enslaved people with them, uprooting them from those they loved. The effects of such movement were described by Thomas Jefferson in 1803 when ordering the sale of a slave he regarded as incorrigible to a "quarter so distant as never more to be heard of among us." This, he explained, "would to the others be as if he were put out of the way by death."[23] The development of active long-distance markets in enslaved people made them much more valuable to their owners while giving masters a powerful new weapon to use in controlling the enslaved. Long-distance domestic slave markets began to appear during the Early Republic and would come to loom over Upper Southern slave communities later in the

---

[21] Robert Sutcliffe, *Travels in Some Parts of North America in the Years 1804, 1805, and 1806* (York: W. Alexander, 1811), 50.

[22] Sidbury, *Ploughshares into Swords*, 55–117; Douglas Egerton, *Gabriel's Rebellion: The Virginia Slave Conspiracies of 1800 and 1802* (Chapel Hill: University of North Carolina Press, 1993), 50–79; Michael L. Nicholls, *Whispers of Rebellion: Narrating Gabriel's Conspiracy* (Charlottesville: University of Virginia Press, 2012).

[23] Thomas Jefferson to Thomas Mann Randolph, 8 June 1803, https://founders.archives.gov/documents/Jefferson/01-40-02-0383.

nineteenth century. This was the lot of many of the enslaved friends and family that Harry Washington must have left on and near Mt. Vernon when he ran to the British.[24]

The story in the Lower South echoed that in the Chesapeake, though there were differences. John Laurens' antislavery beliefs notwithstanding, white Carolinians did not evince even the mild antislavery sentiment that was so prominent in Virginia. In fact, rather than offering freedom to enslaved people who would join to fight the British, South Carolina's government offered a signing bounty of an enslaved person to white Carolinians who enlisted. The war itself did more to disrupt life in the Lowcountry than in Virginia, because the British army occupied both Charles Town and Savannah, and it took longer for white Carolinians to re-establish the old order following the Treaty of Paris. Small maroon settlements were established in relatively inaccessible swamps, and plantation communities had to be convinced, often with violence, to resume their work in the rice swamps. But the old order was indeed re-established in the Lowcountry, and by 1790 rice production exceeded pre-war levels. But the big transformation for Black Carolinians during the decades following the war – a transformation that hit the Lower South sooner and harder than it did the Upper South – was the explosion of cotton cultivation with the proliferation of the cotton gin.

The upcountry of South Carolina and Georgia was the first region in North America to turn to short-staple cotton. It was in part to supply the needs of aspiring cotton planters that South Carolina re-opened the Atlantic slave trade from 1803 to 1808, initiating an orgy of slave importation during which roughly 10 percent of all of the victims of the Atlantic trade who were sold to North America arrived. Cotton began to supplant rice as the most important staple in the Lower South. Before the revolution most enslaved people in Carolina and Georgia were assigned daily tasks to complete in rice swamps, they lived in parishes with large Black majorities, and they had relatively extensive garden plots on which they produced crops to eat and to market into Charles Town or Savannah. After the revolution, most enslaved people lived on cotton plantations in the upcountry, they lived amid many more white people, and they were forced to work in gangs. This began

---

[24] Brenda E. Stevenson, *Life in Black and White: Family and Community in the Slave South* (New York: Oxford University Press, 1996), 206–57; Steven Deyle, *Carry Me Back: The Domestic Slave Trade in American Life* (New York: Oxford University Press, 2005), 245–75; Michael Tadman, *Speculators and Slaves: Masters, Traders, and Slaves in the Old South* (Madison: University of Wisconsin Press, 1989), 133–78.

during the Age of Revolutions and would accelerate through the Antebellum era. It strengthened slavery politically in the new nation and transformed the lives of the enslaved for the worse.[25]

Turning to the Caribbean, the age of the French Revolution looms much larger than that of the American Revolution. If the American Revolutionary War exacerbated the hardships experienced by those enslaved on British islands, the French and Haitian revolutions introduced a fundamentally new level of instability and possibility into the region. The 1791 uprising on Saint-Domingue's Northern Plain and the revolution that grew out of it constitutes the most obvious source of that instability, but it is difficult to disentangle the intertwined effects of the Haitian Revolution, imperial warfare, and metropolitan reform movements on the lives of African-descended people in the British Caribbean between 1790 and 1804.

The French Revolution's effects were felt most directly and profoundly on the Caribbean's richest colony – Saint-Domingue. In 1791, thousands of enslaved people rose up and began what became the only successful slave revolution in recorded human history. The course of the revolution was complicated and is covered in detail elsewhere in this volume, but the bare outline will help to explain what happened on British islands. The massive uprising in the north soon morphed into a conflict pitting royalists against republicans. Black, free colored, and white people fought on both sides, but the French Republic abolished slavery and won the support of Toussaint Louverture and his Black army, which consolidated control first of the colony and then of the entire island of Hispaniola. To do so, Louverture's forces, which were dominated by men freed in 1794, had to defeat French royalists, an invading British expeditionary force, a free colored-dominated regime in the colony's south, and expel the Spanish from the eastern half of Hispaniola. At the same time, France began to use the promise of emancipation to prosecute the wars of the French Revolution in the Caribbean theater. This created conditions that made the 1790s a tumultuous time for African and African-descended slaves living on British islands.[26]

The tumult did not, however, take the form of a string of uprisings inspired by the upheaval on Hispaniola. White Jamaicans, still haunted by

---

[25] Morgan, *Slave Counterpoint*, 179–203; Sven Beckert, *Empire of Cotton: A Global History* (New York: Random House, 2014), 83–97.

[26] Julius S. Scott, *The Common Wind: Afro-American Currents in the Age of the Haitian Revolution* (London: Routledge, 2018), 118–201; Laurent Dubois, *Avengers of the New World: The Story of the Haitian Revolution* (Cambridge, MA: Harvard University Press, 2004).

memories of 1760, created a secret committee to investigate potential French subversion. It found ample evidence that enslaved Jamaicans knew about and discussed the significance of events on their neighboring island. White Jamaicans, caught up in paranoia about the uprising on Hispaniola, even transformed a routine conflict with a maroon community into the Second Maroon War. Nonetheless, committee members found no credible evidence of planned insurrectionary activity. The reasons are not difficult to discern. Black Jamaicans might have found Saint-Domingue inspiring, but war with France brought a large influx of British troops to Jamaica and other islands, significantly raising the always long odds against a successful rebellion. Historians disagree about the long-term effects of the Haitian example on the politics of Africans enslaved on British islands, but heightened planter surveillance combined with a growing military presence helped to push any immediate effects underground. After consolidating his control of Saint-Domingue, Louverture opted against attempts to export emancipation, going so far as to betray a French plan to invade Jamaica in return for a British promise not to interfere with Saint-Domingue's commerce.[27]

If, however, the revolution occurring in Saint-Domingue provided inspiration to slaves on British islands rather than practical support, the war with France had more immediate effects on Blacks living on some British islands. The French Republic sent Victor Hugues to Guadeloupe where he built an army of former slaves who sought to export the revolution throughout the Caribbean. The most tangible effect of his efforts to destabilize Britain's Caribbean empire took the form of efforts by francophone Blacks in Grenada, Dominica, and St. Vincent – islands the British had taken from the French at the end of the Seven Years' War – to overthrow the British and join the newly abolitionist French Republic. These were not strictly slave uprisings – they were led by free people of color – but British planters understood them as a threat to the slave order, and it seems likely that enslaved people living on British islands hoped the same. The British state increased its military presence in the Caribbean to counter threats emanating from Saint-Domingue and Guadeloupe, including a move to institutionalize the arming of slaves by creating what became the West India Regiments. These were regiments formed of men purchased from slavers and then enrolled in the armed forces where they were charged with defending the

---

[27] Philippe Girard, *Toussaint Louverture: A Revolutionary Life* (New York: Basic Books, 2016), 179–85; David Geggus, "The Enigma of Jamaica in the 1790s: New Light on the Causes of Slave Rebellions," *William and Mary Quarterly* 44 (1987), 274–99.

islands against foreign invasion or domestic insurrection. In many ways, the West India Regiments embody the ambiguous effects of the upheaval surrounding the French Revolution on enslaved people in the British Caribbean. They became a permanent military presence on the islands, and thus an important source of stability, but the decision to arm and train newly imported Africans to fight in the British armed forces undercut the racial order at a moment when opposition to slavery and the slave trade was gaining momentum in the metropole.[28]

The unrest that was directly attributable to the French Revolution was relatively short-lived. By 1804, Jean-Jacques Dessalines had declared the independence of the second nation-state in the Americas, and Haiti had assumed standing as a symbol of Black liberation and equality. Nonetheless, he and his successors generally followed Louverture's lead in eschewing efforts to export Black revolution. Napoleon had achieved power in France, rescinded the 1794 abolition law, and Hugues had carried out new orders to reinstate slavery in the French Caribbean with the same enthusiasm he had brought to subverting it. White planters in Jamaica, Dominica, Grenada, and St. Vincent escaped the looming threat of foreign invasion and the promise that they feared a foreign invasion would offer to the enslaved. In addition, Great Britain had taken the formerly French island of St. Lucia, and the Spanish islands of Trinidad and Tobago, expanding the empire's control of the Caribbean. The large island of Trinidad was the biggest prize, and over the next decade the British transported almost 20,000 Africans to jump-start large-scale sugar planting there. When viewed from one angle, British West Indian planters appear to have come out of the chaos of the French Revolution in the Caribbean with a strengthened hand. Such was not the case.

In fact, because of the growing strength of metropolitan reformers fighting the slave trade and the slipping clout of the West India interest in Parliament – factors tied up with, but not reducible to the American, French, and Haitian revolutions – the enslaved in the British Caribbean were

---

[28] Laurent Dubois, *A Colony of Citizens: Revolution and Slave Emancipation in the French Caribbean, 1787–1804* (Chapel Hill: University of North Carolina Press, 2004); Kit Candlin, *The Last Caribbean Frontier, 1795–1815* (London: Palgrave Macmillan, 2012), 1–23; David Lambert, "'[A] Mere Cloak for Their Proud Contempt and Antipathy towards the African Race': Imagining Britain's West India Regiments in the Caribbean, 1795–1838," *Journal of Imperial and Commonwealth History* 46 (2018), 627–50; David Barry Gaspar and David Patrick Geggus, eds., *A Turbulent Time: The French Revolution and the Greater Caribbean* (Bloomington: University of Indiana Press, 1997), esp. Chapters 1, 3, 4, 9.

on the cusp of a series of victories that would have seemed inconceivable prior to 1776. Parliament outlawed the slave trade in 1807. It also passed a series of laws regulating West Indian masters' authority over the enslaved. Such regulations were often observed in the breach, which lessened the intended effects of "amelioration" on the day-to-day lives of the enslaved. But even ineffective efforts to control masters' "excessive" cruelty informed slaves that they had allies in London. British sugar planters appeared to have entered the nineteenth century having weathered the storms created by revolution and in a strengthened position, because Saint-Domingue, their greatest competitor, no longer produced a significant amount of sugar. But in retrospect it is clear that the enslaved had gained new weapons in their fight for emancipation.

Haiti's place in this process was ambiguous. The specter of slave revolution, and the militarization of the Caribbean in response to warfare on Hispaniola and other islands worked in the short term to blunt metropolitan reformers' attempts to legislate against the slave trade; it led West Indian planters to clamp down with a harsher surveillance regime on the enslaved. Nonetheless, the bloody road to Dessalines' declaration of Haitian independence at Gonaïves in 1804 offered inspiration to Blacks throughout the Anglo-American world and helped convince many white Britons of the need for amelioration.[29]

Aftermath

In the decades following the Haitian Revolution, superficial similarities between the histories of antislavery and the enslaved in the United States and the British Caribbean can conceal a fundamental divergence. Black people on the mainland and the islands continued to struggle against their enslavers. Antislavery movements continued to develop in both the British metropole and the northern United States. These movements won almost simultaneous legislative victories that both outlawed the Atlantic slave trade in the Anglophone Atlantic in 1808, and sought to pressure slaveholders and slaveholding in plantation regions. Notwithstanding those parallels, a key structural difference pushed Britain's former American mainland colonies

---

[29] Roberts, *Slavery and the Enlightenment*, 44–53, 78–9; Michael Craton, *Testing the Chains: Resistance to Slavery in the British West Indies* (Ithaca, NY: Cornell University Press, 1982), 241–321; Robin Blackburn, "Haiti, Slavery, and the Age of the Democratic Revolution," *William and Mary Quarterly* 63 (2006), 643–74.

and its remaining Caribbean possessions in very different directions. For all the vaunted influence of the West India interest in Britain's Parliament, influence rooted in the continuing profitability of sugar planting in the Atlantic world, the Caribbean's influence over British politics waned as England grew into the world's first industrial power. Antislavery forces mobilized and continued to win parliamentary victories against the slavocracy, victories that kept enslaved sugar workers aware of internal divisions that they could use in their fight for freedom. The antislavery movement in the United States found it much more difficult to win national legislative victories following the closing of the Atlantic slave trade, and the enslaved perceived many fewer and less promising divisions among those in power. As a result, the closing decades of the Age of Revolutions brought freedom to Blacks in the British Caribbean, while they left those enslaved in the United States fighting a battle that seemed increasingly hopeless.

From many perspectives – though certainly not from those of the enslaved – British antislavery moved remarkably quickly from its victory in the fight against the Atlantic slave trade to a general triumph over Caribbean slavery. Parliamentary investigation had been a key tool in closing the slave trade, and Parliament continued to investigate Caribbean slavery after 1808. This led to the passage of laws that created formal registers of enslaved people and extended limited rights to the enslaved in an effort to ameliorate what metropolitan consensus had come to see as a too-brutal institution. One practical effect of amelioration was to communicate to the enslaved that they had powerful allies in their struggles against their masters. This changed the way that they approached collective resistance.

Between 1808 and 1833 slaves in the British West Indies engaged in many acts of collective resistance, but three stand out for their size and for their influence on the abolition of slavery in the British Atlantic. Barbados in 1816, Demerara in 1823, and Jamaica in 1831 witnessed uprisings among the enslaved on a scale that had not been approached since Tacky's Revolt in 1760. Each grew out of complicated and idiosyncratic local conditions, but in each case the enslaved calibrated their strategies and actions with an awareness that they were not alone in their battle for freedom. This is most clearly conveyed by a brief survey of white casualties in these uprisings. Hundreds of enslaved people rose to demand freedom in Barbados and they destroyed a great deal of property. They killed two Whites. Thousands rose up in Demerara. Two or three Whites were killed by the insurgents. Tens of thousands took part in the Jamaica rebellion of 1831. Fourteen Whites were killed in the fighting. This compares with more than sixty Whites killed during Tacky's Revolt, and fifty in the comparatively tiny uprising led by Nat Turner in Southampton, Virginia, in 1831. White West Indians did not reciprocate, opting instead to enact mass executions and brutal physical punishment on the slave rebels. The contrast undermined proslavery arguments that Africans were "uncivilized brutes" and played an important role in the passage of the Slavery Abolition Act in 1833.[30]

Enslaved people living in the southern United States had no analogous signs of a national antislavery movement that might prevail in Congress. There was, of course, a growing movement of black and white activists fighting against slavery in the United States. They won important victories in the decades following the American Revolution, though the federal structure of the union pushed the battles into state legislatures, rendering those victories less obviously inspirational to those who remained enslaved in the South. That lack of inspiration was exacerbated by the ascendance of white southern interests in the national government, an ascendance that ensured that any outside intervention in cases of conflict between masters and slaves would come in support of, not in opposition to, slavery. The conspiracy described by witnesses at the Denmark Vesey trials in Charleston in 1822 called for the enslaved to kill Whites indiscriminately. When Turner led the uprising in southeastern Virginia in 1831, that is what he and his followers did. One need not think enslaved North Americans more or less savvy, more revolutionary or more pragmatic, or more attracted to violence than their West Indian counterparts. They simply lived in a society in which even a vibrant northern antislavery movement offered no realistic chance for a peaceful, legislative path to emancipation.

The growth of slavery following the revolution makes clear why the enslaved would have known that. There were thirteen slave states when the Declaration of Independence was signed. The significance of northern emancipation takes on a less pleasing hue in light of the fact that there were twelve slave states in the United States in the 1820s, thirteen in the 1830s, and fifteen in the 1840s. Furthermore, revolutionary-era antislavery did not lead to a decline in the number of people suffering enslavement: between 1790 and 1860 the number of people enslaved in the United States increased roughly sixfold (from almost 700,000 to almost 4 million). Of the seven men who served as President of the United States during the Age of Revolutions,

---

[30] Craton, *Testing the Chains*, 125–39; Vincent Brown, *Tacky's Revolt*, 129–207; Christopher Tomlins, *In the Matter of Nat Turner: A Speculative History* (Princeton: Princeton University Press, 2020), 93–126.

five were slave-owning planters. Numbers tell only part of the story: abundant scholarship has established that prior to the Civil War the slave-owning South exercised disproportionate – often dominant – influence on the national government. If the American Revolution created the divided house that would erupt into Civil War in 1861, it also greatly strengthened the hold of slavery on the southern wing of that house.[31]

The Age of Revolutions came to an end in very different ways for Blacks living in the United States and those living in Britain's Caribbean islands. On the islands, the formerly enslaved had won a great victory and faced the challenge of defining what freedom would mean in an Atlantic culture that was growing increasingly committed to racist thought. In the United States, free Black people in the North faced that same challenge, while fighting a battle that seemed increasingly futile against the expansion of slavery to the south and west. Those who remained bound to labor in the plantation South faced an even more daunting reality. Upper Southern families and communities lived under constant threat from the interstate slave trade. Lower Southern people faced increasing pressure to produce more and more cotton to feed the looms of Manchester and New England. The Age of Atlantic Revolutions had transformed their lives, but only for the worse.

---

[31] Robert Parkinson, *The Common Cause: Creating Race and Nation in the American Revolution* (Chapel Hill: University of North Carolina Press, 2016); David Waldstreicher, *Slavery's Constitution: From Revolution to Ratification* (New York: Hill & Wang, 2009); William W. Freehling, *The Road to Disunion*, 2 vols. (New York: Oxford University Press, 2007 [1991]).

16
Life, Land, and Liberty: The Native Americans' Revolution

COLIN G. CALLOWAY

As American colonists fought a war of independence against Britain on the Atlantic coast, Native Americans on the far western edge of the Atlantic world waged their own wars of independence, primarily against American colonists. The Declaration of Independence accused King George III of unleashing "on the inhabitants of our frontiers, the merciless Indian Savages whose known rule of warfare, is an undistinguished destruction of all ages, sexes and conditions." While Americans fought for their rights and freedom, it seemed, Native Americans fought against them, the vicious pawns of a tyrannical king. However, the Indian people who fought in the revolution also fought for their rights and freedom. Some fought for the Americans but most sided with the British. The subsequent experiences of Indigenous peoples elsewhere suggest that Native Americans would not have fared much better in the British empire than in the American republic.[1] But most Indian people at the time saw aggressive Americans pushing on their borders as posing a greater threat to Indigenous lands and ways of life than did a distant king; some said the Americans were intent on destroying them.[2] The revolution in Indian country became increasingly a race war in which American assaults on Indian villages were marked by "an undistinguished destruction of all ages, sexes and conditions." Native Americans did not fight against freedom in the revolution; like the American Patriots, they fought to defend their lives, land, and liberty.

The collapse of an old imperial order and the birth pangs of an expansive new nation brought upheaval and new levels of violence in Indian

---

[1] Gregory Evans Dowd, "Indigenous Peoples without the Republic," *Journal of American History* 104 (2017), 19–41.
[2] Jeffrey Ostler, *Surviving Genocide: Native Nations and the United States from the American Revolution to Bleeding Kansas* (New Haven: Yale University Press, 2019), Chapter 2.

country. Local struggles for power, authority, and resources often took precedence over the larger conflict between the crown and the colonies. Frontier populations that rebelled against the king also contested the government of eastern elites and struggled to build new societies on their own terms.[3] Amid the chaos, however, the revolution was also, quite simply, a war over Indian land. Speculators like George Washington had worked long and hard to get their hands on the best western lands; western settlers sought to rid those lands of Indian neighbors (frontier militia attacking Indian villages and Indian warriors raiding frontier settlements sometimes knew the people they were fighting), and Congress and the individual states needed land to fulfill the bounties and warrants they issued in lieu of pay during the war. Tribal nations struggled to preserve their land and, increasingly, their existence.

Neutrality to Conflict

The American Revolution exacerbated but did not create a culture of racial violence and Indian-hating on the frontier. Despite recurrent conflict, Indians and colonists in some areas had managed to maintain relationships of coexistence and accommodation until the mid-eighteenth century, when increasing encroachments on Indian land, escalating ethnic, social, and political tensions, and the Seven Years' War produced bloodshed, terror, and fear.[4] At the end of that war, flushed with victory over France, the British behaved like conquerors in Indian country, occupying former French posts and terminating gifts, which served to cement alliances and ensure good-faith relationships in Indian diplomacy. Pontiac of the Ottawas, Guyasuta of the Senecas, and other war chiefs forged a multitribal coalition in the Ohio Valley and Great Lakes that waged a

---

[3] Patrick Griffin, *American Leviathan: Empire, Nation, and Revolutionary Frontier* (New York: Hill & Wang, 2007); Daniel P. Barr, *A Colony Sprung from Hell: Pittsburgh and the Struggle for Authority on the Western Pennsylvania Frontier, 1744–1794* (Kent, OH: Kent State University Press, 2014), 175–93; Patrick Spero, *Frontier Rebels: The Fight for Independence in the American West, 1765–1776* (New York: W. W. Norton, 2018).

[4] James H. Merrell, *Into the American Woods: Negotiators on the Pennsylvania Frontier* (New York: W. W. Norton, 1999); Jane T. Merritt, *At the Crossroads: Indians and Empires on a Mid-Atlantic Frontier, 1700–1763* (Chapel Hill: University of North Carolina Press, 2003); Peter Silver, *Our Savage Neighbors: How Indian War Transformed Early America* (New York: W. W. Norton, 2008); Kevin Kenny, *Peaceable Kingdom Lost: The Paxton Boys and the Destruction of William Penn's Holy Experiment* (New York: Oxford University Press, 2009); Matthew C. Ward, *Breaking the Backcountry: The Seven Years' War in Virginia and Pennsylvania, 1754–1765* (Pittsburgh: University of Pittsburgh Press, 2003).

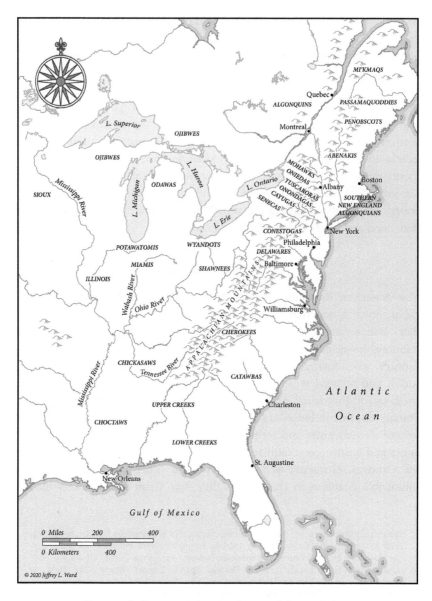

Map 16.1 Indigenous nations on the eve of the revolution.

war of independence against the British empire a dozen years before American colonists did.[5] The government in London responded by declaring the Appalachian Mountains the boundary between British settlement and Indian lands. The Royal Proclamation Line, as it was known, was never intended to be permanent and it barely slowed encroachment on to Indian lands. The army could not enforce it, settlers often ignored it, and land speculators who had hoped to get rich by selling trans-Appalachian lands to westward-moving settlers lobbied against it. Designed to bring order to the American frontier, the Proclamation instead initiated a chain of events that helped to bring about the revolution, especially after Britain imposed taxes in the colonies to help pay for keeping an army in America and administering its new empire.[6]

In subsequent treaties – with the Iroquois at Fort Stanwix in 1768, and with the Cherokees at Hard Labor in 1768 and Lochaber 1770 – the British negotiated new boundary lines that opened up huge swaths of territory in the heart of Indian country. Nevertheless, General Thomas Gage, the commander-in-chief of the British forces in North America, feared that no matter what boundaries Britain made, "the Frontier People are too Numerous, too Lawless and Licentious ever to be restrained." Britain could not keep American colonists off Indian lands and Indian chiefs could not control young warriors angered by the invasion.[7] "These settlers generally set out with a general Prejudice against all Indians and the young Indian Warriors or Hunters are too often inclined to retaliate," said Sir William Johnson, the British superintendent of Indian affairs in the north.[8] "We find your people are very fond of our rich land," Delawares, Munsees, and Mahicans told the governors of Virginia, Pennsylvania, and Maryland in 1771 as colonial settlers pushed west relentlessly; "unless you can fall upon some method of governing your people who live between the Great

---

[5] Gregory Evans Dowd, *War under Heaven: Pontiac, the Indian Nations, and the British Empire* (Baltimore, MD: Johns Hopkins University Press, 2002); David Dixon, *Never Come to Peace Again: Pontiac's Uprising and the Fate of the British Empire in North America* (Norman: University of Oklahoma Press, 2005); Richard Middleton, *Pontiac's War: Its Causes and Consequences* (New York: Routledge, 2007).

[6] Colin G. Calloway, *The Scratch of a Pen: 1763 and the Transformation of North America* (New York: Oxford University Press, 2006); Woody Holton, *Forced Founders: Indians, Debtors, Slaves, and the Making of the American Revolution in Virginia* (Chapel Hill: University of North Carolina Press, 1999), Chapter 1.

[7] James Sullivan et al., eds., *The Papers of Sir William Johnson*, 14 vols. (Albany, NY: University of the State of New York, 1921–1965), vol. VI, 212; vol. XII, 710.

[8] Edmund B. O'Callaghan, ed., *Documents Relating to the Colonial History of the State of New York*, 15 vols. (Albany, NY: Weed, Parsons, 1853–1857), vol. VIII, 396.

Mountains and the Ohio River and who are now very numerous, it will be out of the Indians' power to govern their young men, for we assure you the black clouds begin to gather fast in this country." Having seen nation after nation destroyed, the Indians feared that "it must be soon their turn also to be exterminated."[9]

Their fears were not unfounded. While colonists in the east protested against taxation and resisted imperial restraints, many settlers in the west "wanted to be free of Indians as much as they wanted to be free of their imperial overlords." Resentful of eastern elites who seemed to govern in their own interests and of British officials who seemed to put protecting Indian land and Indian trade before the safety of frontier families, groups like the "Black Boys" were motivated by fear and loathing of Indians as much as by ideals of rights and liberty.[10] Irish trader and agent George Croghan said frontier people had "too great a Spirit ... for killing Indians."[11] That spirit showed itself in the spring of 1774 when frontier thugs murdered thirteen women and children, the family of a Mingo chief Tachnedorus, also known as Logan. The victims included Logan's Shawnee wife and his pregnant sister. Logan's grief became immortalized in a speech attributed to him, most notably the version recorded by Thomas Jefferson in *Notes on the State of Virginia*. When Logan took his revenge on Virginian settlers, Virginia's governor, Lord Dunmore, went to war against the Shawnees.[12] Outnumbered and outgunned by Virginian forces at the Battle of Point Pleasant in October 1774, the Shawnees were compelled to make peace and accept the loss of their hunting lands south of the Ohio River. Shawnee chiefs told the Virginians the following year "we are often inclined to believe there is no resting place for us and that your Intentions were to deprive us entirely of our whole Country."[13]

---

[9] K. G. Davies, ed., *Documents of the American Revolution, 1770–1783 (Colonial Office Series)*, 21 vols. (Shannon: Irish University Press, 1972–1981), vol. III, 254–55 ("black clouds"), vol. V, 203; Colonial Office Records, Series 5, National Archives, Kew, England, C.O. 5/90: 78 ("exterminated").

[10] Spero, *Frontier Rebels*, xxvi.

[11] "Letters of Colonel George Croghan," *Pennsylvania Magazine of History and Biography* 15 (1891), 437–8.

[12] *Notes on the State of Virginia by Thomas Jefferson, with Related Documents*, ed. David Waldstreicher (Boston, MA: Bedford Books, 2012), 124; Reuben Gold Thwaites and Louise Phelps Kellogg, eds., *Documentary History of Dunmore's War, 1774* (Madison: Wisconsin Historical Society, 1905).

[13] Robert L. Scribner et al., eds., *Revolutionary Virginia, The Road to Independence: A Documentary Record*, 7 vols. (Charlottesville: University of Virginia Press, 1973–1983), vol. VII, 770.

The contest for Indian lands merged into the fighting of the revolution. At the Treaty of Sycamore Shoals in Tennessee in March 1775, the Overhill Cherokee chief Attakullakulla, principal headman Oconostota, and the Raven of Chota sold 27,000 square miles of land between the Kentucky and Cumberland rivers – most of modern Kentucky – to Judge Richard Henderson and a group of North Carolina land speculators known as the Transylvania Land Company in exchange for a cabin full of trade goods. Attakullakulla's son, a war chief named Tsi'yu-gûnsini, or Dragging Canoe, reputedly stormed from the treaty council in disgust, vowing to make the ceded lands "dark and bloody." He blamed the older chiefs "who he said were too old to hunt and who by their poverty had been induced to sell their land" and declared that he and his young warriors "were determined to have their land."[14]

In May 1776, fourteen delegates from northern nations – Shawnees, Delawares, Mohawks, Nanticokes, and Ottawas – arrived at Chota on the Little Tennessee River and urged the Cherokees to join in a united war of resistance against the Americans. "Better to die like men than diminish away by inches," declared one of the Shawnees and he offered the Cherokees a 9-foot long wampum belt, painted red as a sign of war. Dragging Canoe and his followers accepted the belt and struck the war post with their hatchets, seizing the opportunity to drive American trespassers from their land and asserting their independence from the older chiefs who would normally have guided the Cherokees in such critical decisions. Attakullakulla, Oconostota, and their generation remembered that British troops had burned their crops and villages the last time the Cherokees went to war, and they did not want war with the Americans now. But years of land sales had eroded their authority, and "instead of opposing the rashness of the young people with spirit, [they] sat down dejected and silent."[15]

As Spain, Britain, and the United States competed for the allegiance of Indian nations near the Gulf of Mexico, the Choctaws, Chickasaws, and Creeks sought to preserve their independence and their trade. At first, most Creeks favored neutrality. Between February 1775 and March 1776, a dozen Creek delegations traveled to Havana to make a commercial alliance with Spain 'to offset the decline in the deerskin trade caused by the

---

[14] *The Colonial and State Records of North Carolina*, 30 vols. (Raleigh, NC: P. H. Hale, 1886–1907), vol. x, 764.

[15] Davies, *Documents of the American Revolution*, vol. xii, 203–4; *Colonial and State Records of North Carolina*, vol. x, 777–80.

British–American conflict. Chiefs Emistiguo and Alexander McGillivray, the son of a Loyalist Scottish trader and a Creek mother, came to regard siding with the British as the best way to maintain their Creek lands and preserve ample trade for manufactured goods, although they did not and could not speak for the whole Creek confederacy, which comprised about fifty semi-autonomous towns scattered across the southeast. Creeks responded to the outbreak of the revolution according to the goals and perceived interests of individual towns and individual leaders. The situation was complicated by an on-going conflict between the Creeks and Choctaws, which British agents now worked to end.[16]

With a population of perhaps 30,000 in 1775, the Choctaws occupied a key strategic position on the lower Mississippi, and they played off Spanish and British rivals as a way to maintain trade with both and independence from both. The Six Towns region, closest to New Orleans, leaned toward Spain but the majority of Choctaws supported King George. Their northern neighbors, the Chickasaws had ties to the British. Chief Payamataha preferred a carefully preserved neutrality, although the Chickasaws made it clear that they did so not out of fear: when the Americans employed threats to try and pressure them into making an alliance, they responded: "Take care that we don't serve you as we have served the French before with all their Indians, [and] send you back without your heads."[17]

British agents operating out of Detroit and American agents at Fort Pitt competed for the allegiance of the Indian nations in the Ohio country. The Shawnee chief Cornstalk had led his warriors in Dunmore's War, but when the revolution broke out he worked for peace and counseled a neutral stance. Unfortunately, neutrality was not a viable option for the Shawnees.[18] "All our lands are covered by the white people, and we are jealous that you still intend to make larger strides," Cornstalk told American agent George Morgan to tell Congress. "We never sold you our Lands which you now possess on the Ohio between the Great Kanawha and the Cherokee River, and which you are settling without ever asking our leave, or obtaining our

---

[16] Claudio Saunt, *West of the Revolution: An Uncommon History of 1776* (New York: W. W. Norton, 2014), 188–203 (Creeks to Cuba); Ethan A. Schmidt, *Native Americans in the American Revolution* (Santa Barbara, CA: Praeger, 2014), 94–103.

[17] Kathleen DuVal, *Independence Lost: Lives on the Edge of the American Revolution* (New York: Random House, 2015); Colin G. Calloway, *The American Revolution in Indian Country: Crisis and Diversity in Native American Communities* (Cambridge: Cambridge University Press, 1995), 44 (Choctaws), 226 (Chickasaw quote).

[18] Gregory Evans Dowd, *A Spirited Resistance: The North American Indian Struggle for Unity, 1745–1815* (Baltimore, MD: Johns Hopkins University Press, 1992), Chapter 3.

consent."[19] The war party gained strength and Cornstalk could not restrain his warriors. Then, in 1777, American militia seized Cornstalk under a flag of truce at Fort Randolph on the Kanahwa River. A month later they murdered him, together with his son and another Shawnee whose body was "terribly mangled." Shawnee runners carried news of the killings, and war belts, through Indian country. Shawnee warriors made common cause with the British, who had been warning them that the Americans intended to annihilate them. Shawnee warriors raided settlements in Kentucky and effectively closed the Ohio River to American traffic.

Like their Shawnee neighbors, Delawares living in the Ohio country were divided in their responses to the revolution. White Eyes, war captain of the Turtle clan, advocated gradual acculturation as the path to the future and peace with the Americans as the best strategy for Delaware security, and he developed a working relationship with George Morgan. Some Delawares had embraced Christianity, and both White Eyes and Gelemend or John Killbuck, chief of the Turtle clan, supported the work of Moravian missionaries and favored a neutral and then pro-American stance. The Delaware chief Buckongahelas, on the other hand, was openly hostile to the missionaries and their teachings, and Hopocan or Captain Pipe of the Wolf clan and his followers distanced themselves from the missions and the Americans.[20]

Reluctant to give direct military assistance to either side, the Delawares initially endeavored to maintain their traditional role and historic reputation as peacemakers and alliance-builders. In 1778, the United States made its first two treaties – with France in March and with the Delawares in September. At the Treaty of Fort Pitt, a Delaware delegation led by White Eyes and commissioners from the Continental Congress agreed to a defensive alliance. But other Delawares complained that the treaty was "wrote down false ... & contain'd Declarations and Engagements they never intended to make or enter into." Two months later, during General Lachlan McIntosh's ineffectual campaign against Detroit, American militia murdered White Eyes, their guide and their best friend in the Ohio Indian country. Like the Shawnees in the aftermath of Cornstalk's murder, most Delawares now made Britain's

---

[19] Cornstalk's speech to Congress, 7 November 1776, in "Letter Book of George Morgan 1776," reprinted in Colin G. Calloway, ed., *Revolution and Confederation*, in *Early American Indian Documents: Treaties and Laws, 1607–1789*, Alden T. Vaughan, gen. ed., 20 vols. (Bethesda, MD: University Publications of America, 1979–2004), vol. XVIII, 147.

[20] Hermann Wellenreuther and Carola Wessel, eds., *The Moravian Mission Diaries of David Zeisberger, 1772–1781* (University Park: Pennsylvania State University Press, 2005), 35–6, 319–21, 608–10; Hermann Wellenreuther, "White Eyes and the Delawares' Vision of an Indian State," *Pennsylvania History* 68 (2001), 139–61.

war their own.[21] Hopocan and his people moved north to Sandusky, closer to the British at Detroit.

For much of the eighteenth century the Six Nations of the Iroquois League in upstate New York – the Mohawks, Oneidas, Onondagas, Cayugas, Senecas, and Tuscaroras – had pursued a foreign policy of official (if not always actual) neutrality, playing off rival colonial powers and exerting their influence in colonial and intertribal diplomacy.[22] Patterns of coexistence and cultural accommodation between colonial and Indian communities had persisted on the borders of Iroquois country even as racial war had produced bloodshed and revenge killings on the frontiers of Pennsylvania and Virginia in the middle of the century.[23] Even the Seneca chief Guyasuta, who had played a leading role in Pontiac's War, tried to avoid getting pulled into this one: "We must be Fools indeed to imagine that they regard us or our Interest who want to bring us into an unnecessary War," he said.[24] But the revolution shattered the peace of the region and the unity of the League. "Times are altered with us Indians," an Onondaga sachem named Tenhoghskweaghta, explained. "Formerly the Warriors were governed by the wisdom of their Uncles the Sachems but now they take their own way ... we wish for peace and they for war."[25] Mohawks, led by war chief Joseph Brant, supported the crown, due in no small measure to the influence of Sir William Johnson, who functioned as the pivotal figure in British–Mohawk relations until his death in 1774. The Mohawks' neighbors, the Oneidas, leaned toward the colonists. Samuel Kirkland, their Presbyterian missionary, favored breaking with the Church of England, and the Oneidas opted to side with the Americans rather than incur their hostility. At the Battle of Oriskany in 1777, Oneidas allied with the Americans fought Mohawks and Senecas who were allied with the British, a devastating development for people who shared clan and kinship ties.[26] In the

---

[21] Amy C. Schutt, *Peoples of the River Valleys: The Odyssey of the Delaware Indians* (Philadelphia: University of Pennsylvania Press, 2007), 163–8; Colin G. Calloway, ed., *The World Turned Upside Down: Indian Voices from Early America* (Boston, MA: Bedford Books, 1994), 156, 190–3.

[22] Timothy J. Shannon, *Iroquois Diplomacy on the Early American Frontier* (New York: Penguin, 2008).

[23] David L. Preston, *The Texture of Contact: European and Indian Settler Communities on the Frontiers of Iroquoia, 1667–1783* (Lincoln: University of Nebraska Press, 2009).

[24] Quoted in Calloway, *American Revolution in Indian Country*, 29–30.

[25] Speech of Tenhoghskweaghta, 10 March 1778, Philip Schuyler Papers, New York Public Library, reel 7, box 14.

[26] Alan Taylor, *The Divided Ground: Indians, Settlers, and the Northern Borderland of the American Revolution* (New York: Alfred Knopf, 2006); Barbara Graymont, *The Iroquois in the American Revolution* (Syracuse, NY: Syracuse University Press, 1972); Joseph T.

spring of 1778, a group of Oneidas carried stores of dried corn to Washington's beleaguered army at Valley Forge.[27]

In New England, the Mohegan preacher Samson Occom wished the Whites would leave the Indians alone and not drag them into the fighting; "what have they to do with your Quarrels?" he asked.[28] However, despite the assertion in the Declaration of Independence that the king had unleashed savage warriors against innocent families, the first Indians to fight in the war appear to have joined the Americans and were from New England. Some fought alongside their colonial neighbors at Bunker Hill. Indian men from Stockbridge in western Massachusetts, a mission community of some two or three hundred Mohican, Housatonic, and Wappinger people, volunteered as Minutemen even before the outbreak of the fighting. The revolution and its rhetoric offered them hope that their history of indebtedness and land loss might be reversed. "If we are conquered our Lands go with yours," Captain Solomon Uhhaunauwaunmut told American commissioners, "but if we are victorious we hope you will help us recover our just Rights." Seventeen Stockbridge warriors joined Washington's army besieging Boston.[29]

Wars of Independence in Indian Country

George Washington's experience as commander of the Virginia militia defending his colony's western frontier in the Seven Years' War had convinced him that the only way to stop Indian raids was to stamp them out at source – in other words, to invade Indian country, burn Indian villages, and destroy food supplies. The French had waged such campaigns against the Iroquois in the seventeenth century, the British had done so against the Cherokees in 1760–1761, and Washington and his contemporaries did so now. The revolution in the west is often portrayed as a rearguard action fought by beleaguered settlers and militia against Indian raiders who struck suddenly and

---

Glatthaar and James Kirby Martin, *Forgotten Allies: The Oneida Indians and the American Revolution* (New York: Hill & Wang, 2006).

[27] Karim M. Tiro, *The People of the Standing Stone: The Oneida Nation from the Revolution through the Era of Removal* (Amherst: University of Massachusetts Press, 2011), 39–40; Glatthaar and Martin, *Forgotten Allies*, 203–8.

[28] Occom to John Thornton, 1776, Dartmouth College, Rauner Library, Ms. 776900.2. Joanna Brooks, ed., *The Collected Writings of Samson Occom, Mohegan* (New York: Oxford University Press, 2006), 113.

[29] Calloway, *American Revolution in Indian Country*, 92, 94; Papers of the Continental Congress, 1774–1789, National Archives, Washington, DC, Microfilm 247, reel 144, item 134: 43; *Documents Relating to the Colonial History of the State of New York*, vol. VIII, 626.

then slipped back into the forests; in reality, the revolution in the west also produced repeated American expeditions into Indian country that targeted fields and villages, the domain of Native women, and sought plunder as well as revenge.[30]

The war was a disaster for the Cherokees. As soon as Dragging Canoe's warriors launched their attacks, militia armies from Virginia, North and South Carolina, and Georgia swept through Cherokee country. "Cut up every Indian corn field and burn every Indian town," William Henry Drayton, chief justice of South Carolina, instructed the troops, assuring them that every Indian they captured would be "the slave and property of the taker." The goal of the campaign was clear and simple: "that the nation be extirpated, and the lands become the property of the public." Thomas Jefferson wanted to see the Cherokees "driven beyond the Mississippi." American soldiers destroyed crops, burned towns, and drove the inhabitants into the woods.[31] Faced with massive destruction, the older chiefs reasserted their influence and sued for peace. At the Treaty of DeWitt's Corner with Georgia and South Carolina in May 1777 and the Treaty of Long Island on the Holston with Virginia and North Carolina in July, the Cherokees lost more than 5 million acres as the price of peace.[32]

Dragging Canoe stayed away from the treaty talks. He and his followers moved south and west lower down the Tennessee River, built new towns along Chickamauga Creek, and continued the fight. In April 1779, while most of the warriors were away attacking frontier settlements in Georgia and South Carolina, Colonel Evan Shelby led a large Virginian force down the Tennessee and attacked the Chickamauga towns. The women and children escaped into the woods, but Shelby burned eleven towns and destroyed some 20,000 bushels of corn. Dragging Canoe and his followers retreated farther downriver and rebuilt their towns, which continued to attract "the young and active, more or less from every town in the nation."[33] Born fighting, the Chickamauga towns existed on a war footing. About one hundred Shawnees also joined the Chickamaugas and some Chickamaugas

---

[30] See, for example, Susan Sleeper-Smith, *Indigenous Prosperity and American Conquest: Indian Women of the Ohio River Valley, 1690–1792* (Chapel Hill: University of North Carolina Press, 2018).

[31] Drayton quoted in Tom Hatley, *The Dividing Paths: Cherokees and South Carolinians through the Era of Revolution* (New York: Oxford University Press, 1993), 192; Julian P. Boyd, ed., *The Papers of Thomas Jefferson* (Princeton: Princeton University Press, 1950–), vol. 1, 494.

[32] Draper Mss., State Historical Society of Wisconsin (microfilm), 4QQ, 151–54.

[33] Walter Lowrie and Matthew St. Clair Clarke, eds., *American State Papers, Class II: Indian Affairs*, 2 vols. (Washington, DC: Gales & Seaton, 1832), vol. 1, 432.

moved north to live and fight with the Shawnees. The Chickamaugas' struggle merged into a broader Indian war for independence in the west.

When Chickamauga warriors raided the American frontier and retreated to their strongholds, Americans often retaliated against the more accessible towns of those Cherokees who were attempting to live at peace and presented an easier target. Troops under Arthur Campbell and John Sevier invaded Cherokee country in late 1780 and 1781, burning towns and destroying food supplies. The Raven of Chota said the soldiers "dyed their hands in the Blood of many of our Woman [sic] and Children," and "our families were almost destroyed by famine."[34] The assaults drove more warriors into the Chickamauga ranks.

At the beginning of the war Choctaw warriors patrolled the Mississippi River, giving the British warning and protection against American attacks downriver. When Spain declared war on Britain in 1779, hundreds of Choctaw warriors helped the British defend Mobile in 1780 and Pensacola in 1780–1781.[35] Most Chickasaws allied with the British. Confronted with aggressions by Georgia, many Creek warriors eventually turned out for British campaigns against both the Americans and the Spaniards, but they were cautious participants in a war they would have rather avoided.[36]

George Rogers Clark, a Virginian with a reputation as an Indian fighter, led a campaign into the Illinois country in 1778–1779 and offered the Indians of the region a simple choice between a white wampum belt of peace and a "bloody belt" threatening destruction. He captured Vincennes by a forced winter march, and took prisoner Lieutenant Governor Henry Hamilton of Detroit, whom Americans accused of buying scalps from the Indians. Declaring that "to excel them in barbarity was and is the only way to make war upon Indians," Clark tomahawked Indian captives and tossed their bodies into the river in plain view of the garrison.[37] The British remained in control at Detroit and Clark's power and presence in the area

---

[34] Calloway, *American Revolution in Indian Country*, 50; Raven quoted in James H. O'Donnell, *The Southern Indians in the American Revolution* (Knoxville: University of Tennessee Press, 1973), 118–19.

[35] Greg O'Brien, *Choctaws in a Revolutionary Age, 1750–1830* (Lincoln: University of Nebraska Press, 2002), provides broader consideration of Choctaw experiences.

[36] Calloway, *American Revolution in Indian Country*, 45–6.

[37] James Alton James, ed., *George Rogers Clark Papers, 1781–1784* (Springfield: Illinois State Historical Society, 1926), 144, 167, 189; Milo M. Quaife, ed., *The Conquest of the Illinois by George Rogers Clark* (Chicago: R. R. Donnelley, 1920), 166–8.

soon disappeared, but his so-called conquest of the Illinois country strengthened the United States' bargaining position at the peace negotiations in Paris.[38]

Clark also invaded Shawnee country, crossing the Ohio River with a force of 1,000 men in 1780. Kentucky militia had burned the Shawnee town at Chillicothe the year before.[39] This time the Shawnees evacuated and burned the town themselves. At Piqua on the Mad River, they stood their ground until Clark turned his artillery on the village council house where many of the people had taken refuge. Shawnee losses were slight, but the Americans killed some old people they found hiding in the cornfields and spent three days burning the crops. Some men dug open Shawnee graves for burial goods and scalps.[40] Kentucky militia crossed the Ohio River almost every year to burn Shawnee villages and crops and bring back scalps and plunder. Thomas Jefferson wanted the Shawnees exterminated or driven from their lands and he advocated turning other tribes against them.[41] The war of attrition took a toll. As one Shawnee told the British, they had been fighting the Virginians "upwards of Twenty Years."[42] Many Shawnees migrated west into present-day Missouri, which was claimed by Spain, rather than live with continual warfare and recurrent invasions in Ohio.

Like the Shawnees and Cherokees, many Iroquois lost their homes during the revolution. Mohawks migrated to Canada and Oneidas took refuge in camps around Schenectady, New York. In 1779, Washington dispatched General John Sullivan to conduct a scorched-earth campaign in Iroquois country. "The immediate objects are the total destruction and devastation of their settlements and the capture of as many prisoners of every age and sex as possible," he instructed Sullivan. "It will be essential to ruin their crops now in the ground and prevent their planting more." As the army cut through Iroquois country, Sullivan was to detach parties "to lay waste all the settlements around" so that the country was "not be merely overrun but

---

[38] Randolph C. Downes, *Council Fires on the Upper Ohio* (Pittsburgh: Pittsburgh University Press, 1940), 229.
[39] Louise Phelps Kellogg, ed., *Frontier Advance on the Upper Ohio, 1778–1779* (Madison: Wisconsin State Historical Society, 1916), 365.
[40] Accounts of the expedition are compiled in J. Martin West, ed., *Clark's Shawnee Campaign of 1780: Contemporary Accounts* (Springfield, OH: Clark County Historical Society, 1975).
[41] Boyd, *Papers of Thomas Jefferson*, vol. III, 259, 276.
[42] *Collections of the Michigan Pioneer Historical Society*, vol. X, 462–65.

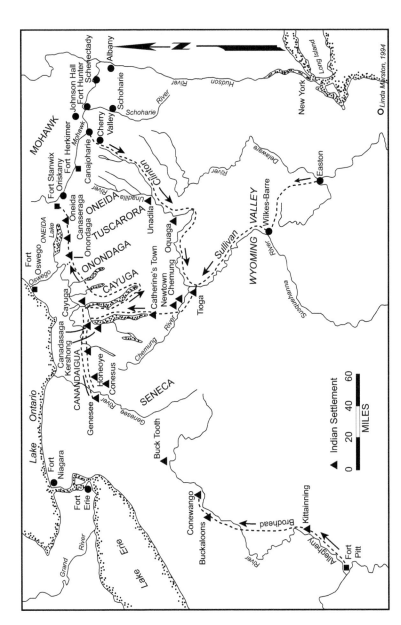

Map 16.2 Sullivan's expedition, 1779. Published in Colin G. Calloway, *The American Revolution in Indian Country: Crisis and Diversity in Native American Communities* (Cambridge University Press, 1995).

destroyed." Employing terror tactics, inflicting severe "chastisement," and driving the Iroquois as far as possible from the American frontier was the only way to achieve peace and security, Washington said, and he forbade Sullivan to listen to any peace overtures until he had "very thoroughly completed the destruction of their settlements."[43] Sullivan did as Washington ordered. In town after town, soldiers burned houses, destroyed fields and stores of corn, and cut down orchards. Sullivan estimated that his army destroyed forty towns, 160,000 bushels of corn, and vast quantities of fruit trees and vegetables.[44] Without food and shelter, several thousand Iroquois people fled to Niagara, creating a refugee crisis at the British fort. Niagara lay at the end of a long supply line that was closed during the winter months when vessels from Montreal and Quebec could not navigate the ice-bound Great Lakes. The refugees endured exposure, starvation, and sickness during one of the coldest winters on record. Come spring, Iroquois warriors resumed their attacks on the frontiers of New York and Pennsylvania with renewed vigor, to take grain and cattle as well as scalps and captives.[45]

Washington and most historians have explained the Sullivan–Clinton campaign and other invasions of Indian country as war measures, to avenge and terminate Indian attacks on the frontier. But the American assaults were also measures to prepare for peace. Once France entered the fray, the war was likely to end with a negotiated peace that included independence, but Washington had no way of knowing what that victory would mean in territorial terms when peace was signed. After all, the British government had included the Ohio country within the new borders of Quebec in 1774 and Quebec did not rebel. What if Britain insisted on keeping the Ohio country as part of Quebec? During peace talks in Europe, mediating neutral powers suggested letting each side keep the territory it controlled at

---

[43] W. W. Abbot et al., eds., *The Papers of George Washington: Revolutionary War Series*, 23 vols. (Charlottesville: University of Virginia Press, 1985–), vol. XX, 717–18; Otis G. Hammond, ed., *Letters and Papers of Major General John Sullivan*, 3 vols. (Concord: New Hampshire Historical Society, 1939), vol. III, 48–53.

[44] Frederick Cook, ed., *Journals of the Military Expedition of Major General John Sullivan against the Six Nations* (Auburn, NY: Knapp, Peck & Thomson, 1887); Max M. Mintz, *Seeds of Empire: The American Revolutionary Conquest of the Iroquois* (New York: New York University Press, 1999); Joseph R. Fischer, *A Well-Executed Failure: The Sullivan Campaign against the Iroquois, July–September 1779* (Columbia: South Carolina University Press, 1997); *Papers of George Washington: Revolutionary War Series*, vol. XXII, 533; Hammond, *Letters and Papers of Major General John Sullivan*, vol. III, 134.

[45] Calloway, *American Revolution in Indian Country*, Chapter 5.

the time peace was made.⁴⁶ Indians controlled the Ohio country and Britain might, as it did in later years, propose establishing the trans-Appalachian West as an Indian buffer against American expansion, something France and Spain also favored.⁴⁷ Washington understood that prospects for the growth and even the survival of the young republic looked bleak if it won independence but remained confined to the land along the Atlantic coast with no opportunity for expansion westward. Being able to claim the fertile lands of Iroquois country and the Ohio Valley on the basis of conquest during the war would be essential to American success at the peace talks. The United States lacked authority in the west, and it needed military strikes in the region – either conducted by federal forces or outsourced to local militias – to establish its claim to the western lands that Washington knew the independent states would need if they were to grow into a nation.⁴⁸ Consequently, Americans continued their assaults on Indian lands and communities long after Lord Cornwallis surrendered to Washington and his French allies at Yorktown in 1781.

The Delawares had tried to avoid war at the beginning of the revolution, but they bore its brunt at the end. Colonel Daniel Brodhead at Fort Pitt believed that, although some Delawares remained friendly to the United States, most now favored the British. In April 1781, he assembled a force of 300 Continental soldiers and Pennsylvania militia, marched against the Delaware capital at Coshocton, and "completely surprised" the town. Finding only fifteen young warriors there, the militia took them prisoner, tried them, found them guilty of raiding and killing, and sentenced them to death. They then bound, tomahawked, and scalped them. They took another twenty or so noncombatants prisoner and burned the town. The plunder they brought back sold for about £80,000, Brodhead said. Indians denounced it as an unprovoked massacre; Brodhead tried to pass it off as a battle (in which, strangely, "I had not a man killed or wounded") and blamed the atrocities on the militia whom he said he could not control.⁴⁹

---

⁴⁶ John Thomas Flexner, *George Washington in the American Revolution* (Boston, MA: Little, Brown, 1967), 423.
⁴⁷ François Furstenberg, "The Significance of the Trans-Appalachian Frontier in Atlantic History," *American Historical Review* 113:3 (2008), 647–77: 655.
⁴⁸ A. C. Flick, ed., "New Sources on the Sullivan–Clinton Campaign in 1779: The Indian–Tory Side of the Campaign," *Quarterly Journal of the New York State Historical Association* 10 (1929), 194 (quote); Colin G. Calloway, *The Indian World of George Washington: The First President, the First Americans, and the Birth of the Nation* (New York: Oxford University Press, 2018), 259, 280–1.
⁴⁹ C. A. Weslager, *The Delaware Indians: A History* (New Brunswick, NJ: Rutgers University Press, 1989, [1972]), 314; Louise Phelps Kellogg, ed., *Frontier Retreat on the*

The Delawares who lived at Gnadenhütten, a village founded by Moravian missionaries in the upper Muskingum Valley, were pacifists. Unfortunately, their neutrality rendered them suspect in the eyes of militants on both sides. In March 1782, Colonel David Williamson and 200 Pennsylvania militia marched to Gnadenhütten. They rounded up the inhabitants, separated the men and the women and children into two houses, and debated how to put them to death. The next day, as the Indians prayed and sang hymns, the militia bound them together in pairs, systematically bludgeoned them to death with wooden mallets, and then scalped and burned them. Ninety-six men, women, and children perished.[50] Gnadenhütten means "Huts of Grace."

When not surprised in their villages, Indian warriors inflicted defeats on American expeditions in the west. Delawares exacted revenge for the massacre of their relatives at Gnadenhütten three months later when they defeated an American expedition heading for Sandusky. They captured and ritually tortured to death Colonel William Crawford, a friend and business associate (read: fellow land speculator) of George Washington. Reports of Crawford's grisly fate provided powerful anti-Indian propaganda and fueled anti-Indian sentiment. In the disorder and chaos of the revolution on the Ohio Valley frontier, revenge killings multiplied. In historian Patrick Griffin's words, racist violence became "the new basis of society in the West."[51]

Shawnee and other warriors routed a force of Kentuckians at the Battle of Blue Licks in August 1782. Daniel Boone was in the battle and one of his sons was among the dead. In the fall, Boone and George Rogers Clark retaliated with another invasion of Shawnee country. They burned five villages, "entirely destroyed their corn and other fruits, and spread desolation through their country." The Shawnees suffered few casualties, but accused "the white Savages Virginians" of committing atrocities.[52] Many Shawnees pulled back

Upper Ohio, 1779–1781 (Madison: Wisconsin State Historical Society, 1917), 265–6, 342–4, 352–53, 376–81, 399; *Pennsylvania. Archives*, 1st series, 12 vols., vol. IX, 161–2 (no casualties).

[50] Paul A. W. Wallace, *Thirty Thousand Miles with John Heckewelder or Travels amoung the Indians of Pennsylvania, New York & Ohio in the 18th Century* (Lewisburg, PA: Wennawoods, 1998) (original edition, Pittsburgh: University of Pittsburgh, 1958), 189–200; *Pennsylvania. Archives*, 1st series, vol. IX, 524–5; Papers of the Continental Congress, 1774–1789, National Archives, Washington, DC, Microfilm 247, reel 73, item 59, vol. III, 49–51.

[51] Griffin, *American Leviathan*, 154.

[52] "Journal of Daniel Boone," *Ohio Archaeological and Historical Publications* 13 (1904), 276; Draper Mss., 1AA 276–77.

from the Ohio River where they were vulnerable to American assaults and congregated with their allies in new refugee towns on the Auglaize and Maumee rivers in northeastern Ohio, communities that were created by war and became the center of the continuing Indian war for independence.[53]

The war had a searing impact in Indian country and on Indian communities, regardless of which side they supported. New England Indians who served the Patriot cause did so at great cost. Stockbridge, a town of about 300 people, lost about forty men in the course of the war. William Apess, a Pequot writing in the next century, said that the Indian town of Mashpee on Cape Cod sent twenty-six men to fight and all but one "fell martyrs to liberty in the struggle for Independence." The Pequots themselves lost about half of the men who went to war. Their Mohegan neighbors suffered heavily as well: Mohegan Rebecca Tanner lost five sons serving in the American army.[54] Mohegan minister Samon Occom reckoned the revolution "has been the most Distructive to poor Indians of any wars that happened in my Day."[55]

American forces killed between two and four times as many Indians during the revolutionary war as British and colonial forces did during the Seven Years' War and Pontiac's War. "[N]ever before had Europeans destroyed so many Indian towns over such a wide area – from the Carolinas to New York – as Americans did during their war to obtain independence from Britain."[56] Indians told the British, "if we had the means of publishing to the World the many Acts of Treachery & Cruelty committed by them on our Women & Children, it would appear that the title of Savages would with much greater justice be applied to them than to us."[57] Indians told the Spanish governor in St. Louis that the revolution was "the greatest blow that could have been dealt us."[58]

Added to the toll taken by war, a familiar killer reappeared in war-torn environments. During the course of the revolution smallpox struck

---

[53] Calloway, *American Revolution in Indian Country*, Chapter 6.
[54] Ibid., 28, 34; Barry O'Connell, ed., *On Our Own Ground: The Complete Writings of William Apess, a Pequot* (Amherst: University of Massachusetts Press, 1992), 239–40; George Quintal, Jr., *Patriots of Color: African Americans and Native Americans at Battle Road and Bunker Hill* (Boston, MA: Boston National Historical Park, 2002), 30–1; *African American and American Indian Patriots of the Revolutionary War* (Washington, DC: National Society Daughters of the American Revolution, 2001).
[55] Brooks, *Collected Writings of Samson Occom*, 119.
[56] Ostler, *Surviving Genocide*, 75–6.
[57] Correspondence and Papers of Governor General Sir Frederick Haldimand, 1758–91, British Museum, London, Additional Manuscripts, 21779: 111–12.
[58] Quoted in Calloway, *American Revolution in Indian Country*, vi, 281.

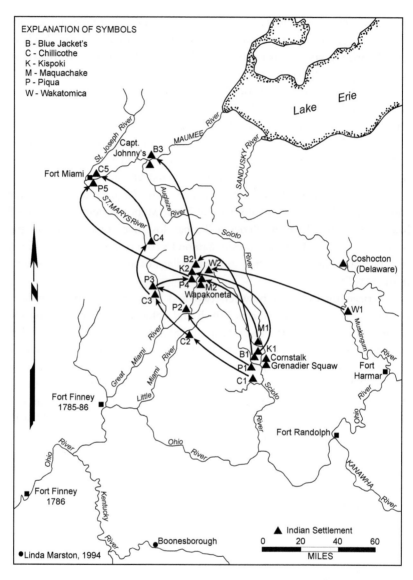

Map 16.3 The Shawnee migrations, 1774–1794. Published in Colin G. Calloway, *The American Revolution in Indian Country: Crisis and Diversity in Native American Communities* (Cambridge University Press, 1995).

Mohawks, Oneidas, Onondagas, Senecas, Creeks, Cherokees, and many other Indian communities, killing hundreds of people and adding to the miseries of the war in the east. In the west, a smallpox epidemic broke out in Mexico City in September 1779, spread north across the Great Plains, and reached Hudson Bay by the end of the war, killing thousands of people in its path.[59]

The Continuing Revolution in Indian Country

At the Treaty of Paris in 1783, Britain recognized the independence of the United States and transferred its claims to all the territory between the Atlantic and the Mississippi and between the Great Lakes and Florida. Britain returned Florida to Spain, but the boundary line between Spanish Florida and the new United States remained vague. The treaty brought no peace to Indian country. Indians were furious and incredulous when they learned that their British allies had given away their lands. Not having been present at or party to the Treaty of Paris, they rejected and resisted American assertions of sovereignty over their homelands. The Americans told them "Your Fathers the English have made Peace with us for themselves, but forgot you their Children, who Fought with them, and neglected you like Bastards."[60] It was difficult for Indians to disagree. Nevertheless, fully expecting another war with the young republic, the British in Canada maintained alliances with Indians for years after the revolution and continued to warn them that Americans intended to take their lands and destroy them as a people.[61] It was difficult for Indians to disagree with that either.

The revolution changed forever American relations with the imperial power across the Atlantic, but it also revolutionized power relations on the continent of North America as "American rebels forwarded their own varieties of independence at the expense of others."[62] Having won

---

[59] Elizabeth A. Fenn, *Pox Americana: The Great Smallpox Epidemic of 1775–82* (New York: Hill & Wang, 2001); Colin G. Calloway, *One Vast Winter Count: The Native American West before Lewis and Clark* (Lincoln, NE: University of Nebraska Press, 2003), 415–26.
[60] Correspondence and Papers of Governor General Sir Frederick Haldimand, 21779: 117.
[61] Colin G. Calloway, *Crown and Calumet: British–Indian Relations, 1783–1815* (Norman: University of Oklahoma Press, 1987); Timothy D. Willig, *Restoring the Chain of Friendship: British Policy and the Indians of the Great Lakes, 1783–1815* (Lincoln, NE: University of Nebraska Press, 2008).
[62] DuVal, *Independence Lost*, xxiv.

independence from the British empire the United States created a different kind of empire and governed its own colonial territories. A post-colonial republic became simultaneously a settler empire, but imperialism and republicanism could be deemed compatible if the lands into which the nation expanded were "vacant" and "domestic space." The federal government might disparage the treaty-breaking assaults of settler colonists on Indian lives and lands – and George Washington decried their lawless occupation of lands to which he claimed title – but nation-building and settler colonialism went hand-in-hand. As the late Patrick Wolfe explained, settler colonialism operated on the "logic of elimination," removing or destroying Indigenous people to make their land available. The United States government absorbed frontier settlers' takeovers of Indian land; sanctioned, turned a blind eye to, or lamented their killing of Indian people; invoked on-the-ground "settler sovereignty" to exert jurisdiction and control over Indian country, and increasingly shaped the pace and patterns of settlement.[63] The American victory in the revolution unleashed a flood of settlers down the Ohio River who drove out the Indians, built towns on sites once occupied by Indian villages, and reduced Indian people to hunger. Native American wars for independence continued long after the American colonists had won their independence.

Efforts to restore peace and social order on the frontier in the wake of the bloody revolutionary war proved futile. The new federalist government confronted the same difficulties that had plagued the British imperial administration in its efforts to impose some restraints on its citizens as they flooded Indian lands, and federalist officials and Indian civil chiefs both struggled to restrain their warriors from violence.[64] The United States government found, as had the British in 1763, that proclaiming order on a distant frontier was a far cry from being able to secure it.

---

[63] Carroll Smith-Rosenberg, *This Violent Empire: The Birth of an American National Identity* (Chapel Hill: University of North Carolina Press, 2010); Mark Rifkin, *Manifesting America: The Imperial Construction of U.S. National Space* (New York: Oxford University Press, 2009), 8–10, 38; Bethel Saler, *The Settlers' Empire: Colonialism and State Formation in America's Old Northwest* (Philadelphia: University of Pennsylvania Press, 2015); Patrick Wolfe, "Settler Colonialism and the Elimination of the Native," *Journal of Genocide Research* 8 (2006), 387–409; Lisa Ford, *Settler Sovereignty: Jurisdiction and Indigenous People in America and Australia, 1788–1836* (Cambridge, MA: Harvard University Press, 2010); Paul Frymer, *Building an American Empire: The Era of Territorial and Political Expansion* (Princeton: Princeton University Press, 2017).

[64] David Andrew Nichols, *Red Gentlemen and White Savages: Indians, Federalists, and the Search for Order on the American Frontier* (Charlottesville: University of Virginia Press, 2008).

The future, perhaps even the survival, of the new nation depended on expansion and the acquisition of Indian lands. The United States government had no money after the long war; its only resource was the land Britain had ceded at the Treaty of Paris – Indian land which, transformed into "public land," could be sold to settlers to help fill the treasury. James Wilson, who signed both the Declaration of Independence and the Constitution, the two foundational documents of the United States, also recognized the foundational role of Indian land in the growth of a nation fueled by European immigration. The United States had immense quantities of land but lacked labor and capital, he wrote; Europe had an abundance of labor and capital but lacked land. Migration on to Indian land would benefit both Europe and the United States.[65]

Beginning with the Declaration of Independence, the United States endeavored to stake its place as a new nation by diplomatic dealings with the existing nations of the world. That involved dealing with Indian nations to the west as well as with European nations to the east.[66] But the dealings with Indian nations were about Indian land. At Fort Stanwix with the Iroquois in 1784, at Fort McIntosh with the Ohio tribes in 1785, and at Fort Finney with the Shawnees in 1786, American commissioners dictated terms based on the assumption that the United States had already acquired Indian territory by right of conquest from Britain. At Fort McIntosh, they told the Indians that since the English king had made no provision for them, they were "left to obtain peace from the U. States ... upon such conditions as seem proper to Congress." Indians' objections that these lands had been handed down to them by their ancestors were of no consequence, the Americans said, *"because we claim the country by conquest; and are to give not to receive."* At the Treaty of Fort Finney in 1786, George Rogers Clark adopted his usual hardline stance; the American commissioners rode roughshod over the old rituals of wampum diplomacy and offered the Shawnees a blunt choice between acquiescence and destruction.[67]

---

[65] Quoted in Robert Alexander, *The Northwest Ordinance: Constitutional Politics and the Theft of Native Land* (Jefferson, NC: McFarland, 2017), 53.

[66] Eliga H. Gould, *Among the Powers of the Earth: The American Revolution and the Making of a New World Empire* (Cambridge, MA: Harvard University Press, 2012); Leonard J. Sadosky, *Revolutionary Negotiations: Indians, Empires, and Diplomats in the Founding of America* (Charlottesville: University of Virginia Press, 2010).

[67] Downes, *Council Fires on the Upper Ohio*, 294 (quote; italics in original). The three treaties and related documents are reprinted in Calloway, *Revolution and Confederation*, ch. 4.

There was no peace even for those who signed the treaties. Within months after the Treaty at Fort Finney, Kentucky militia were back in Shawnee country raiding and burning villages. They found only old men, women, and children in the towns who, according to one report, "made no resistance; the men were literally murdered."[68] Moluntha, an elderly chief who had signed the treaty, met the Americans clutching a copy of the treaty in his hand and died with an American axe in his skull.[69] The Treaty of Hopewell with the United States in 1785 ostensibly secured Cherokee boundaries, but Dragging Canoe did not attend and many frontier settlers ignored its terms: "Your people settle much Faster on our Lands after a Treaty than Before," the Cherokee chief Old Tassel reflected bitterly.[70] Old Tassel worked for peace but American militia murdered him under a flag of truce in 1788.

Nor did the American assault on Indian land spare those who had served the Patriot cause. Stockbridge Indians, who had joined their American neighbors in a shared struggle for land and liberty, lost their land to those same neighbors. Most migrated from western Massachusetts and took up residence on Oneida lands in New York.[71] The Oneidas lost most of their homeland to New York State and New York land speculators in a series of fraudulent treaties and shady deals.[72]

Choctaws and Chickasaws recognized the potential for playing off Spanish and American rivals, as they had previously played off rival colonial powers. After Britain surrendered Mobile and Pensacola to Spain, Choctaws had to secure trade from Spain, the United States, or the several states to their east. Their predicament was heightened by the precipitous decline of the white-tailed deer population as Choctaw hunters harvested

---

[68] "Logan's Campaign: 1786," *Ohio Archaeological and Historical Publications* 22 (1913), 520–1; *The Military Journal of Major Ebenezer Denny* (Philadelphia, PA: Lippincott, 1859), 94.
[69] Calloway, *American Revolution in Indian Country*, 175–7.
[70] Quoted in Calloway, *American Revolution in Indian Country*, 209.
[71] Calloway, *American Revolution in Indian Country*, 100–7; David J. Silverman, *Red Brethren: The Brothertown and Stockbridge Indians and the Problem of Race in Early America* (Ithaca, NY: Cornell University Press, 2010), 118–20.
[72] Glatthaar and Martin, *Forgotten Allies*, Chapter 13; Taylor, *Divided Ground*, Chapter 5; Laurence M. Hauptman, *Conspiracy of Interests: Iroquois Dispossession and the Rise of New York State* (Syracuse, NY: Syracuse University Press, 1999), Chapters 2–4; Franklin B. Hough, ed., *Proceedings of the Commissioners of Indian Affairs Appointed by Law for the Extinguishment of Indian Affairs Appointed by Law for the Extinguishment of Indian Titles in the State of New York*, 2 vols. (Albany, NY: Joel Munsell, 1861), vol. 1, 84–108, 122–4, 241–6; Calloway, *Revolution and Confederation*, 332–8, 472–4.

thousands of deerskins to purchase manufactured goods and rum.[73] A chief named Franchimastabé made a treaty with Spain at Mobile in June 1784; another chief, Taboca, led a delegation over hundreds of miles to attend the Hopewell treaty with the United States early in 1786.[74] Likewise, a Chickasaw chief named Ugulayacabe or Wolf's Friend and other Chickasaw delegates at the Mobile treaty secured continued access to manufactured goods by granting Spain a monopoly on their trade, while a rival Chickasaw chief, Piominko, granted the same trade monopoly to the United States at Hopewell.[75] Piominko and Ugulayacabe were both determined to preserve Chickasaw land and independence; they differed over how to do it. The United States represented one source of trade and protection; Spain offered another. American and Spanish officials trying to follow shifting Choctaw and Chickasaw foreign policies saw only the tips of intratribal politics as one party or another reached out to them and made agreements.[76]

Creeks were shocked by the news of the Treaty of Paris. One chief dismissed it as "a Virginia Lie." McGillivray denounced it as a shameful act of betrayal: Britain had made its own peace and divided Creek lands between the Spaniards and Americans. The king had no right to give up a country he never owned.[77] Spain, the United States, Georgia, and North Carolina all claimed territory north of the 31st parallel and east of the Mississippi, as of course did the Indian nations who lived there.[78] Americans, Spaniards, and British all vied for control of Creek country and influence within the Creek Nation. The United States took the position that most Creeks lived on American soil, and Georgia claimed the Mississippi as its western boundary. But Spain viewed the Tennessee River as the northern limit to its territory and tried to use the tribes who lived there as buffers against its aggressive new republican neighbor.

---

[73] Richard White, *The Roots of Dependency: Subsistence, Environment, and Social Change among the Choctaws, Pawnees, and Navajos* (Lincoln: University of Nebraska Press, 1983), Chapters 4–5.
[74] O'Brien, *Choctaws in a Revolutionary Age*, Chapter 4.
[75] Calloway, *Revolution and Confederation*, 424; *Indian Affairs: Laws and Treaties*, vol. II: *Treaties*, comp. Charles J. Kappler (Washington, DC: Government Printing Office, 1904), 15–16.
[76] Calloway, *Revolution in Indian Country*, 234.
[77] C.O. 5/82: 368 ("Virginia Lie"), 372–3, 405, 432; C.O. 5/110: 70–1; C.O. 5/560: 71–4; John Walton Caughey, *McGillivray of the Creeks* (Norman: University of Oklahoma Press, 1938), 73–4, 90–3.
[78] Caughey, *McGillivray of the Creeks*, 70 (quote).

McGillivray and the Creeks adjusted to the new international situation and charted new foreign policies. "As a free Nation we have an undoubted right to chuse what Protection we think proper," McGillivray told Esteban Miró, the Spanish governor of Louisiana. Although he preferred "the protection of a great Monarch ... to that of a distracted Republic," McGillivray made the best of the new situation and made treaties with both Spain and, at New York in 1790, the United States.[79]

In the North, confronted by a nation on the move, Indians rebuilt multi-tribal coalitions and fought to contain American expansion at the Ohio River for a dozen years after the revolution. The Northwestern Indian confederacy repelled an American invasion in 1790, and the following year obliterated the only army the United States had.[80] Not until General Anthony Wayne rebuilt the army and defeated the allied tribes at the Battle of Fallen Timbers in 1794 did the Indians make peace. At the Treaty of Greenville in 1795, chiefs who had fought the Americans since the days of the revolution ceded most of Ohio to the United States. But the Greenville treaty boundary was no more effective in checking American expansion than the Proclamation or Fort Stanwix boundaries had been. "Scarcely anything short of a Chinese Wall, or a line of Troops will restrain Land Jobbers, and the Incroachment of Settlers, upon the Indian Territory," said George Washington.[81]

Washington, Secretary of War Henry Knox, Thomas Jefferson, and other founding fathers wrestled with the question of how they could deal honorably with Indian people at the same time as they built a nation on Indian homelands. The Northwest Ordinance of 1787 spelled out the dilemma. In establishing the territorial system of the United States, the Ordinance laid out a blueprint for national expansion on Indian lands. The same document pledged that the United States would deal fairly and justly with Indian people. Washington and Jefferson resolved the dilemma to their satisfaction by initiating and implementing policies of "civilization": Native Americans would give up their hunting territories and hunting economy as Americans encroached and game diminished, but they would enjoy a better life by adopting sedentary agrarian lifestyles on smaller plots of land. So-called

---

[79] Caughey, *McGillivray of the Creeks*, 73–4 (quote); Calloway, *The Indian World of George Washington*, Chapter 15.
[80] Colin G. Calloway, *The Victory with No Name: The Native American Defeat of the First American Army* (New York: Oxford University Press, 2015).
[81] John C. Fitzpatrick, ed., *The Writings of George Washington from the Original Manuscript Sources, 1745–1799*, 39 vols. (Washington, DC: Government Printing Office, 1931–1944), vol. xxv, 112.

civilization policies operated to promote and perpetuate dispossession rather than curtail it or cushion its impact.

Viewed from Indian country, the United States won independence from the British empire in the east only to create its own empire in the west.[82] Jefferson called it "an empire of liberty," but it was built on Indian lands at the expense of Indian liberties and justified by a systematic and sustained assault on Indian ways of life. Native Americans fought for their independence during the revolution and they struggled to preserve their lands, cultures, and sovereignty in the nation that the revolution created. It proved to be a struggle without end.

---

[82] Calloway, *Indian World of George Washington*, Chapter 14.

17
Shaping the Constitution

MAX M. EDLING

Introduction

On the morning of 18 September 1787, William Jackson left Philadelphia by stagecoach for New York City and the Second Continental Congress. Formally the government of the American union, Congress was in practice a spent force that struggled to even reach a quorum. Jackson had been the secretary of the Constitutional Convention, and his task was to inform Congress that after a long summer of debates the convention had hammered out a proposal for a new constitution for the union. Along with the proposal, Jackson also carried a covering letter signed by George Washington, the convention's president, which outlined the rationale behind the Constitutional Convention and the aims of the new constitution. Reform-minded "friends of our country," the letter said, had long realized that "the power of making war, peace and treaties, that of levying money and regulating commerce, and the correspondent executive and judicial authorities should be fully and effectually vested in the general government of the Union." But for such powers to be safely entrusted to Congress it was necessary to reorganize the national government.

By investing these powers in the national government, the states relinquished part of their sovereignty. The letter conceded that it was difficult to "draw with precision the line between those rights which must be surrendered, and those which may be reserved; and on the present occasion this difficulty was encreased by a difference among the several States as to their situation, extent, habits, and particular interests." Yet "each State in the Convention" accepted that stronger union was the means to "prosperity, felicity, safety," and even "national existence." Hence, they were led "to be less rigid on points of inferior magnitude, than might have been otherwise expected; and thus the Constitution, which we now present, is the result of a spirit of amity, and of that mutual deference and concession which the peculiarity of our political situation rendered indispensable." Because the states could relinquish their sovereignty only by a voluntary act, and in order to secure the sanction of popular consent to the new compact of union, a separate letter from the Convention recommended that the proposed constitution be "submitted to a Convention of Delegates, chosen in each State by the People thereof" for ratification or rejection.[1]

In our own time the American Constitution is viewed as the fundamental law of a federal state, in which the federal government is the primary locus of political life. This is the result of two centuries of centralization of political authority driven by modernization and international competition, and close to a century of rapid federal government growth. Historians of the Age of Revolutions have contributed to this understanding of the Constitution by presenting it as a milestone in the transition to representative democracy, rule by law, and civic rights, which became organizing principles of political life in several nations on both sides of the Atlantic Ocean in the decades around 1800, and the aspiration of political radicals in many more. But although the insertion of the Constitution into a narrative of the rise of liberal democracy makes sense when looking back at the period from present times, it offers little insight into the intentions of the Constitution's framers, who were looking forward and saw a highly uncertain future for their experiment in republican government.

The letters from the Philadelphia Convention to Congress turn our attention to an alternative understanding of the Constitution as a compact of federal union between sovereign republics: a union that served as a means for the states to maintain their independence and promote their interests; a union that was the outcome of a negotiation between states with different and sometimes conflicting interests, rather than between social classes; a union that was sanctioned by "the peoples" of these states rather than by "the people" of the United States; a union created by a grant of power from the states to the national government, in a move that involved the difficult matter of how to "draw the line" between state and national authority.

The American founders were steeped in early modern political theory, which viewed republics as inherently weak and unstable polities at risk from foreign domination and conquest. If the security dilemma of republics was

---

[1] "The President of the Convention to the President of Congress, 17 September," in Merrill Jensen, John P. Kaminski, and Gaspare J. Saladin, eds., *The Documentary History of the Ratification of the Constitution*, 37 vols. (Madison: Wisconsin Historical Society Press, 1976–), vol. 1, 305–6.

widely recognized in this literature, so was its solution. By pooling resources, federal union allowed republics to combine the internal advantages of their republican form of government with the external strength of monarchies. To American statesmen of the revolution, federal union was therefore a necessary appendage to independence. Necessary to convince European powers that American independence represented a viable state-building project and necessary to furnish the means for the colonies to defeat Britain in the War of Independence. It was therefore perfectly natural that Congress' decision in May 1776 to declare the colonies independent was accompanied by a decision to create a federal union. But whereas the Declaration of Independence was produced and delivered quickly, the Articles of Confederation were presented to Congress only in 1777 and brought into effect only by the ratification of Maryland in 1781. Long before that day, the flaws in the Articles had become apparent. By 1787, a significant reform movement was afoot to reform a union that seemed unable to safeguard the independence, security, and prosperity of the American states. Reform or dissolution of the union into smaller confederacies seemed at that point a real possibility.

The Foundations of Union

The American union was not only a theoretical construct but also grew out of the practice of opposition against the British Parliament that began after the conclusion of the Seven Years' War. The new fiscal and commercial regulations introduced by Parliament made no attempt to discriminate between, and thereby divide, Britain's Atlantic colonies. Unwittingly, the imperial center thus created a shared interest in the peripheries. This shared interest fostered intercolonial coordination of protests. At key moments, such as in the aftermath of the Boston Tea Party of December 1773, the leaders of the revolution managed to maintain intercolonial solidarity.

Intercolonial unity had limits that have not been fully explored by historians. The common claim that Britain lost its American empire in the Treaty of Paris in 1783 is a misrepresentation. Britain in fact retained half of its transatlantic empire and the colonies it kept mattered more than the colonies it lost.[2] Caribbean dependencies such as Jamaica were economically far more important than those on the North American mainland. Nova Scotia, East Florida, and St. Kitts had greater military significance to the protection of the

---

[2] See, on the same point, Trevor Burnard, Chapter 9 in this volume.

most valuable American possessions of the British empire than any of the original thirteen states. Many American revolutionaries hoped that the impulse toward independence would reach beyond the thirteen colonies. They expected that Britain's Caribbean dominions and the province of Quebec, recently conquered from the French, would join the protests against the Stamp Act in 1765, and some did. As late as 1777, Congress inserted in the Articles of Confederation an open invitation for "Canada" to join the American union. But the British West Indies remained loyal to the empire because the planter class believed that they had more to gain from maintaining the imperial connection. In the north, a history of intermittent conflict with their Yankee neighbors inspired little faith in the Québécois that the United States would respect their religion and civic rights. They, too, chose to put their trust in the British empire. Intercolonial unity in fact arose only when geographic proximity was coupled with a common identity based on the Protestant religion and the British constitution, and a common sense that English liberties were endangered.[3]

The thirteen colonies coordinated their opposition to Britain in continental congresses and correspondence societies. In these fora a shared interpretation of what was at stake in the conflict with Britain and a shared understanding of the political identity of the colonies emerged, laying the foundation for a primitive concept of American nationhood distinctive from both individual colonies and Britain. These institutions also created new sources of political legitimacy because they claimed to speak in the name of the united colonies. This supra-colonial authority began competing with the imperial government for the allegiance of the inhabitants in the mainland colonies, but far from everyone accepted their authority.[4]

The practice of protest against Britain thus gave rise to proto-national institutions and a proto-national authority in North America. But the struggle itself was framed as the protection from imperial initiatives not of the rights of America, but of the corporate rights of the individual colonies. When the struggle began, neither the precise nature of the colonies as bodies politic, nor their rights, were fully articulated. The intellectual history of the

---

[3] Andrew Jackson O'Shaugnessy, *An Empire Divided: The American Revolution and the British Caribbean* (Philadelphia: University of Pennsylvania Press, 2000).

[4] Edmund S. Morgan and Helen M. Morgan, *The Stamp Act Crisis: Prologue to Revolution* (Chapel Hill: University of North Carolina Press, 1953); David Ammerman, *In the Common Cause: American Response to the Coercive Acts of 1774* (Charlottesville: University of Virginia Press, 1974); Edmund S. Morgan, *Inventing the People: The Rise of Popular Sovereignty in England and America* (New York: Norton, 1988), 239–62.

American Revolution is in large part the working out of the status of the colonies in the British empire. Thanks to continental congresses, correspondence societies, and the circulation of print, the ideology of the revolution became intercolonial. It found expression in the formal declarations and correspondence of colonial assemblies and continental congresses, and in pamphlets and newspaper essays. The series of essays penned by John Dickinson under the title *Letters from a Farmer in Pennsylvania* is a good case in point. The series first appeared in installments in a Philadelphia newspaper, but was eventually reprinted in all but four colonial newspapers. Three pamphlet editions were printed in Philadelphia, two in Boston, and other editions appeared in New York, Williamsburg, and far-away Dublin and Paris.[5]

The so-called "commonwealth" conception of the British empire that was articulated by revolutionary ideologues in the 1760s and 1770s envisioned the empire as a conglomeration of sovereign and formally equal polities held together by their voluntary subjection to the rule of the same monarch. This distinctive theory of empire shaped protests against Britain but also the federal union that came to replace the British empire. The theory stressed the corporate status and rights of the colonies against the right of Parliament to legislate for Britain's American dependencies. It was premised on the idea that the constituent parts of the empire were all sovereign and equal. The colonies were presented as distinctive bodies politic and were equipped with a history that stretched back to their first settlement. On settling in America, transplanted Englishmen chose to "continue their union" with England, said Thomas Jefferson, "by submitting themselves to the same sovereign, who was thereby made the central link connecting the several parts of the empire thus newly multiplied." The colonies had never been under the authority of Parliament, however, because they were sovereign polities that soon created their own legislative assemblies, which, according to John Adams, "have, and ought to exercise, every power of the house of Commons."[6]

---

[5] Robert Middlekauff, *The Glorious Cause: The American Revolution, 1763–1789*, 2nd edition (New York: Oxford University Press, 2005), 161.

[6] Alexander Hamilton, "The Farmer Refuted, &c.," in Harold C. Syrett, ed., *Papers of Alexander Hamilton*, 27 vols. (New York: Columbia University Press, 1961–1987), vol. 1, 81–165; Thomas Jefferson, "Draft of Instructions to the Virginia Delegates in the Continental Congress (MS Text of A Summary View, &c.), [July 1774]," in Julian P. Boyd, ed., *The Papers of Thomas Jefferson*, 45 vols. (Princeton: Princeton University Press, 1950–), vol. 1, 121–37; John Adams, "Novanglus VII: To the Inhabitants of the Colony of Massachusetts-Bay, 6 March 1775," in Robert J. Taylor, Gregg L. Lint, and C. Walker, eds., *Papers of John Adams*, 19 vols. (Cambridge, MA: Harvard University Press, 1977–), vol. 11, 307–27. See Jack P. Greene, *The Constitutional Origins of the American Revolution* (New York: Cambridge University Press, 2011).

Although American ideologues denied that Parliament had any right to legislate over the internal affairs of the colonies, they did accept that it had the right to regulate trade within and without the empire. But this arrangement, said Adams in words that signal his understanding of the empire as a federal union, "may be compared to a treaty of commerce, by which ... distinct states are cemented together, in perpetual league and amity." At least in the abstract Adams seems to have accepted the potential problem that such states might pursue their own "particular interests" to the detriment of the common good of the whole. A "superintending power" might therefore be necessary to ensure that all states acted in concert, at least in the event of war or commercial conflicts. Nevertheless, Adams claimed that serious conflicts of interests were unlikely and called for the continuation of the status quo "by letting parliament regulate trade and our own assemblies all other matters." This division of labor between a central authority governing trade and external matters and colonial or state authorities governing "all other matters" would survive independence to become an organizing principle of the American union.[7]

The notion that Britain's colonies were in effect self-governing polities bound together in union with the mother country for purposes of trade and defense colored the flurry of formal plans for imperial reform that appeared as the American crisis unfolded in the 1770s. According to one count as many as thirty-seven of these appeared between 1774 and 1777 alone.[8] It also served to guide and legitimate colonial protests. When colonial governors and Parliament tried to quell resistance to British legislation by dissolving colonial assemblies, the revolutionaries responded by forming new representative assemblies. Technically extra-legal, their political authority was founded on the principle of popular sovereignty. Looking back at the chaotic situation of the mid-1770s from the distance of two decades, St. George Tucker commented that even though the provisional assemblies of Virginia had not even "the shadow of a legal, or, constitutional form about [them]" they embodied *"the people themselves,"* who were "impelled to assemble from a sense of common danger, consulting for the common good, and acting in all things for the common safety." Tucker never bothered to define who the "people" were, but the provisional assemblies to which he referred

---

[7] John Adams, "Novanglus VII," in Taylor, Lint, and Walker, *Papers of John Adams*, vol. II, 320–2.
[8] Heather Schwartz, "Re-Writing the Empire: Plans for Institutional Reform in British America, 1675–1791," PhD dissertation, SUNY Binghamton, 2011, appendix A, 245–55.

represented property-owners rather than a cross-section of Virginia inhabitants. Tucker's interpretation of events presented the electorate of Virginia and the other colonies as sovereign nations or "states," the latter the more common term at the time. According to revolutionary ideologues, imperial action could dissolve colonial governments but not the American bodies politic. Faced with the threat of losing their government, the sovereign people possessed the "unlimited and unlimitable authority and capacity" to create new governments according to its will.⁹

At the same time that provisional assemblies in the colonies claimed to express the popular will when creating new governments, the continental congresses claimed authority to speak in the name of the American people when recommending all colonies to formalize their provisional governments by writing new state constitutions. Eleven colonies did so in the period from 1775 to 1777. All of them claimed independent statehood and instituted a republican form of government founded on popular sovereignty. The two exceptions were Connecticut and Rhode Island where the colonial charters already embodied republican principles and could therefore be retained once all references to the English monarch had been excised. The ideology of the American Revolution thus introduced a nebulous concept of popular sovereignty, which somehow existed both at state and national level. It was a malleable source of political legitimacy that often proved to be helpful in overcoming theoretical conundrums thrown up by both the commonwealth conception of empire and the subsequent American union. But it also inserted into American political life a fundamental tension between local and national authority that remained unresolved until the Civil War.¹⁰

---

⁹ Kamper v. Hawkins, in Report of a Case, Decided on Saturday, the 16th of November, 1793, in the General Court of Virginia; Wherein Peter Kamper, Was Plaintiff, against Mary Hawkins, Defendant; On a Question Adjourned from the District Court of Dumfries, for Novelty and Difficulty, Touching the Constitutionality of an Act of Assembly; Together with Arguments and Opinions of the Respective Judges at Large, and the Order of the Court Thereon (Philadelphia, PA: McKenzie & Co., 1794), 40, 41, 44; St. George Tucker, "Of the Constitution of Virginia," in Clyde N. Wilson, ed., Tucker, View of the Constitution of the United States, With Selected Writings (Indianapolis, IN: Liberty Fund, 1999), 88, 91.

¹⁰ Merrill Jensen, The Founding of a Nation: A History of the American Revolution, 1763–1776 (New York: Oxford University Press, 1968); Willi Paul Adams, The First American Constitutions (Chapel Hill: University of North Carolina Press, 1980); Richard L. Bushman, King and People in Provincial Massachusetts (Chapel Hill: University of North Carolina Press, 1985); Morgan, Inventing the People; John E. Selby, The Revolution in Virginia, 1775–1783 (Williamsburg, VA: Colonial Williamsburg Foundation, 1988).

Shaping the Constitution

Independence and the First American Union

Independence was declared on 4 July 1776, only after a prolonged debate in which the Second Continental Congress considered the consequences of breaking with Britain. Abiding by the commonwealth concept of the empire, the revolution's leaders first turned to George III for support against Parliament's alleged usurpation of power. But the king shared neither their view of the empire nor of the British Constitution. When Congress' Olive Branch Petition was met by the King's Proclamation for Suppressing Rebellion and Sedition, which declared his North American subjects to be in a state of rebellion, the Declaration of Independence followed. Armed conflict had then been ongoing for more than a year.

The Declaration was the work of a committee appointed by Congress on 11 June, on a day when Congress appointed two additional committees "to prepare and digest the form of a confederation to be entered into between these colonies" and "to prepare a plan of treaties to be proposed to foreign powers." A month earlier, on 10 May, Congress had sent its recommendation to write and adopt new constitutions to the colonies. These four acts – declaring independence, creating a union, establishing relations with foreign powers, and writing state constitutions – were closely intertwined steps in the process toward the creation of an independent union of republics.[11]

By writing and adopting state constitutions the colonies claimed the status of sovereign states. Several of the new constitutions incorporated Congress' declaration of independence in whole or in part, thus illustrating how legitimate authority was based on popular sovereignty simultaneously expressed at national and local level. By writing and adopting the Articles of Confederation, the new sovereign states entered into a union to secure their independence through the defeat of Britain. But independence could succeed only if the American states established diplomatic relationships with foreign powers by entering into international agreements. By declaring their independence to "a candid world," finally, the American colonists signaled that they were in earnest about their decision to free themselves from British rule and that rebellion against their lawful monarch was justified

---

[11] Journals of Congress, 10 May 1776, in Worthington C. Ford et al., eds., *Journals of the Continental Congress*, 34 vols. (Washington, DC: Government Printing Office, 1904–1937), vol. IV, 342, 7 June 1776, vol. V, 425; Jack N. Rakove, *The Beginnings of National Politics: An Interpretative History of the Continental Congress* (New York: Knopf, 1979), 135–91; Leonard J. Sadosky, *Revolutionary Negotiations: Indians, Empires, and Diplomats in the Founding of America* (Charlottesville: University of Virginia Press, 2009), 59–89.

by George III's systematic disregard for the law and for the British Constitution.

Ideally, these four actions should have happened in the correct sequence. Americans should have first established sovereign republics in place of colonies, next these republics should have confederated and the confederation be declared independent, after which the confederation should have entered into treaties and alliances with foreign powers. But the pressure of events jumbled the process. A month before independence was declared, political insider John Adams wrote that it was impossible to "proceed systematically." "We shall be obliged to declare ourselves independent States before we confederate, and indeed before all the Colonies have established their Governments. It is now pretty clear, that all these Measures will follow one another in rapid Succession, and it may not perhaps be of much Importance, which is done first."[12] Adams was right. The states began writing constitutions early in 1776, but only four states had new constitutions in place on 4 July. Four more followed before the end of the year. The United States signed its first international treaty of significance with France in 1778, before the Articles of Confederation had been ratified. Confederation was the last act to be completed. Although the Articles were presented to Congress in 1777, they were only ratified and formally put into effect in 1781.

The American independence process was driven by pressure from the international state-system. The language of the Articles of Confederation makes clear that the management of foreign relations and war were the central purposes behind the formation of the first American union. In the Declaration of Independence, the state-republics each claimed the "full Power to levy War, conclude Peace, contract Alliances, establish Commerce, and to do all other Acts and Things which Independent States may of right do." Articles VI and IX of the Articles of Confederation transferred the power of making war and peace, sending and receiving ambassadors, and entering into treaties and alliances from the states individually to "the united states in congress assembled." Congress was also invested with the power to arbitrate interstate conflicts among the members of the union, to facilitate their commercial intercourse by determining the value of coins and fixing weights and measures, and to regulate member states' relations with American Indian nations.

---

[12] John Adams to Patrick Henry, 3 June 1776, in Taylor, Lint, and Walker, *Papers of John Adams*, vol. IV, 234–5.

The United States thus originated as an organizational solution to the security concerns of thirteen small and weak republics. Union allowed them to defend their independence and interests collectively by pooling their resources. The Articles of Confederation followed the precepts of early modern political theorists closely by investing powers over war and international matters in a congress of states, while reserving to the individual state governments their right to govern their own internal affairs. Despite the fact that Congress was charged with very extensive duties, the Articles created little in the way of national governmental institutions. And although the concept of a sovereign American people can perhaps be gleaned from the Declaration of Independence, the Articles recognized no such body and provided no method to collect the popular will other than channeled through the thirteen member states. Hence, although the Articles presented the United States as a "nation" laying claim to membership in the international system of states, and recognition in the eyes of the law of nations that governed it, the American union did not become a nation-state. There was no mechanism to make the national will anything other than the sum total of the interests of the member states. At the same time, union was believed to be necessary if the states were to survive and flourish as independent polities. Independence and union were mutually dependent and became the "Staatsräson" of the American federation of republics.[13] To a degree not always appreciated, this understanding of the federal union survived the transition from the Articles of Confederation to the Constitution.

War and the Dissolution of Union

During the War of Independence (1775–1783), the Articles of Confederation fell considerably short of their intended aim to allow the states in Congress assembled to pursue the war with efficiency and dispatch. Congress struggled to raise and supply troops, to command resources, and to borrow money. But at least the pressure of war kept the union together. Once independence was secured, centripetal forces set in. Congress failed to deal with several pressing issues that gradually corroded the American union. By winter and spring of 1787, many political leaders and many citizens had come to see the future as a stark choice between reform of the union or the dissolution of the United States.[14]

---

[13] David C. Hendrickson, *Peace Pact: The Lost World of the American Founding* (Lawrence: Kansas University Press, 2003), xii.

[14] George W. Van Cleve, *We Have Not a Government: The Articles of Confederation and the Road to the Constitution* (Chicago: University of Chicago Press, 2017).

The main problems identified by politicians pushing to reform the Articles of Confederation stayed the same from the War of Independence to the meeting of the Constitutional Convention. They were four in number. The first concerned commerce and shipping. The American economy was heavily dependent on the income from international trade, shipping services, and fishing, especially in the middle and northern states. As British colonies, Americans had traded within an extensive imperial common market. With independence, the United States was excluded from several important British markets, while France and Spain continued their pre-independence policy of denying Americans access to their marts. Because the Articles of Confederation left the authority to formulate trade policy to the state governments, it proved to be difficult to coordinate a response to European trade restrictions. Several attempts were made to amend the Articles to invest the power to regulate commerce in Congress.

The second problem concerned the public finances. During the War of Independence Congress had racked up a very substantial public debt to domestic and foreign creditors. The former went unpaid and the United States struggled to maintain its international credit. By 1787, the union was on the verge of bankruptcy. This had serious implications for the American state-building project. In an age when war was fought on credit, defaulting on the debt would severely undermine the union's capacity for war-making. Yet Congress could do little to redress the problem. The Articles of Confederation gave Congress the right to borrow but not to tax. Reflecting the revolution's origin in a tax rebellion of the periphery against the impositions of the metropole, the American union left taxation the exclusive preserve of the state governments. Congress could requisition funds from the states, but when their response fell short it could not coerce the states to fulfill their obligations to the union.

The third problem was the management of the western regions of the United States. The Treaty of Paris awarded the Americans an enormous territory in the continental interior between the Appalachian Mountains and the Mississippi River. Several states had territorial claims in this area that rested on their colonial charters. In a process that began soon after the peace, state governments began the voluntary transfer of their claims to Congress. This made governing trans-Appalachia the responsibility of the union. Potentially an enormous resource, it was an asset hard to cash in on. The region was controlled by powerful American Indian confederacies and only sparsely populated by European Americans. Settling the western territory required organizing the region politically and transferring land rights from

Congress to settlers. The latter issue was resolved by the Land Ordinance of 1785, the former by the Northwest Ordinance of 1787. The Northwest Ordinance was adopted by Congress when the Constitutional Convention was still sitting thanks to members of the convention traveling to New York City to resume their seats in Congress. It was almost certainly part of a deal between northern and southern interests in the convention, and along with the Constitution the Northwest Ordinance formed an integral part of the reform of the American union.

The fourth problem was coercion of the states. The flawed organizational structure of the union underlay and exacerbated the difficulties with managing commerce, finances, and the west. The Articles of Confederation gave Congress wide-ranging authority on paper but little real power to implement decisions. The union was designed to make the state governments the executive arm of Congress. Hence, the state governments had almost all power of implementation and in practice this gave them the power to veto congressional decisions within their jurisdictions. When a state could or would not comply with a congressional decision, that decision could be ignored without consequences. Thus, Congress could declare and conduct war, but not recruit or supply an army; it could borrow money, but not provide for its repayment; it could enter into treaties with foreign powers, but not prevent its own citizens from violating those international agreements. On paper, Congress' powers were formidable; in reality, they were feeble.

Because of the failure of Congress to address problems facing the American union, the War of Independence and the immediate post-war years saw national authority and prestige contract. But not all government did. Whereas the central government became weaker, the state governments became stronger. States expanded their coercive powers to police and suppress dissent. When the revolution broke out, the legitimacy of both independence and the new state governments was questioned by people who remained loyal to the crown and Parliament. There were also many people reluctant to commit themselves either for or against the revolutionary cause. Revolutionaries accepted neither dissent nor neutrality, however, and used the terror of the state to force allegiance to the new regimes. In Pennsylvania, for example, the property of Loyalist dissenters was confiscated. All male citizens were required to muster for the militia and take an oath of allegiance to the new state. So-called "Commissioners of Allegiance" and county lieutenants were empowered to arrest anyone suspected of endangering "the preservation" of the Commonwealth of Pennsylvania and were given immunity from prosecution in the courts.

Violence and murder often accompanied the enforcement of loyalty. All over the United States new jails and prison ships were created to house those who refused to take the oath of allegiance to the new republics and their federal union. The use of the death penalty rose sharply. Between 1777 and 1783, Pennsylvania executed more people than the colonial government had done in the thirty-seven years preceding the revolution.[15]

But the revolution also created conditions for the state governments to play a more positive role in social and economic life by enhancing their ability to respond to constituency demands. The collapse of the empire created an institutional vacuum soon filled not by Congress but by the new states. Although the colonists had vehemently opposed Parliament's attempt to legislate over the colonies, Americans were not averse to government as such. To the contrary, they wanted more, not less, government intervention in society and the economy, but they wanted government intervention under their own control. American independence terminated the Privy Council's power to review and overrule colonial legislation and Parliament's contested right to legislate for the colonists. This freed up the American assemblies to be much more active than in the past. During and after the revolution, state governments redrew election districts, incorporated boroughs and counties, secured land claims, promoted roads, canals, bridges, and ferries, regulated health and hygiene, and supported education.[16] As a consequence, the state governments emerged from the War of Independence as the principal political organization of the American union, whereas the value and effectiveness of the union that had been furnished by the Articles of Confederation were increasingly questioned.

---

[15] Christopher Ryan Pearl, *Conceived in Crisis: The Revolutionary Creation of an American State* (Charlottesville: University of Virginia Press, 2020), Chapter 6; Joshua Canale, "'When a State Abounds in Rascals': New York's Revolutionary Era Committees for Public Safety, 1775–1783," *Journal of the Early Republic* 39:2 (2019), 203–38.

[16] William J. Novak, "A State of Legislatures," *Polity* 40:3 (2008), 340–47; Douglas Bradburn, *The Citizenship Revolution: Politics and the Creation of the American Union, 1774–1804* (Charlottesville: University of Virginia Press, 2009), 47. For more on the rise of the state legislatures in the revolutionary period, see Christopher Tomlins, *Law, Labor, and Ideology in the Early American Republic* (New York: Cambridge University Press, 1993), 35–59; James Henretta, "Magistrates, Common Law Lawyers, Legislators: The Three Legal Systems of British America," in Christopher Tomlins and Michael Grossberg, eds., *The Cambridge History of Law in America*, 3 vols. (Cambridge: Cambridge University Press, 2008), vol. 1, 586–9; Douglas Bradburn, "The Rise of the States: Governance, Institutional Failure, and the Causes of American Independence," unpublished paper presented at the conference on Political Economy and Empire in the Early Modern World, Yale University, May 2013, 14–36; Pearl, *Conceived in Crisis*.

Reforming the Union

The Constitutional Convention convened in Philadelphia in May 1787. The Convention was preceded by numerous attempts to amend the Articles of Confederation, which had begun before they were even ratified. Such amendment proposals invariably addressed the four issues identified above as the scourge of the union: state compliance with congressional demands; revenue and public finance; retaliation against commercial discrimination; and the organization of the trans-Appalachian west. Only the question of the management of the west saw any progress. Reforms addressing the other issues faltered either because sectionalism prevented the existence of sufficient support in Congress or because the unanimous state approval of amendments demanded by the Articles of Confederation could not be reached. When reform through amendments seemed impossible, reform-minded politicians turned from Congress to the states to bring about change. In 1785, Virginia and Maryland negotiated rights of navigation on their shared waterways and later invited Delaware and Pennsylvania to join the agreement. In 1786, delegates from five states met in Annapolis to discuss the national regulation of commerce, but limited attendance prevented them from conducting any business. However, the Annapolis Convention recommended calling another convention the following summer to "devise such further provisions as shall appear to them necessary to render the constitution of the Foederal Government adequate to the exigencies of the Union." There was at first scant support for the idea but gradually the states came round and began to appoint delegates to the Philadelphia Convention. Congress reluctantly sanctioned the meeting, but restricted its mandate to "the sole and express purpose of revising the Articles of Confederation."[17]

Fifty-five delegates from twelve states, only Rhode Island chose not to participate, attended the Constitutional Convention, which sat with only short breaks between 25 May and 17 September 1787. The delegates were appointed by the state legislatures rather than by popular election. Even had the latter mode of appointment been chosen, it would have excluded the majority of US inhabitants from participation in the election as most states restricted voting rights to white, property-owning males. Critics have argued

---

[17] "Proceedings and Report of the Commissioners at Annapolis, Maryland," 11–14 September 1786, in Jensen, Kaminski, and Leffler, *Documentary History of the Ratification of the Constitution*, vol. 1, 184; "Confederation Congress Calls the Constitutional Convention," 21 February 1787, in Jensen, Kaminski, and Leffler, *Documentary History of the Ratification of the Constitution*, vol. 1, 187.

that the appointment process made sure that elite interests were far better represented than the "popular feeling" in Philadelphia. Other critics have questioned the legitimacy of the Constitution. By accepting a set of resolutions submitted by the Virginia delegation, the Convention immediately decided to go beyond its mandate to revise the Articles of Confederation to instead establish a national government with a separate legislature, judiciary, and executive. Their decision to radically reform rather than to amend the federal Constitution, and their circumvention of Congress by a direct appeal for popular support for their action, form the basis of the charge that the Constitution amounts to a *coup d'état* of dubious legality.[18]

The Virginia resolutions did not really challenge ideas about the purpose of the union. Instead, they argued that the "articles of Confederation ought to be so corrected & enlarged as to accomplish the objects proposed by their institution; namely, 'common defence, security of liberty and general welfare.'" In an accompanying speech, Virginia's governor, Edmund Randolph, made clear that the "defects" of the Articles were the familiar financial and commercial difficulties that had plagued the union for a decade. The solution was a national government that could "secure 1. against foreign invasion: 2. against dissentions between the members of the Union, or seditions in particular states: 3. to p[ro]cure to the several States various blessings, of which an isolated situation was i[n]capable: 4. to be able to defend itself against incroachment: & 5. to be paramount to the state constitutions." Although the third item sounds far-ranging, Randolph had quite specific blessings in mind, such as "a productive impost," "counteraction of the commercial regulations of other nations," and the ability to increase American commerce "ad libitum."[19]

Scholars typically seek to establish the meaning of the Constitution by interpreting the extant records from the Constitutional Convention, above all the extensive notes taken by James Madison. A recent scrutiny of Madison's notes has exposed them as a deeply problematic source, however, neither complete nor contemporary with the Convention, and certainly not

---

[18] Charles A. Beard, *An Economic Interpretation of the Constitution of the United States* (New York: Macmillan, 1913), 64–72, 217–25 (quote at 66). The most recent so-called Progressive interpretation is Michael J. Klarman, *The Framers' Coup: The Making of the United States Constitution* (New York: Oxford University Press, 2016).

[19] "The Virginia Resolutions," in Jensen, Kaminski, and Leffler, *Documentary History of the Ratification of the Constitution*, vol. 1, 243–5; Max Farrand, ed., *The Records of the Federal Convention of 1787*, 4 vols., 2nd edition (New Haven: Yale University Press, 1966 [1937]), vol. 1, 18–19, 20.

impartial.[20] A safer method to investigate the meaning and significance of the Constitution to North American and Atlantic history is therefore to compare the Constitution with the Articles of Confederation in order to identity both the nature of the reform of the American union and the consequences of that reform.[21]

Such comparison reveals the transition from the Articles of Confederation to the Constitution to be a story of both change and continuity. Adoption of the Constitution signified important changes to the legitimating principles and structure of the union. The authority of the Constitution rested on popular sovereignty, whereas the Articles of Confederation had been an agreement between states. In contrast to the Articles, which were ratified by the state governments, the Constitution was adopted by the people of the states, through their representatives in special state ratifying conventions. The Constitution also created a national government that could act independently of the states, whereas the Continental Congress had depended on the state governments to execute its decisions. Furthermore, the Constitution invested in Congress new powers to regulate commerce and to tax (Art. I, § 8), and it circumscribed certain powers of the states, most significantly by forbidding them from issuing paper money and from "impairing the obligation of contracts" (Art. I, § 10). But in other respects, there was continuity. The principle remained that the union and the national government were designed primarily to govern the common affairs of the states – for example, interstate matters, the western territories, and foreign affairs, including commerce – rather than the domestic affairs of the states. In the words of one perceptive commentator, the framers were critical of the confederation for "its failures to achieve the ends for which it was instituted, not its failure to seek ends beyond these."[22] Nor did the Constitution

---

[20] Mary Sarah Bilder, *Madison's Hand: Revisiting the Constitutional Convention* (Cambridge, MA: Harvard University Press, 2015).

[21] I present my understanding of the convention at greater length in Max M. Edling, *Perfecting the Union: State and National Authority in the US Constitution* (New York: Oxford University Press, 2021), Chapter 2. The best analytical works on the convention are Lance Banning, *The Sacred Fire of Liberty: James Madison and the Founding of the Federal Republic* (Ithaca, NY: Cornell University Press, 1995), 1–191; Bilder, *Madison's Hand*; Cathy D. Matson and Peter S. Onuf, *A Union of Interests: Political and Economic Thought in Revolutionary America* (Lawrence: University Press of Kansas, 1990), 101–23; Jack N. Rakove, *Original Meanings: Politics and Ideas in the Making of the Constitution* (New York: Knopf, 1996); Michael P. Zuckert, "A System without Precedent: Federalism in the American Constitution," in Leonard W. Levy and Denis J. Mahoney, eds., *The Framing and Ratification of the Constitution* (New York: Macmillan, 1987), 132–50.

[22] Michael P. Zuckert, "Federalisms and the Founding," *Review of Politics* 48:2 (1986), 174.

challenge the principle that the union was primarily a political organization created to further the interests of the states. Despite significant changes, the Constitution should therefore be seen as a reform of the organization of the federal union, not of its rationale or aims.

Reading the Constitution alongside the Articles of Confederation makes it plain that the new federal Constitution aimed to solve the problems that Congress had so consistently failed to address under the old constitution. The authority to regulate trade was transferred from the states to the national government, which was given a monopoly over trade legislation. The national government was invested with almost unrestricted fiscal powers, some exclusive, some concurrent with the state governments. The Northwest Ordinance, adopted on 13 July 1787, created a framework for the government of the western territories and their gradual incorporation into the union. The problem of state delinquency, finally, was resolved by the creation of a separate national government – equipped with a legislative, judicial, and executive branch, and with authority over a set of enumerated policy areas – existing in parallel to the state governments. This made it possible for the national government to operate largely independently of the states to implement its decisions.

Writing in *The Federalist* a few months after the adjournment of the Constitutional Convention, Madison claimed that "[i]f the new Constitution be examined with accuracy and candour, it will be found that the change which it proposes consists much less in the addition of NEW POWERS to the Union than in the invigoration of its ORIGINAL POWERS." Under the Articles of Confederation, Congress already possessed the powers over war and peace, the military, diplomacy, and "finance." The authority to regulate commerce, Madison conceded, was "a new power; but that seems to be an addition which few oppose, and from which no apprehensions are entertained." Arguing that the core of the reform was the creation of a separate national government apparatus, Madison concluded that the Constitution did not add powers to the union, "it only substitutes a more effectual mode of administering them."[23]

It was an analysis both insightful and disingenuous. Madison accurately identified the heart of the reform, but he deliberately misconstrued the response to the Constitution both within the Convention and without. National trade regulation was a point of contention between northern and

---

[23] James Madison, "Federalist 45," in *The Federalist*, ed. Jacob E. Cooke (Middletown, CT: Wesleyan University Press, 1961), 314.

southern state delegations in Philadelphia and was later much protested. Taxation was less controversial in the Convention, but once the Constitution was made public, opposition to federal property, poll, and excise taxes became central elements of Antifederalist objections. In Philadelphia, and in the ratification debate that followed, many critics worried about the creation of a national government able to exercise military and fiscal power regardless of state cooperation. Some worried that the national government would turn its coercive power against the states, others that it would monopolize all important government business and make the states redundant. In quoting from the twenty-year-old *Letters from a Farmer in Pennsylvania*, Antifederalist writer "Centinel" suggested that the battle over the Constitution repeated the struggle against an overbearing imperial parliament that led to the American Revolution. With the power to tax, regulate trade, conduct diplomacy, and provide for defense in the hands of the national government, nothing "would be left for [the state governments] to do, higher than to frame bye-laws for the empounding of cattle or the yoking of hogs."[24]

"Centinel's" complaint was based on the generally accepted view that authority over war, diplomacy, and taxation were key elements of political sovereignty and were of a higher order than other governmental duties. From this perspective, it was hard to deny that lodging these powers in the national government, in contrast to asking Congress to coordinate state efforts, diminished the sovereignty of the states. The concern over the future of the states was further heightened by the vague and sweeping "necessary and proper" and "general welfare" clauses, which seemed to herald the continuous expansion of national government activity into the internal affairs of the states.

In the Constitutional Convention, Madison had in fact attacked the state governments as the principal cause of the union's dysfunctions and had seemingly favored dramatically curbing their status and power. He denied that the states were sovereign political bodies by describing them as "corporations" with merely the authority to pass "bylaws," thereby implying that the states were subordinate creations of either a sovereign Congress or a nation. Madison's proposal for a "negative" on – that is, national oversight of – state

---

[24] "Centinel" II, in Jensen, Kaminski, and Leffler, eds., *Documentary History of the Ratification of the Constitution*, vol. XIII, 460–1. "Centinel's" quote from Dickinson's *Letters from a Farmer in Pennsylvania* indicates how the perception of an inherent conflict between center and periphery survived independence.

legislation aimed to formalize precisely this relationship. The objections from Convention delegates show that, just like "Centinel," they could envision an all-encompassing national government supervising state affairs, but also that they refused to create such an institution. "Is no road or bridge to be established without the Sanction of the General Legislature?" Madison was asked. "Is this to sit constantly in order to receive & revise the State laws?"[25]

Because the majority of the Convention did not share Madison's extreme nationalist sentiment the finished Constitution instead protected the corporate identity and rights of the states as distinctive bodies politic by guaranteeing their territorial integrity and self-determination. Large states could not be subdivided, and small states could not be merged with other states without their consent (Art. IV, § 3). States were protected from invasion and rebellion and guaranteed a "Republican Form of Government" (Art. IV, § 4). The states were made essential elements of the federal government structure by the provision for equal state representation in the Senate (Art. I, § 3, and further protected by Art. V), but also by creating a House of Representatives elected by "the People of the several States" (Art. I, § 2) and an executive chosen by state electors appointed "in such Manner as the Legislature [of each state] may direct" (Art. II, § 1).

Yet arguably the most important protection of the corporate identity of the states was the framers' design of a national government of limited and enumerated powers, which was geared toward the management of diplomacy, international trade, and war, but left domestic matters mostly alone. Federal government powers were explicitly listed in Article I, § 8 of the Constitution. Powers not enumerated there were reserved to the states or the people. This principle was made explicit in the ratification debates soon after the Constitution became public and it remained a crucial part of the Federalists' defense of the new order.[26] It was eventually codified in the Tenth Amendment, which states that "[t]he powers not delegated to the United States by the Constitution, nor prohibited by it to the States, are reserved to the States respectively, or to the people." Such division of government duties meant that the states retained the right to regulate property; to determine the nature and extent of civic rights, including the legality of slavery; to promote the economy through incorporation and

---

[25] Bilder, *Madison's Hand*, 100; Farrand, *Records of the Federal Convention*, vol. II, 390.
[26] "James Wilson: Speech at a Public Meeting in Philadelphia 6 October," *Pennsylvania Herald*, 9 October 1787, in Jensen, Kaminiski, and Leffler, eds., *Documentary History of the Ratification of the Constitution*, vol. II, 167–8.

infrastructural investment; to support religion and institutions of learning; and to watch over the health and morals of their populations without interference from the national government.

Negotiations between state delegations in the Convention also led to the Constitution providing both explicit and implicit protection for state economic interests. The slave states were strikingly successful in getting explicit protections written into the document, guaranteeing numerical advantage in the House of Representatives (Art. I, § 2) and presidential elections (Art. II, § 1) as a result of the "three-fifths clause," which counted 60 percent of the slave population for purposes of representation; return of escapee slaves in the fugitive clause (Art. IV, § 2); and a continuation of the slave trade to at least 1808 (art. I, § 9; Art. V). The Constitution also banned export duties (Art. I, § 9), which would have affected southern staples such as rice and tobacco, and introduced a comity clause (Art. IV, § 1) that forced nonslave states to recognize the legality of slavery in the South. So pronounced was the southern victory that recent interpretations have placed protection of slavery at the center of the American federal treaty, vindicating an understanding once embraced by radical abolitionists and slaveowners alike that the Constitution was a pro-slavery document.[27]

The support northern states gained for the shipping interest was much more limited. Northern delegates defeated the slave states' demand that a qualified majority be required for Congress to pass navigation acts, but a two-thirds majority in the Senate was nevertheless required to ratify commercial treaties (Art. II, § 2). The Northwest Ordinance banned slavery north of the Ohio River and ensured that the federal territory would be a free-soil region. But if the Northwest Territory thereby became an attractive destination for migrants from the northern states, the ordinance implied slavery's legality in future territories to be created south of the Ohio River. North and South, the argument was also made that economic interests would be promoted by the creation of a stronger national government with the power to conclude beneficial trade agreements in the Atlantic marketplace and to pacify Indigenous nations in the western borderlands.

Of equal importance to explicit guarantees for state economic interests was the realization in the Constitutional Convention and the ratification

---

[27] David Waldstreicher, *Slavery's Constitution: From Revolution to Ratification* (New York: Hill & Wang, 2009), 57–105; George William Van Cleve, *A Slaveholders' Union: Slavery, Politics, and the Constitution in the Early American Republic* (Chicago: University of Chicago Press, 2011), 103–83.

debate that state interests had to be balanced with the need to preserve the union. This involved accepting that the interests of other states were real and that their pursuit of self-interest was legitimate. Up to a point, the framers argued that claims about sectional antagonism – based on slave, shipping, and agricultural interests centered in the south, north, and west – were exaggerated and that the sections could coexist in a harmonious "union of interests." But whenever state interests clashed, compromise alone, achieved by bargaining, could prevent disunion. This acceptance laid the foundation for a distinctive American style of politics, as the statesmen of the Antebellum era became adept at developing the art of the sectional compromise.

A More Perfect Union

The Constitution was ratified by special state conventions amidst a public print debate of unprecedented proportions that pitted Federalist friends of the Constitution against Antifederalist critics. From early December 1787 to early January 1788, five states accepted the new compact of union. In Massachusetts, the Constitution was ratified by a slim margin only after the Federalist majority had agreed to ratification with amendments aimed to strengthen the rights of individuals and to limit the new national government's power over the states. After the Massachusetts convention, ratification with amendment became the norm. On 21 June, New Hampshire became the ninth state to ratify thereby formally bringing the Constitution into effect. But the success of the reform was only sealed with Virginia's ratification four days later and New York's on 26 July. North Carolina and Rhode Island at first rejected the Constitution and existed outside the union until November 1788 and May 1790, respectively. The Antifederalist amendment proposals eventually led to the adoption of the first ten amendments shepherded through Congress by James Madison. Despite the significance often ascribed to them by historians and others, they did not address the main objections of the Antifederalists who dismissed them as a ruse. It is significant that no one called them the Bill of Rights at the time, an appellation that became common only during the Second World War.[28]

---

[28] Pauline Maier, *Ratification: The People Debate the Constitution, 1787–1788* (New York: Simon & Schuster, 2010); Kenneth R. Bowling, "'A Tub to the Whale': The Founding Fathers and Adoption of the Federal Bill of Rights," *Journal of the Early Republic* 8 (1988), 223–51; Gerald N. Magliocca, *The Heart of the Constitution: How the Bill of Rights Became the Bill of Rights* (New York: Oxford University Press, 2018).

In *The Federalist*, Hamilton remarked that "it seems to have been reserved to the people of this country, by their conduct and example, to decide the important question, whether societies of men are really capable or not, of establishing good government from reflection and choice, or whether they are forever destined to depend, for their political constitutions, on accident and force."[29] Popular ratification struck contemporary observers as a novel phenomenon and latter-day observers have largely agreed. The degree to which the process was "democratic" and "popular" has long been contested, however. It is a matter unlikely to ever be resolved. There was no single agreed meaning of these terms in the late eighteenth century, nor is there one now. It is therefore more fruitful to ask why the ratification process took the form it did and what role the process played in the evolution of modern democratic government.

The fact that all but two state constitutions had been written by regular legislative assemblies or irregular provisional assemblies, and that none had been adopted by popular vote, made American politicians question if and how the revolutionary state constitutions were binding on state assemblies. This became a pressing matter because Americans were diverging from the evolving British view, expressed most trenchantly by William Blackstone, that because political sovereignty rested in Parliament, Parliament's interpretation of the British Constitution *was* the constitution. The emerging American position, in contrast, held that a constitution represented a higher form of law than statutory law and was therefore binding on the legislature. From this position it followed that a regular legislative assembly could neither adopt nor alter the constitution. Such actions could be performed only by the sovereign, which in the American republics meant "the people." In its combination of a popularly elected constitutional convention and ratification through township meetings and popular vote, the Commonwealth of Massachusetts developed a procedure that gave practical form to the expression of popular sovereignty and thereby bestowed legitimacy on its 1780 constitution.[30]

In 1787, the Constitutional Convention decided on popular approval through ratifying conventions early in the proceedings. If adopted, the Constitution would create a national government of enumerated powers

---

[29] Alexander Hamilton, "Federalist 1," in Cooke, *The Federalist*, 3.
[30] Willi Paul Adams, *The First American Constitutions: Republican Ideology and the Making of the State Constitutions in the Revolutionary Era* (Chapel Hill: University of North Carolina Press, 1980).

that acted directly on individual citizens, thereby cutting out the states in the administration of its duties. Committed to a republican form of government, such a government would be legitimate to Americans only if it rested on the consent of the people – although we should notice that "the people" was conceptualized at state rather than national level, and that no mechanism was provided to make ratification depend on the majority will of an American "people" rather than on the approval of nine states. But there were also pragmatic reasons for avoiding ratification by Congress or the state legislatures. The convention had exceeded its mandate to do no more than to revise the Articles of Confederation and there was concern that their proposal would therefore meet with resistance by congressmen and state legislators.[31]

Like other popular elections at the time, the right to vote for delegates to state ratifying conventions was limited to property-owning adult males and was sometimes also restricted by race. Turnout among eligible voters was low. Restrictions and abstentions meant that the Constitution was adopted by conventions appointed by only a small minority, perhaps no more than five percent, of the total population. Had it been possible to calculate the popular vote exactly, the result might have pointed to rejection. This was the outcome in Rhode Island, where the legislature refused to call a ratifying convention and the citizens rejected the Constitution in a popular referendum by 2,714 votes to 238 (out of a total population of close to 70,000). In the other states the active management of the press, of elections to ratifying conventions, and of the conventions themselves secured a Federalist majority. Critics have pointed to the undue haste with which the Constitution was adopted, to the restriction of the choice open to the people to either adopt or reject the plan in toto, and to the improprieties, including bribes, committed by the Federalists to secure ratification.[32] If such political management, which sometimes turned into manipulation, means that the adoption of the Constitution was not in fact a "popular" act ultimately depends on the criteria used to define democracy and popular elections. But at the very least, the adoption of the Constitution represents a novel means of registering the popular will and an important step toward the modern understanding of a constitution as a higher law equally binding on the citizens and the government.

---

[31] Rakove, *Original Meanings*, 94–130.
[32] This critique of the ratification process was present already in Beard, *Economic Interpretation*, 217–52.

The first Congress assembled in the fall of 1789 and continued the work begun in the Constitutional Convention by transforming the clauses of the Constitution into government institutions and policies that would address the problems facing the American union. Three administrative departments were set up to handle foreign affairs, finances, and defense, together with a post office. A diplomatic corps, a small army, a more substantial revenue service, and a sprawling post office network were the main field services. The Judiciary Act of 1789 organized the federal judiciary and specified its jurisdiction. The federal territories in the west were managed jointly by the three departments. The War Department was responsible for the US Army and so-called "Indian affairs." Land sales took place through Land Offices that were part of the Treasury Department. Territorial government, finally, was the responsibility of the State Department.

Although these federal bodies were pitifully small by modern standards, they were remarkably successful. After initial setbacks, the powerful Indian confederacy in the Northwest Territory was defeated at the Battle of Fallen Timbers in 1794 and forced to surrender much of its territory in the Treaty of Greenville the following year. The fiscal apparatus was remodeled to secure a stable income from customs duties. Public finances were reformed and public credit restored. By 1794, Congress was able to borrow to finance war against Native Americans and to suppress a tax rebellion in the western borderlands. In the nineteenth century, tax income and loans would finance the nation's spectacular expansion through wars and territorial purchase. In 1795, major treaties were concluded with Britain and Spain. They signaled that the United States was at long last regarded as a "treaty-worthy" nation that was able to abide by the law of nations that bound together Europe's "civilized" family of nations. Jay's Treaty made Britain give up its strategic forts in Indian territory and Pinkney's Treaty made Spain open the Mississippi River to American trade. Both measures were needed for successful settlement of the trans-Appalachian west.

The fiscal, military, and administrative resources that the Constitution invested in the new federal government made possible the gradual transformation of the west into republics that were admitted as new member states of the American union. In the train of federal soldiers came surveyors and land agents, followed by settler colonists. Between 1791 and 1810, treaties with Native American nations transferred some 170,000 square miles of land – an area almost two and a half times the size of New England – to the United States, the bulk of which was passed on to white settlers. They filled up the land quickly. In 1790, there were 110,000 settler colonists living in what became the states of Kentucky and Tennessee. By the turn of the eighteenth century, that figure had almost tripled. An additional 50,000 settlers resided in territories that would become Ohio and Indiana. Of the Kentucky residents in 1800, some 40,000 were enslaved persons forcefully removed from the Chesapeake, thus highlighting how western expansion was also slavery's expansion. This peopling of the west was made possible only by the violent removal of the Native American proprietors of the land and the disciplining of the ethnically and culturally mixed borderlands population that chose to remain.[33]

The activism of the federal government abroad and in the western borderlands conformed to the principle that the national government should concentrate on international and intra-union affairs but abstain from meddling in the domestic politics of the states. Outside the western territories, the federal government did little to regulate social and economic affairs but left such activities to the state governments. For example, the federal government spent $60 million on transportation projects and incorporated two banks between 1790 and 1860. In the same period, the state governments invested more than $450 million in transportation and incorporated thousands of banks. What is more, such state action was often controversial and gave rise to political struggles that furthered the democratization of

---

[33] Charles J. Kappler, ed., *Indian Affairs: Laws and Treaties*, vol. II: *Treaties* (Washington, DC: Government Printing Office, 1904); *Eighteenth Annual Report of the Bureau of American Ethnology to the Secretary of the Smithsonian Institution 1896–97*, Part II: *Indian Land Cessions in the United States 1784–1894*, 56th Congress, 1st Session, H.R. doc. no. 736/3, 56th Congress, 1st Session (1899), US serial set no. 4015; *Indians Removed to West Mississippi from 1789*, H.R. doc. 147, 25th Congress, 3rd Session (1838), Statement B, 9; US Bureau of the Census, *Historical Statistics of the United States, Colonial Times to 1970*, bicentennial edition, 2 vols. (Washington, DC: Government Printing Office, 1975), vol. I, 24–37. Peter Onuf interprets this process in Peter S. Onuf, *Jefferson's Empire: The Language of American Nationhood* (Charlottesville: University of Virginia Press, 2000), 18–52, 147–88; Peter S. Onuf, "The Empire of Liberty: Land of the Free and Home of the Slave," in Andrew Shankman, ed., *World of the Revolutionary American Republic* (New York: Routledge, 2014), 195–217. See also Bernard W. Sheehan, *Seeds of Extinction: Jeffersonian Philanthropy and the American Indian* (Chapel Hill: University of North Carolina Press, 1973); Peter S. Onuf, *Statehood and Union: A History of the Northwest Ordinance* (Bloomington: Indiana University Press, 1987); Bernard W. Sheehan, "The Indian Problem in the Northwest: From Conquest to Philanthropy," in Ronald Hoffman and Peter J. Albert, eds., *Launching the "Extended Republic": The Federalist Era* (Charlottesville: University of Virginia Press, 1996), 190–222; John Craig Hammond, "Slavery, Sovereignty, and Empires: North American Borderlands and the American Civil War, 1660–1860," *Journal of the Civil War Era* 4:2 (2014), 264–98; Reeve Huston, "Land Conflict and Land Policy in the United States, 1785–1841," in Andrew Shankman, ed., *The World of the Revolutionary American Republic* (New York: Routledge, 2014), 324–45; Bethel Saler, *The Settlers' Empire: Colonialism and State Formation in America's Old Northwest* (Philadelphia: University of Pennsylvania Press, 2014).

American government.³⁴ Adhering to the principle of state self-government, the federal government also conscientiously abstained from interfering with the legality of slavery.

The National Archives Rotunda in Washington, DC, is the holy temple of America's civic religion. Its shrine is dedicated to the Declaration of Independence, the Constitution, and the Bill of Rights, a trinity of sacred texts held to express the meaning and purpose of the United States. Like most nationalist myths, the official assertion that these documents are "Charters of Freedom" is deeply problematic. American independence prolonged slavery, the Constitution sanctioned it, and the federal government secured its expansion. The transfer of the west from Britain to the United States in the Treaty of Paris and the creation of a stronger federal government under the Constitution accelerated the displacement and dwindling of the Native American population in a process that some modern scholars label a genocide. The so-called Bill of Rights did nothing to secure or expand civic rights before the acceptance of the doctrine of incorporation in the twentieth century, and little before the 1950s. For the vast majority of the population, the founding was not an era of emancipation. Women, children, servants, "nonwhites," the destitute, vagrants, and "idlers" continued to be oppressed and discriminated against by state constitutions, state laws, and state police regulations that kept in place a social hierarchy that was rooted in the colonial era but survived the transition to independence.³⁵

At the same time, the Constitution and the federal government did enhance the power of the American "people." In the 1790s and early nineteenth century, property restrictions on civic rights were removed to give way for universal white male citizenship.³⁶ In their state and federal governments the American citizenry found powerful means to shape society to their liking. The unsettling fact about this development is the frequency with which white male citizens used the instrument of government to exploit and dispossess non-citizens. By this process, the national "Charters of Freedom" laid the foundation for a democratic social order that combined unsurpassed equality and opportunity with institutionalized inequality and oppression.

---

[34] John Joseph Wallis, "The Other Founding: Federalism and the Constitutional Structure of American Government," in Douglas A. Irwin and Richard Sylla, eds., *Founding Choices: American Economic Policy in the 1790s* (Chicago: University of Chicago Press, 2011), 177–213.

[35] For a powerful analysis of the discriminatory nature of nineteenth-century United States, see Barbara Young Welke, *Law and the Borders of Belonging in the Long Nineteenth Century United States* (New York: Cambridge University Press, 2010).

[36] Alexander Keyssar, *The Right to Vote: The Contested History of Democracy in the United States* (New York: Basic Books, 2000), 53–76, 340–67.

18

Reform and Rebellion in Spanish America at the Time of the American Revolution

ANTHONY MCFARLANE

The British monarchy was not alone in confronting colonial rebellion at the time of the American Revolution. In 1765, when British colonial subjects rioted against the new duty imposed by the Stamp Act, the people of Quito also protested against government changes to taxation, in riots which turned into a state of rebellion. In 1767, riots also broke out in New Spain, linked to the expulsion of the Jesuits. Unlike the Stamp Act riots, these civil disorders in Spanish America did not lead to the development of a wider movement against government policy during the ensuing decade. They did, however, foreshadow a formidable challenge to Spanish authority in 1780 and 1781. Then, while Britain's North American colonies were fighting for their independence and establishing a new republic, several regions in the Spanish viceroyalties of Peru and New Granada were beset by rebellions of an unprecedented scale and power.

The first of these, known as the rebellion of Túpac Amaru, broke out in November 1780. It began among the indigenous peasantry in the region south of Cuzco, but subsequently spread over the southern Andes, interacting with other rebellions in Upper Peru and bringing thousands of Indian peasants into a bloody internal war. The other major rebellion, which started in March in 1781, was at the center of the viceroyalty of New Granada. Known as the revolt of the Comuneros, it began with rioting in small provincial towns but developed into a regional rebellion that challenged the royal authorities in Bogotá, before dissolving peacefully.

That these rebellions do not share a place in world history alongside the American Revolution is perhaps not surprising. They did not end European rule in Spanish America or lead directly toward the establishment of independent states, nor do they seem at one with the "democratic" or "Atlantic" revolutions of the United States and France. They are nonetheless of considerable historical interest, in themselves and comparatively.[1] In the first place, the rebellions of Quito, Túpac Amaru, and the Comuneros reflect important changes in the character of the Spanish monarchy during the later eighteenth century, when, under pressure from rival powers, Bourbon kings accelerated efforts to enlarge their power over Spain's American territories. The rebellions are important, too, for what they reveal about society and political culture in Spanish America. Not only do they illuminate social divisions and conflicts, but they also throw light on the nature of authority, political participation, ideas, and attitudes toward Spanish rule, and the potential for radical change at the time when the first American republic was emerging in North America.

Spanish America under Bourbon Rule

The rebellions of Spanish America began, like those in British America, as reactions against reforming policies adopted after the Seven Years' War. Reform initially focused on the Spanish Caribbean, where Cuba's defenses and administration were reorganized, and Havana and other island ports opened to direct trade with Spain. It extended into New Spain, too, where José de Gálvez conducted a *visita general* (general inspection). Gálvez's *visita* (1765–1771) focused mainly on the royal treasury, with measures for increasing returns from taxes on production and trade and building income streams from royal monopolies of tobacco and aguardiente. It also had an important political dimension. For, in seeking to replace American Spaniards (creoles) with European Spaniards (peninsulars) in government posts and recommending the installation of an intendancy system, Gálvez started a "revolution in government" that was to extend throughout Spanish America.[2]

This shift toward closer control and higher taxation caused friction in several regions. While creole patricians in Mexico City objected to Gálvez's

---

[1] For comparisons of the New Granada and Peruvian rebellions, see Scarlett O'Phelan Godoy, "Rebeliones andinas anticoloniales. Nueva Granada, Peru y Charcas entre el siglo XVIII y XIX," *Anuario de Estudios Americas* 49 (1992), 395–440; for comparisons of Quito, New Granada, Peru, and Mexico, see Anthony McFarlane, "Rebellions in Late Colonial Spanish America: A Comparative Perspective," *Bulletin of Latin American Research* 14:3 (1995), 313–39; for comparisons of the American Revolution and the rebellions of Túpac Amaru and the Comuneros, see J. H. Elliott, *Empires of the Atlantic World: Britain and Spain in the Americas* (New Haven: Yale University Press, 2006), Chapter 11.

[2] On the "revolution in government," David A. Brading, "Bourbon Spain and Its American Empire," in Leslie Bethell, ed., *Cambridge History of Latin America* (Cambridge: Cambridge University Press, 1984), vol. 1, 397–409.

moves to centralize power and reduce their role in government, people in New Spain's northern provinces reacted against increases in taxation, militia reforms, and, in 1767, objected to the expulsion of the Jesuits, sometimes in violent civil disorders.[3] However, the first instance of large-scale resistance to the Caroline reforms was in the heart of Spanish South America. In 1764, the viceroy of New Granada sent a special envoy to the city of Quito with plans to bring the collection of the *alcabala* (sales tax) and aguardiente monopoly under direct royal administration; in 1765, the city responded with riot and rebellion.

The Rebellion of Quito

Opposition in Quito emerged first among the city's patricians, who denounced the new measures as detrimental to the *bien común* (common good) and called a *cabildo abierto* (an emergency city council meeting) to petition for their reversal. When the viceroy refused to relent, peaceful dissent orchestrated by the creole patriciate gave way to popular rioting. In May 1765, people from the city's neighborhoods attacked and destroyed the premises of the *alcabala* administration; thus began the "rebellion of the barrios" which, for several months, nullified royal government in the city.[4]

At first, it seemed that order would be rapidly restored. Royal officials had insufficient forces to impose their will and decided to conciliate by suspending the new sales tax, cancelling street patrols, and granting a general pardon. However, people in the barrios continued to assert themselves in acts of defiance, such as emptying the city jail, and when the authorities sought to forestall further rioting, another great tumult occurred on 24 June, the feast of St. John. Thousands poured onto the streets and rioting escalated into a violent assault on the audiencia palace, the city's principal seat of government. In the ensuing battle, many of the rioters were killed but, when reinforcements arrived from Indian villages in the city's hinterland, the authorities decided to surrender. The crowds had moved from riot to urban insurrection, leaving the authorities with little option but to negotiate. At a

---

[3] On the creole response, David A. Brading, *The First America: The Spanish Monarchy, Creole Patriots, and the Liberal State* (Cambridge: Cambridge University Press, 1991), 480–3. On riots in Mexico in 1767, Felipe Castro Gutiérrez, *Nuevo Ley y Nuevo Rey: Reformas borbónicas y rebelión popular en Nueva España* (Zamora: Colegio de Michoácan, 1996).

[4] Anthony McFarlane, "The 'Rebellion of the Barrios': Urban Insurrection in Bourbon Quito," *Hispanic American Historical Review* 69 (1989), 283–330.

public meeting in the central square, the audiencia announced the suspension of the new taxes, the expulsion of certain European Spaniards, and the concession of a general pardon, sealed by the acclamation "Long live the King."

This did not restore the *status quo ante*. To rebuild order, the audiencia judges allowed the barrios to choose prominent creoles as their "captains" in an "aristocratic government" which side-lined the audiencia. These captains secured popular approval by appointing plebeian leaders, chosen by the barrios, to minor posts in municipal government. Thus, although the audiencia remained in formal control, power shifted into the hands of the people and their tribunes. Radical ideas circulated, such as the demand that a prominent *quiteño* aristocrat should be made king of Quito, and the city's poor enjoyed an unusual freedom. Radicalization of the rebellion was prevented, however, by creole leaders who cooperated with the audiencia in gradually recouping its authority. When in September 1766, the viceroy sent soldiers from Bogotá, they entered the city unopposed, and, with an amnesty for the population, Quito returned to normal.

The Quito rebellion was partly driven by economic grievances. Landowners rejected changes to the aguardiente monopoly and the *alcabala*, on the ground that they threatened to damage a community already in economic distress, due to environmental problems and the contraction of its textile industry. Amongst the populace, dislike of *alcabala* reform was widespread, due to fears that the new tax regime would end traditional exemptions, to the detriment of houseowners, small traders, and artisans.[5] Opposition to the reforms had an important political dimension, too, because they were implemented in a manner that ran counter to long-standing conventions. Leading members of the social and political hierarchy argued that the viceroy's abrupt revision of tax rules was inconsistent with what they regarded as the constitution of the Spanish monarchy, inculcated under Habsburg rule. The procurator of the Quito *cabildo* contended that, when making policy, the crown had to take account of local practices and customs; indeed, he likened the customs of Quito to the *fueros* of the Basque and Aragonese, the *ordenanzas* of Peru, and the municipal laws of the Indies. A senior *oidor* (judge) of Quito's audiencia took a similar view and, appealing to legal traditions and unimpeachable jurists, concluded that laws had to be

---

[5] Kenneth J. Andrien, "Economic Crisis, Taxes and the Quito Insurrection of 1765," *Past and Present* 129 (1990), 104–31.

adapted to the customs and well-being of the societies for which they were enacted.

These arguments reflect the norms of contemporary Hispanic political culture. Habsburg kings had always allowed regional elites a substantial measure of autonomy, on the understanding that, while the kingdoms and provinces that formed Spain's "composite monarchy" owed unquestioning allegiance to the king, they preserved their own forms of government and law. Within this framework, the sovereign's prime responsibility was to provide justice for his subjects under the relevant body of law (the "Laws of the Indies" in Spanish America), rather than to govern in the modern sense.[6] The maintenance of order was largely in the hands of the many corporate bodies which structured social and political life (religious confraternities, guilds, mercantile associations, universities, the cabildos of Indian and Spanish towns, and so on).[7] These provided an experience of self-regulation which underpinned the belief that, in the larger constitutional order of monarchy, matters of law and policy should be subject to processes of corporate consultation and negotiation. The monarchy also offered its subjects other forms of participation: first, by allowing American subjects to petition the king directly and, second, by making room for local elites to hold government office. Creoles were routinely appointed to the offices of church and state, and they were sometimes in the majority on Spanish American audiencias. Creole patricians also exercised influence indirectly, by forming family and business relationships with Spanish officials. And, although Spanish Americans had no representative institutions directly comparable to the Anglo-American assemblies, the cabildos of Spanish America's many towns and cities provided vehicles for local elites to exercise power in the name of their community. Indeed, when Quito's political elite convoked a *cabildo abierto*, they presented themselves as the representatives of the *bien común* or *bien público*, engaged in a legal response to the viceroy's breach of customary political practice.[8]

---

[6] Pedro Cardim, Antonio Feros, and Gaetano Sabatini, "The Political Constitution of the Iberian Monarchies," in Fernando Bouza, Pedro Cardim, and Antonio Feros, eds., *The Iberian World, 1450–1820* (London: Routledge, 2020).

[7] On the role of corporations, see Annick Lempérière, *Entre Dios y el Rey: La ciudad de México de los siglos XVI al XIX* (Mexico City: Fondo de Cultura, 2013), Chapters 1–2.

[8] This was not the first rebellion to use the *bien común* and the *cabildo abierto* in defense of local interests against crown policies. Both were found in earlier rebellions in Paraguay and Venezuela. See James Schofield Saeger, "Origins of the Rebellion of Paraguay," *Hispanic American Historical Review* 52:2 (1972), 215–29; Adalberto López, *The Colonial History of Paraguay: The Revolt of the Comuneros, 1721–1735* (New York: Routledge, 2005);

This sense of legitimate opposition in defense of the community was also reflected in the behavior of those who participated in the riots. In Quito's first riot, the rioters targeted their attack on government offices, avoiding indiscriminate violence or plunder. The second was much more violent but still concentrated on specific targets, rather than becoming a destructive rampage by an infuriated mob. The plebeians of Quito thus displayed a key characteristic found in the behavior of rioters and rebels in other civil disorders of the period: namely, a commitment to defend a "moral economy" by direct but disciplined action against abuses of power, violations of custom, or abnormal exploitation.[9]

The "rebellion of the barrios" did not spread beyond the city. There were some small-scale protests in neighboring areas but, despite the paralysis of government in the capital, there was no general challenge to Spanish authority. The rebellion was, however, only one sign of opposition to Bourbon reform in these years. In Spain itself, the populace of Madrid and other cities rose in violent rioting in 1766, encouraged by opponents of reform in the ranks of government and the nobility. To stem the disorder, Charles III dismissed the Marqués de Esquilache, his chief minister; then, to save face, he blamed the Jesuits and expelled them from his realms in 1767. This caused considerable disquiet in Spanish America, where the expulsion forced creole Jesuits into exile and deprived American elites of the colleges which educated their sons; in New Spain it also triggered rioting in several towns, which Gálvez put down by violent repression.

The riots and rebellions of the mid-1760s were all reactions against Bourbon policies but were otherwise unconnected. None became the basis for the prolonged transregional network of opposition that emerged from the Stamp Act riots in North America. Nor did they discourage the crown from continuing with reform; indeed, after the Esquilache riots in Spain, ministers were even more inclined to pursue reform in Spanish America. Their opportunity came in 1776, when Britain's war with its North American colonies altered the international situation. Faced with the strong possibility that Spain would join France in war against Britain, plans for tightening control over Spanish America took on greater urgency. The resumption of

---

Jesse Cromwell, *The Smugglers' World: Illicit Trade and Atlantic Communities in Eighteenth-Century Venezuela* (Chapel Hill: University of North Carolina Press, 2018).

[9] Anthony McFarlane, "Civil Disorders and Popular Protests in Late Colonial New Granada," *Hispanic American Historical Review* 64:1 (1984), 17–54. On the relevance of the concept of "moral economy," see McFarlane, "Rebellions in Late Colonial Spanish America," 327–30.

reform started when Charles III appointed Moniño, now Conde de Floridablanca, as minister of state and José de Gálvez as minister of the Indies.[10]

Emblematic of Bourbon determination to sharpen defenses and government in Spanish America was the creation in 1776 of the Viceroyalty of the Río de la Plata. Pivoted on Buenos Aires, the new viceroyalty strengthened Spain's military and commercial presence in the South Atlantic but dismembered the old Viceroyalty of Peru. While Lima's political and economic importance diminished, the Andean regional economy connected to the mining center of Potosí was damaged by the diversion of trade to Buenos Aires. Even more disruptive was the deployment of the *visita general* as a device for driving rapid reform. Gálvez appointed *visitadores generales* for Chile, Quito, New Granada, and Peru in 1777, and, in the two latter territories, provoked widespread opposition.

Rebellion in Peru and Upper Peru

The stage for rebellion in Peru was set by the *visitador general* José Antonio de Areche, who made his presence felt with unpopular fiscal measures. He increased the *alcabala* from 4 percent to 6 percent, raised the price of liquor by making new charges on aguardiente production, imposed taxes on groups which had previously been exempt, and pushed ahead with measures to enlarge the number of those liable for tribute payment. To maximize returns, he ordered rigorous enforcement of the fiscal rules and created a new system of customs houses and excise officials to ensure collection.[11]

These fiscal reforms provoked riots in cities and rural areas. The city of Arequipa saw an early instance of urban protest when, in mid-January 1780, rioters attacked the customs house and tax officials, backed by a cross-section of society from creole patricians to mixed-race plebeians. This alliance soon broke down, when attacks on the city's jail and against the *corregidor* and his business associates, together with the spread of rebellion to Indian villages, caused creoles to fear a wider breakdown of social discipline. They formed militia companies to beat off an invasion from the peasantry of neighboring villages, then conducted an armed repression in the countryside with many

---

[10] Allan J. Kuethe and Kenneth J. Andrien, *The Spanish Atlantic World in the Eighteenth Century: War and the Bourbon Reforms, 1713–1796* (Cambridge: Cambridge University Press, 2014), 287–304.

[11] John R. Fisher, *Bourbon Peru, 1750–1824* (Liverpool: Liverpool University Press, 2003), 29–33.

arrests and several executions.[12] Thus, like the rebellion of Quito in 1765, the Arequipa revolt subsided when the local patriciate took fright at plebeian mobilization and rallied to defend the established order. However, the turmoil in Arequipa and other cities was the prelude to the far greater challenge to Spanish rule that appeared in Andean Peru and Upper Peru in 1780–1782, when rural insurrections took place in the regions of Cuzco, the north of Potosí, and the area around La Paz. These arose separately but interacted to generate a formidable anticolonial insurgency that spread over a huge area of the southern Andes.[13]

The rebellion near Cuzco was a key part of the insurgency. It sprang from the actions of José Gabriel Condorcanqui, a mestizo *cacique* who, taking the title of Túpac Amaru, proclaimed himself heir to the Inca throne and raised an insurrection among indigenous rural communities in the Vilcanota Valley, south of Cuzco. He started the revolt on 4 November 1780 by seizing Antonio de Arriaga, the *corregidor* of Canas y Canchis, and proclaiming some extraordinary reforms. He decreed the abolition of the *alcabala* and the customs houses where the tax was collected; ended the *reparto de mercancías* (which forced Indian communities to buy goods from Spanish merchants); the *mita de Potosí* (which compelled communities to provide forced labor for the silver mines); and ordered the destruction of the *obrajes* (textile mills), which used Indian forced labor. Claiming that he had secret instructions from the king and the highest authorities in Peru, Túpac Amaru put Arriaga on trial and ordered his public execution. He then raised recruits throughout the Quechua-speaking peasant communities of the provinces of Canas y Canchis and Quispicanchis, where his followers, often led by caciques with whom he had kinship connections, spread the rebellion and built a force capable of attacking Cuzco.[14]

At first, Túpac Amaru hoped to build a political coalition across social and cultural boundaries. Given the widespread dislike of Areche's reforms, the idea of such a coalition was not unrealistic; indeed, Túpac Amaru's initial cohort of leaders included creoles and mestizos. His hopes of merging social

---

[12] David Cahill, "Taxonomy of a Colonial 'Riot': The Arequipa Disturbances of 1780," in John R. Fisher, Allan J. Kuethe, and Anthony McFarlane, eds., *Reform and Insurrection in Bourbon New Granada and Peru* (Baton Rouge: Louisiana State University Press, 1990), 255–91.

[13] For an illuminating synthesis, see Sergio Serulnikov, *Revolution in the Andes in the Age of Túpac Amaru* (Durham, NC: Duke University Press, 2013).

[14] Charles F. Walker, *The Tupac Amaru Rebellion* (Cambridge, MA: Harvard University Press, 2014), Chapters 4–6, 8, provides an essential introduction to the social character of the rebellion and its development as an armed movement.

groups behind common goals soon foundered, however. Cuzco's political elite, including almost all Inca nobles and caciques in the city's region, turned against him, followed by much of the populace. His plan for taking Cuzco was further damaged by failings in military organization. Although he had as many as 40,000 followers, his forces were unsuited to fighting battles and, weakened by disease and desertion while massing near Cuzco, they were swiftly defeated when military columns sent from Lima reinforced Cuzco's militias. In January 1781, Túpac Amaru retreated to his home base; by late March, royal forces had the upper hand, pushing into rebel territory amidst growing violence. In April, Túpac Amaru was betrayed, captured, and taken to Cuzco; there, after interrogation under torture, he suffered an execution of extraordinary cruelty, in a public spectacle designed to terrify the Indian population and cow the rebels into submission.

After Túpac Amaru's death, his insurrection continued under the leadership of his cousin Diego Cristóbal Túpac Amaru and other family members, who moved their operations southwards into the basin of Lake Titicaca. The rebellion now entered a more radical and violent phase, as its leaders abandoned hopes of alliance with creoles, and engaged in overtly anti-Hispanic warfare. Radicalization was matched by military success. Diego Cristóbal besieged the city of Puno in April–May 1781 and the authorities were forced to retreat to Cuzco, along with many refugees. Andrés Mendigure, Túpac Amaru's nephew, moved into Upper Peru, where he gathered a force of several thousands, took the town of Sorata, and massacred its inhabitants. And, while the Tupamaristas gained the upper hand in the Titicaca region, rebellion was spreading in Upper Peru, where other indigenous insurgents raised a war against Hispanic towns and cities.

The first of these rebellions was in Chayanta, in the region north of Potosí. In August 1780 (months before Túpac Amaru's rebellion) the cacique Tomás Katari had, after a long legal campaign for redress of Indian grievances, started a movement to restore community governance. The rebellion started peacefully, as Indian communities adopted self-government under their chosen leaders and Tomás Katari insisted on his loyalty to Charles III. However, the movement changed in early 1781, after Tomás was arrested and killed. His brothers Nicolás and Dámaso Katari reacted by launching a violent assault on Hispanic society. Rebel groups mobilized across their region, looting haciendas and attacking whites and mestizos, and, in February 1781, Dámaso Katari led a large force to attack the city of La Plata, the regional center of Hispanic authority. He tried to link up with Túpac Amaru but, due to divisions among his followers, suffered defeat at La

Plata; shortly after, the movement disintegrated. Handed over to the authorities by those who had once followed them, the brothers suffered grisly executions and most of the region fell back into an uneasy peace.[15]

Another uprising, stirred by news of the rebellions in Chayanta and Cuzco, broke out in the city of Oruro in early February 1781, at around the time of the siege of La Plata. The rebellion was started by a group of creole mine owners who, in pursuit of their dispute with Spanish merchants, tried to advance their own political agenda by making common cause with plebeian and Indigenous groups within the city. Events soon outran their control, when they were overrun by rural Indians who demanded that the city's people adopt Indigenous dress and manners. Within a few weeks, the creoles had resumed control and, faced with continuing Indian unrest in the countryside, they accepted the return of the royal authorities as the lesser of two evils. Thus ended the only major urban rebellion among the several strands of insurrection that spread over the southern Andes, and one for which creole leaders were later to suffer severe punishment.[16]

In the same month, a large-scale rural insurrection threatened the city of La Paz. Led by Julián Apaza (who called himself Túpac Katari in honor of Túpac Amaru and Tomás Katari), peasants from Aymara-speaking communities took control of large rural areas, besieged La Paz in March 1781, and challenged the authority of royal government in the audiencia of Charcas.[17] When Túpac Katari's forces were joined by Tupamaristas at the second siege of La Paz in August–October 1781, it appeared that an alliance of insurgents would take the city and dominate the strategic territory between Cuzco and Potosí, with its rich resources and crucial role in commerce and communications.

At this point, Indigenous rebellion seemed to pose an existential threat to Spanish governance and the society on which it rested. However, rather than driving the Spanish out, the rebels were defeated by military repression and internal division. Túpac Amaru's rebellion faded when Diego Cristóbal

---

[15] For the rebellion in Chayanta, see Sergio Serulnikov, *Subverting Colonial Authority: Challenges to Spanish Rule in Eighteenth-Century Southern Andes* (Durham, NC: Duke University Press, 2003).

[16] On the Oruro rebellion, see Oscar Cornblit, *Power and Violence in the Colonial City: Oruro from the Mining Renaissance to the Rebellion of Tupac Amaru (1740–1782)* (Cambridge: Cambridge University Press, 1995).

[17] On Túpac Katari's rebellion, María Eugenia del Valle de Siles, *Historia de la rebelión de Túpac Catari, 1781–82* (La Paz: Editorial Don Bosco, 1990), provides a detailed narrative. Sinclair Thomson, *We Alone Will Rule: Native Andean Politics in the Age of Insurgency* (Madison: Wisconsin University Press, 2002), throws new light on its origins and character.

Túpac Amaru and his relatives entered peace negotiations in early 1782 and accepted royal pardons; meanwhile, royal forces killed the Katari brothers and Túpac Katari, and repressed the rebellions in Upper Peru. Surviving members of the Túpac Amaru family were subsequently eliminated too, and the authorities mounted a campaign to eradicate symbols of Inca history and culture. Thus, the great rebellion faded, leaving a bitter memory among Indian communities that had suffered great loss of life (possibly as many as 100,000 deaths) together with the destruction of their villages and economic resources.

To understand the causes of the great rebellion that swept across the southern Andes is to be aware, above all, of the widespread sense of injustice among the Indigenous peasantry, arising from the effects of economic exploitation and cultural alienation. In theory, Indian communities had a special, protected position within the monarchy, based on the sixteenth-century idea that the king's subjects constituted two separate political communities, each with its own social hierarchy. The *república de españoles* encompassed those of Spanish, mixed, and African descent; the *república de indios* was the social and political sphere of Indigenous communities. In this system, Indians were to be segregated in their own towns and villages, under ethnic leaders (caciques) who administered local justice, delivered the tribute owed to the crown, together with the labor drafts demanded by the settler economy, notably for the silver mines at Potosí. This relationship was regarded as a reciprocal pact. The Indians were treated as free subjects (albeit under special laws); in return they paid tribute and labor levies, delivered by ethnic leaders to the *corregidor de indios* (the royal official responsible for collecting taxes, ensuring justice, and regulating relations between Indian communities and outsiders).

This "colonial pact" initially allowed Indigenous societies to retain autonomy under their own ethnic lords in return for delivering economic resources to the crown and Spanish settlers. Gradually, however, this system was replaced by another, more attuned to a mercantile society. By the early eighteenth century, tribute payments were a head tax owed by all Indians rather than a collective payment made by ethnic groups, and goods which had been produced and consumed within ethnic economies were increasingly commercialized.[18] However, while the Indigenous communities

---

[18] Luis Miguel Glave, "Republic of Indians in Revolt (c. 1680–1790)," in Frank Salomon and Stuart B. Schwartz, eds., *The Cambridge History of the Native Peoples of the Americas* (Cambridge: Cambridge University Press, 1999), vol. III, Part II, 502–55.

adapted to the market economy, they continued to bear the burdens of tribute payment and labor levies. The Potosí *mita* was particularly onerous; even more so was the *reparto de mercancías*, a practice that enabled *corregidores* (provincial magistrates) to force Indian communities to buy goods on adverse terms. Legalized in 1756, the *reparto* inflicted economic damage on Indigenous communities by draining them of money and burdening them with debt, often against a background of land shortages and falling agricultural prices. As protests mounted, Bourbon officials recognized the need to reform the *reparto*, as part of a wider plan to rationalize taxation. Attempts to extend crown control in the rural world were, however, fraught with difficulties and produced unintended consequences. Plans to reform tribute collection, for example, aroused opposition in communities accustomed to organize payment according to their own criteria, rather than an official set of rules. Indeed, reorganization of the tribute system was particularly delicate because it was invariably based on local negotiations between corregidores and caciques, and managed by caciques in negotiation with their communities. Bourbon plans to curtail the contributions which Indians made to the clergy added to the disruption, for, by generating conflict within the governing elites over how the new rules should be applied, they provided Indian communities with opportunities to contest existing arrangements.[19]

The establishment of the Viceroyalty of the Río de la Plata (1776) and the advent of Areche's *visita general* (1777) imposed further strains. The transfer of Upper Peru to the jurisdiction of a new viceroy upset political and economic connections traditionally linked to Lima; it also disrupted long-established commercial networks by redirecting the silver trade toward Buenos Aires and increasing European imports into Andean markets previously dominated by local producers.[20] More importantly, the reforms introduced by *visitador general* Areche aroused antagonisms across social ranks. Tax changes, state intrusion into Church affairs, plans to overhaul the system of government and to give greater prominence to European Spaniards: all contributed to generating political turbulence by provoking dissent among the privileged, the plebeians, and the peasantry.

---

[19] On the crisis of cacique authority in regions of Upper Peru; Serulnikov, *Subverting Colonial Authority*, Chapters 2–3; Thomson, *We Alone Will Rule*, Chapters 3–4.

[20] On these economic stresses in the region of Túpac Amaru's rebellion and their relation to other contributing factors, see Ward Stavig, *The World of Túpac Amaru: Conflict, Community and Identity in Colonial Peru* (Lincoln: University of Nebraska Press, 1999), Chapter 8.

In this world, occasions for conflict multiplied. From the mid-eighteenth century, Indigenous revolts became more frequent and widespread, with the tempo rising toward the 1770s. They were usually protests of the "moral economy" type, in which Indian peasants took violent action against abusive officials, often after they had failed to secure legal redress of their grievances.[21] These small-scale revolts sometimes voiced anticolonial attitudes by repudiating the Spanish king and making demands for Indian equality with whites and autonomy in government, but they were too localized to constitute a direct threat to Spanish rule.[22] However, as discontents proliferated, ideas which envisaged the overthrow of the existing system of Spanish rule gained wider currency, especially among Indigenous peoples who wanted equality with, even ascendancy over, the Hispanic society which demanded their deference.

Critiques of Spanish rule and ideas for alternatives were far from new. One important critical discourse emerged from within Hispanic society, among Andean intellectuals (mostly mestizo priests and caciques) who denounced the mistreatment of the Indians and called for reform of their government. Drawing on neo-Thomist political thought, Spanish law, and Christian theology, they advocated a *república de indios* that was equal to the *república de españoles*, in which the Indians were governed by their own native lords, took spiritual guidance from an Indigenous Christian priesthood, and had direct access to the king in Spain. This discourse was neither explicitly anti-Spanish nor antimonarchical. However, by calling for Indian autonomy, it fueled more radical challenges, notably in the Lima conspiracy and Huarochirí revolt of 1750, and the rebellion of Túpac Amaru in 1780.[23]

Another ideological challenge to Spanish rule emanated from Andean Indigenous cultures, in a discourse that blended elements of Christian and pre-Christian religious belief. Both Quechua and Aymara cultures retained a cyclical view of time, in which great cataclysms driven by divine forces periodically overturned the existing world and returned it to the past. In the popular culture of Andean communities, this worldview nurtured the myth of *Inkarrí*, a resurrected Inca who would return the world to a golden age of harmony and justice. First found in the Indigenous resistance

---

[21] Scarlett O'Phelan Godoy, *Rebellions and Revolts in Eighteenth Century Peru and Bolivia* (Cologne: Böhlau Verlag, 1985), Part III.

[22] For examples, see Thomson, *We Alone Will Rule*, 144–62.

[23] Alcira Dueñas, *Indians and Mestizos in the "Lettered City": Reshaping Justice, Social Hierarchy, and Political Culture in Colonial Peru* (Boulder: University Press of Colorado, 2010), 108–28.

movements of late sixteenth-century Peru, this millenarian vision acquired a new prominence during the eighteenth century, when the concept of an Inca restoration was taken up by opponents of Spanish government.[24] In 1738–1739, for example, the creole leader of a rebellion in Oruro spoke of restoring the old kings and expelling the Spanish. During the 1740s, Juan Santos Atahualpa, a Jesuit-educated Indian, stirred a rebellion among Indigenous peoples on Peru's eastern frontier and, claiming descent from the Inca Atahualpa, promised to restore an Inca kingdom throughout Peru. In 1750, the idea of an Inca revival resurfaced in a conspiracy at Lima and in the Huarochirí revolt that followed. It appeared again in the 1770s, in the Inca heartland of Cuzco. In 1777, conspirators spread rumors of a prophesized apocalypse that would restore an Inca king; in 1780, the Cuzco Silversmiths' Conspiracy envisaged an anti-Spanish rebellion led by creoles and Indian nobles, with an Inca at its head; and, finally, Túpac Amaru raised the greatest of the Andean insurrections on his claim to be an Inca king.[25]

The notion of an Inca restoration was widely disseminated among the insurgents of 1780–1781, but was most closely associated with the rebellion led by Túpac Amaru. A movement that reflected the society and culture of the Quechua-speaking peoples in the old Inca heartlands, Túpac Amaru's rebellion was strongly inflected by Inca revivalism, primarily because Cuzco and its hinterland retained powerful reminders of Inca rule. Not least of these was the presence of a wealthy Indian nobility that claimed descent from Inca royal clans and reinforced its prestige by marrying into elite creole families, owning property, and asserting an entitlement to social privilege. Inca nobles claimed equivalence with the Castilian nobility, defended their lineages

---

[24] On the sources of these ideas and their influence on the great rebellions, see John Rowe, "El movimiento nacional inca en el siglo XVIII," in Alberto Flores Galindo, ed., *Túpac Amaru II – 1780: Sociedad colonial y sublevaciones populares* (Lima: Retablo del papel, 1976); Leon Campbell, "Ideology and Factionalism during the Great Rebellion, 1780–1782," in Steve J. Stern, ed., *Resistance, Rebellion and Consciousness in the Andean Peasant World, 18th to 20th Centuries* (Madison: University of Wisconsin, 1987), 110–43; Jan Szyminski, "Why Kill the Spaniard? New Perspectives on Andean Insurrectionary Ideology in the 18th Century," in Steve J. Stern, ed., *Resistance, Rebellion and Consciousness in the Andean Peasant World, 18th to 20th Centuries* (Madison: University of Wisconsin, 1987), 166–92; Alberto Flores Galindo, *In Search of an Inca: Identity and Utopia in the Andes* (New York: Cambridge University Press, 2010), Chapters 1–4; Thomson, *We Alone Will Rule*, Chapter 5.

[25] On Juan Santos Atahualpa, see Steve J. Stern, "The Age of Andean Insurrection, 1742–1782: A Reappraisal," in Steve J. Stern, ed., *Resistance, Rebellion and Consciousness in the Andean Peasant World, 18th to 20th Centuries* (Madison: University of Wisconsin, 1987), 34–93. On the Huarochirí rebellion, see Karen Spalding, *Huarochirí: An Indian Society under Inca and Spanish Rule* (Stanford: Stanford University Press, 1984), 270–93. On the 1777 plot, see Walker, *Tupac Amaru Rebellion*, 32–3.

assiduously, and performed their position by taking a prominent part in the city's political and religious life; they also cultivated an Inca identity in paintings, regalia, and religious festivals. They did not advocate an end to Spanish rule; their aspiration was to share the privileges of Hispanic elites and they scorned Túpac Amaru's pretensions.[26] Nevertheless, the presence of Inca lords and Inca imagery in Cuzco had a wider significance among Indian commoners, for, by keeping alive memories of a glorious past, they stimulated hopes of restoring an idealized past, free from Spanish dominance.

Túpac Amaru's sudden appearance as the prophesized Inca king transformed these hopes into a political project. His status as a hereditary cacique with a claim to noble lineage, his charisma and ability to move between cultures, his kinship networks among community leaders, and his ability to communicate in Quechua, all underpinned his ability to mobilize caciques and commoners. He knew how to navigate between cultures, especially in shaping the idea of an Inca restoration to fit with Indigenous Christian culture. In his proclamations, Túpac Amaru frequently invoked the Bible and suggested that the restored Inca might rule in conjunction with the Catholic king in Spain; he also referred to European notions of kingship, presenting himself as the rightful claimant to the throne of a native monarchy whose "natural lords" the Spanish conquerors had illegally overthrown.[27]

Túpac Amaru's claim to Inca kingship seems revolutionary, since it announced an alternative sovereignty. Whether he aimed at replacing Spanish rule with an Indigenous kingdom remains uncertain, however, as his political statements were ambiguous. On the one hand, his proclamations prompted Indigenous peoples to imagine the replacement of the Spanish king; on the other, he adopted a discourse that blended readily with that of Spanish constitutionalism. Using the lexicon of Hispanic political thought, he accepted the Spanish king as a *señor natural*, respected social hierarchy, and, by proclaiming to represent all *peruanos*, aimed to build alliances with creoles and mestizos in a sovereignty shared with Spain. Here, he displayed an affinity with the Hispanic political thinking learned in his education as an Indian noble and cultivated during the decade he had spent in seeking to obtain a Spanish aristocratic title. He counted whites among his friends, including priests, and evidently shared the entrenched creole belief, shaped

---

[26] On Cuzco's Inca nobility, Peter T. Bradley and David Cahill, *Habsburg Peru: Images, Imagination and Memory* (Liverpool: Liverpool University Press, 2000), Chapters 8–9; David T. Garrett, *Shadow of Empire: The Indian Nobility of Cusco, 1750–1825* (Cambridge: Cambridge University Press, 2005), 76–86, 97–102.

[27] Walker, *Tupac Amaru Rebellion*, Chapter 2.

by the conventions of the Habsburg monarchy, that Americans were entitled to participate in the governance of their *patrias*. Túpac Amaru also courted Church support, by playing on rifts between crown and clergy. He understood that recognition from the clergy was vital to his cause and presented himself as a champion for the Church, at the head of Indian followers who were good Christians, unlike the European Spaniards whom he disparaged as morally corrupt and anti-Church.

The rebellions in Upper Peru that flanked the Tupamarista movement and interacted with it had their own characteristics and dynamics. In Chayanta, the uprising led by the cacique Tomás Katari and his brothers developed out of a long legal struggle by Indian communities to curb exploitation by corregidores and to restore their corporate rights, especially the choice of their own leaders. This was not a rejection of Spanish rule; although they refused to cooperate with district officials, communities continued to pay their dues to the crown. However, the assassination of Tomás Katari moved politics onto a new plane, from hopes of reforming the system to plans for its overthrow. Influenced by the messianic ideas stirred by Túpac Amaru's rebellion, Katari's brothers launched a war against whites and mestizos, in anticipation of the *pachacuti* that would sweep Hispanic society away and return the world to the Indians; indeed, their escalation of violence was taken as a sign that the *pachacuti* had begun.[28]

The influence of millenarian beliefs was also evident in the movement led by Túpac Katari in the La Paz region, perhaps the most explicitly anti-Spanish and anticolonial of the Andean rebellions. This insurrection was not based on communities led by caciques in the way of Chayanta and Cuzco; nor did its participants follow Túpac Amaru's search for alliances with other social groups. Instead, Túpac Katari's followers killed creoles and mestizos, attacked towns and undertook prolonged sieges of La Paz, the major regional center of Hispanic power and culture. Based in a peasantry with a record of violent resistance against local officials, this insurrection was more overtly radical than Túpac Amaru's. For, stirred by hopes of taking over government in their localities and recouping control of their resources, the rebels immediately attacked the social and cultural pillars of Spanish colonialism. They killed white and mestizo property owners, including clerics, and they asserted their cultural equality by forcing non-Indians to wear Indian costume and adopt Indian ways. In this, they expressed aspirations for a new

---

[28] Serulnikov, *Subverting Colonial Authority*, Chapter 6.

political order, an inversion of the hierarchy of colonial society and its replacement by Indigenous supremacy.[29]

Taken together, these rebellions were a new phenomenon, in that they developed simultaneously and threatened to merge into a concerted attack on Hispanic government and society. All were Indigenous movements with strong anticolonial implications; all involved attacks on the symbols and institutions of Hispanic domination; all embraced Indigenous forms of Christianity, while denouncing Spaniards as bad Christians; all spurned Spanish domination, albeit without entirely rejecting connections to the Spanish monarchy. They did not, however, form a uniform or unified movement. The rebellions in the Cuzco, Potosí, and La Paz regions had distinctive social and cultural characteristics and, although they were aware of each other, they did not come together in a military and political alliance capable of challenging the Spanish state.

Túpac Amaru's vision of a political revolution that embraced different social groups initially seemed a realistic alternative, but it evaporated when creoles and mestizos failed to provide active support. And, as the rebellion became synonymous with Indigenous violence against creoles and mestizos, so the possibility of attracting their support diminished. Indigenous communities were also divided amongst themselves. In Cuzco and its region, Túpac Amaru was rejected by Inca nobles and allied caciques, who organized Indigenous forces to fight against the rebels, alongside white and mestizo militias and royal troops. In Upper Peru, the Katari brothers and Túpac Katari were able to dominate rural areas and occasionally convene large forces for attacks on cities, but their movements were unstable and connections with the Tupamaristas were complicated by social and cultural differences. Aymara rebels in Upper Peru, for example, embraced the idea of Túpac Amaru as a native king but, given that the Incas had been historic enemies, they did not envisage unification under Inca sovereignty. Unity among Aymaras was also fragile. There were moments when their forces threatened to overturn Spanish domination, but disputes over local power tended to take priority over ambitions to overthrow the Spanish social and political order as a whole. Insurrection was, moreover, drained by the armed struggle. When Túpac Amaru, the Katari brothers, and Túpac Katari

---

[29] On the character of Túpac Katari, his movement and the reasons for its violence, see Thomson, *We Alone Will Rule*, Chapter 6. On the role of Indigenous millenarianism in the great Andean rebellion, see Nicholas A. Robin, *Insurgencies and the Genocidal Impulse in the Americas* (Bloomington: University of Indiana Press, 2005), 36–51, 74–84, 102–41, 147–51.

mobilized large forces for assaults on towns and cities they did not create effective armies; their forces were too lightly armed, ill-disciplined, and prone to desertion, and they tended to suffer heavy casualties. The forces of counterinsurgency also suffered serious setbacks but, backed by well-armed forces led by professional soldiers and financed by the resources of colonial treasuries, they were better positioned to prevail.

Crushed by armed force, the rebels' military defeat was the prelude to a longer social repression. Indian leaders, even those who had fought on the side of the authorities, were regarded with suspicion and deprived of power; the use of Inca regalia and symbols was banned; schools for Indian nobles were closed; Quechua was no longer allowed as a language for education. Indeed, the idea of the Indian republic was officially relegated, along with the traditional system of governance by corregidores, who were replaced by regional intendants. Thus, after the rebellions, a new form of government took shape, disconnected from the traditions of Hispanic–Andean society and distant from Indian dreams of restored territorial and communal rights.

The Comunero Rebellion in New Granada

The other large-scale revolt that took place in Spanish America at the time of the American Revolution was in the eastern highlands of New Granada, in a region close to the viceregal capital of Bogotá. Like Túpac Amaru's rebellion in Peru, it stemmed from reforms introduced by an emissary of Gálvez, in this case the *visitador general* Antonio Gutiérrez de Piñeres. Installed in Bogotá, he raised the rate of the sales tax, extended the range of goods it covered, tightened regulations over the sale of aguardiente and the cultivation and sale of tobacco, and introduced a more efficient system for tax enforcement; to these increases, he added the demand that all free adult males make a "voluntary" donation to pay for the war against Britain. Moreover, like Areche in Peru, Gutiérrez de Piñeres followed Gálvez's plans to reduce the influence of creoles in government, both by replacing creole judges on the audiencia of Santa Fe and planning for the introduction of intendants.[30]

---

[30] The following account draws on John Phelan, *The People and the King: The Comunero Revolution in Colombia* (Madison: University of Wisconsin, 1978); Mario Aguilera Peña, *Los Comuneros: Guerra social y lucha anticolonial* (Bogotá: Universidad Nacional de Colombia, 1985); Anthony McFarlane, *Colombia before Independence: Economy, Society and Politics under Bourbon Rule* (Cambridge: Cambridge University Press, 1993), 208–22, 251–64.

Popular protest swiftly followed, launching a revolt driven from below. It started among small farmers who objected to bans on tobacco cultivation, then spread to country parishes, before finally taking on a more focused form in a series of riots in the town of Socorro. These started on 16 March 1781, when the public announcement of new sales tax regulations triggered a riot among the crowds gathered for the town's weekly market. In the days that followed, rioting broke out in the nearby parishes of Simacota and Pinchote and the town of San Gil, where restrictions on tobacco cultivation directly affected small farmers. Then, when resistance to increases in the *alcabala* combined with protests against the tobacco monopoly, the constituency of protest broadened. Socorro rioted again, on 30 March, and a surge of discontent swept through neighboring settlements in early April, in a chain of riots against the personnel and property of the local tobacco and aguardiente monopoly administrations. In mid-April, after a third major riot in Socorro, the crowds acclaimed four prominent citizens as their "captains-general," chosen to defend the interests of the *común*, and a concerted regional movement came into being.

The royal government made some conciliatory gestures while making ready for repression. When they mobilized a small military contingent, they found the Comunero "captains-general" ready for armed confrontation. On 2 May, these captains established a "Supreme Council of War" under the command of Francisco Berbeo and expanded their forces with militias sent by towns and villages under local "captains." Shortly afterward, the expeditionary force sent by the government surrendered, giving up arms and funds without resistance. Emboldened by this success, the patrician–plebeian alliance in Socorro gained both confidence and fresh recruits, drawn from an increasingly broad network. The adhesion of the city of Tunja and neighboring town of Sogamoso was particularly important; so, too, was the broadening of the social base by inclusion of the Indigenous communities of Santa Fe, Tunja, Vélez, and Sogamoso, after Ambrosio Pisco, the mestizo cacique who was their titular leader, accepted a position as a "captain" of the Comuneros.

After revealing its military weakness, the Bogotá government changed strategy. The *visitador general* fled to Cartagena to join the viceroy, and authority temporarily passed to a committee composed of audiencia judges, senior officials, clerics, and representatives of the Bogotá cabildo. Meanwhile, the rebellion continued to spread. It even reached the distant Llanos, where, from mid-May, a group of creoles raised an Indian rebellion and allied themselves to the Socorro movement by taking titles and commissions from

Berbeo's Supreme Council of War. While growing numbers mobilized in defiance of government, Berbeo further extended the area under rebel control and isolated the capital from communication with the viceroy. He sent José Antonio Galán into the Upper Magdalena valley to raise support and impede communication between Bogotá and the coast. In late May, he stationed 20,000 men near the town of Zipaquirá, en route to the capital, and sent a force of Indians from nearby villages to guard the entry to Bogotá. The Indians were withdrawn under protest from the authorities, but the tactic was a clever one. By displaying his Indian allies, Berbeo exploited racial fears, thereby heightening tensions in the capital and forcing government to consider his terms. It was in these circumstances that the rebellion moved toward its climax during the first week of June 1781.

As the rebels gathered near Zipaquirá, the stage was set for the seizure of Bogotá and the overthrow of the audiencia. In the event, the invasion was averted due to disagreements among the rebels. The plebeians from the Socorro area regarded capture of the capital as the best means to ensure that their demands were honored; leaders from Tunja and Sogamoso, who were anxious to avoid any further disturbance, preferred to seek a negotiated conclusion. Their opinion prevailed and negotiations with the envoys of the government, led by the archbishop of Santa Fe, Antonio Caballero y Góngora, opened on 5 June 1781.

The rebels presented their demands in a *plan de capitulaciones* (terms of settlement) composed of thirty-five clauses. Fearing that the rebels would invade Bogotá, Archbishop Caballero y Góngora and his commissioners promised to implement all their terms on the understanding that the Comuneros would demobilize and return to their homes. Some pockets of resistance remained: José Antonio Galán refused to surrender his arms and from his base in Ambalema he tried to raise rebellion in the previously undisturbed areas of Mariquita, Neiva, and the province of Antioquia. Resistance also persisted in the Llanos, and from July until October, rioting against officials occurred in widely dispersed settings throughout New Granada, as far south as Pasto.[31] But, if these local riots and revolts were inspired by the example of the Comuneros, they were of a very different social character to the original movement and did not achieve the same

---

[31] Jane M. Loy, "Forgotten Comuneros: The 1781 Revolt in the Llanos de Casanare," *Hispanic American Historical Review* 61:2 (1981), 235–57; Rebecca Earle Mond, "Indian Rebellion and Bourbon Reform in New Granada: Riots in Pasto, 1780–1810," *Hispanic American Historical Review* 73:1 (1993), 99–124: 105–10.

degree of regional mobilization or cross-class organization. As for Galán's breakaway rebellion, it was short-lived. He and his few followers were arrested, snuffing out the possibility that the rebellion might reignite.

Like the rebellions in Quito and Peru, the Comunero rebellion began as a reaction against administrative and tax reforms, and originated in communities linked by a network of social ties and a sense of communal solidarity. The social milieu of the Comunero rebellion was, in one key respect, closer to the Quito rebellion than to Túpac Amaru's, being built on a white and mestizo population with little Indian participation. Comunero recruits were mostly farmers, artisans, and small traders who produced and traded food crops, tobacco, and cotton for local and regional markets. Their regional society was also distinctive, being based on relatively recent colonization and vigorous growth, in which the foundation of new parishes and towns had stimulated political life and fostered a sense of shared identity. Not all towns joined the Comuneros, but there were sufficient to create a large movement linked by a common cause. Crucial, too, was the willingness of the local gentry to take positions of leadership. For, in a hierarchical society, the assumption of leadership by local notables was an important endorsement of the rioters' claim to be acting in benefit of the *común*.

Francisco Berbeo, who emerged as the Comuneros' *caudillo*, exemplified the social character of the movement's leadership. His father was a Spaniard who had been notary of Socorro and his brothers held municipal office; he was himself a modest landowner but had traveled outside the region, had some military experience from campaigns on the Indian frontier, and had contacts in influential creole circles in Bogotá. His respect for authority was reflected in the Comuneros' structure of command. He assumed a quasi-official title, as *superintendente y comandante*, and recruited as "captains" men of similar social rank. Of the other thirty-four captains in the Socorro region, the great majority – some twenty-eight – were of similar social standing. Most were literate whites who, as relatively wealthy landowners and members of the local "municipal aristocracies" of officeholders and tax-farmers, jealously guarded the local social and political preeminence of their families.

The rebels were motivated primarily by anger at new taxes, but once the rebellion was underway, other grievances appeared. The first written expression of a common set of complaints came in the shape of a satirical poem, probably written by a Dominican friar from Bogotá. Composed of roughly rhyming stanzas, the poem spoke in colloquial language and crystallized popular resentments in verses that expressed outrage at new taxes, dislike of peninsular Spaniards, and emotions of local patriotism. It also infused the rebellion with the dignity of a wider political meaning, defining the *socorranos* in quasi-biblical terms as a "chosen people," whose "enterprise" was a shining inspiration to all who opposed tyranny in New Granada. Easily communicable, it became a kind of manifesto for the Comuneros, stating their grievances and justifying their demands.[32]

A clearer sense of the Comuneros' grievances and ideas is found in the *capitulaciones* which their leaders presented to the authorities. These were in large part economic grievances, assembled in an unstructured way, and reflecting the participation of different social groups. In addition to rejection of the *visitador general*'s tax reforms, the economic burdens imposed by the Church came under attack, with calls for a reduction in the charges made by clerics, and for abolition or fairer regulation of charges made by tithe collectors. Indian grievances also found a place in calls for the tribute to be halved, for the alleviation of Indian exploitation by corregidores and clergy, and for the restoration of their *resguardos* (community lands) in the form of individual holdings.

The Comuneros program primarily reflects the economic concerns of the free peasantry and modest landowners of Socorro and its adjoining region of Tunja. The interests of small producers and traders surfaced in calls for the sale of Indian community lands, for improving roads and bridges, ending private tolls, allowing freedom to pasture animals on roadsides, and ensuring fairer regulation of weights and measures by town councils. Some of the *capitulaciones* demanded changes in local government; others had wider political implications. Thus, when the rebels called for the expulsion of the *visitador general*, they also insisted on the abolition of the *visita general* as an institution. Even more striking was their statement that "in offices of first, second and third levels, the nationals of this America should be given preference and privilege over Europeans," on the grounds that the latter lacked sufficient knowledge of and sympathy for local concerns, and because "as we are all subject to the same King and Lord, we should live together in fraternal harmony."[33] This idealized harmony also required the removal of "foreigners," all of whom should be expelled within two months. Finally, to ensure that their demands were met, the Comuneros insisted that the royal

---

[32] For the text, see Pablo Cárdenas Acosta, *El movimiento comunal de 1781 en el Nuevo Reino de Granada*, 2 vols. (Bogotá: Editorial Kelly, 1960), vol. I, 121–30; for analysis, see Phelan, *The People and the King*, 71–8.
[33] Cárdenas Acosta, *El movimiento comunal*, vol. II, 18–29.

government confirm all appointments in the rebel command structure and allow Comunero forces to be maintained as militias, while also granting a general pardon to seal the pact and restore normal relations.

The Comuneros' demands reflected political beliefs and attitudes that were similar to those of rebels in Quito and Cuzco. They did not challenge the God-given authority of kings nor demand secession from the Spanish monarchy; their intention was to defend the political and fiscal status quo against Bourbon innovations, and their rhetoric echoed the old contractualist doctrine which gave subjects the right to appeal to the king for justice over the heads of his ministers, by force if necessary. Hence, the Comunero slogan of "Long live the King and down with bad government," a cry that was characteristic of *ancien régime* rebellions. While they accepted the authority of the king, the Comuneros evidently believed in an "unwritten constitution" that allowed the king's subjects a voice in matters important to their political community, expressed through the social and political hierarchy.[34]

By reforming government and taxation without consulting the creole elites and favoring peninsulars over creoles in high office, Charles III disturbed this constitutional arrangement at more than one level. Not only were audiencias purged of creoles, but Gálvez's policies threatened the political power which local notables enjoyed in their home areas. By placing power in the hands of officials who did not belong to local political factions, these measures damaged ties of clientelism and thereby diminished the standing of local authorities. For the local notables, this was of itself a powerful motive for involvement in the rebellion. Here, then, was a crucial cause of creole intervention in the Comunero rebellion and the reason why popular revolt extended into a wider coalition, incorporating the leading sectors of provincial society. While peasants and plebeians protested new taxes, the provincial gentry sought to defend its local political prestige and authority, also in the name of the common good.[35]

Defense of the status quo restricted the political reach of the rebellion. Creole patricians wanted to restore and preserve the traditional order, and, having much to lose from prolonged political upheaval, they curbed its radicalization. Thus, the Comunero rebellion did not create a revolutionary situation comparable with that of the great rebellion in the southern Andes, nor did it reflect or induce an analogous shift in political consciousness. Held together by vertical alliances between gentry and plebeians, rather than grouped in horizontal alliances based in social class or ethnic groups, the Comuneros aimed to defend

---

[34] Phelan, *The People and the King*, 79–88.
[35] McFarlane, *Colombia before Independence*, 266–7.

local autonomy, not overthrow Spanish rule. Their rebellion was, in essence, a regional movement structured around the local politics in the Socorro area, in alliances bonded by kin and clientelism. Such politics reflected a sense of local identity and separateness, expressed in the claim that "nationals of this America" should have preference in the disposition of local office. This was, however, still an idea of "nation" within the Spanish monarchy, not a rallying cry for independence. The Comunero rebellion ended, as it had begun, as a protest within the political system, not a demand for its overthrow.

Connections and Comparisons

The rebellions that took place in North and South America between 1765 and 1783 shared some political similarities. In 1766, the fiscal attorney of Quito made a comment about the city's rebellion that would have resonated with contemporary British officials in North America: namely, that "there is no American who does not reject any novelty whatsoever in the management of taxation."[36] In 1781, another official drew a direct comparison between the rebellions in British North America and those in New Granada and Peru, stating that, just as "the rebellion of the English colonies had its origins in taxes, that of Lima (sic) had the same beginning, and that of Santa Fe also."[37] Associated with this similarity was another: the idea that tax increases dictated from the imperial center were unconstitutional (in the sense of breaking time-honored political conventions), and, if legal representations failed, could justifiably be opposed by action outside the law.

There were, however, few direct linkages between the rebellions in British North America and Spanish South America. Some cross-fertilization of images and ideas may have taken place: Túpac Amaru, for example, possibly learned of the North American rebellion while residing in Lima in 1777, when one of his confidantes was Miguel Montiel, a merchant who in the 1760s and 1770s had traveled in Spain, France, and England, and greatly admired the English. Montiel, it was said, believed that Spanish rule was illegitimate and encouraged Túpac Amaru to take the throne, with the aid of the English if Indigenous support was insufficient.[38] The Comunero leaders were probably also aware of events in British America: Viceroy Flórez of New Granada said that "the

---

[36] Quoted by McFarlane, "Rebellion of the Barrios," 287.
[37] Francisco de Saavedra, *The Journal of Don Francisco Saavedra de Sangronis, 1780–1783*, ed. Francisco Morales Padrón, trans. Aileen Moore Topping (Gainesville: University of Florida Press, 1989), 259–61.
[38] Walker, *The Tupac Amaru Rebellion*, 27–8.

form of independence won by the British colonies of the North is now on the lips of everyone ... in the rebellion."³⁹ Rumors circulated, too, that the British might intervene to support rebellions, though these might simply reflect the long-standing myth (which originated in the sixteenth century) that the English would release Indian peoples from subjugation to Spain. It is unlikely, however, that the rebellions in Spanish America had any direct connection to the ideas and actions of North American revolutionaries. News of the rift between Britain and its colonies no doubt reached Spanish America via port cities and government capitals but, without newspapers to report events or comment upon them, such news could not spread far.

Contemporary critics of the rebellions detected the corrosive influence of Enlightenment ideas, stimulating subversion.⁴⁰ Joaquin de Finestrad, for example, denounced the Comuneros for being in thrall to the "system of reason" which undermined religion and authority and had led them astray with subversive ideas.⁴¹ In Peru, Areche also condemned Enlightenment ideas, blaming clerics, among whom "there are many Voltaires, many Rousseaus, many Raynalds (sic) and many others who have sacrilegiously opposed in their writings the authority of Kings ..."⁴² In fact, such heterodox political ideas had scarcely been seeded in Spanish America at the time of the American Revolution. Creoles trained in law might recognize the concept of independence from Emer Vattel's *Law of Nations* (1758), but ideas for radical political change remained on the margins of creole political thinking until after the French Revolution, when some creole intellectuals began to see North American independence as an example they might follow.

The absence of external ideological influences does not mean that the Spanish American rebellions of the 1780s were devoid of revolutionary ideas. The autonomy of self-governing communities sought by the Chayanta rebels could coexist with Spanish sovereignty, but required major changes in social relations. Millenarian beliefs had even more revolutionary implications, given that the desire to restore a mythical Andean utopia required the overthrow of

---

³⁹ Quoted by Jonathan I. Israel, *The Expanding Blaze: How the American Revolution Ignited the World* (Princeton: Princeton University Press, 2017), 437.
⁴⁰ For a view which sees the Túpac Amaru rebellion as a stimulus to Enlightenment political thinking in Peru and detects signs of Enlightenment thinking in the Comunero rebellion, see Jonathan I. Israel, *Democratic Enlightenment: Philosophy, Revolution and Human Rights, 1750–1790* (Oxford: Oxford University Press, 2012), 497–502, 530–2.
⁴¹ Joaquín de Finestrad, *El vasallo instruido en el estado del Nuevo Reino de Granada y en sus respectivas obligaciones*, transcription and introduction Margarita González (Bogotá: Universidad Nacional de Colombia, 2001), 42–3.
⁴² Quoted by Walker, *Rebellion of Tupac Amaru*, 84.

the existing social and political order. The Comuneros had a radical component too, albeit amongst the small group who followed Galán. However, if these social rebels envisaged the overthrow of the established order, they lived in societies where the legitimacy of the Spanish monarchy and the social hierarchy on which it rested were generally unquestioned. Whereas the North American rebellion developed in a context where rapid demographic and economic growth had weakened social hierarchy and respect for the British king, the Spanish American rebellions took place in societies where political cultures were firmly anchored to throne and altar and corporate structures were strong. In such settings, the idea of creating independent states that proclaimed the rights of the individual in republican constitutions had no foundation. Indeed, unlike the rebels in North America, those in Peru and New Granada did not systematically criticize the Spanish king nor reject the concept of monarchy. While the North American Declaration of Independence of 1776 included specific criticisms of George III's behavior, the texts that emitted from the Comuneros and Túpac Amaru treated the king as the natural head of the body politic, contained no personal criticisms of Charles III, and did not imagine a republican alternative. Nor did the rebels in Peru and New Granada seek to establish an independent state or seek support from foreign powers. They had no equivalent to the Continental Congress or Washington's Continental Army, no external financial and military aid, nor any vision of a future within the international concert of states.

In short, the Spanish American rebellions lacked radical ideological input of the kind injected into the American Revolution by the Declaration of Independence, Paine's *Common Sense*, and the Pennsylvania Constitution of 1776. Their revolutionary potential had very different sources, in the neo-Inca and millenarian ideas which stimulated a struggle against an oppressive social hierarchy and its government. However, although Andean rebels imagined a different social order, they did so in the terms of the Andean rather than the Atlantic cultural world and, together with the Comuneros, were confined within political cultures that were as yet largely untouched by modern ideas. The influence of such ideas and the example of the American Revolution had to wait at least another generation, until after the French Revolution and the ensuing crisis of the Spanish monarchy.[43]

---

[43] On political developments after the rebellions of the 1780s, see Anthony McFarlane, "The American Revolution and Spanish America, 1776–1814," in Gabriel Paquette and Gonzalo M. Quintero Saravia, eds., *Spain and the American Revolution: New Approaches and Perspectives* (Abingdon: Routledge, 2020), 47–56.

19
International Warfare and the Non-British Caribbean

WIM KLOOSTER

If the echo of the American Revolution in the British Caribbean was faint, its ideological impact in the rest of the Caribbean was even smaller. The chain of events set in motion by the first clash of arms in Lexington and Concord did, however, have powerful consequences in those non-British islands in other ways. Especially during the first three years of the revolutionary war, the French colonies of Martinique and Saint-Domingue and the Dutch island of St. Eustatius played an active role in furnishing arms and ammunition to the Patriots. The subsequent formal declarations of war by France and Spain against Great Britain moved the war's center of gravity to the Caribbean and the Gulf of Mexico.[1] What military and social effects did this shift have in the Caribbean?

Procuring War Supplies

The outbreak of the American Revolutionary War was not wholly unexpected. In different locations, the Patriots had prepared for armed struggle before the actual fighting began. Gathering in October 1774, Massachusetts' first Provincial Congress led the way by appointing a committee that surveyed the amount of gunpowder and ordnance stores required for the province and what had to be procured at short notice. In February 1775, a Committee of Safety in Virginia offered a £20 reward for the first person in the colony who made 5,000 pounds of powder. Small successes were recorded in attempts to secure arms and ammunition. A raid netted large quantities of gunpowder and arms in the harbor of Portsmouth, New

---

[1] Agustín Guimerá Ravina, "La stratégie navale et la navigation espagnole vers les Antilles et le Golfe du Mexique (1759–1783)," in Olivier Chaline, Philippe Bonnichon, and Charles-Philippe de Vergennes, eds., *Les Marines de la guerre d'Indépendance américaine (1763–1783)*, 2 vols. (Paris: Presses de l'université Paris-Sorbonne, 2018), vol. II, 67–90: 87.

Hampshire, while a group of Patriots in Boston succeeded in stealing a British cannon from under the noses of the artillery guard.[2] What gave a real boost to the search for weapons and their production were the skirmishes in Lexington and Concord in April. On the same day that news about the events in Massachusetts arrived in New York, local Patriots broke into City Hall and made off with five hundred muskets and a supply of gunpowder. Similarly, in Savannah, Georgia, a mob stole most of the gunpowder from the town's public magazine. Everywhere, the rebels began to gather military stores, confiscate guns, and start the production of musket balls and gunpowder for the benefit of the militias and the Continental Army.[3]

The arms industry had to overcome a range of obstacles. Iron ore for the production of gun barrels and lead for shot were abundantly available, but two of the three ingredients for gunpowder – sulfur and saltpeter (the other one being charcoal) – were in very short supply. All sulfur had to be imported from continental Europe. Another problem was that powder mills that had operated in the seventeenth and eighteenth centuries had fallen into disrepair after the Seven Years' War. Not a single powder mill was operating when the revolutionary war broke out. There were gunsmiths, but they worked on their own or aided by one or two apprentices. Powder mills and saltpeter refineries were now erected at a rapid pace, with existing mills being converted for the sake of wartime industries. The result was that American powder mills manufactured about one-third of the gunpowder used by the Patriots during the first two years of the war.[4]

Domestic production was necessary because import of war supplies got going slowly, jeopardizing the Patriots' war effort at Boston. Soldiers involved in the Battle of Bunker Hill (17 June 1775) were ordered to wait

---

[2] William Lincoln, ed., *The Journals of Each Provincial Congress of Massachusetts in 1774 and 1775, and of the Committee of Safety, with an Appendix* (Boston, MA: Dutton & Wentworth, 1838), 30; Donald E. Reynolds, "Ammunition Supply in Revolutionary Virginia," *Virginia Magazine of History and Biography* 73:1 (1965), 56–77: 56; Robert A. Gross, *The Minutemen and their World* (New York: Hill & Wang, 1976), 68.

[3] Roger J. Champagne, "New York's Radicals and the Coming of Independence," *Journal of American History* 51:1 (1964), 21–40: 22; Sheldon S. Cohen, "The Odyssey of Ebenezer Smith Platt," *Journal of American Studies* 18:2 (1984), 255–74: 258; Alan D. Watson, "The Committees of Safety and the Coming of the American Revolution in North Carolina, 1774–1776," *North Carolina Historical Review* 73:2 (1996), 131–55: 148.

[4] Neil L. York, "Clandestine Aid and the American Revolutionary War Effort: A Re-examination," *Military Affairs* 43:1 (1979), 26–30: 26–7; David L. Salav, "The Production of Gunpowder in Pennsylvania during the American Revolution," *Pennsylvania Magazine of History and Biography* 99:4 (1975), 422–42: 423, 424, 431, 441.

until the last moment before unleashing a volley in light of the modest gunpowder supply. A month later, General George Washington found to his horror that his army had a mere ninety barrels of gunpowder left, which translated to nine cartridges per man. What enabled his army to keep fighting was the capture by a Georgia privateer of a British ship en route to Florida with firearms, bullets, and a large quantity of gunpowder on board, 5,000 pounds of which were sent to Washington's army besieging Boston.[5] In addition, the army depended on what provincial congresses could spare and what supplies could be purchased from private traders.[6]

It was just as well that the winter of 1775–1776 did not see large-scale battles. At the start of the new year, Washington remarked that it made no sense to equip a force "without any money in our treasury, powder in our magazines, arms in our stores ..."[7] When the thaw came, however, a growing number of military supplies began to arrive from various non-British Caribbean islands, and especially the island of Martinique. Following the British occupation during the Seven Years' War, the island had been restored to French rule and transformed into the principal French naval base in the Caribbean. To that end, supplementary fortifications were constructed and improvements were made in coastal defense.[8] The island's role as an arms supplier to the North American insurgents was the result of initiatives by a select number of North American rebel agents, men such as Silas Deane and William Bingham.

Virtually all these supplies originated in France, but direct imports from there to North America were forbidden by the French government, which, despite being well-disposed vis-à-vis the rebels, preferred covert support in order not to anger Great Britain. Transferring the supplies to American vessels was supposed to shield the French from exposing their involvement.

Silas Deane arrived in France in May 1776 as the first agent of the Continental Congress to strike deals with weapon producers. By December, he had already shipped 80,000 pounds of saltpeter and 200,000

---

[5] Nathaniel Philbrick, *Bunker Hill: A City, a Siege, a Revolution* (New York: Viking, 2013), 220; Donald Barr Chidsley, *The Siege of Boston: An on-the-Scene Account of the Beginning of the American Revolution* (New York: Crown, 1966), 116; Cohen, "The Odyssey of Ebenezer Smith Platt," 258–9.
[6] Erna Risch, *Supplying Washington's Army* (Washington, DC: Center of Military History, United States Army, 1981), 341.
[7] Orlando W. Stephenson, "The Supply of Gunpowder in 1776," *American Historical Review* 30:2 (1925), 271–81: 276.
[8] R. J. Singh, "L'importance stratégique des colonies antillaises dans la politique française de l'après-guerre (1763–1770)," *Revue d'histoire de l'Amérique française* 28:1 (1974), 27–43: 37.

pounds of gunpowder from France by way of Martinique. William Bingham was active in Martinique itself as agent of the Continental Congress. His first task was to secure 10,000 good muskets, which he had to dispatch not in a single shipment to the eastern seaboard, but to distribute in small lots among swift sailing vessels. In that way, the risk of seizure by the numerous British privateers was reduced.[9]

French officials walked a fine line as they attempted to allow the illegal trade with the rebels to proceed without publicly acknowledging it. Some ministers in Paris played down reports presented to them by the British ambassador, until they were shown undeniable evidence of the sale of British prizes (ships captured by privateers) at the French colonies, which led to a prohibition of such sales. Covert French aid seemed to be additionally jeopardized by the arrival in Martinique of a new governor general of the French Antilles in 1777. The Marquis de Bouillé placated British anxieties by acknowledging Britain's right to search French Caribbean vessels for produce from North America, which was commonly paid for in French military stores. In reality, Bouillé not only allowed ammunition to leave the French islands with great frequency, he gave vessels departing for the mainland the protection of a warship until they were clear of the islands. Nor did he object to the steady stream of Patriot privateers anchoring at Martinique's ports.[10]

In order to carry out his duties, Bingham created a network of agents across the Caribbean, appointing agents in Saint-Domingue, Guadeloupe, St. Eustatius, and Curaçao. In Martinique, he was joined by young Americans representing Pennsylvania, Georgia, and Maryland. One of them was Richard Harrison, who had offered his services to the Maryland Convention when he heard about its plan to send grain and tobacco to the French and Dutch colonies in exchange for arms and ammunition. In response, the Convention asked him by return mail to become its agent in Martinique.[11]

Virginia-born Arthur Lee, one of four brothers who served the American Revolution as diplomats, arranged for the import from the French port of Nantes of 15,000 firearms and the shipments of more war materials under the

---

[9] York, "Clandestine Aid," 28; Margaret L. Brown, "William Bingham, Agent of the Continental Congress in Martinique," *Pennsylvania Magazine of History and Biography* 61:1 (1937), 54–87: 56.

[10] Brown, "Bingham," 68–70. During the French Revolution, Bouillé would be one of the architects of King Louis XVI's attempted flight abroad, which ended at Varennes.

[11] Myron J. Smith, Jr. and John G. Earle, "The Maryland State Navy," in Ernest McNeill Eller, ed., *Chesapeake Bay in the American Revolution* (Centreville, MD: Tidewater, 1981), 204–60: 212, 214.

cover of the Atlantic slave trade. Lee also took part in negotiations that led to the most impressive contribution to the American independence movement by the French government: the extension of aid worth 1 million livres in the form of war supplies, an amount soon matched by the Spanish crown. To camouflage the French government's role, a fictitious company headed by Pierre-Augustin Caron de Beaumarchais took responsibility for the shipments. The French polymath, an ardent supporter of the Patriots' cause, only requested payments in kind. A stream of French-produced uniforms, tents, artillery pieces, and muskets got underway.[12]

The ubiquity of British privateers, many of them fitted out in Dominica and other British Leeward Islands, combined with uncertainty about the stance of the French and Dutch colonial governments, made the voyages of North American vessels to the Caribbean hazardous affairs in the early part of the American Revolutionary War. A ship captain who was sent on a "powder voyage" in late 1775 to the French island of St. Lucia, just south of Martinique, was instructed that it was probable that some merchants on that island would take his cargo and furnish the powder at another island. In case no business could be conducted at St. Lucia, he was to sail to Martinique, Guadeloupe, or any other French, Spanish, or Dutch island. However, "if after Cruizing over all the foreign West Indies, and no Gun Powder to be had ... you must then Endeavour to purchase what Salt Petre, and Sulphur you possibly can ..."[13]

As in Martinique, trade in war supplies was soon set up in Saint-Domingue, once again in response to North American initiatives. The French part of Hispaniola had probably become the world's most valuable colony by the time the American Revolution broke out, attracting legal and illicit trade with the Thirteen Colonies. These connections were solidified by North American help after an earthquake (1770) and two hurricanes (1772) hit Saint-Domingue. In August 1776, the Committee of Secret Correspondence, which had been established by Congress to import arms and ammunition, wrote to Saint-Domingue's governor requesting the permanent residence of an agent and the free admission of North American vessels. Letters also arrived from the "president" of Georgia and Patriot

---

[12] Patrick Villiers, "Rodrigue, Hortalez et Cie," in Gregory Fremont Barnes and Richard Alan Ryerson, eds., *The Encyclopedia of the American Revolutionary War: A Political, Social, and Military History*, vol. III (Santa Barbara, CA: ABC-CLIO, 2006), 1088–91.

[13] "Instructions to Captain Thomas Peverly for a Powder Voyage," in William Bell Clark, ed., *Naval Documents of the American Revolution*, vol. III (Washington, DC: United States Navy Department, 1968), 270.

general Charles Lee, which asked for two ship captains to be received in Cap Français – Saint-Domingue's chief port – for the purchase of war stores. Without consulting Paris, the governor agreed, inviting the North Americans to buy whatever merchandise they desired, and promising their vessels protection. Trade with the North Americans prospered like never before in the years that followed. The large number of masts, spars, knees, rafters, and thick planks that entered Cap Français in return for war supplies made the port self-sufficient in naval stores. Besides, more than enough foodstuffs were introduced.[14]

Until the declaration of war against Britain in June 1778, official French policy continued to be articulated to counter British accusations of massive French services to aid the rebels. North Americans were not to load arms or ammunition onto their vessels, and American privateers could only remain in port for a few days and only to obtain provisions or repair their ships. Prizes they brought in could not be protected or sold in the French Caribbean.[15] It was all part of a strategy to conceal the truth.

Starting in 1775, Cap Français thus became the main nexus in the arms trade between France and the united colonies. The embarkation of war supplies in Môle St. Nicolas, another port in Saint-Domingue, was soon hampered by the Royal Navy, which stationed two frigates off that port in early 1776. Although the Royal Navy captured many a vessel, some slipped through the blockade, such as the *Lexington*, fitted out by the Patriots' Continental Navy. During its return voyage, begun in December 1776, the ship was captured by a navy frigate, whose officers made the mistake of taking off only *Lexington*'s officers and a few crew members due to the high sea. The British sailors probably discovered the rum stored below deck, because they soon found themselves locked in the hold by *Lexington*'s crew, who steered the ship to Baltimore, where the military stores were unloaded. Congress expressed thanks to the crew with two months' pay.[16]

French shipments of war supplies to North America were also routed through the tiny Dutch island of St. Eustatius. Although it had a small plantation sector, the island's economy mainly revolved around inter-imperial trade.

---

[14] Frostin, "Saint-Domingue et la révolution américaine," 83–5, 101; Trevor Burnard and John Garrigus, *The Plantation Machine: Atlantic Capitalism in French Saint-Domingue and British Jamaica* (Philadelphia: University of Pennsylvania Press, 2016), 198–9.

[15] L. Rouzeau, "Aperçus du rôle de Nantes dans la guerre d'indépendance d'Amérique (1775–1783)," *Annales de Bretagne* 74:2 (1967), 217–78: 235–6.

[16] Nathan Miller, "Chesapeake Bay Ships and Seamen in the Continental Navy," in Ernest McNeill Eller, ed., *Chesapeake Bay in the American Revolution* (Centreville, MD: Tidewater, 1981), 133–69: 145.

Business was especially brisk during the War of Jenkins' Ear (1739–1748) and the Seven Years' War, when Dutch neutrality paid off, although British privateers ceased respecting that neutrality during the latter war. Dutch supplies of war materials to the Patriots began even before Lexington and Concord. In August 1774, a ship from Nantucket sailed to Amsterdam, where the captain bought 300,000 pounds of gunpowder. It was the start of a sustained export of military supplies from Dutch port cities to North America, most of which were transferred to American ships at St. Eustatius. The Dutch shipowners used various ruses to fool British observers. Some ships supposedly sailed to Africa, but actually set sail for St. Eustatius, often officially carrying cargoes of items such as tea, although their holds were filled with ammunition. Upon arrival, the goods were bought by American agents. None of this eluded the British, one of whose agents in Rotterdam noted that in May 1776, no fewer than eighteen ships had departed from Amsterdam to St. Eustatius, all laden with powder and ammunition. British pressure had led the Dutch States General to adopt a resolution in 1775, which was extended in the two following years, forbidding the export of war ammunition, gunpowder, cannon, guns, and balls in ships domiciled in English territories. That ban, which was aimed at the American rebels, would be honored in the breach by dozens of Dutch firms.[17] The invaluable aid to the rebels by St. Eustatius was summed up later by British admiral George Rodney, the man who would later capture the island: "This rock [St. Eustatius] of only six miles in length and three in breadth has done England more harm than all the arms of her most potent enemies and alone supported the infamous American rebellion."[18]

That the trade in military stores was so brisk at St. Eustatius was shown in June 1775, when just one barrel of gunpowder was left on the island, the rest having all been shipped to North America.[19] Shipments of gunpowder from St. Eustatius were increasingly jeopardized by the British yachts and tenders cruising off the island, which reduced the shipping traffic in 1775 and 1776

---

[17] Wim Klooster and Gert Oostindie, *Realm between Empires: The Second Dutch Atlantic, 1680–1815* (Ithaca, NY: Cornell University Press, 2018), 46–8, 77; Daniel A. Miller, *Sir Joseph Yorke and Anglo-Dutch Relations, 1774–1780* (The Hague: Mouton, 1970), 39, 41; Friedrich Edler, *The Dutch Republic and the American Revolution* (Baltimore, MD: Johns Hopkins University Press, 1911), 26–7.

[18] J. Franklin Jameson, "St. Eustatius in the American Revolution," *American Historical Review* 8:4 (1903), 683–708: 695.

[19] Lord George Townshend to Lord Dartmouth, Rainham, 21 July 1775, in William Bell Clark, ed., *Naval Documents of the American Revolution*, vol. 1 (Washington, DC: United States Navy Department, 1964), 1333.

compared with earlier years.[20] Virtually none of the products introduced by the North Americans were consumed on the island. The provisions from New England and the Middle Colonies that were disembarked made their way to nearby British and French islands, while Chesapeake tobacco and South Carolina indigo were carried by Dutch or French vessels to Europe.[21] These shipments were also increasingly risky. In 1777, forty-four ships en route from St. Eustatius to Amsterdam ended up in British hands.

St. Eustatius' supply of military supplies became even more significant in the late 1770s after France entered the war against Britain. While French ships could no longer pose as neutrals, the Dutch maintained their neutrality. The roadstead at Oranjestad – St. Eustatius lacked a port – may have been the busiest trading place in the Americas at the time, as the island enjoyed an even closer connection to Martinique than before and firms in France opted for the Dutch colony as the first destination for their cargoes (military or otherwise). The Bordeaux company of David Gradis, for example, shipped salted beef and flour via London to St. Eustatius, from where a British firm transported the cargo to Martinique.[22]

Warfare Afloat and Ashore

The outbreak of the American Revolution had a powerful impact on the ties between British America and the French Caribbean. The French colonies in the West Indies had been commercially linked to Britain's mainland colonies since the first quarter of the century. Merchants from New England and New York had forged these links, eager to sell their fish, flour, bread, butter, and building materials in exchange for sugar, rum, and molasses. Not even the Seven Years' War severed these connections, nor did the American Revolution, although it did introduce changes in the relationship. The Royal Navy blocked North America's eastern seaboard, while the British Caribbean colonies, which had in the past served as intermediaries in the trade between New Englanders and the French islands, remained attached to the metropole. Deprived of trade with the mainland, the British islands were

---

[20] W. R. Menkman, "Sint Eustatius' gouden tijd," *West-Indische Gids* 14 (1932/33), 369–96: 372–3.
[21] Michael Jarvis, *In the Eye of All Trade: Bermuda, Bermudians, and the Maritime Atlantic World, 1680–1783* (Chapel Hill: University of North Carolina Press, 2010), 403.
[22] P. Butel, "Le trafic européen de Bordeaux, de la guerre d'Amérique à la Révolution," *Annales du Midi* 78:76 (1966), 37–82: 67.

forced to buy provisions from the French islands with cash crops of their own, reversing the previous relationship.[23]

This new relationship did not last, in part because of the privateering war that soon began in Caribbean waters. After Massachusetts pioneered the issuance of privateering commissions in November 1775 and other provinces had followed suit, the Continental Congress started granted its own commissions in March 1776. Having initially exempted British Caribbean vessels from capture, Congress changed course in July of the same year. Henceforth, property of residents of the British West Indies could be confiscated. Numerous North Americans responded by cruising around the British islands, soon accompanied by French ships based at Martinique, whose captains had obtained blank commissions issued on that island by William Bingham.[24] For rebel privateers based on the eastern seaboard, French collaboration reduced the risks of Caribbean navigation. They no longer had to fear French warships, which halted their efforts to clamp down on illegal trade with the French Caribbean, and were allowed to seek refuge in French colonial ports in case of distress.[25] Exposed to "American" privateers, merchants in the British islands armed their ships against these enemies, first in Antigua and Tortola and later everywhere else. Likewise, the British islands fitted out numerous privateers that targeted rebel vessels.[26]

The British Navy also became involved. Shortly after the French entry in the war, one British squadron blockaded the coast off Saint-Domingue, aided by the feared privateers from Jamaica. By late 1778, 200 enemy vessels had fallen into this trap at Cap Français alone. The Royal Navy reinforced the British position in the Caribbean by capturing St. Lucia, from where ship movements to and from Martinique's main port of Fort Royal (present-day Fort-de-France) could be watched. On the other hand, the French conquest of the poorly defended island of Dominica in September of that year dealt a heavy blow to British privateering. French vessels based in Cap Français also destroyed the salt pans at the Turks and Caicos Islands, where Bermudians

---

[23] Patrick Villiers, *Le commerce colonial atlantique et la Guerre d'Indépendance des États-Unis d'Amérique 1778–1783* (New York: Arno, 1977), 203.

[24] Andrew Jackson O'Shaughnessy, *An Empire Divided: The American Revolution and the British Caribbean* (Philadelphia: University of Pennsylvania Press, 2000), 154–6.

[25] Jonathan R. Dull, *The French Navy and American Independence: A Study of Arms and Diplomacy, 1774–1787* (Princeton: Princeton University Press, 1975), 58, n. 7.

[26] Charles Frostin, "Saint-Domingue et la révolution américaine," *Bulletin de la société d'histoire de la Guadeloupe* 22 (1974), 73–114: 77; Florence Lewisohn, *The American Revolution's Second Front: Persons & Places Involved in the Danish West Indies & Some Other West Indian Islands* ([St. Thomas]: Caribbean Research Institute, College of the Virgin Islands, 1976), 10.

had been raking salt. Here French interests did not align with those of the Patriots, who highly valued salt shipments from Bermuda. The contemporaneous wrecking by Spanish forces of the saltworks at Salt Tortuga created serious salt shortages in parts of the Chesapeake and the Carolinas.[27]

Unsurprisingly, the Royal Navy also targeted St. Eustatius, whose trade had tested the British government's patience. In 1780, cruisers were dispatched to search and seize Dutch vessels in large numbers. At year's end, Great Britain issued a declaration of war against the Dutch Republic, which was in no small measure inspired by the trade at Oranjestad. One of the war's first acts was the British conquest of St. Eustatius on 3 February 1781.

The island had been left undefended after the departure two days before of a homeward-bound Dutch squadron, which was seized by the same British fleet that captured St. Eustatius. The officer in charge of the fleet, Admiral George Rodney, confiscated 200 ships, emptied all warehouses, and arrested over 2,000 North Americans. One historian has called what happened next "one of the greatest auction sales in history. Naval stores were sent to Antigua, provisions to Jamaica, and West Indian and American produce to the home country, but all goods of European origin were put on the block."[28] Rodney wasted so much time on raiding mercantile wealth that he missed the French fleet bound for Martinique and failed to intercept it again when it sailed from Saint-Domingue to Virginia. This was the fleet that would defeat the British fleet in the Battle of the Chesapeake, which enabled the Patriot victory at Yorktown.[29]

That battle underlined how much the international balance of power had changed since the days of British maritime superiority during the Seven Years' War. France and Spain combined had more ships than their foe, which prevented Britain from dominating in European or American waters.[30] British naval successes in these theaters were consequently few and far

---

[27] Frostin, "Saint-Domingue et la révolution américaine," 98–9; Piers Mackesy, *The War for America, 1775–1783* (Cambridge, MA: Harvard University Press, 1964), 227, 230–2; Jarvis, *In the Eye of All Trade*, 402.

[28] Lowell Joseph Ragatz, *The Fall of the Planter Class in the British Caribbean, 1763–1833: A Study in Social and Economic History* (New York: Century, 1928), 161.

[29] Andrew Jackson O'Shaughnessy, *The Men Who Lost America: British Leadership, the American Revolution, and the Fate of the Empire* (New Haven: Yale University Press, 2013), 297–302; Victor Enthoven, "'That Abominable Nest of Pirates': St. Eustatius and the North Americans, 1680–1780," *Early American Studies: An Interdisciplinary Journal* 10 (2012), 239–301: 292–3.

[30] Jeremy Black, "Naval Power in the Revolutionary Era," in Roger Chickering and Stig Förster, eds., *War in an Age of Revolution, 1775–1815* (Washington, DC: German Historical Institute; Cambridge: Cambridge University Press, 2010), 219–41: 231.

between. In 1782, St. Kitts, Montserrat, and Nevis fell into French hands, leaving all British Leeward Islands in enemy possession except for Antigua. Likewise, St. Vincent, Grenada, and Tobago were lost to France.[31] However, the plan for a Franco-Spanish fleet to subdue Jamaica was prevented by Admiral Rodney's defeat of a French fleet en route from Europe to Saint-Domingue off Dominica at the Battle of the Saintes (9–12 April 1782), which would have disembarked French soldiers.

Three years before the Battle of the Saintes, Spain had allied with France by signing the Treaty of Aranjuez. Although Spain stopped short of entering into a treaty with the Patriots, it did declare against Britain two months later. The decision to go to war had been a long time coming. Having initially remained neutral, by late 1776 the Spanish government sent secret orders to its Caribbean colonies to admit ships, including privateers, flying British or American colors.[32] What is more, the government also decided to ship military supplies to the Patriots by way of Havana and New Orleans.[33] For their part, the Patriots responded to Spain's commencement of hostilities by sending a large amount of flour to Havana, Spain's military nerve center in the Americas. Technically, it was the task of the viceregal government in Mexico City to both finance Spain's defenses in the Caribbean and supply flour to Havana, home to a large garrison. The latter task had only been recently assigned to Mexico, which had to assume responsibility for a role that had traditionally been reserved for the metropole. However, due to the royal monopoly on flour exports from New Spain and the lack of regular transport vessels, Mexican flour supplies remained woefully inadequate. Hence, the Spanish wish to start imports from North America. When the Continental Congress approved such shipments, wealthy Spanish merchant Juan de Miralles and Philadelphia entrepreneur Robert Morris closely collaborated to create a commercial network that connected Maryland, Virginia, and the Carolinas to Cuba. Flour shipments from the eastern seaboard totaled six times those from New Spain in the years 1779–1783 and dwarfed those from Europe. But the scale of the sudden North American involvement in Cuba went beyond flour, extending to naval stores and the re-export of salted beef from the Río de la Plata. On the mainland, New Orleans and

---

[31] Ragatz, *Fall of the Planter Class*, 162.
[32] Alberto A. García Menéndez, "El Caribe Hispánico y la Revolución Americana," *Revista Interamericana* 5 (1975/76), 583–608: 597.
[33] Johanna von Grafenstein Gareis, *Nueva España en el Circuncaribe, 1779–1808: Revolución, competencia imperial y vínculos intercoloniales* (Mexico City: Universidad Nacional Autónoma de México, 1997), 150.

Mobile after its capture by Spanish troops (1780) were also provisioned by the eastern seaboard.³⁴

The massive flour shipments to Havana were badly needed after an expeditionary army of 12,000 men arrived there from Cádiz in the summer of 1780. The army's size indicated the ambition of Spanish policymakers. The geopolitical situation offered possibilities for Spain to reconquer territories lost to Britain as recently as 1763 (Florida) and as long ago as 1655 (Jamaica), to halt British expansion in Central America, and to put an end to British hegemony in the Gulf of Mexico. One step in that direction was the conquest of Mobile in March 1780, which reduced the British military presence in West Florida to Pensacola. In 1781, Spanish troops and their French allies successfully laid siege to that town as well, completing the conquest of West Florida in May of that year. This was followed by Spanish forces dislodging the British from Roatan Island in the Bay of Honduras.

Food Shortages and Marronage

As active participants in the American Revolutionary War, the non-British Caribbean islands had to cope with its fallout. Privateering and British naval blockades cut off or interfered with the regular supply of foodstuffs to the islands. Even islands that remained neutral were affected. Soon various islands faced food shortages, such as Guadeloupe and Saint-Domingue in 1779, with dramatic, often deadly, consequences for the enslaved population. In Guadeloupe, the suffering was somewhat relieved by imports of provisions from St. Thomas, the neutral Danish island that was most likely also the supplier of enslaved workers to the French islands in the following years.³⁵ In Puerto Rico, there were acute food shortages as well. The island was supposed to be sustained by Havana, but the Mexican flour stored there

---

[34] Carlos Marichal, "Las guerras imperiales y los préstamos novohispanos, 1781–1804," *Historia Mexicana* 39:4 (1990), 881–907: 882; James A. Lewis, "Anglo-American Entrepreneurs in Havana: The Background and Significance of the Expulsion of 1784–1785," in Jacques A. Barbier and Allan J. Kuethe, eds., *The North American Role in the Spanish Imperial Economy, 1760–1819* (Manchester: Manchester University Press, 1984), 112–26: 113–14; Nikolaus Böttcher, "Juan de Miralles: Un comerciante cubano en la guerra de independencia norteamericana," *Anuario de Estudios Americanos* 57 (2000), 171–94: 185–6; Grafenstein Gareis, *Nueva España en el Circuncaribe*, 151–2; Peggy K. Liss, *Atlantic Empires: The Network of Trade and Revolution, 1713–1826* (Baltimore, MD: Johns Hopkins University Press, 1983), 112, 115.

[35] Jacques Coquille to the governor and intendant of Guadeloupe, 13 July 1782, in Anne Pérotin-Dumon, *La ville aux Iles, la ville dans l'île: Basse-Terre et Pointe-à-Pitre, Guadeloupe, 1650–1820* (Paris: Karthala, 2000), 748–9; Svend E. Green-Pedersen, "The Scope and Structure of the Danish Negro Slave Trade," in George F. Tyson, ed.,

had rotted by the time it arrived in Puerto Rico.[36] Merchants here and elsewhere did all they could to procure food from other islands, but the war was a major impediment. The Dutch island of Curaçao, which relied on food imports from British North America, was on the brink of disaster in 1779. One local trader wrote that the flour supply would not last for another two days and that a loaf of bread cost six times as much as in Amsterdam. Among both the free and enslaved residents, fatalities were recorded each day, which may have fueled the authorities' fear of a slave revolt.[37]

That was certainly true in Saint-Domingue, where food prices also soared, with the price of wine doubling and flour almost tripling by early 1779. Other staples such as olive oil, soap, and candles were not even available anymore. Food conditions, worsened by drought conditions, had swelled the ranks of the maroons since the start of the revolutionary war. Enslaved men and women abandoned plantations where almost every square meter was devoted to cash-crop production to take to the mountains, forming small groups and living off raids. Arguing that lack of sustenance was what caused slaves to run away and that neighboring islands were not likely to provide badly needed provisions under the prevailing conditions of war, the colony's rulers attempted to halt marronage by implementing a careful scheme of planting subsistence crops in 1776. For every twenty slaves, one *carreau* of land (1.292 hectares) had to be planted with potatoes and yams, and for every single slave, plots of manioc and banana had to be sown. Twice a year, inspections by militia officers were to take place. The scheme failed to have the desired effect, since planters predictably continued to use as much land as possible to cultivate profitable crops. Consequently, by late 1779, slaves in at least one area in Saint-Domingue ("Cul de Sac") began to die from malnutrition. To survive, slaves stole lead from the roofs of hold houses to sell as rifle shot. They stole chickens and other livestock, ran away, and set fire to real estate.[38] It would be wrong, however, to view this marronage as a harbinger of the Haitian Revolution. As historian David Geggus has argued, Saint-Domingue's

---

Bondmen and Freedmen in the Danish West Indies: Scholarly Perspectives (US Virgin Islands: Virgin Islands Humanities Council, 1996), 18–53: 32.

[36] Grafenstein Gareis, *Nueva España en el Circuncaribe*, 133, 141–2, 157–8.

[37] Mark Häberlein and Michaela Schmölz-Häberlein, *Die Erben der Welser: Der Karibikhandel der Augsburger Firma Obwexer im Zeitalter der Revolutionen* (Augsburg: Wißner, 1995), 55–6.

[38] Bernard Foubert, "Le marronage sur les habitations Laborde à Saint-Domingue dans la seconde moitié du XVIIIe siècle," *Annales de Bretagne et des Pays de l'Ouest* 95:3 (1988), 277–310: 298–9; Frostin, "Saint-Domingue et la révolution américaine," 79–80, 99; Paul Cheney, "A Colonial Cul de Sac: Plantation Life in Colonial Saint-Domingue, 1775–1782," *Radical History Review* 115 (2013), 45–64: 57.

plantation system stopped producing runaways just a few years later and certainly several years before the start of the rebellion near Cap Français in 1791 that started the revolution. Nor did the rebel leaders – with one exception – have a maroon past.[39]

Marronage also increased in other parts of the Caribbean as a result of international warfare. At the start of Franco-British hostilities, French troops from Martinique captured Dominica, located between Guadeloupe and Martinique and a French colony until 1763 but since then under British rule. In this island, where slaves made up seven-eighths of the population, the French occupiers gave muskets, bayonets, and encouragement to those men and women who (had) fled from their predominantly British masters into the interior. Well-armed, they built camps from where they raided plantations, seizing provisions and spawning an exodus of planters. Their goal, which they continued to pursue after the British restoration, was to set up their own independent nation. A British counteroffensive in 1785 reduced maroon numbers and destroyed their dreams.[40]

While Dominica's maroons never asked for French help, the Indigenous Caribs of St. Vincent did, upset as they were about the vast expansion of the island's sugar industry since the British takeover in 1763. French troops did indeed disembark on the island in 1779 for the start of a four-year occupation. Like Dominica, Grenada, and Tobago, St. Vincent belonged to the Ceded Islands, which France had ceded to Britain after the Seven Years' War. In 1795, at the next stage of the Age of Revolutions, the Caribs would attempt to shake off British rule by building a coalition with French settlers, the enslaved population, and French forces at Guadeloupe, but their endeavor was not crowned with success.[41]

Free People of Color

Another path to freedom for enslaved men in the French colonies, less risky than marronage, was provided by militia service. Men could enter a militia

---

[39] David Geggus, "Saint-Domingue on the Eve of the Haitian Revolution," in David Patrick Geggus and Norman Fiering, eds., *The World of the Haitian Revolution* (Bloomington: Indiana University Press, 2009), 3–20: 4–5.

[40] Thomas Atwood, *The History of the Island of Dominica: Containing a Description of Its Situation, Extent, Climate, Mountains, Rivers, Natural Productions, &c. &c.* (London: J. Johnson, 1791), 228–32; Joseph A. Boromé, "Dominica during French Occupation, 1778–1784," *English Historical Review* 84:330 (1969), 36–58: 41, 54; Neil C. Vaz, "Maroon Emancipationists: Dominica's Africans and Igbos in the Age of Revolution, 1763–1814," *Journal of Caribbean History* 53:1 (2019), 27–59: 38–42.

[41] Julie Chun Kim, "The Caribs of St. Vincent and Indigenous Resistance during the Age of Revolutions," *Early American Studies* 11:1 (2013), 117–32: 127–9.

company comprised of people of color once their master and the commander of that district had agreed to it. After serving for a specified amount of time, the new recruits were allowed to shed their condition as slaves.[42] This practice increased the number of free men of color, whose militias had acquired a reputation in the course of the eighteenth century for their military prowess. Free men of color from Saint-Domingue confirmed this reputation during the War of American Independence. Their service began after a French fleet arrived in Cap Français in 1779. For the purpose of helping the North American rebels lay siege to British-held Savannah (Georgia), the fleet's admiral – the Count d'Estaing, former governor of Saint-Domingue – set up two volunteer units in the colony, one of which was made up of free men of color. For that unit, 545 men presented themselves, although by no means all voluntarily. Among them were men who would make a name for themselves during or after the Haitian Revolution, such as André Rigaud and Henri Christophe. This episode occurred as the size of the free population of color was approaching that of the Whites and as white interest in serving on militias was waning. Free men of color were seen by some Whites as so successful in their militia duties, one of which was to hunt down maroons, that they proposed turning them into full-time soldiers and accordingly endowing them with civil rights. Following the failed siege of Savannah, during which the free soldiers of color were largely used as auxiliary troops, 150–200 of them were sent to serve in Grenada. At the same time, an attempt to conscript free colored men into regular service in Saint-Domingue miscarried. Dreading the prospect of leaving their homes, many of them did not show up for duty, enabling marronage to thrive. Protected by their white officers, the refusal of free men of color eventually paid off, and their militias were reinstated. The lesson that the freed people of color could learn from this was that they were indeed free at the end of the day, a lesson that would be confirmed by the French revolutionaries' insistence on equality.[43]

---

[42] Frédéric Régent, "Armement des hommes de couleur et liberté aux Antilles: Le cas de la Guadeloupe pendant l'Ancien régime et la Révolution," *Annales historiques de la Révolution française* 348 (2007), 41–56.

[43] John D. Garrigus, "Catalyst or Catastrophe? Saint-Domingue's Free Men of Color and the Battle of Savannah, 1779–1782," *Review/Revista Interamericana* 22 (1992), 109–25; Boris Lesueur, "Les paradoxes de la liberté par les armes (Antilles, XVIIIe siècle)," in Dominique Rogers and Boris Lesueur, eds., *Sortir de l'esclavage: Europe du Sud et Amériques (XIVe–XIXe siècle)* (Paris: Karthala, CIRESC, 2018), 209–10. See also Chapter 23 in Volume II of this book by John Garrigus.

Free people of color were also given an increasingly important role in Martinique and Guadeloupe. When the war with Britain got underway, Martinique's governor announced that he counted for the defense of the island on 850 militiamen of color, although the total number of free colored men who could serve was not even 650. It meant that he also expected armed assistance from the so-called *libres de fait*, those who claimed to be free, some of whom did indeed try to obtain legal freedom through militia service, even if that would take eight to ten years.[44] Guadeloupe's free men of color were charged with the somewhat contradictory task of both policing the slave population and helping to uphold a system in which as many men as possible were released from slavery at their masters' wish. Since 1768, against the backdrop of continuing Anglo-French rivalry, French policy aimed at stimulating manumission of skilled slaves and thereby boosting the ranks of free militiamen. In addition, a force of "Free Volunteers of Guadeloupe" was formed at the start of the war in 1778, in which 527 men would be enrolled. For the first time, men of color were not simply a police force, but a military combat unit. While they could thus showcase their loyalty and conscientiousness, the outbreak of the French Revolution would reveal that their quest for equal rights trumped their commitment to royal rule. In 1792 and 1793, free people of color enthusiastically greeted the changing of the guards in Martinique and Guadeloupe.[45]

The number of free colored people in Grenada, another of the Ceded Islands which changed hands more than once in the second half of the century, almost equaled that of the white population. At the time of the American War of Independence, 57 percent of the island's militia was free colored.[46] Ever since Britain had assumed power on the island after the Seven Years' War, they had found themselves increasingly discriminated against. While they had previously been able to inherit and bequeath property, marry in the Catholic Church, and serve on the militia, the British governor feared the negative influence of the francophone majority on their anglophone counterparts and issued an order for the island's free colored foreigners (most of whom were French-speaking) to be exiled from

---

[44] Abel A. Louis, *Les libres de couleur en Martinique*, 3 vols. (Paris: L'Harmattan, 2012), vol. 1, 127.

[45] Régent, "Armement des hommes de couleur," 43–4; Laurent Dubois, *A Colony of Citizens: Revolution and Slave Emancipation in the French Caribbean, 1787–1804* (Chapel Hill: University of North Carolina Press, 2004), 119–23.

[46] Baptiste Bonnefoy, "Les langages de l'appartenance: Miliciens de couleur et changements de souveraineté dans les îles du Vent (1763–1803)," *L'Atelier du Centre de recherches historiques* 20 (2019), https://journals.openedition.org/acrh/9607.

the island or arrested as vagabonds. The French takeover of the islands in 1779 marked the start of a four-year interlude during which white and black francophones showed themselves subservient to the new rulers. After the British restoration of 1783, they were chastised for their conduct by being excluded from public life and having their political and religious rights curtailed. Their ostracism helps to explain why free people of color were eager in 1795 to help launch Fédon's Rebellion, in which 6,000 slaves took part, although the free coloreds were later singled out for punishment.[47]

On the Caribbean islands under French rule, the defenses increasingly relied on the free colored militia in the decades after the close of the Seven Years' War at the same time that a whole range of discriminatory measures were adopted that aimed to keep the free colored populations in check. Historian Frédéric Régent has argued that once this process was completed, segregation from the white population had become systematic, obeying the logic of slave societies.[48] Unsurprisingly, the 1790s then saw free colored people use different strategies to challenge this system.

By contrast to the Ceded Islands, free men of color in Cuba were unwilling to enter into an alliance with an invasion force. Instead, they attempted to improve their condition as subjects of the Spanish king by distinguishing themselves militarily, especially in the years 1780–1782 when they took part in Spanish conquests of British strongholds. They notably contributed to the defeat of the British forces defending Mobile (West Florida), and reinforced the Hispano-French siege of Pensacola, where 3,239 regular (white) troops were flanked by 378 *pardos* (mulattoes) and *morenos* (Blacks).[49] The conquest of the Bahamas was achieved with the help of 202 free colored militiamen along with 3,174 white regulars, veterans, and laborers.[50] Two free black companies involved in the fighting at Pensacola and Mobile had been formed

---

[47] Tessa Murphy, "Reassertion of Rights: Fedon's Rebellion, Grenada, 1795–96," *La Révolution française* 14 (2018), 8, 10–14, http://journals.openedition.org/lrf/2017; Edward L. Cox, "Fedon's Rebellion, 1795–96: Causes and Consequences," *Journal of Negro History* 67:1 (1982), 7–19: 10–11.

[48] Frédéric Régent, *La France et ses esclaves: De la colonisation aux abolitions, 1620–1848* (Paris: Éditions Grasset & Fasquelle, 2007), 197.

[49] Allan J. Kuethe, *Cuba, 1753–1815: Crown, Military, and Society* (Knoxville: University of Tennessee Press, 1986), 104, 106, 107; Gustavo Placer Cervera, *Ejército y Milicias en la Cuba colonial (1763–1783)* (Havana: Ediciones de Ciencias Sociales, 2015), 167, 176.

[50] Kuethe, *Cuba, 1753–1815*, 117–18. Kuethe confuses New Providence (the Bahamas) with Providence Island. For the conquest by Spanish and American Patriot forces, see Ross Michael Nedervelt, "Securing the Borderlands/Seas in the American Revolution: Spanish–American Cooperation and Regional Security against the British Empire," in Gabriel Paquette and Gonzalo M. Quintero, eds., *Spain and the American Revolution: New Approaches and Perspectives* (London: Routledge, 2020), 171–83.

at the request of two Cuban corporals, a *moreno* and a *pardo*.[51] Serving in the militia was so popular among Cuba's free colored population that by 1770, one in five males was a member of the militia, and in Havana, two of every three men served in it by 1776.[52] In that capacity, they were not paid (except for high-ranking officers), but enjoyed *fuero* rights, which, historian Matt Childs has written, "included access to military courts, exemptions from certain taxes, tribute payments, and labor levies, and the right to bear arms, something long denied to the population of African ancestry."[53] Men who had served for more than twenty years could ask for retirement and had the right to a small pension.

Despite the crown's insistence on the extension of the *fuero* on an equal basis to free nonwhite militiamen, their plight worsened in the years ahead due to a combination of economic, social, and demographic changes. If most islanders were still white in 1774, the enslaved population rose steadily afterwards. As British warships gave way to British slave ships, enabling the island's transformation to one of the global giants in sugar production, slaves' quest for freedom was made harder, while free people of color were subjected to new rules, including the need to carry a license. As international wars held off, the free coloreds were deprived of opportunities to prove their worth on the battlefield.[54]

Unrest among the enslaved and free colored populations in the non-British Caribbean was, then, partly a result of the military developments to which the American Revolution gave rise. It was certainly not a consequence of the embrace by nonwhites of principles or policies associated with the revolution. Unlike in Massachusetts, where petitioning Blacks increasingly insisted on their rights, nonwhites in the Caribbean did not appropriate the discourse of the insurgents for their own cause.[55] The contrast to the reverberations of the French Revolution, especially among free people of color across the

---

[51] Joseph P. Sánchez, "African Freedmen and the Fuero Militar: A Historical Overview of Pardo and Moreno Militiamen in the Late Spanish Empire," *Colonial Latin American Historical Review* 3:2 (1994), 165–84: 183–4.
[52] Herbert S. Klein, "The Colored Militia of Cuba: 1568–1868," *Caribbean Studies* 6:2 (1966), 17–27: 21; Federica Morelli, *Free People of Color in the Spanish Atlantic: Race and Citizenship, 1780–1850* (New York: Routledge, 2020), 39.
[53] Matt D. Childs, *The 1812 Aponte Rebellion in Cuba and the Struggle against Atlantic Slavery* (Chapel Hill: University of North Carolina Press, 2006), 83.
[54] Elena A. Schneider, *The Occupation of Havana: War, Trade, and Slavery in the Atlantic World* (Williamsburg, VA: Omohundro Institute of Early American History and Culture; Chapel Hill: University of North Carolina Press, 2018), 297–303.
[55] Chernoh M. Sesay Jr., "The Revolutionary Black Roots of Slavery's Abolition in Massachusetts," *New England Quarterly* 87:1 (2014), 99–131.

Caribbean in the 1790s, is conspicuous.[56] The equality enshrined in the Declaration of the Rights of Man and Citizen was evidently more appealing than the uproar about unfair taxation in the rebellious British colonies. Unfamiliar with the metaphor of slavery that North American activists frequently used to describe their plight, Caribbean nonwhites were unable to borrow it for their own purposes. The revolutionary struggle in the Thirteen Colonies was a distant feud which, it would seem, offered no hope for them.

Conclusion

The British war with France and Spain led to a new stage in the American Revolution, which entailed the involvement of the non-British Caribbean. But even before the start of formal hostilities, a few non-British islands actively took part in the battle between Britain and the North American rebels by providing war materiels to the Patriots. Once the war had partly shifted to Caribbean waters, combined French and Spanish naval power more than matched that of Britain, leading to the conquest of several British islands. In the non-British slave societies, the war had two significant unintended consequences. It created military possibilities for the growing group of free men of color and, by reducing food supplies, induced marronage. Free and enslaved nonwhites thus engaged in their own quest for freedom and equality in the shadow of the North American independence war.

---

[56] See Chapters 27 and 28 in Volume II of this book by Jessica Pierre-Louis and Cristina Soriano, respectively.

20

Interpreting a Symbol of Progress and Regression: European Views of America's Revolution and Early Republic, 1780–1790

LLOYD KRAMER

The American Revolution's influence on late eighteenth-century European politics and culture has been analyzed across the North Atlantic world since the 1780s. This chapter explores some early themes in this long-developing, cross-cultural analysis by examining how various European writers perceived America's revolution and its new republican government as symbols of human progress. It also emphasizes, however, that optimistic Europeans already feared in the 1780s that the political and social progress of the emerging American republic was threatened by regressive social forces that could well destroy their hopes for what the historian Durand Echeverria famously called the "Mirage in the West."[1]

The looming dangers to the optimistic European "mirage" of American progress appeared most conspicuously in the regressive contradictions of the racist slave system and in the growing wealth inequalities that could transform American society into a disappointing reproduction of European social hierarchies. Both the supportive and critical themes in early European narratives often reappeared in later accounts of the new nation's revolutionary transitions to a republican government; and European interpretations of the complex tensions between progress and regression in the United States have continued down to our own time. Although these recurring themes suggest the enduring influence of late eighteenth-century writers, this chapter looks specifically at European perceptions in the 1780s to expand the analysis that Echeverria and other modern historians have developed in their accounts of transnational exchanges during the Age of Atlantic Revolutions.

---

[1] Durand Echeverria, *Mirage in the West: A History of the French Image of American Society to 1815*, with a foreword by Gilbert Chinard (Princeton: Princeton University Press, 1957).

Historians have shown how ideas circulated in this era as travelers, book publishers, newspaper editors, and political actors exchanged news through transatlantic communications. Revolutionary events in North America became important for European readers, and at least twenty-five books on American subjects were published in three or more European languages between the 1770s and 1790.[2] Numerous other commentaries were published in pamphlets or newspapers, and pro-American perspectives on the revolutionary war or the emerging republic appeared in the Netherlands, Ireland, Germany, and Italy, as well as in France and England. There were, of course, also critical accounts of the American Revolution in the English press and in the commentaries of French writers such as Simon Linguet (1736–1794), who edited the conservative French journal *Annales politiques, civiles et littéraires du 18ᵉ siècle*.[3] The critics of America's revolutionary movement nevertheless failed to counter the influential tide of pro-American writings that gained particular influence in France and other places where political theorists and activists were agitating for political change.

Some writers visited the emerging American republic, but many other Europeans advocated the American cause without ever leaving home. My discussion of these cross-cultural perceptions focuses mainly on two travelers and on two theorists who lived only in Europe. The Marquis de Chastellux (1734–1788) and Jacques-Pierre Brissot (1754–1793) wrote books about their experiences as they traveled through diverse American states. Chastellux was a high-ranking general in the French army that reached Rhode Island in 1780 and contributed decisively to the American military victory at Yorktown in the following year. Brissot visited America in 1788 (with support from bankers) to explore possible French investments in the United States. In addition to the narratives of these two French travelers, this chapter also examines the optimistic views of the Parisian philosophe Nicolas de Condorcet (1743–1794) and of the English clergyman Richard Price (1723–1791), both of whom wrote about America's revolutionary

---

[2] Valuable analysis of these transatlantic exchanges can be found in Janet Polasky, *Revolutions without Borders: The Call to Liberty in the Atlantic World* (New Haven: Yale University Press, 2015); Wim Klooster, *Revolutions in the Atlantic World: A Comparative History* (New York: New York University Press, 2018 [2009]); Joanna Innes and Mark Philp, eds., *Re-imagining Democracy in the Age of Revolutions: America, France, Britain, Ireland 1750–1850* (Oxford: Oxford University Press, 2013); R. R. Palmer, *The Age of the Democratic Revolution: A Political History of Europe and America, 1760–1800*, 2 vols. (Princeton: Princeton University Press, 1964 [1959]). For a summary of European books on America in this era, see Palmer, *Age of Democratic Revolution*, vol. 1, 243–5.
[3] Linguet's critiques are summarized in Echeverria, *Mirage in the West*, 62–3.

changes by drawing on first-hand reports from others rather than by crossing the Atlantic themselves. Although Price wrote in English, his translated interpretations of the American Revolution quickly reached readers in France and the Netherlands, where they reinforced pro-American perspectives throughout the 1780s. Other writers, such as Anne Robert Jacques Turgot (1727–1781) in France, Joan Derk van der Capellen (1741–1784) in the Netherlands, and William Drennan (1754–1820) in Ireland, also praised American ideas and actions in texts that will be noted briefly as examples of the wider European response to the United States' struggle to create new institutions for self-government.

Pro-American writers described the American Revolution as a major event in the political and social *progress* of world history, with a specific emphasis on: (1) the political progress that emerged from the new nation's defense of freedom, human rights, and constitutional government; (2) the socioeconomic progress that developed through commercial creativity and a new social mobility that also offered some autonomy for single women; (3) the cultural progress that became possible when enlightened leaders understood the value of reason, education, and religious tolerance; and (4) the moral progress that shaped the virtuous actions of humble farmers and merchants, as well as the wise leadership of Benjamin Franklin and George Washington. Moral progress was viewed as an essential foundation for all other aspects of historical progress.

Optimistic European writers thus portrayed the emerging European–American society as an historical forerunner of the more enlightened sociopolitical systems that they expected to see eventually in the Old World. But this new American republic, as even the most optimistic writers described it, could not really achieve its potential for historical progress until it abolished its *regressive* agricultural system of enslaved labor and recognized growing economic inequalities that encouraged wasteful spending on unneeded luxury goods. The contradictions of slavery and economic inequality endangered the long-term progress of the new republic and created a threatening gap between the American society that actually existed and the progressive future that European writers envisioned for people throughout the Atlantic world.

Political Progress: Human Freedom, Human Rights, and Constitutional Government

The political achievements of the American Revolution were widely viewed as the emerging republic's most significant contribution to historical progress. European accounts of this new political culture therefore always emphasized American ideas about human freedom, human rights, and constitutionalism. The radical-minded Jacques-Pierre Brissot asserted on the first page of *New Travels in the United States of America, 1788* (1791) that Americans understood and defended the inviolable existence of personal and collective freedom. "It is the condition in which man is subject only to the laws he has himself made," Brissot explained. "Coercion is dishonorable to free men and is virtually nonexistent in a true state of freedom," which he claimed to have found in the emerging American nation. Projecting his most idealistic aspirations onto people whom he met on his travels, Brissot announced that his book would show "the prodigious effects of liberty on morals, on human industry, and on the improvement of mankind ... You will find here the Free American who now knows no boundaries but those of the universe and no constraints or prohibitive restrictions but the laws made by his own representatives."[4]

Brissot's idealized description of American freedom was especially remarkable because he wrote about his actual travel through the United States, but the same optimism appeared in the works of people who only imagined the New World from their Old World homes. Richard Price's *Two Tracts on Civil Liberty* (first edition, 1776) offered one of the earliest, armchair European narratives of the American Revolution as a campaign for a "civil government" that would be freely created by "the people" it represented.[5] Price sent his *Two Tracts* to Benjamin Franklin, who shared the pamphlet with influential French leaders such as the economist Turgot. As a former government minister and ally of the French king, Turgot's social identity differed profoundly from the position of wandering writers such as Brissot, yet Turgot joined the chorus of praise of the Americans' unique political progress. "They are the hope of the world," Turgot wrote in a letter to Price. "They may become a model to it. They may prove ... that men can be free and yet tranquil ... They may [also] exhibit an example of political liberty, of religious liberty, of commercial liberty, and of industry."[6]

---

[4] J. P. Brissot de Warville, *New Travels in the United States of America, 1788*, trans. Mara Soceanu Vamos and Durand Echeverria, ed. Durand Echeverria (Cambridge, MA: Belknap Press of Harvard University Press, 1964 [1791]), 3, 13.

[5] Richard Price, "Two Tracts on Civil Liberty: The War with America, and the Debts and Finances of the Kingdom" [1776], in Richard Price, *Political Writings*, ed. D. O. Thomas (Cambridge: Cambridge University Press, 1991), 23.

[6] A. R. J. Turgot to Richard Price, 22 March 1778, appendix to "Observations on the Importance of the American Revolution," in *Richard Price and the Ethical Foundations of the American Revolution: Selections from His Pamphlets with Appendices*, ed. Bernard Peach

Price endorsed Turgot's views and expanded his own early praise for American achievements in his even more sympathetic *Observations on the Importance of the American Revolution* (1785), which described recent revolutionary events as one of the great turning points in world history. Assuring his readers that Americans had established "forms of government more equitable and more liberal than any the world has yet known," Price went on to place their political achievements in a truly millennial perspective. "Perhaps I do not go too far," Price noted in the text that was immediately translated into French, "when I say that, next to the introduction of Christianity among mankind, the American revolution may prove the most important step in the progressive course of improvement. It is an event which may ... become the means of setting free mankind from the shackles of superstition and tyranny."[7]

The converging optimism of Brissot, Price, and Turgot shows how the American Revolution symbolized the human freedom and human rights that sympathetic Europeans saw as the main goals for progressive political change. These overarching abstractions nevertheless required the kind of specific, substantive evidence that writers such as Condorcet and Chastellux provided in their more detailed analyses of America's state and national constitutions. The Americans had created constitutional structures that demonstrated how human rights could be defended far more effectively by representative institutions than by monarchical regimes. Condorcet summarized these foundational principles in his *Ideas on Despotism* (1789) as the rights to security, freedom, and legal equality that must be protected for all persons and their property.[8]

This insistence on universal rights gave Condorcet a strong interest in the declarations of rights that emerged from America's Continental Congress and also appeared in various state charters. As he noted in another important essay, *Influence of the American Revolution in Europe* (1786), the American "Declaration of Independence is a simple and sublime exposition of these rights, so sacred and so long forgotten. No nation has known them so well or

(Durham, NC: Duke University Press, 1979), 222. Price translated and published this letter to show how his views converged with the ideas of leading French thinkers.

[7] Richard Price, "Observations on the Importance of the American Revolution and the Means of Making It a Benefit to the World" [1785], in Price, *Political Writings*, 117, 119.

[8] Nicolas de Condorcet, "Ideas on Despotism: For the Benefit of Those Who Pronounce This Word without Understanding It" [1789], in *Condorcet: Writings on the United States*, ed., trans., and introduction, Guillaume Ansart (University Park: Pennsylvania State University Press, 2012), 74–5.

preserved them with such perfect integrity."⁹ He also believed that forceful American statements about such rights were "useful to all others despite the differences in climate, manners, and constitutions." The recent American declarations still needed improvements that might set better limits on criminal punishments or correct the problems of unequal taxation or eliminate state support for church expenses, but Condorcet was certain that the new republic marked a major milestone on the long historical journey of political progress.¹⁰

General theories of human rights therefore contributed most directly to historical change when these broad principles were carefully translated into specific constitutions and governing institutions. Chastellux explained in his *Travels in North America* (1786), for example, that America's government institutions were evolving in different ways, yet every state shared similar commitments to representative government. "Although their constitutions are not all alike," he noted, "there is in all of them a democratic government and a government by *representation*, in which the people express their will through their delegates." These legislative systems attracted Chastellux's interest and respect because he believed they embodied "everything that reason alone might dictate, in such an enlightened age as this, to peoples who were choosing the type of government best suited to them."¹¹ Where Europeans would expect to find such reasonable actions among only elite social classes, both Chastellux and Brissot reported that men from diverse (but all white) social groups were elected to the legislative chambers. Brissot described a visit to the Pennsylvania General Assembly, where he saw some fifty legislators sitting on wooden chairs and dressed with a "simplicity" that might seem scandalous to Parisians. One of the delegates was a "nondescript" farmer who "wore common clothes yet displayed great talent and eloquence."¹² Here, then, was a new kind of government that represented common people, expressed reasonable conceptions of equal rights, and deliberated in modestly furnished public buildings.

---

⁹ Nicolas de Condorcet, "Influence of the American Revolution on Europe" [1786], in ibid., 25.

¹⁰ Ibid., 26; Condorcet, "Ideas on Despotism," in ibid., 76–77. Like most French theorists, Condorcet saw bicameral legislatures as an obstacle to fair representation of the people's rights and political will because upper chambers steadfastly protected elite interests.

¹¹ Marquis de Chastellux, *Travels in North America in the Years 1780, 1781 & 1782*, ed. Howard C. Rice, Jr., 2 vols. (Chapel Hill: University of North Carolina Press, 1963 [1786]), vol. II, 533–4.

¹² Brissot, *New Travels in the United States*, 202.

Condorcet never actually entered an American legislative chamber, and he began to lose some of his political optimism as the United States moved from the Articles of Confederation to the new Constitution in 1787. He believed that the revised political system placed too much power in the national government – a problem that was exacerbated by a division of legislative power that enhanced the power of elites and gave smaller state populations (through the Senate) a disproportionate influence on national policies.[13] The new American Constitution weakened the popular majority's power to shape laws and undermined some of the political progress that Condorcet admired in the earlier declarations of human rights and construction of representative state governments. The national Constitution thus needed numerous improvements, but Condorcet believed it still reflected the "knowledge and wisdom" of judicious men who must have had "powerful reasons" to accept a document that retained flaws and "imperfections."[14]

Although writers such as Condorcet and Chastlellux contributed especially to discussions of American constitutionalism within France and a wider community of French-reading philosophes, other Europeans also referred to the emerging American republic as they called for political reforms and constitutions in their own countries. The American rejection of Britain's imperial system attracted particular attention in the Netherlands and Ireland because the "patriot" parties in these societies viewed America's revolution as a model for their own anti-British campaigns. The Dutch writer Joan Derk van der Capellen, for example, published an influential *Address to the People of the Netherlands on the Present Alarming ... Situation of the Republic of Holland* (1782) in which he vehemently attacked the pro-English Stadtholder, William V, with language that echoed America's recent Declaration of Independence. Emphasizing that "all men are born free" and that free people must assert their "national rights," van der Capellen urged his compatriots to emulate the American revolutionaries by supporting "fellow-citizens" who would promote "public liberty and prosperity" against the self-interested policies of Holland's ruling elites. "Arm yourselves: choose your commanders," he wrote, and "follow the example of the people of

---

[13] Nicolas de Condorcet, "Supplement to Filippo Mazzei's Researches on the United States," in Ansart, *Condorcet: Writings on the United States*, 52–3. This supplement was added to Mazzei's book, but scholars generally agree that Condorcet was the main author.
[14] Ibid., 57–9.

America ... [to] act with prudence, wisdom and moderation."[15] This pro-American language resonated in Dutch political culture as the Patriot party soon rose up against William V and eventually created a Batavian Republic in the 1790s.

Praise for the American revolutionary movement also spread across Ireland when political activists mobilized new opposition to British imperial control during the 1780s. William Drennan became one of the leading advocates for Irish autonomy by publishing demands for a "free *constitution*" that could assure institutional respect for "life, liberty, and property." Calling himself an "Irish Helot" (1785), Drennan evoked the language from America's Declaration of Independence to argue that Ireland must not be taxed without parliamentary representation and that the Irish people must defend their inherent constitutional rights because "no governments, except those in America" currently allowed the self-representation that protected the people's freedom. "What is the distance between an Irishman and a Freeman?" Drennan asked in one of his polemical letters. "Not less than three thousand miles."[16] Those miles suggest why the Americans gained a political independence that eighteenth-century Irish activists could never achieve, but Drennan's reference to this distant freedom also suggests how American claims for constitutional rights influenced Irish writers at the same time that many other Europeans were drawing on American examples to affirm their own collective aspirations for political progress.

Political writers in each European society described the distinctive aspects of their own national cultures, and, like Condorcet, they often recognized "imperfections" in America's emerging constitutional system. Despite the perceived need for continuing reforms in the United States, Europe's pro-American writers remained confident that the new republic's state and national constitutions offered frameworks for political progress that could be replicated in other places. The Americans had shown political writers in France, England, the Netherlands, and Ireland how new constitutions could construct governing institutions that represented a whole nation. These new political institutions became the American achievement that evoked the widest European interest, yet the writers who looked most carefully at

---

[15] Joan Derk van der Capellen, *An Address to the People of the Netherlands on the Present and Most Dangerous Situation of the Republic of Holland ... by a Dutchman*, trans. from Dutch (London: Stockdale, 1782), 40, 42, 137.

[16] William Drennan, *Letters of Orellana, an Irish Helot* ... (Dublin: Constitutional Society of Dublin, 1785), reprinted in William Drennan, *Selected Writings*, ed., Brendan Clifford, 3 vols. (Belfast: Athol, 1998), vol. 1, 195–7.

American society believed that the new republic's success would also depend on future socioeconomic progress as well as the cultural and moral progress that would be essential for more enlightened national states.

Economic Progress: Commerce, Equality, and the Social Role of Women

Europeans were highly aware of American commerce and the transatlantic trade that had developed over the eighteenth century, and travelers who actually visited American cities and farms also noted the impressive expansion of the new nation's commerce. Brissot went to the United States specifically to examine commercial opportunities for French investors, so his reports focused especially on the booming international trade in Boston, New York, and Philadelphia. Describing the commercial activity in New York City, Brissot explained that economic growth was creating an American prosperity that homebound Europeans could scarcely imagine. "Let those who doubt the prodigious effects of liberty on man and on his industry come to America! What miracles they will witness! While almost everywhere in Europe towns and villages are falling into ruin, here new buildings are rising on every hand ... The activity which reigns on all sides announces the prosperity of the future."[17]

Brissot constantly linked the political liberty and economic vitality of American society to personal or social virtues, which he found particularly salient among the Quakers of Philadelphia. "*Without private virtue,*" he wrote in one of his generalizations, "*there can be no public morality, no civic spirit, and no liberty.*"[18] The people of Pennsylvania showed how prosperity could be traced "to the Quakers' simplicity and thrift; to their firm virtues; and to their industry." Although some travelers (including Chastellux) condemned the Quakers for their pacifism and inward-looking social life, Brissot portrayed this religious community as a real-world demonstration of how personal virtues led to economic success as well as wise public policies. France could therefore assure its own economic progress, Brissot advised, by emulating the moral virtues of Pennsylvania merchants and farmers, removing all barriers to American trade, and welcoming American ships to its ports. "It is difficult even to enumerate all the manufacturing goods now shipped abroad by Americans," he explained in a typical magnification of American

---

[17] Brissot, *New Travels in the United States*, 145.
[18] Ibid., 8. Brissot italicized the words in this quotation.

achievements; and this trade would inevitably grow because Americans were also "destined to become the greatest 'maritime carriers' in the world."[19]

Condorcet and Chastellux also described America's economy as a foundation for social progress and international influence. The resources and social mobility in this new society offered what Condorcet called "attractive hopes to industry," and he expected that America's political liberty would enhance the country's economic life and facilitate global trade. Americans, in other words, could become a progressive commercial model for the whole world.[20] Chastellux's first-person account of his American travels also stressed the rapid development of commerce and agriculture. Rural families helped each other build farms in the wilderness, Chastellux explained, transforming vast forests into a landscape that was now "peopled with three million inhabitants." Americans were a hardworking, moral people whose "recompense" for collegial labor was often a "cask of cider drunk in common, and with gaiety, or a gallon of rum."[21]

The moral order of this new American society, as Chastellux and Brissot both explained, depended partly on the impressive talents and freedom of women. Brissot reported that American women traveled freely with men in public coaches and that single women had the kind of freedom they had once enjoyed in republican Geneva. Contrasting New England social mores with the gendered deceits in France, Brissot explained in another utopian generalization that "almost all marriages" in America were "happy" and "pure."[22] The casual relations between unmarried men and women also impressed Chastellux, who found that an "extreme liberty ... prevails in this country between the two sexes as long as they are not married."[23]

Americans carried their virtues from the home into commerce and public action. Although women did not participate equally with men in the public sphere, the natural, unaffected qualities of family life encouraged men and

---

[19] Ibid., 261, 396, 398, 404. Brissot had strongly condemned Chastellux's criticisms of American Quakers in a pre-journey review (1787) of Chastellux's *Travels in North America*. Brissot's praise for Quaker virtues thus shows how his own narrative evolved partly as a critical, dialogical response to Chastellux's earlier work. For more on the diverging views of Chastellux and Brissot, see Iris de Rode, *François-Jean de Chastellux (1734–1788): Un soldat-philosophe dans le monde atlantique à l'époque des Lumières* (Paris: Honoré Champion, 2022), 484–95.

[20] Condorcet, "Influence of the American Revolution," 27, 36–8.

[21] Chastellux, *Travels in North America*, vol. 1, 80–1. Like most European visitors, Chastellux said very little about the Indigenous peoples who had long lived in the American "wilderness."

[22] Brissot, *New Travels in the United States*, 85–6, 154.

[23] Chastellux, *Travels in North America*, vol. 1, 120.

women alike to pursue virtuous behavior far outside their own households. "Licentious manners ... ," Chastellux reported after a stopover at a Connecticut tavern, "are so foreign in America that conversation with young women leads no further, and that freedom itself there bears a character of modesty unknown to our affected bashfulness and false reserve."[24] Europeans thus interpreted America's flourishing commerce, innovative workers, virtuous farmers, and free-spirited, unmarried women as evidence to confirm the new nation's socioeconomic progress – which became even more impressive when it overlapped with new contributions to human knowledge.

Cultural Progress: Education, Religious Tolerance, and Intellectual Freedom

European theorists assumed that political and economic progress depended on the progressive development of education and cultural enlightenment. As Richard Price argued in a typical political–cultural linkage, "Liberty is the soil where the arts and sciences have flourished and the more free a state has been, the more have the powers of the human mind been drawn forth into action."[25] This belief in the connections between liberty and human knowledge gave European writers a strong desire to show how the American desire to create a new kind of enlightened society depended also on broad commitments to education and scientific studies.

Condorcet offered a typical argument for America's intellectual progress by emphasizing (optimistically) that more people in America would be able to acquire advanced education because social distinctions did not impede access to the best schools. Social mobility was a fact of American life that could transform knowledge as rapidly as it transformed the economy. "Therefore," Condorcet wrote, "there is reason to hope that a few generations from now, America, by producing almost as many men who will be busy adding to the extent of our knowledge as all of Europe, will at least double its progress or make it twice as fast. Such progress will include the useful arts as well as the speculative sciences."[26]

Condorcet imagined the future development of education, but Chastellux found that the American desire for enlightened education and academic institutions was already generating impressive cultural progress. He was

---

[24] Ibid., 68.   [25] Price, "Two Tracts," 29.
[26] Condorcet, "Influence of the American Revolution," 35.

pleased to report, for example, that the library at Harvard contained "very handsome editions of the best authors" and that the university's president understood the complexities of the most recent scientific knowledge. Americans therefore had no reason to worry about the inferiority of their education or scholars. "I must here repeat," Chastellux noted after his visit to Harvard, "what I have observed elsewhere, that in comparing our universities and our studies in general, with those of the Americans, it would not be in our interest to call for a decision of the question, which of the two nations should be considered an infant people."[27]

In addition to fostering education the Americans were making cultural progress because, as sympathetic Europeans described them, they had implemented the enlightened ideals of religious tolerance and intellectual freedom. Chastellux described America as "the only country possessing true tolerance, that absolute tolerance, which has ... triumphed over superstition."[28] Brissot emphasized this same tolerance in an account of Boston's churches, where he discovered that the "tolerance born with American independence" led to the banishment of "dogmatic preaching."[29] Idealized reports from other travelers who wrote about the new nation's religious diversity convinced Condorcet that the American model of religious tolerance would lead eventually to an official tolerance for all religions in France. "The dogma dearest to Americans," Condorcet wrote in 1786, "the one they value most, is the dogma of religious tolerance or rather religious freedom;" and this kind of freedom became possible because Americans were "governed more than any other by reason alone."[30]

Religious tolerance was an essential precondition for intellectual freedom, but free thought also required a free press in which all ideas could be openly debated. Here again the Americans were leading others toward future cultures in which controversial ideas would not be suppressed. "Freedom of the press is established in America," Condorcet noted in his essay on the influence of the American Revolution, "and there the right to say and hear truths that are considered useful has been regarded with just reason as one of the most sacred rights of humankind."[31]

The cultural advances of education, religious tolerance, and a free press therefore overlapped with the new political system and commercial

---

[27] Chastellux, *Travels in North America*, vol. II, 504; he also described a visit to Princeton, in ibid., vol. I, 122–3.
[28] Ibid., vol. II, 547.   [29] Brissot, *New Travels in the United States*, 87.
[30] Condorcet, "Influence of the American Revolution," 39.   [31] Ibid., 27.

expansion to support the virtuous behavior of good people; and the lives of both obscure and famous persons further confirmed America's progressive contributions to future world history.

The Moral Progress of Human Virtue: Exemplary People and Enlightened Leaders

All pro-American writers portrayed the emerging nation's political, economic, and cultural achievements as evidence of broad historical transitions, but they also liked to connect these public processes to the moral virtues of America's common people as well as the most prominent leaders. The moral progress of Americans became a sustaining force for all of their other political, economic, and cultural progress. European optimists therefore projected their utopian stereotypes onto people they scarcely knew to demonstrate the character of enlightened citizens. "The habitual practice of reason," Brissot wrote in a typical explanation, "produces in America a large number of what are called 'principled men.'" These reasonable people lived with a "simplicity" that Brissot admired in both the houses and clothing of people he met almost everywhere (except among the large landowners in Virginia). "When men have this simplicity," Brissot noted, "they are worthy of liberty, and they are sure to enjoy it a long time."[32] He thus emphasized this distinctive social "simplicity" whenever he praised American virtues, but he was especially impressed by the lifestyles of Pennsylvania Quakers.

In contrast to Chastellux's critique of Quakers for "concealing their indifference to the public welfare under the cloak of religion," Brissot quoted George Washington himself to confirm that Quaker communities expressed key values of America's emerging republican culture. Washington's respect for Quakers, according to Brissot, was all the more striking because he had initially agreed with the Patriot critique of Quakers who would not support military action for the revolutionary cause. The general had gradually changed his views, however, when he recognized how Quaker social practices actually converged with the political aspirations of the revolution. "He told me that because of their simple way of life, their thrift, their fine moral standards, the excellent example they set, and their support of the Constitution," Brissot reported, "he considered them to be the strongest pillars of the new government, which requires of its citizens both full loyalty

---

[32] Brissot, *New Travels in the United States*, 14, 104.

and frugality."³³ Brissot thus expanded on Voltaire's praise for Pennsylvania Quakers in his influential *Letters on England* (1733) to suggest that this small religious sect embodied a sociocultural vanguard for the historical march toward future social virtues, personal simplicity, and republican equality. "If we love the good of mankind," Brissot advised his readers, "let us pray that this peaceful society will spread over the whole world, or at least that its humane principles will be universally adopted."³⁴

Although Brissot's praise for Quaker virtues did not become a notable theme among other pro-American French writers, the connections between simplicity and philosophical wisdom frequently reappeared in descriptions of exemplary Americans. Chastellux's hostility to Quaker values has been noted, yet he shared Brissot's appreciation for the down-to-earth qualities of America's revolutionary soldiers and leaders. The American reliance on citizen-soldiers rather than professional military officers exemplified a less hierarchical approach to military ranks, which seemed strange to Europeans when they learned that "nothing is more common in America than to see an innkeeper [serve as] a colonel." Such commanders were "chosen by the militia themselves," and they came to their positions because they were respected as the "most esteemed citizens" in their communities. Knowing that French elites would view such commanders as incompetent or unqualified, Chastellux explained that these unprofessional soldiers regularly accomplished impressive military feats and also built fortifications that matched the best work of experienced European generals. After visiting the defensive works at West Point, for example, he noted that the entire structure was built by people "who six years before had scarcely ever seen cannon."³⁵

Wise and virtuous citizens could thus be found at every level of American society, but European writers liked to focus on Benjamin Franklin and George Washington to show the exceptional virtues of republican leadership. Condorcet's eulogy for Franklin at the French Academy of Sciences (13 November 1790) provided a typical summary of the philosophical talents that shaped both his personal character and his contributions to the public

---

[33] Ibid., 330; for an example of Chastellux's critique of Quakers, see his *Travels in North America*, vol. 1, 166.

[34] Brissot, *New Travels in the United States*, 327. The early French praise for Quakers emerged most notably in Voltaire, *Letters on England*, trans. Leonard Tancock (London: Penguin, 1980 [1733]), 23–36. A few Italians also wrote about the progressive values of Quakerism, see Stefani Buccini, *The Americas in Italian Literature and Culture, 1700–1825*, trans. Rosanna Giammanco, foreword Franco Fido (University Park: Pennsylvania State University Press, 1997), 111–17.

[35] Chastellux, *Travels in North America*, vol. 1, 84, 91.

good. "He preferred the good obtained through reason to the one expected from enthusiasm," Condorcet explained in his eulogistic comments. The American philosopher/scientist was a wise leader who always believed "in the power of reason and the reality of virtue, and who had wished to become the educator of his fellow citizens before being called to be their legislator."[36] Franklin's wisdom, as Condorcet described it, thus grew out of a tolerance for religious diversity and a deep respect for the scientific knowledge that would lead human societies to a more enlightened future.

Although Franklin represented an idealized image of American science and philosophy, pro-American Europeans regularly portrayed George Washington as the all-important exemplar of America's military and political achievements. Chastellux's important position in the French army brought him into numerous meetings with Washington, whom he characterized as "brave without temerity, laborious without ambition, generous without prodigality, noble without pride, [and] virtuous with severity."[37] Brissot also reported memorable conversations with Washington, though he visited the general at his Mount Vernon home instead of a military camp. "His modesty is astonishing," Brissot wrote, "particularly to a Frenchman." Washington may not have been the greatest military leader, yet Brissot reported that he had "all the qualities and the virtues of the perfect republican," which gave Washington his exalted place in American and world history.[38] Yet even the esteemed Washington was unable to escape the central flaw in American society because he owned some 300 enslaved persons at Mount Vernon. Although Washington told Brissot that American liberty was threatened by deep national "schisms," he would not call for the abolition of slavery. "It would undoubtedly be fitting that such a lofty, pure, and disinterested soul be the one to make the first step in the abolition of slavery in Virginia . . . But he did not conceal the fact that there are still many obstacles and it would be dangerous to make a frontal attack on a prejudice which is beginning to decrease."[39]

Recognizing that even America's greatest leader could not see how or when black freedom could be achieved, Brissot's optimism collided with the

---

[36] Nicolas de Condorcet, "Eulogy of Franklin: Read at the Public Session of the Academy of Sciences, 13 November 1790," in Ansart, *Condorcet: Writings on the United States*, 105. Condorcet stressed Franklin's respect for science and religious tolerance in ibid., 83–4, 102–3.

[37] Chastellux, *Travels in North America*, vol. 1, 113.

[38] Brissot, *New Travels in the United States*, 344–5.   [39] Ibid., 238, 344.

fundamental contradictions that would discredit the aspirations for American progress from the time of the Revolution down to the twenty-first century: how could America be a truly free nation and a symbol of human rights when Black people were enchained in a racist slave system or blocked from equal rights even when they escaped from enslavement? This question led to a permanent counternarrative that challenged the story of American progress by focusing on the regressive denial of Black people's freedom, the brutalities of systemic racism, and the social inequalities that violated America's claim to defend liberty and justice for all.

The Regressive Realities of American Slavery and Racism

Every European advocate for American progress condemned the persistence of a slave system that blatantly contradicted the American declarations of human rights. From the emerging nation's first post-colonial decade, European supporters recognized this key flaw in the society they wanted always to defend: the slave system and the racist laws that extended beyond slavery created a racialized hierarchy of rights (or denial of rights). These inequalities produced regressive sociopolitical structures and undermined the nation's exemplary status for anyone who wanted to celebrate the American Revolution's distinctive contributions to progressive political and social change. Free white Americans argued eloquently for freedom and universal human rights while keeping most Black people enslaved (especially in the South). There was no coherent, nonracist response to this obvious injustice, and some disappointed Europeans soon learned that slaveholding Americans did not even want to talk about their systematic denial of basic rights to other human beings.

Richard Price vehemently condemned slavery as a painful betrayal of the cause he had otherwise defended against all British critics. "The Negro trade cannot be censured in language too severe," he wrote in his *Observations on the American Revolution* (1785). "It is a traffic which ... is shocking to humanity, cruel, wicked, and diabolical." Americans must therefore abolish slavery and the slave trade, because the continuation of slavery meant that Americans apparently did not "deserve the liberty for which they have been contending."[40] After sending his abolitionist proposal to political leaders in

---

[40] Price, "Observations on the American Revolution," 150.

South Carolina, however, he learned that they immediately rejected all of his recommended "measures for preventing too great an inequality of property and for gradually abolishing the Negro trade and slavery." Describing this unfortunate response in a letter to Thomas Jefferson, Price noted that such attitudes made him "fear that I have made myself ridiculous by speaking of the American Revolution in the manner I have done; it will appear that the people who have been struggling so earnestly to save themselves from slavery are very ready to enslave others." Indeed, he began to worry that America's great revolutionary events "which had raised [European] hopes will prove only an introduction to a new scene of aristocratic tyranny and human debasement."[41] The real meaning of American liberty, Price belatedly recognized, would depend on how the new nation actually defended and promoted human freedom in the post-colonial era.

Condorcet made the same critique in his mainly supportive analysis of the progressive meaning of the American Revolution (1786). The abolition of slavery had to become the next American task, Condorcet insisted, because "all enlightened men feel the shame, as well as the danger, of slavery, and soon this blemish will no longer sully the purity of American laws."[42] Meanwhile, in contrast to both the Americans and the French, retreating British forces in Virginia had given valuable support to basic human rights by helping enslaved people leave the country and settle in other places. Although Condorcet almost surely did not know the precise policies that guided the French army's actions in 1781–1782, the need for support from white Virginians forced Chastellux to compromise his own enlightened ideas by prohibiting French assistance for runaway slaves. When the Virginia governor William Harrison wrote to French military commanders to ask if their army was hiding people who escaped from local slaveholders, Chastellux responded on behalf of General Rochambeau to assure the governor that the "laws and property" of Virginia would be respected and that French soldiers would not shelter persons who fled from their enslavement.[43] In this same letter, however, Chastellux praised the Virginians for their many efforts in the campaign to assure their own liberty, thereby

---

[41] Richard Price to Thomas Jefferson, 2 July 1785, in Peach, *Richard Price and the Ethical Foundations of the American Revolution*, 330–1.

[42] Condorcet, "Influence of the American Revolution," 25; he noted the British aid for people who escaped from slavery in the "Supplement to Mazzei," in ibid., 48.

[43] Marquis de Chastellux to Governor Harrison, 6 July 1782, in Edwin Martin Stone, *Our French Allies: Rochambeau and his Army* (Providence, RI: Providence Press, 1884), 503.

describing the main contradictions of the American Revolution on the very ground where it was won.

Chastellux stated his personal opposition to slavery in his philosophical reflections on the agricultural system in Virginia, where he saw that enslaved people were "ill-lodged, ill-clothed, and often overwhelmed with work."[44] He therefore condemned slavery abstractly as a regressive social institution, but like many theorists of the era he did not challenge the racism that undergirded the brutal, systemic denial of human rights. The more radical Brissot, however, went beyond Chastellux and most French intellectuals in rejecting racist ideas as well as the whole structure of the slave system. He had met militant British abolitionists during a trip to England in 1787, and he later joined with Lafayette, Condorcet and others in establishing the Parisian Société des Amis des Noirs in February 1788.[45] Brissot thus condemned slavery wherever he traveled, but he also criticized the deep racism in American society, which posed a discrediting threat to the broader American campaign for liberty, virtue, and human progress.

Although slavery was declining in most northern states, the anti-Black racism that supported it was ubiquitous. While traveling through Newport, Rhode Island, for example, Brissot saw white people mocking a young Black child and reinforcing destructive racist attitudes. "It was an indication of the contempt in which Negroes are still held," Brissot explained, "a contempt which Americans, above all others, must renounce if they wish to be consistent." Brissot therefore found that regressive racist ideas afflicted social life in both the North and South, creating an "humiliating barrier" that blocked Black people from their fundamental human rights and impeded "all the efforts they make to elevate themselves. This discrimination is apparent everywhere."[46] He never met anyone in the South who praised European antislavery organizations or read the works of abolitionists, but he constantly encountered racist claims about how Blacks were "intellectually inferior" to Whites. Brissot criticized and strongly challenged such racism throughout his narrative, in part by describing the talents or creativity of Black students and workers who lived freely in some American cities. He insisted that "the mental capacity of Negroes is equal to any task," though (like all human beings) they needed freedom and education to utilize their

---

[44] Chastellux, *Travels in North America*, vol. II, 439.
[45] For a brief summary of Brissot's role in the Société des Amis des Noirs, see Echeverria's introduction to Brissot, *New Travels in the United States*, xvi–xvii. See also Chapter 4 in Volume II of this book by Erica Johnson Edwards.
[46] Brissot, *New Travels in the United States*, 134, 233.

Interpreting a Symbol of Progress and Regression

Figure 20.1 Declaration of Independence, painting by John Trumbull, 1819. Courtesy of United States Capitol.

diverse skills and ambitions. Reporting on his visit to a Philadelphia school where free Black children flourished, Brissot emphasized that the students' obvious abilities to read, write, and learn mathematics clearly demonstrated how "Negroes, by their virtue and diligence, disprove the slanderous lies which their oppressors utter about them elsewhere."[47]

Brissot therefore recognized the pervasive racial discrimination that contradicted and overwhelmed America's theoretical aspirations for political and legal equality, but he and others also criticized new inequalities that were reshaping American social relations as people turned toward the corruptions of wealth and luxury.

The Regressive Realities of America's Economic Inequalities

European narratives about the progress of American society often described social relations that were far more egalitarian than the social hierarchies in long-established Old World societies. European writers thus began to worry

[47] Ibid., 217, 231, 237.

Figure 20.2 "The Old Plantation," South Carolina, c. 1790. Enslaved Gullah workers asserted their own identities by dancing and playing musical instruments derived from Africa. Unknown artist. Public domain.

that a growing American desire for luxury goods would create the kind of permanent social inequalities that generated so much unhappiness and social instability in their own countries. The idealized American simplicity was thus threatened by *regressive* social–economic developments which (like slavery) could well destroy the post-colonial nation's exceptional historical progress.

Condorcet summarized one strand of concerns about emerging economic dangers when he criticized a new embrace of "mercantilist" trade policies that impeded the free flow of goods into American states. Arguing that unhindered free trade was the only economic policy that ensured economic prosperity, Condorcet warned that the "wealth inequality" which disrupted "public tranquility" in Europe would soon develop in America if the government blocked or taxed the import of certain goods from Europe. Such policies would serve special commercial interests and lead to dangerous concentrations of wealth. Americans were thus weakening their distinctive egalitarian social practices because "on the important and closely related subjects of taxation and trade, they seem to have retained some remnants of the prejudices of the English nation." Condorcet thus feared that Americans would create destabilizing social inequalities by succumbing to European economic ideas at the very moment when their own progressive conceptions of liberty were spreading across Europe.[48]

Other writers were less interested in trade laws, though they shared Condorcet's concerns about the rise of new socioeconomic inequalities in

---

[48] Condorcet, "Influence of the American Revolution," 40–1.

American society. Chastellux worried, for example, that economic disparities could threaten the much-desired political equality in governing institutions. Reporting on a conversation with Samuel Adams in Philadelphia, Chastellux summarized his concerns about how economic inequalities could well overwhelm the theoretical aspirations for permanent political equality:

> Success of trade, and even of agriculture, will introduce riches among you, and riches will produce inequality of fortunes and property. Now, wherever this inequality exists, the real force will invariably be on the side of property; so that if the influence in government be not proportional to that of property, there will always be a contradiction, a struggle between the form of government and its natural tendency [equal rights vs. power of property]; the right will be on one side, and the power on the other; hence the balance can only exist between the two equally dangerous extremes of aristocracy and anarchy.[49]

Chastellux's concerns about the political consequences of unequal wealth thus identified a socioeconomic threat that could soon weaken or even destroy the institutional structures of republican equality. Adams responded to Chastellux's warnings about future economic inequalities with optimistic assurances that legislative divisions of power between upper and lower houses would ensure the proper political balance between the people and propertied elites, but Chastellux clearly doubted that "mixed government" could actually solve the real-world challenges of concentrated wealth.[50]

The dangers of economic inequality, as Europeans perceived it, became all the more striking when the quest for luxury goods distracted people from the ethical actions of a virtuous personal life. "Luxury begins," Brissot explained in a typical defense of simplicity, "where utility ends." Although most Americans had previously shown little interest in consuming useless luxuries, their post-revolutionary behavior was changing – and even the virtuous Quakers were buying fine cloth and expensive furniture. Projecting his own conceptions of moral virtue on to Americans who were *supposed* to act in "simple" ways, Brissot wanted Americans to avoid the luxuries that created personal obsessions with social status and made once-free citizens

---

[49] Chastellux, *Travels in North America*, vol. 1, 161.
[50] Ibid., vol. 1, 163. Chastellux also expressed his ongoing concerns about wealth inequality in a question he posed to the president of the College of William and Mary. If the gap between wealthy elites and artisans continued to grow, Chastellux asked, "Do you believe that your principles are democratic enough so that the landholders and the opulent would still continue to regard [artisans] as their equals?" Ibid., vol. II, 536.

dependent on others. A person who eschewed the quest for luxuries was "free to vote as he pleases and to criticize any public official." The costly desire for luxury goods, however, changed citizens into consumers who flattered wealthy, powerful people so they could buy expensive, unneeded things. "You who aspire to independence," Brissot declared with moral fervor, "then renounce luxury! Inspire in your children ... an aversion to it; teach them to love simplicity and orderliness in all their doings and all their occupations."[51]

Richard Price also raised questions about Americans' troubling desire for dangerous luxuries as he wrote post-revolutionary letters about America's disappearing "simplicity." There was already disturbing evidence by 1785, he noted in a letter to Jefferson, that a "threatening" luxury trade was transforming coastal cities, and this corrupting consumerism could soon alter the political system he so deeply admired. "If the people deviate from simplicity of manners into luxury, the love of show, and extravagance, the governments must become corrupt and tyrannical." The awful virus of luxury, in Price's view, was endangering the whole society because it would "spread among the body of the people till the infection becomes general and the new governments are rendered images of our European governments."[52]

The mirage of an exceptional American nation thus began to look different when Europeans discussed economic inequalities and status-driven consumerism as well as the institutional structures of slavery and white racism. Indeed, Price concluded his own exuberant praise for the American Revolution with a confession that he felt "mortified more than I can express by accounts which have led me to fear that I have carried my ideas of [Americans] too high and deceived myself with visionary expectations." Despite its great historical promise, the American republic could fall far short of its anticipated goals; and "the consequence will be that the fairest experiment ever tried in human affairs will miscarry and ... become a discouragement to all future efforts in favour of liberty and prove only an opening to a new scene of human degeneracy and misery."[53] The tensions and flaws within American society might ultimately turn the grand historical hope for human progress into the painful reality of human disappointments.

---

[51] Brissot, *New Travels in the United States*, 302–3, 307.
[52] Richard Price to Thomas Jefferson, 21 March 1785, in Peach, *Richard Price and the Ethical Foundations*, 327.
[53] Price, "Observations on the American Revolution," 151.

Conclusion: The Unending American Contradictions of Progress and Regression

America lost its symbolic role as the vanguard of human progress after the French Revolution began to transform European politics and society in the early 1790s. France became the new symbol of progressive historical change, and the most prominent pro-American writers of the 1780s were all dead by 1794 (Brissot and Condorcet were two of the French Revolution's most famous victims). The themes of early European narratives about American progress never disappeared, however, and American nationalists often incorporated similar ideas into their own accounts of American exceptionalism. The United States was described as the "exceptional" homeland of freedom, constitutional government, and human rights. Equally important, it represented the progress of modern commerce and social mobility, the cultural achievements of religious and intellectual freedom, and the egalitarian value of personal virtues that shaped less hierarchical social relations.

Yet the European writers who praised American progress throughout the 1780s were never as naïve or optimistic as their idealistic themes suggested. The most optimistic accounts of the emerging American republic also described the *regressive* dangers of a racist slave system and the *regressive* power of economic inequalities or the luxury trade. The idealists all condemned the disturbing contradictions of a liberty-loving people who enslaved other human beings and who ignored the anti-egalitarian dangers of great wealth. Europe's most pro-American writers feared that political, economic, and cultural flaws could destroy their hopes for America and carry the new nation into the age-old history of abusive power and social injustice. Their counternarrative of America's very unexceptional racism and social inequalities emerged within the same narratives that told the stories of American progress and national exceptionalism. This early European projection of deep fears as well as forward-looking aspirations has never disappeared, and the multilayered contradictions of American society continually generate new anxieties among even its most sympathetic European interpreters.

Index

Figures and maps are indicated by fig. and map, respectively.
Footnotes are indicated by n. after the page number.

Abad y Queipo, Manuel, 112
Abascal y Souza, José Fernando, Viceroy of Peru, 113
abolitionism. *See* slavery abolition
Adams, Abigail, 388, 394
Adams, Charles Francis, 191–2
Adams, John
  "American Revolution" term pondered by, 55–6, 161–2
  on Boston Massacre, 351, 380
  on British Parliament's role, 452–3
  on rights and natural law, 20, 63, 65
  on social happiness, 66–7
  other mentions, 76, 122, 286
Adams, Samuel, 539
Adelman, Jeremy, 219
African Americans
  in American Revolution. *See* enslaved and free Black people in American Revolution
  US discourse on, 72–4, 390–1, 404, 421
Agustín I of Mexico, 33
Alembert, Jean le Rond d', 92, 102
Allen, Ethan, 327
Alzate y Ramírez, José Antonio, 112
American Revolution. *See also* British North America; United States
  "American Revolution" term, 55–6, 78–9, 161–4
  Articles of Confederation. *See* Articles of Confederation
  British West Indies perspective on, 177, 239, 255–60, 408–9
  censorship in, 14, 147–8, 349–51
  cities and citizenship in. *See* cities and citizenship in American Revolution
  cultural practice reforms, 147–9, 234–5
  Declaration of Independence. *See* Declaration of Independence
  economic equality demands, 25, 26
  Enlightenment ideas. *See* Enlightenment and the American Revolution
  enslaved and free Black people in. *See* enslaved and free Black people in American Revolution
  European writers on. *See* European writers' accounts of American Revolution
  French and Spanish support. *See* French and Spanish support for American Revolution
  imperialist dimension, 49–50, 254
  international influence. *See* international influence of American Revolution
  Loyalists in. *See* Loyalists in American Revolution
  millenarian ideology, 3
  Native Americans in. *See* Native American peoples; tribe names
  political violence of. *See* political violence of American Revolution
  Revolutionary War. *See* American Revolutionary War
  royalist v. republican sentiment, 31–2, 34, 77, 452–3
  tax resistance triggering. *See* tax resistance pre-American Revolution
  white women in. *See* white women in American Revolution
American Revolutionary War
  bandits in, 39
  Canadian theater, 178–9, 257

542

Index

Caribbean theater, 280, 291–3, 507–11, 518
Central American theater, 288–9
cities in, 241–4, 337–8. *See also* particular cities
civilians, treatment of, 30, 333, 336–42, 384, 386–7
desertions from armed forces, 39–40
Franco-American operations, 179, 283, 288, 289–91
Franco-Spanish operations, 285–9, 291–3, 310, 511, 516–17
Loyalists in. *See* Loyalists in American Revolution
military supplies, domestic production, 500–2
military supplies, French provision, 270–1, 502–7
militia groups, 339–41, 359, 361
Native Americans in. *See* Native American peoples; tribe names
outline of, 178–80, 241, 257
particular battles and sieges. *See under* place names
political violence analyzed. *See* political violence of American Revolution
prisoners, treatment of, 333–6
Treaty of Paris 1783, 180, 184, 185, 244, 294, 434–41, 450–1
Amory, Thomas and John, 214, 216
Andrews, Charles, 198n
Antioquia, Constitution of, 43–4
Apaza, Julián (Túpac Katari), 483, 489–91
Apess, William, 439
Aquinas, St. Thomas, 106–7, 124
Areche, José Antonio de, 480, 485–6, 491–2, 498
Arendt, Hannah, 76
Arequipa Revolt, 480–1
Argüelles, Agustín, 116
Aristotle, 75
Arnold, Benedict, 257, 327
Arriaga, Antonio de, 481
Articles of Confederation. *See also* Declaration of Independence; United States Federal Constitution
  drafting and adoption of, 450, 455–6
  Federal Constitution compared with, 462–4
  international relations under, 456–7
  weaknesses of, 180, 275, 457–9
Artigas, José, 26
arts and culture. *See* cultural practices and revolutionary politics

Atlantic trade system
  Britain's economic dependence on, 219, 250
  British Parliament's role, Adams on, 452–3
  British tax policies, 174, 221–5
  resistance to. *See* tax resistance pre-American Revolution
  cities, emergence and development, 212, 229–34
  corruption, 198–9, 215–16
  creole peoples. *See* creole peoples
  cross-Atlantic warfare, 218–21
  entanglement of, 209–13, 219–20, 225–6, 227, 238
  exchange of information and ideas, 56–60, 216–18, 238
  French and Spanish administrative reforms, 223–4, 226
  introduction to study, 207–9
  new money, 216
  piracy, 194–5
  slave trade. *See* slave trade
  smuggling. *See* smuggling
  white women, impact on, 373–9
Attakullakulla, 427
Attucks, Crispus, 406
Auslander, Leora, 152–3

Babeuf, Gracchus, 100
Bacon, Francis, 84
Bahamas, 260, 293, 407, 516
Baker, Keith, 94
bandits and guerilla fighters, 26–7, 38–9, 330–1
Banneker, Benjamin, 412
Baquíjano y Carrillo, José, 112
Barbados, 193–4, 201, 230, 266, 399–402, 419
Barbé-Marbois, François, 68
Barère, Bertrand, 48
Barnes, Christian, 385
Barrington, Samuel, 280
Barry, James, fig. 1.1
Bastidas, Micaela, 143
Batavian Republic, 14–15, 22, 526. *See also* Dutch Republic
Bayle, Pierre, 88
Bayly, C. A., 1–2
Beaumarchais, Pierre-Augustin Caron de, 270–1, 504
Beckford, William, 250
Belich, James, 268
Bennett, Richard, 199

543

Index

Berbeo, Francisco, 492, 494
Bergosa y Jordán, Antonio, 113
Berkeley, William, 199
Berlin, Ira, 411
Bilād al-Sūdān, 35–6
Bilder, Mary Sarah, 202–3
Bill of Rights (US), 59–60, 126, 183, 468–9, 473
Billaud-Varenne, Jacques-Nicolas, 25
Bingham, William, 503, 508
Black Pioneers corps, 362–3, 398
Blackstone, William, 469
Blickle, Peter, 43
Bloch, Marc, 85
Bloch, Ruth H., 3
Boissy d'Anglas, François Antoine, 19
Bolívar, Simón, 18, 26–7, 33–4, 123, 130, 207
Bolivia. *See* Upper Peru
Bonaparte, Napoleon, 47, 185, 417
Boston
  in American Revolutionary War, 178–9, 243, 277–8, 326, 328–9
  Boston Massacre, 145, 351, 379–80, 406
  charter, 246
  colonial era, 212, 214, 233–4, 235, 236, 237
  free Black community in, 410
  Powder Alarm, 324
  tax resistance, 177, 240, 258, 320–2
Bouillé, François Claude Amour, Marquis de, 503
Brandywine, Battle of, 274, 332
Brant, Joseph (Thayendanegea), 357, 358, 359, 364, 368, 430
Brant, Mary (Koñwatsiʼtsiaiéñni), 357–9, 364
Braudel, Fernand, 85
Brazil
  gold mined in, 213
  Portuguese royal family's escape to, 117
  religious tolerance, 9
  revolution in, 13–14, 41, 44–5, 48, 124–5
  royalist v. republican sentiment, 32–3, 127
  social reform demands unsuccessful, 20–1
  voting rights, 16, 17–18
Breen, T. H., 145, 324–5, 351
Brenner, Robert, 85
Brewer, Holly, 202–3
Brissot, Jacques-Pierre
  on economic inequality in United States, 539–40
  in French Revolution, 541
  optimistic views of American Revolution, 520, 522, 524–5, 527–8
  on Quaker virtues, 527, 531–2, 539
  on slavery and racism in United States, 536
  on George Washington, 533
British East India Company, 171–2, 194
British North America. *See also* American Revolution; British West Indies; Canada; United States
  Atlantic trade system. *See* Atlantic trade system
  British colonial governance system, 172–4, 248, 254–5, 266, 294–5
    "salutary neglect" policy. *See* British North America, "salutary neglect" policy myth
  cities, emergence and development, 212, 229–34
  colonization of, 162, 163
  creole peoples. *See* creole peoples
  economy and population size, 162–5, 210–11, 237
  Loyalists in. *See* Loyalists in American Revolution
  Native Americans. *See* Native American peoples
  Seven Years' War, American theater, 170–1, 220–1, 423, 431
  slave trade. *See* slave trade
  tax resistance in. *See* tax resistance pre-American Revolution
  territories (in 1763), map 5.1
  territories retained after American Revolution, 180, 181
British North America, "salutary neglect" policy myth
  arguments in summary, 9–10, 190–1, 193, 204, 250
  Burke's coinage of term, 189–90, 197, 205–6, 227
  corruption, 198–9, 215–16
  customs controls, 195–8, 222
  English law and courts, 202–4, 299, 374–5
  exemplary episodes of colonial power, 199–202
  historians' use of term, 191–3, 198n
  navy, trade route protection use, 194–5
  slave trade, reliance on imperial force, 193–5
  sovereign and parliamentary power, 197–8, 201–2, 257
  trade companies as vehicles of colonial power, 171–2, 194

544

British West Indies. *See also* particular jurisdictions
  after American Revolution, 249–50, 260, 268, 407
  American Revolution, perspective on, 177, 239, 255–60, 408–9
  American Revolutionary War, Caribbean theater, 280, 291–3, 507–11, 518
  cities, emergence and development, 229–30, 231
  colonial government in, 174
  economy and population size, 164–6
  free ports establishment, 223
  Glorious Revolution, impact in, 201
  Loyalist migrations to, 369
  planter class. *See* planter class
  in Seven Years' War, 170–1
  slavery abolition, 415–20
  slavery economy, 165–6, 193–4, 400–2
  territorial acquisitions in Napoleonic Wars, 248–9, 263, 265, 416–17
Brodhead, Daniel, 437–8
Brown, Ephraim, 379
Brown, Howard, 30
Brown, Wallace, 366
Brownlow, William, 304
Buckongahelas, 429
Buenos Aires, 32, 48, 128, 480
Buffon, Count de (Georges-Louis Leclerc), 68
Bunker Hill, Battle of, 329, 353, 431, 501–2
Burgoyne, John, 332, 358
Burke, Edmund
  on British "salutary neglect" of North America, 189–90, 197, 205–6, 227
  other mentions, 80, 203, 314
Burlamaqui, Jean-Jacques, 69
Bustamante, Carlos María de, 111
Butler's Rangers, 359
Byles, Mather, 366
Byrd, Mary Willing, 387

Caballero y Góngora, Antonio, Archbishop of Bogotá, 493
cabildos (municipal councils of Spanish America), 127–8, 478–9
Cádiz, Constitution of, 7–8, 16, 43–4, 123, 128
Caldas, Francisco José, 119
Calonne, Charles Alexandre de, 96–7, 98
Campomanes, Pedro Rodríguez de, 114
Canada. *See also* British North America
  after American Revolution, 180, 181, 244, 249–50, 266, 268, 451
  American Revolutionary War, Canadian theater, 178–9, 257
  Lower Canada Rebellion (1837), 267
  Loyalist migrations to, 260–2, 266–8, 367–8
  Native American peoples in, 267–8, 364, 368, 372, 441
  Quebec. *See* Quebec
  Seven Years' War, Canadian theater, 170
Cano, Melchor, 106
Cantillon, Richard, 93
Capellen, Joan Derk van der, 521, 525–6
capitalism
  Atlantic trade system. *See* Atlantic trade system
  Dutch and British transition to, 84–5, 86, 89
  US capitalism, European writers' concerns, 23–4, 537–41
Carcassonne, Elie, 90, 94, 95–6, 97
Caribbean. *See* British West Indies; particular jurisdictions
Carleton, Guy, 257
Carlisle Commission, 279, 332–3, 360
Carlos IV of Spain, 47, 117, 128
Carmichael, William, 273
Carroll, Charles, 204–5
Carvalho e Melo, Sebastião José de, Marquês de Pombal, 109, 117
Cassirer, Ernst, 82
Castelli, Juan José, 112
Castries, Charles Eugène Gabriel de La Croix, Marquis de, 293
Catherine the Great of Russia, 77
Catholicism and Catholic Church
  absolutist monarchs, support for, 7–8, 88–9, 113, 129–30
  Catholic colonies of Great Britain. *See* Ireland; Quebec
  Catholic states, religious tolerance policies, 8–9
  education provision, 137
  Enlightenment philosophy condemned by, 47–8, 118
  French Revolution, anti-clericalism, 7, 89, 111
  Jacobitism in Great Britain, 302, 309
  Protestant states, anti-Catholic policies, 6–7, 203, 515–16
caudillos (Spanish American warlords), 26–7, 39
Ceded Islands. *See* Dominica; Grenada; St. Vincent; Tobago

censorship. *See also* press freedom
  in American Revolution, 14, 147–8, 349–51
  Enlightenment philosophy works, 47–8, 118
  in French Revolution, 143, 147–8
  in New Spain, 14
  in Spain, 7, 36–7
"Centinel" (antifederalist writer), 465, 466
Central American theater of American Revolutionary War, 288–9
Ceylon, 293
Charles II of Great Britain, 229
Charles III of Spain, 77, 479–80, 496, 499
Charleston (formerly Charles Town), South Carolina
  in American Revolutionary War, 243–4, 312, 341, 356–7
  charter, 246
  colonial era, 212, 230, 231, 235, 401
  Stono Rebellion, 402
Chartier, Roger, 83, 102
Chastellux, François Jean, Marquis de
  in American Revolutionary War, 520, 533, 535–6
  on economic inequality in United States, 23–4, 539
  optimistic views of American Revolution, 524, 528–30, 532
  Quakers criticized by, 527, 531
  slavery, opposition to, 536
Cherokee War (1759–61), 171
Cherokees in American Revolution
  early mobilization, 329–30, 355, 356–7
  entry into war, 427
  genocide and territorial loss, 49, 432–3, 444
  smallpox epidemic, 439–41
Chesapeake, Battle of the, 288, 290–1, 509
Chesapeake colonies. *See* Maryland; Virginia
Chickasaws in American Revolution, 427, 428, 433, 444–5
Childs, Matt, 517
Chile, 14, 29, 39, 41
Choctaws in American Revolution, 427, 428, 433, 444–5
Christophe, Henri, 32, 514
cities and citizenship in American Revolution. *See also* particular cities
  cities in Revolutionary War, 241–4, 337–8
  citizenship idea, 23, 228, 235–7, 319, 389–90, 396
  colonial cities, emergence and development, 212, 229–34
  Committees of Safety established in, 240, 324–5
  model form cities, 228–9
  republican cities, 244
  social life of cities, 141–2, 234–5
  tax resistance in cities. *See* tax resistance pre-American Revolution
  urban disorder, 237
  women traders in, 375
Civil Constitution of the Clergy (France), 7
civilians in American Revolutionary War
  violence toward, 30, 333, 336–42, 384, 386–7
  white women. *See* white women in American Revolution
Clark, George Rogers, 433–5, 443–4
Clarke, William, 170
Clausewitz, Carl von, 318
Clavijero, Francisco Javier, 111
climate theory of civilization, 68–9
Clinton, Henry, 354–5, 360
Clive, Robert, 251
clubs and societies, 135–7, 141–2, 234–5
Cochin, Augustin, 80, 82
coffeehouses and salons, 135–7, 141–2, 234–5, 395–6
Colombia. *See* New Granada, viceroyalty of
Comay, Rebecca, 103–4
Commager, Henry Steele, 54
Comuneros Rebellion, New Granada, 110, 474, 491–8
Concord and Lexington, Battles of, 270, 326–7, 329, 382, 501
Condorcanqui, José Gabriel. *See* Túpac Amaru (José Gabriel Condorcanqui)
Condorcet, Nicolas de
  on economic inequality in United States, 538
  on Benjamin Franklin, 532–3
  in French Revolution, 541
  optimistic views of American Revolution, 520–1, 523–4, 528, 529, 530
  slavery, opposition to, 535, 536
  on US Federal Constitution, 525, 526
Congress of Vienna, 32
Constant, Benjamin, 80
Constitution of the United States. *See* United States Federal Constitution
Conway, Stephen, 258, 335
Conyngham, Gustavus, 273
Copley, John Singleton, 216, 345

Coram, Robert, 25
Corbin, Margaret, 388
Córdova, Luis de, 282, 286, 292
Cornbury, Lord (Edward Hyde), 196
Cornstalk, 428–9
Cornwallis, Charles, 179, 290, 336–7
counter-revolutionaries, 36–7, 112–13, 124, 155, 257–8. *See also* Loyalists in American Revolution
Cournand, Antoine de, 24–5
Crawford, William, 438
Creeks in American Revolution, 427–8, 433, 439–41, 445–6
creole peoples
  French and Spanish administrative reforms affecting, 223–4, 226, 475–6, 479–80, 496
  generally, 49–50, 145, 221
  global traders, 215, 216
  planters. *See* planter class
  tax resistance by. *See* tax resistance pre-American Revolution
  urban v. provincial and rural elites, 231–2, 236–8
Crillon, Duke de (Louis des Balbes de Berton de Crillon), 286
Croghan, George, 426
crowds, fear of, 20, 237
Cuba
  in American Revolutionary War, 288, 292, 510–11, 516–17
  Bourbon administrative reforms, 475
  in Seven Years' War, 251
  slavery in, 215, 517
cultural practices and revolutionary politics
  cause and effect paradigms
    cultural change as revolution, 151–3
    cultural practices as vehicles for political ideas, 153–6, 157
    cultural practices causing revolutions, 141–7
    revolutions changing cultural practices, 147–51, 157
  European writers on, 529–31
  everyday practices
    clothing and hairstyles, 150–1, 240–1, 380, 382, 383–4
    eating and drinking, 12–13, 137–9, 147, 240–1
    religious worship, 144–6
    weights and measures, 150
    women as consumers and traders, 373–4, 376–9, 382–3

fine arts, 139–41, 147–8, 149, 155
introduction to study, 132–4
social arts
  letter-writing, 13, 135–6, 149, 154–5, 156, 381–2
  music and dancing, 140–1, 155
  print media development, 12, 57–8, 143–4, 218, 234
  salons, clubs and societies, 135–7, 141–3, 234–5, 395–6
Curaçao, 503, 512

Dam, Isaac van, 270
David, Jacques-Louis, 147
Davidson, Neil, 86
Deane, Silas, 272–3, 278–9, 502–3
Declaration of Independence. *See also* Articles of Confederation
  Charles Carroll (signatory) interviewed about, 204–5
  drafting and adoption of, 450, 455
  international influence, 42, 58, 523–4
  international relations under, 456
  list of grievances, 59, 63, 330, 422, 499
  Loyalist critique of, 352–3
  nature and natural law ideas, 5, 60, 65
  "pursuit of happiness" idea, 67
  reason, discourse of, 70–1
  sovereign powers claimed under, 272
Declaration of the Rights of Man and of the Citizen
  critical views on, 5, 90
  international influence, 42, 118, 123, 126, 517–18
  provisions, 93, 97–8
Deep South of America. *See* Lower South American states
Delawares in American Revolution, 427, 429–30, 437–8
Demerara, 419
democracy. *See* popular sovereignty
Descartes, René, 84, 87
desertions from armed forces, 40
Dessalines, Jean-Jacques, 9, 32, 404, 417
Díaz de Gamarra, Benito, 111–12
Dickens, Charles, 247
Dickinson, John, 272
Dickson, John, 452
Diderot, Denis, 18, 92, 100
District of Columbia, 247
Dom Pedro I of Brazil, 33, 125
Dom Pedro II of Brazil, 33
Dominica, 280, 416, 508, 513

Dragging Canoe (Tsi'yu-gûnsini), 357, 427, 444
Drayton, William Henry, 432
Drennan, William, 521, 526
du Motier, Gilbert, Marquis de Lafayette, 272–3, 279–80, 289, 536
du Pont de Nemours, Pierre Samuel, 55
Duane, James, 69–70
Dumont, Étienne, 11–12
Dunmore, Earl of (John Murray), 241, 329, 342, 354–5, 403–4, 426
Duquesnoy, Adrien, 18
Dutch Republic
  British declaration of war against, 292, 293, 509
  capitalism, Anglo-Dutch transition to, 84–5, 86
  Caribbean colonies. *See* Curaçao; St. Eustatius
  Dutch Revolt, 86–7
  popular sovereignty interpreted, 10, 37
  rebellions and revolutionary thought in, 11, 13, 142–3, 525–6

Eacott, Jonathan, 193
Eardley-Wilmot, John, 369–70
East India Company, British, 171–2, 194
Echeverria, Durand, 519
economic (in)equality, 23–7, 537–41
Edelstein, Dan, 88, 102
education, public. *See also* literacy
  American Revolution and (European writers' views), 529–30
  Catholic institutions, 7, 137
  for free Black children, 537
  representative democracy and, 18–19, 50
  for white women, 23, 74–5, 393–4
Elliott, J. H., 144
Emistiguo, 428
Encyclopédie, 80, 90, 92, 98, 102, 120
English law and courts, 202–4, 299, 374–5
Enlightenment and the American Revolution
  citizenship idea, 23, 228, 235–7, 319, 389–90, 396
  Enlightenment literature, North American reception, 56–60, 217–18
  European writers' responses to revolution. *See* European writers' accounts of American Revolution
  introduction to study, 53–6
  Loyalists' Enlightenment thinking, 345
  nature and natural law discourse, 53, 60–6, 69, 72–4

Phoenix, or the Resurrection of Freedom (Barry), fig. 1.1
  popular sovereignty interpreted, 10, 15, 297, 453–5
  progress and happiness discourse, 66–70, 75–6
  reason discourse, 70–5
  revolution discourse, 75
  salon and club debates, 141–2, 234–5, 395–6
  women, ideas applied to, 377
Enlightenment and the French Revolution
  early revolution and "moderate" Enlightenment ideas, 96–9
  Encyclopédie, 80, 90, 92, 98, 102, 120
  entwinement thesis, 102
  First Republic as "radicalized" Enlightenment, 99–102
  Israel's "Radical Enlightenment" thesis, 82–3, 89–90, 97, 99, 100, 104, 116
  long nineteenth century views, 80
  Mornet's refutation, 80–1, 96
  Revisionist interpretation, 81–2
  non-French origins of Enlightenment philosophy. *See* Enlightenment philosophy, origins
  phases of enlightened political thought, 90–6
  salon and club debates, 141–2
Enlightenment and the Ibero-American revolutions
  contemporary critics' views, 498
  Enlightenment literature, Ibero-American reception, 110–12, 119, 131, 143–4
  ilustrados and revolutionaries, links between, 117–23, 130–1
  influence disputed, 110, 498–9
  introduction to study, 106–8
  liberalism, Enlightenment influence, 123–5
  Loyalists' Enlightenment thinking, 112–13
  monarchies and Enlightenment ideology, 108–10, 113–17
  popular sovereignty in new republics, 10, 125–30, 131
Enlightenment philosophy
  condemnations of, 47–8, 118
  cross-border dissemination, 4, 43, 54–5, 57, 110–12, 131, 143–4, 217–18
  on economic equality, 24–5
  "enlightened despot" monarchs, 76–8, 101, 108–10
  on mass education, 19

548

Index

natural law discourse. *See* natural law discourse
origins. *See* Enlightenment philosophy, origins
on popular sovereignty, 17, 18, 94–5, 99
revolutions, influence on. *See* Enlightenment and the American Revolution; Enlightenment and the French Revolution; Enlightenment and the Ibero-American revolutions
rights, ideal view of, 4–5, 61–2, 65
Enlightenment philosophy, origins
capitalism, transition to, 84–5, 86, 89
classical antiquity, 75, 84
Dutch Revolt, 85–8
emergence of "Enlightenment" term, 81–2
Glorious Revolution, 86–7, 172, 197, 200–1, 225
medieval thought, 115–16, 124
Renaissance and Reformation thought, 83–4, 88–9, 106–7
Scientific Revolution, 60, 84, 87, 111–12, 117–18, 119
enslaved and free Black people in American Revolution. *See also* Loyalists in American Revolution; slave trade; slavery in United States
antislavery activism by, 72–3, 406
Caribbean slaves, starvation and malnutrition, 408–9, 511–13
escapes by, 386, 387, 398, 405, 414, 535–6
as French and Spanish soldiers, 416, 513–18
introduction to study, 398–9
migrations after revolution, 260–1, 342, 365, 368–9, 372, 398, 407–8
neutrality or British loyalism, 40, 257, 260–1, 362–3, 398, 404–7
as patriot soldiers, 405–7
slave revolts (actual or rumored), 329, 342, 354–5, 403–4, 408, 512–13
slaves given to white enlistees, 414
Escarano, Francisco Antonio, 280–1
Espejo, Eugenio, 118
Esquilache riots, Spain, 479
Estaing, Charles Henri Hector d', 67, 275, 277–8, 280, 291–2, 514
European writers' accounts of American Revolution. *See also* international influence of American Revolution
as cultural progress, 529–31
economic inequality, concerns about, 23–4, 537–41

as economic progress, 527–9
introduction to study, 519–21
as moral progress, 531–4
as political progress, 521–7
slavery and racism condemned, 521, 533–4, 541
everyday practices. *See under* cultural practices and revolutionary politics

Fallen Timbers, Battle of, 446, 471
Faneuil, Peter, 233
Fergus, Claudius, 264
Ferguson, Adam, 67–8
Fernández Sebastián, Javier, 7–8
Fernando VII of Spain, 47, 127, 129
Ferrone, Vincenzo, 104
feudalism abolition in France, 20, 27, 30, 45, 97
Fichte, Johann Gottlieb, 103
Fick, Carolyn, 145
fine arts, 139–41, 147–8, 149, 155
Finestrad, Joaquín de, 498
First Nations people. *See* Native American peoples
Fleury, André Hercule de, Cardinal, 91, 92
Florida
British colonial rule, 171, 174, 275
Revolutionary War, West Florida theater, 286–8, 511, 516–17
Spanish colonial rule, 180, 181, 185, 294, 441
Floridablanca, Count of (José Moñino), 36–7, 114, 275, 281–2, 479–80
Foronda, Valentín de, 116
Forster, Georg, 25
France. *See also* French Revolution; Napoleonic Wars
American Revolution, support for. *See* French and Spanish support for American Revolution
Bourbon monarchy, 85–6, 88–9
Enlightenment *philosophes* on, 91–2, 95
British nationals expelled from, 48–9
capitalism, delayed transition to, 84–5
Caribbean colonies. *See* particular jurisdictions
Louisiana Purchase, 69, 185–7
North American colonies, 170–1, 212–13, 219
salons, 135–7, 141–2
Seven Years' War, implications for, 92, 269–70, 273, 296
territories lost to Great Britain, 280, 416–17

549

Franchimastabé, 445
franchise extension, 15–18, 23, 390, 392
Franklin, Benjamin
  diplomatic work, 279–80
  moral leadership praised by European writers, 521, 532–3
  writings of, 170, 218
  other mentions, 207, 238–9, 351, 522
Frederick the Great of Prussia, 77–8
free Black people in American Revolution. *See* enslaved and free Black people in American Revolution
freedom of the press. *See* press freedom
freedom to profess one's religion. *See* religious freedom
French and Spanish support for American Revolution
  British Loyalist support, effect on, 258, 303–4, 359–60
  consequences for colonial powers, 294–5
  diplomatic contacts, 272–5, 278–80, 284–5
  enslaved people as militia members, 416, 513–18
  espionage, 271–2
  finance and supplies, 270–1, 502–7, 510–11
  Franco-American operations, 179, 283, 288, 289–91
  Franco-Spanish operations, 285–9, 291–3, 310, 511, 516–17
  French aims, 273, 276
  French naval operations, 273–8, 280, 283, 288, 290–1, 509–10
  illustrations depicting, fig. 10.1, fig. 10.2
  introduction to study, 269–70
  military impact, 41, 179, 282–4, 360–1, 436
  peace treaties, 293–4
  Spanish ambivalence, 274–5, 280–1
  Spanish entry into war, 281–3, 510
French Revolution
  anti-clericalism, 7, 89, 111
  censorship in, 143, 147–8
  cultural practice reforms, 147–51
  Declaration of the Rights of Man and of the Citizen. *See* Declaration of the Rights of Man and of the Citizen
  economic equality demands, 24–5
  feudalism abolition, 20, 27, 30, 45, 97
  food shortages, 145
  ideology, 3–4, 5, 42–3, 48, 49
    Enlightenment ideas. *See* Enlightenment and the French Revolution
  international influence. *See* international influence of French Revolution
  popular sovereignty interpreted, 10, 15, 16–17, 18
  Protestant and Jewish emancipation, 7, 8
  public opinion as political force, 11–12
  royalist v. republican sentiment, 31, 98–9
  strategic interests in, 14
  Vendée War, 36, 38–9
  violence in, 29, 30–1
  women's equality rights, 22–3
Fréron, Elie Cathérine, 102
Friesland, 14–15
Frölich, Carl Wilhelm, 25–6

Gabriel's Conspiracy, 412–13
Gage, Thomas
  before American Revolutionary War, 206, 321, 324, 325, 425
  in American Revolutionary War, 326, 328–9
Galán, José Antonio, 493–4
Galloway, Grace Growden, 385
Galloway, Joseph, 351
Gálvez, Bernardo de, 286–7
Gálvez, José de, 475, 479, 480, 496
Gálvez, Matías de, 289
Gardoqui, Diego, 270
Gay, Peter, 82, 88
Geggus, David, 45, 512–13
Gelemend (John Killbuck), 429
Geneva Revolution, 41
geographical scope of revolutions, 1–2
George I of Great Britain, 192, 198
George II of Great Britain, 77, 192
George III of Great Britain, 31, 205, 206, 257, 282, 371, 455
George, David, 260–1
Georgia. *See* Lower South American states
Gérard de Rayneval, Conrad, 277, 278–9
Germain, Lord George, 305
German states, 14, 25–6, 45–6
Gibraltar, 275, 285–6, 294
Glorious Revolution, 86–7, 172, 197, 200–1, 225
Godoy, Manuel de, 116
González Carvajal, Ciriaco, 113
Görres, Joseph, 50
Gouges, Olympe de, 22
Gould, Eliga, 192, 222, 269
Gournay, Vincent de, 93
"Government" concept, 63, 75
Grafton, Anthony, 87, 88

Grasse, François Joseph Paul, Count de, 179, 288, 289, 290–3
Gratton, Henry, 305–6
Graves, Thomas, 288, 290–1
Gravier, Charles, Count de Vergennes, 273, 278
Great Awakening evangelical revival, 377–8
Great Bridge, Battle of, 382
Great Britain
  anti-Catholic policies, 6–7
  Atlantic trade system. *See* Atlantic trade system
  British Isles, Franco-Spanish attack on, 285, 310
  British Isles in 1775, map 11.1
  capitalism, Anglo-Dutch transition to, 84–5, 86
  cities of, 228–9, 230, 308–9
  colonial governance system, 172–4, 248, 253–5, 266, 294–5
    "salutary neglect" policy. *See* British North America, "salutary neglect" policy myth
  colonies. *See* British North America; British West Indies; Canada; India; Ireland
  economic reform movements, 313–16, 317
  Glorious Revolution, 86–7, 172, 197, 200–1, 225
  parliamentary reform movements, 307–13, 317
  salons and coffeehouses, 135–7
  Seven Years' War, implications for. *See under* Seven Years' War
  slave trade. *See* slave trade
  territorial acquisitions in Napoleonic Wars, 248–9, 263, 265, 416–17
Green, Jacob, 25
Greene, Nathanael, 338, 384
Grenada, 253, 265–6, 280, 416, 510, 515–16
Grenville, George, 308
Griffin, Patrick, 250, 438
Grotius, Hugo, 69, 87, 107
Guadeloupe, 44–5, 416, 503, 511, 513, 515
guerilla fighters and bandits, 26–7, 38–9, 330–1
Guichen, Luc Urbain de Bouëxic, Count de, 292
Guitteau, William, 191
Gustav III of Sweden, 77
Gutiérrez de Piñeres, Antonio, 491–2
Guyasuta, 430

Habermas, Jürgen, 133–4, 135, 146, 234
Hadfield, Joseph, 376
Haitian Revolution. *See also* Saint-Domingue
  Declaration of Independence, 404
  ideology, 42–3
  international influence, 42–5, 262–5, 412, 415–18
  Louisiana Purchase, relationship with, 185
  Louverture's letter-writing in, 155
  Maroons in, 39
  Masonic lodges in, 142
  outline of, 415
  royalist v. republican sentiment, 32
  violence in, 28, 29–31
  women in, 22
Haldimand, Frederick, 364, 368
Hall, Prince, 406, 410
Hamilton, Alexander, 72, 122, 187–8, 469
Hancock, John, 214, 216
happiness discourse, American Enlightenment, 66–70, 75–6
Harrison, Richard, 503
Hart, Nancy, fig. 14.2
Harvey, William, 87
Hastings, Warren, 280
Haudenosaunee. *See* Iroquois Confederacy
Havana. *See* Cuba
Hays, Mary Ludwig, 388
Hazard, Paul, 82, 87
Hébrard, Véronique, 11
Hegel, Georg Wilhelm Friedrich, 103–5
Helvetic Republic, 6, 8
Helvétius, Claude Adrien, 92, 100
Henretta, James, 192–3, 199
Heron, Sir Richard, 303–4
Herrejón, Carlos, 112
Hidalgo, Miguel, 8, 112
Hilliard d'Auberteuil, Michel René, 53
Hobbes, Thomas, 61, 87, 94
Holbach, Paul-Henri Thiry, Baron d', 18, 92
Home, Henry, Lord Kames, 67–8, 71
Honduras, 275, 288, 289
Hoock, Holger, 39, 335, 337
Hood, Samuel, 292
Hopocan, 429, 430
Hotham, William, 280
Howe, Richard, 277
Howe, William, 331
Hughes, Edward, 280
Hugo, Victor, 80, 105
Hugues, Victor, 44, 416, 417

Hulliung, Mark, 99
Hulsebosch, Daniel, 202
human rights. *See* rights
humanism, 87, 88, 106–7
Hume, David, 60, 107n
Hungary, 42
Hunt, Lynn, 82, 153–4
Hutcheson, Francis, 71
Hutchinson, Thomas, 28, 352–3, 381–2
Hyde, Edward, Lord Cornbury, 196

Iberian America. *See* Portuguese America; Spanish America
Iberian wars, 116–17, 121, 295
India, British colonial era, 171–2, 179, 251, 280, 293
Indian colonial pact (Spanish and Portuguese America), 34–5, 484–5
Indians/Indigenous nations. *See* Native American peoples
international dimension of revolutions
  American Revolution, influence of. *See* international influence of American Revolution
  anti-imperialist sentiment, 48–9, 187
  Enlightenment ideas, cross-border dissemination, 4, 43, 54–5, 57, 110–12, 131, 143–4, 217–18
  French Revolution, influence of. *See* international influence of French Revolution
  Haitian Revolution, influence of, 42–5, 262–5, 412, 415–18
  military support. *See* French and Spanish support for American Revolution
  slavery abolition, international impact, 42–5, 49
international influence of American Revolution. *See also* European writers' accounts of American Revolution
  in Britain and Ireland generally, 316–17
  British economic reform movements, 313–16, 317
  British parliamentary reform movements, 307–13, 317
  Declaration of Independence, 42, 58, 523–4
  in Dutch Republic, 525–6
  Irish reform movements, 301–2, 304–7, 526
  Palmer's thesis, 56, 296–8
  in Spanish America, 497–8

international influence of French Revolution
  in Europe, 42, 43, 45–6, 541
  with Haitian Revolution, 42–5, 262–5, 415
  in Spanish America, 42, 118, 123, 126, 498
Intolerable Acts, 240, 320–2
Iredell, James, 59–60
Ireland
  anti-British sentiment in, 49, 255, 302, 525, 526
  British Isles in 1775, map 11.1
  Burke on British policies in, 190, 205
  Catholic elites in, 302–3
  colonial government in, 223, 250, 254, 266, 299–300
  North American migration from, 210, 267
  Protestant elites in, 297–304, 306–7
  reform movements (1778–83), 301–2, 304–7, 317
  revolutionary violence in, 28, 29
Iroquois Confederacy
  British relations with, 425
  entry into war, 430
  generally, 354, 368
  revenge attacks, 436–40
  Sullivan Expedition against, 359, 434–40
  territorial loss, 443
Israel, Jonathan
  on Miranda as *ilustrado*, 120
  "Radical Enlightenment" thesis, 82–3, 89–90, 97, 99, 100, 104, 116
  other mentions, 87, 96, 108
Italy, 12, 26, 38, 46–7
Iturbide, Agustín de, 33

Jackson, William, 448
Jacobinism, 19, 25, 99–100
Jacobitism, 302, 309
Jacobs, Margaret, 82, 89
Jainchill, Andrew, 100–1
Jamaica
  in American Revolutionary War, 292–3, 408
  Baptist churches founded on, 407
  Haitian Revolution, impact in, 415–16
  in Napoleonic Wars, 259
  planter class in, 231, 255–6, 258–60, 262–3
  slave revolts in, 171, 251–3, 266, 402–3, 408, 419–20
  slavery economy, 400
James II of Great Britain, 197, 200, 229
Jasanoff, Maya, 260, 367
Jaucourt, Louis de, 98
Jay, John, 28, 181–2, 278, 284–5

Jefferson, Martha, 384–5
Jefferson, Thomas. *See also* Declaration of Independence
  in American Revolutionary War, 336–7
  Federal Constitution, role in drafting process, 180–1
  Louisiana Purchase, 69, 185–7
  Native Americans, attitude toward, 432, 434, 446–7
  on natural law and natural rights, 65, 73–4, 79
  slave ownership, 412, 413
  US political economy, vision of, 187–8, 452
  Virginia, concerns for, 68–9
Jewish emancipation in France, 7, 8
João VI of Portugal, 32–3, 117
Johnson, Sir John, 357, 358
Johnson, Sir William, 357, 425, 430
Johnston, William Martin, 361–2, 364–5
Jones, Colin, 151–2
Jones, T. Cole, 334–5
Jovellanos, Gaspar Melchor de, 109–10, 112, 114

Kalb, "Baron" Johann de, 271, 272–3
Kamensky, Jane, 345
Kames, Lord (Henry Home), 67–8, 71
Kant, Immanuel, 78, 79, 82, 84, 103
Katari, Nicolás and Dámaso, 482–3, 484, 489, 490–1
Katari, Tomás, 482, 489
Killbuck, John (Gelemend), 429
King, Martin Luther, 42–3
Kirkland, Samuel, 430
Klooster, Wim, 86
Kongo, 35
Koñwatsiʔtsiaiéñni (Mary Brant), 357–9, 364

La Mettrie, Julien Offray de, 92
Ladies Association of Philadelphia, 384
Lafayette, Marquis de (Gilbert du Motier), 272–3, 279–80, 289, 536
Lafrance, Xavier, 93n
Lancaster, Joseph, 19
Laurens, Henry, 278, 406
Laurens, John, 406, 414
League of Armed Neutrality, 283
Leclerc, Georges-Louis, Count de Buffon, 68
Lee, Arthur, 272, 274, 278, 503–4
Lee, Charles, 504–5
Lee, Jean, 336
Lee, Jeremiah, 270
Lee, Richard Henry, 272

Leibniz, Gottfried Wilhelm, 87
Lender, Mark, 361
Leonard, Daniel, 348–9
letter-writing, 13, 135–6, 149, 154–5, 156, 381–2
Levy, Jacob, 91
Lexington and Concord, Battles of, 270, 326–7, 329, 382, 501
Linebaugh, Peter, 196n
Linguet, Simon, 520
literacy. *See also* education, public
  Enlightenment goal of, 19
  letter-writing, 13, 135–6, 149, 154–5, 156, 381–2
  print media development, 12, 57–8, 143–4, 218, 234
Llano, José María Queipo de, Conde de Toreno, 116
Locke, John
  "common sense" theory, 71
  depicted, fig. 1.1
  habit theory, 132, 157
  on Native American peoples, 61
  on natural law and natural rights, 61–2, 64, 391
  other mentions, 84, 87, 205–6
Logan (Tachnedorus), 426
Loménie de Brienne, Étienne Charles de, 96–7
Louis XIV of France, 85–6, 88–9
Louis XVI of France, 11, 32, 92, 93–4, 95, 96, 295
Louisiana Purchase, 69, 185–7
Louverture, Toussaint, 9, 155, 415, 416
Lovejoy, Paul, 35–6
Lowell, James Russell, 191
Lower Canada Rebellion (1837), 267
Lower South American states. *See also* British North America; United States
  in American Revolutionary War, 179, 243–4, 286–8, 312, 356–7, 510–11
  cities, emergence and development, 230. *See also* Charleston; Savannah
  Federal Constitution, responses to, 184–5
  Loyalists in, 354–5, 361–4
  in Seven Years' War, 171
  slavery abolition resisted in, 414–15, 420
  slavery economy, 168, 179, 211, 400–1
  trade regulation, colonial era, 198
Loyalists in American Revolution
  Declaration of Independence, Loyalist critique, 352–3
  diaspora of, 260–2, 364–70, 406–8
  disaffection during war, 39–40, 363–4

553

Loyalists in American Revolution (cont.)
  enslaved people. *See* enslaved and free Black people in American Revolution
  French and Spanish support for revolution, effect on, 258, 303–4, 359–60
  generally, 257–8, 344–6, 370–2
  geographical distribution in war, 353–5, 361–4
  historians' accounts of, 371
  Irish loyalists, 302–4
  Native American peoples. *See* Native American peoples
  numbers of, 346–7
  political punishment of, 351–2
  property confiscated from, 396–7, 459
  religious dissenters, 366
  strategic interests of, 13, 40, 260–1, 356, 422–4, 426–7
  views of, 37, 258–60, 345, 347
  violence toward, 344–5, 348–51, 355–6, 380, 385
  white women, 382–4, 385, 396–7
Luttrell, John, 288
Lynch, John, 119

Mably, Gabriel Bonnot de, 48, 94–5, 99, 100
Machiavelli, Niccolò, 78
Mackesy, Piers, 361
Madison, James, 59, 182, 237, 462–3, 464, 465–6, 468
Maher, John, 119–20
Maier, Pauline, 322
Marat, Jean-Paul, 102–3
Mariana, Juan de, 107
Maria-Theresa, Holy Roman Empress, 77
marronage. *See* slave revolts
Marshall, P. J., 258, 267, 268
Martin v. Massachusetts, 396–7
Martin, James Kirby, 361
Martin, Joseph, 339
Martínez Compañón, Baltasar Jaime, 111
Martinique, 280, 292, 502–4, 507, 515
Marxism, 67, 82, 142n
Maryland. *See also* British North America; United States
  in American Revolutionary War, 336, 354, 510
  economy and population, colonial era, 166–7, 169, 170
  Glorious Revolution, impact in, 200–1
  provincial congress, 325
  slavery abolition resisted in, 411–12, 420
  slavery economy, 166–7, 400, 401
  trade regulation, colonial era, 198, 231
Mason, George, 65
Masonic movements, 142, 406, 410
Maxwell, Kenneth, 110
McDonnell, Michael, 329, 355
McGillivray, Alexander, 428, 445–6
McMahon, Darrin, 102
Melon, Jean-François, 93
Mendigure, Andrés, 482
Mexican uprising. *See also* New Spain, viceroyalty of
  bandits and guerilla fighters, 38
  ideology, 8, 111
  royalist v. republican sentiment, 33, 127
  Spanish nationals, expulsion of, 48
  violence during, 28–9
Middle Colonies of America. *See also* British North America
  cities, emergence and development, 230. *See also* New York City
  economy and population, 167–8, 169
  Loyalists in, 354
  Saratoga, Battles of, 178–9, 274, 310, 332, 358, 359–60
Milan, 46, 47
militia groups in American Revolutionary War, 339–41, 359, 361
Mill, James, 122
Millar, John, 67–8
millenarian ideology
  American Revolution, 3
  Spanish American rebellions, 486–7, 498–9
Miller, Andrew, 339
Minorca, 275, 294
Mirabeau, Honoré Gabriel Riquetti, Count de, 102
Miralles, Juan de, 284, 510
Miranda, Francisco de, 119–23, 128
Mohawks in American Revolution
  at Battle of Oriskany, 430
  Mary and Joseph Brant, profiles of, 357–9
  Covenant Chain alliance membership, 354
  entry into war, 427, 430
  genocide and territorial loss, 434–40
  smallpox epidemic, 439–41
Molina, Luis de, 107
Moluntha, 444
Molyneux, William, 299–300, 307
monarchies
  British colonies, sovereign power over, 197, 201–2, 257
  Catholic Church support for absolutist monarchs, 7–8, 88–9, 113, 129–30

Dutch Revolt, 85–8
"enlightened despot" monarchs, 76–8, 101, 108–10
France, Bourbon monarchy, 85–6, 88–9
Enlightenment *philosophes* on, 91–2, 95
Glorious Revolution of Great Britain, 86–7, 172, 197, 200–1, 225
Ibero-American, Enlightenment ideology and, 108–10, 113–17
Jacobitism in Great Britain, 302, 309
royalist v. republican sentiment. *See* royalist v. republican sentiment
Moñino, José, Count of Floridablanca, 36–7, 114, 275, 281–2, 479–80
Montesquieu
influence of, 77–8, 93, 109, 127, 130
monarchy, views on, 87, 91–2
natural law theory, 63–4, 127
Montgomery, Richard, 257
Montiel, Miguel, 497
Moore, Sir Henry, 252
Mora, José María Luis, 35
Morelly, Étienne-Gabriel, 92, 100
Moreno, Mariano, 112
Mornet, Daniel, 80–1, 90–1, 93–6
Morris, Gouverneur, 3–4
Morris, Richard, 283–4
Morris, Robert, 284, 510
Mounier, Jean-Joseph, 10
Murray, Elizabeth, 383, 386
Murray, John, Earl of Dunmore, 241, 329, 342, 354–5, 403–4, 426
Murray, Judith Sargent, 74, 394
Murrin, John, 254
Mutis, José Clemente, 119

Namier, Lewis, 199
Napoleon, 47, 185, 417
Napoleonic Wars
British territorial acquisitions, 248–9, 263, 265, 416–17
Enlightenment philosophy condemned during, 47–8
Haitian Revolution. *See* Haitian Revolution
Iberian wars, 116–17, 121, 295
Louisiana Purchase, 69, 185–7
sister republics of Napoleonic France, 45–7
war of 1812, 185, 257, 261–2, 342, 372, 405
Nariño, Antonio, 118–19, 129
Nath, Kimberly, 22

Native American peoples. *See also* Loyalists in American Revolution
British relations with, colonial era, 174, 227, 423–6
in Canada, 267–8, 364, 368, 372, 441
Cherokee War (1759–61), 171
everyday practices, 139, 145–6
Locke on, 61
smallpox epidemic in war, 439–41
strategic interests in American Revolution, 356, 422–4, 426–7
territorial losses, American Revolution, 49, 423–4, 427, 431, 432–40
territorial losses, colonial era, 170, 174, 423–6
territorial losses, republican era, 183–4, 185, 411–12, 413, 434, 471–2
tribal experiences in American Revolution. *See* Cherokees; Chicasaws; Choctaws; Creeks; Delawares; Iroquois Confederacy; Mohawks; Oneidas; Senecas; Shawnees
viewed as uncivilized, 68–9, 357, 422
violence toward, 342, 345–6, 356–7, 432–5, 437–9
natural law discourse
American Enlightenment, 53, 60–6, 69, 72–4
Burke's "salutary neglect" thesis using, 189–90
counter-revolutionaries rejecting, 37, 43
generally, 101
natural rights, 5, 61–2, 72, 101, 108, 391
Renaissance era, 106–7
in Spanish America, 125–6, 127
tax resistance justified by, 64–5, 225
Necker, Jacques, 94
Netherlands. *See* Dutch Republic
New England. *See also* British North America; United States
in American Revolutionary War. *See* New England in American Revolutionary War
Boston. *See* Boston
economy and population, colonial era, 166, 169
global trade (licit and illicit), 214
Glorious Revolution, impact in, 200
Newport. *See* Newport, Rhode Island
provincial congress, 325–6
religion in, 6, 146, 176, 303
in Seven Years' War, 137

New England (cont.)
  social arts in, 137
  tax resistance, 176–7, 240, 258, 320–2
  violence (late 1774), 322–3, 324
New England in American Revolutionary
    War
  Boston, 178–9, 243, 277–8, 326, 328–9
  Bunker Hill, Battle of, 329, 353, 431,
    501–2
  Lexington and Concord, Battles of, 270,
    326–7, 329, 382, 501
  Loyalists, 347–9, 352–3, 385, 396–7
  standard narrative, 353–4
New Granada, viceroyalty of
  Comuneros Rebellion, 110, 474, 491–8
  legal system reforms, 127
  Nariño's sedition trial, 118–19
  popular sovereignty interpreted, 10, 43–4,
    126–7, 129
  rebellions against Bourbon reforms,
    19–20, 223–4, 476–9
  religious tolerance, 9
  royalist v. republican sentiment, 32, 33–4,
    496
New Spain, viceroyalty of, 14, 16, 474, 475,
    479. *See also* Mexican uprising
New York City
  in American Revolutionary War, 243, 244,
    337, 340, 354, 355
  colonial era, 232–3, 235, 237
  free Black community in, 410
  as refugee center, 367
  republican era, 246–7, 527
  Rivington (Loyalist printer) persecuted in,
    349–51
Newport, Rhode Island
  in American Revolutionary War, 67, 242,
    243, 277–8, 279, 289, 354
  charter, 246
  colonial era, 230, 231
  free Black community in, 410, 536
  tax resistance in, 238
newspapers. *See* censorship; press freedom
Newton, Isaac, 60, 84, 87, 119
nonideologically committed combatants,
    13–14, 37–40
Norfolk, Virginia, 230, 231, 241, 246, 329, 336
North, Frederick, Lord North, 291, 293, 305,
    314, 332
North Carolina. *See* Lower South American
    states
Northwest Ordinance (1787), 181, 184, 185,
    446–7, 458–9, 464, 467

Occom, Samson, 431, 439
Odell, Jonathan, 360
Olavide, Pablo de, 109, 112, 116
Oliver, Peter, 348, 380
Oneidas in American Revolution, 358,
    430–1, 434–41, 444
Oriskany, Battle of, 358, 430–1
O'Shaughnessy, Andrew Jackson, 253–5,
    288, 408
Otis, James, 64–5, 255
Ottoman empire, 2

Paape, Gerrit, 22
Paine, Thomas
  in American Revolutionary War, 278
  on representative democracy, 18–19
  revolution, arguments for, 24, 31, 71, 76,
    272, 318
Palmer, R. R., 1, 56, 296–7, 365
Paris, Treaty of (1783), 180, 184, 185, 244,
    294, 434–41, 450–1
Parker, Hyde, 280
Pauw, Cornelius de, 68, 110
peasantry
  agrarian capitalism, transition to, 85
  Brazil, social reform demands
    unsuccessful, 20–1
  elite view of, 11, 18
  France, feudalism abolition, 20, 27, 30, 45,
    97
  France, Vendée War, 36, 38–9
  private property abolition, calls for, 25–6
  revolutions, limited impact on, 14–15, 150
  in sister republics of France, 45–6
Penn, William, 229, 232, 351
Pennsylvania. *See also* British North
    America; United States
  economy and population, colonial era,
    167–8, 169, 211
  Loyalists in, 351, 459
  Philadelphia. *See* Philadelphia
  religion in, 6
  republican era, 459–60, 524–5, 527–8,
    531–2
Pensacola, Siege of, 287–8, 511, 516–17
Peru, viceroyalty of. *See also* Upper Peru
  Arequipa Revolt, 480–1
  counter-revolutionaries in, 37
  crowd mobilizations, 20
  Indigenous groups in, 484–7, 491
  international dimension of revolution, 41
  Río de la Plata viceroyalty creation,
    impact on, 480

Spanish nationals expelled from, 48
Túpac Amaru Rebellion. *See* Túpac
  Amaru (José Gabriel Condorcanqui)
Peters, Thomas, 362–3, 365, 368–9, 372
Pétion, Alexandre, 32, 45
Petley, Christer, 263, 264, 265
Petty, William, Earl of Shelburne, 293–4, 306, 314
Phelan, John Leddy, 110
Philadelphia
  in American Revolutionary War, 241, 242–3, 332, 338, 340–1, 354
  charter, 246
  colonial era, 229, 231, 232, 234–5, 237
  Fort Wilson incident, 244–5
  free Black community in, 410
  Ladies Association of Philadelphia, 384
  Quakers in, 232, 527–8, 531–2
  tax resistance in, 238–9, 320
  Young Ladies' Academy of, 393–4
Physiocracy, 93, 97
Pinckney, Eliza Lucas, 375, 386
Pincus, Steve, 86
Piominko, 445
piracy, 194–5
Pisco, Ambrosio, 492
Pitt, William (the Younger), 264, 312, 314–15
planter class. *See also* creole peoples; slave trade
  American Revolution, perspective on, 258–60
  American revolutionaries' view of, 255–6
  city dwellers, suspicion of, 231–2, 236–8
  Haitian Revolution, perspective on, 262–5
  slavery abolition, perspective on, 259, 263, 264–5
  tax resistance, perspective on, 176, 177, 239, 258–9
  wealth and political power, 165, 216, 250–1, 262, 263, 419
  women planters, 375–6, 387
Point Pleasant, Battle of, 426
Polasky, Janet, 144
political violence of American Revolution.
  See also American Revolutionary War; tax resistance pre-American Revolution
  intimidative and catalytic violence, 320–30
  introduction to study, 30, 318–20
  militias' war and retaliatory violence, 340–1, 361–2
  regular and logistical violence, 330–40

toward civilians, 30, 333, 336–42, 384, 386–7
toward enslaved people and Native Americans, 341–2, 345–6, 356–7, 432–5, 437–9
toward Loyalists, 344–5, 348–51, 355–6, 380, 385
toward prisoners, 333–6
Polybius, 75
Pombal, Marquês de (Sebastião José de Carvalho e Melo), 109, 117
Pontiac's War, 174, 423–5
Poor, John, 393
popular sovereignty
  citizenship idea, 23, 228, 235–7, 319, 389–90, 396
  counter-revolutionary rejection of, 124, 266
  interpretations of, 10–11, 15, 297, 313, 453–5, 524–5
  public opinion as political force, 11–12, 19–21, 41–2
  representative democracy, 16–20
  Rousseau and Mably on, 16–17, 94–5, 99
  in Spanish American republics, 10, 125–30, 131
  US Federal Constitution, popular ratification process, 468–71
  voting rights, 15–18, 23, 390, 392
Portuguese America
  Brazil. *See* Brazil
  Enlightenment influence in. *See* Enlightenment and the Ibero-American revolutions
  Indian colonial pact, 34–5
  monarchy, reforms resisted, 109
Powder Alarm (Boston), 324
Premo, Bianca, 108
press freedom. *See also* censorship
  American Revolution and (European writers' views), 530
  generally, 12
  print media development, 12, 57–8, 143–4, 218, 234
  in Spain, 7
Price, Richard, 520–3, 529, 534–5, 540
prisoners in American Revolutionary War, 333–6
Privy Council, 202–3
progress discourse, American Enlightenment, 66–70, 75–6
property, private
  abolition, calls for, 25–6
  confiscated from Loyalists, 396–7, 459

property, private (cont.)
  women's ownership rights, 374–5, 391–3, 394, 396–7
Protestantism
  in American states, 6–7, 146, 176, 303, 377–8
  dissenters, 366, 527–8, 531–2
  anti-Catholic policies in Protestant states, 6–7, 203, 515–16
  Dutch Revolt and English revolutions, 85–8
  France, Protestant emancipation, 7
  Ireland, Protestant elites in, 297–304, 306–7
  religious tolerance policies of Catholic states, 8–9
public education. *See* education, public
public opinion as political force, 11–12, 19–21, 41–2
Puerto Rico, 511–12
Pufendorf, Samuel von, 69, 107
Pybus, Cassandra, 405

Quakers, 232, 366, 527–8, 531–2, 539
Quebec
  after American Revolution, 267, 451
  in American Revolutionary War, 257, 436–7
  British acquisition of, 251
  British colonial governance, 174, 177, 253, 302–3, 347
  Quebec Act 1774, Virginia's response, 178
  in Seven Years' War, 170
Quintana, Manuel Josef, 116
Quito Junta, 118, 128
Quito Revolt (Rebellion of the Barrios), 474, 476–9

Racine, Karen, 119
Ragatz, Lowell Joseph, 509
Ramsay, David, 75–6
Randolph, Edmund, 462
Randolph, Edward, 195–6
Rao, Gautham, 192
rapes during revolutions, 29, 30, 333, 337, 341–2, 387
Raphael, Ray, 323
Rathell, Jane, 383
Rawdon, Francis, Lord, 387
Raynal, Guillaume Thomas François, 47–8, 62–3, 75, 110
reason discourse, American Enlightenment, 70–5
Rebellion of the Barrios (Quito Revolt), 474, 476–9

Reed, Esther de Berdt, 384
Régent, Frédéric, 516
Reid, Thomas, 71
religious freedom
  American Revolution and (European writers' views), 530
  anti-Catholic policies in Protestant states, 6–7, 203, 515–16
  France, restrictions on, 7
  Spain, opposition to, 7–8
  tolerance policies in Catholic states, 8–9
representative democracy, 16–20. *See also* popular sovereignty
republican v. royalist sentiment. *See* royalist v. republican sentiment
"revolution" term, 75, 101
Riaño, José Antonio, 112
Rigaud, André, 514
rights
  alternative conceptions, 5–6
  economic equality, 23–7, 537–41
  Enlightenment ideal, 4–5, 61–2, 65
  fears of escalating demands, 20, 73–4, 390–1, 397
  natural rights discourse, 5, 61–2, 72, 101, 108, 391
  press freedom. *See* press freedom
  religious freedom. *See* religious freedom
  slavery abolition. *See* slavery abolition
  US Bill of Rights, 59–60, 126, 183, 468–9, 473
  voting rights, 15–18, 23, 390, 392
  women's equality, 5, 22–3, 74–5, 108, 390–1
Río de la Plata, viceroyalty of, 26, 127, 274, 480, 485
Rivington, James, 349–51
Roberts, Bartholomew ("Pyrate Roberts"), 194
Roberts, Justin, 401
Robertson, Ritchie, 89
Robertson, William, 67–8, 110
Rochambeau, Count de (Jean-Baptiste Donatien de Vimeur), 289–90
Rockingham, Charles Watson-Wentworth, Marquess of, 291, 293, 305–6, 314
Rodney, George, 179, 292, 293, 506, 509, 510
Rodríguez de Mendoza, Toribio, 112
Roland, Jeanne-Marie, 143
Rousseau, Jean-Jacques
  on economic inequality, 24
  on natural law, 61
  on popular sovereignty, 16–17, 94, 99

Panthéon internment, 80, 102–3
other mentions, 47–8, 77–8, 100
Royal African Company, 194, 214
royalist v. republican sentiment
  in American Revolution, 31–2, 34, 77, 452–3
  in French Revolution, 31, 98–9
  in Portuguese America, 32–3, 127
  in Spanish America, 32–4, 127, 129–30, 496, 499
Rush, Benjamin, 72, 161
Russell, Thomas, 49
Russo, Vincenzio, 18

Saavedra, Francisco, 114
Saint-Domingue. *See also* Haitian Revolution
  British Navy blockade of, 508
  Dutch and British smuggling trade, 213
  French administrative reforms, 223–4, 226
  French militia members from, 514
  military supplies to American revolutionaries via, 504–5
  religious tolerance, 7, 9
  slave revolts, 3, 145, 512–13, 514
  slavery abolition, 44
  wheat imports, 139
Saintes, Battle of the, 293, 510
salons and coffeehouses, 135–7, 141–2, 234–5, 395–6
"salutary neglect" policy. *See* British North America, "salutary neglect" policy myth
Sampson Gannett, Deborah, 388–9
San Martín, José de, 33
Santos Atahualpa, Juan, 487
Saratoga, Battles of, 178–9, 274, 310, 332, 358, 359–60
Savannah
  British occupation in American Revolutionary War, 242, 243–4, 341, 414
  gunpowder seized from, 327–8, 501
  Loyalists in, 361–4, 389
  siege of, 280, 514
Schlemmer, Joseph, 46
Schuyler, Catherine, 386
Schuyler, Peter, 358
Scientific Revolution, 60, 84, 87, 111–12, 117–18, 119
Scott, Jonathan, 86
Seelye, James, 192
Selby, Shaw, 192
Senecas in American Revolution, 423–5, 430, 434–41

Senegal, 276
Seven Years' War
  American cities, impact on, 237
  American theater, 170–1, 220–1, 423, 431
  Dutch neutrality in, 506
  France, implications for, 92, 269–70, 273, 296
  Great Britain, implications for
    colonial holdings, 92, 248, 251, 254–5, 300
    economic impact, 171, 173–4, 220–1, 296, 300, 378
    Jacobite hopes ended, 302, 309
  Spain, implications for, 269–70, 296
Sewell, William, 89, 93, 95–6, 97
Sharp, Granville, 255
Shawnees in American Revolution
  Chickamaugas, alliance with, 432–3
  entry into war, 426–9
  genocide and territorial loss, 434, 438–9, 443–4
Shelburne, Earl of (William Petty), 293–4, 306, 314
Shy, John, 353
Sierra Leone, 261, 342, 368–9, 372, 398, 407
Sieyès, Emmanuel Joseph, 17, 97
sister republics of Napoleonic France, 45–7
Six Nations. *See* Iroquois Confederacy
slave revolts
  after slave trade abolition, 419–20
  in American Revolutionary War (actual or rumored), 329, 342, 354–5, 403–4, 408, 512–13
  in Dominica, 513
  Fédon's Rebellion, Grenada, 265–6, 516
  generally, 402
  in Saint-Domingue, 3, 145, 512–13, 514.
    See also Haitian Revolution
  Stono Rebellion, South Carolina, 402
  Tacky's Revolt, Jamaica, 171, 251–3, 402–3, 419–20
slave trade. *See also* Atlantic trade system
  abolition, 412, 419. *See also* slavery abolition
  economic significance, 165–70, 179, 211, 230, 250
  entanglement of, 214–15, 227, 399–402
  French aspirations for, 276
  planters. *See* planter class
  regulation of, 193–5, 252–3, 402
  Somerset case, 256–7
  suspension during American Revolutionary War, 408–9

slavery abolition
  British Government's perspectives, 263–4, 419
  in British West Indies, 415–20
  emancipatory discourse, 42–4, 73, 108, 412
  Haitian and French revolutions, impact on, 262–5, 412, 415–18
  international impact, 42–5, 49
  planter class's perspective, 259, 263, 264–5, 419
  Saint-Domingue, abolition and reinstatement, 415, 417
  in United States. See slavery in United States
slavery in United States. See also enslaved and free Black people in American Revolution
  abolition, north of Mason-Dixon Line, 72–3, 409–11, 467
  abolition resisted, southern states, 44, 411–12, 414–15, 420
  African American activism for abolition, 72–3, 410, 412–13
  British loyalism of enslaved people, threat posed by, 404–5
  constitutional protection for, 182–3, 467
  European writers on, 521, 533–4, 541
  everyday practices of enslaved people, 145
  long-distance domestic slave markets, 413–14
  manumission laws, 411
  natural law arguments justifying, 73–4
  slave trade abolition, 412, 419
  western expansion, impact on, 472
Smith, Adam, 220, 244
smuggling. See also Atlantic trade system
  American revolutionaries supplied by, 270–1
  anti-smuggling rationale of tax policies, 176, 198, 222
  British toleration of, 205
  entanglement of Atlantic system illustrated by, 212–14
  as tax resistance, 225
social arts. See under cultural practices and revolutionary politics
societies and clubs, 135–7, 141–2, 234–5
"society" concept, 61–3
Socorro Rodríguez, Manuel del, 111
Solano, José, 287, 292
Somerset case, 256–7
Sonenscher, Michael, 83n, 98, 99–100

South Carolina. See Lower South American states
Souza Coutinho, Rodrigo de, 114, 117
sovereignty, popular. See popular sovereignty
Spain
  American Revolution, support for. See French and Spanish support for American Revolution
  Bourbon monarchy, 116
  Cádiz constitutional system, 7–8, 16, 43–4, 123–4, 128
  censorship, 7, 36–7
  Esquilache riots, 479
  Napoleonic Wars in, 116–17, 121, 295
  religious intolerance, 7–8
  royalist v. republican sentiment, 34, 127
  Seven Years' War, implications for, 269–70, 296
  Spanish Inquisition, 36–7, 116, 120
  tertulias (conversation societies), 136–7
  voting rights, 16
Spanish America. See also particular jurisdictions
  banditry, 26–7, 39
  Bourbon administrative reforms, 223–4, 226, 475–6, 479–80, 496
  cabildos (municipal councils), 127–8, 478–9
  censorship, 14
  colonization, 162
  Indian colonial pact, 34–5, 484–5
  Miranda's Projects for independence, 120, 121–2
  rebellions. See Spanish American rebellions
  royalist v. republican sentiment, 32–4, 127, 129–30, 496
  Seven Years' War impact, 171, 251, 269
  slavery in, 215
  smuggling in, 213
  tertulias (conversation societies), 136–7, 142
  women's equality rights opposed, 23
Spanish American rebellions
  American Revolution, influence of, 497–8
  Bourbon administrative reforms triggering, 223–4, 226, 475–6, 479–80, 496
  Comuneros Rebellion, New Granada, 110, 474, 491–8
  cross-border dimension, 41–4, 48, 484–7

560

Enlightenment ideas. *See* Enlightenment and the Ibero-American revolutions
French and Haitian revolutions, influence of, 42, 45, 118, 123, 126, 498
introduction to study, 474–5
Mexican uprising. *See* Mexican uprising
millenarian ideology, 486–7, 498–9
"moral economy" commitment, 479
pardos, strategic interests in, 37–8
plebeian mobilization in, 19–20
popular sovereignty interpreted, 10, 125–30, 131
Quito Revolt (Rebellion of the Barrios), 474, 476–9
royalist v. republican sentiment, 32–4, 127, 129–30, 496, 499
Túpac Amaru Rebellion, Peru. *See* Túpac Amaru (José Gabriel Condorcanqui)
Upper Peru rebellions (1780–1781), 482–4, 489–91
violence of, 28–9
Spanish Inquisition, 36–7, 116, 120
Spinoza, Baruch, 82, 84, 87
St. Clair, Sally, 389
St. Eustatius, 270, 292, 505–7, 509
St. Kitts, 293, 450–1, 510
St. Lucia, 280, 293, 417, 504, 508
St. Vincent, 280, 416, 510, 513
Stäfner Memorial, 6
Stamp Act (1765), resistance to. *See* tax resistance pre-American Revolution
Starkey, Armstrong, 335
state of nature discourse. *See* natural law discourse
Steffens, Henrik, 4
Steinberg, Mark D., 3
Stiles, Ezra, 78–9
Stono Rebellion, South Carolina, 402
strategic interests in revolutions, 13–14, 37–40, 356
Stuart, John, 364
Suárez, Francisco, 107
suffrage, 15–18, 23, 390, 392
Suffren, Pierre André de, 293
Sugar Act (1764), resistance to. *See* tax resistance pre-American Revolution
Sullivan Expedition, 359, 434–40

Taboca, 445
Tachnedorus (Logan), 426
Tacky's Revolt, Jamaica, 171, 251–3, 402–3, 419–20
Taine, Hippolyte, 80, 82

tax resistance pre-American Revolution
British response, 226, 321–2
city-based, 238–41
French and Spanish support for. *See* French and Spanish support for American Revolution
intercolonial unity fostered by, 450–2
Ireland, influence in, 301–2
narrative of, 347
natural law and natural rights arguments, 64–5, 225
in New England, 176–7, 240, 258, 320–2
paradoxical logic of, 225–6
planter class's perspective, 176, 177, 239, 258–9
political violence analyzed. *See* political violence of American Revolution
rationale of tax policies, 174, 221–5, 308, 378
in Virginia, 177–8, 256
by women, 378–81
Taylor, Alan, 256, 261–2
Taylor, Simon, 258–60, 262–3
Tenhoghskweaghta, 430
tertulias (Spanish-style conversation societies), 136–7, 142
Thayendanegea (Joseph Brant), 357, 358, 359, 364, 368, 430
Thibaud, Clément, 10, 42, 45, 126
Thomism, 106–7
Thompson, E. P., 144–5
Thomson, Charles, 66
Thornton, John, 35
timeframe of revolutions, 1–2
Tobago, 292, 417, 510
Tocqueville, Alexis de, 80, 82, 204–5
Toreno, Conde de (José María Queipo de Llano), 116
Torres, Camilo, 121, 129
Townshend Acts, resistance to. *See* tax resistance pre-American Revolution
Trinidad, 121, 417
Trumbull, John, 352
Trumbull, Joseph, 338
Tryon, William, 336
Tsi'yu-gûnsini (Dragging Canoe), 357, 427, 444
Tucker, Frances Bland Randolph, 375–6
Tucker, St. George, 453–4
Túpac Amaru (José Gabriel Condorcanqui)
Inca kingship claim, 487–9
Indigenous group opposition to, 35, 490
possible influences on, 110, 497
rebellion led by, 120, 474, 481–2, 490

Túpac Amaru, Diego Cristóbal, 482, 483–4
Túpac Katari (Julián Apaza), 483, 489–91
Turgot, Anne Robert Jacques, 93, 98, 270, 521, 522–3
Turner, Nat, 420

Ugulayacabe (Wolf's Friend), 445
Uhhaunauwaunmut, Solomon, 431
United Kingdom. *See* Great Britain
United States. *See also* American Revolution; British North America
  African Americans, discourse on, 72–4, 390–1, 404, 409–11, 421
  cities in early republican era, 244
  civilization and political survival, concerns for, 67–70, 76
  economic inequality in, 23–4, 537–41
  economy and population size, 163–4, 180–1, 182n, 187–8
  European writers on. *See* European writers' accounts of American Revolution
  "exceptionalism" praised by nationalists, 541
  Federal Constitution. *See* United States Federal Constitution
  first American Union, acts of. *See* Articles of Confederation; Declaration of Independence
  first American Union, dissolution of, 457–61
  Indian territory acquisitions, 183–4, 185, 411–12, 413, 434, 471–2
  Louisiana Purchase, 69, 185–7
  Native Americans. *See* Native American peoples
  religion in, 6, 146, 527–8, 531–2, 539
  slavery in. *See* slavery in United States
  Treaty of Paris 1783, terms, 180, 184, 185, 244, 294, 434–41, 450–1
  union of states, foundation of, 450–5
  war of 1812, 185, 257, 261–2, 342, 372, 405
  white women in. *See* white women
United States Federal Constitution
  Articles of Confederation compared with, 462–4
  Bill of Rights, 59–60, 126, 183, 468–9, 473
  "Charter of Freedom" claim, 473
  competing state interests, compromise politics, 467–8
  Condorcet on, 525, 526
  Constitutional Convention, convening of, 461–2

  debates and controversies, 182–3, 464–6
  federal bodies established under, 471
  federal–state governmental relations under, 466–7, 472–3
  introduction to study, 448–50
  language of, 59–60
  Lower South states' view of, 184–5
  natural law influence on, 69
  ratification by state conventions, 468–71
  slavery, protections for, 182–3, 467
  on territorial acquisitions, 185
  Virginia Plan, 182, 462
Upper Peru. *See also* Peru, Viceroyalty of
  Indigenous groups in, 40, 484–7, 491
  rebellions (1780–1781), 482–4, 489–91
  Río de la Plata viceroyalty creation, impact on, 485

Van Kley, Dale, 88–9, 92–3, 99
Vanegas, Isidro, 110n
Vattel, Emer de, 69, 107, 498
Vaughn, James, 251
Vendée War, 36, 38–9
Venezuela
  First Republic, 122–3
  Miranda's expedition to (1806), 122, 128
  public opinion as political force, 11
  republican conspiracy (1797), 8
Venturi, Franco, 82
Vergennes, Count de (Charles Gravier), 273, 278
Villanueva, Joaquín Lorenzo, 124
Vimeur, Jean-Baptiste Donatien de, Count de Rochambeau, 289–90
violence of revolutions, 27–31. *See also* political violence of American Revolution
Virginia. *See also* British North America; United States
  in American Revolutionary War. *See* Virginia in American Revolutionary War
  cities, emergence and development, 229–30, 231. *See also* Norfolk
  civilization and political survival, Jefferson's concerns for, 68–9
  Declaration of Rights, 65
  economy and population, colonial era, 166–7, 169, 170, 211
  Gabriel's Conspiracy, 412–13
  Glorious Revolution, impact in, 201
  House of Burgesses, 199–200, 322
  law restricting right to testify in court, 203

Point Pleasant, Battle of, 426
religion in, 6, 146
salons and coffeehouses, 137
slavery abolition resisted in, 411–12, 420
slavery economy, 166–7, 400, 401, 404
Somerset case, 256–7
tax resistance in, 177–8, 256
trade regulation, colonial era, 195–6, 198
Virginia in American Revolutionary War
  destructive violence, 241, 329, 336–7
  failed French operation, 289–90
  flour shipments to Cuba, 510
  Great Bridge, Battle of, 382
  Native Americans, violence toward, 356–7
  slave revolts and escapes, 329, 342, 354–5, 403–4, 535–6
  Yorktown, siege of, 179, 290–1, 331
Virginia Plan, 182, 462
Viscardo, Juan Pablo, 120–1
Vives, Juan Luis, 106
Voltaire
  Panthéon internment, 80, 102–3
  other mentions, 47–8, 77–8, 91, 532
voting rights, 15–18, 23, 390, 392

Wahrman, Dror, 151–2
Walpole, Robert, 197–8, 201, 205
Walsh, Lorena, 401
war of 1812, 185, 257, 261–2, 342, 372, 405
War of Independence. *See* American Revolutionary War
War of Spanish Succession, 215, 218, 285
warfare, cross-Atlantic, 218–19
Warren, Mercy Otis, 381–2
Washington, George
  Constitutional Convention, letter to, 448–9
  Continental Army formation, 178
  customs of war upheld by, 333–5
  Franco-American operations, 278, 279, 283, 289–90
  military tactics, 331–2, 502
  moral leadership praised by European writers, 521, 533–4
  Native Americans, attitude toward, 49, 423, 431, 436, 442, 446–7
  Quakers, attitude toward, 531–2
  slave ownership, 398, 406, 533
  other mentions, 284, 330, 335, 338
Washington, Harry, 398–9, 404, 405, 407, 414
Washington, Martha, 384–5
Weber, Eugen, 150
Weed, Elizabeth, 383

West, Benjamin, 369–70
West Florida theater of American Revolutionary War, 286–8, 511, 516–17
West Indies. *See* British West Indies; particular jurisdictions
Wheatley, Phillis, 406
White Eyes, 429
white women
  in American Revolution. *See* white women in American Revolution
  Atlantic trade consumer revolution and, 373–9, 382–3
  citizenship idea applied to, 23, 236, 389–90, 396
  education of, 23, 74–5, 393–4
  Enlightenment and evangelical ideas applied to, 377–8
  equality rights demands, 5, 22–3, 74–5, 108, 390–1
  investments by, 394–5
  moral authority afforded to, 393, 395, 397, 528–9
  planter class, 375–6, 387
  political activism, 392–3, 395–6
  property ownership rights, 374–5, 391–3, 394, 396–7
  social arts of, 135, 140–1, 395–6
  voting rights, 390, 392
white women in American Revolution
  "camp followers", 388
  everyday practices imbued with politics, 380–6
  fundraising by, 384–5
  household management during War, 387–8
  introduction to study, 21–2, 373
  Loyalists, 382–4, 385, 396–7
  rape and other violence toward, 30, 333, 337, 341–2, 384, 386–7
  soldiers (disguised as men), 388–9
  tax resistance, 378–81
White, Alexander, 395
Whitefield, George, 218
Whitman, James, 331
Wilberforce, William, 122, 259, 264–5
Wilkes, John, 308, 310
William III of Great Britain, 178, 200, 201, 206
William V, Prince of Orange, 525–6
Williams, Eric, 262
Williamson, David, 438
Wilson, James, 244–5, 443
Wolfe, James, 251

Wolfe, Patrick, 442
Wolff, Christian, 107
Wolf's Friend (Ugulayacabe), 445
Wollstonecraft, Mary, 22, 75
women, white. *See* white women
Wood, Gordon, 65
Woolman, John, 72

Wootton, David, 89
Wright, James, 355, 361, 363

Yorktown, siege of, 179, 290–1, 331

Zea, Francisco Antonio, 118, 119
Ziegenhagen, Heinrich, 26